THE HAMBURG DR
BY G.E. LESSING

While eighteenth-century playwright and critic Gotthold Ephraim Lessing made numerous contributions in his lifetime to the theater, the text that best documents his dynamic and shifting views on dramatic theory is also that which continues to resonate with later generations – the *Hamburg Dramaturgy* (*Hamburgische Dramaturgie*, 1767–69). This collection of 104 short essays represents one of the eighteenth century's most important critical engagements with the theater and its potential to promote humanistic discourse. Lessing's essays are an immensely erudite, deeply engaged, witty, ironic, and occasionally scathing investigation of European theatrical culture, bolstered by deep analysis of Aristotelian dramatic theory and utopian visions of theater as a vehicle for human connection.

This is the first complete English translation of Lessing's text, with extensive annotations that place the work in its historical context. For the first time, English-language readers can trace primary source references and link Lessing's observations on drama, theory, and performance not only to the plays he discusses, but also to dramatic criticism and acting theory. This volume also includes three introductory essays that situate Lessing's work both within his historical time period and in terms of his influence on Enlightenment and post-Enlightenment theater and criticism.

The newly translated *Hamburg Dramaturgy* will speak to dramaturgs, directors, and humanities scholars who see theater as a medium not only for entertainment, but also for philosophical and political debate.

Gotthold Ephraim Lessing (1729–81) was a playwright, critic, and philosopher of the German Enlightenment. His plays include *Miss Sara Sampson*, *Minna von Barnhelm*, *Emilia Galotti*, and *Nathan the Wise*. In addition to the *Hamburg Dramaturgy*, Lessing is known for his masterpiece of aesthetic theory, *Laocoon: An Essay on the Limits of Painting and Poetry*.

Wendy Arons is professor of drama at Carnegie Mellon University. She is the author of *Performance and Femininity in Eighteenth-Century German Women's Writing: The Impossible Act* (Palgrave Macmillan, 2006) and coeditor, with Theresa J. May, of *Readings in Performance and Ecology* (Palgrave Macmillan, 2012).

Sara Figal's research centers on eighteenth-century German literature and history. She is the author of *Heredity, Race, and the Birth of the Modern* (Routledge, 2011 and 2008) and coeditor, with Mark Larrimore, of *The German Invention of Race* (SUNY Press, 2007 and 2006).

Natalya Baldyga's research focuses on theater historiography, cultural identity, and the performing body in eighteenth-century Europe. Her published essays include "Sensate Cognition and Properly Feeling Bodies: G. E. Lessing, Acting Theory, and Emotional Regulation in Eighteenth-Century Germany" (*Theatre Survey*, 2017).

THE HAMBURG DRAMATURGY BY G.E. LESSING

A New and Complete Annotated English Translation

Translated by Wendy Arons and Sara Figal
Edited by Natalya Baldyga

Routledge
Taylor & Francis Group

LONDON AND NEW YORK

First published 2019
by Routledge

2 Park Square, Milton Park, Abingdon, Oxon OX14 4RN
and by Routledge
605 Third Avenue, New York, NY 10017

First issued in paperback 2021

Routledge is an imprint of the Taylor & Francis Group, an informa business

British Library Cataloguing-in-Publication Data
A catalogue record for this book is available from the British Library

Library of Congress Cataloging-in-Publication Data
Names: Lessing, Gotthold Ephraim, 1729-1781, author.
Title: The Hamburg dramaturgy / by G.E. Lessing.
Other titles: Hamburgische Dramaturgie. English
Description: Milton Park, Abingdon, Oxon ;
New York, NY : Routledge, 2019. |
Includes bibliographical references and index.
Identifiers: LCCN 2018023957 | ISBN 9780415662451
(hardback : alk. paper) | ISBN 9780203072400 (ebook)
Subjects: LCSH: Drama—Technique. | Aristotle. Poetics.
Classification: LCC PN1664 .L413 2019 | DDC 808.2—dc23
LC record available at https://lccn.loc.gov/2018023957

ISBN 13: 978-1-03-209445-8 (pbk)
ISBN 13: 978-0-415-66245-1 (hbk)

Typeset in Bembo
by Apex CoVantage, LLC

Cover image title: Portrait of Gotthold Ephraim Lessing (ca. 1767-68)
Artist: Attributed to Anna Rosina Lisiewska (1713-83)
Permission to reproduce from: Gleimhaus Halberstadt – Museum der deutschen Aufklärung (Museum of the German Enlightenment)

To the spirit of Gotthold Ephraim Lessing and all
those who tenaciously pursue humanistic inquiry in
challenging times.
And in memory of Eric Arons (1968–2013), who, like
Lessing, loved a good intellectual argument.

CONTENTS

Preface   *xi*
Acknowledgments   *xiii*
List of contributors   *xvi*
A note on the original author   *xviii*

1   Missions, misunderstandings, and mythologies: the relationship
    between the *Hamburg Dramaturgy* and the Hamburg
    National Theater   1
    Natalya Baldyga

2   "We have actors, but no art of acting": performance theory
    and theatrical emotion in the *Hamburg Dramaturgy*   13
    Natalya Baldyga

3   The legacy of the *Hamburg Dramaturgy*   23
    Michael M. Chemers

4   Note on the translation   31
    Wendy Arons and Sara Figal

    Volume I   35
       Notice 35
       Essay 1 37
       Essay 2 40
       Essay 3 42

Contents

Essay 4 45
Essay 5 48
Essay 6 51
Essay 7 54
Essay 8 57
Essay 9 60
Essay 10 62
Essay 11 64
Essay 12 67
Essay 13 69
Essay 14 72
Essay 15 75
Essay 16 77
Essay 17 80
Essay 18 82
Essay 19 85
Essay 20 87
Essay 21 90
Essay 22 92
Essay 23 95
Essay 24 97
Essay 25 100
Essay 26 102
Essay 27 105
Essay 28 108
Essay 29 111
Essay 30 113
Essay 31 115
Essay 32 118
Essay 33 120
Essay 34 123
Essay 35 126
Essay 36 128
Essay 37 131
Essay 38 134
Essay 39 136
Essay 40 139
Essay 41 142
Essay 42 145
Essay 43 147
Essay 44 150
Essay 45 153

Essay 46 156
Essay 47 158
Essay 48 161
Essay 49 164
Essay 50 166
Essay 51 169
Essay 52 172

Volume II   175

Essay 53 175
Essay 54 178
Essay 55 180
Essay 56 183
Essay 57 185
Essay 58 188
Essay 59 190
Essay 60 193
Essay 61 196
Essay 62 199
Essay 63 202
Essay 64 206
Essay 65 209
Essay 66 213
Essay 67 216
Essay 68 220
Essay 69 223
Essay 70 225
Essay 71 228
Essay 72 231
Essay 73 233
Essay 74 236
Essay 75 239
Essay 76 241
Essay 77 244
Essay 78 246
Essay 79 249
Essay 80 251
Essay 81 254
Essay 82 257
Essay 83 259
Essay 84 262
Essay 85 264

Contents

Essay 86 267
Essays 87 and 88 269
Essay 89 274
Essay 90 277
Essay 91 279
Essay 92 282
Essay 93 284
Essay 94 286
Essay 95 288
Essay 96 291
Essay 97 293
Essay 98 296
Essay 99 298
Essay 100 301
Essays 101, 102, 103, and 104 304

Paralipomena   313

Notes to essays 1–104   *322*
Notes to the Paralipomena   *396*
Works cited   *402*
Subject index   *425*
Name index   *433*
Title index   *442*

PREFACE

This project had its origins over a cup of coffee in Phoenix at the 2007 annual conference of the American Society for Theatre Research (ASTR), when Michael Chemers expressed an ardent wish for a new translation of the *Hamburg Dramaturgy*, one that would include an editorial apparatus situating the text within its historical context and in relation to Lessing's other writings. Wendy Arons agreed that a new translation was sorely needed, noting that the extant translation was difficult to read and lacked the spirit and wit of the original. Natalya Baldyga, whose research focused on the *Hamburg Dramaturgy*, concurred with both concerns and then contributed some remarkable data: the only English translation available – produced by Helen Zimmern in 1879 and reprinted regularly since – entirely omitted 19 of Lessing's 104 essays and excised an additional 30 percent of the text from the essays it did include. Casual conversation led to the strong scholarly conviction that this seminal text of theater history needed an update: a new translation that was engaging, complete, and annotated.

A Domestic Exchange grant from ASTR in 2010 funded initial work on the project, which produced the realization that translating a text of this magnitude was a job for more than one person. Wendy Arons persuaded Sara Figal, a Germanist with expertise on Lessing and the German eighteenth century, of the project's importance, and Sara joined the team as co-translator in 2011. Later that year, we were impressed by the open peer review model developed by MediaCommons Press and were inspired to propose this work for online pre-publication. We imagined that if Lessing had been alive in the twenty-first century, the *Hamburg Dramaturgy* might have emerged as a series of blog posts, and we were certain that he would have liked the idea of engaging in dialogue with readers through live comments on his writing. A contract from Routledge Press and a major "Scholarly Editions and Translations" grant from the National Endowment for the Humanities launched this project in earnest, and we began publishing the translated essays "serially," as we completed them, just as Lessing had originally intended to do with his essays. The online "rough draft" version of this book – which has minor errors and issues that have been corrected in this print volume – remains available at http://mcpress.media-commons.org/hamburg/.

The *Hamburg Dramaturgy* represents one of the eighteenth century's most important critical engagements with the theater and with its potential to promote humanistic discourse and inquiry. Lessing's essays are an immensely erudite, deeply engaged, witty, ironic, and occasionally scathing investigation of German and European theatrical culture, bolstered by deep analysis of Aristotelian dramatic theory and utopian visions of theater as a vehicle for human connection. Lessing's reflections range far beyond merely literary concerns: he explores, among other topics, acting theory and technique, French cultural hegemony, the character of the German people, theatrical illusion, audience reception and the psychology of emotional response, the potential reform of the German theater, and the role of the arts within a framework of sentimental philosophy. The *Hamburg Dramaturgy* thus maintains an extraordinary relevance for dramaturgs, directors, and humanities scholars who see theater as a medium for philosophical and political debate as well as for entertainment. Our new, complete, and annotated English translation removes the major obstacle – the language barrier – that has kept English-speaking scholars and students from investigating the full depth and breadth of Lessing's critical and philosophical thinking in the *Hamburg Dramaturgy*.

We have had a long journey since that initial coffee shop conversation, one filled with challenges and discoveries, frustration and delight. We are grateful to have had the opportunity, a rare one these days, to spend years engaged in the deep study of a single, highly complex work. The process has been illuminating and valuable to our scholarship as a whole. We hope that our work will allow others to enjoy their own adventurous peregrinations through Lessing's idiosyncratic and inspiring contribution to the history, theory, and practice of the theater.

Wendy Arons, Natalya Baldyga, and Sara Figal
May 2018

ACKNOWLEDGMENTS

This project has been seven years in the making. Over that time, many people and institutions have provided assistance in many forms. We are enormously grateful, to begin with, to the National Endowment for the Humanities "Scholarly Editions and Translations" program for the multi-year grant that helped fund the bulk of the work on this project, and to NEH program officers Daniel Sack and Stefanie Walker for their assistance and support throughout the process. Routledge Press also provided seed funding for this project in the early stages; we thank Routledge acquisitions editor Talia Rodgers for having shepherded this project through the initial contracting process and editors Ben Piggott and Laura Soppelsa for carrying it through to its final stages. Additional significant funding was provided by Dan Martin (the Stanley and Marcia Gumberg Dean of the College of Fine Arts at Carnegie Mellon University) and Peter Cooke (head of the School of Drama at Carnegie Mellon University). Thanks are also due to Dan Martin and Peter Cooke for supporting a year-long sabbatical leave that provided the time to produce a first draft of the translation of the text. The Carnegie Mellon University Berkman Faculty Development Fund supplemented the NEH grant with funding for travel, which allowed us to engage in regular working retreats. At Carnegie Mellon University, Liz Fox, Rachael Swetnam, Jenn Joy Wilson, Keith Marsh, and Gina Kuhn provided administrative support for this project at many levels; thank you all for patiently walking us through how to write a budget and for keeping track of expenses. We are also grateful to the American Society for Theatre Research for the receipt of a Domestic Exchange Grant and to Monika Fick and the Lessing Society for providing funding for us to present our work at a special conference on the *Hamburg Dramaturgy* in Wolfenbüttel, home of the Herzog August Bibliothek and the Lessing House Museum.

We were the beneficiaries of the skills, expertise, and generosity of many scholars, artists, and students who answered the call when we needed help. Beatrix Brockman, Karen Jürs-Munby, and Elisabeth Krimmer served as translation consultants on the project – we thank them for generously sharing their time and expertise. We are also grateful to Stephen Brockmann, Erhard Friedrichsmeyer, Peter Erickson, and Hans-Joachim Jürs for lending their fluency in German to making our translation more accurate and clear. Peter Erickson also graciously shared his expertise on Cronegk's play *Olint and Sophronia* and the Christian tragedy in general. Willi Goetschel took time out of his busy schedule to help us think through the best way to deal with the term *Affekt*. Stephen C. Carlson and Michael Anthony Bruni-Fowler helped us to translate challenging passages and phrases from ancient Greek into English, and Michael Hoffman did the same with Latin. France and French are everywhere in the *Hamburg Dramaturgy*, and although all of us can read a fair amount of French, we at times depended on the kindness of experts. Matthew McMahan, as well as vetting the occasional translation, read and researched a wide range of eighteenth-century French sources in order to answer questions for us; Sebastien Dubreil and Daniel Smith provided translations of tricky passages from French into English; and John Golder answered a last minute "cold call" for help in fact-checking a bit of trivia from French theater history that enabled us to sleuth out the origin of Lessing's claim, in Essay 36, that Pierre Corneille had a seat reserved for him on the stage – such are the research rabbit holes a project like this engenders! Other rabbit hole questions were answered by Patrick King, who tracked down several obscure items (including performing marmots), and by Linda Ross Girard, who drew on her costuming expertise in historical dress styles. Playwright Savannah Reich provided a dialect for us to use in translating *Plattdeutsch* into English for the dialogue Lessing quotes in Essay 28, Erik Butler produced a translation of the annotations from the *Werke und Briefe* edition for reference purposes, and William G. Henry was our go-to expert on editorial questions large and small – of which there were many.

Others provided additional assistance that was vital to our success. Caitlin Cox spent many hours adding alphabetical bookmarks to PDFs of eighteenth-century German-English dictionaries, which thereby saved us countless more hours scrolling through thousands of pages looking for words. Brandi Wilkins Catanese generously took the time to download and email a 600-page source that was only accessible through the UC Berkeley library so that we could verify a quote. Yizhou Huang swiftly scanned and sent excerpts from Voltaire's *Commentaries on Corneille* for use during an out-of-town marathon work session. The UC Santa Cruz library provided online access to the entire 12-volume *Gotthold Ephraim Lessing Werke und Briefe*, which was not in the collections of any of our institutional libraries. Kathleen Fitzpatrick facilitated the publication of the project online through MediaCommons Press and responded rapidly whenever we had questions about the interface or needed help troubleshooting an issue with the website. Many colleagues in the field logged onto that website and offered helpful comments, suggestions, and queries; they include (in alphabetical order) Elizabeth Coen, Heather Gibson, Lilia Hinojosa, Jack Riley, Leah Schatz, Nitsan Scharf, Morgan Scott, Aaron C. Thomas, and Yu Wang. Mary Helen Dupree, Beate Allert, and Magda Romanska invited us to present our work at ASECS and at LMDA; we are grateful to them for the opportunity to publicize the project more widely. We also express thanks to our many friends and colleagues who provided other less quantifiable – but by no means less valuable – support, in the form of conversation, questions, and encouragement.

Last, but certainly not least, we owe a debt to our respective families for making it possible for us to devote substantial time and attention to this years-long endeavor. Gerald Figal and Michael Perdriel kept us well-fed and well-beveraged during our regular marathon retreats in Nashville and Pittsburgh, and they graciously took care of other matters domestic so that we could focus on our work. From the earliest days of the project, Ryan J. Wheeler provided his unwavering support and, during crunch times and retreats, bore the brunt of caring for the small person whose birth coincided with the launching of this massive endeavor. Thanks also to Safa, Henry, Avalon, Leda, Philip, and Leo, our collective children, who tolerated the frequent absences this project engendered and who were warm and welcoming hosts during our peripatetic work sessions. Spending time with all of you was an unexpected and delightful side benefit of working on this project.

CONTRIBUTORS

Wendy Arons (translator) is a professor of drama and head of the dramaturgy option at the Carnegie Mellon University School of Drama. Her research interests include eighteenth- and nineteenth-century theater history, feminist theater, and performance and ecology. She is the author of *Performance and Femininity in Eighteenth-Century German Woman's Writing: The Impossible Act* (Palgrave Macmillan, 2006) and coeditor, with Theresa J. May, of *Readings in Performance and Ecology* (Palgrave Macmillan, 2012). She has published articles in numerous journals as well as chapters in a number of anthologies, including "Ecodramaturgy in/and Contemporary Women's Plays" (coauthored with Theresa J. May) in *Contemporary Women Playwrights* (Palgrave Macmillan, 2014, ed. Penny Farfan & Leslie Ferris) and "Beyond the Nature/Culture Divide: Challenges from Ecocriticism and Evolutionary Biology for Theatre Historiograpy" in *Theatre Historiography: Critical Questions* (University of Michigan Press, 2010, ed. Henry Bial & Scott Magelssen). She is also author of a Pittsburgh-based arts and culture blog, *The Pittsburgh Tatler*.

Natalya Baldyga (editor) has taught theater history at Tufts University and the Florida State University. Her research focuses on theater historiography, cultural identity, and the performing body in eighteenth-century Europe. Her published essays include "Sensate Cognition and Properly Feeling Bodies: G. E. Lessing, Acting Theory, and Emotional Regulation in Eighteenth-Century Germany" (*Theatre Survey* 2017) as well as articles on eighteenth-century German, Polish, and English theater in journals such as *The Eighteenth Century: Theory and Interpretation* and in the anthologies *Staging Nationalism: Essays on Theatre and National Identity* (McFarland & Co., 2005) and *Public Theatres and Theatre Publics* (Cambridge Scholars, 2012). In addition, she contributed all entries on eighteenth- and nineteenth-century German actors for the *Cambridge Encyclopedia of Stage Actors and Acting* (Cambridge University Press, 2015). Dr. Baldyga also works as a freelance theater director and translator. Her original translation and adaptation of Carlo Gozzi's *King Stag* had its world premiere at Tufts University in 2017.

Michael M. Chemers (contributor) holds a Ph.D. in theater history and criticism (2001, University of Washington) and an MFA in playwriting (1997, Indiana University). He was the founding director of the BFA in production dramaturgy program at Carnegie Mellon University's School of Drama from 2007 to 2012. He is the author of several books and more than 60 scholarly articles on theater history, adaptation of classical texts, and dramaturgy; one of which (*Ghost Light: An Introductory Handbook for Dramaturgy*, Southern Illinois University Press, 2010) has been translated into Korean and Farsí. He has worked as a dramaturg all over the United States and abroad for more than 20 years. He is also the editor of the English translation of Alexander Iliev's *Towards a Theory of Mime* (Routledge, 2014). He is currently a professor of dramatic literature at the University of California Santa Cruz.

Sara Figal (translator) is a former faculty member at Vanderbilt University whose area of specialization is German literature and culture of the long eighteenth century. She has received numerous awards for her work, including the Goethe Society of North America's Essay Prize in 2010 and the Max Kade Award for the Best Article in *The German Quarterly* in 2006; she has also been the recipient of Fulbright, DAAD, and National Endowment of the Humanities grants, among others. She is the author of *Heredity, Race, and the Birth of the Modern* (Routledge, 2008 and 2010) and coeditor, with Mark Larrimore, of *The German Invention of Race* (SUNY Press, 2006 and 2007). She has published articles on eighteenth-century German literature, science, and culture in journals including *Lessing Yearbook*, *Eighteenth-Century Studies*, *German Quarterly*, and *Women in German Yearbook*, as well as in various essay collections. Dr. Figal was named one of Nashville's "Women of Influence" in 2017.

A NOTE ON THE ORIGINAL AUTHOR

Gotthold Ephraim Lessing (1729–81) was a playwright, humanist scholar, critic, and philosopher of the German Enlightenment. In addition to producing a wide range of literary and theological works, Lessing founded several journals, including the *Beyträge zur Historie und Aufnahme des Theaters* [*Contributions to the History and Development of the Theater*] (1750) and the *Theatralische Bibliothek* [*Theatrical Library*] (1754–58). As a playwright, Lessing added to a growing body of original German-language dramatic literature; his plays include the masterworks *Miss Sara Sampson* (1755), *Minna von Barnhelm* (1767), *Emilia Galotti* (1772), and *Nathan the Wise* (1779). In his dramatic works and theory, Lessing challenged French neoclassical models and provided new interpretations of Aristotle. Other important contributions include not only the *Hamburg Dramaturgy* (1767–69) but also his masterpiece of aesthetic theory, *Laocoon: An Essay on the Limits of Painting and Poetry* (1766). Eschewing dogmatism in all forms, Lessing promoted, through his art and scholarship, a discourse of religious and intellectual tolerance.

1

MISSIONS, MISUNDERSTANDINGS, AND MYTHOLOGIES

The relationship between the *Hamburg Dramaturgy* and the Hamburg National Theater

Natalya Baldyga

In the spring of 1767, the Hamburg National Theater was preparing to open. The experimental enterprise, meant to promote theatrical reform and the legitimacy of German drama, had procured financial backing, a brand-new performance space, and star talent. What it lacked was cultural capital – specifically, a distinguished literary figure whose presence could lend the new theater an air of respectability. As luck would have it, Gotthold Ephraim Lessing (1729–81) was in need of employment. A popular playwright, highly esteemed (and even feared) as a critic, Lessing nevertheless had failed, due to various contretemps, to secure his dream position as the royal librarian in Berlin. Financially, the celebrated author was in desperate straits. It was at this moment that he received an offer to join the Hamburg National Theater as its "official theater poet." Although the Hamburg endeavor appealed to him, Lessing, who frequently had significant difficulties meeting deadlines, wisely rejected the offer to serve as the theater's resident playwright. An alternative was suggested: join the theater as an in-house critic and author a serial publication for the theater's patrons. Lessing accepted. The Hamburg National Theater had succeeded in adding a celebrity author to its roster. After careful deliberation, Lessing chose to call his new journal the *Hamburgische Dramaturgie*, intending his essays to be a didactic supplement to the Hamburg theater experiment, in the form of a *kritisches Register* (a critical register) to the plays performed by the Hamburg company ("Notice" 36).

   As originally conceived by Lessing, the *Hamburg Dramaturgy* was meant to contribute to a growing German interest in dramatic theory, to assess the work of playwrights

1

and actors, and to educate the taste of the public ("Notice" 36–7). In practice, however, the *Hamburg Dramaturgy* differed considerably in form and function from its original theoretical conception. Lessing's commentary hardly serves as a critical register to the performances: a significant number of plays are never discussed, and some are barely mentioned, while the discussion of others extends over five, ten, or even seventeen essays. When one reads the *Hamburg Dramaturgy*, the discrepancy between theory and practice quickly becomes apparent: by the time that Lessing concludes his commentary about the theater's premiere performance in his seventh essay, the Hamburg National Theater had been open for over a month.[1] By the end of the first year of the Hamburg enterprise, Lessing's journal had little association with the theater to which it was ostensibly attached. Lessing's commentary in the *Hamburg Dramaturgy* ends with the theater's 52nd evening, which occurred on 28 July 1767, even though the Hamburg National Theater continued performances until early 1769.[2] In his final installment of essays, issued on Easter 1769, shortly after the theater's closing performance, Lessing admits that his writings were "not exactly what [he] promised" ("Essays 101–104" 306).

Yet it was Lessing's shift in focus from practical staging matters to dramatic theory that most likely ensured the position of the *Hamburg Dramaturgy* as a seminal text of the European – and specifically, German – theater, as nineteenth- and early twentieth-century scholarship prioritized dramatic theory over discussions of acting and performance and later twentieth-century scholars turned to the text for evidence of incipient German nationalist discourse. Today, in library catalogs, one finds the work listed under the subject headings "Drama – Technique," "Aristotle – Poetics," and, occasionally, "Drama – History and criticism." Such headings elide the scope and complexity of Lessing's project. So too do the brief synopses in theater history textbooks, which describe the *Hamburg Dramaturgy* as a treatise in which Lessing challenged French neoclassical interpretations of Aristotle and professed his admiration for Shakespeare. Although both of these statements are true, they nevertheless provide an erroneous understanding of the form and function of Lessing's journal by presenting it as a cohesive and premeditated literary endeavor, when it was in actuality rather disjunctive and improvisational in nature. Additionally, the origins of Lessing's journal have been significantly mythologized, which has colored how the *Hamburg Dramaturgy* has been viewed. As is often the case, the full story is rather messier than the sanitized hagiographies that prevail in textbooks. Both in Lessing's time and in ours, people's expectations regarding the *Hamburg Dramaturgy* seldom align with the realities of its production, and its contents are often less – and sometimes more – than originally promised. These disparities make greater sense when one considers Lessing's journal in relation to his larger interest in cultural reform and the founding and brief life of the Hamburg National Theater.

Lessing followed a circuitous path to his role as one of Germany's most influential literary critics. Born in Saxony in 1729, Lessing was the son of a Lutheran pastor-scholar. Scholarships allowed him to attend the University of Leipzig, propelling him into an eighteenth-century German mecca of culture, literature, and learning (and gateway to European Enlightenment thinking). Although enrolled as a theological student, Lessing frequented lectures on literature, philology, classical studies, and philosophy. These years also marked Lessing's first serious engagement with the theater, an interest that developed early and persisted despite the active disapproval of his parents, actors being considered social outcasts by reputable citizens. Lessing fraternized with actors in Leipzig and attended the theater often, translating plays as a means of gaining admission to performances. Later, as Lessing's fortunes as a journalist, critic, translator, traveling companion, and independent writer waxed and waned, he would shuttle between Leipzig and Berlin, with time in Wittenberg, Breslau, Amsterdam, and other cities as well. Before his move to Hamburg to join its new National Theater, Lessing had obtained a master's degree in philosophy, scraped together a living from all manners of clerical work, published an acclaimed six-volume collection of his plays, poetry, criticism, and theological and philosophical works, and founded several journals, including the *Beyträge zur Historie und Aufnahme des Theaters* [*Contributions to the History and Development of the Theater*] (1750), the first German periodical to focus on drama and theatrical performance.[3]

Much of Lessing's prolific output was related to the theater. His second periodical, the *Theatralische Bibliothek* [*Theatrical Library*] (1754–58), was meant, much like the *Beyträge*, to provide a scholarly discussion of drama and theater history accessible to the general public. Lessing's thinking about theater and performance was further developed by his conversations (in person and in letters) with his wide range of talented and illustrious friends and acquaintances, and in particular with the philosopher Moses Mendelssohn (1729–86) and the bookseller and entrepreneur Friedrich Nicolai (1733–1811). Together, the three friends published the *Briefe, die neueste Litteratur betreffend* or *Litteraturbriefe* [*Letters Concerning the Most Recent Literature* or *Letters on Literature*] (1759–65) and maintained a running epistolary dialogue that addressed contemporary aesthetic and philosophical debates (including dramatic and theatrical matters) for over a quarter of a century. Moreover, in addition to his vast and influential critical writings, Lessing was also a celebrated playwright who added to the growing body of original German-language plays aimed at a domestic audience. Before moving to Hamburg, Lessing had already written two of his masterworks, the domestic tragedy *Miss Sara Sampson* (1755) and his controversial political comedy *Minna von Barnhelm* (1767), in addition to other minor plays.

If Lessing was attracted by the mission statement of the Hamburg National Theater, which emphasized the reform of the German theater and the development of its literature, he was, as yet, unaware of the mixed and sometimes conflicting aims of those involved in the establishment of the new theater.[4] The impetus for the Hamburg enterprise is often ascribed to a "group of art-loving citizens," a narrative founded more on the promotional hyperbole surrounding the new theater's inauguration than on fact.[5] Although Hamburg, by the 1760s, had at one time or another housed the most important German acting companies of the early to mid-eighteenth century, not all of Hamburg's populace was pleased that their city served as a locus for theatrical entertainment. Theater in the German lands had not yet gained the status of a respectable pastime. In order to understand the experimental nature of the Hamburg National Theater and the situation in which Lessing found himself, one needs to know something of the turbulent history of the eighteenth-century German theater.

At the time of the Hamburg National Theater's founding, German troupes were largely relegated to town halls and temporary stages or performing booths (*Spielbude*) that were torn down after performances. Large opera houses built in the seventeenth century in Germany had up-to-date neoclassical scenery and stage machinery but were used for Italian opera and occasionally for visiting French acting companies; German troupes did not have access to them. Appropriately known as *Wanderbühnen* (traveling players), German actors remained permanently on tour, leading a vagabond existence in conditions that ranged from difficult to appalling. The main fare of the early eighteenth-century German companies was improvisational comedy featuring the boisterous "German harlequin" Hanswurst (Jack Sausage), Italian opera libretti, and the *Haupt- und Staatsaktionen* (chief and state plays), sensational tragedies adapted from English, French, and Spanish plays. Although these mixed entertainments were well attended, the boisterous non-literary repertoire of the *Wanderbühnen*, their itinerant status, the nature of their performance spaces, and the widely held preconception of actors (and especially actresses) as people of loose morals all contributed to the impression held by the educated middle-classes and lower gentry that theater was a suspect pastime, perhaps appropriate for the lower classes but not for respectable citizens.

The Hamburg National Theater can be seen as the direct descendant of earlier efforts to reform the German theater, which began in earnest in the first third of the eighteenth century with the partnership between professor and critic Johann Christoph Gottsched (1700–66) and actress-manager Friederike Karoline Neuber (1697–1760) in Leipzig.[6] The performance of original German-language works was rare at this time, and there were few available for companies to perform. In his search for a new German literature, Gottsched looked to the strict rules and order of French neoclassicism as his model for German playwriting. Beginning in 1727, Gottsched and Neuber worked to establish a new theatrical repertoire, which included not only French tragedies by Corneille and Racine but also plays by German authors such as Johann Elias Schlegel (1719–49), Johann Christian Krüger (1722–50), and even a young Lessing, then a student at the university.[7] Gottsched and Neuber combined their respective talents – scholarship and performance – in the attempt to convert the public to their views. The Gottsched-Neuber repertoire was initially successful in Leipzig, but interest palled and their partnership began to disintegrate; it eventually came to a final and acrimonious end in 1741 when Neuber lampooned Gottsched onstage. Both the Neuber-Gottsched dramatic repertoire and its attendant acting style (the "Leipzig style") were passed down by the leading actor-managers who had begun as members of Neuber's troupe. Their companies, as well as Neuber's, brought the experiments in theater reform begun in Leipzig to the theater-going public in Hamburg.[8] The company of Johann Friedrich Schönemann (1704–82) supplemented Neuber's French neoclassical repertoire with pastorals, *Haupt- und Staatsaktionen*, and bourgeois dramas such as Lessing's *Miss Sara Sampson* (1755), performing this adapted repertoire in Hamburg throughout the 1740s and early 1750s. Schönemann's repertoire was in turn inherited by Konrad Ernst Ackermann (1712–71), a performer in Schönemann's troupe who established his own company in Hamburg in 1764. It was Ackerman's company that would be coopted by theater critic and theatrical reformer Johann Friedrich Löwen (1727–71) in order to form the Hamburg National Theater.[9]

Ackermann not only presented English, Italian, and German works alongside the standard French neoclassical plays but also provided the public with highly popular ballets and pantomimes. In 1765, Ackermann constructed a new theater in Hamburg which, although small (and deemed a fire hazard by the city authorities), was preferable to the space he had previously leased, and hired Löwen, an erstwhile academic and theater critic, as a literary advisor. The appointment did not prove congenial. Ackermann came to resent Löwen's criticism of his management of the theater and replaced him. In 1766, Löwen secured backing for a new Hamburg theatrical endeavor, which was intended to replace Ackermann's company. In actuality, Löwen leased the theater building from Ackermann, merely changing its name, while retaining most of the in-house company, including Ackermann himself. Having secured a theater, Löwen now set his sights on obtaining a company playwright, with a view toward promoting German-language plays.

At the time of the founding of the Hamburg National Theater, some playwrights were writing in the German language, but there was no established school of German playwriting. In 1755, when Lessing wrote his first major play, the immensely popular domestic tragedy *Miss Sara Sampson*, most German playwrights were still focusing their efforts on translating or adapting classical or foreign works. J. C. Gottsched's six-volume *Die Deutsche Schaubühne* [*The German Stage*] (1741–45), for example, contained primarily translations of French neoclassical works, which his own plays strove to emulate. Gottsched was not the only playwright to rely on French dramaturgical models.[10] Johann Elias Schlegel, for example, wrote most of his plays in alexandrines, despite his interest in other potential models for German playwriting, including both the ancient Greeks and Shakespeare.[11] Lacking a unifying poetics, German dramatists explored a wide range of styles and modes of playwriting. In the *Hamburg Dramaturgy*, Lessing positively evaluates both the Saxon "comedy of types" (*sächsische Typenkomödie*) of J. E. Schlegel, which he feels is representative of German customs and character, and the new sentimental comedy (*rührendes Lustspiel*) by authors such as Christian Fürchtegott Gellert (1715–69). He is surprisingly hard, however, on his longtime friend, Christian Felix Weisse (1726–1804), a talented playwright whose works were regularly performed, and is especially unkind to the translator and playwright Luise Kulmus Gottsched (1713–62), whom some have called the "mother of modern German comedy."[12] These were not the only German playwrights of Lessing's age, although they were some of the most prominent during the years that Lessing and others sought to promote the growth of German drama.[13]

Both Lessing and Löwen were aware that the German theater required significant structural changes before it could truly promote German-language plays. Löwen stressed the need for public support of standing, permanent theaters; better training of actors through acting academies; the shifting of the management of theater from actors to professional managers; and incentives, in the form of prize competitions, for new German plays.[14] He therefore outlined a lofty agenda for the new Hamburg theater, promising a theatrical academy that would train actors and provide lecture-demonstrations on "physical eloquence" and tragic declamation, annual prizes for the best new German tragedy and comedy, and benefit performances for local charities. Löwen, however, proved unable to deliver on his promises. By the time of the theater's opening on 22 April 1767, most of his proposed reforms had been dropped from the program.

Löwen's program may have been overambitious, but one can see why Hamburg might have seemed an excellent location for a new and respectable German-language theater for middle-class audiences. Rather than answering to a ruling monarch, Hamburg was a "free city," whose inhabitants were governed by a senate made up of private citizens. Since the theater in Hamburg did not rely on aristocratic patronage, it was not tied to the theatrical tastes of the nobility, which, at the time, predominately favored the French theater and its imitators. In Berlin, Frederick the Great extended his patronage to the great French luminary Voltaire and showed no interest in promoting art or literature in German, a language he referred to as "coarse and almost barbaric" (Frederick II 224).[15] In Hamburg, however, the city was run by the bourgeoisie, and its merchant government was responsible for approving or rejecting new cultural endeavors. As a vital and cosmopolitan port city, Hamburg perceived itself as a major cultural center, with numerous citizen groups dedicated to learning and the arts and all manner of voluntary associations, clubs, and political organizations. At the same time, however, the absence of a centralized cultural style (as one might find in a court-controlled state) and the reliance on market forces could also be inimical to certain cultural endeavors.[16] Indeed, the entirely commercial nature of the Hamburg National Theater would ultimately be its downfall. Mercantile sponsorship dictated the scope and goals of the project, and, without the full support of the Hamburg senate, it was unable to secure a monopoly on theatrical performance that might have protected it from foreign and domestic competitors.[17] That which made Hamburg inviting for a new theater – its lack of a court, with no need to appeal to a particular reigning head – was also responsible for its demise, as the theater required the support of a varied constituency with differing tastes and concerns.

In fact, Hamburg's leading bourgeois citizens were not involved in the running of the theater; nor were they committed to Löwen's ideological project. Rather than being a coalition of art-loving citizens or – as Lessing describes in his opening "Notice" – "a society of Friends of the Theater," the founders of the Hamburg National Theater were a "consortium" of 12 businessmen whom Löwen gathered to support the endeavor; they were outsiders in Hamburg society and had varying motives for financing the theater (36). Löwen's chief financial backers, Abel Seyler, Johann Martin Tillemann, and Adolf Siegmund Bubbers, had entrepreneurial reasons for signing on, although Seyler and Bubbers were both admirers of principal actress Sophie Friederike Hensel (1738–89), and it has often been suggested that the Hamburg National Theater was established to provide a theatrical home for her.[18] The other investors played no active role, and indeed the Consortium was primarily a one-man affair – all funds for the new theatrical enterprise were controlled by Seyler (whose own business was on the verge of bankruptcy). Despite its new financing, new name, and new management, the theater would in fact continue to be run much as it had been under Ackermann's direction. Given the circumstances of its founding – a disgruntled would-be manager, a profusion of ego and intrigue, and a lack of broad support from the citizenry – it is perhaps not surprising that the Hamburg National Theater would meet its demise through fiscal mismanagement, poor leadership (Löwen was not a strong personality), and considerable personal conflict.

These factors were unknown to Lessing, however, when he was invited to join the theater. On paper it would have seemed like a good match. The cultural and aesthetic aims of the Hamburg National Theater's mission, as articulated by Löwen, would have appealed to Lessing, as would have Hamburg's status as a free city.[19] Both as a center of theatrical activity and in its open cosmopolitanism, Hamburg seemed like an excellent location for Lessing to contribute to a theater whose ideology was in line with the literary and cultural ideals he espoused.

The Hamburg National Theater's mission is outlined in the prologue that was spoken at the theater's opening night performance on 22 April 1767.[20] Following the arguments of other proponents of theater for the educated middle classes, the prologue claims that theater can benefit all ranks of humanity, even rendering the barbarian humane, by stirring "the dullest of feelings to keenest compassion," and that even the "angry, wild man" might be changed into a "human being, citizen, friend, and patriot" for the benefit of the state. These statements echo Lessing's earlier writings on drama and performance that describe compassion as a civilizing force, emphasizing the salutary effect of a theater that "awakens us to pity, compassion, and generosity" ("Essay 6" 52). In its ideals, at least, the Hamburg National Theater aligned with Lessing's views, and Lessing was prepared to further its mission through his critical expertise. "Not every enthusiast is a connoisseur," he explains, and "not every person who perceives the beauty of one play or the correct performance of one actor can thereby also judge the value of all others," but "[i]f we want to instill good taste in someone of sound judgment, we only need to make apparent to him why he did not like something" ("Notice" 36).

Regardless of whether the audience was ready to be instructed by Lessing, members of the theater's company were not. Principal actress Susanne Mecour (1738–84), for reasons unknown, made it a specific condition of her employment that she would not be reviewed by Lessing (Daunicht 227). Sophie Hensel objected to Lessing's criticism, apparently complaining that Lessing milled about noisily, spending entire acts at the buffet instead of in the theater, and only occasionally popped his head through the door of the *parterre* to view performances (Oehlke 2: 20). Leading actor Konrad Ekhof (1720–78), on the other hand, might have been considered an ally. A proponent of the more naturalistic acting style emerging in the mid- to late-eighteenth century, Ekhof had established a brief-lived "acting academy" in Schwerin that considered acting matters both practical and theoretical.[21] Actors, Ekhof had counseled, should desire learning and self-improvement. At the Hamburg National Theater, however, Ekhof was in no position to pursue reform. Because of Löwen's insufficiencies, he was forced to become the theater's de facto actor-manager, juggling not only difficulties with the theater's financial backers but also the complaints of disgruntled company members (who were sometimes intriguing with the financial backers).

If one considers the situation of the Hamburg actors from their point of view (as few historians have seemed willing to do), their general resistance to Lessing and Löwen is actually quite understandable. Many of the principal actors had achieved their fame through roles that Lessing would have rendered obsolete. Although Sophie Hensel, for example, had starred successfully in new dramas such as Lessing's *Miss Sara Sampson* and *Minna von Barnhelm*, she had made her name playing great queens from the French theater, including Voltaire's Sémiramis, Zayre, and Mérope, and Pierre Corneille's Cleopatra. If Lessing had had his way with the repertoire of the Hamburg National Theater, popular French neoclassical roles would have been greatly reduced or expunged. Actors of both genders "owned" certain roles; this correlation was extremely important to an actor's self-identity and ability to obtain employment. Performers were therefore understandably possessive about the roles with which they were associated. Given the connections between the actors and their traditional repertoire, the shaky nature of the theater's finances, and the precarious nature of the profession as a whole, asking the actors to gamble on new and untested roles was not a small request.

Lessing and Löwen were also calling for changes that significantly reduced the ability of the actor to control his or her conditions of employment. Both write that actors' lives would be improved through their greater financial security as members of a permanent commercial theater. Replacing the itinerant companies with permanent companies, Lessing and Löwen each argued, would allow German literature to develop while freeing actors from the stresses of money-making; actors could then approach acting as an art rather than as a business, improving their performances and their personal conduct. In return, however, actors would have to cede control over repertoire and other production matters to a business manager.[22] One can understand how actors accustomed to artistic autonomy might wish to maintain control over decisions regarding plays, performances, and casting, which explains in part their refusal to submit to Löwen's management and their resistance to the new repertoire promised by his mission statements. One month after the new theater's opening, Lessing confided his uneasiness with the venture to his brother Karl, writing that no one was certain who was in charge ("Brief an Karl Lessing" 467). The disconnect between the theater's promotional program and its company created difficulties for Lessing as well as Löwen, leading to the first significant alteration to the *Hamburg Dramaturgy*'s aims. After the journal's 25th entry, Lessing ceases to write performance reviews, thus abandoning his stated intention to assess the work of the actors for the benefit of spectator and actor alike.[23]

Although Lessing stopped reviewing performances, he continued his attempts to shape audience tastes by shifting his emphasis to literary analysis and dramatic theory. Indeed, the question of taste informs the *Hamburg Dramaturgy* as a whole. Regardless of the changes that occurred in its form and function, Lessing's journal continually returns to interconnected questions of aesthetic, national, and cultural tastes in order to articulate how and why particular texts or performances appeal to German tastes, as opposed to those of other lands, most notably England and France. Although Lessing specifically addresses the citizens of Hamburg in his opening notice, the majority of the essays in *Hamburg Dramaturgy* speak in fact to a more general audience of German readers and spectators, and the public Lessing addresses becomes increasingly more theoretical as he disengages with the actual theatrical activities occurring on the stage of the struggling Hamburg National Theater.

Lessing's "erratic and tenuous" relationship with the Hamburg National Theater is evidenced by the fact that the essays of the *Hamburg Dramaturgy* address only the first 14 weeks that the theater was open, from 22 April until 28 July 1767, covering less than a third of the plays performed by the company; the dates Lessing attaches to individual essays are often specious, as he began publishing his essays in batches due to their being pirated by disreputable publishers.[24] Lessing abandoned his promise to provide a critical register of all the plays performed partly because of his customary issues with deadlines and partly because the theater did not follow its originally proposed program. The actual repertoire of the Hamburg National Theater was hardly cutting-edge or experimental. Each evening's tragedy or comedy (usually five acts) was followed either by a shorter dramatic piece (a farce or one-act comedy) or by non-dramatic fare such as musical entertainments, pantomimes, or ballets. This lineup of mixed attractions was the norm for theater companies in the German lands (as it was in England and across Europe), and the Hamburg National Theater did not skimp on popular non-literary material, which included ballets, harlequinades (originally banned by Löwen), and even Italian intermezzi. None of these entertainments are given a single mention in the *Hamburg Dramaturgy*.

If these non-literary entertainments reveal that commercial necessities impacted the mission of the Hamburg National Theater, so too do the plays chosen for production, which represent a fairly standard breakdown for German theater companies of the day. French works dominated the Hamburg stage, as they did elsewhere in Germany. Of the 502 performances given by the Hamburg National Theater, fully 308 were of 70 individual French plays. The German works meant to form the lynchpin of the enterprise were significantly underrepresented (with 176 performances of 40 German plays, many of which were based on French plays or written in the French style).[25] Practically the entire repertoire was made up of tried and true works from Ackermann's company or those of others, with very few premieres. The repertoire was impacted not only by audience tastes but also by the costume and properties inventory that came with the leased theater; these made it expedient to stage lavish French hits such as Pierre Corneille's *Rodogune*.[26] The actors also wanted to repeat roles for which they were known, which placed an emphasis on known and popular French and German works rather than on new German plays.[27]

These statistics might be disheartening for those wishing to see the Hamburg National Theater as a pioneering enterprise, but, as a commercial endeavor, the theater had to answer to its material operating circumstances. And, in comparison to other companies, the number of German plays it presented is actually fairly healthy. Lessing has many complaints in the *Hamburg Dramaturgy*, but he does not condemn the company's repertoire *per se*, although his criticism of popular works can be biting. In the final essay of the *Hamburg Dramaturgy*, he directs his ire at the audience who failed to support the theater, rather than at the theater itself, unlike those who have since blamed the theater for failing to measure up to Lessing's ideals. Practically speaking, it is hard to see how the theater could have followed the program outlined by Löwen. The most famous German theatrical experiments in the eighteenth and nineteenth centuries, those of Weimar (1791–1817) and Meiningen (1866–90), were backed by court sponsorship; the Hamburg National Theater had none of the resources available to Goethe or the Duke of Saxe-Meiningen. One wonders what might have come of the Hamburg enterprise had its audiences actually clamored for a new German theater.

"For a long time [the theatrical muse] has sought a stage in vain / In Hamburg she found protection: here is her Athens!" So proclaimed the Hamburg National Theater's opening night prologue, describing theater as an art that awakens its audience "to pity, compassion, and generosity" ("Essay 6" 53). Is not, it asked, this "model of decorum that teaches every virtue . . . worth your favor and your patronage?" ("Essay 6" 52). Swelling with optimism and pride, the prologue offers the citizens of Hamburg the opportunity to serve as a model for other German lands by supporting a civilized and civilizing theater that could equal that of classical Athens and rival that of modern France and England. Unfortunately, Hamburg's citizens did not accept the challenge. Or rather, not all of them did: there were multiple audiences in Hamburg, and the theater could not appeal to all of them simultaneously. Some of the theater-going public was interested in literary drama, but a greater majority merely desired popular entertainment. Additionally, aficionados of dramatic literature were often highly suspicious of the theater itself – some who read plays never actually entered a playhouse.[28] And, in fact, as Lessing's essays became less connected to actual performances at the Hamburg National Theater, they were increasingly addressed less to spectators in the Hamburg theater and more to readers interested in discussions about the form and function of dramatic literature.

As quickly as the Hamburg National Theater left behind the ideological program upon which it was founded, the *Hamburg Dramaturgy* relinquished its original purposes. The focus of the *Hamburg Dramaturgy* became that for which it is known, the analysis of playwriting and dramatic theory. Yet Lessing never fully abandoned his original preoccupations. The subject of "German taste" remained critical throughout the remainder of Lessing's essays, so that the *Hamburg Dramaturgy* continued to serve as an instrument of cultural reform, even if that reform became a long-term rather than an immediate prospect. Moreover, Lessing's thinking about performance and reception informed how that cultural reform might be achieved, by insisting that theater can generate a communal experience. The *Hamburg Dramaturgy*, for all its imperfections and idiosyncrasies, sought to do the same, working to foster communal identity and serving as an agent of change, in the service of a German theater and culture that Lessing could envision – even if it remained, at that moment, out of reach.

Notes

1 In that month the company had performed over a dozen other plays, with their accompanying afterpieces or ballets.

2 That is, Lessing purports to discuss the 52nd evening, claiming that it featured *Die Brüder* [*The Brothers*] (1763) by Karl Franz Romanus. The mainpiece of the 52nd evening was in fact Voltaire's *Nanine* (1749).

3 The *Beyträge* was co-founded and co-edited by Christlob Mylius, a relation of Lessing's.

4 The misleading term "national theater" had a different implication in eighteenth-century Hamburg – the arbitrary designation was used to indicate a theater that offered German-language plays rather than housing foreign touring companies; see Carlson, *The German Stage in the Nineteenth Century* 2.

5 Löwen presented his rationale for the theater's founding and its goals in his "Vorläufige Nachricht" ["Preliminary Announcement"]. Lessing's statement that the new theater's aims "have been received with approval both here and abroad by the more refined public" should be seen as an appeal to the Hamburg citizenry – rather than as an accurate description of the situation on the ground; see Lessing, "Notice" 35.

6 Neuber, one of the earliest actress-managers, cofounded her company with her husband.

7 *Der junge Gelehrte* [*The Young Scholar*] (1748).

8 Heinrich Gottfried Koch and Karl Gottlieb Döbbelin, both Neuber protégées, brought their companies to Hamburg between 1741 and 1763.

9 Ackermann and his wife, Sophie Charlotte Schröder, were progenitors of an acting dynasty and promoted the developing trend toward greater stage realism. After the Hamburg National Theater's collapse, Ackermann regained control and ran the company with his stepson, the great actor Friedrich Ludwig Schröder.

10 Although initially influential, Gottsched was challenged in the 1740s by Swiss scholars Johann Jakob Bodmer and Johann Jakob Breitinger. Lessing took exception to both camps.

11 The German language was not served well by attempts to shoehorn it into Alexandrine verse.

12 Luise V. A. Gottsched (née Kulmus), a prolific translator as well as an author, has been overshadowed by her husband, J. C. Gottsched, despite her immense contribution to his projects; this oversight has begun to be rectified in current scholarship. See, for example, Ball, et al., *Diskurse der Aufklärung*; Kord, *Little Detours,* and Brown, *Luise Gottsched the Translator.*

13 See also Johann Christian Krüger and Hinrich Borkenstein. Female playwrights and actress-managers such as Karoline Neuber, Sophie Hensel, and Sophie Charlotte Ackermann also wrote for the stage; see Goodman, *Amazons and Apprentices*; Dupree, *The Mask and the Quill*; and Becker-Cantarino, *Der lange Weg zur Mündigkeit.*

14 For Löwen's description of hindrances to and solutions for the development of the German theater, see his "Geschichte des deutschen Theaters" ["History of the German Theater"] and "Vorläufige Nachricht" ["Preliminary Announcement"].

15 The Gallomania affecting the German lands was Lessing's bête noire. Most German aristocrats were devotees of French arts, literature, and, mores, and their tastes were imitated by the up-and-coming middle classes.

16 Hamburg did not always support cultural enterprises, and scholars from various disciplines have begun to reconsider its reputation as a unique site of political and cultural autonomy; see, for example, articles by Hohendahl, Lindemann, and McCarthy in Hohendahl, *Patriotism, Cosmopolitanism, and National Culture.*

17 The founders of the theater were outsiders, which affected their relationship with the Hamburg Senate; see McCarthy, "Lessing and the Project of a National Theater in Hamburg" 83–4.

18 Hensel and Seyler married in 1772; after the demise of the Hamburg National Theater, Seyler founded his own company.

19 Lessing was opposed to absolutism in all forms, but was also freshly smarting from a recent and painful snub by Frederick the Great, who had denied him the post of librarian/archivist at the Royal Library in Berlin, even though he was the most qualified candidate; see J. G. Robertson 117, and Nisbet 330.

20 Reprinted in full in Lessing's sixth essay.

21 Ekhof, the "father of German acting," remains one of the most important actors of the German stage; he promoted German-language and bourgeois dramas (including Lessing's), new acting methods, and a greater social acceptance of the acting profession. See Piens, *Conrad Ekhof und die erste deutsche Theater-Akademie.*

22 See Löwen, "Geschichte des deutschen Theaters" 63, and "Vorläufige Nachricht" 908.

23 Lessing left no official explanation; scholars have assumed that pressure from Hensel and the other actors led Lessing to abandon performance reviews. For Lessing's original goals, see his opening "Notice."

24 The phrase is Nisbet's. On the piracy that plagued the book industry in general and Lessing in particular, see Reemtsma 22–33 and Nisbet 379–82.

25 Other nations in the repertoire included England (17 performances of four plays), Italy (20 performances of five plays), and a single performance of one Dutch play.

26 For a list of all plays produced by the Hamburg National Theater, see J. G. Robertson 44–7.

27 "Until the performance of [Lessing's] *Minna von Barnhelm* some five months after the 'Enterprise' was inaugurated," J. G. Robertson writes, "it is difficult to point to a single play the

choice of which was due to a desire to serve literature" (41). Actors had practical reasons for repeating roles: the actress Karoline Schulze-Kummerfeld, for example, claimed in her memoirs that in 1783 she appeared on stage 120 times in 63 roles, 39 of which were newly learned (Schulze-Kummerfeld, *Lebenserinnerungen* 2: 121).

28 For more on Lessing's audience, see Nisbet 372.

Works cited

Ball, Gabriele, Helga Brandes, and Katherine R. Goodman. *Diskurse der Aufklärung: Luise Adelgunde Victorie und Johann Christoph Gottsched.* Wiesbaden: Harrassowitz, 2006. Print.

Becker-Cantarino, Barbara. *Der lange Weg zur Mündigkeit: Frauen und Literatur in Deutschland von 1500 bis 1800.* Munich: Deutscher Taschenbuch Verlag, 1989. Print.

Brown, Hilary. *Luise Gottsched the Translator.* Rochester, NY: Camden House, 2012. Print.

Carlson, Marvin. *The German Stage in the Nineteenth Century.* Metuchen, NJ: Scarecrow Press, 1972. Print.

Daunicht, Richard, ed. *Lessing im Gespräch: Berichte und Urteile von Freunden und Zeitgenossen.* Munich: W. Fink, 1971. Print.

Dupree, Mary Helen. *The Mask and the Quill: Actress-Writers in Germany from Enlightenment to Romanticism.* Lewisburg, PA: Bucknell University Press, 2011. Print.

Frederick II (King of Prussia). "Des Moeurs, Des Coutumes, de L'Industrie, des Progrès de L'Esprit Humain dans les Arts et dans les Sciences." 1750. In *Oeuvres de Frédéric le Grand.* Ed. J .D. E. Preuss. Vol. 1. Berlin: Rodolphe Decker, 1846. Print.

Goodman, Katherine. *Amazons and Apprentices: Women and the German Parnassus in the Early Enlightenment.* Rochester, NY: Camden House, 1999. Print.

Hohendahl, Peter Uwe. *Patriotism, Cosmopolitanism, and National Culture: Public Culture in Hamburg, 1700–1933.* New York: Rodopi, 2003. Print.

Lessing, Gotthold Ephraim. "Brief an Karl Lessing." 22 May 1767. Letter 373. In *Werke und Briefe in zwölf Bänden.* Ed. Wilfried Barner with Klaus Bohnen, et al. 12 vols. Frankfurt-am-Main: Deutscher Klassiker Verlag, 1985–2003. 11/1: 466–8. Print.

Lindemann, Mary. "Fundamental Values: Political Culture in Eighteenth-Century Hamburg." In *Patriotism, Cosmopolitanism, and National Culture.* Ed. Peter Uwe Hohendahl. New York: Rodopi, 2003. 17–32. Print.

Löwen, Johann Friedrich. "Geschichte des deutschen Theaters." In *Johann Friedrich Löwens Schriften.* Vol. 4. Hamburg: Bock, 1766. 3–66. Print.

———. "Vorläufige Nachricht von der auf Ostern 1767 vorzunehmenden Veränderung des Hamburgischen Theaters." 1766. In Lessing, G. E. *Werke und Briefe in zwölf Bänden.* Ed. Wilfried Barner with Klaus Bohnen, et al. 12 vols. Frankfurt-am-Main: Deutscher Klassiker Verlag, 1985–2003. 6: 906–11. Print.

McCarthy, John. "Lessing and the Project of a National Theater in Hamburg." In *Patriotism, Cosmopolitanism, and National Culture.* Ed. Peter Uwe Hohendahl. New York: Rodopi, 2003. 71–90. Print.

Nisbet, Hugh Barr. *Gotthold Ephraim Lessing: His Life, Works, and Thought.* Oxford: Oxford University Press, 2013. Print.

Oehlke, Waldemar. *Lessing und seine Zeit.* Vol. 2. Munich: C. H. Beck'sche Verlagsbuchhandlug, 1929. Print.

Piens, Gerhard. *Conrad Ekhof und die erste deutsche Theater-Akademie.* Heidenau: Mitteldeutsche Kunstanstalt, 1956. Print.

Reemtsma, Jan Philipp. *Lessing in Hamburg.* Munich: Beck, 2007. Print.

Robertson, John George. *Lessing's Dramatic Theory.* New York: Benjamin Blom, 1936. Cambridge: Cambridge University Press, 1965. Print.

Schulze-Kummerfeld, Karoline. *Lebenserinnerungen der Komödiantin Karoline Schulze-Kummerfeld.* Ed. Emil Benezé. 2 vols. Berlin: Selbstverlag der Gesellschaft für Theatergeschichte, 1915. Print.

2

"WE HAVE ACTORS, BUT NO ART OF ACTING"

Performance theory and theatrical emotion in the *Hamburg Dramaturgy*[1]

Natalya Baldyga

Most Anglophone readers know Gotthold Ephraim Lessing (1729–81) for his dramatic theory and his major plays, *Miss Sara Sampson* (1755), *Minna von Barnhelm* (1767), *Emilia Galotti* (1772), and *Nathan the Wise* (1779). Fewer, however, are familiar with his acting theory and his long association with actors, an association that began in his college years and which so disturbed Lessing's father that the respectable pastor lured the wayward student home by falsely claiming that Lessing's mother was ill (Nisbet 39).[2] During his university days, Lessing translated plays for the troupe of Karoline Neuber (1697–1760) and socialized with the company's actors; over time he would continue to accrue significant firsthand knowledge of theatrical performance, not only through his frequent theater going but also through the coaching of his own plays. This familiarity with actors and acting informed not only Lessing's performance theory, but his dramatic theory as well, including that which one finds in the *Hamburg Dramaturgy*.

In Anglophone studies of Lessing's journal, however, one rarely sees Lessing's dramatic theory placed in conversation with his acting theory, reception theory, or performance reviews.[3] Due to the short and contentious life of the Hamburg National Theater, historical narratives more often focus on Lessing's strained relations with the performers in the Hamburg acting company. Such a focus, however, neglects the fact that Lessing's acting theory supports his wider ideas about how theater might function as a force for social change. Although Lessing ceased to review the performances at the Hamburg National Theater after his 25th essay, the *Hamburg Dramaturgy* remains inflected by his career-long interest in the acting process, and this interest is a critical component of Lessing's agenda for theatrical and cultural reform. To construct his unique understanding of performance and reception, Lessing borrows from French and English contemporaries, as well as the German philosopher Moses Mendelssohn (1729–86). Negotiating larger eighteenth-century international debates about physiology and performance, Lessing argues that theatrical emotion can be controlled and adjusted through a mechanistic regulation of the actor's body.

Lessing's interest in the technique of acting was somewhat unusual for his time. Most, if not all, critical discourse on the subject of acting in the eighteenth-century German lands focused less on the style and methods of German acting than on the morally questionable status of actors; theater reformers themselves, including Karoline Neuber and Johann Friedrich Löwen (1727–71), sought to make unimpeachable moral behavior a condition of employment for company members. Konrad Ekhof (1720–78), for example, included in his "Grammatik der Schauspielkunst" ["Rules for Acting"] (1753) admonitions to actors regarding their comportment.[4] This critical emphasis on actors' morals, rather than on their technique, when coupled with the unstable position of the theater in Germany, resulted in a dearth of serious German discourse on acting. Whereas England and France had produced important works of acting theory in both the seventeenth and eighteenth centuries, in the German lands, where the theater was still largely viewed as a disreputable pastime, the goals and methods of acting were for the most part left unexplored until the middle of the century.

Lessing's more accepting view of the acting profession was connected to his belief in the theater's potential as a civilizing force. In the preface to his journal *Beyträge zur Historie und Aufnahme des Theaters* [*Contributions to the History and Development of the Theater*] (1750), Lessing suggests that performance is a necessary component of dramatic poetry, with its own rules of "corporeal eloquence" (*Beredsamkeit des Körpers*); these can benefit not only actors, he suggests, but all those whose occupations require physical eloquence – including ministers (*Beyträge* 730). Ultimately, the moral conduct of individual actors was of less interest to Lessing than the theater's larger potential to serve as a "school of the moral world," within which the actor could serve as a catalyst for feeling and, in particular, as a catalyst for the spectator's compassion, which for Lessing was at the heart of morality and ethical human behavior ("Essay 2" 40). For Lessing, it is impossible to think about theatrical reform and the attendant goal of creating a respectable, literary German theater without addressing the art of theatrical performance.

Hence Lessing's need to wrestle with what constitutes good acting. Lessing notes in his opening notice to the *Hamburg Dramaturgy* that the art of the actor is always difficult to evaluate, due to its transitory and ephemeral nature ("Notice" 36–7). Moreover, since, for most of the eighteenth century, German acting, like German dramatic literature, answered to no particular system, critics in the German lands faced additional challenges. Whereas Lessing's contemporaries in England or France could refer to rules of performance that had grown up alongside specific dramatic traditions, Lessing had no German equivalent to which he could refer. Actors learned their craft informally, essentially training themselves while on the job. "We have actors," Lessing laments in the *Hamburg Dramaturgy*, "but no art of acting" ("Essays 101–104" 306). As long as actors lack a formalized system of acting, Lessing writes, they will continue to rely on their established lines of business, resulting in hit-or-miss performances that may or may not move the audience emotionally.

Lessing's concerns regarding the affective qualities of the theater and the extent to which an actor is responsible for an audience's emotional experience were hardly new. Theater practitioners and theorists have wrangled over the nature and function of theatrical emotion for centuries. A central question of these debates has always been whether an actor must experience emotion him- or herself in order to stimulate the emotions of the audience. In other words, are actors' performances more effective if they actually feel the emotion they are representing for the audience? This question took on a particular importance in eighteenth-century Europe. New models of playwriting (such as bourgeois drama, sentimental comedy, and domestic tragedy) were becoming increasingly popular. Playwrights such as Lessing, Denis Diderot (1713–84), and George Lillo (1691/93–1739) were introducing middle-class characters as objects for audience sympathy and exploring a greater illusionism than their predecessors. These new dramatic forms, coupled with influential discourses of sentimental and natural philosophy, required that critics rethink the nature of theatrical performance and audience reception vis-à-vis the "sensible qualities" of the actor.[5]

As Lessing points out in the *Hamburg Dramaturgy*, however, the sensible qualities of an actor are notoriously difficult to identify ("Essay 3" 43–5).[6] How can we be *certain* as to the presence of feeling on the part of the actor? After all, sensibility is elusive and hard to define. An actor, Lessing explains,

> can have truly abundant feeling, and at the same time appear to have none. Among an actor's abilities, feeling is undoubtedly always the most questionable. It can exist where one does not perceive it; and one can believe that one sees it where it does not exist.
>
> ("Essay 3" 43)

The crux of the trouble, Lessing decides, is that "feeling is something interior, which we can only judge by its outward manifestations" ("Essay 3" 43). This theatrical conundrum reflects an Enlightenment preoccupation with human character and its exterior signs. Social reform efforts privileged emotional transparency, and thus the dissimulation of emotion remained a troublesome topic for proponents of the theater who suggested it could serve as an instrument of moral reform. Larger questions regarding theater's ability to serve as a means of moral and social reform therefore drive Lessing's concern regarding the expression and reception of emotion in performance.

Concurrent with the rise of sentimental philosophy, eighteenth-century proponents of the theater argued that its ability to stir the emotions of the audience proved that it could function as a force for social good, while its opponents worried about the potentially "infectious nature" of emotions aroused during a performance.[7] According to the theater's supporters, the better the actor's performance, the greater the salutary effects of the theater on the audience members. If, however, as Lessing suggests in Essay 3 of the *Hamburg Dramaturgy*, the ability of the actor to feel and to accurately represent the passions remains questionable, and if an actor's affective performance is prone to erroneous readings, how then might one continue to support the idea of a sentimental, morally useful theater? Lessing's solution is to propose an intriguing synthesis of eighteenth-century theories of performance, suggesting that the affective experience of the actor and audience members can be systematically adjustable. This approach, both mechanical and sentimental in nature, allows for a shared emotional experience in the theater that is capable of regulation, thus permitting the theater to serve as a healthy mechanism for moral humanitarian advancement. What distinguishes Lessing from his contemporaries is the manner in which his model of acting and reception draws from opposing theoretical camps without forming a clear allegiance to either.

In the *Hamburg Dramaturgy*, Lessing demonstrates that competing eighteenth-century approaches to stage acting fail to fully address the illusive nature of the actor's sensibility within a theater that calls for the perfect expression and reception of emotional signs. Throughout the century, acting theorists would suggest different means through which such a difficulty might be overcome, some privileging the imitation of models and others the actor's imagination.[8] Acting theorists from these two opposing camps were united in some regards, complicating what might otherwise be seen as a strict dichotomy, but their fundamental disagreement centered on whether acting was something that should be approached externally or internally. In the *Hamburg Dramaturgy* and other writings, Lessing directly and indirectly applies theories from both camps to his writing about the acting process.[9]

In Essays 3–5, for example, in which he reviews performances by leading actors Konrad Ekhof and Sophie Hensel (1738–89), Lessing reveals his long-held interest in the externals of an actor's performance (gesture and the actor's delivery), to which he returns repeatedly over the course of his career.[10] Both Lessing's early thoughts about acting and his writing about gesture in the *Hamburg Dramaturgy* draw on the theoretical works of art critics and "externalist" acting theorists, notably those of Antoine-François (Francesco) Riccoboni (1707–72), William Hogarth (1697–1764), and Charles Le Brun (1619–90).[11] Writers who focused on the external figure of the actor believed that an affective theatrical experience could be generated best by the actor's physical replication of universal signs of emotion, through which both the body and face could provide a transparent and universal register of authentic emotion. Their theories promoted an acting method predicated on the systematic study and imitation of such signs, which the externalists saw as being scientifically determinable.[12] Externalists therefore codified physical expression and created a register of "natural" universal emotional expression that could be studied and copied, and, theoretically, allow an audience to correctly read the emotional signs performed by actors.[13] The codification of emotion supported the argument that an authentic signification of the passions was possible and addressed concerns such as Lessing's about a lack of correspondence between internal feeling and its external expression.[14] According to externalist theory, regardless of what an actor actually feels, if he or she accurately performs these universalized expressions of emotion, the audience will share "the same idea at first sight" (Riccoboni 36).

Despite his long-standing attention to gesture and the external expression of emotion, however, Lessing's acting theory also relies on the actor's own experience of emotion and is indebted to the work of the "internalists," that is, those who favored the actor's imagination over the imitation of physical signs. Although both internalist and

externalist acting theorists of the eighteenth century drew on a mechanistic understanding of the body derived from Descartes and those who followed him, those
favoring an internalist approach dismissed what they perceived as an overly mechanical approach to acting. "What the actor himself does not feel," wrote John Hill
(1714–75) in 1755,

> he will never make the audience feel, tho' he copy ever so perfectly the best
> player who every pronounced a sentence. We see it is a mechanical exhibi-
> tion in which nature has no part; and feeling nothing, we know he feels
> nothing.
>
> (92)

Because they believed that imitative methods diminished the affective power of acting,
internalists argued against what they saw as a misguided focus on physical externals
and sought instead a means by which the actor's emotion might best be internally
generated, asserting that audiences would respond most strongly to spontaneous and
individualized emotive expression rather than to the imitation of universal signs.
Internalists such as Pierre Rémond de Sainte-Albine (1699–1778) argued that the
actor needed to stimulate his or her own emotions in order to affect an audience.
The key for these theorists was the actor's imagination, which, they suggested, could
trigger an appropriate internal and authentic emotional experience if the actor was
capable of sympathizing with his or her character and that character's circumstances.[15]

In his own writing about affective performance, Lessing relies heavily on the work
of the internalists, although not without reservations. Sainte-Albine, for example, is
essential to both Lessing's early acting theory and discussions of performance in the
Hamburg Dramaturgy. Analyses of specific performances by the Hamburg actors often
echo Sainte-Albine, as does Lessing's emphasis on an actor's need for plasticity. Despite
his reliance on the French theorist, however, Lessing ultimately concludes that, "the
whole principle of [Sainte-Albine] should be reversed" ("Auszug aus dem Schauspieler" 310). The problem, Lessing believes, is that theatrical performance requires
more than just an individualized and everyday expression of emotion. In the theater,
Lessing explains, "one wants to see sentiments and passions expressed in the most
perfect way" ("Auszug aus dem Schauspieler" 310). The need for a perfect expression
of the passions leads Lessing to his own theoretical approach to the acting process,
which integrates externalist and internalist ideas into a holistic model of affective performance – one in which the imitation of natural signs triggers an involuntary experience of authentic emotion for both the audience and the actors themselves. Lessing's
theory is driven in part by his recognition that German actors possess unequal talent
and training. He proposes that it is possible to circumvent the weaknesses of individual actors through the imitation of a perfect model, ensuring a natural representation
and regulated experience of the passions.

Ultimately, "corporeal eloquence" is the key that provides a solution to the troublesome question of the actor's emotion. Lessing suggests that an outward manipula-
tion of the actor's body can effect internal changes, so that the external expression of
a specific emotion generates an authentic physiological experience of that emotion

within the body of the actor. Instead of relying on the actor's soul for a perfect external expression of the passions, Lessing proposes that the physical markers of emotion, when embodied through performance, can generate the appropriate passion within the soul of the actor. The benefit of this "outside – in" approach is that focusing on the external performance of universal and natural signs of emotion allows one to circumvent differing aptitudes for empathy or imagination. So long as one has an appropriate model available for imitation, actors of lesser abilities can produce an authentic affective performance – they need only copy the physical expressions of a more gifted actor such as a Garrick or an Ekhof ("Essay 3" 43–4).[16] Thus, in Essay 3, Lessing tells his reader that "modifications of the soul that bring about certain changes in the body can in return be produced by those changes to the body" (43). This mechanically generated emotion may not be as powerful as that which is produced naturally by the imagination of the mind/soul but will be nonetheless "powerful enough in the moment of performance to bring about some of the involuntary changes in the body from whose presence alone we believe we can dependably infer a person's inner feelings" ("Essay 3" 43). These signs, although mechanically induced, are, according to Lessing, natural, universal, and authentic, allowing them to be immediately comprehended by the audience.

This mechanical production of authentic feeling within the actor is what distinguishes Lessing's theory from that of his contemporaries and informs his broader thinking about theatrical performance, its reception, and its possible social benefits. Unlike Diderot in his *Paradoxe*, Lessing does not insist that the actor remain reflective and insensible. Neither does he intend that the actor function as a mere copyist or mechanical automaton. Rather, by relying on a type of "sensate cognition," Lessing suggests that the body has its own form of intelligence, which is corporeal rather than rational. This sensate cognition resides in the bodies of both actor and spectator; both therefore respond to what Lessing believes to be natural and universal signs of emotion, which is why his essays in the *Hamburg Dramaturgy* so frequently return to (and address so specifically) the topic of gesture or other externals of performance.[17] Passions may be universal, but an actor's individualized experience of them must be coordinated with a natural and *idealized* expression of the passion's physical signs if his or her performance is to reach its highest affective potential. In the theater, nature must be aided by scientific study in order to communicate clearly to an audience. Paradoxically, an actor's attention to physical performance can ensure that his expression of a passion is "more natural" than his natural experience of it. The determination of a correct model, one that can be reproduced by an actor, whether "feeling" or "unfeeling," allows for a performance that is both natural and capable of external regulation. Because the audience cannot help but respond to natural signs, the regulation of an actor's emotion concomitantly allows for the regulation of the audience's emotion.

Lessing's model of acting, which relies on a shared affective experience between actor and audience, challenges antitheatrical views that emotional stimulation in the theater could be harmful to the spectator, while supporting sentimental approaches to the theater that argued for the beneficial social effects of compassion. Lessing's "aesthetics of compassion" (*Mitleidsästhetik*; also referred to as his *Mitleidsdramaturgie*), which also underlies much of his dramatic theory in the *Hamburg Dramaturgy*, combines "corporeal eloquence" with compassion to suggest that theatrical performance creates a "sympathetic vibration" between the organisms of actor and spectator rather than creating a situation in which actors impose emotion upon the audience. Developed through his long-running epistolary dialogue with the philosopher Moses Mendelssohn and the bookseller and entrepreneur Christoph Friedrich Nicolai (1733–1811), Lessing's *Mitleidsästhetik* refutes the "infectious" model of acting upheld by detractors of the theater, who argued that emotion in the theater was contagious and subjected audiences to excessive emotional stimulation.[18] In Lessing's model, the bodies of actor and spectator are contained and impermeable, so that the relationship between them is one of resonance rather than imposition and infection.[19]

Lessing explains that regardless of the emotions represented onstage, the only "primary affect" is compassion (*Mitleid*), which is internally originated through the audience member's sympathetic reaction to a performance rather than being transmitted from performer to spectator.[20] "This affect (compassion)," Lessing explains, "is not felt by the playing persons . . . rather it arises in us originally from the effect of the objects on us; it is not a communicated secondary affect" ("Brief an Moses Mendelssohn" 714). Lessing suggests that this relationship is analogous to the sympathetic vibration between two strings in a single musical instrument and that this "string metaphor" (*Saitenmetapher*) illustrates how an actor's experience of the passions stimulates a reaction in the spectator, even though both bodily spaces are separated from each other and remain impermeable. "It is known," he writes, "that when one gives two strings the same tension, and the first is made to sound through a touch, the other will sound with it, without having been touched itself" ("Brief an Moses Mendelssohn" 713). The sensibilities of actor and spectator function like these strings in that their sympathetic resonance causes an emotional reaction distinct from that which triggered it. In Lessing's metaphorical example, the vibration of the first string affects the other only when the two share a particular correspondence through their tuning; the first string does not force the other to sound the same note but rather stimulates the other to sound its *own* note. When extended into the theater and applied to the acting process, the *Saitenmetapher* suggests that an actor, the "first string," is able to stimulate, through the "sounding" of his passion, a sympathetic reaction in the audience's body (the "second string"). Lessing establishes the bodies of actor and performer as discrete sites of emotional experience but nevertheless allows for the actor to have an emotional effect on the spectator.

The ability to stir the emotions of audience members through mechanical methods has important implications for how one views Lessing's larger efforts toward theatrical, social, and cultural reform. Lessing's discussion of actors and their art in the *Hamburg Dramaturgy* serves his attempt to forge a German theater distinct from neo-classicism and popular forms of theatrical entertainments, but it also allows for the development and regulation of "proper feeling" in the audience, not only through the individual stimulation of compassion but also through the shared experience of that compassion. In this model, the theater functions as a form of moral gymnasium because of its ability to stimulate sympathetic emotion. "*Der mitleidigste Mensch ist der beste Mensch,*" Lessing famously insisted – "The man of empathy is the most perfect man" ("Brief an Nicolai" 671).[21] Theatrical performance, therefore, by providing a physiological strengthening exercise for humankind's moral muscle, increases the potential for a person of ordinary human feeling to become a better human being and citizen. Human beings may have different levels of judgment, writes Lessing, but regardless of education, natural aptitude, or other factors, all human beings by definition have sensibility. Love for our fellow human beings is always present, it "smolders unceasingly, hiding itself under the ashes of other, stronger feelings, awaiting only a favorable gust of misfortune and pain and ruin to fan it into a flame of compassion" ("Essay 76" 243). As an art form centered on the stimulation of empathy, theatrical performance was central to the eighteenth-century civilizing process of which Lessing was a part; Lessing's writing about acting suggests that the systematization and regulation of emotion can promote a new social community founded on compassion. Controlling the actor's performance of emotion becomes the first step in that process.

Notes

1 "Wir haben Schauspieler, aber keine Schauspielkunst" ("Essays 101–104" 306). This chapter is excerpted from a longer article, "Corporeal Eloquence and Sensate Cognition: G. E. Lessing, Acting Theory, and Properly Feeling Bodies in Eighteenth-Century Germany," which provides a more detailed explanation of Lessing's *Mitleidsästhetik* (aesthetics of sympathy), as well as a greater exploration of the eighteenth-century acting theorists from whom Lessing draws; see Baldyga, "Corporeal Eloquence and Sensate Cognition."

2 Nisbet's biography is the definitive source for details of Lessing's life and works.

3 For a list of those conducting excellent studies (both German and Anglophone) in this area, see Baldyga 181.

4 A theorist and practitioner, Ekhof, who is referred to as the "father of German acting," sought for a systematic approach to acting and to better the status of the acting profession. In 1753, while in Schwerin, Ekhof established a short-lived acting "academy" made up of members of Schönemann's troupe. For 13 months, he and his colleagues met every two weeks to consider practical matters as well as the nature of the acting process.

5 Within an eighteenth-century context, the sentimental theater was that which engaged the human faculties of "sensibility" (generally speaking, this implies one's capacity to feel emotion, and especially compassion) and "sentiments" (impressions of emotion examined through reason) as a means of moral improvement.

6 Lessing is discussing Konrad Ekhof's performance in Johann Friedrich von Cronegk's *Olint und Sophronia* (1764).

7 The dangers of theatrical emotion, according to antitheatricalists dating back to Plato, include the potential overstimulation of spectators' emotions and the possibility that spectators could be "infected" by onstage emotions, arguments that Jean-Jacques Rousseau employs in his *Lettre a M. d'Alembert sur les spectacles* [*Letter to D'Alembert on the Theatre*] (1758).

8 Some, such as Diderot, would reverse their original positions; Lessing would not have read his *Paradoxe sur le comédien* (written 1773–7 and published posthumously in 1830), which privileges the "unfeeling actor" of "equal aptitude."

9 Lessing drew on an extensive list of sources in his writing about performance and reception; in addition to works noted in this essay, Lessing's sources included the seminal *Pratique du théâtre* [*The Whole Art of the Stage*] (1657) by François Hédelin, the Abbé d'Aubignac, and Diderot's *Lettre sur les sourds et muets* [*Letter on the Deaf and Dumb*] (1751), as well as his plays *Le Fils naturel* [*The Natural Son*] (1757) and *Le Père de Famille* [*The Father of the Family*] (1758), which Lessing translated, along with their accompanying *Entretiens sur Le Fils Naturel* [*Conversations on the Natural Son*] and *Discours sur la poésie dramatique* [*Discourse on Dramatic Poetry*].

10 Lessing's preoccupation with gestural language and its effects can be traced back to early uncompleted projects: "Abhandlung von den Pantomimen der Alten" ["A Treatise on the

Pantomime of the Ancients"] (dated 1749–50) and "Der Schauspieler: Ein Werk worinne die Grundsätze der ganzen körperlichen Beredsamkeit entwickelt werden" ["The Actor: A Work Wherein the Basic Principles of All Physical Eloquence Will Be Developed"] (dated 1750–54).

11 François Riccoboni's seminal treatise on acting, *L'Art du théâtre* [*The Art of Theatre*] (1750), issued one of the first and most influential challenges to those who claimed that actors needed to experience emotion onstage.

12 "Universality" was the lynchpin of much eighteenth-century dramatic theory.

13 Lessing argues that actors can learn genuine and unaffected movement through the methodological consideration and application of "scientific" studies of gesture. Lessing also longs for the days of ancient oratory, when actors' gesticulations followed a regularized system in which hand and arm movements had specific meanings; see "Essay 4" 45–6.

14 Acting theorists, and especially externalists, struggled with the idea that the representation of emotion could be feigned, as this undermined the moral mission of the sentimental theater.

15 The acting theory of the internalists, with its emphasis on what we might call imagined circumstances, can sound, to the twenty-first century reader, like contemporary psychological theories of acting. However, although this approach may remind modern readers of Stanislavsky's system, or of Method acting and other approaches attendant on the actor's psychology, eighteenth-century acting debates are rooted in an Enlightenment understanding of physiology. Emotion, when conceived of in terms of "the passions of the soul," is simultaneously psychological, physiological, and metaphysical, according to a model of interactive dualism inherited from the seventeenth century.

16 Ultimately, says Lessing, the actor who feels much but does not appear to be feeling is much less useful to the theater than the actor of "indifference and coldness" who produces the illusion of feeling ("Essay 3" 43).

17 See, for example, Essay 3, in which Lessing describes the proper delivery of moral truisms.

18 Lessing contradicts himself in this (and other) matters; there are shades of "emotional contagion" in his discussion of Hamlet's ghost (see Essay 11).

19 Lessing's thinking about the emotional experience of the spectator is most fully developed in those essays in which he wrestles with Aristotle's concept of *catharsis*, and in particular with the terms *phobos* (fear) and *eleos* (pity). See Essay 32 and Essays 74–78.

20 Parsing Lessing's use of *Mitleid* is not always an easy task, and the word is variously translated as "pity," "sympathy," or "compassion"; see the Translator's Note in [32.6].

21 Lessing italicized this sentence for emphasis.

Works cited

Baldyga, Natalya. "Corporeal Eloquence and Sensate Cognition: G. E. Lessing, Acting Theory, and Properly Feeling Bodies in Eighteenth-Century Germany." *Theatre Survey* 58.2 (2017): 162–85. Print.

Diderot, Denis. *Entretiens sur Le Fils Naturel*. In *Oeuvres de Denis Diderot*. 6 vols. Paris: Desrey & Deterville, 1798. 4: 109–238. Print.

———. *Le Fils Naturel*. In *Oeuvres de Denis Diderot*. 6 vols. Paris: Desrey & Deterville, 1798. 4: 10–108. Print.

———. "De la Poésie Dramatique, à Monsieur Grimm [Discours sur la poésie dramatique]." In *Oeuvres de Théâtre de M. Diderot, Avec un Discours sur la Poésie dramatique*. 2 vols. Paris: chez la Veuve Duchesne, 1771. 2: 229–394. Print.

———. *Lettre sur les sourds et muets*. Paris: [publisher unknown], 1751.

———. *Paradoxe sur le comédien*. Paris: A. Sautelet, 1830.

———. *Le Père de Famille*. In *Oeuvres de Théâtre de M. Diderot, Avec un Discours sur la Poésie Dramatique*. 2 vols. Paris: chez la Veuve Duchesne, 1771. 2: 1–226. Print.

Hédelin, François (Abbé d'Aubignac). *La Pratique du Théâtre*. 1657. Vol. 1. Amsterdam: J. F. Bernard, 1715. Print.

Hill, John. *The Actor: A Treatise on the Art of Playing. Interspersed with Theatrical Anecdotes, Critical Remarks on Plays, and Occasional Observations on Audiences.* 1750. New York: Benjamin Blom, 1971. Print.

Lessing, Gotthold Ephraim. "Abhandlung von den Pantomimen der Alten." 1750. *Werke und Briefe* 1: 711–21. Print.

———. "Auszug aus dem *Schauspieler* des Herrn Remond von Sainte Albine." 1754. *Werke und Briefe* 3: 304–11. Print.

———. *Beyträge zur Historie und Aufnahme des Theaters.* 1750. *Werke und Briefe* 1: 725–950. Print.

———. "Brief an Moses Mendelssohn." 2 February 1757. Letter 115. "Briefwechsel über das Trauerspiel zwischen Lessing, Mendelssohn, und Nicolai." *Werke und Briefe* 3: 711–15. Print.

———. "Brief an Nicolai." 13 November 1756. Letter 103. *Werke und Briefe* 3: 668–73; also 11/1: 116–22. Print.

———. "Der Schauspieler: Ein Werk worinne die Grundsätze der ganzen körperlichen Beredsamkeit entwickelt werden." 1750–1754. *Werke und Briefe* 3: 320–9. Print.

———. *Werke und Briefe in zwölf Bänden.* Ed. Wilfried Barner with Klaus Bohnen, et al. 12 vols. Frankfurt-am-Main: Deutscher Klassiker Verlag, 1985–2003. Print.

Nisbet, Hugh Barr. *Gotthold Ephraim Lessing: His Life, Works, and Thought.* Oxford: Oxford University Press, 2013. Print.

Riccoboni, François (Francesco). *L'art du Théâtre: Suivi d'une Lettre de M. Riccoboni Fils à M*** au Sujet de L'art du Théâtre.* 1750. Geneva: Slatkine Reprints, 1971. Print.

Rousseau, Jean-Jacques. *Lettre à M. d'Alembert sur les spectacles.* 1758. *Oeuvres Complètes de J. J. Rousseau.* Vol. 16. *Sciences, Arts, Et Belles-Lettres.* Vol. 2. Paris: Poinçot, 1791. Print.

3

THE LEGACY OF THE
HAMBURG DRAMATURGY

Michael M. Chemers

> I demand just a voice in this company, where so many who claim one would be more
> silent than fish if they had not learned to parrot what this or that foreigner had said.
> –G. E. Lessing, *Hamburg Dramaturgy* "Essays 101–4" 308

Perspicacious as he was, Lessing could hardly have understood the impact his Hamburg National Theater gazettes would have on the development of theatrical aesthetics over the ensuing 250 years. Read separately, the essays are notable for their erudite
(if scathing) indictment of contemporary German aesthetic culture and their bold
(if ill-timed) assault on French neoclassicism in general and Voltaire in particular.
But when they were collected and published in two volumes in 1769, something
extraordinary emerged – an Enlightened model of critical engagement with theatrical
aesthetics that would prove compelling to centuries of theater artists not limited to
playwrights, actors, and directors. Lessing's "demand" for "a voice in this company"
inaugurated the position of dramaturg in Western theaters.

Many factors contribute to the longevity of the *Hamburg Dramaturgy*'s influence,
but there are three that his readers found particularly engaging. The first is Lessing's
use of Shakespeare to support his claim that French neoclassicism derived from a poor
reading of the *Poetics* of Aristotle. The argument that Shakespeare was a better Aristotelian than Voltaire was shocking, but it represented an aesthetic frontier of the brutal,
bloody, and intercontinental Seven Years' War (1756–63) in which the German states
allied with England against France.[1] Shakespeare had suffered critical ambivalence in
his native land since 1660, when Charles II brought Parisian neoclassicism with him
from his exile, but in 1769 (the same year the *Hamburg Dramaturgy* was published) the
British victory revels included an immense "Shakespeare Jubilee" in London that
ridiculed French culture (and included personal mockery of Voltaire), presented by
David Garrick (Mason 174–5). Shakespeare was reinvented as a national (and nationalist) hero. That same year Jean-François Ducis presented a popular French adaptation

of *Hamlet* at the *Comédie Française*, albeit a neoclassical one without any ghost to speak of (Flatter 5). Insulted and horrified that Shakespearean aesthetics might corrupt French taste, Voltaire waged a literary crusade against Shakespeare that backfired, insofar as it only made him a better target for the emerging international cult of "bardolaters" as well as aesthetic revolutionaries like Lessing (Mason 174–5; Chemers, "Later classicism"). Voltaire waned while Shakespeare waxed, and Lessing waxed with him.

A second impactful trait of the *Hamburg Dramaturgy* is its treatment of serious theater as a tool for engaging in progressive social discourse. Lessing's first major intervention into this kind of criticism appears in *Laocöon* (1766), which deals with painting, sculpture, and poetry, but in the dynamism and dialectical nature of live performance Lessing had already found a medium more conducive to his ideas. In 1756, Lessing wrote to his friend Christoph Friedrich Nicolai:

> the power of tragedy is this: it should broaden *our capacity to feel compassion*.
> [. . .] Anyone who makes us compassionate makes us better and more virtuous, and the tragedy that achieves the former also achieves the latter, or – it does the former in order to do the latter.[2]

The *Hamburg Dramaturgy* contains Lessing's most cogent argument that a theater presented without critical engagement is one that cannot take best advantage of its power to transform individuals (and, by and by, societies) by deepening their capacity for compassion, thus advancing humanistic discourse toward a more just and harmonious society. In pursuit of this goal, the *Hamburg Dramaturgy* advances the notion of a "bourgeois tragedy" uncoupled from the Aristotelian insistence on aristocratic protagonists – in France, Diderot and Marmontel were already busy waging this war (see Essay 6).

The third significant element of the *Hamburg Dramaturgy* that would appeal to later dramatists is Lessing's appreciation for the totality of the theatrical experience. Although predominantly focused on text, the *Hamburg Dramaturgy* provides investigations of acting theory and technique, gesture, the illusion of authenticity on stage, the effect of performers on specific audiences (and, significantly, vice versa), and many other factors. These investigations provide insight on, and likely helped to foster, the naturalistic experiments conducted by the Hamburg National Theater's Konrad Ekhof and others that would contribute to the emergence of a performance style that continues to dominate Western theater 250 years later (Jürs-Munby 19–20). Lessing seeks to engage with the total process of creating theater in order to enrich its dialectical virtues; this notion remains central for modern theater artists.[3] The theory of performance that thereby develops implicitly suggests that the development of a new mode of theatrical culture necessitates an equally original style of staging – he therefore presciently recognizes the extent to which "the medium is the message." The major transformation the *Hamburg Dramaturgy* incited was this: the reimagining of the theater from a site of entertainment to one of edification, philosophical disputation, acculturation, and the promulgation of values (Luckhurst 40).

The impact of the *Hamburg Dramaturgy* in the German states was rapid and spawned imitators. Three prominent and politically allied Enlightenment thinkers

(Otto Heinrich von Gemmingen-Hornberg, Adolph Freiherr von Knigge, and Heinrich Christoph Albrecht) published their own dramaturgies shortly afterwards (respectively the *Mannheimer Dramaturgie* in 1775; the *Dramaturgische Blätter* in 1788; and the *Neue Hamburgische Dramaturgie* in 1791) (Schechter 19; Romanska 2). The *Hamburg Dramaturgy*'s transmission of Shakespeare is generally credited for inciting the German *Sturm und Drang* and the subsequent Romantic movement in drama by directly inspiring the critic Johann Gottfried Herder (1744–1803) and writer Johann Georg Hamann (1730–88) and the aesthetic philosophies of Georg Wilhelm Friedrich Hegel (1770–1831).[4] Friedrich Schiller (1759–1805) echoed Lessing's notions of aesthetics and compassion, his rehabilitation of Shakespeare and reframing of Aristotle, and his insistence on the potential for theater to become "the public mirror of human life" (Beiser 193). Ludwig Tieck (1773–1853) was hired as "dramaturg" at the Dresden Theater in 1824 and explicitly referred to himself by that title in writings throughout his life (Zeydel 258).[5] In 1828, Johann Wolfgang von Goethe (1749–1832) wrote: "Lessing would not allow himself the lofty title of a genius; but his permanent influence bears witness against him" (Oxenford 2: 42). In his 1861 essay "Zukunftsmusik" ["Music of the Future"], Richard Wagner (1813–83) applied Lessing's ideas to music.

By the end of the nineteenth century the *Hamburg Dramaturgy*'s influence had expanded beyond Germany, influencing, for instance, the work of Norwegian playwright Henrik Ibsen (1828–1906) (Johnston 74). In 1895, the British playwright and Ibsen devotee George Bernard Shaw described Lessing as "the most eminent of dramatic critics," who was known "for not only cutting off his victim's heads but holding them up afterwards to show that there were no brains in them" (258). In 1924, the legendary Russian director Konstantin Stanislavski (1863–1938) placed Lessing among the greatest influences in Western drama (166). The twentieth-century American masters wrestled to shape the bourgeois tragedy of the eighteenth century into a modern "tragedy of the common man" and viewed as their responsibility Lessing's call that the theater be a site for the advancement of personal enlightenment and social justice (e.g. Miller, "Tragedy and the Common Man").

But in Germany of the late nineteenth century, right-wing scholars and critics committed to promulgating the works of eminent German nationalists also wrestled with modernizing Lessing according to their own terms. After the fall of Napoleon, Lessing was regularly cited by German conservatives as anti-French (despite his numerous admiring references to Molière, Diderot, Marmontel, and even Voltaire), and by the end of the century a strange revisionist historical movement managed to cast Lessing as a militant champion of the very racism and intolerance against which he had perpetually battled. By the end of World War I, schoolchildren in Germany were introduced to a Lessing who appeared in lockstep with the most reactionary right-wing elements of German society (Nisbet 662). It was in some part against this distortion of Lessing that the prolific intellectual and translator Helen Zimmern (1846–1934), a British subject of German-Jewish descent, engaged in the first English translations and biographies of Lessing, excoriating Germany for its departure from Lessingian humanism. Until now, Zimmern's incomplete 1879 translation of the *Hamburg Dramaturgy* was the only version available to English readers.[6]

German dramaturgy's relationship with Lessing grew even more muddled in the twentieth century. As Hitler's propaganda master Joseph Goebbels (1897–1945) extolled the *Hamburg Dramaturgy* as a model for filmmaking, *Nathan the Wise* (Lessing's masterpiece drama of tolerance and acceptance) suffered protests and demonstrations from the right. At the same time, Goebbel's apprentice Rainer Schlösser (1899–1945), who as *Reichsdramaturg* [National Dramaturg] enforced complete control over German theater activities from 1933 to 1945, applied Lessing's teachings in reverse. Schlösser did not merely eliminate anti-Nazi political theater – he eliminated all political theater, offering instead copious state subsidies for grand productions of Romantic drama and the bourgeois drama Lessing had advocated (and authored) while obfuscating Lessing's writings on humanist social justice (particularly toward Jews) in plays, theology, and criticism. Schlösser went so far as to ban dramatic criticism in 1936 (Turner and Behrndt 106). In 1939, J. G. Robertson concluded his important English study of the *Hamburg Dramaturgy* by lamenting that German criticism had fallen away from Lessing's clarity, and that therefore the text had become little more than a valuable historical artifact, out of touch with modern aesthetics – he does not mention the growing humanitarian crisis in Germany (489–91). But humanist playwrights like Erwin Piscator and Bertolt Brecht drew upon many key concepts from the *Hamburg Dramaturgy*, including those of the *Gestus* [gest] and the *gemischte Charaktere* [internally contradictory character].[7] Indeed, a dramaturg appears as a character in Brecht's play *Dialoge aus dem Messingkauf* [*Messingkauf Dialogues*] (written between 1939 and 1942).

During his tenure as *Reichsdramaturg*, Schlösser led a purge of prominent Jewish theater artists and intellectuals whom he forcibly reformed into an alliance known as the *Kulturbund Deutscher Juden* [Cultural Association of German Jews], a segregated network of all-Jewish theater artists and audiences; ostensibly a safe place for theatrical Jews but actually a heavily regulated tool for ghettoizing Jewish cultural influence and for lulling Jews into a false sense of security, since it was eventually used to turn theaters into concentration camp deportation centers. The *Kulturbund* inaugurated its extraordinary existence in 1933 with a grand production of *Nathan the Wise*. The *Kulturbund* changed the play's ending, however: instead of the utopian reconciliation of Christianity, Islam, and Judaism that Lessing envisioned, the Jewish protagonist Nathan is left isolated, unable to participate in the harmony he created for non-Jews (Rovit 1). By way of repudiation of the Nazis, the first postwar theatrical production in Germany was *Nathan the Wise* at the Berlin Deutsches Theater on September 7, 1945, starring Paul Wegener (an actor who had trained with German-Jewish director Max Reinhardt but also had collaborated with the Nazis) in the title role. Brecht's mentor Erwin Piscator presented a *Nathan the Wise* in Marburg in 1953 that used projected images of concentration camps and film footage from the Nazi era. *Nathan* remains a prominent feature of German theater to this day, and Lessing is celebrated (particularly in Hamburg) as a courageous Enlightenment humanist (Eckhardt 63–5).

As Europe reconstructed itself in the aftermath of the war, the position of dramaturg experienced various levels of popularity in different countries and periods, and even the job description of the dramaturg has been fluid between companies. The conventional professional dramaturg has evolved from the ones that worked in the theaters of Piscator and Brecht into two general types: in Europe and in Central and South America, the position's portfolio includes selecting a repertoire, investigating and developing new works, providing research and analytical support for a play's director, and providing content for notes in the program, designed, more or less like the essays of the *Hamburg Dramaturgy*, to place the current production into historical context and ongoing discourses of aesthetics or politics (Stegemann 45). Among the most influential of these was Heiner Müller, dramaturg and eventual artistic director of the Berliner Ensemble, who established dramaturgical training as integral for developing playwrights. In the UK, however, the dramaturg developed a different profile as more of a "literary manager," charged with investigating and developing new writing for production, including helping playwrights revise their work. The most prominent of these was Kenneth Tynan, who became literary manager of the National Theatre in 1963.

In the United States, dramaturgy became prominent with emergence of important regional theaters, like the Guthrie and the American Conservatory Theatre, that were charged to develop new writing and so required a specialist on staff. Yale's prestigious School of Drama began training students in theater criticism in 1966 and graduated the first Master of Fine Arts in Dramaturgy in 1977 (Turner and Behrndt 8). Americans were ambivalent about dramaturgs, but the position made significant inroads, and in 1985, the Literary Managers and Dramaturgs of the Americas society was founded to support dramaturgs in the US, Canada, and Mexico. In the 1990s, the Yale School of Drama's dramaturgy programs flourished under the leadership of Mark Bly, generating influential American dramaturgs trained in the Lessing style who would become the progenitors of a vigorous international movement.

In the twenty-first century, dramaturgy has enjoyed both increasing respect from theater makers and interest from scholars in the English-speaking world, and the field continues to be shaped in direct reference to Lessing's work. Several important recent publications have helped to support the establishment of undergraduate and graduate dramaturgy programs; these texts invariably ascribe the origin of the modern dramaturg to the *Hamburg Dramaturgy* (Pavis 124).[8] Globally, dramaturgy as an artistic practice continues to adapt to sociocultural forces. India enjoys an unbroken tradition of dramaturgy millennia old (dating at least as far back as Bharatamuni's *Natyasastra*), but the presence of an in-house dramaturg has only recently been seen as important (see Datta). Dramaturgy in Latin America, France, Poland, and Russia likewise has a vibrant tradition, but is only now starting to see itself as functionally distinct from playwriting.[9] In Eastern Europe (including in the Czech Republic where, in 1993, the dramaturg and playwright Václav Havel became the first democratically elected president), dramaturgy often wrestles with the post-Soviet de-politicization of the theater; while in countries like Iran and China, where all theatrical production is under state control, some dramaturgs enforce censorship while others attempt to subvert it (see Moosavi; Sun). Dramaturgs in countries with brutal colonial legacies (particularly Chile, Australia, South Africa, and Brazil) work to employ theater in service of coping with national trauma and the formation of new national identities.[10] In Japan, dramaturgs work to blend indigenous performance styles with Western imports.

Although the dramaturg is not universally welcome in all theaters, nor can be said to have a single consistent job description, some of the most celebrated theatrical directors and playwrights at the time of this writing have extolled the virtues of Lessing-style dramaturgy, prompting Edward Kemp to refer to Lessing as "the patron saint of dramaturgs" in his 2003 translation of *Nathan the Wise* (3). Dramaturgs are also widely utilized as translators. Dramaturgs increasingly are experts on critical theory as applied to the drama, as a means of linking the work more directly to social discourses. Springing from this base, dramaturgs are now making significant forays into opera, dance, film and television, and with the rise of digital media and the internet, into games, artificial intelligence, and social robotics.[11]

Lessing's mark on this tradition is indelible. In the words of Dr. Martine Kei Green-Rogers, President of the Literary Managers and Dramaturgs of the Americas,

> We are indebted to Lessing's advocacy of the field without being beholden to how he originally thought of the work and theory of dramaturgy. That, I think, is the brilliance of the field he helped forefront. He realized the true value of dramaturgy may only manifest if we are on the "front lines" with the-aters so that the field of dramaturgy may grow in tandem with the art itself.[12]

Notes

1 Particularly since Shakespeare was all but unknown to Germany in Lessing's youth, and his exposure to the Bard likely came mostly through his reading of Voltaire; see Lamport 59; 153; and Brennecke 11.

2 G. E. Lessing, "Briefwechsel über das Trauerspiel" ["Correspondence on Tragedy"] (Letter 103) dated [13] November 1756, *Werke und Briefe* 3: 671. Emphasis in original. Translation by Wendy Arons. Original reads: "die Bestimmung der Tragödie ist diese: sie soll *unsere Fähigkeit, Mitleid zu fühlen,* erweitern. [. . .]. Wer uns also mitleidig macht, macht uns besser und tugendhafter, und das Trauerspiel, das jenes tut, tut auch dieses, oder – es tut jenes, um dieses tun zu können."

3 Including, for example, Eugenio Barba; see Turner and Behrndt 31.

4 Carlson 171; Joeres 182–3. A more traditional formulation of this argument is expressed in *Shakespeare und der deutsche Geist* (1911) by Friedrich Gundolf, the first recipient of the Hamburg Lessing Prize in 1930.

5 Zeydel chronicles at length Tieck's self-acknowledged debt to Lessing and describes Tieck's duties in Dresden as "1. Giving the director advice and aid in his literary tasks (selection of plays), 2. Training the younger and less experienced actors," but Zeydel himself refers to the dramaturg as "the man of letters who rashly interferes in the business of theatre" (261). Tieck authored his own *Dramaturgische Blätter* (1826).

6 Her translation first appeared in 1879 as "Dramatic Notes" in *Selected Prose Works of G.E. Lessing,* ed. Edward Bell; this translation was reproduced, essentially unaltered, by Dover Books in 1962, ed. Victor Lange; Dover reprinted the text again unchanged in 1982.

7 See Spolders; White 229; and Willett 181.

8 A list of more recent English texts that tie modern dramaturgy to Lessing includes, but is not limited to: Bly, *Production Notebooks* v. I and II; Jonas, Proehl, and Lupu, *Dramaturgy in the American Theatre;* Rudakoff and Thompson, *Between the Lines;* Chemers, *Ghost Light;* Irelan, Fletcher, and Dubiner, *The Process of Dramaturgy;* and Romanska, *Routledge Companion to Dramaturgy.* See also Lehmann, *Post-Dramatic Theatre:* although committed to dramaturgy as a practice, Lehmann argues that Lessing's approach must evolve to encompass more sub-versive and nontraditional theatrical aesthetics (25).

9 See, for example, Espada; Bredeson; and Dabek. Note the difference between the Spanish terms *dramaturgo* (playwright) and *dramaturgisto* (dramaturg).

10 See, for example, Ward.
11 See, for example, Carpenter; Profeta; Warner; Eckersall, Grehan, and Scheer; and Chemers, "Lyke Unto."
12 Personal Interview, 23 March 2018.

Works cited

Beiser, Frederick C. *Schiller as Philosopher*. Oxford: Oxford University Press, 2005. Print.
Bly, Mark. *The Production Notebooks*. 2 vols. New York: Theatre Communications Group, 1995–2001. Print.
Bredeson, Kate. "The Making of *La Dramaturgie* in France." In *The Routledge Companion to Dramaturgy*. Ed. Magda Romanska. Oxford: Routledge, 2015. 50–56. Print.
Brennecke, Ernest. *Shakespeare in Germany 1500–1700*. Chicago: University of Chicago Press, 1964.
Carlson, Marvin. *Theories of the Theatre: A Historical and Critical Survey, from the Greeks to the Present*. Ithaca, NY: Cornell University Press, 1993.
Carpenter, Faedra Chatard. "Reading and (Re)Directing 'Racial Scripts' on and beyond the Stage." In *The Routledge Companion to Dramaturgy*. Ed. Magda Romanska. Oxford: Routledge, 2015. 145–50. Print.
Chemers, Michael M. *Ghost Light: An Introductory Handbook for Dramaturgy*. Carbondale, IL: Southern Illinois University Press, 2010. Print.
———. "Later Classicism in the Drama: How Shakespeare's Ghosts Came to Haunt the Eighteenth Century." *The Routledge Research Companion to Shakespeare and Classical Literature*. Ed. Sean Keilen and Nick Moschovakis. Oxford: Routledge, 2016. 245–57. Print.
———. "Lyke Unto a Lively Thing: Theatre History and Social Robotics." In *Theatre, Performance, and Analogue Technology*. Ed. Kara Reilly. London: Palgrave Macmillan, 2013. 232–49. Print.
Dabek, Agata "Dramaturgy and the Role of the Dramaturg in Poland." In *The Routledge Companion to Dramaturgy*. Ed. Magda Romanska. Oxford: Routledge, 2015. 57–61. Print.
Datta, Ketakai. "Dramaturgy in Indian Theatre: A Closer View." In *The Routledge Companion to Dramaturgy*. Ed. Magda Romanska. Oxford: Routledge, 2015. 94–8. Print.
Eckersall, Peter, Helena Grehan, and Edward Scheer. *New Media Dramaturgy: Performance, Media, and New-Materialism*. London: Palgrave Macmillan, 2017. Print.
Eckhardt, Jo-Jacqueline. *Lessing's* Nathan the Wise *and the Critics, 1779–1991*. Columbia, SC: Camden, 1993. Print.
Espada, Margaret. "Collaborative Dramaturgy in Latin American Theatre." In *The Routledge Companion to Dramaturgy*. Ed. Magda Romanska. Oxford: Routledge, 2015. 30–4. Print.
Flatter, Richard. *Hamlet's Father*. New Haven: Yale University Press, 1949. Print.
Green-Rogers, Martine Kei. Personal Interview with Michael Chemers. 23 March 2018.
Gundolf, Friedrich. *Shakespeare und der deutsche Geist*. Berlin: Georg Bondi, 1911. Print.
Irelan, Scott, Anne Fletcher, and Julie Felise Dubiner. *The Process of Dramaturgy: A Handbook*. Newburyport, MA: Focus, 2010. Print.
Joeres, Ruth-Ellen Boetcher. "The German Enlightenment (1720–1790)." In *The Cambridge History of German Literature*. Ed. Helen Watanabe-O'Keilly. Cambridge: Cambridge University Press, 1997. 147–201. Print.
Johnston, Brian. *The Ibsen Cycle: Design of the Plays from* Pillars of Society *to* When We Dead Awaken. Altoona, PA: Penn State University Press, 1992. Print.
Jonas, Susan, Geoff Proehl, and Michael Lupu, eds. *Dramaturgy in American Theatre: A Source Book*. Orlando, FL: Harcourt Brace, 1997. Print.
Jürs-Munby, Karen. "Of Textual Bodies and Actual Bodies: G. E. Lessing's Abjection of Performance." *Theatre Research International* 30.1 (2005). 19–35. Print.
Lamport, F[rancis] J. *Lessing and the Drama*. Oxford: Oxford University Press, 1981. Print.
Lehmann, Hans-Thiess. *Postdramatic Theatre*. Trans. Karen Jürs-Munby. Oxford: Routledge, 2006.

Lessing, Gotthold Ephraim. "Briefwechsel über das Trauerspiel zwischen Lessing, Mendelssohn, und Nicolai." In *Werke und Briefe in zwölf Bänden.* Ed. Wilfried Barner with Klaus Bohnen, et al. Frankfurt-am-Main: Deutscher Klassiker Verlag, 1985–2003. 3: 662–736. Print.

———. *Nathan the Wise.* Trans. Edward Kemp. London: Nick Hern, 2003. Print.

Luckhurst, Mary. *Dramaturgy: A Revolution in Theatre.* Cambridge: Cambridge University Press, 2006. Print.

Mason, Haydn T. "Voltaire vs. Shakespeare: The Lettre à L'Académie Française (1776)." *Nineteenth Century Studies* 18.2 (1995). 173–84. Print.

Miller, Arthur. "Tragedy and the Common Man." *New York Times* 27 February 1949. *New York Times: Books Online.* www.nytimes.com/books/00/11/12/specials/miller-common.html. Web. 5 January 2018.

Moosavi, Marjan. "Dramaturgy in Post-Revolution Iran: Problems and Prospects." In *The Routledge Companion to Dramaturgy.* Ed. Magda Romanska. Oxford: Routledge, 2015. 68–74. Print.

Nisbet, Hugh Barr. *Gotthold Ephraim Lessing: His Life, Works, and Thought.* Oxford: Oxford University Press, 2013. Print.

Oxenford, John, ed. and trans. *Conversations of Goethe with Eckermann and Soret.* 2 vols. London: Smith, Elder, & Co., 1850. Print.

Pavis, Patrice. *Dictionary of the Theatre: Terms, Concepts, and Analysis.* Toronto: University of Toronto Press, 1998. Print.

Profeta, Katherine. *Dramaturgy in Motion: At Work on Dance and Movement Performance.* Madison: University of Wisconsin Press, 2017. Print.

Robertson, John G. *Lessing's Dramatic Theory.* Cambridge, UK: Cambridge University Press, 1939. Print.

Romanska, Magda, ed. *The Routledge Companion to Dramaturgy.* Oxford, UK: Routledge, 2015. Print.

Rovit, Rebecca. *The Jewish Kulturbund Theatre Company in Berlin.* Iowa City: University of Iowa Press, 2012. Print.

Rudakoff, Judith, and Lynn Thompson. *Between the Lines: The Process of Dramaturgy.* Toronto: Playwrights Canada Press, 2002.

Schechter, Joel. "In the Beginning, There Was Lessing . . . Then Brecht, Müller, and Other Dramaturgs." In *Dramaturgy in American Theatre: A Source Book.* Ed. Susan Jonas, Geoff Proehl, and Michael Lupu. Orlando, FL: Harcourt Brace, 1997. 16–24. Print.

Shaw, George Bernard. "Told You So." In *Dramatic Opinions and Essays: With an Apology.* London: Brentano's, 1906. 258. Print.

Spolders, Sascha. *Lessing und Brecht: Zwei Dramenreformmodelle in Vergleich.* Munich: Grin Verlag, 2008. Print.

Stanislavski, Konstantin. *My Life in Art.* New York: Routledge, 1952. Print.

Stegemann, Bernd. "On German Dramaturgy." *The Routledge Companion to Dramaturgy.* Ed. Magda Romanska. Oxford: Routledge, 2015. 45–9. Print.

Sun, William Huizhu. "Official and Unofficial Dramaturgs: Dramaturgy in China." *The Routledge Companion to Dramaturgy.* Ed. Magda Romanska. Oxford: Routledge, 2015. 81–6. Print.

Turner, Cathy, and Synne K. Behrndt. *Dramaturgy and Performance.* Houndmills: Palgrave Macmillan, 2008. Print.

Wagner, Richard. "Zukunftsmusik." In *Richard Wagner's Prose Works.* Trans. William Ashton Ellis. Vol. 3. London: Kegan Paul, Trench, Trübner & Co., 1894. 293–347. Print.

Ward, Julie Ann. "Documentary Dramaturgy in Brazil." In *The Routledge Companion to Dramaturgy.* Ed. Magda Romanska. Oxford: Routledge, 2015. 35–9. Print.

Warner, Vessela. "Borderless Dramaturgy in Dance Theatre." In *The Routledge Companion to Dramaturgy.* Ed. Magda Romanska. Oxford: Routledge, 2015. 348–53. Print.

White, John. *Bertolt Brecht's Dramatic Theory.* New York: Rochester University Press, 2010. Print.

Willett, John, ed. *Brecht on Theatre: The Development of an Aesthetic.* Trans. John Willett. New York: Hill and Wang, 1977. Print.

Zeydel, Edwin. *Ludwig Tieck, the German Romanticist: A Critical Study.* Princeton: Princeton University Press for the University of Cincinnati, 1935. Print.

Zimmern, Helen, trans. "Dramatic Notes." In *Selected Prose Works of G. E. Lessing.* Ed. Edward Bell. London: George Bell and Sons, 1889. 227–493. Print.

4

NOTE ON THE TRANSLATION

Wendy Arons and Sara Figal

To date there has been only one translation into English of G. E. Lessing's *Hamburg Dramaturgy*: the selectively abridged version produced by the German-born British author/translator Helen Zimmern (1846–1934). Zimmern's translation was first published in 1879 in *Selected Prose Works of G. E. Lessing*, and, despite its dated prose style, has been regularly reprinted over the past century. That edition has been the sole source of access for English-language readers to this seminal work of dramatic theory and criticism since Lessing published the collected essays in 1769. Zimmern's translation was never intended to convey the entirety of Lessing's endeavor: Edward Bell, the editor of that volume, explains in his preface that her version of the text (which appeared under the title "Dramatic Notes") is "somewhat abridged by the omission of passages unlikely to interest readers of the present day."[1] But that phrase "somewhat abridged" vastly understates the extent to which Zimmern edited Lessing's work: her edition omits 19 of the 104 essays in their entirety, and also cuts about 30 percent of the text from among the included essays. Moreover, although Zimmern was a prolific translator (from both German and Italian) who made many otherwise inaccessible texts available to English readers, she writes in an antiquated Victorian style that can be off-putting to the contemporary reader.[2] Her fustiness as a writer does a particular injustice to Lessing, a master prose stylist whose contribution to the German language itself is much celebrated. Within the *Hamburg Dramaturgy*, Lessing deftly employs a range of voices, from highly formal (particularly in the "Notice" and earlier essays) to quite personal (particularly in his final diatribe in Essays 101–104 over the piracy of his work and against his critics). His observations about current social norms and his frequent jabs at literary rivals are often laugh-out-loud funny. Our goal with this new translation, then, has been two-fold: first, to provide a complete and accurate translation of the text into English so that readers will have access to Lessing's impressive scope of thought; and second, to develop a style of translation that would convey to English-language readers the range of rhetorical styles and sharp wit that marks Lessing's prose. In his own day, Lessing's dramaturgical essays conveyed a freshness and urgency that we were eager to capture – at the very least, we were determined to prevent those qualities from being suffocated by now-antiquated diction. In order to achieve those twin goals – accuracy and replication of style – we have had to make many artistic and methodological choices. This note briefly sketches out some of the choices we made and the rationale behind them.

To begin with, we sought, wherever appropriate, to use the active voice in English. Readers of German will appreciate that this decision is tantamount to throwing down a gauntlet. German – both now and in the eighteenth century – has a grammatical structure that differs in several significant ways from English, and one example is that the passive voice, generally avoided in English as indirect and rather flat, can, in German, be quite vigorous. Our aim was to convey the vividness and energy of Lessing's writing, and we discovered that replicating his use of the passive voice in English not only made his ideas unnecessarily opaque, but the text itself became cumbersome, lacking idiomatic finesse and sounding quite clumsy. In such instances, we decided to honor what we identified as the spirit of Lessing's style rather than adhere to a precise translation of his sentence structures into English. This may well provoke some healthy scholarly debate, but we hope it will also introduce the sheer delight of reading Lessing to a new Anglophone audience.

For similar reasons, we often split long, complex sentences into two shorter sentences, in order to render the expressed ideas into English with greater clarity. We also punctuated according to modern usage in English, choosing semi-colons where Lessing might place a comma, and restoring quotation marks around quotes that are unmarked as such in his text.[3] Finally, although we were careful to avoid anachronisms (for example: terms like "empathy" or "lifestyle" that were not available in 1769), we did strive to use words, phrases, and sentence rhythms that would sound natural to a twenty-first century reader. While we strove for clarity, we also sought to accurately convey the complexity of Lessing's writing and thinking. In a few instances this led us to reproduce ambiguities of meaning we perceived in the original German.

We also had to make significant decisions concerning the translation of key terms. Our intention with this translation has not been to weigh in definitively on the philological debates over the precise meaning of terms such as *Mitleid, Wahrscheinlichkeit, das Wunderbare, Genie, Affekt, Empfindung*, etc., many of which Lessing was in the process of defining and clarifying as he wrote the *Hamburg Dramaturgy*. Rather, we aimed in each instance to choose an English term that we felt best conveyed Lessing's meaning.[4] In such cases, we provide a translator's note to explain our choice of English term for the German and trust that interested readers will look more deeply into the etymological significance of those key terms.

Throughout the *Hamburg Dramaturgy*, Lessing quotes extensively from foreign languages – he excerpts dramatic and theoretical texts in French, Spanish, Italian, Greek, Latin, and English. To complicate matters, his quotes and references are not always completely accurate. Our source text, published in the scholarly *Werke und Briefe in zwölf Bänden*, faithfully replicates Lessing's misspelling and Germanization of many names and titles (i.e., Lessing gives Ben Jonson's name as Johnson and omits the accents in Molière and *Cénie*, to give only a few examples), and it also reproduces errors in Lessing's quotations from foreign-language texts. We have silently corrected such misspellings and restored missing accents, unless the replication of an error was important to Lessing's analysis of the text, in which case we note the salient difference in our annotations. We provide translations into English of all of the foreign-language quotes and phrases that appear in the body of Lessing's writing in our annotations; but, with a few exceptions, we leave the foreign-language quotes that Lessing added to his own footnotes untranslated, on the principle that this reproduces, for the reader of our English text, the experience of Lessing's original reader, who would have encountered a text that offered foreign-language source text in the footnotes.[5] Where Lessing translates, into German, a text that was originally written in English, we restore the original (rather than translating his German back into English) and note the source in our annotations.

Titles of plays, as well as character names from plays, posed another set of challenges. In deciding how to translate titles of plays or character names that Lessing mentions in the *Hamburg Dramaturgy*, we began by first determining whether or not the given play already had an extant English translation; if so, we opted to use the title of the English translation and the character names as they appeared in that translation, on the principle that our reader might wish to consult the English version of the text, which we list in our bibliography. Where no English version of a play exists, we gave our own translation of the title, and, in general, we anglicized character names.

Our edition of the *Hamburg Dramaturgy* differs in another significant way from Zimmern's 1879 translation: we provide annotations to the text to help contextualize the many references to historical and contemporary writers and works that Lessing mentions along the way. Entire books have been written about some of the ideas Lessing raises in the course of these essays, and it was tempting to write long discursive endnotes explaining the debates surrounding many of the issues he addresses. We resisted that urge. Although we explain the significance of important terms and seek to situate Lessing's discussions within the context of both his own earlier works and larger eighteenth-century debates, we are primarily concerned with giving the reader the most immediate information necessary for understanding a particular essay. We have provided, for curious readers, references to both primary and secondary sources, should they wish to pursue a topic further. Within our endnotes, cross-references to other essays appear as a number in square brackets (e.g., [12] refers the reader to Essay 12; [12.3] refers the reader to endnote 3 of Essay 12).

While we are the primary authors of this translation, we had a great deal of help on many fronts. In particular, the *Plattdeutsch* dialogue that appears in Essay 28 challenged our comprehension; we are grateful to Karen Jürs-Munby and her father, Hans-Joachim Jürs, for their help decoding the dialect, and to playwright Savannah Reich for suggesting an English equivalent. Helen Zimmern's 1879 English translation of the text remained, despite its flaws and omissions, an important reference text for us; an equally helpful resource was Jean Valentin's 2010 translation of the *Hamburg Dramaturgy* into French. Beatrix Brockman reviewed our translation and offered many suggestions that improved both the accuracy and the stylistic consistency of our work; we are also grateful to Stephen Brockmann, Peter Erickson, and Daniel Smith for catching errors and infelicities in the version of this translation published online on MediaCommons Press.[6] The text is much improved as a result of input from this community of scholars; any lingering errors or infelicities are, of course, are own.

It is our hope that this new, modern, complete, and annotated translation of the *Hamburg Dramaturgy* will not only offer to Anglophone readers previously unavailable access and insight into Lessing's thinking about the theater and drama but also provide a sense of his wit, erudition, and (for lack of a better word) personality. We continue to find delight in the humor Lessing brought to his endeavor, and it's our hope that this translation will invite a new generation of readers to take pleasure in Lessing's invitation to wrestle with the aesthetic and social power of the theater.

Notes

1 Bell, "Preface" in *Selected Prose Works of G. E. Lessing.*
2 See Creffield.
3 Our source text for this translation was the edition prepared by Klaus Bohnen in *Gotthold Ephraim Lessing Werke und Briefe in zwölf Bänden* 6: 181–714. We chose this version because it is the most recent and definitive edition of the text to date and was prepared in accordance with modern standards for scholarly editions.
4 Our most controversial decision, perhaps, is in our choice to translate *Mitleid* as "compassion" instead of "pity"; see [32.6].
5 The footnotes Lessing included in his text are indicated, in ours, by a superscript symbol (*, †, §, ‡, etc.) Our own annotations appear as endnotes, and are referenced with superscript Arabic numerals.
6 The online version of our translation remains open for commentary at http://mcpress. media-commons.org/hamburg/.

VOLUME I

Notice

It will be readily apparent that the catalyst for this present publication is the new administration of our local theater.

The ultimate aim of the publication corresponds with the good intentions that we cannot help but associate with the men who intend to take on the management of this theater. They have explained their aims sufficiently themselves, and their statements have been received with approval both here and abroad by the more refined public. This is approval that every voluntary promotion of the common good both deserves and should expect in our day.

To be sure, there are always and everywhere people who, because they know themselves so well, see nothing but ulterior motives in every good undertaking. We could gladly grant them this with respect to themselves: however, when they these supposed ulterior motives to attack the undertaking itself, and when their spiteful envy, in seeking to block these motives, also derails the project, then they really ought to understand that they are the most despicable members of human society.

Happy is the place where such miserable people do not set the tone; where the majority of well-meaning citizens keeps them within the boundaries of respectful behavior and does not allow the better part of the whole to fall victim to their intrigues, or patriotic intentions to become the object of their sneering lunacy!

May Hamburg be so happy in everything that concerns its well-being and freedom, for it deserves to be so happy!

When Schlegel made recommendations for the improvement of the Danish theater (a German writer for the Danish theater!) – a matter that will long serve as a subject of reproach to Germany, which gave him no opportunity to make such recommendations for the improvement of our own – this was the first and foremost recommendation: "that the concern of working for a profit or loss must not be left to the actors alone."[1] The troupe leaders among them have reduced an art form to a trade, which the master carries out more or less perfunctorily or self-servingly, depending on the degree to which his customers – his buyers – promise him basic necessities or luxury.

Even if nothing more has occurred here, than that a society of Friends of the Theater has put itself to the task and committed itself to work on a plan for the common good, a great deal has been achieved just by doing this. For all of the other improvements that our theater needs will arise easily and quickly from this initial change, even with only a modest encouragement from the audience.

Certainly nothing will be spared in terms of effort or money; only time will tell whether taste or discretion are lacking. And does the audience not have the power to remedy and improve whatever it might find lacking here? It needs only to come, to watch and listen, to consider and judge. Its voice will never be summarily dismissed, its judgment will always be heard with deference!

However, not every little fault-finder should fancy himself The Audience, and someone whose expectations are disappointed needs to stop and think a bit about the nature of those expectations. Not every enthusiast is a connoisseur; not every person who perceives the beauty of one play or the correct performance of one actor can thereby also judge the value of all others. A person who has only a biased taste has no taste; but he is often therefore more partisan. True taste is general and extends to beautiful things of every kind, but it does not expect more pleasure or delight from them than can be afforded by their particular nature.

There are many steps an emergent theater must climb in order to reach the pinnacle of perfection; but a corrupted theater is of course even further removed from this height, and I greatly fear that the German theater is more of this latter sort than the former.

Thus not everything can happen all at once. But although we may not see something growing, we do, after some time, find it grown. The slowest person who never loses sight of his goal always goes faster than one who wanders around aimlessly.

This *Dramaturgy* will maintain a critical register of all of the plays that will be produced, and it will follow every step here that is relevant to the art of both the writer and the actor. The choice of the plays is no small thing: but choice presupposes quantity, and if masterpieces are not always produced, one can readily see where the fault lies. In the meantime, it is a good thing if a mediocre play is not made out to be anything more than what it is, and the dissatisfied audience member can at the very least learn to judge from it. If we want to instill good taste in someone of sound judgment, we only need to make apparent to him why he did not like something. Certain mediocre plays must also be retained because they have certain excellent roles in which this or that actor can demonstrate his full strength. Similarly, one does not immediately reject a musical composition just because its accompanying text is wretched.

The great discernment of the drama critic lies in his ability to distinguish, whenever he feels pleasure or displeasure, to what extent that feeling should be credited to the writer or to the actor. For to rebuke one for something the other has caused is to ruin both of them. The first will be discouraged while the other becomes over-confident.

The actor in particular demands that we maintain the greatest rigor and impartiality in this regard. The vindication of the writer can be undertaken at any time; his work remains present and can be brought before our eyes time and again. But the art of the actor is transitory in its effects. His good and bad moments of performance rush past with equal speed, and often the momentary mood of the spectator is more responsible than the actor himself for why the good or the bad left the more vivid impression.

A beautiful figure, a captivating face, an expressive eye, a charming walk, a mellifluous tone, a melodic voice: these are all things that are not easily expressed in words. But these are neither the only nor the greatest perfections of the actor. They are valuable gifts of nature, necessary to his profession, but they are far from sufficient for his work! He must constantly think with the writer, and when something all too human overtakes the writer, he must think *for* him.

We have every reason to expect many examples of this from our actors. – But I do not want to raise the audience's expectations any higher. Both he who promises too much and he who expects too much does himself a disservice.

Today marks the opening of the theater. The opening will determine much, but it should not determine everything. In the first few days there will no doubt be a crossing of opinions. It would take effort to be heard calmly. – For this reason, the first installment of this publication will not appear before the beginning of next month.

Hamburg, April 22, 1767

Essay 1

1 May 1767[1]

The theater celebrated its successful opening on the 22nd of last month with the tragedy *Olint and Sophronia.*[2]

No doubt they really wanted to begin with a German original, which would also have the appeal of novelty. The intrinsic value of this play could not make any claims to such recognition. The choice would warrant criticism, if it were clear that something better could have been found.

Olint and Sophronia is the work of a young writer, and it is his unfinished posthumous work.[3] Cronegk certainly died too young for our stage; but in truth, his fame is based upon what he might have achieved, according to the judgment of his friends, rather than upon what he actually accomplished. And what dramatic writer, from any era or nation, could have died in his twenty-sixth year without leaving an equally ambivalent assessment of his true talent?

The subject matter is the well-known episode from Tasso.[4] It is not easy to reshape a brief, touching story into a touching drama. It may take little effort to invent new entanglements and to expand isolated feelings into entire scenes. But to know how to prevent these new developments from weakening the interest or compromising the appearance of truth; to be able to shift oneself from the perspective of narrator to the authentic position of each and every person; to avoid describing passions and instead to let them develop before the eyes of the audience and grow smoothly with such illusory continuity that the audience must sympathize, whether it wants to or not: that is what is necessary.[5] That is what the genius does unconsciously, without explaining everything to death. And it is what the merely clever wit torturously tries to imitate, but in vain.

In his Olint and Sophronia, Tasso seems to have had Virgil's "Nisus and Euryalus" in mind.[6] Where Virgil portrayed the power of friendship in his work, Tasso wanted to depict the power of love. In Virgil, it is the heroic sense of duty that triggers the test of friendship. In Tasso, it is religion that gives love the opportunity to show its true power. But religion, which is just the means through which Tasso shows love at work, becomes the central theme of Cronegk's version. Cronegk wanted to ennoble the triumph of love through the triumph of religion. Certainly, a pious improvement – but nothing more than pious! For it has misled him into taking the simple, natural, true, and human in Tasso and rendering it so complicated, fanciful, wondrous, and heavenly that it is devoid of meaning.

In Tasso, it is a magician – a man who is neither Christian nor Muslim but rather someone who has woven together his personal belief out of both religions – who advises Aladin to move the miraculous image of Mary from the Temple to the Mosque.[7] Why did Cronegk turn this magician into a Mohammedan priest? The priest could give such advice only if he were as ignorant of his own religion as the playwright seems to be. Muslims do not permit any images in their mosques. Cronegk reveals in numerous places that he possesses a very mistaken conceptualization of the Muslim faith. The most negligent mistake, however, is that he makes this religion guilty of polytheism when it is perhaps more than any other committed to a singular God. He refers to the mosque as "the seat of false gods," and he has the priest cry out:

> Will you not arm yourselves with vengeance and punishment, oh Gods?
> Strike down, destroy the brazen Christian people!

So the dutiful actor tried to observe the precise mode of dress in his costume, from head to toe; and then he had to speak such nonsense![8]

In Tasso, the image of Mary disappears from the mosque without anyone knowing whether it was taken by human hands or whether a higher power was involved. Cronegk makes Olint responsible. It is true that he transforms the image of Mary into "an image of the Lord on the Cross."[9] Nevertheless, an image is an image, and this miserable superstition creates a despicable side to Olint's character. One cannot forgive him for being willing to risk leading his people to the brink of destruction through such a small act. When he later freely confesses, it is only out of guilt and not magnanimity. Tasso has him take this step out of love: he wants to save Sophronia or die with her. Die with her, simply to die with her – he can do nothing more. Unable to share a bed, they share a pyre; bound at her side to the same stake, certain to be consumed by the same fire, he feels nothing but the happiness of such a sweet proximity. He does not give a thought to what awaits him beyond the grave and wishes for nothing more than that the proximity be even closer and more intimate, that he press his breast against her breast and be allowed to breathe out his spirit upon her lips.

This superb contrast between a sweet, gentle, romantic, effusive young woman and a fiery-tempered, lusty young man is entirely lost with Cronegk, where they are both driven by the coldest singularity of intent: both have nothing but martyrdom in mind. And it is not enough that *they* both want to die for the sake of religion; Evander also wants to, and even Serena seems to have no small desire to do so.[10]

Here I would like to make a two-fold argument that, if well heeded, will protect an aspiring tragic playwright from great missteps. The first point has to do with tragedy in general. If heroic sentiments are to evoke admiration, then the playwright must not use them promiscuously.[11] People stop marveling at what they hear and see too often. Cronegk crossed this line badly with his *Codrus*.[12] The love for the land of one's birth and the willingness to die for its sake should have been embodied by Codrus alone.[13] He should have stood as the only example of a very particular type, in order to make the impression that the playwright intended. But Elisinde and Philaide and Medon (and how many others?) are all equally ready to sacrifice their lives for their homeland.[14] Our admiration is divided, and Codrus gets lost in the crowd. The same occurs here. In *Olint and Sophronia*, all those of Christian faith appear to regard being martyred as if it were no more than drinking a glass of water. We hear such pious bravado so often, from so many mouths, that it loses all of its power.

The second observation has to do with the Christian tragedy in particular. Heroes of these plays are usually martyrs. Now, however, we live in a time in which the voice of healthy reason calls out too loudly to allow every madman to claim the title of martyr just because he willingly and unnecessarily hurtles toward death with no thought to his civic obligations. We now know all too well how to distinguish the false martyrs from the true; we despise the former as much as we revere the latter, and the most they can do is squeeze from us a melancholy tear over the blindness and stupidity of which humanity is evidently all too capable. However, this tear is not the pleasurable sort that tragedy wants to stimulate. When the playwright chooses a martyr as his hero, he must give him the clearest and most effective motivations! Place him in conditions of utter necessity, so that he must take the step that puts him in danger! Do not let him seek death lightly or arrogantly will it! Otherwise, his pious hero will become an object of our disgust, and religion itself – that which the playwright wants to honor – may suffer. I have already touched upon the fact that only a worthless superstition, like the one we despise in the magician Ismenor, could drive Olint to take the image out of the mosque. It does not excuse the playwright that there have been times when such superstition was common and existed alongside many positive traits, and that there are still lands where such superstition accords with pious simplicity. But he did not write his play for those times, any more than he intended it to be produced in Bohemia or Spain.[15] The good writer, regardless of genre – if he is not writing merely to demonstrate his wit or his erudition – always has the best and most enlightened people of his time and place in mind, and he deigns only to write what will appeal to them, what can move them. Even the dramatic writer, if he sinks to the level of the masses, only condescends in order to enlighten and improve, and not to confirm them in their prejudices and ignoble ways of thinking.

Essay 2

5 May 1767[1]

Yet another observation, also concerning the Christian tragedy, might be made with regard to Clorinda's conversion.[2] While we may always wish to be convinced of the direct effects of grace, it can please us but little in the theater, where everything that belongs to the personality of the characters must spring from the most natural causes.[3] In the theater we tolerate miracles only in the physical world; in the moral realm, everything has to keep to its proper course, because theater should be the school of the moral world.[4] The motives for each decision, for each change in even the most minor thoughts and opinions, must be precisely weighed for consistency with the character as it has already been presented, and they must never provoke more than they could according to the strictest truth. The writer might possess the art of seducing us into overlooking incongruities of this type through beautiful details; but he deceives us only once, and as soon as we have cooled down, we take back the applause he wheedled from us. Applying this to the fourth scene of the third act, we see that Sophronia's speeches and behavior might indeed have moved Clorinda to compassion, but they are far too ineffectual to have the effect of conversion on a person who is not at all disposed to enthusiasm.[5] In Tasso, Clorinda also embraces Christianity, but only in her last hour, only after she has discovered that her parents had embraced this faith: these are subtle, weighty circumstances, through which the impact of a higher power is interwoven into a series of natural events.[6] No one has better understood how far one may go with this subject on stage than Voltaire.[7] After the sensitive, noble soul of Zamor has been assaulted and shaken to its core by example and pleading, by magnanimity and exhortations, Voltaire allows him more to suppose than actually to believe the truth of the religion whose converts display so much greatness.[8] And perhaps Voltaire would have also suppressed this supposition, if something of the sort had not been necessary to assuage his audience.

In view of the above observations, even Corneille's *Polyeucte* is faulty; and since its imitations have all been even worse, we are without doubt still waiting for the first tragedy deserving to be called Christian.[9] By that I mean a play in which, for the first time, the Christian interests us as a Christian. – But is such a play even possible? Isn't the character of the true Christian somehow completely untheatrical? Don't his most characteristic traits – quiet tranquility and consistent gentleness – somehow conflict with the entire business of tragedy, which seeks to purify passions through passions?[10] Doesn't his expectation of a rewarding happiness in the next life contradict the selfless altruism with which we wish to see all great and good actions on the stage undertaken and performed?

Until a work of genius incontestably refutes these concerns – for experience has shown us that genius can overcome many difficulties – my advice would be: do not stage any of the Christian tragedies written to date.[11] This advice, which is derived from the requirements of art and can deprive us of nothing except very mediocre plays, is none the worse for coming to the aid of those weaker souls who feel I-know-not-what kind of horror when they hear sentiments spoken in the theater that they are only prepared to encounter in a holier place. The theater should offend no one, whoever they may be; and I wish that it also could and would forestall any offenses to anyone.

Cronegk had only managed to get his play to nearly the end of the fourth act. The rest was added by a pen in Vienna; a pen – for the work of a mind is not very evident in it.[12] Apparently the wielder of the pen ended the story completely differently than Cronegk planned. Death best solves all complications; thus, he allows both Olint and Sophronia to die. In Tasso they both survive, because Clorinda takes up their cause with selfless generosity. But Cronegk had made Clorinda fall in love, and so it was admittedly difficult to guess how he intended to deal with two rivals without calling death to his aid. In a different and even worse tragedy when one of the main characters suddenly died, one member of the audience asked his neighbor: "But what did she die of?" – "Of what? Of the fifth act," answered the other. Truth be told, the fifth act is an evil nasty disease that carries away many a one to whom the first four acts had promised a much longer life.

But I don't want to go to any greater lengths with my criticism of the play. As mediocre as it is, it has been exceptionally produced. I am not talking about the external splendor, because this improvement of our theater requires nothing other than money. The arts that require this sort of help have the same level of excellence here as in every other country; it is just that our artists wish to be paid as well as those in every other country.

One should be satisfied with the production of a play if among four or five people a few have performed excellently and the others well. He who is so offended by a beginner or some substitute in a minor role that he turns up his nose at the whole thing should travel to Utopia and visit the perfect theater there, where even the candlesnuffer is a Garrick.[13]

Herr Ekhof was Evander; although Evander is in fact Olint's father, he essentially functions as not much more than a confidant.[14] This actor, however, can make what he wants of a role; even in the smallest role we always recognize him as the finest of actors and regret not being able to see him play all of the other roles in addition to his own. One talent completely unique to him is that he knows how to deliver moral adages and sweeping observations, those boring digressions of an awkward writer, with such grace and inner fire that in his mouth the most trivial phrases are imbued with novelty and dignity, the coldest phrases with fire and life.

The interspersed morals are Cronegk's strength. Both here and in his *Codrus* he has expressed quite a few with such a lovely and emphatic brevity that many of his verses deserve to be kept as aphorisms and taken up by the general public as part of the prevailing wisdom in everyday life.[15] Unfortunately, he also often tries to peddle colored glass for precious stone and witty antitheses for common sense. Two lines of that kind in the first act had a particular effect on me.[16] The first,

Heaven can forgive, but a Priest cannot.

The second,

He who thinks badly of others is himself a villain.

I was struck by a general movement in the *parterre* and noticed that murmuring through which applause expresses itself when the audience's attentiveness does not allow it to fully break out. On the one hand, I thought: Wonderful! These people love morality; this audience has a taste for maxims; a Euripides could earn fame on this stage, and Socrates would happily visit it. On the other hand, it also occurred to me how cockeyed, how false, how offensive these supposed maxims were, and I very much wished that disapproval might have had the largest share in that murmuring. There has only been one Athens, there will only ever be one Athens, where even among the rabble moral sentiment was so fine and sensitive that actors and playwrights ran the risk of being driven out of the theater because of corrupt morality! I am well aware that in the drama sentiments must correspond with the assumed character of the person who expresses them; they therefore cannot bear the stamp of absolute truth. It is enough if they are poetically true, if we must admit that this character, in this situation, in this state of passion, could not have judged otherwise. But on the other hand, even this poetic truth must approach the absolute, and a writer must never think so unphilosophically as to imagine that a person could want evil for evil's sake, that a person could act according to vicious principles, recognize the viciousness of those principles, and even boast about them to himself and others. Such a person is a monster, as hideous as he is uninstructive, and he is nothing but the miserable last resort of an insipid mind who thinks glittering tirades are the highest achievement in tragedy. If Ismenor is a cruel priest, then are all priests Ismenors?[17] One must not argue that we are talking about priests of a false religion. No religion in this world has ever been so false that its teachers necessarily had to be fiends. Priests have wreaked havoc in false religions as well as in true ones, not because they were priests, but because they were villains who would have abused the privileges of any social position in the service of their evil inclinations.

When the stage indulges the expression of such ill-considered judgments against priests, is it any wonder that among them there are some foolish enough to proclaim the stage a high road to hell?[18]

But I am falling again into criticism of the play, and I wanted to speak of the actors.

Essay 3

8 May 1767[1]

So how does this actor (Herr Ekhof) manage to please us even when speaking the most ordinary truism?[2] What is it exactly that another actor could learn from him, so that we would find that actor equally captivating in such cases?

All moral truisms have to come from the abundance of the heart, which then finds its way over the lips; one must appear neither to think long about them nor to be ostentatious about them.[3]

It is self-evident that the moralistic passages have to be particularly well memorized. They have to be spoken without faltering, without the slightest stumbling, in an unbroken flow of words, and with an ease that makes them seem to be spontaneously inspired by the immediate situation rather than a strenuous regurgitation of memory.

It also follows that no false emphasis should make us suspect that the actor is babbling something he does not understand. He has to convince us through the truest, most confident tone that he comprehends the full significance of his words.

But correct emphasis can, in a pinch, be taught to a parrot. There is a tremendous gulf between the actor who merely understands a passage and one who also feels it! Words that have been committed to memory and whose meaning one has grasped can be recited quite correctly even if one's soul is preoccupied with entirely different things; but there will be no possibility of feeling. The soul must be entirely present; it must direct its attention solely and entirely to its speech, and only then –

But also then the actor can have truly abundant feeling, and at the same time appear to have none. Among an actor's abilities, feeling is undoubtedly always the most questionable. It can exist where one does not perceive it; and one can believe that one sees it where it does not exist. For feeling is something interior, which we can only judge by its outward manifestations. It is quite possible that certain things in the construction of the body either simply do not allow for these manifestations, or they weaken them and render them ambiguous. The actor could have a particular facial structure, particular facial expressions, or a particular tone that we tend to associate with completely different capacities, different passions, and different sentiments than those he ought to express and demonstrate at a given moment. In such a case, regardless of how much he feels, we will not believe him, because he is in a state of contradiction with himself. On the other hand, a different actor could be so felicitously built, he could possess such decisive features, all of his muscles could respond so easily and swiftly to his command, he could control such fine and varied inflections of his voice – in short, he could be so blessed with all of the gifts necessary for acting in such a high degree that he will appear to us to be inspired by the most profound feeling, even in those roles that he performs not from original inspiration but in imitation of some good example and in which everything that he says and does is really nothing more than mechanical mimicry.[4]

This actor, notwithstanding his indifference and coldness, is without question far more useful to the theater than the other. Once he has spent enough time doing nothing more than simply mimicking others, he will have acquired a number of little habits according to which he will begin to behave. And (according to the principle that those modifications of the soul that bring about certain changes in the body can in return be produced by those changes to the body) through observation of those rules, he will attain a kind of emotion that, to be sure, may not have the duration or fire of that which arises from the soul but which is powerful enough in the moment of performance to bring about some of the involuntary changes in the body from whose presence alone we believe we can dependably infer a person's inner feelings.[5] Imagine, for example, that this kind of actor is supposed to convey anger's most extreme fury. Suppose that he does not really understand his role, that he is neither able to comprehend the reasons for the anger sufficiently nor to imagine them vividly enough to inspire anger in his own soul. Nevertheless, I maintain that if he has learned even the crudest expressions of anger from an actor with native sentiment and knows how to imitate them well – the quick pace; the stamping foot; the raw, now shrieking, now grim tone; the play of eyebrows; the trembling lips; the grinding of teeth, etc. – I repeat, if he imitates just these things that can be mimicked and he does so well, then his soul will without question be overtaken by a dark feeling of anger, which will then in turn provoke a reaction in the body and bring about those changes that cannot be controlled by our will: his face will glow, his eyes will flash, his muscles will swell; in short, he will seem to be truly enraged, without actually being so – without understanding in the least bit why he ought to be so.

With these fundamental principles of feeling in mind, I have tried to determine which external characteristics accompany the feelings with which moral observations should be delivered and which of these characteristics are within our control so that any actor, whether or not he has the feelings himself, can portray them. I propose the following:

Every moral truism is a universal axiom or premise that, as such, requires a certain amount of spiritual composure and quiet contemplation. It should be spoken, therefore, dispassionately and with a distinct coldness.

On the other hand, this universal axiom is the result of impressions made by unique circumstances upon the acting persons. It is not merely a symbolic conclusion; it is a generalized feeling, and as such it should be spoken with fire and with a certain zeal.[6]

So with zeal and with dispassion? With fire and with coldness? –

Precisely, with a mixture of both, in which, however, sometimes the one or the other takes precedence according to the nature of the situation.

If the situation is calm, then the soul has to want to inspire itself anew with the help of the moral principle. It must appear to meditate generally on its happiness or on its duties, so that through this generalization, it can enjoy the former with more gusto or keep watch over the latter more willingly and courageously.

If, on the other hand, the situation is tempestuous, then the soul must rein itself in by means of the moral truism (a term that I understand to mean every universal observation). The soul must seem willing to give its passions the appearance of reason and its stormy outbursts the appearance of carefully weighed resolutions.

The former requires a lofty and inspired tone; the latter a measured and solemn tone. In the one, reason must ignite emotion, and in the other, emotion must cool itself through reason.

Most actors get this backwards. In tempestuous situations, they bellow out the universal observations with just as much bombast as the rest of the dialogue, and in calm situations, they rattle off these passages like the rest. And so it comes to pass that the moral does not stand out in either case, and that we find it unnatural in the one case and boring and cold in the other. They never stop to consider that embroidery has to contrast with its background and that gold embroidered on gold is in terrible taste.

Moreover, they ruin everything altogether with their gestures. They neither know when they should make use of them nor to what end. The gestures they do make are usually too many and too meaningless.

When the soul seems to collect itself suddenly in a tumultuous situation in order to reflect upon itself or its circumstances, then the soul will naturally control all movements of the body that are subject to its will. Not only will the voice quiet down; but the limbs will also fall into a relaxed state in order to express that inner calm without which the eye of reason cannot look around. All at once, the advancing foot stands fast, the arms sink, and the entire body gathers itself into equilibrium. A pause – and then comes reflection. The man stands there in solemn silence, as if he doesn't want to hinder himself from hearing himself. Then the reflection is over – another pause – and then, depending on whether the reflection directed him either to temper or to ignite his passions, he either suddenly breaks out, or only gradually sets his body in motion again. The evidence of emotion remains only on the face during the reflection; the facial expression and the eyes remain in motion and on fire, because we do not have sudden and complete control over countenance and eyes the way we do over feet and hands. And so it is here, in the telltale expressions, in these burning eyes and in the utter composure of the rest of the body, that the mixture of fire and coldness is found with which I believe a moral truism can be conveyed in an intense situation.

It should also be conveyed by the same mixture in tranquil situations – but with the difference that the part of the action that was fiery in the previous case will here be cold, and where there it was cold, here it must be fiery. Namely: when the soul has nothing but gentle emotions, it will try to give these emotions a higher degree of liveliness during universal contemplation, and to that end it will also make use of the limbs of the body that are under its direct command. The hands will be in full motion, but the expression of the face cannot follow so quickly, and the calm from which the rest of the body would like to work its way out will still rule the face and eyes.

Essay 4

12 May 1767

But what kind of hand movements should accompany the speaking of a moral truism in quiet situations?[1]

We know very little of the chironomy of the ancients – that is, of the essence of the rules stipulated by the ancients regarding the movements of the hands.[2] But we do know that they had brought the language of the hands to a perfection that – given what our orators are capable of achieving – is nearly impossible to imagine. From this complete language, we seem to have retained nothing other than an inarticulate clamor, nothing other than the capacity to produce movements without knowing how to give those movements a fixed meaning or how to combine them so that they become capable of producing a holistic expression rather than just individual significations.[3]

I am fully aware that when talking of the ancients, we must not conflate the pantomimes with the actors.[4] The actor's hands were not nearly as loquacious as the pantomime's. In the case of the latter, the hands substituted for speech; whereas in the case of the former, the hands served to give increased emphasis to speech and, as natural signs of things, helped to lend truth and life to the corresponding signs of the voice.[5] The pantomime's hand movements were not simply natural signs; many of their movements had a conventional meaning, which the actor had to avoid at all costs.[6]

The actor thus used his hands more sparingly than the pantomime, but just as effectively as the latter. He never gestured unless, in so doing, he could convey or emphasize meaning. He knew nothing of those indifferent gestures through whose continuous and monotonous use so many actors, particularly women, give the perfect impression of being marionettes. When they describe half of a stunted figure eight downwards from the body, first with the right hand, then with the left, or use both hands simultaneously to row the air away from them, they call it acting; and if someone is adept at doing this with a certain dance master's grace – well! He believes he can hold us spellbound.

I know well that even Hogarth instructs actors to learn how to move their hands in beautiful serpentine lines – but to all sides, and with all the possible variations that these lines are capable of in terms of fluctuation, range, and duration.[7] And in the end, he instructs them to learn this primarily as an exercise, to make them adept at acting, to make their arms familiar with graceful curves, and not out of a belief that acting consists only of describing such beautiful lines, always in the same direction.[8]

So away with this meaningless *port de bras*, and in particular during moral passages![9] Grace in the wrong place is affectation and contortion; and that same grace, repeated too many times in a row, becomes cold and ultimately repugnant. When the actor offers me general observations with the same movement one uses to proffer one's hand in a minuet, or offers his moral as if winding a spindle, I see a schoolboy reciting his little verses.

Every movement of the hand in the delivery of moral passages must be meaningful. One may approach the picturesque at times, but only if one avoids pantomime. There may perhaps be an opportunity in the future to elucidate through example the differences and gradations in gesture from meaningful to picturesque and from picturesque to pantomimic. At present this would lead me too far, and I will only note here that among the meaningful gestures, there is one type above all that the actor should mark well, and with which alone he can infuse light and life into the moral. This is, in a word, the individualizing gesture. The moral is a general tenet drawn from the particular circumstances of the characters; by means of its generality, it becomes somewhat distanced from the action; it becomes a digression whose relationship to the present will not be noted or understood by the less observant or less discriminating spectators. If, then, there exists some means to make this relationship evident to the senses, to make the symbolic nature of the moral transparently visible, and if this means consists of certain gestures, then the actor must not fail to use them.[10]

I will be best understood if I offer an example. I use one that occurs to me in the moment; the actor will be able to think of many more enlightening ones with little trouble. – When Olint flatters himself with the hope that God will move Aladin's heart, so that he will not deal as cruelly with the Christians as he has threatened to, then Evander, as an older man, cannot do other than warn him to take to heart the deceitfulness of our hopes:[11]

> Trust not hopes, my son, they betray us!

His son is a fiery youth, and in youth we are particularly inclined to expect only the best from the future.

Because they trust too easily, spirited youth often err.

But then he remembers that the old are no less inclined to the opposite error; he does not want to completely crush the fearless young man. He continues:

Age torments itself, because it hopes too little.

To pronounce these sentences with an indifferent action, accompanied by nothing but a beautiful movement of the arms, would be far worse than saying them with no action at all. The only action appropriate to them is one that narrows their generality back down to the specific. The line,

Because they trust too easily, spirited youth often err.

must be spoken in the tone and with the gesture of fatherly warning for – and to – Olint, because it is Olint's inexperienced, gullible youth that has motivated this observation from the cautious old man. In contrast, the line

Age torments itself, because it hopes too little.

demands the tone and the shrug of the shoulders with which we are in the habit of admitting our own weaknesses, and the hands must necessarily be drawn against the breast, in order to make the point that Evander came by this maxim from his own experience, that he himself is of the age for which it holds true.

It is time that I return from this digression about the representation of moral passages. We have Herr Ekhof's examples to thank for whatever we might find instructive therein; I have done nothing but try to abstract correctly from them. How easy and pleasant it is to study an artist who not only succeeds but also sets a new standard!

The role of Clorinda was played by Madame Hensel, who is unquestionably one of the best actresses the German theater has ever had.[12] Her particular accomplishment is a very accurate declamation; a false accent will scarcely escape her lips; she knows how to say the most confusing, stumbling, murky verse with such lightness and precision that, through her voice, it receives the clearest interpretation and the most perfect commentary. Frequently she couples this with a refinement that testifies to either a very felicitous feeling, or a very correct judgment. In my imagination, I can still hear the declaration of love she makes to Olint:[13]

– Know me! I can no longer remain silent;
Deception or pride belong to baser souls.
Olint is in danger, and I am beside myself –
With admiration I often watched you in war and battle;
My heart, which shied away from discovering itself to itself,
Was in combat against my reputation and my pride.
But your misfortune transported my soul entirely,
And now I finally see how small, how weak I am.

Now when all who once honored you, hate you,
When you are destined for punishment, abandoned by everyone,
Equated with criminals, ill-fated and a Christian,
Near terrible death, and wretched even in death:
Now I dare to confess it: now know my desires![14]

How free, how noble was this outburst! What fire, what ardor animated each tone! With what forwardness, with what an overflowing heart did her compassion speak! With what decisiveness did she begin her admission of love! But then how unexpectedly, how surprisingly, did she suddenly break off and change, all at once, her voice and expression and the whole posture of her body, as the moment came to speak the blunt words of her confession. Eyes cast down toward the earth, after a long sigh, in a fearful, pinched tone of confusion, came finally

I love you, Olint –

and with such truth! Even someone uncertain of whether love would declare itself in such a way must have felt that it ought to declare itself so. As a heroine, she resolved to admit her love; but she confessed it as a tender, bashful woman. As much as she was a warrior, otherwise accustomed to doing everything in a masculine manner, here the feminine kept the upper hand. But no sooner were these words that posed such difficulty to modesty uttered than all at once the outspoken tone was back again. She continued with the most unfettered spirit, in the most reckless heat of passion:

– and proud of my love,
proud, that your life can be saved by my power,
I offer you hand and heart, crown and scepter.

For at this point love manifests itself as generous friendship; and friendship is as bold as love is shy.

Essay 5

15 May 1767

It is undeniable that the actress, by masterfully setting apart the words

I love you, Olint –

gave the passage a measure of beauty for which the playwright – for whom everything rushes by in a torrent of words – cannot be given even the slightest credit.[1] If only it had pleased her to continue with these refinements of her role! Perhaps she was concerned that she would entirely miss the spirit of the playwright; or maybe she feared being accused of performing not what the playwright wrote, but rather what he should have written. But then, what praise could be better than such an accusation? Admittedly, not every actor should imagine earning such praise. If that were the case, things would look bad for the poor playwrights.

Cronegk really turned his Clorinda into an extremely vulgar, unsavory, ugly thing. And yet, she is still the only one of his characters of interest to us. While he totally failed to give her any natural beauty, nevertheless her heavy-handed, uncouth nature has its own effect.[2] That is because the other characters are completely unnatural, and we can more easily sympathize with a battle-axe of a woman than with mystical dreamers. It is only toward the end, when she falls into their overzealous tone, that she becomes just as indifferent and disgusting to us. Everything in her is contradiction, and she continually springs from one extreme to another. No sooner has she declared her love, than she adds:

> Will you spurn my heart? You are silent? –
> Make your decision;
> And if you doubt – then tremble!

Tremble? Olint is supposed to tremble? He, whom she has seen so often in the tumult of battle, unfazed by the blows of death? And he should tremble before her? What is she going to do? Scratch his eyes out? – If only, instead of this unseemly feminine blustering "then tremble," it had occurred to the actress to say: "I tremble!" She could tremble as much as she wanted, finding her love spurned and her pride wounded. That would have been very natural. But to demand it from Olint, to demand love from him with a knife at his throat, is as uncouth as it is laughable.

But then again, what good would it have done to keep the playwright one moment longer within the bounds of propriety and moderation? He then proceeds to have Clorinda rage in the authentic tones of a drunken fishwife; and from that point on, there is no letting up or mincing of words.[3]

The only thing that the actress might yet do for the benefit of the playwright would be, perhaps, not to let herself be so totally carried away by his wild fire, to restrain herself, and to avoid expressing the utmost fury with the utmost strain of the voice or with the most violent gestures.

If Shakespeare was not as great an actor as he was a dramatic writer, he at least knew full well what belonged to the art of the one and what belonged to the art of the other.[4] Perhaps he thought all the more deeply about the art of the former because he possessed such a lesser genius for it. At the very least, every word that he puts into Hamlet's mouth when he instructs the players is a golden rule for all actors who strive for honest acclaim. Among other things, he has him say to the comedians, "Speak the speech, I pray you, as I pronounced it to you, trippingly on the tongue: but if you mouth it, as many of your players do, I had as lief the town-crier spoke my lines. Nor do not saw the air too much with your hand, thus, but use all gently; for in the very torrent, tempest, and, as I may say, whirlwind of your passion, you must acquire and beget a temperance that may give it smoothness."[5]

People talk a lot about the fiery passion of an actor; they argue with each other over whether an actor can have too much fire.[6] Where those who claim that it is possible point out as evidence that an actor was too fierce in the wrong place, or at the very least might have been fiercer than the conditions required; then those who disagree might very well respond that in such cases the actor showed not too much fire but rather too little sense. After all, it really depends on what we understand by the word fire. If shouting and contortions are fire, then it is indisputable that the actor can go too far with it. If fire, however, consists in the speed and liveliness with which all the attributes of the actor combine to give his performance the appearance of truth, then to argue that it is possible for the actor to apply too much fire in this sense is to assume that we do not wish to see the appearance of truth driven to the utmost illusion. It thus cannot be this fire, either, that Shakespeare demands be restrained, even in the flowing current, in the storm, in the whirlwind of passion: he must clearly mean the violence of voice and of movements; and it is easy to see the reason why, in places where the playwright has not observed the slightest moderation, the actor must nevertheless restrain himself in both respects. There are few voices that do not become obnoxious in their most extreme exertion; and all-too-quick, all-too-stormy movements are seldom noble. Neither our eyes nor our ears should be injured; and it is only when actors avoid everything that could be unpleasant to these, in their expression of strong passions, that they will have that smoothness and suppleness that a Hamlet demands of them – even under circumstances in which they are to make the greatest impression and frighten awake the conscience of the unrepentant sinner.

The art of the actor exists midway between the visual arts and poetry.[7] As visible painting, beauty must be its highest principle; but as transitory painting it need not always give its postures that calm that made ancient art works so impressive. Acting should, it *must* often allow itself the wildness of a Tempesta, the audacity of a Bernini; it possesses all of their characteristic expressiveness without the offensiveness that visual art may have because of its static state.[8] But acting must not linger too long in any given posture; it must gradually prepare for each one through the movements leading up to it and resolve each one through the subsequent movements back to a general tone of decorum; moreover, it must never give any posture all of the force to which the playwright, in his handling of the material, can drive it. For although this is a silent poetry, it wants to make itself immediately understood by our eyes; and any sense must be gratified if it is to communicate directly to the soul those concepts that have been entrusted to it.[9]

It could well be that our actors, with an eye to applause, would not be altogether comfortable with the moderation to which art obliges them even in the most extreme passions. – But what applause? – The gallery is admittedly a great lover of noise and bluster, and will seldom fail to respond with loud hands to strong lungs. But even the German *parterre* shares this taste to great degree, and there are actors who are clever enough to take advantage of this.[10] The laziest actor pulls himself together near the end of the scene before he is to exit, suddenly raises his voice, and exaggerates the action without considering whether this greater effort serves the sense of his speech. Often this contradicts the condition in which he should exit; but what does that matter to him? It is sufficient that he has thereby reminded the *parterre* to pay attention to him, and if they would be so kind, to applaud him. They ought to hiss at him! But sadly, the *parterre* on the one hand lacks connoisseurship and on the other hand is too forgiving, and mistakes the desire to please for the accomplishment.

I do not trust myself to say anything about the performance of the remaining actors in this piece. If they must always be occupied with masking mistakes and making the merely adequate seem acceptable, then even the best cannot do any better than appear in a very ambivalent light. Even if we refrain from blaming the actor for the aggravation that the playwright has caused us, we nevertheless cannot calm our irritation enough to do him the justice that he deserves.

The conclusion of the first night was *The Triumph of Times Past*, a comedy in one act, based on the work of the French writer Le Grand.[11] It is one of the three small plays that Le Grand brought to the French stage in 1724 under the general title *The Triumph of Time*, after he had already worked with the same material – garnering little applause – a year previously under the title *The Ridiculous Lovers*.[12] The event that lies at its center is droll enough, and several scenarios are quite ridiculous. But this ridiculousness is of a type better suited to a satiric story than to the theater. The triumph of time over beauty and youth makes for a sad concept; the vain delusion of a sixty-year-old fop and an equally foolish old woman – that time had no power over their own powers to attract – is truly ridiculous; but to see this fop and this fool is more repulsive than comical.

Essay 6

19 May 1767

I still have not mentioned the addresses delivered to the audience before and after the main play on the first evening.[1] They were written by a poet who understands better than any other how to enliven profound ideas with wit and lend an agreeable air of playfulness to serious thought.[2] How could I better enhance these pages, than by sharing them in full with my readers? Here they are. They need no commentary. I only hope that they do not fall on deaf ears!

They were both unusually well delivered; the first with all of the grace and dignity, and the second with all of the warmth, delicacy, and engaging courtesy that the particular content of each demands.

Prologue[3]

(SPOKEN BY MADAME LÖWEN)[4]

Dear friends, who have enjoyed here the manifold display
Of humanity through the art of imitation:
You who gladly weep, you tender, better souls,
How beautiful, how noble your desire to vex yourselves so;
When by and by sweet tears, from melting hearts,
Dissolved in tenderness, steal quietly down cheeks,
When then the soul, assailed, with every nerve aquiver,
Revels in suffering, and trembles with desire!
O say: this art, that so melts your heart,
This stream of passion, that surges through your core,

Which pleases when it's touching, and delights with fear,
Which awakens you to pity, compassion, and generosity;
This model of decorum that teaches every virtue –
Is it not worth your favor and your patronage?

Compassionate Providence sends this art to Earth
To benefit barbarians, so they become humane;[5]
It consecrates art with majesty, with genius, and passion divine,
To be the teacher of princes and kings;
It calls on art to use its power of enthralling us in tears
To sharpen the dullest sense of compassion;
To conquer evil and strengthen souls
Through sweet apprehension and pleasurable dread;
To mold, for benefit of the state, the angry, wild man
Into a person, citizen, patriot, and friend.

Laws may well strengthen the safety of nations,
Like chains binding the hands of injustice:
But craftiness will always hide scoundrels from judges,
And power will often shelter nobility's villains.
Who will avenge innocence, then? Woe to the enfetter'd state,
Whose only virtue is a book of laws!
Laws that merely bridle public crimes,
Laws abused to deliver verdicts of hate,
When selfishness, pride, and prejudice
Impose the spirit of oppression on the spirit of Solon![6]
Then corruption soon seizes the sword of majesty
In order to escape its retribution:
Then the power-hungry, rejoicing in the decay
Of integrity, plant a foot on freedom's neck;
Make noble men languish in irons and shame
And slaughter the innocent with Themis's bloodstained sword.[7]

When he, unpunished by any and punishable by none,
The clever villain, the bloodthirsty tyrant,
When he suppresses innocence, who will defend it?
One is protected by pools of deceit, another armed with terror.
Who is the protector of innocence, who will stand in opposition? –
Who? – That fearless art, which wields both dagger and scourge
And dares to hold the mirror up
To all miscreants of unpunished folly;
Which unveils deception's tangled web,
And tells tyrants that indeed tyrants they are;
Which, fearless, shows its strength before the throne,
And speaks to the hearts of princes in a thunderous tone;
Which frightens crowned murderers, and sobers the ambitious,
Chastens the hypocrite, and laughs the fool wiser;

Which teaches us a lesson by bringing the dead to life:
That great art with which we laugh, or cry.

In Greece Thalia found protection, love, and the desire for learning;
In Rome, in Gaul, in Albion, and – here.[8]
When her tears have flowed with noble tenderness,
You, friends, have often joined in with yours;
You have openly merged your pain with hers,
And cried your applause with full hearts to her:
Like her, you have hated, loved, hoped, and feared,
And through suffering, rejoiced in your humanity.
For a long time she has sought a stage in vain:
In Hamburg she found protection: here is her Athens!
Here, in the bosom of peace, protected by wise patrons,
Encouraged by praise, perfected by the connoisseur,
Here will flourish – yes, I wish, I hope, I predict! –
A second Roscius, a second Sophocles,[9]
Who will revive Greek tragedy for the Germans:
And some of this fame shall be yours, you patrons
O be worthy of the same! Uphold your benefaction,
And remember, O remember, all Germany looks up to you!

Epilogue

(DELIVERED BY MADAME HENSEL)

See here! how resolutely the stalwart Christian dies!
And how coldly he hates, who finds use in delusion,
Who needs barbarity, the better to make his cause,
His vision, his dream, into the word of God.
The spirit of delusion was persecution and violence,
Where blindness was merit, and fear, piety.
Thus the web of lies was protected with the flare
Of majesty, with poison, and with assassination.
Where conviction is lacking, fear steps in:
Truth is condemned, delusion claims blood.
Those whose faith differs from Ismenor's
Must be hunted and converted by the sword.
And many an Aladin, whether conniving or weak, indulges
The dark court of holy murders,
And must use his sword against his friend,
The enemy of fanaticism, the martyr to the truth –
An abominable masterwork of ambition and cunning
For which no name is too harsh, no insult too bitter!
O dogma, that allows abuse of the deity itself,
Allows the dagger of hatred to be plunged into an innocent heart,
You, with your bloody banner so often carried over corpses:

Who will lend me a curse with which to condemn you, you abomination!
You friends, in whose breast the noble voice of humanity
Spoke out for the heroine, as she became an innocent victim
Of the priest's fury and died for the truth:
Be thanked for this feeling, thanked for each tear!
He who errs does not deserve the high price of hate or derision:
The teachings of hatred are no teachings of God!
Oh! Love those who err, who are blind without malice,
Who perhaps are much weaker, but still human beings.
Teach them, tolerate them; do not force to tears those
Who cannot be reproached for anything other than different beliefs!
Righteous the man who, true to his faith,
Forces no one to deceive or viciously to pretend;
Who burns for truth, and, like Olint, never cobbled by fear,
Joyfully seals it with his blood.
Such an example, noble friends, deserves your applause:
What a blessing! if what Cronegk teaches so beautifully,
If the ideas, that have so ennobled him,
Were engraved deep in your hearts by our performance.
The poet's life was beautiful, as is his repute;
He was, and – oh, forgive my tears! – died a Christian.
To posterity he left his magnificent heart in poems,
So that – and what more can one do? – he could teach us even in death.
If Sophronia has moved you here,
Do not withhold from his ashes what they are rightly owed:
The heartfelt sigh that he died, gratitude for his lessons,
And – ah! the sad tribute of a salty tear.
But us, noble friends, encourage with benevolence;
And if we have failed, please rebuke; but forgive.
Forgiveness encourages ever nobler striving,
And delicate reproach teaches how to earn the highest praise.
Remember that this art, with its thousand Quins for just one Garrick,[10]
Has just begun with us;
Do not expect too much, so that we may continue to improve,
And – certainly the privilege to judge is only yours, as ours is to be silent.

Essay 7

22 May 1767

The Prologue presents the theater in its most noble aspect, insofar as drama may be regarded as a supplement to the law.[1] There are matters in the moral comportment of men that, with regard to their direct impact upon the well-being of society, are too insignificant and in themselves too changeable to be worthy or capable of standing under the official purview of the law. There are others, on the other hand, against which all of the power of legislation is too limited, that are so incomprehensible in their driving forces, so egregious in and of themselves, so immeasurable in their consequences, that they either are able to escape the penalty of the law or cannot possibly be punished as they deserve. I will not attempt to reduce these matters by assigning the former to comedy, the genre of the ridiculous, and the latter – as extreme acts in the realm of behavior that shock reason and set the heart in tumult – to tragedy. Genius laughs at all of the categorizations of the critic. But this much is indisputable: drama takes a stand on either one side of the law or the other and handles the particulars of that subject matter only insofar as they get lost in the ridiculous or expand into the despicable.

The Epilogue expounds on one of the primary lessons that is a partial focus of the plot and characters of this tragedy. It was, admittedly, a bit ill-considered for Herr Cronegk to preach tolerance in a play whose subject was taken from that unfortunate period of the Crusades and to try to convey the horrific spirit of persecution through the followers of the Muslim religion. For these Crusades themselves, which in their conception were a political invention of the Popes, were in their execution the most inhumane persecutions that Christian superstition has ever perpetrated. At that time, the majority of the bloodthirsty Ismenors were of the true faith – and to see individual persons who robbed a mosque punished, can that really stand against the disastrous madness that depopulated Europe of righteous believers in order to lay waste to pagan Asia? But what the tragedian presented quite inappropriately, the poet of the Epilogue grasped quite befittingly. Benevolence and gentleness deserve to be commended whenever possible, and, at the very least, no cause for such emotions can ever be so remote that our hearts would not find it natural and compelling.

By the way, I am happy to concur with the touching praise that the poet bestowed upon the late Cronegk. But I will hardly be convinced that he should not also agree with me about the poetic value of the criticized play. I was quite taken aback when I was informed that I might have alienated my readers unwittingly through my candid judgment. If modest freedom, which has no hidden agenda, displeases them, then I run the risk that I will still frequently alienate them. It was never my intention to spoil their reading of a playwright who is recommended for his unpretentious wit, many refined emotions, and clearest morality. These qualities will always make him admirable, even if one faults him for other effects for which he either had no talent or lacked the critical maturity – as death denied him reaching the crucial age. His *Codrus* was given a prize by the editors of the *Library of the Literary Arts* not because it was a good play but rather because it was the best among those that competed for the prize at the time.[2] My judgment does not therefore deny him any honor that the critics bestowed upon him at the time. When limping men run a race, the one who makes it first across the finish line still limps.

One statement in the Epilogue has been the subject of a misconception from which it deserves to be rescued. The poet writes:

> Remember that this art, which has a thousand Quins for just one Garrick,
> Has just begun among us;

Quin, I have heard in response to this, was not a bad actor. − No, certainly not; he was Thomson's best friend, and the friendship that connected an actor with a playwright like Thomson will always awaken in posterity a positive prejudice toward his artistic talents.[3] And Quin had much more than just this prejudice in his favor: we know that he played in tragedies with great dignity, that he knew how to handle Milton's lofty language particularly well, and that in the comic realm he played the role of Falstaff to its greatest perfection.[4] But all this makes him no Garrick; and the misunderstanding rests simply in the fact that people assume the poet wanted to contrast this universal and extraordinary actor with one who was bad and generally recognized as such.[5] But Quin is meant to represent here one of the ordinary types we see every day; a man who always does his job so well that we are happy with him; who also plays certain characters truly superbly as long as his physique, voice, and temperament are suited to the task. Such a man is very useful, and can be called a good actor with complete justification; but he still lacks too much to be considered the kind of Proteus in his art that Garrick has long been universally acclaimed to be.[6] Such a Quin no doubt played the King in *Hamlet* when Tom Jones and Partridge went to the theater;* and there are many Partridges who would not hesitate for a moment to prefer him to a Garrick.[7] "What?" they say, "Garrick the best player? He didn't seem frightened by the Ghost, he actually was. What kind of art is that, to be frightened by a ghost? For certain and true, if we had seen a ghost, we would have looked in the very same manner, and done just as he did. Now the other one, the king, also seemed somewhat moved, but as a good actor he took every possible care to hide it. In addition, he spoke all his words distinctly, and spoke twice as loud as that small, unattractive man that you all make such a fuss about!"

Among the English every new play has a prologue and epilogue that are written by either the playwright himself or one of his friends. They do not use the prologue for the same purpose that the ancients did, that is, to instruct the spectator in various things that will help them to understand more quickly the underlying story of the play.[8] Nevertheless, it is not without purpose. They have a hundred and one ways of saying things in prologues that can predispose the auditorium to the playwright or to his work and can preempt unfair criticism not only against him but also the actors. Still less do they use the epilogue in the way that writers like Plautus sometimes used it, that is, to narrate a complete resolution of a play for which the fifth act did not have room.[9] Rather, they give it a practical application, full of good lessons and fine observations about the morals depicted and about the art used to depict them, and all of it in the most droll and humorous of tones. This tone does not change even in the case of tragedies; and it is not at all uncommon that, after the most bloody and moving of them, the satire provokes such loud laughter, and the wit becomes so boisterous, that it seems the express purpose was to drive away all impressions of good through mockery. It is well known how fervently Thomson railed against this fool's cap jingling after Melpomene.[10] Therefore, if I wish that we would not bring original plays before our public without introduction and recommendation, it is with the understanding that, in the case of tragedies, the tone of the epilogue ought to be more

---

* Part VI, p. 15.

suited to our German seriousness. After comedies it can be as burlesque as it wants to be. Dryden has written masterpieces of this sort in England which are still read with great pleasure, even after the plays for which he composed them have – for the most part – long been forgotten.[11] Hamburg may well have a Dryden nearby; and I need not identify yet again that man among our playwrights who can season morality and criticism with Attic salt as well as the English do.[12]

Essay 8

26 May 1767

The performances of the first evening were repeated on the second.

On the third evening (Friday, the 24th of May), *Mélanide* was performed.[1] This play by Nivelle de la Chaussée is well-known.[2] It belongs to that touching genre that has been given the derisive epithet *larmoyant*.[3] If *larmoyant* refers to something that brings us to the verge of tears, that gives us a strong desire to cry, then several plays of this genre are something more than *larmoyant*, as they will cause a sensitive soul to dissolve in streams of tears; in comparison to such works, the common mass of French tragedies deserves to be called merely *larmoyant*. For really, they only bring us to the point where we recognize that we would be crying if the writer had practiced his craft better.

Mélanide is no masterpiece of this genre; but one still always watches it with pleasure. It has kept its place even in the French theater in which it first played in the year 1741.[4] The subject matter supposedly derives from a novel titled *Mademoiselle de Bontems*.[5] I do not know this novel; but if the situation in the second scene of the third act is also taken from it, then I must envy an unknown person, instead of de la Chaussée, for creating that scene, since it is the reason I would wish to have written a *Mélanide*.[6]

The translation was not bad; it is infinitely better than an Italian translation that is in the second volume of Diodati's *Theatrical Library*.[7] I must offer reassurance to the majority of our translators that their Italian comrades are, for the most part, far worse than they are. To translate good verse into good prose demands something more than correctness; or, I probably should say, something else. Excessive fidelity will make any translation stiff, because it is impossible for everything that is natural in one language to be so in the other. Moreover, the literal translation of verses renders them watery and cockeyed. For where is that fortunate versifier who has never been forced by the meter or rhyme into saying something more or less here, stronger or weaker there, or earlier or later than he would have if he were free from this constraint? Now, if the translator does not know how to discern this, if he does not have enough taste and courage to leave out a digression here, or to use the actual expression instead of a metaphor there, or to fill in for an ellipsis elsewhere, then he will pass on to us all of the faults of the original and will have done nothing more than deprive them of this defense: namely, that they are due to challenges posed by the symmetry and melody of the original language.

The role of Mélanide was played by an actress who, after a nine-year absence from the theater, has reappeared with all those perfections that experts and amateurs, those with and without discretion, have always perceived and admired in her. Madame Löwen combines the silver tones of the most lovely, sonorous voice with the most open, peaceful, and at the same time most expressive face in the world; the finest, quickest emotions; and the surest, warmest sentiment (which, to be sure, is not always as lively as many might wish, but nonetheless always expresses itself with grace and dignity). She accentuates her declamation correctly but not too markedly. A complete lack of marked accentuation brings about monotony; but without accusing her of this, she knows how to use it more sparingly, due to a refinement of which, alas! many actors know absolutely nothing. I want to explain what I mean. We know what tempo means in music; not beat, but the degree of slowness or rapidity with which the beat is played. This tempo is uniform throughout the whole piece; the same degree of speed in which the first beats are played must be sustained for every bar until the last. Such uniformity is necessary to music, because a composition can only express itself in such a way, and without uniformity the combination of different instruments and voices would be impossible. With declamation, on the other hand, things are very different. If we consider a passage composed of many lines to be a special type of musical piece and regard the lines as beats or measures of the same, then even if these lines were all of exactly the same length and consisted of the same number of syllables of equal measure, they should never be spoken with one and the same speed. For since they cannot have the same value and importance, either with regard to enunciation and emphasis or in light of the affect that governs the whole passage, it follows that the voice would utter the least significant lines quickly, slipping over them in a perfunctory and hasty manner, whereas it would linger over the more substantive ones, stretching and honing them and making sure that each word and each letter in each word counts. The degrees of difference are infinite, and even though they do not allow themselves to be fixed by any artificial divisions of time and thereby to be measured against one another, they will still be differentiated by the most unskilled of ears and observed by the most unskilled of tongues – if and when the speech flows from a heart penetrated with feeling and not merely from well-prepared memorization. The effect of this constantly changing movement of the voice is incredible; and when it is combined with absolutely all of the possible changes in tone – not only with respect to high or low, strong or weak, but also to harsh or soft, sharp or round, even clumsy or smooth – at the proper moments, then that natural music occurs to which our heart unfailingly opens, because we sense that it originates in the heart and that art only plays a part in it insofar as art can become nature, too. And with such music, I say, the actress of whom I speak is absolutely splendid; no one compares to her except Herr Ekhof, who brings his declamation to an even higher degree of perfection mainly because he intensely accents individual words (something she makes less effort to do). But perhaps she too has this under her command, and I merely judge her thus because I have not yet seen her in a role in which the touching is elevated to the solemn. I look forward to seeing her in a tragedy – and in the meantime continue with the history of our theater.

On the fourth evening (Monday, the 27th of May), a new German original was produced, titled *Julie, or the Conflict between Duty and Love.*[8] The author is Herr Heufeld from Vienna, who tells us that recently two of his other plays have earned the acclaim of the audience there.[9] I do not know them; but to judge from this one, they are probably not entirely terrible.

The principal features of the story and most of the situations have been taken from Rousseau's *New Heloise.*[10] I would wish that Herr Heufeld had read and studied the evaluation of this novel in the *Letters Concerning the Newest Literature** before he approached this project.[11] He would have worked with a more secure insight into the beauties of the original and might have been more successful in many places.

The value of *The New Heloise*, in terms of originality, is quite minor, and the best of it is totally unsuitable for dramatic adaptation.[12] The situations are commonplace or unnatural, and the few good ones are spaced so far apart that they do not allow themselves to be squeezed into the narrow space of a three-act play without unnatural effort. The story could not possibly conclude on stage as it does in the novel, in which it does not so much wrap up as lose itself. Here, Julie's lover must be happy, and Herr Heufeld allows him to be happy. He gets to marry his pupil. But did Herr Heufeld consider that his Julie is now no longer in any way Rousseau's Julie? Then again, Rousseau's Julie or not – who cares? As long as she is a person who interests us. But that is precisely what she is not; she is nothing but a lovestruck little fool who from time to time chatters agreeably enough, whenever Herr Heufeld recalls a beautiful passage from Rousseau. "Julie," writes the critic whose evaluation I mentioned above, "plays a double role in the story. In the beginning she is a weak and, indeed, somewhat seductive girl; at the end, she becomes a woman who, as a model of virtue, far surpasses all who have ever been invented."[13] She becomes the latter through her obedience, through the sacrifice of her love, and through the control she gains over her heart. But if there is nothing to be seen or heard of all this in the play, what is left of her except, as I already said, a weak seductive girl with virtue and wisdom on her tongue and foolishness in her heart?

Herr Heufeld has rechristened Rousseau's St. Preux as Siegmund. To us, the name Siegmund rather smacks of a domestic servant. I wish that our dramatic poets were a bit more discriminating in such details and strove to capture a more sophisticated tone. – St. Preux is already a very tasteless figure in Rousseau. "They all call him," writes the above-mentioned critic, "the philosopher. The philosopher! I'd like to know what the young man says or does in the whole story that earns him this name? In my eyes he is the most fatuous person in the world, who praises reason and wisdom to the skies with the most generic proclamations and who does not possess the slightest spark of either. He is absurd, bombastic, and extravagant in matters of love, and we do not find the slightest trace of reflection in the rest of his doings. He is proudly confident of his levelheadedness, and yet is not decisive enough to take the tiniest step without his pupil or his friend leading him by the hand."[14] – And yet how far below this St. Preux ranks the German Siegmund!

* Part X, p. 255 ff.

Essay 9

29 May 1767

In the novel, St. Preux has the occasional opportunity to demonstrate his enlightened mind and play the active role of an upstanding man.[1] In the comedy, however, Siegmund is no more than a small, conceited pedant, who makes a virtue of his weakness and is quite offended to find that others do not universally do justice to his tender little heart. His entire impact comes down to a pair of massively idiotic deeds. The boy wants to fight and to stab himself.

The playwright figured out on his own that his Siegmund does not appear to be sufficiently active; but he believes he precludes this criticism when he announces that, "a man of his sort, in a period of twenty-four hours' time, cannot accomplish great things like a king, to whom every moment offers such opportunities. One must simply accept at the outset that he is the upright man he is described to be; and it suffices that Julie, her mother, Clarisse, and Edward – all clearly upright people – have recognized him as such."[2]

In daily life it is right and proper to avoid placing injurious mistrust in the character of others and to place one's faith in the opinions shared among upstanding people. But should the dramatic poet be allowed to get away so easily with fobbing this social convention off on us? Certainly not, even if he could thereby make his own work much easier. On stage, we want to see who people really are, and we can only see that through their actions. The good that we should attribute to them just because others say so cannot possibly interest us; it leaves us utterly indifferent, and when we ourselves do not have even the slightest direct experience of this good, it really just leaves a bad impression of those people whose belief and opinions we are supposed to accept on their word alone. Far be it then that we should be prepared to acknowledge Siegmund as the most splendid and perfect young man just because Julie, her mother, Clarisse, and Edward say so: rather, we are far more likely to develop mistrust in the perspective of all of these other characters if we never see anything with our own eyes that justifies their favorable opinion. It is true that a private person cannot accomplish many great deeds in twenty-four hours. But who is asking for great? A character can reveal himself even in the smallest actions; and only those actions that shine the most light upon character are truly the greatest, according to poetic evaluation.[3] So how did it come to be that twenty-four hours were enough to drive Siegmund to the two most extreme follies that could possibly occur to a man in his circumstances? The playwright might answer that the circumstances are suitable: but this he certainly will not do. Yet even if the circumstances were developed naturally and managed delicately, the follies themselves that we see Siegmund threatening to commit would still not lose their noxious effect on our impression of the tempestuous young pseudo-intellectual. We see for ourselves that he behaves badly; we only hear that he is capable of behaving well, and even then we hear no specific examples but instead only the most general, vacillating descriptions.

The severity that Julie encounters at the hand of her father, because he wants her to marry someone other than her own heart's choice, is barely touched upon by

Rousseau.[4] Herr Heufeld had the courage to present us with an entire scene. I love it when a young poet takes a risk. He has the father throw the daughter to the ground. I was worried about the staging of this action. But without cause: our actors had choreographed it so well, there was so much grace on the part of the father and the daughter, and this grace did so little damage to the truth of the moment, that I had to concede that if any actors could accomplish such a scene, it was these or none. Herr Heufeld demands that when Julie is raised up by her mother, blood should be visible on her face. He can be grateful that this was left out. The physical staging must never be carried to disgusting extremes.[5] It is enough when the heated fantasy imagines seeing blood in such cases, but the eye must not actually see it.[6]

The scene that follows is the most splendid of the entire play. It originates in the Rousseau. I myself cannot explain what kind of displeasure mixes with the feeling of pathos when we see a father begging for something at the feet of his daughter. It offends, it affronts us, to see him to whom nature has given such holy rights brought so low. We have to forgive Rousseau this extraordinary lever: the mass that he has to set in motion is too big. Since no argument will change Julie, since her heart is so constituted that it will only more stubbornly fortify itself in its resolve, she could only be shaken by the sudden surprise of the most unexpected encounter and turned about in a kind of stupefaction. We are to believe that the lover becomes a daughter, and that seductive tenderness transforms into blind obedience. Because Rousseau saw no means to derive these changes from Nature, he felt compelled to contrive them from – or, if you will, force them onto – Nature. There is no other way we could forgive Julie when, in what follows, she supposedly sacrifices the most passionate lover for the coldest husband. But since this sacrifice never transpires in the comedy, since it is not the daughter but the father who finally gives in, should Herr Heufeld not have softened that change of heart? A change that Rousseau merely used to justify what is disturbing in that sacrifice and to shield what is unusual in it from the accusation of being unnatural? – But I could go on and on! If Herr Heufeld had done that, we would have lost a scene that, while not fitting so well with the whole, nonetheless is quite powerful; it would be as if he had painted out of his rendering a source of light that has a tremendous effect, even though we never quite know its origin.[7] The skill with which Herr Ekhof played this scene, the movement by which he brought a shock of gray hair in front of his eyes as he pleaded with his daughter: these alone would make worthwhile the perpetration of a minor indecency that perhaps no one would notice, other than the cold critic analyzing the plot.

The afterpiece of this evening was *The Treasure*, an imitation of Plautus's *Trinummus* in which the playwright sought to concentrate all of the comic scenes of the original into one act.[8] It was performed quite well. The actors all played their roles with the dexterity that low comedy so necessarily demands. If a half-baked gag, an indiscretion, or a play on words is delivered in a slow and stuttering manner, if the characters have to stop and think about poor jokes that could do nothing more than raise a smile, boredom is inevitable. Farces have to be delivered rapid-fire, and the spectator must not have even a moment to consider just how witty or stupid they are. There are no women in this play; the only one who might have been brought in would have been an icy lover, and honestly, it is better to have none than such a one. Otherwise, I would not wish to advise anyone to cultivate this peculiarity. We are too accustomed to the combination of both sexes not to feel that entirely eliminating the more charming of the two leaves something missing.

Previously Cecchi, among the Italians, and more recently Destouches, among the French, brought this same comedy by Plautus back to the stage.[9] They both made it into a long five-act play and were therefore compelled to expand the Roman's plot with their own inventions. The play by Cecchi is called *The Dowry*, and in his history of the Italian theater Riccoboni recommends it as one of the best of those old comedies.[10] The play by Destouches bears the title *The Hidden Treasure* and was performed just once in the year 1745 on the Italian stage in Paris – and even this once was not performed to its end.[11] It found no renown and only first appeared in print after the death of the author, and also after the appearance of the German play *The Treasure*. Plautus himself was not the first inventor of this successful and oft-imitated material; rather it was Philemon, who gave it the simple title to which the German version returned.[12] Plautus had his own unique style in naming his plays, and for the most part he took his titles from the most insignificant incidents. For example, he called this play *Trinummus*, or *The Three Pieces of Money*, because this is what the impostor receives for his efforts.[13]

Essay 10

2 June 1767

On the fifth evening (Tuesday, the 28th of April), the play was *The Unexpected Obstacle, or the Obstacle without Obstacle*, by Destouches.[1]

When we look through the annals of the French theater, we find that the funniest plays by this author are also the ones that have received the least public acclaim. Neither the present play, nor *The Hidden Treasure*, *The Nocturnal Drummer*, or *The Country Poet* have survived; and even when they were new, they were only performed a few times.[2] A great deal hinges on the tone that a writer uses to introduce himself or that he uses to produce his best works. We tacitly assume that he has entered thereby into a commitment never to diverge from this tone, and if he does, we consider ourselves entitled to be confounded by it. We seek the author in the author and believe that we have found something worse the moment we find something different. In his plays *The Married Philosopher*, *The Conceited Count*, and *The Spendthrift*, Destouches produced examples of a finer and higher comedy than even Molière in his most serious plays.[3] The critics, who so gladly classify, immediately identified this as his unique sphere. That which for the poet had perhaps been nothing more than incidental choice was identified by the critics as superb instinct and masterful ability; that which he once or twice had chosen not to do, they declared him incapable of doing, and once he did want to, is it not typical of the critics that they would rather not do him justice than alter their hasty judgment? I am not saying here that the low comedy of Destouches is of the same quality as Molière's. It is really a great deal stiffer; a clever mind is more in evidence than a faithful painter. His fools are seldom the kind of easy fool that comes from nature but more often of the wooden sort that art tends to carve, and overloaded with affectation, with an ill-conceived way of life, with pedantry. As a result, his Schulwitz and his Masures are more chilly than ridiculous.[4] But that notwithstanding – and this is all I wanted to say – his humorous plays are not nearly so lacking in genuine comedy as an overly refined taste might find them to be. They occasionally contain scenes that make us laugh from the heart, and that alone might assure him a considerable rank among the comic poets.[5]

A new comedy in one act followed, called *The New Agnes*.[6]

Madame Gertrude pretends to be a pious prude before the eyes of the world, but secretly she is the obliging, fiery girlfriend of a certain Bernard.[7] "How happy, oh how happy you make me, Bernard!" she cries out in ecstasy – and she is overheard by her daughter. The following morning, the sweet simple girl asks, "But mama, who is this Bernard, who makes people happy?" The mother realizes she is discovered and quickly pulls herself together. "It is the saint whom I have recently chosen, my daughter; one of the greatest in Paradise." Not long afterward, the daughter gets to know a certain Hilary. The good child finds great pleasure in his company, mama gets suspicious, mama sneaks up on the happy pair, and mama hears as lovely a sigh from the darling daughter as this darling daughter recently heard from mama. The mother gets angry, attacks her, rages. "What is all this, dear mama?" the calm girl finally says. "You chose St. Bernard for yourself, and I chose St. Hilary. Why not?" – This is one of the educational little fairy tales that the divine Voltaire in his wise old age bestowed upon the young.[8] Favart found it so edifying that he felt compelled to turn it into a comic opera.[9] He saw nothing objectionable in it beyond the name of the saint, and so he removed this irritation. Out of Madame Gertrude he made a platonic sage, a follower of the teachings of Gabalis, and "Saint Bernard" becomes a sylph, who visits in the name and form of a good friend of the virtuous woman.[10] Hilary also becomes a sylph, and so forth. In short, he wrote the operetta *Isabelle and Gertrude, or the Imagined Sylphs*, which is the foundation for *The New Agnes*. There was an attempt to bring the moral conventions closer to our own, there was an attempt to observe all respectability; the sweet girl possesses the most charming, admirable innocence, and strewn throughout the whole are many good comic ideas, some of which are the German author's own. I cannot go more specifically into the changes that he makes to his original; but people of taste who know it might wish that he had retained the woman next door rather than the father. – The role of Agnes was played by Mademoiselle Felbrich, a young woman who promises to be an excellent actress and thus deserves the warmest encouragement.[11] Age, figure, expression, voice – everything comes together in her; and even if these natural gifts allow her to perform much of this role automatically, one still must concede that she adds many refinements revealing forethought and art – but not more nor less than should be revealed in an Agnes.

On the sixth evening (Wednesday, the 29th of April), M. de Voltaire's *Sémiramis* was performed.[12]

This tragedy was brought to the French stage in 1748, received great acclaim, and was to a certain degree epoch-making in the history of that theater. After M. de Voltaire had delivered his *Zaïre* and *Alzire* and his *Brutus* and *Caesar*, he was confirmed in his opinion that the tragic poets of his nation far overtook the ancient Greeks in many particulars. From us French, he says, the Greeks could have learned a more skillful exposition as well as the grand art of joining scenes together such that the stage is never empty and characters never enter or exit without purpose.[13] From us, he says, they could have learned how rivals in love, male and female, converse with each other in witty repartee, and how the poet must dazzle and astonish with plenty of lofty, brilliant thoughts. From us they could have learned – But of course, what is there that cannot be learned from the French! Here and there a foreigner who has also read a little of the ancients might humbly beg to differ in opinion. He might perhaps object that all of these French merits have in fact no great influence on the substance of tragedy, that these are superficial beauties which the simple greatness of the ancients looked upon with scorn. But what use is it to object to anything M. de Voltaire says? He speaks and people believe. There was only one thing he found lacking in the French theater – that its great masterpieces were not being performed with the kind of magnificence that the Greeks deemed worthy of their trifling attempts at a newly evolving art. The theater in Paris – an old tennis court with decorations of the worst taste, where standing spectators push and shove each other in a dirty *parterre* – rightly offended him; and he was particularly offended by the barbaric practice of tolerating spectators on the stage, where they left the actors barely enough room for their most necessary movements.[14] He was convinced that this unseemly practice alone deprived France of much that doubtless would have been ventured in a sumptuous theater that was more open and accommodating to action. And in order to test this, he wrote his *Sémiramis*.[15] A queen, who gathers together the nobles of her realm in order to announce her marriage; a ghost who climbs out of his crypt to prevent incest and to revenge his own murder; this same crypt, into which a fool enters in order to reemerge as a criminal: all of this was in fact something completely new for the French. It makes as much fuss on the stage, it demands as much pageantry and change of scene as we have only ever been used to in an opera. The playwright thought he had provided the model for a very special genre; and even if that model was made not for the French stage as it was, but rather as he wished the stage to be, in any case it was played on that stage more or less as well as it could be played for the time being. At the first performance, the audience still sat on the stage, and I really would have loved to see an old-fashioned ghost appear in such a gallant circle.[16] Only with the second performance was this blunder remedied. The actors took over their stage, and what was once only an exception for the benefit of such an unusual play has since become the lasting arrangement. But only, for the most part, at the theaters in Paris, for which, as mentioned above, *Sémiramis* was epoch-making. In the provinces they often continue with the old fashion and would rather relinquish all illusions than give up the privilege of being able to step on Zaïre's or Mérope's gown.[17]

Essay 11

5 June 1767

The appearance of a ghost was such an audacious innovation for a French tragedy, and the writer who took this risk justified it with such singular reasoning, that it is worth taking the trouble to dwell on it a bit.[1]

"They wailed and wrote from all sides," says M. de Voltaire, "that no one believes in ghosts anymore, and that in the eyes of an enlightened nation the appearance of the dead can be nothing other than childish. But how?" he counters, "All of the ancient world is said to have believed in this marvel, and should it not be acceptable to conform to the ancients? What? Our religion is supposed to have sanctified similar extraordinary acts of providence, and yet it would be ridiculous to repeat them?"[2]

It seems to me that such proclamations are more rhetorical than substantial. Above all, I would wish to leave religion out of this discussion. In matters of taste and criticism, arguments taken from religion are well and good for silencing an opponent, but they are not really so fit for convincing him. Religion *qua* religion need not decide anything here; it is merely one kind of tradition from antiquity, and as such, its evidence is no more or less valid than any other evidence from the ancient world. And therefore here, too, we would only need to deal with antiquity.

Very well, all of antiquity believed in ghosts. The dramatic poets in the ancient world were justified in exploiting this belief, and if we find one of them bringing the dead back to life on stage, it would be uncharitable of us to condemn him according to our superior understanding. But then does the modern poet, who partakes in our superior understanding, have the same authority? Certainly not. – But what if he sets his story back in those gullible times? Even then, no. For the dramatic poet is no history writer; he does not narrate what people believed and what happened long ago; rather, he allows it to happen once again before our eyes, and does so not for the sake of pure historical accuracy but rather for a very different and higher purpose.[3] Historical truth is not his goal but merely the means to his end; he wants to deceive us and, through deception, move us.[4] If it is then true that we do not believe in ghosts anymore, if this lack of belief would necessarily hinder deception, if without deception we cannot possibly sympathize, then the dramatic poet of today would be working against himself if, notwithstanding all this, he furnished forth such unbelievable fairy tales; all of the art that he might employ would be in vain.

And in consequence? In consequence, should it be wholly impermissible to put ghosts and apparitions on stage? In consequence, must this wellspring of terror and pathos run dry for us?[5] No, that would be too great a loss for poetry. And does poetry not provide many examples in which a genius defies all our philosophies, and things that we sneer at in cold reason manage to appear frightening to our imagination? The consequence must thereby fall out differently, and the premise must be false. We no longer believe in ghosts? Who says this? Even more, what does this mean? Does it mean that we have come so far in our understanding that we can prove their impossibility? Does it mean that certain irrefutable truths that contradict the belief in ghosts are so generally known and universally accepted, even to the most common man, that everything that contests those truths must seem ridiculous and absurd to him? It cannot mean that. The statement that we do not believe in ghosts in the present day can mean only this much: that in this matter, on which as much can be said in favor as against, and which has not and cannot be resolved, the currently dominant mode of thinking has given greater weight to the reasons against. A few people think this way, and many more want to seem as if they do; these people make a lot of noise and set the tone. The greater masses remain silent and behave indifferently, thinking now this, now that, hearing with pleasure as ghosts are derided in the light of day and telling horror stories of them in the dark of night.

But the lack of belief in ghosts according to this understanding cannot and should not keep the dramatic poet from using them. The seed of belief lies in all of us, and most of all in those for whom he primarily writes. It would depend only on his art to germinate this seed, only on the possession of certain skills that quickly set in motion arguments in favor of their reality. If he has this in his power, then we can believe what we want in our daily lives – in the theater we must believe what HE wants us to.

Shakespeare is this kind of writer, and perhaps Shakespeare is the one and only. Faced with his ghost in Hamlet, one's hair stands on end, regardless of whether it covers a credulous or incredulous brain. M. de Voltaire was foolish to appeal to this ghost; it makes him and his ghost of Ninus laughable.[6]

Shakespeare's ghost appears truly to come from that other world; so it seems to us. For it appears at the sacred hour, in the harrowing stillness of the night, fully accompanied by all the sepulchral, mysterious indicators that, from the time we nursed mother's milk, lead us to expect ghosts and with which we are accustomed to thinking of them. But Voltaire's ghost is not even as good as a bogeyman designed to scare children; he is simply a disguised comedian, who has nothing, says nothing, does nothing that he actually could do, if he were what he claimed to be. Moreover, all of the circumstances in which he appears destroy the illusion and reveal him as the creation of a cold playwright who hopes to trick and scare us, without knowing how he should go about it. Consider just this one point: in broad daylight, in the middle of the gathering of nobles of the kingdom, announced by a thunderclap, the Voltairian ghost strides out of his crypt.[7] Where did Voltaire hear that ghosts are so brazen? Could not any old woman have told him that ghosts avoid sunlight and certainly do not tend to visit large gatherings? Of course, Voltaire surely knew this, but he was too fearful, too dainty, to make use of common circumstances. He wanted to show us a ghost, but it had to be a ghost of a nobler sort, and through this attempt at nobility he ruined everything. The ghost that presumes to do things contrary to all tradition, contrary to all good manners among ghosts, strikes me as no proper ghost, and everything here that does not support the illusion destroys the illusion.

If Voltaire had stopped to consider the physical staging, he would have sensed, from yet another perspective, the impropriety of having a ghost appear before a large gathering. Everyone has to express fear and dread at the same time upon seeing it, and everyone has to express this in different ways if the scene is to avoid the mechanical symmetry of the ballet. Go ahead and train a herd of stupid supernumeraries to do this, and, if one has trained them exceedingly well, then imagine the degree to which the diverse expressions of a particular emotion will split our attention and pull it away from the main characters.[8] If these main characters are to make the proper impression on us, not only must we be able to see them, but it is also good if we see nothing but them. With Shakespeare, it is solely Hamlet to whom the ghost appears.[9] In the scene in which the mother is present, she neither sees nor hears it. All of our attention therefore focuses upon Hamlet, and the more we see symptoms of a temperament shattered by horror and terror, the more willing we are to accept the apparition – that which caused this shattering in him – for what he takes it to be. The ghost affects us more through him than it does by itself. The impression that it makes upon him is transferred to us, and the effect is too apparent and too strong for us to doubt the extraordinary cause.[10] How little Voltaire understood this artistic device! His ghost frightens many, but they are not frightened much. Sémiramis cries out once, "O Heaven! I am dying!" And the others make hardly more fuss over this ghost than they would over a friend, believed to be far away, who suddenly enters a room.

Essay 12

9 June 1767

I see yet one more difference between the ghosts of the English poets and those of the French.[1] Voltaire's ghost is nothing but a poetic machine, there only to serve the plot's complication; on its own it does not interest us in the least.[2] Shakespeare's ghost on the other hand is a real and active person whose fate engages our sympathy; not only do we shudder, but we also feel compassion.[3]

Without doubt this difference originated in the two poets' divergent way of thinking about ghosts in general. Voltaire considers the appearance of a dead person to be a miracle; for Shakespeare it is a completely natural occurrence.[4] There should be no question which of the two is the more philosophical thinker, but Shakespeare was the more poetic. Voltaire never considered the ghost of Ninus to be a being who is still capable – even on the other side of the grave – of pleasant and unpleasant feelings, and for whom we thus might feel compassion. His only purpose was for the ghost to demonstrate that the highest Power will make an exception to its eternal laws in order to bring hidden crimes to light and to punish them.

I do not wish to say that it is a mistake for a dramatic writer to arrange his story in such a way that it can serve to explain or confirm some great moral truth. But I will say that this arrangement of the fable is anything but necessary – there can be very instructive and accomplished plays that do not aim at imparting such individual maxims – and we commit an injustice when we focus on the moral statement at the end of many ancient tragedies as if the play only existed for its sake.[5]

Thus, if M. de Voltaire's *Sémiramis* had no other merit than the one of which he is so proud – namely that we will learn to venerate the highest justice, which chooses exceptional methods to punish exceptionally vicious deeds – then in my opinion *Sémiramis* would be only a very mediocre play. Particularly since this moral is hardly the most edifying. For it is without question far worthier of the wisest being when it does not need to resort to these extraordinary methods, and we imagine the punishment of good and evil woven into the proper order of things.[6]

But I will not dwell longer on this play, other than to say a word about the way it was produced here. We have every reason to be satisfied in this respect. The stage is roomy enough to contain without confusion the multitude of characters that the writer puts on stage in several scenes. The decorations are new and in the best of taste, and to the best extent possible they bring together the all-too-frequently changing locations.[7]

On the seventh evening (Thursday, the 30th of April), *The Married Philosopher* by Destouches was performed.[8]

This comedy first appeared in 1727 on the French stage and received so much acclaim that it was performed thirty-six times within one year.[9] The German translation is not the prose version from the Berlin translation of Destouches's collected works; rather, it is in a verse form that several hands have tinkered with and improved.[10] It has many very successful verses, but also many passages that are hard and unnatural. It is impossible to describe how difficult those passages make it for the performers to act, and yet there are few French plays that could ever succeed better on any German stage than this one did on ours. The roles have all been cast to perfection; in particular Madame Löwen plays the moody Céliante masterfully, and Herr Ackermann is excellent as Géronte.[11] I need not talk about the play itself. It is too well known, belonging unquestionably among the masterpieces of the French stage that even we Germans always see with pleasure.

The play on the eighth evening (Friday, the 1st of May), was *The Coffee-house, or the Scotch Woman* by M. de Voltaire.[12]

A long story could be told about this comedy. Its author sent it out into the world as a translation from an English work by Hume, not the historian and philosopher, but rather another of this name who had made himself known to the world through the tragedy *Douglas*.[13] Some of its characters are similar to those in Goldoni's *The Coffee House;* in particular Goldoni's Don Marzio seems to have been the prototype for Frélon.[14] But where in that play he is just a malicious fellow, in this one he is also a miserable writer, whom the author named Frélon so that the interpreter might thus more quickly make the connection to his sworn enemy, the journalist Fréron.[15] The author wished thereby to strike this man down, and no doubt he dealt him a sore blow. We foreigners, indifferent to the spiteful infighting among French intellectuals, look past the identities in this play and find in Frélon simply the faithful depiction of a type of person not unknown among us. We have our Frélons just as the French and English do; they just create less of a sensation here because we generally respond more indifferently to our literature.[16] But even if in Germany we completely fail to appreciate who is represented by the character, the play still has enough interest without him; the honorable Freeport alone could keep us engaged. We love his bumbling magnanimity, and even the English themselves were flattered by this depiction.

In fact, it is only because of this character that they have just recently transplanted the whole tree to what was claimed to have been its original soil. Colman, unquestionably their best comic writer, translated *The Scotch Wife* under the title *The English Merchant* and gave it all of the national coloring that was lacking in the original.[17] As much as M. de Voltaire claims to know English customs, he nonetheless frequently violated them – for example, when he has Lindane live at a coffeehouse. Colman has her rent instead from an honorable woman who has furnished rooms, and this woman is far more suitable as the friend and benefactor to the young abandoned beauty than Fabrice. Colman also sought to shape the characters more strongly to English tastes. Lady Alton is not just a jealous fury; she aspires to be a lady of genius, taste, and education and puts on the appearance of a literary patroness. Colman thereby thought to make a more plausible connection between her and the sorry Frélon (whom he names

Spatter). Above all, Freeport gets another sphere of activity, and he is as passionately concerned for Lindane's father as he is for Lindane herself. What Lord Falbridge does to secure the father's pardon in the French is done by Freeport in the English, and he alone brings everything to a happy end.[18]

English critics found Colman's adaptation to have exquisite sentiments, fine and lively dialogue, and well-drawn characters. But they far prefer Colman's other plays (one of which, *The Jealous Wife*, was previously seen here in the Ackermann theater; those who remember that play can judge for themselves).[19] *The English Merchant* does not have enough action for them. There is not enough in it to feed their curiosity; the whole development of the plot is apparent in the first act. What follows strikes them as having too many similarities with other plays, and the best situations lack originality. Freeport, they claim, should never have felt the least spark of love for Lindane; his good deed would lose all of its merit, etc.[20]

Some of this criticism is not completely unfounded; at the same time, we Germans are quite satisfied that the plot is not richer and more complicated. On this point, the English fashion distracts and wearies us; we love a simple plot that can be taken in at a glance. Just as the English have to cram French plays full of episodes if they want them to succeed on their stage, so we Germans have to unburden English plays of their episodes if we hope to enrich our theaters successfully with them.[21] Their best comedies by Congreve and Wycherley would be unbearable to us without this trimming of their all-too-voluptuous girth.[22] We do better with their tragedies; for the most part, these are not nearly as confusing as their comedies, and some have had success here without even the tiniest change, which is more than I can say of any of their comedies.

The Italians also have a translation of *The Scotch Wife* that appears in the first volume of Diodati's *Theatrical Library*.[23] It follows the original step by step, just as the German does, except that the Italian version has added one more scene to the end.[24] Voltaire said that in his English source Frélon was punished in the end, but as deserved as this punishment was, for Voltaire it seemed to have taken away from the main interest of the play, and he therefore left it out. This excuse did not seem sufficient to the Italian translator, so he supplied a punishment for Frélon out of his own imagination; the Italians are great lovers of poetic justice.[25]

Essay 13

12 June 1767

On the ninth evening (Monday, the 4th of May), *Cénie* should have been performed.[1] But due to an epidemic emergency, more than half of the actors were suddenly rendered incapable of performing, and they had to sort things out as best as possible.[2] They repeated *The New Agnes* and put on the light opera *The Governess*.[3]

On the tenth evening (Tuesday, the 5th of May), *The Young Hypocrite, or the Country Poet* by Destouches was performed.[4]

This play has three acts in French, but five in translation. Without this improvement it did not merit inclusion in *The German Stage* of the erstwhile renowned

Professor Gottsched, and his learned lady friend, the translator, was far too good a wife not to submit blindly to the critical dictums of her husband.[5] How hard can it be to turn three acts into five? You have coffee served in another room, you propose a walk in the garden, and, if push comes to shove, the candlesnuffer can always come out and say: "Ladies and Gentlemen, exit the stage for a bit; intermissions were invented so we can trim the lights, and how does it help your performance if the audience cannot see?" – The translation itself is otherwise not bad, and in particular Professor Gottsched's wife had good success with Masure's doggerel verse, as is fitting.[6] It could possibly be shown by comparison whether or not she was equally successful in those places where she thought she needed to give the circumstances of the original a new turn. I heard others take issue with one such improvement of this sort, notwithstanding the dear lady's good intentions in making it. In the scene in which Henriette acts the foolish strumpet, Destouches has Masures say to her: "You astonish me, mademoiselle; I took you for a *virtuose*."[7] "Oh phooey!" Henriette replies, "What do you take me for? I am a good girl, you should know that." "But indeed," Masures interrupts her, "one can be both a good girl and a *virtuose* at the same time." "No," Henriette says, "I am sure one can't be both. Me, a *virtuose!*" Recall what Madame Gottsched inserted instead of the word *virtuose:* a "wonder."[8] No wonder she did this, people said. She believes herself to be something of a *virtuose* and was angered by the intended jab. But she should not have gotten angry; the Professor's wife could have repeated without pursed lips what the witty, educated Henriette says in the guise of a dumb "Agnes."[9] But perhaps she was simply tripped up by the foreign word *virtuose;* wonder is more German. Among our beauties there are fifty wonders to every *virtuose*. The lady wished to translate clearly and comprehensibly; she was quite justified.

The Dumb Beauty by Schlegel ended the evening.[10]

Schlegel wrote this little piece for the newly established Copenhagen Theater, to be produced there in a Danish translation. Because of this, the customs and morals in it are really much more Danish than German. Nevertheless, it is indisputably our best original comic play written in verse. Schlegel achieves a versification throughout that is as fluid as it is graceful, and it was fortunate for his successors that he did not also write his longer comedies in verse. He could have easily spoiled audiences for them, and then they would not only have had his theories but also his examples working against them.[11] Earlier, he had vigorously defended rhymed comedy, and the more successfully he surmounted its challenges, the more convincing his argument would seem. Yet, as he set himself to work on the task, he no doubt discovered what inexpressible trouble it cost to surmount just a portion of those challenges, and how little the pleasure that came from these victories could compensate for the many small virtues that had to be sacrificed for their sake. At one time the French were so loathsome as to insist on having Molière's prose plays brought into verse after his death; and even now they consider a prose comedy to be the kind of thing any of them could write. The English, on the other hand, would hound a rhymed comedy right out of the theater. Only the Germans are, on this point – shall I say more reasonable, or indifferent? They accept what the poet offers. What would it be like if they began wanting to choose and reject?

The role of the silent beauty has its difficulties. People say that a silent beauty is not necessarily a stupid one, and the actress who plays the role as a silly clumsy strumpet is wrong. But Schlegel's silent beauty is also, in fact, stupid; the reason she does not say anything is that she does not think anything. The trick to it is as follows: one has to make her unsophisticated in every instance where she would have to think in order to appear sophisticated, but at the same time give her all the refinements that are merely mechanical and that she could have without much thought. For example, her gait and her curtsy need not be rustic; they can be as fine and dainty as only a dance master can teach – for why should she have learned nothing from her dance master, if she has been able to learn quadrille?[12] And she must not play quadrille badly, because she counts on winning money from her father. Her clothing, too, must be neither old-fashioned nor frumpy, for Mrs. Lovetotalk specifically says:[13]

> Aren't you nicely dressed? – Let's see!
> Now! – turn around! – That's right, and sit gallantly.
> What does the lunatic mean by saying you have no brain?

The poet has clearly indicated here, with Mrs. Lovetotalk's observations, how he wishes his silent beauty to appear on the outside.

> Let's see, how are you carrying yourself? – Don't stick your head back like that!

Stupidity without breeding will hold the head more forwards than back; the dance master teaches how to hold it back. They must therefore send Charlotte to the dance master, and the more, the better; for this does not damage her beauty – on the contrary, the stiff, dainty, dance-master-manners are precisely those that suit the silent beauty best. They show off her beauty to its greatest advantages, save that they rob her of life.

> Who cares if she has a brain? He should just look at her eyes!

It would be very good to have an actress with big beautiful eyes play this role. But those lovely eyes must hardly move, perhaps not at all; their glances must be slow and vacant; they must want to set us aflame with their immobile points of focus, but they must say nothing.

> Walk about a bit. – Good! Come here! – Bow! There we have it, that's what's missing. No, look! This is how one bows.

One misunderstands these lines if one has Charlotte make an uncouth bow, a stupid curtsy. Her bowing must be learned, and as already mentioned, it must not bring shame upon her dance master. Mrs. Lovetotalk must believe only that it does not have enough affectation. Charlotte curtsies, and Mrs. Lovetotalk thinks she should make it fancier. That is the whole difference, and Madame Löwen observed it quite well, although at the same time I don't believe that Mrs. Lovetotalk is otherwise a good role for her. She is not able to hide the fine lady enough, and certain faces simply cannot manage unworthy actions, like the swapping of a daughter.

On the eleventh evening (Wednesday, the 6th of May), *Miss Sara Sampson* was performed.[14]

One can demand no more of the art than what Mme. Hensel achieves with the role of Sara, and overall the play was very well performed. It is a little too long, and is therefore usually shortened by most theaters. Whether the author is happy with all of this cutting, I have my doubts. We all know how writers are; if you just try to remove a hangnail, they immediately scream: you are murdering me! Admittedly, the excessive length of a play is poorly remedied by simply cutting, and I don't understand how someone can shorten a scene without changing the whole sequence of dialogue. But if the cuts made by others do not sit well with the author, then he should make some himself, if he thinks it is worth the trouble, and if he is not one of those who brings children into the world and then abandons them forever.

Madame Hensel died quite decently, in the most picturesque position, and one feature in particular greatly surprised me. It has been observed of the dying that they begin to pluck at their clothing or bedsheets with their fingers.[15] She availed herself of this observation in the most fortunate manner. In that moment in which the soul departed there was a slight spasm, just in the fingers of her otherwise stiff arm; she pinched her skirt, which was lifted just a bit and then immediately fell back again: the last fluttering of an extinguishing light, the final ray of a setting sun. – Anyone who does not perceive from my description how beautiful this refinement was should lay the blame on my description – but he should see it someday![16]

Essay 14

16 June 1767

The bourgeois tragedy found a strong defender in the French critic who acquainted his country with *Sara.*[*,1] The French otherwise rarely approve of something for which they themselves have no example.

The names of princes and heroes can give a play pomp and majesty, but they contribute nothing to its emotional power.[2] The misfortune of someone whose circumstances come closest to our own must naturally penetrate most deeply into our souls, and, if we have compassion for kings, we have it for them as people rather than as kings. If occasionally their rank makes their misfortunes more important, it does not therefore make them more interesting. Though entire populations may be enmeshed, our sympathy demands a single subject, and a nation is far too abstract a concept for our sentiments.

"We wrong the human heart," says Marmontel, "we misunderstand Nature, if we believe that titles are required to move us and touch us.[3] The sacred names of friend, father, beloved, spouse, son, mother, of human beings in general: these have more

---

* *Journal Étranger*, December 1761. ["*Miss Sara Sampson,* Tragèdie bourgeoise de M. Lessing." – Ed.]

pathos than anything else; they assert their rights always and forever. What difference does social standing, surname, or birth make to the unfortunate man whom seductive example and kindness toward unworthy friends draw into gambling? Whose fortune and honor are destroyed as a result, and who suffers now in prison, torn by shame and regret? If you ask who he is, I would answer: he was an honest man, and, to his torment, a husband and father; his wife, whom he loves and by whom he is loved, now wastes away in utter poverty and can offer her hungry children nothing but tears. Show me, in the history of heroes, a situation that is more touching, more moral, in a word, more tragic! And when this unhappy man finally poisons himself, when he learns, just after he has poisoned himself, that heaven wants to rescue him – what is missing, in this painful, dreadful moment, in which the fear of death is joined with tormenting thoughts of how happily he could have lived – I ask, what is lacking here to be worthy of tragedy? The marvelous, one might say. How so? Is there not marvel enough in the sudden transition from honor to shame, from innocence to crime, from the sweetest peace to despair – in short, in the most extreme unhappiness brought on by mere weakness?"[4]

But no matter how much these Diderots and Marmontels impress their observations upon the French, it does not seem that the bourgeois tragedy will find a niche among them. The nation is too vain, too enamored of titles and other superficial privileges; down to the most common man, they only want to be seen with people of greater distinction, and the company of one's equals is the same as bad company. To be sure, a happy genius can accomplish much among his people; Nature has not given up her rights anywhere, and perhaps she is simply waiting there for the poet who knows how to depict her in all her truth and power. The attempt made by an anonymous writer in a play called *The Picture of Indigence* has beautiful elements, and until the French acquire a taste for it, we should adopt it for our theater.[5]

The aforementioned critic finds faults with the German *Sara* that are not entirely unfounded. But I believe that the author would rather retain his errors than undergo what might prove to be a misbegotten effort toward a complete reworking of the play.[6] He remembers what Voltaire said in a similar situation: "We cannot always do what our friends advise. There are also necessary errors. To cure a hunchbacked man of his hunch, you would have to take his life. My child is hunchbacked, but it is otherwise just fine."[7]

On the twelfth evening (Thursday, the 7th of May) *The Gamester* by Regnard was performed.[8]

This play is undoubtedly the best that Regnard wrote; but Rivière Dufresny, who also brought a *Gamester* to the stage soon after, took him to task regarding its invention.[9] He complained that Regnard stole both the concept and various scenes from him; Regnard shifted the blame back on him, and now we only know this much for certain from the quarrel, that one of the two was a plagiarist. If it was Regnard, then we should thank him for overcoming his better instincts and abusing the trust of his friend; it was for our own good that he appropriated the material, which he anticipated would be ruined. We only would have had a very bad *Gamester* if he had been more scrupulous. But he should have confessed the deed and given poor Dufresny a share of the honor he earned by it.

On the thirteenth evening (Friday, the 8th of May), *The Married Philosopher* was repeated; the evening concluded with *The Lover, Author and Servant*.[10]

Cérou is the author of this short, clever play; he was a law student in 1740 when he gave the play to the Italians in Paris to perform. It succeeds uncommonly well.

On the fourteenth evening (Monday, the 11th of May), *The Coquette Mother* by Quinault and *The Village Lawyer* were produced.[11]

Experts count the former among the best plays of the French theater from the previous century. There truly is much fine comedy in it, the likes of which Molière might have been proud. But the fifth act and the whole resolution could have been much better; the old slave, who is mentioned several times in the previous acts, does not appear, and the play ends with cold narration after we had been prepared for theatrical action.[12] Otherwise the play is notable within the history of French theater because the ridiculous marquis is the first of his type. *The Coquette Mother* is also not the best possible title, and Quinault could have let the second title, *The Quarreling Lovers*, suffice.

The Village Lawyer is actually an old farce from the fifteenth century that received extraordinary acclaim in its day.[13] It earned it, too, due to the singular merriment and the fine comedy that arises from the action itself and from the character's situations, and is not just based on gags. Brueys gave it a new language and put it into the form that is currently being produced. Herr Ekhof was absolutely superb in the role of the lawyer Patelin.

On the fifteenth evening (Tuesday, the 12th of May), Lessing's *The Freethinker* was presented.[14]

It is known here under the title *The Ashamed Freethinker*, because people wanted to differentiate it from the tragedy by Herr von Brawe that bears the very same title.[15] In truth, one cannot really say that a person who betters himself is ashamed. Adrast is also not the one and only freethinker; there are, rather, several persons who share this role. The vain impulsive Henriette, the mischievous Johann, and Lisidor, who is indifferent to truth or falsehood – all of these are types of freethinkers, who together must live up to the title of the play.[16] But of what consequence is the title? It is enough that the performance merited much acclaim. Without exception the roles are well cast, and in particular Herr Böck plays Theophan with all of the friendly decency that this character requires in order to set off in contrast his eventual indignation over Adrast's obstinacy in misjudging him, on which the play's whole resolution depends.[17]

The evening concluded with a pastoral play by Herr Pfeffel called *The Treasure*.[18]

Besides this short play, this writer has made himself a bit of a reputation through another work, *The Hermit*.[19] In *The Treasure* he has tried to put in more interest than is usual in our pastoral plays, since their entire substance is trifling love. His writing, however, is often a bit too strained and precious, so that the already too rarefied sentiments acquire a highly unnatural air and become nothing but frosty plays of wit. This is particularly true of his *Hermit*, which is intended to be a short tragedy that could be used to follow a poignant play in lieu of a comic afterpiece. The intention is all to the good, but we would much rather proceed from crying to laughing than to yawning.

Essay 15

19 June 1767

On the sixteenth evening (Wednesday, the 13th of May), *Zaïre* by M. de Voltaire was performed.[1]

"Those who love literary history will be pleased to know how this play originated," M. de Voltaire says.[2] "Certain ladies had accused the author of not having enough love in his tragedies. He answered them that, in his opinion, tragedy was not the most fitting place for love, but if they absolutely had to have amorous heroes, he would gladly make some as good as the next writer. The play was completed in eighteen days and was a great success.[3] In Paris they called it a Christian tragedy, and it is often performed instead of *Polyeucte*."[4]

We have the ladies to thank for this play, then, and it will long remain the ladies' favorite. A young fiery monarch, subject only to love; a proud victor, conquered only by beauty; a sultan without polygamy; a seraglio, transformed into the freely accessible abode of a sovereign governess; an abandoned girl, raised to the highest degree of happiness through nothing but her beautiful eyes; a heart caught between affection and religion, divided between its god and its idol, and willing to be pious, if only it does not have to stop loving; a jealous man who recognizes his injustice and takes it out on himself – if such pleasing ideas do not dazzle the fair sex, what will they be dazzled by?

"Love itself dictated *Zaïre* to Voltaire," a critic courteously claims.[5] More correctly, he should have said: "Gallantry."[6] I only know of one tragedy whose work was helped by love itself, and that is Shakespeare's *Romeo and Juliet*. It is true, Voltaire has his enamored Zaïre express her feelings very delicately, very properly – but what is this expression when compared to that living picture of all the smallest, most secret intrigues that love uses to steal into our souls, of all the imperceptible advantages it gains thereby, of all the stratagems it uses to bring every other passion under its sway, until it becomes the sole tyrant of all we desire and detest? If I may put it this way, Voltaire has an excellent understanding of the court-style of love, that is, the language and tone that love employs when it wishes to express itself in the most careful and measured manner, when it wishes to say only what it can justify to the priggish lady sophist or the cold critic.[7] But even the best court clerk does not always know the most about the secrets of the government; or, in any case, if Voltaire has the same deep insight into the nature of love that Shakespeare did, then he does not seem to have wanted to display it here, and the poetry has remained far beneath the abilities of the poet.

Pretty much the same can be said about jealousy. In contrast to Shakespeare's jealous Othello, the jealous Orosman is a very threadbare character. And yet apparently Othello was the model for Orosman.[8] Cibber says that Voltaire has usurped the fire that lights Shakespeare's tragic pyre.*[9] I would have said – a flame from that burning

---

* From English Plays, Zara's French author fir'd
  Confess'd his Muse, beyond herself, inspir'd;
  From rack'd Othello's rage, he rais'd his style
  And snatch'd the brand, that lights this tragic pile.

pyre, and moreover one that smokes more than it illuminates or warms. We hear Orosman speak the words of a jealous man, we see him commit the rash deed of a jealous man, but of jealousy itself we learn nothing more or less than we already knew. Othello, on the other hand, is a perfect primer for this sad delirium; we can learn from him everything about it, everything that awakens it, and how to avoid it.

But some of my readers will ask, is it always and forever Shakespeare who has understood everything better than the French? That irritates us; we cannot read him. – I take this opportunity to remind the public of something that it seems to deliberately wish to forget. We have a translation of Shakespeare. It has just barely been finished, and already no one pays it any attention. The critics have said many bad things about it. I have a good mind to say many good things about it.[10] Not to contradict these learned men, nor to defend the mistakes that they have noted in it, but rather because I believe that they should not have made such a fuss over those mistakes. The undertaking was difficult; someone other than Herr Wieland would have blundered more often in haste and have omitted even more out of ignorance or laziness, but no one could improve on what he did well. His presentation of Shakespeare remains a book that cannot be recommended enough among us. We will continue to learn from the beauties it provides us for a long time before the blemishes that come with it offend us so much that we require a better translation.

But back to *Zaïre*. The author brought it to the Paris stage in 1733, and three years later it was translated into English and also played in London at the Theater in Drury Lane.[11] The translator was Aaron Hill, himself a playwright, and not the worst kind.[12] Voltaire was very flattered by this, and what he wrote about it (in his distinctive tone of proud modesty) in his dedication of the play to the English statesman Fawkener deserves to be read.[13] Only we must not assume everything he says is true. Woe to the person who does not generally read Voltaire's writing with the skeptical spirit in which he wrote much of it!

For example, he says to his English friend: "Your writers have a custom to which even Addison[†] submitted, for custom is as powerful as reason and law.[14] This rather unreasonable custom demanded that every act end in verses that were in a completely different taste than the rest of the play; moreover, these verses also necessarily had to contain a comparison. Phèdre, as she exits, compares herself very poetically to a deer, Cato compares himself to a rock, and Cleopatra herself to children who cry themselves to sleep.[15] The translator of *Zaïre* is the first who has dared to assert the rights of nature against a taste so foreign to it. He abolished this custom, perceiving that passion must speak its own true language, and the poet must hide himself everywhere in order to allow us to recognize the hero."[16]

There are no more than three falsehoods in this passage, and for M. de Voltaire that is actually not many. It is true that since the time of Shakespeare, and perhaps

---

[†] "Le plus sage de vos ecrivains," Voltaire adds. How should that best be translated? Sage means wise; but "the wisest of English playwrights" – who would identify Addison as such? I recall that the French also call a girl *sage* who cannot be accused of any indiscretion, or at least of any of the rude indiscretions. Perhaps this meaning would fit here. And accordingly, one could probably translate this as: Addison, the one among your writers who most resembles us harmless, sober French.

even longer, the English have had the custom of ending acts that are in unrhymed blank verse with a few rhymed lines. But to say that these rhymed lines contained only comparisons – that they necessarily had to be comparisons – this is completely wrong, and I do not understand how M. de Voltaire can rub such a thing in the face of an Englishman whom he would have to presume had also read the tragic poets of his country. Second, it is simply not true that Hill has abolished this custom in his translation of *Zaïre*. It is in fact almost unbelievable that M. de Voltaire should not have looked more closely at the translation of his play than I or any other person. Nonetheless, it must be, for as surely as it is in blank verse, just as surely each act ends with two or four rhymed lines. True, they do not contain comparisons, but as noted, among all such rhymed passages with which Shakespeare, and Jonson, and Dryden, and Lee, and Otway, and Rowe, and all the rest conclude their acts, there are plenty that also do not have them.[17] What has Hill done that is so special, then? And if he had really done this unique thing that Voltaire claims he did, then thirdly, it would not be true that his example had the influence that Voltaire gives it. Even now there are just as many plays whose acts conclude with rhymed verses as those whose acts do not (although the plays nowadays are not tragedies). Hill himself has not completely relinquished this old fashion in any one of the various plays he wrote after his translation of *Zaïre*. And what difference does it make, if we hear rhymes or not in the end? If they are there, they can perhaps still be of use to the orchestra, namely as a signal to pick up their instruments, a signal that would thus be taken more suitably from the play itself than that given by the whistle or some other sign.[18]

Essay 16

23 June 1767

The English actors were a bit too unnatural in Hill's time.[1] In particular their tragic acting was extremely wild and exaggerated; when they had to express strong passions they screamed and gestured like they were possessed, and they sang out the rest with a stiff, strutting solemnity that betrayed the actor in every syllable. Thus, when he endeavored to have his translation of *Zaïre* produced, he entrusted the role of Zaïre to a young woman who had never before performed in a tragedy.[2] He reckoned thusly: this young woman has feeling, voice, figure, and grace; she has not yet adopted the false tone of the theater; she does not need to unlearn any bad habits; if she can just convince herself for a couple of hours that she really is what she pretends to be, then she needs only to speak naturally and everything will go well. It did, too, and the theater pedants, who had argued against Hill that only a very practiced and experienced person could do justice to such a role, were shamed. This young actress was the wife of the actor Colley Cibber, and her first effort, at the age of eighteen, was a masterpiece.[3] It is an odd coincidence that the French actress who first played Zaïre was also a beginner. The young, charming Mademoiselle Gaussin was made famous overnight, and Voltaire himself was so enamored of her that he miserably regretted his age.[4]

The role of Orosman was taken on by a relative of Hill's who was not an actor by profession but rather a gentleman.[5] Acting was his hobby, and he did not have the least scruples about performing in public in order to demonstrate a talent that is as valuable as any other. It is not rare in England to see such examples of distinguished people occasionally performing for their own enjoyment. "What is surprising about this," M. de Voltaire says, "is that it surprises us. We should consider that everything in the world depends on custom and opinion. In the past, the French court danced with opera performers on the stage, and no one found anything unusual in it, except that this type of entertainment is no longer in fashion. Is there any difference between these two arts, other than the fact that the one is superior to the other in the same way that abilities of the mind are superior to mere physical skills?"[6]

Count Gozzi translated *Zaïre* into Italian, very precisely and very gracefully; it can be found in the third volume of his *Works*.[7] In what language could tender complaints sound more moving than in this one? But we can hardly be pleased with the single freedom that Gozzi took toward the end of the play. After Orosman stabs himself, Voltaire has him say just a few more words to reassure us about Nérestan's fate.[8] But what does Gozzi do? The Italian doubtless felt it too cold to let a Turk die so undramatically. Thus he puts yet another tirade into Orosman's mouth, full of proclamations, whining, and despair. Because it is hard to find, I reprint it below.*[9]

It is curious how distant German taste is in these matters from Italian taste! For the Italians, Voltaire is too short; for us Germans, he is too long. Orosman has scarcely said "honored and avenged," he has scarcely killed himself with a deadly thrust, and we let the curtain fall.[10] But is it really true that German taste demands this? We cut many plays along similar lines, but why? Do we really want a tragedy to end like an epigram? Always with the point of a dagger or with the last sigh of the hero? Where do we calm, serious Germans get such flittering impatience that we do not want to listen to anything more after the execution is done, even if just a few indispensable words to fully round out the play? But I search in vain for the cause of a thing that

---

* Questo mortale orror che per le vene
  Tutte me scorre, omai non è dolore,
  Che basti ad appagarti, anima bella.
  Feroce cor, cor dispietato, e misero,
  Paga la pena del delitto orrendo.
  Mani crudeli – oh Dio – Mani, che siete
  Tinte del sangue di sì cara donna,
  Voi – voi – dov'è quel ferro? Un' altra volta
  In mezzo al petto – Oimè, dov'è quel ferro?
  L'acuta punta –
  Tenebre, e notte
  Si fanno intorno –
  Perchè non posso –
  Non posso spargere
  Il sangue tutto?
  Sì, sì, lo spargo tutto, anima mia,
  Dove sei? – piu non posso – oh Dio! Non posso –
  Vorrei – vederti – io manco, io manco, oh Dio!

does not exist. We could be cold-blooded enough to hear the poet to the end, if the actor would trust us. We would gladly hear the last orders of the courageous sultan, gladly share the awe and the compassion of Nérestan, but this is not to be. And why not? I really have no reason. Is it the fault of the actors who play Orosman? It would be easy enough to understand why they wanted to have the last word. Stabbed and applauded! We must forgive artists their small vanities.

Zaïre found no sharper critic anywhere than among the Dutch. Frederik Duim, who may be related to the famous actor by this name at the Amsterdam Theater, found so much to criticize in the play that he thought he might as well write a better one.[11] And he really did write one, which is different in that the conversion of Zaïre is the primary focus, and which ends with the Sultan overcoming his love and sending the Christian Zaïre to her native land with all the pomp warranted by her elevated status. The old Lusignan dies of joy. Who needs to know more? The one unforgivable flaw of a tragic poet is this: that he leaves us cold. If he engages us, he can do whatever he wants with the small technical rules. The Duims of the world may well find fault, but they should not presume to draw Ulysses' bow. I say all this because I do not want to imply anything about the merits of his criticism merely because his improvement was inept. Duim's criticism is in many places well grounded: he notes with particular astuteness how Voltaire is a bit clumsy in his presentation of place, and how he fails to provide sufficient motivation for character entrances and exits. Additionally, the contradictions in the sixth scene of the third act do not escape his attention. "Oros-man," he notes, "comes to fetch Zaïre in the Mosque; Zaïre refuses to go with him, failing to provide the least shred of an excuse for her refusal; she leaves, and Orosman is left standing there like a dolt (*als eenen lafhartigen*). Is this really suitable for one of his dignity? Does this correspond well with his character? Why does he not press Zaïre to explain herself? Why does he not follow her into the Seraglio? Is he not allowed to follow her there?"[12] – My good Duim! If Zaïre had explained herself sufficiently, where would the rest of the acts have come from? Wouldn't the entire tragedy have been ruined? – Precisely! The second scene of the third act is equally misconceived: Orosman comes again to Zaïre, Zaïre again walks off without providing the slightest justification, and Orosman, the decent fellow (*dien goeden hals*), consoles himself with a monologue.[13] But as I already said, the entanglements or uncertainties have to last until the fifth act; and if the whole plot hangs on a hair, many more important things in the world hang on nothing stronger.

This last-mentioned scene is otherwise one in which the actor playing Orosman can show his finest skills in all their unassuming brilliance and which only an equally refined connoisseur is capable of perceiving. He has to transition from one emotion to another, and he has to know how to make this transition look so natural through body language that the audience is not jolted but pulled along through swift but gradual progression. At first the noble Orosman reveals himself willing to forgive Zaïre when he thinks her heart is set, as long as she is honorable enough not to keep it a secret from him any longer. But then his passion reawakens, and he orders the sacrifice of his rival. He is tender enough to ensure her of his favor at this point. But when Zaïre insists on her innocence, despite what he believed was such clear evidence, he is overcome with the most intense displeasure. And so he goes from pride to tenderness, and from tenderness to bitterness. All that Rémond de Saint-Albine wants to see achieved in *The Actor* is accomplished by Herr Ekhof in such a magnificent way that one could believe he alone was the model for the critic.[14]

Essay 17

26 June 1767

On the seventeenth evening (Thursday, the 14th of May), *Sidney* by Gresset was performed.[1]

This play first came to the stage in 1745. A comedy against suicide did not meet with great success in Paris. The French said: this is a play for London. But I am not so sure, for the English might find *Sidney* a bit too un-English: he does not get down to business quickly enough; he philosophizes too much before he commits the deed and too little after he thinks he has done it; his remorse could look like shameful cowardice; indeed, to be fooled by a French servant might be thought by many to be a humiliation worthy of death.

But as it stands, the play seems just right for us Germans. We like to cloak a frenzy in a little philosophy, and we do not feel our honor compromised if someone keeps us from doing something stupid and gets us to admit that we have philosophized wrongly. Thus even though Dumont is a French braggart, we like him so well that the etiquette the playwright observes with him is offensive. For when Sidney finally learns that due to Dumont's precautions he is no nearer to death than the healthiest of people, Gresset has him call out: "I can hardly believe it! – Rosalie! – Hamilton! – and you, whose fortunate zeal etc."[2] Why this hierarchy? Might manners not be sacrificed to thankfulness? The servant has saved him; the first word, the first expression of joy should go to the servant, no matter how far below his master and his master's friends he may be. If I were an actor, I would boldly take the liberty here to do what the writer should have done. If I could not go against his specifications and direct the first word to my rescuer, then at least I would deliver the first emotional look his way and rush to him with the first thankful embrace; and then I would turn to Rosalie and Hamilton, and then come back to him. It should always be more in our interest to show humanity than manners!

Herr Ekhof played Sidney so excellently – it is unquestionably one of his strongest roles. One can hardly express with more art or with greater truth the enthusiastic melancholy, the feeling of an utter lack of feeling, if I may put it that way, that makes up Sidney's entire state of mind. Ekhof has such a cornucopia of expressive gestures, through which, so to speak, he embodies general statements and makes his innermost feelings concrete and visible! And what a rousing tone of conviction! –

The evening concluded with a play in one act, based on the French play by L'Affichard, with the title: *Is he a member of the family?*[3] One guesses right away that it must feature a fool since it mainly concerns the old aristocracy. A young person, well-bred but of doubtful parentage, courts the stepdaughter of a Marquis. The consent of the mother depends on the clarification of this point. The young man believes that he is only the foster-child of a certain bourgeois Lisander, but it turns out that Lisander is his real father. Now the marriage would be inconceivable, if Lisander himself had not been forced down into the bourgeois class by mischance. In fact he is as noble as the Marquis: he is the Marquis's son, driven from the family estate because of youthful indiscretions. Now he wants to use his son to reconcile with his father. The reconciliation succeeds and makes the end of this play very moving. But because the overarching tone is more moving than comic, shouldn't the title have us expect more of the former than the latter? The title is really a tri-fling thing, but in this case I would not have based it upon one ridiculous character. It need not indicate nor exhaust the content; it should, however, not lead us astray. And this one does that a bit. What is easier to change than the title? The rest of the deviations the German author made from the original redound more to the play's advantage and give it the local flavor that nearly all of the plays taken from French theater lack.

On the eighteenth evening (Friday, the 15th of May), *The Ghost with the Drum* was performed.[4]

This play is adapted from the English play by Addison. Addison wrote only one tragedy and one comedy. Dramatic poetry in general was not his strength. But a smart man can pull anything off, and so both his pieces at least have some merits that make them valuable works, even if they are not the best of their genres. He tried with both the comedy and the tragedy to incorporate French rules, but even twenty more Addi-sons could never make these rules suit English taste. He who settles for them knows no higher beauties!

Destouches, who had personal contact with Addison in England, gave the Eng-lishman's comedy more of a French turn. We now perform it using this revision, which is actually much finer and more natural but also somewhat colder and less powerful. If I am not mistaken, Madame Gottsched, who wrote the German transla-tion, had the English original to hand and used it to good advantage.

On the nineteenth evening (Monday, the 18th of May), *The Married Philosopher* by Destouches was repeated.

Democritus by Regnard was the play performed on the twentieth night (Tuesday, the 19th of May).[5]

This comedy teems with errors and inconsistencies, and yet it pleases. The con-noisseur laughs just as heartily as the least educated among the masses. What do we make of this? That the beautiful qualities it does possess must be true and universal, and that perhaps the errors only involve arbitrary rules that can be set aside more eas-ily than a critic might like to admit. He did not adhere to the unity of place – be that as it may. He got rid of everything familiar – all the same. His Democritus does not resemble the real Democritus in any way, and his Athens is an entirely different Ath-ens than the one we know. So fine, just take away Democritus and Athens, and replace them with invented names. Regnard certainly knew as well as anyone that there are no deserts, tigers, or bears around Athens; that at the time of Democritus, it had no king, etc. But he did not want to know all of this here; his purpose was to depict the customs of his land in foreign disguise. This depiction – and not historical truth – is the primary task of the comedic poet.

Other errors may be harder to excuse: the lack of interest, the scant complications, the multitude of tiresome persons, and the tasteless chatter of Democritus – tasteless not only because it contradicts the image that we hold of Democritus but also because it would still be nonsense in any other mouth, regardless of what the poet named him. But what won't we forgive when we are having the kind of fun that Strabo and Thaler create for us? The character of Strabo is hard to pin down: you don't know what you should make of him; he changes his tone with everyone he meets. First he is a refined and clever wit, and then he is a simple prankster, now a prissy intellectual, and then an unabashed dandy. His encounter with Cleanthis is incredibly funny but implausible. The art with which Mademoiselle Beauval and la Thorillière first played this scene has spread from one actor and actress to another.[6] It involves the most despicable grimaces; but they have become sanctified in France and Germany by tradition, so that no one would think to change anything, and I will take good care not to say that we should really barely tolerate them in the most trivial of farces. The best, funniest, and most developed character is Thaler, a real country farmer – if anything too roguish, too full of angry muttering – and the one who – from a poetic perspective – is anything but episodic, since he is as indispensable to the final resolution as he is suited to it.

Essay 18

30 June 1767

On the twenty-first evening (Wednesday, the 20th of May), Marivaux's comedy *The False Confessions* was performed.[1]

Marivaux wrote for the theater in Paris for nearly half a century; his first play dates from 1712, and he died at the age of seventy-two in 1763.[2] The number of his comedies adds up to about thirty, of which more than two-thirds feature a Harlequin because he produced them for the Italian stage.[3] *The False Confessions* belongs to this group. It was first performed in 1763 without great acclaim, but revived two years later and then received so much more.

As rich as his plays are in characters and complications, they still seem very similar to each other. All have the same shimmering, often farfetched humor; the same metaphysical analysis of the passions; and the same flowery language, full of neologisms.[4] His plots are small in scale but, as a true Callippides of his art, he understands how to traverse their tight confines with such tiny and yet remarkably distinct steps that at the end we imagine we have traveled quite a distance alongside him.[5]

Ever since Frau Neuber publicly banned Harlequin from her theater under the auspices of his Magnificence, Herr Professor Gottsched, all of the German theaters striving to conform to the rules seem to have joined in this banishment.[6] I say "seem," because in reality they abandoned only the colorful little jacket and the name but kept the fool.[7] Neuber herself put on a number of plays in which Harlequin was the main character. But in her theater Harlequin became "Little Hans" and wore all white instead of motley. A great triumph for good taste, indeed!

The False Confessions has a Harlequin, too, who has become "Peter" in the German translation. Neuber is dead, Gottsched is also dead: I'd think we could put his little jacket back on him. – Seriously, though, if he can be tolerated under a strange name, why not under his own? "He is a foreign creation," they say. So what? I wish all the fools among us were foreigners! "He dresses in a way no person among us would dress." Well, then, he need not waste a lot of time introducing himself. "It is preposterous to allow the same individual to appear each day in another play." We should not consider him to be an individual, but rather a type. It is not Harlequin who appears today in *Timon*, tomorrow in *The Falcon*, the day after in *The False Confessions*, like a real jack-of-all-trades; rather, these are Harlequins.[8] The type supports a thousand variations. The one in *Timon* is not the same as the one in *The Falcon;* the former lived in Greece, the latter in France, and it is only because the characters share some of the same main traits that we give them the same name. Why should we be more contemptuous, more picky about our amusements, and more susceptible to hollow nitpicking – I will not say, than the French and Italians are, but rather – than the Romans and Greeks were themselves? Was their Parasite something other than a Harlequin?[9] Did he not have his own special costume, in which he appeared play after play? Didn't the Greeks have a special drama into which Satyrs had to be woven, whether or not they belonged in the story of the play?[10]

A few years ago Harlequin defended his cause before the bench of true criticism with as much whimsy as thoroughness. I recommend Herr Möser's essay on the grotesque-comical to all of my readers who do not yet know it; I already have the support of those who do know it.[11] It speaks in passing of a certain author who possesses enough insight to become Harlequin's eulogist someday. "Now he has achieved it!" people will think. But no: he has always been so. He cannot remember ever having made the objection against Harlequin that Herr Möser puts in his mouth; indeed, he cannot remember ever having even thought it.[12]

Another servant besides Harlequin appears in *The False Confessions*, one who leads the whole intrigue. Both roles were played very well; overall, when it comes to servant roles, our theater has few actors from whom it could demand more than Herr Hensel and Herr Merschy.[13]

On the twenty-second evening (Thursday, the 21st of May), M. de Belloy's *Zelmire* was performed.[14]

The name de Belloy cannot be unknown to anyone who knows anything about recent French literature. The author of *The Siege of Calais*![15] If this play did not earn all the clamor the French made over it, nonetheless the clamor itself brings honor to the French. It shows them to be a nation jealous of its fame, still impressed by the great deeds of its ancestors, and one that, convinced of the value of a poet and of the influence of theater on virtue and manners, does not count the former among its useless members and the latter as an object that only concerns men of leisure. How far behind the French in this matter are we Germans! To say it plainly: in comparison to them, we are still veritable barbarians. More barbaric than our barbaric ancestors, for whom a troubadour was a highly estimable man, and who, for all their indifference regarding arts and sciences, certainly would have considered the question: "Who is the more useful citizen, a poet or a man who deals in bearskins and amber?" to be the question of a fool! – Look wherever I might in Germany, a city has yet to be built that might be expected to show a German poet even a thousandth part of the respect and recognition that Calais had for de Belloy.[16] We always take this for French vanity; how far we have yet to go before we are capable of such vanity! And is it any wonder? Our scholars themselves are so small-minded that they reinforce our nation's contempt for anything that does not directly fill the purse. You may speak of a work of genius, any you like; you may talk about encouraging artists; you may express the wish that a rich, flourishing city might, merely by taking an interest, assist in establishing not only the most respectable recreation for men who must bear the stress and heat of their daily business, but also the most useful pastime for those who don't want any business at all (the theater is this at least, is it not?) – and just look and listen to the reply. It's not just the usurer Albinus who cries out "Thank heaven our citizens have more important things to do!"[17]

> – *Eu!*
> *Rem poteris servare tuam!* –[18]

More important? More profitable, I'll concede. Of course, among us profitability has no connection to the liberal arts. But

> – *haec animos aerugo et cura peculî*
> *Cum semel imbuerit* –[19]

But I forget myself. What does all this have to do with *Zelmire?*

De Belloy was a young man who wanted – or was supposed – to study law. "Was supposed to" is probably more likely, for the love of theater kept the upper hand: he laid Bartolus aside and became an actor.[20] He performed for some time with the French troupe in Braunschweig, wrote several plays, returned to his native country, and thanks to a couple of tragedies quickly became as happy and famous as legal scholarship ever could have made him, even if he had become a Beaumont.[21] Woe to the young German genius wanting to pursue this path! Contempt and beggary would be his most certain fate!

De Belloy's first tragedy was *Titus*; *Zelmire* was his second.[22] *Titus* found no favor and was performed only once. But *Zelmire* found much greater acclaim; it was performed fourteen times in a row, and the Parisians still could not get enough of it. The subject matter is of the author's own invention.[23]

A French critic took the opportunity on this occasion to declare himself generally against tragedies of this type.[24] "We would have preferred," he writes, "material taken from history. After all, the annals of the world are rich enough in notorious crimes, and tragedy is specifically intended to present the great actions of real heroes for our admiration and imitation. In paying the tribute posterity owes to their ashes, tragedy also inspires those living today with the noble desire to be like those heroes. One should not argue that *Zaïre, Alzire, Mahomet* are also just fabrications of fiction.[25] The names of the first two are invented, but the basis for their stories is historical. There really were Crusades, in which Christians and Turks hated and slaughtered each other for the glory of God, their common father. The conquest of Mexico necessarily brought to light the fortuitous and sublime contrasts between European and American morals, between fanaticism and true religion. And as for *Mahomet*, it is the extraction, the quintessence, so to speak, of the whole life of this deceiver; it is fanaticism in action, the finest and most philosophical portrait that has ever been made of this dangerous monster."[26]

Essay 19

3 July 1767

Everyone is entitled to his own taste, and it is laudable for someone to attempt to give an account of his taste.[1] But to give the reasons that account for one's taste a universal character and to thereby establish that taste as the only true taste: this signals that one is exceeding the limits of the inquiring admirer and setting oneself up as an intractable lawmaker. The aforementioned French author begins with a modest, "We would have preferred," and then goes on to such generally binding principles that we are to believe this "we" has come directly from the mouth of Criticism itself. The true critic of art does not follow rules dictated by his own taste, but rather forms his taste upon rules demanded by the nature of the subject.

Long ago Aristotle determined the degree to which the tragic poet should concern himself with historical truth: he should engage it only insofar as it resembles a well-constructed fable that he can suit to his purposes. He does not need a story because it happened, but because it happened in such a way that it would be difficult for him to invent something better for his present purposes. If by chance he finds something suitable in a true event, he welcomes it, but it is not worth his effort to spend a great deal of time searching for such events in the history books. And how many people do know what happened? If we only want to believe it is possible for something to happen because it has happened, then what keeps us from taking a completely made-up story for a real historical occurrence that we had never heard about? What is the first thing that makes a history believable to us? Is it not that it intrinsically appears true?[2] And does it really matter if this appearance of truth cannot be confirmed by witnesses or traditions, or if it is confirmed by those whom we do not even know? It is assumed without reason that one purpose of the theater is to preserve the memory of great men; but this is what history is for, not theater. In the theater we should not study what this or that single person did but rather what any person of a certain character would do under certain given circumstances. The purpose of tragedy is far more philosophical than the purpose of history, and we diminish its true value when we make it into a mere panegyric for famous men or misuse it to feed our national pride.

This same French critic's second objection to de Belloy's *Zelmire* is more important. He condemns it for being almost nothing more than a web of various miraculous coincidences that, pressed together into the narrow confines of twenty-four hours, would be incapable of producing any illusion. One oddly isolated situation after another! One unexpected *coup de théâtre* after another![3] So much happens! What a lot to keep in mind! When there are so many events clustered together, it is difficult to prepare them all properly. When there are so many surprises, some will disconcert us more readily than they will surprise us. "Why, for example, does the Tyrant have to reveal himself to Rhamnès?[4] What forces Anténor to divulge his crimes to him? Doesn't Ilus seem to drop from heaven? Isn't Rhamnès' change of heart far too rapid? Up until the moment he stabs Anténor, he is a committed participant in his master's crimes, and if he ever seemed to feel regret, he immediately suppressed it. What trifling causes does the poet often give to the most important matters! For instance, when Polidore returns from battle and wants to hide in the tomb, he has to turn his back to Zelmire, and the poet has to carefully impress this trivial circumstance upon us.[5] For if Polidore had gone another way, if he had turned his face instead of his back to the princess, she would have recognized him, and the ensuing scene, in which the tender daughter unknowingly delivers her father to his executioners – this striking scene that makes such a great impression on the whole audience – would have had to be scrubbed. Anyway, would it not have been far more natural if Polidore, in seeking refuge in the tomb, had noticed Zelmire, called out to her, or even just given her a glance? Of course it would have been more natural than basing the entire final act on the path Polidore takes and whether he turns his back this way or that way. Azor's note is the same case: if, in the second act, the soldier had brought the note with him as he should have, then the tyrant would have been exposed and the play would have ended."[6]

The translation of *Zelmire* is only in prose.[7] But who would not rather hear a concise, pleasant sounding prose than flat, mangled verse? Of all our rhymed translations there are hardly half a dozen that are bearable.[8] And do not take me literally and ask me to name them! I would rather know where to stop than where to start. The best among them is dark and ambiguous in many places. The Frenchman is already not the greatest verse writer – he dabbles and cobbles; the German is even less of one, and naturally, because he took pains to translate the successful and unsuccessful lines from his original with equal faithfulness, what was just padding or tautology there often becomes absolute nonsense here. The diction is for the most part so base, and its construction so perverse, that the actor needs all his nobility to elevate it and all his understanding to prevent it from missing the mark. Absolutely no thought was given to making his declamation easier!

But is it really worth the trouble to expend so much effort on French verse when all that results are verses in our own language that are just as watery and punctilious and just as grammatically frigid? On the other hand, even if we translate all the poetic ornament of the French into prose, the result will still not make our prose very poetic. We will still not achieve that hybrid tone that has emerged in the prose translations of English poets, in which the use of the boldest tropes and figures together with a tightly cadenced syntax makes us think of drunks who dance without music. The locution will, at most, be no more elevated over everyday speech than theatrical declamation should be over the normal tone of social conversation. And thus I would wish our prose translators ever so many successors, even though I absolutely do not share Houdar de la Motte's opinion that meter is a childish constraint to which the dramatic poet should submit least of all.[9] For here it comes down to choosing the lesser of two evils – either to sacrifice reason and emphasis to versification, or vice versa. Houdar de la Motte should be forgiven for his opinion. He had a language in mind in which the poetic meter only tickles the ear and can contribute nothing to the intensification of an expression. In our own language, however, it is something more, and we can come a great deal closer to the Greeks, who were able to suggest the passions expressed in their verses through the rhythm alone. French verses have nothing in their favor but the merit of difficulties overcome, a very miserable merit indeed.

Herr Borchers played the role of Anténor uncommonly well, with all of the self-assurance and serenity that seems natural for a villain of great intelligence.[10] No failed attempt will confound him; he has an inexhaustible supply of new intrigues, he hardly stops to recollect himself, and even the most unexpected stroke, one that threatens to expose him, gets a twist that only stamps his mask on more firmly. It is absolutely necessary for the actor to possess the most exacting memory, the most mature voice, and the most free and casual movement if he is not to ruin this character. Over all, Herr Borchers has many general talents, and the sole fact that he is as happy to perform older roles as younger ones must awaken prejudice in his favor. This is proof of his love of the art, and connoisseurs readily distinguish him from so many other young actors who want only to shine on the stage and whose petty vanity to be ogled and admired in nothing but the roles of gallant lovers is their primary, and often their only, calling to the stage.[11]

Essay 20

7 July 1767

On the twenty-third evening (Friday, the 22nd of May), *Cénie* was performed.[1]

This excellent play by Grafigny had to fall into Frau Gottsched's hands for translating. Given the confession she herself made, "that she considered the honor one could earn through the translation, or even through the production, of theatrical plays to be only very mediocre," it is easy to suppose that she expended only a very mediocre effort to obtain this mediocre honor.[2] I have done her the justice of noting that she has in fact not ruined a few comic plays by Destouches. But how much easier it is to translate a funny tale than a feeling! The witty or unwitty can parrot the ridiculous, but only someone with a heart can match the language of the heart. It has its own rules; and it will lose its vibrancy if we misinterpret those rules and instead subordinate that language to the rules of grammar, attempting to equip it with all the cold perfection and boring clarity that we demand from a logical sentence. For example, Dorimond intends to give Mericourt a respectable marriage along with a quarter of his wealth. But Mericourt is after much more; he refuses the generous offer and wants to appear to have refused it out of unselfishness. "What for?" he says. "Why do you want to rob yourself of your wealth? Enjoy your goods yourself – they cost you danger and labor enough." "J'en jouirai, je vous rendrai tous heureux," Grafigny has the dear kindhearted old man answer: "I shall enjoy it, I shall make all of you happy."[3] Superb! Precision in every word! The truly effortless brevity of a man, for whom benevolence has become second nature, speaking of his own benevolence, if speak of it he must! To enjoy his own good fortune, to make others happy: both are one and the same to him. One is not merely a result or a part of the other; for him, one is entirely the other. In the same way that his heart does not recognize any difference between them, his mouth cannot create a difference. He speaks as if he said the same thing twice, as if both sentences were true tautological sentences, perfectly identical sentences, without the slightest conjunction. O the wretch who does not feel the connection, who needs a particle to make that connection! And how do you think Frau Gottsched translated these eight little words? "Only then will I begin finally, truly to enjoy my wealth – when I will have made you both happy through it."[4] Unbearable! The sense is perfectly translated, but the spirit is gone: a torrent of words has suffocated it. This "only then" with its tail of "when"; this "finally," this "truly," this "through it": blunt specifications that give outpourings of a heart the ponderousness of deliberation and transform a warm sentiment into frosty speech.

To those who understand me, I will simply say that the entire play is translated roughly along these lines. Every refined inclination has been paraphrased into healthy common sense, every touching expression has been broken into the dead components of its meaning. Add to this the dreadful tone of ceremony in many places; showy proclamations of honor contrast with the natural exclamations of emotion in the most nauseating manner. When Cenie recognizes her mother, she cries, "My Lady Mother! O what a sweet name!"[5] The name "mother" is sweet, but "My Lady Mother" is pure honey with lemon juice. A heart opening itself to sentiment closes back up against this awful title. And in the moment that she finds her father, she throws herself into his arms with, "My Gracious Lord! May I be worthy of your favor!"[6] "Mon père!" becomes, in German: My Gracious Lord. What a respectful child! If I were Dorsainville, I would have preferred not to have found her again rather than being greeted with this speech.

Madame Löwen plays Orphise. One cannot play her with more nobility and sentiment. Every expression conveys the quiet awareness of her unacknowledged worth, and she succeeds in revealing gentle melancholy with just her glance and her tone.

Madame Hensel is Cenie. Not a single word falls flat. What she says is not memorized: it seems to come from her own mind, from her own heart. Whether or not she is speaking, she is always acting. I know of only one flaw; it is a very rare flaw, a very enviable flaw. The actress is too big for the role. I feel like I am watching a giant perform drills with the rifle of a cadet.[7] Just because I can do something excellently doesn't mean I would always choose to do so.

Herr Ekhof, in the role of Dorimond, is completely Dorimond. Such a combination of gentleness and gravity, of tenderheartedness and austerity, either is genuine in this kind of a man or is found in no one. When at the end of the play he says of Mericourt, "I will give him enough that he can live in that great world that is his homeland, but I wish never to see him again!"[8] – who taught the man to show us in one gesture, merely with a pair of raised fingers moving slightly, with just a mere turn of the head, what kind of a land this is, this homeland of Mericourt's? A dangerous, evil land!

Tot linguae, quot membra viro! –[9]

On the twenty-fourth evening (Friday, the 25th of May), Herr Weisse's *Amalia* was produced.[10]

Connoisseurs consider *Amalia* to be this writer's best comedy. Indeed, it really does have more interest, better-developed characters, and more lively and thoughtful dialogue than his other comic plays. The roles are very well cast here; in particular, Madame Böck plays Manley (the disguised Amalia) with great charm and a casual lightness without which we might find it somewhat improbable to see a young woman go unrecognized for so long.[11] In general, disguises of this type give a dramatic play a novelistic quality, but by the same token it is also inevitable that they should occasion not only comedic scenes but also really quite interesting ones.[12] The fifth scene of the final act is of this type, in which I might counsel my friend to soften a few of the brushstrokes that are too boldly sketched and to blend them into a more harmonious relationship with the rest.[13] I do not know if such a thing happens in the world, if someone might really speak to a woman in such an importunate manner. I will not investigate how far female modesty could go in handling certain matters so roughly, even when in disguise. I will leave unspoken the idea that perhaps this is not at all the correct way to corner a Lady Freemann; that a true Manley probably could have begun the matter more subtly; that one must not insist on wanting to swim in a straight line over a rushing stream; that – as I said, I will leave these ideas unspoken, for in such dealings there could easily be more than one correct way. Given these circumstances, even then, it is by no means certain that this woman, on whom this first attempt has miscarried, will resist all other attempts. I will merely acknowledge that personally, I would not have had courage enough to handle a similar scene. I would have been as afraid of the one cliff – of showing too little experience – as of the other – of betraying too much. Indeed, if I were sensible of a more-than-Crébillonian capacity in myself to steal between both cliffs, I still do not know if I would not have preferred a completely different path.[14] Especially since this other path opens on its own here. Manley, or Amalia, knows full well that Freemann is not legally wed to his alleged wife. So why could he not use this as an excuse to seduce her away from Freemann, and offer himself not as a gallant only interested in fleeting signs of favor but rather as a serious lover, ready to share his fate with her? His propositions would then have been – I will not say inculpable, but certainly less culpable; he would have been able to insist on them without insulting her to her face; the test would have been that much more enticing, and her resolve that much more decisive in favor of her love for Freemann. At the same time, we would have seen a proper plan on the part of Amalia instead of being unable to guess what she might have done had she been unfortunately fortunate in her seduction.

Saint-Foix's short comedy *The Financier* followed after *Amalia*.[15] It comprises approximately a dozen scenes that are wondrously lively. It would be difficult to squeeze more healthy morals, more characters, and more interest into such tight confines. This likable writer's manner is well-known. Never has a poet ever known how to make such a small, precious entirety as well as he.

On the twenty-fifth evening (Tuesday, the 26th of May), *Zelmire* by de Belloy was repeated.

Essay 21

10 July 1767

On the twenty-sixth evening (Friday, the 29th of May), Nivelle de la Chaussée's *School for Mothers* was performed.[1]

This is the story of a mother who receives a just comeuppance for her biased tenderness toward a worthless, sycophantic son. Marivaux has a play with the same title.[2] But his tells the story of a mother who, in order to turn her daughter into a properly obedient child, raises her in total innocence, giving her no knowledge of the world and no experience; and how does that go? Just as one might readily guess. The sweet girl has a sensitive heart, she does not know how to avoid danger because she is unaware of any danger, she falls in love with the first who comes along without asking mama, and mama can thank heaven that things go as well as they do. In that *School* there are many serious observations to be made; in this one there is more to laugh at. One is the counterpart to the other, and I believe it would be an additional pleasure for connoisseurs to be able to see one after the other on the same evening. They are also formally suited to such a pairing: the first play has five acts, and the second has one.

On the twenty-seventh evening (Monday, the 1st of June), M. de Voltaire's *Nanine* was performed.[3]

"*Nanine*?" asked so-called critics, when this comedy was first published in 1749. "What kind of title is that? What is one to think of it?" – Nothing more and nothing less than one should think of a title. A title does not have to be a menu. The less it reveals of the content, the better it is. Both writers and spectators are best served this way; moreover, the ancient Greeks rarely gave their comedies anything other than meaningless titles. I hardly know of three or four that indicated the main character or gave away any hint of the plot. Plautus's *Miles Gloriosus* is one of these.[4] How is it that no one has noticed that only half this title belongs to Plautus? He simply called his play *Gloriosus*, just as he called another *Truculentus*.[5] *Miles* must have been the addition of a grammarian.[6] It is true, the braggart that Plautus depicts is a soldier, but his swaggering is not only related to his rank and his military deeds. He is just as boastful on the subject of love; he prides himself not only on being the bravest but also the most handsome and charming of men. Both of these can reside in the word *gloriosus*, but as soon as one adds *miles* the *gloriosus* is limited to the first. Perhaps a passage from Cicero* misled the grammarian who made this addition, but in this instance he should have paid attention to Plautus instead of Cicero.[7] Plautus himself writes:

> Alazon *Graece huic nomen est Comoediae*
> *Id nos latine* Gloriosum *dicimus* –[8]

Moreover, it is by no means certain that the passage from Cicero is discussing Plautus's play. The character of the boastful soldier appeared in several plays. Cicero could just

---

* *De Officiis* Book I. Chap. 38.

as well have meant Terence's Thraso.[9] – But all this is incidental. I recall that I have already expressed my general opinion about the titles of comedies. It could be that the matter is not so insignificant. Many a bungler has written a bad comedy under a beautiful title, simply on account of the title.

I would prefer a good comedy with a bad title. If you look into all the character types that have been explored, you will hardly be able to think of one after whom a play has not been named (particularly by the French). "That one has already been around for a long time!" someone cries. "That one too! That one's been borrowed from Molière, and that other one from Destouches!" Borrowed? That is what comes from beautiful titles. What kind of ownership does a poet have over a certain character type just because he took his title from it? If he had made tacit use of the character, then I might also tacitly use it, and no one would make me out to be an imitator as a result. But for example, let someone dare just once to write a new play about a misanthrope. Even if he does not take a single characteristic from the Molière, his misanthrope will still be called just a copy. It is enough that Molière was the first to use the name. The new writer is to blame for living fifty years later, and because language does not have infinite names for the infinite varieties of human dispositions.

Although the title *Nanine* tells us nothing, the subtitle does say more: *Nanine, or Prejudice Overcome*. And why shouldn't a play have two titles? We human beings also have two or three names. The names exist to differentiate; it is harder to confuse people with two names than with one. With the second title, M. de Voltaire appears to be unsure of himself. In the same edition of his works he calls it on one page "*Prejudice Overcome*," and on another, "*The Man without Prejudice*."[10] Of course, they are not very far apart. The play is about the prejudice that a proper marriage requires equality of birth and social standing. In short, the story of *Nanine* is the story of *Pamela*.[11] M. de Voltaire certainly did not want to use the name Pamela, since several years earlier a couple of plays already appeared under this name and had no great success. The *Pamela* of Boissy and that of de la Chaussée are also rather barren pieces, and Voltaire did not even need to be Voltaire in order to make something far better.[12]

Nanine is a sentimental comedy. It has, however, quite a few funny scenes; Voltaire only seems to tolerate these in comedy when the funny scenes alternate with the touching ones. An entirely serious comedy, where no one ever laughs or even smiles, where one only wants to cry, is a monstrosity for him. On the other hand, he finds the transition from the sentimental to the comedic, and from the comedic to the sentimental, very natural. Human life is nothing other than a constant chain of such transitions, and the comedic genre should be a mirror of human life. "What is more familiar," he says, "than a house in which the angry father stomps around, the infatuated daughter sighs, the son considers himself superior to both of them, and each relative feels something different within the same scene? In one room, they make fun of what is extremely moving in another room; and it is not uncommon that within a quarter of an hour, the same person both laughs and cries over the same situation. A venerable matron sat at the bedside of one of her daughters who was dangerously ill, and the entire family had gathered around her. She wanted to dissolve into tears, she wrung her hands and cried, 'O God! let me, let me keep this child, just this one, even if you take all of the others from me in exchange!' At this point a man who had married one of her other daughters stepped forward, tugged at her sleeve, and asked: 'Madame, the sons-in-law, too?' The deadpan, comical tone with which he spoke these words made such an impression on the distressed lady that she couldn't help bursting into laughter. Everybody followed suit and laughed; the sick girl herself, when she heard it, nearly choked with laughter."[13]

"Homer," he says at another point, "has the gods themselves laugh at Vulcan's adorable sense of decorum as they are deciding the fate of the world. Hector laughs at the fear of his young son while Andromache weeps bitter tears. It really can happen, in the middle of the horrors of battle, in the middle of the terrors of a conflagration or some such tragic doom, that a thought or a casual joke, despite all the anxiety, despite all the compassion, provokes uncontainable laughter. At the Battle of Speyer, a regiment was ordered to show no mercy. A German officer begged for pardon, and the Frenchman whom he addressed answered: 'Ask whatever you will, my good man; just do not ask for your life. I am unable to help you with that!' This *naiveté* instantly made the rounds; they laughed and butchered. Think how much more readily laughter can follow touching sentiments in comedy. Does Alcmena not touch us? Does Sosia not make us laugh? What sorry and futile work, to fight against experience."[14]

Indeed! But doesn't M. de Voltaire fight against experience when he declares serious comedy as a flawed and boring genre? Perhaps not at the time when he wrote that. At that time there was not yet a *Cénie*, not yet a *Father of the Family*; a genius has to make something first, so that we can perceive it as possible.[15]

Essay 22

14 July 1767

On the twenty-eighth evening (Tuesday, June 2nd), *The Village Lawyer* was repeated, and the evening ended with Herr Gellert's *The Sick Woman*.[1]

Of all our comic playwrights, Herr Gellert is without doubt the one whose plays are the most originally German. They are true family portraits in which we feel immediately at home. Every spectator imagines recognizing in them a cousin, a brother-in-law, or an auntie from his or her own family. They also provide proof that there is no shortage of original fools among us; it is just that they show themselves in their true light to relatively few eyes. Our follies are more observable than observed: in everyday life we look past many of them out of kindheartedness, and our *virtuosi* have become accustomed to using a one-dimensional style in imitating them. The actors bear a resemblance to fools but do not bring them to life. They affect, but because they do not know how to shine an advantageous light on their subject, their portrait lacks rounding, corporality. We see only one side, which we quickly tire of looking at, and when we try to imagine its other sides, its all-too-sharply defined contours immediately remind us that we are watching an illusion. Fools the world over are flat and cold and disgusting; if they are going to make us laugh, the poet must give them something of himself. He must not bring them onto the stage in their everyday dress, in the dirty carelessness in which they absently wander their own little world. They must reveal nothing of the narrow sphere of worrisome concerns from which each might want to work his way out. He has to clean them up; he has to lend them wit and understanding in order to be able to cover up their miserable follies; he has to give them enough ambition to want to shine.

"I have no idea," said one of my female acquaintances, "what kind of a couple this is, this Herr Stephan and this Frau Stephan! Herr Stephan is a rich man and a good man. Nevertheless his beloved Frau Stephan has to make such a fuss about a shabby Adrienne dress.[2] Granted, we often get sick over nothing, but not over such a big nothing. A new Adrienne! Can she not simply send out, choose, and have one made? The husband will pay, of course; he must."

"Absolutely right!" says another. "But I have something else to add. The writer was writing during our mother's time. An Adrienne! What tailor's wife still wears an Adrienne? Might the actress not help the good man out a bit? Could she not substitute Robe Ronde, Benedictine, Respectueuse instead!?"[3] – (I have forgotten the other names, I would not know how to spell them anyway) – "Just imagining myself in an Adrienne could make me sick. If Madame Stephan is coveting the newest things, it has to be the newest style of dress. How else are we to find it probable that she has become sick over it?"

"And I," said the third (this was the most learned of them), "find it very improper that the Stephan woman tries on a dress that was not tailor-made for her. But we can easily see what forced the author into this – what should I call it? – misunderstanding of our delicacy. The unity of time! The dress has to be finished, Stephan must try it on, and a dress cannot be finished in twenty-four hours. In fact he could barely permit himself twenty-four hours for a little afterpiece. For Aristotle says – " And here my critic was interrupted.

On the twenty-ninth evening (Wednesday, the 3rd of June), *The Man of the Clock, or the Regular Man* was performed after de la Chaussee's *Mélanide.*[4]

The author of this piece is Herr Hippel, from Danzig. It is full of funny incidents; too bad that as soon as we hear the title we predict them all. It is also sufficiently national, or rather more provincial. And this can easily become the other extreme into which our comedic playwrights fall when they wish to depict real German customs. I fear that each may treat the paltry habits from the corner of the world in which he was born as the authentic custom of our common fatherland.[5] But whose job is it to discover how often one eats green cabbage during the year in this place or that?

A comedy can have a double title; but it is a given that each says something different. This is not the case here: *The Man of the Clock, or the Regular Man* – these say basically the same thing, except for that the first is roughly a caricature of the second.

On the thirtieth evening (Thursday, the 4th of June), Thomas Corneille's *Earl of Essex* was performed.[6]

This tragedy is perhaps the only one of the impressive number of plays by the younger Corneille that survives on the stage. And I believe it is performed even more frequently in the German theater than in the French. It was written in 1678, forty years after Calprenède had already worked on the same story.[7]

"It is well known," writes Corneille, "that the Earl of Essex stood in particular favor with Queen Elizabeth. He was proud by nature. The great services that he rendered England swelled him up even more. His enemies accused him of conspiring with the Earl of Tyrone, who was chosen to lead the rebels in Ireland. The suspicion that attached to him on this account caused him to lose command of the army. He was embittered, came to London, stirred up the populace, was thrown into prison, was condemned, and – after he refused to beg for pardon – was beheaded on the 25th of February 1601. This much I gleaned from history. I am very much surprised to be charged with falsifying an important historical point because I did not make use of the incident with the ring that the Queen had given the Earl as a token of her unfailing favor, in case he should ever be found guilty of treason. I am assured that this ring is an invention of Calprenède, at least I can say I have never read the slightest thing about it by any historian."[8]

In any case, Corneille was free to use or not to use this incident with the ring; but he went too far when he identified it as a poetic invention. Its historical accuracy has recently been acknowledged to be nearly without doubt, and those most cautious, skeptical writers of history, Hume and Robertson, have included it in their works.[9]

When Robertson writes in his *History of Scotland* about the melancholy into which Elizabeth fell before her death, he says: "The most common opinion at that time and perhaps the most probable was that it flowed from grief for the Earl of Essex. She retained an extraordinary regard for the memory of that unfortunate nobleman; and though she often complained of his obstinacy, seldom mentioned his name without tears. An accident happened soon after her retiring to Richmond, which revived her affection with new tenderness, and imbittered her sorrows. The Countess of Notting-ham, being on her death bed, desired to see the Queen, in order to reveal something to her, without discovering which, she could not die in peace. When the Queen came into her chamber, she told her, that while Essex lay under sentence of death, he was desirous of imploring pardon in the manner which the Queen herself had prescribed, by returning a ring, which during the height of his favour she had given him, with a promise that, if in any future distress, he sent that back to her as a token, it should intitle him to her protection; that Lady Scroop was the person he intended to imploy in order to present it; that by a mistake, it was put into her hands instead of Lady Scroop's; and that she having communicated the matter to her husband, one of Essex's most implacable enemies, he had forbid her either to carry the ring to the Queen, or to return it to the Earl. The Countess, having thus disclosed her secret, begged the Queen's forgiveness; but Elizabeth, who now saw both the malice of the Earl's enemies, and how unjustly she had suspected him of inflexible obstinacy, replied, 'God may forgive you, but I never can;' and left the room in great emotion. From that moment, her spirit sunk entirely; she could scarce taste food; she refused all the medicines prescribed by her physicians; declaring that she wished to die, and would live no longer. No intreaty could prevail on her to go to bed; she sat on cushions, during ten days and nights, pensive, and silent, holding her finger almost continually in her mouth, with her eyes open, and fixed on the ground. The only thing to which she seemed to give any attention, were the acts of devotion, performed in her apartment, by the Archbishop of Canterbury; and in these she joined with great appearance of fervour. Wasted, at last, as well by anguish of mind, as by long abstinence, she expired without a struggle, on Thursday the 24th day of March, in the 70th year of her age, and in the 45th of her reign."[10]

Essay 23

17 July 1767

M. de Voltaire criticized *Essex* in a peculiar way.[1] I should not like to contradict him by claiming that *Essex* is a first-rate play, but it is easy to show that many of the errors he condemns in it are either not found there at all or are such irrelevant trivialities as to imply a concept of tragedy that is neither the best nor the worthiest.

One of M. de Voltaire's weaknesses is that he wants to be a very profound historian. With *Essex* he leapt onto this warhorse of his and exercised it violently. It is only a shame that all of the deeds he accomplishes thus mounted are not worth the dust he raises.

He claims Thomas Corneille knew little of English history, and it was fortunate for the poet that the audience of the time knew even less. Now, he says, we know Queen Elizabeth and the Earl of Essex better; nowadays a poet who made similar gross offenses against historical truth would be more sharply reproached.[2]

And what, then, are these offenses? Voltaire has calculated that the Queen was sixty-eight years old at the time that she had the Earl put on trial. It would thus be ridiculous, he says, for someone to imagine that love could have played the least part in this episode.[3] Why? Does nothing ridiculous ever happen in the world? Is it so ridiculous to imagine that something ridiculous might have happened? After the verdict over Essex was pronounced, Hume writes, the Queen was in a state of "most real agitation and irresolution. She felt a perpetual combat between resentment and inclination, pride and compassion, the care of her own safety and concern for her favourite; and her situation, during this interval, was perhaps more an object of pity, than that to which Essex himself was reduced. She signed the warrant for his execution; she countermanded it; she again resolved on his death; she felt a new return of tenderness. Essex's enemies told her, that he himself desired to die, and had assured her, that she could never be in safety while he lived: It is likely, that this proof of penitence and of concern for her would produce a contrary effect to what they intended, and would revive all the fond affection, which she had so long indulged toward the unhappy prisoner. But what chiefly hardened her heart against him was his supposed obstinacy, in never making, as she hourly expected, any application to her for mercy; and she finally gave her consent to his execution."[4]

Why should Elizabeth, in her sixty-eighth year, not still have loved, she who so loved to be loved? She who was so flattered when someone extolled her beauty? She who liked it so much when someone seemed to wear her chains? The world has likely never seen a more vain woman in this respect. Her courtiers all pretended to be in love with her and employed, with all appearance of earnestness, manners of the most ridiculous gallantry when addressing Her Majesty. When Raleigh fell into disgrace, he wrote a letter to his friend Cecil – which he doubtless intended to be shown to the Queen – in which he called the Queen a Venus, a Diana, and I don't know what else.[5] This goddess was nevertheless sixty years old at the time. Five years later Henry Unton, her emissary in France, conducted the same discourse with her.[6] In short, Corneille was perfectly justified in attributing to her all the weaknesses of being in love, which allowed him to bring the tender woman into such interesting conflict with the proud Queen.[7]

Furthermore, he neither distorted nor falsified the character of Essex. Essex, Voltaire claims, was not the hero Corneille makes him out to be; he never did anything remarkable.[8] But even if he was no hero, he certainly believed himself one. The destruction of the Spanish Armada and the capture of Cadiz – events in which Voltaire believes he played little or no part – he held to be so very much his own work that he could not stand it when anyone else claimed the least bit of honor from them. He offered to prove with sword in hand that these honors belonged to him alone, in single combat against the Earl of Nottingham (under whom he had held his command), or his son, or any of his relatives.[9]

Corneille has the Earl speak very disparagingly of his enemies, particularly Raleigh, Cecil, and Cobham.[10] Voltaire disapproves of this as well. It is not permitted, he says, to falsify modern history so grossly and to abuse men of such noble birth and great merits so undeservingly.[11] But it does not matter here what these men were, only what Essex thought they were, and Essex was proud enough of his own merits not to allow them any whatsoever.

When Corneille has Essex say that the only thing keeping him from ascending the throne himself was a lack of will, he certainly has him say something that is quite far from the truth.[12] But even so, Voltaire had no need to exclaim over it: "What? Essex on the throne? By what right? Under what pretexts? How would that have been possible?"[13] For Voltaire should have remembered that Essex descended from the royal house on his mother's side and that he in fact had supporters who were imprudent enough to count him among those who could make a claim to the crown. Consequently, when he entered into secret negotiations with King James of Scotland, the first thing he did was to reassure the king that he himself had never had such ambitions. What he distances himself from here is not considerably different from what Corneille has him imply.[14]

Thus, while Voltaire finds nothing but historical inaccuracies throughout the whole play, he perpetrates some himself that are not insignificant. Walpole* has already made fun of one of them.[15] Namely, when Voltaire goes to name the favorites of Queen Elizabeth, he names Robert Dudley and the Earl of Leicester.[16] He did not know that they were both the same person and that one could with the same justification make two different persons out of the poet Arouet and the Chamberlain de Voltaire.[17] Just as unforgiveable is the *hysteron proteron* he lapses into with the slap in the face the Queen gave Essex.[18] It is false that he received it after his unsuccessful expedition in Ireland; he had received it long before then. Moreover, it is just as untrue that at the time he tried to soften the Queen's anger through any humility; rather, he expressed his feelings about the matter both verbally and in writing in the most lively and noble

---

* *The Castle of Otranto*, Preface.

manner. He also did not take the first step toward his own pardon; the Queen had to take it.[19]

So to what degree does M. de Voltaire's historical ignorance concern me? As little as Corneille's historical ignorance should have concerned him. And actually I just want to defend the latter against the former.

Corneille's whole tragedy is a fiction: if it is moving, does it then become less moving because the poet has made use of real names?

Why does the tragic playwright choose real names? Does he take his characters from these names, or does he take these names because the characters that history attributes to them are more or less similar to the characters that he has undertaken to show in his story? Here I am speaking not of the way that most tragedies probably have originated, but rather of how they really should originate. Or, to express myself in better accordance with the usual praxis of poets: does the writer choose one given incident over another because of the mere *facta*, the circumstances of the time and place, or because of the character of the persons through whom those *facta* become real? If it is because of the characters, then does that not immediately decide the question of how far the writer can depart from historical truth? As far as he wants in everything that does not concern the characters. Only the characters are sacred to him: to strengthen these, to show these in their best light, is all he may be permitted to do on his own. The smallest substantial change would void the reasons why they have these names and not others, and nothing is more offensive than something for which we ourselves cannot give a reason.

Essay 24

21 July 1767

If the character of Corneille's Elizabeth is the poetic ideal of the true character that history attributes to the Queen bearing this name; if there we find depicted in true colors the indecision, contradictions, fear, regret, and desperation into which a proud and tender heart like Elizabeth's – I will not say "has degenerated" but merely "could be believed to have degenerated" – then the writer has done everything it behooves him to do as a writer.[1] To scrutinize his work with a chronology in hand, to take him before the court of history in order to make him prove every date, and every incidental reference – even those to people about whom history itself has doubts: this is to misunderstand both the poet and his profession. And when it comes from someone who cannot be accused of such a misunderstanding, it is, in a word, chicanery.

To be sure, in the case of M. de Voltaire it could easily be neither misunderstanding nor chicanery. For Voltaire himself is a tragic poet and unquestionably a far greater one than the younger Corneille. It seems that one can be master of an art and yet still have false ideas about the art. And as to chicanery – the whole world knows that this is not his style. That which seems to resemble it here and there in his writings is nothing other than caprice: from time to time he plays the historian in poetry, the philosopher in history, and the wit in philosophy, all from mere caprice.

Should it be for nothing that he knows Elizabeth was sixty-eight when she had the Earl beheaded? Still in love, still jealous, in her sixty-eighth year! Add to this Elizabeth's big nose, and what kind of hilarious ideas must arise!² Of course, these hilarious ideas are written in the commentary on a tragedy; that is, just where they do not belong. The writer would have been justified to say to his critic: "My dear Mr. Notetaker, these droll stories belong in your general history, not below my text. For it is not true that my Elizabeth is sixty-eight years old. Show me where I say that. What is in my play that keeps you from assuming she is approximately the same age as Essex? You say: 'But she was not the same age.' Which she? Your Elizabeth in Rapin de Thoyras?³ That might be. But why did you read Rapin de Thoyras? Why are you so learned? Why do you mix up his Elizabeth with mine? Do you seriously believe that a spectator's memory of reading Rapin de Thoyras will be more vivid than his experience of the sensuous performance of a well-formed actress in her best years in the theatre? He sees my Elizabeth and his own eyes will convince him that this is not your sixty-eight-year-old Elizabeth.⁴ Or will he believe Rapin de Thoyras better than his own eyes?"

The poet could similarly explain the role of Essex. "Your Essex in Rapin de Thoyras," he could say, "is just the embryo of mine. What he believes himself to be in yours, he really is in mine. What he perhaps might have done for the Queen under happier circumstances, mine has done. Indeed, you hear that the Queen herself admits this; do you not want to trust my Queen as much as you trust Rapin de Thoyras? My Essex is a great and worthy man, but also proud and inflexible. Yours was in reality neither so great nor so inflexible: so much the worse for him. Enough for me, that he was in fact still great enough and inflexible enough to lend his name to the character I abstracted from him."

In short: tragedy is not history rendered into a dialogue. For tragedy, history is nothing but a repertory of names with which we are accustomed to associate certain characters. If the poet finds historical details that are convenient to the embellishment and individualization of his material, then good, he should use them. Except he should neither be praised for this nor persecuted for the opposite!

Aside from this point about historical truth, I am very prepared to subscribe to the rest of M. de Voltaire's criticism. *Essex* is a mediocre play with regard to both its plot and its style. To make the Earl into Irton's sighing lover, to have him end up on the scaffold more out of despair that he cannot be hers than from a gallant pride that will not allow him to stoop to excuses and pleas – this was the most unfortunate idea that Thomas could have had, but one which, as a Frenchman, he probably had to have.⁵ The style is weak in the original language; in the translation it often becomes cringeworthy. But, in general, the play is not without interest and has successful verses from time to time; these are, however, more successful in French than in German. "Actors," adds M. de Voltaire, "particularly those in the provinces, play the part of Essex far too gladly because they can appear in it with an embroidered ribbon under the knee and a big blue ribbon over the shoulders. The Earl is a hero of the first class who is dogged by envy: that makes an impression. Besides, the number of good tragedies from all nations in the world is so small that those that are not completely bad always draw an audience just so long as they are supported by good actors."[6]

He defends this general judgment with several specific comments that are as correct as they are perceptive and which we may want to recall with pleasure at a repeat performance. Thus I share the best of them here, in the firm belief that criticism does not compromise enjoyment and that those who have learned to judge a play most sharply are always those who visit the theater most diligently.

"The role of Cecil is a minor role, and a very cold minor role. To paint such a groveling flatterer, one must have the same colors in one's paint box as Racine used to portray Narcissus."[7]

"The fictional Duchess of Irton is a rational, virtuous woman who, in her love for the Earl, wants neither to bring the Queen's disfavor upon herself nor to marry her lover. This character would be very beautiful if it had more life and if it contributed more to the complication; but here she merely fills the place of a friend. This is not sufficient for the theater."[8]

"It seems to me that everything that is said and done by the persons in this tragedy remains very cockeyed, confused, and uncertain. The plot must be clear, the entanglements must be understandable, and every sentiment must be plain and natural: those are the first and most essential rules. But what does Essex want? What does Elizabeth want? What is the Earl's crime? Is he guilty, or has he been falsely accused? If the Queen holds him innocent, then she must help him. But if he is guilty, then it is very unreasonable to have the confidant say that he will never again plead for mercy, that he is far too proud for that. This pride is well suited to a virtuous innocent hero, but not to a man who has been convicted of high treason. The Queen wants his subservience. But if she loves him, is that really the attitude she would have? Once he has subjugated himself; when he has accepted her forgiveness, will Elizabeth then be more loved by him than before? The Queen says: 'I love him a hundred times more than I love myself.' Ah, Madame, if it has come to this, if your passion has become so fierce, then you should investigate the accusations against your beloved yourself and not allow his enemies to persecute him and oppress him in your name, the way they do throughout the whole play, without any cause."[9]

"We also cannot figure out whether the Earl's friend Salisbury thinks he is guilty or innocent. He suggests to the Queen that appearances often deceive, and that one should take heed of the partisanship and unfairness of his judges. Nonetheless he seeks refuge in the Queen's mercy. Why would he need this if he believes his friend not to be guilty? But what should the audience member believe? He does not know what to make either of the Earl's conspiracy or of the Queen's tenderness toward him."[10]

"Salisbury informs the Queen that someone has forged the Earl's signature. But it does not occur to the Queen to investigate such an important circumstance more closely. Nonetheless she was bound to do so, as Queen and as lover. She doesn't even respond to this disclosure, which she should have seized with the greatest eagerness. She merely replies that the Earl is far too proud, and that she absolutely desires him to plead for mercy."[11]

"But why should he plead for mercy if his signature was forged?"[12]

Essay 25

24 July 1767

"Essex himself protests his innocence, but why would he rather die than convince the Queen of it?[1] His enemies have maligned him; with one word he can strike them down, and he does not. Is that in keeping with the character of such a proud man? If he should be acting so absurdly out of love for Irton, then the writer should have shown him more ruled by his passion throughout the whole play. The tumult of emotion can excuse everything; but we do not see him in such a tumult."[2]

"The Queen's pride is in continuous conflict with Essex's pride; such a conflict can be easy to enjoy. But if it is only this pride that causes them to act, then it is nothing but obstinacy on the part of both Elizabeth and the Earl. He should beg me for mercy; I will not beg her for mercy: it is the same old story, again and again. The spectator has to forget that Elizabeth is either very vulgar or very unjust when she demands that the Earl ask forgiveness for a crime that he has not committed and that she has not investigated. He has to forget it, and he really does forget it, in order to concern himself only with the feeling of pride that is so flattering to the human heart."[3]

"In brief: there is not a single role in this tragedy that is what it should be: all of them are flawed, and nevertheless the play has pleased. What is the cause of this pleasure? It is apparently due to the situation of the characters, which in itself is moving. – A great man about to be executed will always be of interest, and the representation of his fate will make an impression even without any help from poetry – just about the same impression that reality itself would make."[4]

For the tragic playwright, so much depends on the choice of material. The weakest and most confused plays can find some form of success through this alone, and I do not know how it is that good actors are the most appealing in such plays. It is rare that a masterpiece is performed as masterfully as it is written; actors always fare better in mediocre plays. Perhaps this is because they can put more of themselves into mediocre plays, or perhaps because mediocre plays leave us more time and ease to notice their acting, or perhaps because in the mediocre work everything rests on one or two prominent persons – unlike in a more accomplished play, in which every person must be a first-rate actor, and if they are not, they help ruin all the others by botching their own roles.

All of these reasons and more come together in *Essex*. Neither the Earl nor the Queen has been portrayed by the author with such power that they could not become much more powerful through performance. Essex does not speak so proudly that the actor could not make him prouder with his every gesture and facial expression. It is in fact an essential feature of pride that it often expresses itself less through words than through other behavior. His words are often modest, and we can only see, not hear, that his is a proud modesty. This role must necessarily gain something in performance. Moreover, the secondary roles cannot have any negative influence on him; the more deferentially Cecil and Salisbury are played, the more Essex will stand out. I thus need not write at length about how excellently an Ekhof must play this role, which even the most indifferent actor could not completely ruin.

Things are not quite the same with the role of Elizabeth, but it too would be difficult to spoil completely. Elizabeth is as tender as she is proud; I am willing to believe that a woman's heart can be both at the same time, but I do not quite comprehend how an actress can perform both well at the same time. In nature, we do not expect tenderness from a proud woman, nor pride from a tender one. We do not expect this, I say, because the signs of one contradict the signs of the other. It is a miracle when a woman experiences both equally; but if only one of the two is mainly in her power, then although she may indeed feel the passion expressed by the other, it will be difficult for us to believe that she feels it as much as she claims. And how can an actress go further than nature? If she has a majestic stature, if her voice has a fuller and more masculine timbre, if her look is bold, her movement quick and lively, then she will have excellent success with the proud passages; but what about the tender ones? If, on the other hand, her figure is less imposing, if her countenance is ruled mainly by gentleness, her eyes by a modest glow, if her voice is more melodious than emphatic, if her movement contains more grace and dignity than strength and spirit, then she will accomplish the tender passages with the greatest satisfaction; but what about the proud ones? She will not ruin them, certainly not; she will contrast them sufficiently, we will see her play an offended angry lover – just not an Elizabeth who was man enough to send her general and lover home with a slap in the face. I mean that the actresses who could successfully play a wholly two-sided Elizabeth might be even more rare than such an Elizabeth herself; and we can and must be content if only one half is played fairly well and the other is not completely neglected.

Madame Löwen pleased mightily in the role of Elizabeth; but, to apply those general observations to her, she let us see and hear more of the tender woman than the proud monarch. Her figure, her voice, her modest acting, all lead us to expect nothing else, and it seems to me we did not enjoy her performance any less. For if one necessarily overshadows the other, if it cannot be otherwise that either the Queen must give way to the lover or the lover to the Queen, then I believe it is more advantageous that something of the pride and of the Queen be lost rather than of the lover and her tenderness.

When I criticize thusly, it is not just idiosyncratic taste; even less is it my intent to pay a compliment to a woman who would still be a master of her art even if she had not succeeded in this role.[5] I know how to pay only one compliment to an artist, be that a person of my own sex or the other, and that consists in assuming that he is so far removed from all vanity that art is more important to him than anything else, that he likes to be criticized freely and loudly, and that he would rather be judged falsely from time to time than hardly at all. Regarding anyone who does not understand this flattery: I acknowledge myself mistaken in him, and he is not worthy of our attention. The true virtuoso will not even believe that we recognize and feel his perfections, no matter how much noise we make over them, unless he also sees that we perceive and feel his weaknesses. He will mentally scoff at any unconditional admiration and appreciate only the praise of those he knows will not refrain from criticizing him.

I wanted to say that there are reasons why it is better if the actress expresses more of the tender than the proud Elizabeth. She has to be proud, that is a given; and we will hear that she is proud, indeed. The question is only whether she should seem more tender than proud or more proud than tender; whether, if we had to choose between two actresses, we would be better off taking the one who is able to embody the offended Queen, with all of the threatening seriousness and dreadfulness of vengeful majesty, or the one who is more suited to the jealous lover, with all of her mortifying feelings of unrequited love, with all her readiness to forgive the beloved wretch, and all her anxiety about his obstinacy and sorrow over his loss? And I say: this second one.

In the first place, this would prevent the doubling of the same character. Essex is proud, and if Elizabeth should also be proud, then she must at least be so in a different way. If in the case of the Earl tenderness must be subordinate to pride, then in the case of the Queen tenderness must outweigh pride. If the Earl gives himself a more elevated air than he deserves, then the Queen must appear somewhat less than she actually is. To have both of them strutting about on stilts with their noses in the air, both looking down on everything around them with contempt: this would be the most irritating uniformity. We must not be able to believe that if Elizabeth were in Essex's place she would act just as he does. The ending proves that she is more yielding than he; thus, from the very beginning she must not act as haughtily as he does. Someone who is able to hold himself aloft through external power needs to expend less effort than one who must do so through his own inner strength. Along these lines, we always know that Elizabeth is the Queen, even if at the same time Essex attempts to act more majestically.

In the second place, it is more suitable in a tragedy if the characters rise rather than fall in their attitudes. It is more suitable for a tender character to have moments of pride, than for a proud character to be carried away by tenderness. The former appears to ascend; the latter, to sink. To take a serious Queen – with a furrowed brow, and a look that makes everyone around her shy and trembling, and a tone of voice that alone could command obedience – and make her indulge in love-sickness and sigh over the trivial urges of her passion is almost laughable. A lover, on the other hand, who is reminded by her jealousy that she is Queen rises above herself, and her weakness becomes dreadful.

Essay 26

28 July 1767

On the thirty-first evening (Wednesday, the 10th of June), the comedy by Madame Gottsched, *The French Housekeeper, or the Mamsell*, was performed.[1]

This play is one of the six original works that were bequeathed to Germany in 1744 through Gottschedian midwifery, with the fifth volume of *The German Stage*. They say that when it was new it played here and there to acclaim. There was a desire to see what kind of acclaim it could still get, and it received what it deserved: none at all.[2] *The Last Will*, by the same author, has something to it, but *The French Housekeeper* is nothing at all.[3] Even less than nothing, for it is not only base, and dull, and cold, but on top of that dirty, disgusting, and offensive to the highest degree.[4] It is inconceivable to me how a lady could write such stuff. I can only hope that all this will be proven by someone. –

On the thirty-second evening (Thursday, the 11th of June), M. de Voltaire's *Sémiramis* was repeated.

Because the orchestra takes the place of the ancient chorus in our plays to a certain extent, connoisseurs have long wished that the music performed before, during, and after the play would correspond better to its content.[5] Herr Scheibe is the first among musicians to note here an entirely new art form.[6] Because he perceived that each play demands its own musical accompaniment if the audience's emotion is not to be weakened and interrupted in an unpleasant manner, he not only tried, as early as 1738, to produce symphonies specific to the plays *Polyeucte* and *Mithridate*, which were performed by the Neuber troupe here in Hamburg, in Leipzig, and in other places, but he also held forth at elaborate length, in a special issue of his *Critical Musician*, about what, in general, the composer should consider if he wants to earn renown in this new genre.[7]

"All symphonies," he says, "produced for a play should relate to its type and content. Thus a different kind of symphony belongs with a tragedy than with a comedy. In the same way that tragedies and comedies differ from each other, so must the music for each differ. In particular, however, because there are different sections of music within the plays, one must pay attention to the nature of the passage to which each musical section pertains. Hence the overture must relate to the first act of the play. The symphonies that occur between the acts, however, must partly accord with the end of the previous act, and partly with the beginning of the subsequent act; just as the final symphony must be in accord with the end of the final act."[8]

"All symphonies for tragedies must be stately, fiery, and spirited. In particular, though, one must take notice of the main characters and the main topic and arrange one's creation to accord with them. This is of no mean consequence. We find tragedies in which the main matter is sometimes one particular virtue of a hero or heroine, and sometimes another. Compare *Polyeucte* to *Brutus*, or *Alzire* to *Mithridate*, and you see immediately that there is no way the same music would suit both.[9] A tragedy in which the hero or heroine's religion and piety accompany all their vicissitudes also demands the kind of music that reflects, to a certain extent, the magnificence and solemnity of church music. But if generosity, valor, or steadfastness dominate all manner of misfortunes in the tragedy, then the music must be much more passionate and lively. The tragedies *Cato*, *Brutus*, and *Mithridate* are of this latter sort.[10] But *Alzire* and *Zaïre* demand a somewhat varied music, because the events and characters in these plays are of a different nature and show more variance in emotions."[11]

"Similarly, comic symphonies must overall be free, flowing, and at times also playful; in particular, however, they must take their cue from the individual content of a given comedy. Just as the comedy is now more serious, now more amorous, now more jocular, the symphony must be composed accordingly. For example, the comedies *The Falcon* and *The Double Inconstancy* would require completely different symphonies than *The Prodigal Son*.[12] And the symphonies that would well suit *The Miser* or *The Imaginary Invalid* would not befit *The Irresolute Man* or *The Absent-Minded Lover*.[13] The former must be merrier and more playful, the latter more peevish and serious."[14]

"The overture must relate to the whole play; but at the same time it must prepare for the beginning and thus accord with the first scene. It can have two or three movements as the composer sees fit. – But the symphonies between the acts might most naturally have two movements, because they should be determined by the end of the preceding act and the beginning of the following one. In the first movement one can refer more to the previous act, and in the second more to the following one. But such a thing is only necessary when the emotions of each are very much opposed, otherwise one can probably just make one movement if it has sufficient length to allow all of the needs of the performance to be taken care of, such as lamp trimming, costume changes, etc. – The final symphony must agree most exactly with the end of the play, in order to allow its events to make that much stronger an impression on the audience. What is more ridiculous than when a hero has lost his life in an unfortunate manner, and a playful and lively symphony follows? And what is more absurd than following the happy end of a comedy with a heavy, emotionally moving symphony?" –[15]

"Moreover, because the music for plays is purely instrumental, a change in instrumentation is necessary in order to more securely hold the spectators' attention, which might be lost if they were always to hear the same instrumentation. It is, however, pretty much a necessity that the overture be strong and fully orchestrated so that it makes the strongest impression on the ear. Thus the change in instrumentation must appear primarily in the interval symphonies. One must judge carefully which instruments are most suitable for the material and most surely express what one ought to express. One must make a reasonable choice here if one wishes to achieve one's purpose with skill and certainty. In particular, however, it is bad when one uses the same instrumentation in two consecutive *entr'actes*. It is always better and more pleasant when one avoids this failing."[16]

These are the most important rules necessary to bring the art of music and the art of poetry into a more precise association. I wanted to convey them in the words of a musician, and in particular of the one who had the honor of inventing them, rather than in my own. For musicians frequently accuse poets and critics of expecting and demanding far more from them than the art is capable of achieving. Most of them must first hear from one of their artistic colleagues that the goal is achievable before they will give it the least attention.

True, it was easy enough to make the rules themselves; they only teach what should happen, without saying how it should happen. The expression of the passions, which is what it all comes down to, is still solely the work of genius. For even though there are and have been musicians who have been amazingly successful in this, we still have not as yet had a philosopher who has learned their methods from them and deduced general principles from their examples. But the more of these examples there are, the more material that accumulates from which such deductions can be made, the sooner we can look for them. And I must be very mistaken if a great step in that direction could not happen as a result of the zeal of musicians in composing dramatic symphonies of this kind. In vocal music, the text helps enormously – the weakest and shakiest music is clarified and strengthened through the words; in instrumental music, on the other hand, this help disappears, and the music says absolutely nothing if it does not directly say what it wants to say. Thus the artist will have to apply his utmost powers, and from among the various sequences of notes that could express an emotion, he will have to choose only those that express it most clearly. We will hear this more often, we will be able to compare them to each other more often, and by noticing what they have in common we will discover the secret to expression.

Every person can conceive for himself how much our enjoyment of the theater would increase thereby. From the very beginning of the new administration of our theater we have thus not only made a general effort to improve the orchestra, but have also found worthy men who were ready and willing to get down to work to create models of this sort of composition that have exceeded all expectations. Herr Hertel has already produced special symphonies for Cronegk's *Olint and Sophronia*, and the second performance of *Sémiramis* was presented with similarly special music by Herr Agricola of Berlin.[17]

Essay 27

31 July 1767

I want to try to give a sense of Herr Agricola's music.[1] Not, of course, of its effects, for the more lively and fine a sensual pleasure is, the less it allows itself to be described in words. One really cannot do much more than fall into general praise, vague proclamations, and cries of amazement, and these are as uninstructive for the amateur as they are repulsive to the virtuoso whom one means to honor. Rather, I want merely to give a sense of the intentions the maestro had and of the general means he wished to use to achieve them.

The overture consists of three movements. The first movement is a *largo* with violins, oboes, and flutes; the bass line is augmented by bassoons. Its expression is serious, at times even wild and stormy; the spectator should assume that the play will be of a similar tenor. But not just this tenor alone; tenderness, remorse, troubled conscience, and submission play a part in it, and the second movement, an *andante* with muted violins and bassoons in concert, deals with dark and pitiful laments. In the third movement, agile musical phrases intermix with proud ones, as the curtain opens to reveal a stage dressed with more than usual splendor. Sémiramis is nearing the end of her magnificence, and the ear should perceive this magnificence as much as the eye does. The character of the movement is *allegretto*, and the instruments are the same as in the first, except that the oboes, flutes, and bassoons have a few special short passages that they play together.

Throughout the whole, the music between the acts consists of only one movement whose expression refers to the action that has just occurred. Herr Agricola does not seem to approve of a second movement that refers to what will follow. I tend to be very much of the same taste in this matter. For the music should not ruin anything for the poet; the tragic poet loves what is unexpected and surprising more than anything else, and he does not like to allow his course to be guessed easily in advance. The music would betray him if it revealed the next emotion. The case of the overture is different; it cannot refer to anything that preceded it, and yet it must only set the general tone of the play, nothing stronger or more definite than the title might reveal. One may show the spectator where one wants to lead him, but the various paths he will need to take to reach the destination must remain completely hidden from him. This argument against a second movement between the acts derives from its advantage to the writer, and it is strengthened by a second that comes from the limits of music. For if the passions that dominate two consecutive acts were to be completely contradictory to each other, then of necessity the two musical movements would have to be of similarly conflicting nature. Now I understand quite well how a playwright can bring us from any one passion to its opposite, to its complete contradiction, without unpleasant violence; he does it bit by bit, slowly, slowly, climbing the whole ladder rung by rung, either up or down, without making the least little jump at any point. But can the musician do this, too? He might be able to do this as well in one piece of the requisite length. But in two completely distinct pieces, the jump – from, for example, the calm into the stormy, or from the tender into the cruel – must necessarily be very noticeable, and have all the offensive qualities that every sudden transition in nature from one extreme to another tends to have, e.g. from dark into light, from cold into heat. Now we are melting in sorrow, and suddenly we are supposed to rage. How? Why? Against whom? Against the person toward whom our souls were entirely sympathetic? Or against some other? Music cannot ascertain all this, it leaves us in uncertainty and confusion. We feel, without apprehending a correct sequence of our feelings; we feel as if in a dream, and all of these disorderly feelings are more exhausting than captivating. Poetry, on the other hand, never lets us lose the threads of our feelings; not only do we know what we should be feeling but also why we should feel it, and only this "why" makes the sudden transitions not only bearable but pleasant. In fact, this motivation of sudden transitions is one of the greatest advantages that music draws from the union with poetry, perhaps the greatest of all. For it is really not so necessary to use words to restrict general undefined feelings of music, like joy, to a certain single object of joy, because the dark shifting feelings are still very pleasant. But it is very necessary to join separate, conflicting feelings through clear concepts that only words can furnish, in order to weave these feelings into a whole in which one does not just perceive their diversity but also recognizes their harmony. With double movements between the acts of a play, however, this connection would only be made in retrospect; we would only come to know afterward why we had to leap from one passion to an entirely opposite one, and as far as the music is concerned, it would be the same as if we never knew at all. The leap has already had its negative effects and does not offend us any less because we now see that it was not supposed to offend us. One should not believe, however, that this means all symphonies must be condemned, because all of them consist of several movements that can be distinguished from one another, each expressing something other than the rest. They express something other, but not something different; or rather, they express the same thing but only in another way. A symphony that expresses different, conflicting passions in its various movements is a musical monstrosity. In one symphony, only one passion must dominate, and each individual movement must resound with, and try to awaken in us, this very same passion, just with different modifications, according to the degree of its strength and liveliness or according to the amount it coalesces with other related passions. The overture fully had this quality; the turbulence of the first movement dissolves into the lamentation of the second, which is then raised to a kind of solemn majesty in the third. A composer who allows himself more in his symphonies, who stops the affect after each movement in order to begin a completely new affect with the subsequent one, and then lets this one go, too, in order to throw himself into a third, equally different one, will have wasted much art to no avail; he can surprise, intoxicate, titillate, but he just cannot move us. The composer who wishes to speak to our hearts and awaken sympathetic feelings in them must pay attention to coherence as much as the one who reckons to entertain our reason and teach us. Without coherence, without the inner connection of each and every part, the best music is a vain heap of sand, incapable of any lasting impression. Only connectedness renders it into a solid marble on which the artist's hand can immortalize itself.

The movement after the first act thus seeks only to sustain what the poet has focused on in that act: Sémiramis's worries and fears, which are as yet still mixed with some hope; an *andante mesto*, with only muted violins and violas.

In the second act, Assur plays too important a role not to determine the expression of the music that follows.[2] An *allegro assai* in G major – with bugles reinforced by flutes, oboes, and bassoons playing along with the contrabass – expresses the pride of this faithless, power-hungry official, a pride that is continually revived despite bouts of fear and doubt.

The ghost appears in the third act. I have already taken the opportunity in my discussion of the first performance to observe how minimal an impression Voltaire has his ghost make on those present. But the composer rightly ignores this; he makes up for what the poet failed to do, and an *allegro* in E minor – with the same instrumentation as the previous movement, except that E horns alternate with G horns – depicts no mute dull amazement but rather the true wild panic that such an apparition must provoke among people.

Sémiramis's fear awakens our compassion in the fourth act; we are sorry for the remorseful woman, even though we know her to be a guilty criminal. And so the music strikes a note of compassion and pity, in a *larghetto* in A minor, with muted violins, violas, and oboes in concert.

Finally, just one movement follows the fifth act, an *adagio*, in E major, with violins, violas, horns, reinforced by oboes and flutes, and with bassoons playing with the contrabass. It expresses a grief appropriate to the persons of the tragedy, raised to the sublime, with some due regard, it seems to me, to the last four lines, in which Truth gravely and powerfully raises a voice of warning against the powerful on earth.

To notice the aims of the composer is to acknowledge that he has achieved them. His work should not be a puzzle whose solution is as difficult as it is capricious. Whatever a healthy ear hears most quickly in a work of music is what it intended to say, and nothing else. Its praise increases with its comprehensibility – the more easy and general the latter, the more deserved is the former. – It is no great credit to me to have heard correctly; rather, the credit to Herr Agricola is all the greater because nobody heard anything different than I did in his composition.

Essay 28

4 August 1767

On the thirty-third evening (Friday, the 12th of June), *Nanine* was repeated, and the evening ended with *The Farmer Inherits a Fortune*, from the French play by Marivaux.[1]

This short play suits our taste here and thus always gives great pleasure. Jürge returns from the city, where he has buried a rich brother from whom he inherited a hundred thousand marks.[2] Luck changes both status and manners: now he wants to live the way genteel people live; he elevates his Lise to a Madame, quickly finds respectable matches for his Hans and his Grete, everything is good; but then the bad news arrives. The agent who held the hundred thousand marks is bankrupt, Jürge is once again nothing but Jürge, Hans gets dumped, Grete is jilted, and the end would be sad if fortune could take more than it has given. But they were healthy and satisfied before, and healthy and satisfied they remain.

Anyone could have invented this story, but few would have known how to make it as entertaining as Marivaux does. The most droll humor, the most amusing wit, the most mischievous satire have us beside ourselves with laughter, and the naïve rural dialect gives the whole thing its own special piquancy. The translation is by Krüger, who has translated the French *patois* masterfully into the local low dialect.[3] It is only a shame that the printing of several passages was garbled and full of errors. Many needed to be corrected and expanded in the performance. For example, the following, which is in the very first scene:

JÜRGE: Hey, hey, hey! Gimme five schillins change, alls I got is gulden 'n' dollahs.

LISE: Hey, hey, hey! Five schillins, you crazy? Whatcha wannit fer?

JÜRGE: Hey, hey, hey! Jus' gimme five schillins cuz I said so.

LISE: What fer, John Fool?

JÜRGE: Fer this guy that carried m' pack all the way up the whole road to our village, 'n' I was jest walkin' all light 'n' easy.

LISE: You walk'd here?

JÜRGE: I did. It was real comf't'ble.

LISE: Here's a mark.

JÜRGE: That's good. How much is that now? That much. She gimme a mark: there, there it is. Take it, that's right.

LISE: Yer gonna waste five schillins on some guy who carried your pack?

JÜRGE: Yeah! I gotta give 'im a tip.

VALENTIN: Are those five schillings for me, Mr. Jürge?

JÜRGE: Sure are, pal!

VALENTIN: Five schillings? A rich heir! Five schillings, a man of your standing? And where is the grandeur of the soul?

JÜRGE: Oh! I don't care 'bout all that, ask anyone. Go on, woman, throw 'im another schillin'; that's how we reckon 'round here.

How is that? Jürge came on foot because it is more comfortable? He asks for five schillings, and his wife, who did not want to give him five schillings, gives him a mark? The wife is supposed to toss another schilling to the boy? Why doesn't he do it himself? There was change left over from the mark, after all. Without the French text it is hard to get one's bearings. Jürge did not come on foot, but in a coach; that is what his "It was real comf't'ble" refers to. But the coach probably only went past his village, and he had his pack carried from where he got off to his house. This is what he gives the boy five schillings for. His wife does not give him a mark; rather, that is what he had to pay for the coach, and he just tells her how swiftly he dealt with the coachman concerning the payment.[*,4]

On the thirty-fourth evening (Monday, the 29th of June), Regnard's play *The Absent-Minded Lover* was produced.[5]

I doubt our grandfathers understood the German title of this play. Even Schlegel translated *Distrait* as *Dreamer*.[6] To be absent-minded, a scatterbrain, is simply to make an analogy to the French term. We do not want to investigate who had the right to coin these words; rather, we want to use them after they have already been coined. As of now we all understand them, and that is enough.[7]

Regnard brought his *Absent-Minded Lover* to the stage in 1697, and it did not have the least success. But thirty-four years later, when the comedians brought it out again, it fared much better.[8] Which audience was right? Perhaps neither was wrong. That earlier, rigid audience rejected the play for not being a good conventional comedy, which is doubtless what the writer claimed it to be.[9] This more sympathetic one took it for nothing more than what it is: a farce that is supposed to make us laugh. We laughed and were thankful. The first audience thought:

— *non satis est risu diducere rictum*
Auditoris —[10]

---

* BLAISE: Eh! Eh! Eh! Baille-moi cinq sols de monnoye, je n'ons que de grosses pièces.

CLAUDINE *le contrefaisant*: Eh! Eh! Eh! Di donc, Nicaise, avec tes cinq sols de monnoye, qu'est-ce que t'en veux faire?

BLAISE: Eh! Eh! Eh! Baille moi cinq sols de monnoye, te dis-je.

CLAUDINE: Pourquoi donc, Nicodême?

BLAISE: Pour ce garçon qui apporte mon paquet depis la voiture jusqu'à cheux nous, pendant que je marchois tout bellement et à mon aise.

CLAUDINE: T'es venu dans la voiture?

BLAISE: Oui, parce que cela est plus commode.

CLAUDINE: T'a baillé un écu?

BLAISE: Oh bian noblement. Combien faut-il? Ai-je fait. Un écu, ce m'a-t-on fait. Tenez, le vela, prennez. Tout comme ça.

CLAUDINE: Et tu dépenses cinq sols en porteurs de paquets?

BLAISE: Oui, par manière de recreation.

ARLEQUIN: Est-ce pour moi les cinq sols, Monsieur Blaise?

BLAISE: Oui, mon ami. &c.

And this one:

> – *& est quaedam tamen hic quoque virtus.*[11]

This comedy cannot have been a great deal of trouble for Regnard to write, other than the versification, which happens to be careless and full of errors. He found the character of his protagonist fully conceptualized in La Bruyère.[12] He did not have to do anything other than take the most prominent traits and bring them out, partly through the action and partly through narration. What he added of his own matters little.

There is no objection to be made to this criticism, but there is an objection to be made against another criticism that attacks the writer from the standpoint of morality.[13] An absentminded person should not be the subject of a comedy. Why not? The claim is that absentmindedness is an illness, a misfortune, and not a vice. An absentminded person does not deserve to be laughed at any more than someone who suffers headaches. Comedy must only deal with faults that can be corrected. But someone who is absentminded by nature can be as scarce corrected through mockeries as someone who limps.

But is it in fact true that distraction is a deficiency of the soul that our best efforts cannot remedy? Is it really more a natural deficiency than a bad habit? I cannot believe that. Are we not masters of our own attention? Do we not have it in our power to compel or withdraw it at will? And what is absentmindedness if not an improper use of our attention? The absentminded person thinks; he just does not think about what he ought to think about according to his present sensual impressions. His mind is not asleep, not stupefied, not put out of action; it is just absent, busy elsewhere. But as good as it can be there, it can be here: the mind's natural calling is to be present to the sensual changes of the body. Effort is required to wean it from this calling, so should it really be impossible to reacquaint it with that calling?

Let us assume absentmindedness is incurable: where is it written that we should only laugh at moral faults or correctable bad habits in comedies? Every absurdity, every contrast between imperfections and reality is laughable. But laughter and derision are very far apart.[14] We can laugh about a person, and on occasion laugh at him, without deriding him in the least. As uncontested and well-known as this difference may be, nevertheless all of the chicanery Rousseau has recently resorted to in his attack on the value of comedy only arose because he did not take this difference into proper consideration.[15] For example, he says that Molière makes us laugh at the misanthrope even though the misanthrope is the honest man in the play; Molière thus proves himself an enemy of virtue by making the virtuous man the object of scorn. But no: the misanthrope does not become contemptible; he remains who he is, and the laughter, which derives from the situations the playwright puts him in, does not take away the least bit of our admiration for him. Likewise with the absentminded one: we laugh about him, but do we despise him because of it? We value his other good qualities as we should value them; indeed, without them we would not be able to laugh at his absentmindedness. Give this absentmindedness to an evil, worthless man and see if it will still be laughable. It will be repugnant, loathsome, ugly – not laughable.

Essay 29

7 August 1767

Comedy aims to improve us through laughter, but not through derision, exactly; not through those flaws at which it makes us laugh, and even less through those people in whom these flaws are found.[1] Its true and universal value lies in laughter itself: in the exercising of our ability to identify the laughable, to quickly and easily find it under the cloak of passion and of fashion, in all combinations with yet worse or with good qualities, even in the wrinkles of ceremonial gravitas.[2] Granted, Molière's *Miser* never improved a miser, and Regnard's *Gamester* never improved a gambler.[3] Conceded, laughter could never improve these fools: so much the worse for them, but not for comedy. It suffices for comedy that if it cannot heal hopeless illnesses, it can shore up health in the healthy. The *Miser* is instructive to the generous man; the *Gamester* is illuminating even to one who never gambles; others with whom they must coexist have the follies that they do not have. It is beneficial to know those with whom one might come into contact; beneficial to protect oneself against all impressions of the example. Preventative medicine is also valuable medicine; and morality in its entirety has nothing more powerful or potent than that which produces laughter.

The Puzzle, or, What Best Pleases the Ladies, a comedy in one act by Herr Löwen, brought this evening to an end.[4]

If Marmontel and Voltaire had not written stories and fairy tales, the French theater would have missed out on a great deal of novelty. The comic opera has profited the most from these sources. Voltaire's *What Pleases the Ladies* provided the material for a comedy in four acts with interspersed arias, produced in December 1765 by the Italian comedians in Paris under the title *The Fairy Urgele*.[5] Herr Löwen would appear to have had the actual story by Voltaire, rather than this play, at hand. If one judges a statue based on the block of marble from which it was made; if the raw form of this block can explain why this or that limb is too short, or why this or that position is too forced: then we have to dismiss the criticism that would be leveled against Herr Löwen on account of the structure of his play. Take a fairy tale about a witch and turn it into something more realistic, if you can! Herr Löwen himself offers his *Puzzle* as nothing more than a little pleasantry that can be enjoyed in the theater if it is well performed. Transformation and dance and song all contribute to this end; and it would be blatant obstinacy to resist finding any pleasure in it. Pedrillo's attitude is, of course, not original, but well done.[6] It just seems to me that a weapon carrier or a groom who recognizes the tastelessness and insanity of the irrational knightly class does not fit so well into a story that bases itself on the reality of magic and that accepts courtly adventures as commendable actions of a responsible and brave man. No matter – as already noted, this is a pleasantry, and one should not dissect pleasantness.

On the thirty-fifth evening (Wednesday, the first of July), Pierre Corneille's *Rodogune* was performed in the presence of His Royal Highness of Denmark.[7]

Corneille professed that he thought this tragedy was his best, that he regarded it as far superior to his *Cinna* and *Cid*, that his other plays had few strengths that were not found united in this one: a good plot, completely new fictions, strong verses, a solid conceptual basis, powerful passions, and dramatic interest that develops from act to act.[8]

It is only fitting that we dwell for a bit on the great man's masterpiece.

The history it is based on is told by Appianus Alexandrinus toward the end of his book about the Syrian war:[9] "Démétrius, surnamed Nicanor, undertook a campaign against the Parthians, and lived for a time as prisoner of war at the court of their King Phraates, whose sister, Rodogune, he married. In the meantime, Diodotus, who had served the previous kings, seized the Syrian throne and placed upon it a child, the son of Alexander Rothus, under whose name, as regent, he initially ruled. Soon, however, he pushed the young king aside, took the crown for himself, and gave himself the name Tryphon. When Antiochus, the brother of the imprisoned king Démétrius, heard of his fate and of the subsequent unrest in the kingdom, he returned to Syria from Rhodes, where he was staying, vanquished Tryphon with much difficulty, and had him executed. From there he turned his weapons against Phraates and demanded the liberation of his brother. Phraates, fearing the worst, did let Démétrius go; but nonetheless there was still an encounter between himself and Antiochus, in which the latter lost and killed himself in despair. After Démétrius returned to his kingdom, he was killed by his wife, Cleopatra, out of hatred for Rodogune, even though in anger over that marriage Cleopatra herself had married that same Antiochus, Démétrius's brother. She had two sons with Démétrius; the oldest one, named Séleucus, who had ascended the throne after the death of his father, she shot to death with an arrow with her own hands, either because she worried that he would revenge the death of his father on her, or because her generally cruel disposition prompted her to it. The youngest son, named Antiochus, followed his brother in rule, and forced his abominable mother to drink the cup of poison that she had intended for him."[10]

There is material for more than one tragedy in this story. It would not have taken much more invention on the part of Corneille to make a *Tryphon*, an *Antiochus*, a *Demetrius*, or a *Seleucus* out of it than it took for him to create a *Rodogune*. What excited him primarily about all this was the aggrieved wife who believed she could not avenge the usurped rights of her rank and bed gruesomely enough. Therefore this is what he extracted from it, and it is indisputable that as a result the play should not be called *Rodogune* but rather *Cleopatra*.[11] He admitted this himself, and it was only because he worried that the spectator would confuse this queen from Syria with that famous Egyptian queen of the same name that he preferred to take the title from the one person rather than from the other. "I thought to allow myself this freedom," he says, "all the more because I had noted that the ancients themselves did not consider it necessary to name a play for its hero and would not even hesitate to name it after the chorus, which played even less of a role and appeared more intermittently than Rodogune; for example, Sophocles named one of his tragedies *The Women of Trachis*, which today would hardly be titled anything other than *The Dying Hercules*."[12] This observation is correct in and of itself; the ancients considered the title wholly unimportant; they did not believe in the least that it should reveal the content; it sufficed if it served to distinguish one play from another, and for this purpose the smallest feature is adequate. That said, I hardly believe that Sophocles would have wanted to give the title *Deianira* to the play he called *The Women of Trachis*. He did not hesitate to give it an insignificant title, but he would have been far more cautious about giving it a seductive title that points us in the wrong direction. Besides, Corneille's concerns went too far: anyone who knows the Egyptian Cleopatra also knows that Egypt is not Syria, and that many kings and queens had the same names; anyone who does not know this is not going to confuse one for the other.[13] At the very least Corneille should not have avoided the name Cleopatra so carefully in the play itself; the clarity suffered in the first act, and the German translator did well to dismiss this trivial hesitation.[14] No writer, even less a poet, should assume his reader or his auditor to be so completely ignorant; he ought more likely to think from time to time – if they do not know, they should ask!

Essay 30

11 August 1767

In the history, Cleopatra kills her husband, shoots one of her sons, and tries to poison the other.[1] Without doubt one crime followed upon the other, and essentially they all had one and the same origin. At least we can assume with some probability that this singular jealousy could turn a raging wife into an equally raging mother. To see herself set aside in favor of a second wife and made to share the love of her husband and the grandeur of her rank quickly brought resolve to her sensitive and proud heart not to possess at all what it could not possess alone. Démétrius must not live because he does not wish to live for Cleopatra alone. The guilty husband falls; but with him falls a father, who leaves behind vengeful sons. In the heat of her passion, the mother had not thought of them, or she had only thought of them as her sons, of whose devotion she was assured, or at least whose childish zeal would, if it had to choose between parents, unfailingly declare itself in favor of the party that was injured first. But she found this was not so; the son became king, and the king did not see the mother in Cleopatra, only the regicide. She had everything to fear from him, and, from that moment on, he had everything to fear from her. Jealousy still boiled in her heart; the faithless husband still remained in his son; she began to hate everything that reminded her she once loved him; self-preservation strengthened this hatred; the mother was better prepared than the son, the offender better prepared than the offended; she committed the second murder in order to escape punishment for the first; she perpetrated it against her son and consoled herself with the idea that she had only perpetrated it on someone who was fixed upon her own ruin, that she did not actually murder but only preempted her own murder. The fate of the older son would also have been the fate of the younger; but the latter was swifter or luckier. He forces the mother to drink the poison that she had prepared for him; one inhumane crime revenges the other, and it just comes down to circumstances to determine whether we ought to feel more disgust or compassion for one side or the other.

   This triple murder would make up only one action that has its beginning, middle, and end in the same passion of the same person. What is still missing as material for a tragedy? For the genius, nothing is missing; for the bungler, everything. There is no love, no complication, no recognition, no unexpected miraculous event; everything goes its natural way. This natural way inspires the genius, and it frightens the bungler. Genius concerns itself only with incidents that are grounded in each other, with chains of cause and effect. To trace one back to another, to weigh one against another, to consistently exclude chance, to let everything that happens happen in such a way that it could not happen otherwise: this is his task when he works in the field of history, in order to transform the useless hoards of memory into nourishment for the spirit. On the other hand, if a wit attempts the kind of work that should be reserved to genius alone, because he is not concerned with events that are grounded in each other but rather only with what is similar or dissimilar, he dwells on events that have nothing more in common with each other than that they happen at the same time. The only thing the wit can do is join these together, weaving and tangling their threads so that from one moment to the next we lose one among the others and are toppled from one perplexity into another. From this constant intersecting of such threads of wholly different colors a fabric emerges that is to art what the weavers call *changeant*: a material that we cannot call blue or red, green or yellow; it is both, it seems one thing from one side, and something else from the other.[2] A toy for fashion, trick-attire for children.

Now to judge whether the great Corneille adapted his material more like a genius or like a wit. The only thing needed for this judgment is to apply a principle that no one would doubt: the genius loves simplicity, the wit, complexity.

In the history, Cleopatra kills her husband out of jealousy. "Out of jealousy?" thought Corneille: that would be a very common woman indeed. No, my Cleopatra must be a heroine, who might have gladly lost her husband but never the throne. The fact that her husband loves Rodogune would not hurt as much as Rodogune becoming queen like her; that is much grander. –

Precisely: far grander – and much less natural. For one thing, pride is essentially a less natural, more artificial vice than jealousy. Secondly, the pride of a woman is even less natural than the pride of a man. The female gender is equipped by nature for love, not for violence – it should awaken tenderness, not fear; it should be powerful only through its attraction; it should rule only through caresses and should not wish to rule any more than it can enjoy. A woman who likes to dominate simply for the sake of dominance, whose every desire is subordinate to ambition, who knows no other happiness than to order, to tyrannize, and to place her foot upon the neck of an entire populace: such a woman may once, even more than once, have really existed, but she is nevertheless an exception, and whoever depicts an exception definitely depicts something less natural. Corneille's Cleopatra, who is just such a woman, who indulges all crimes to satisfy her ambition, her wounded pride, who flings about nothing but Machiavellian maxims, is a monster of her sex, and in comparison Medea is virtuous and loveable.[3] For all of the horrors that Medea commits are committed out of jealousy. I will forgive a tender, jealous woman everything; she is just as she should be, only more intense. But one's whole heart rises up against a woman who perpetrates crimes out of cold pride, out of calculated ambition; and all the art of a playwright cannot make her interesting to us. We gape at her as we gape at a monster; and when we have satisfied our curiosity, we then thank heaven that nature only errs thus once in a thousand years, and we are annoyed by the poet who wants to pass off such miscreants as human beings as if knowing about them might benefit us. Look through all of history: among fifty women who toppled their husbands from a throne and murdered them, there is hardly one concerning whom we could not prove that only wounded love drove her to this act. Hardly a one went so far as to seize the scepter that a loving husband held merely out of naked desire to rule, out of pure pride. Many of these injured spouses, after having seized power, went on to govern the realm with masculine pride; this is true. They had learned all too well from their cold, ill-tempered husbands how mortifying subservience was; so much so that their subsequent independence, achieved only with utmost risk, would have been that much more precious to them. But surely no one ever thought or experienced what Corneille has his Cleopatra say about herself: the most preposterous bravado of vice. The greatest villain tries to justify himself, tries to persuade himself that the evil he commits is not such a great evil, or that unavoidable necessity forces him to commit it. It flies in the face of nature that he would pride himself on vice as vice; and we should chastise the playwright who, out of a desire to say something dazzling and strong, leads us to misread the human heart, as if its basic tendencies could tend toward evil for the sake of evil.

No playwright gives us such misshapen characters, such shocking tirades more frequently than Corneille, and it could well be that this is the basis in part for his epithet, "the Great." It is true, everything he does breathes heroism; but that includes vice, which should not be capable of heroism and which is really not capable of it. One should have named him "the Behemoth," "the Gigantic," but not "the Great." Nothing is great that is not true.

Essay 31

14 August 1767

Cleopatra revenges herself only on her husband in Appianus's history; she could not or would not revenge herself on Rodogune.[1] When the play opens, the revenge upon her husband is already in the distant past; Démétrius's murder is simply narrated, and all of the action of the play centers on Rodogune. Corneille does not abandon his Cleopatra with the job half done; she must not believe that she has had her revenge at all until she also revenges herself on Rodogune. It is absolutely natural for a jealous woman to be even more unforgiving toward her rival than she is toward her faithless husband. But as already mentioned, Corneille's Cleopatra does not possess much, if any, jealousy; she is simply ambitious, and the revenge of an ambitious person should never resemble the revenge of a jealous one. The two passions are too different for their effects to be the same. Ambition is never without a kind of nobleness, and revenge conflicts too much with decency for the revenge of the ambitious person to lack all restraint or purpose. As long as he pursues his goal, his revenge knows no limits; but as soon as he has reached it, as soon as he has gratified his passion, his revenge starts to become colder and more deliberate. He proportions his revenge not so much according to the disadvantages already suffered but rather according to those yet to be feared. He forgets that a person has harmed him if that person cannot cause him further harm. He despises anyone he does not need to fear, and anyone he despises is unworthy of his revenge. Jealousy, on the other hand, is a kind of envy; and envy is a petty, sneaky vice that knows no other gratification than the complete destruction of its object. Jealousy rages forth in a fiery manner; nothing can placate it. Because the offense that awakened it never stops being the same offense and because it continues to grow the longer it lasts, jealousy's thirst for revenge can never be quenched and will sooner or later be carried out with equal fury. This is precisely what Cleopatra's revenge in the Corneille play resembles, and the discordance between her revenge and her character can only be extremely offensive. Her proud attitudes and unbridled desire for honor and independence lead us to view her as a great and elevated soul who deserves our admiration. But then her spiteful resentment, her malicious vindictiveness against a person from whom she has nothing more to fear, whom she has in her power and would have to forgive had she the least spark of nobility, and the recklessness with which she not only commits crimes herself but also brazenly and matter-of-factly asks others to commit the most senseless crimes – all these make her so small that we cannot despise her enough. In the end, this disdain will invariably erode any admiration, and then nothing else remains of Cleopatra but an ugly disgusting woman who is always spluttering and raging and who deserves the first place in the madhouse.

But it is not enough for Cleopatra to revenge herself on Rodogune; the playwright insists she do so in a wholly exceptional way. How does he manage this? If Cleopatra gets rid of Rodogune on her own, the whole matter is far too natural; for what is more natural than to kill one's enemy? What if her murder were, at the same time, the execution of a mistress? And what if she were executed by her lover? Why not? Let us imagine that Rodogune never actually married Démétrius; let us imagine that after his death, both sons fell in love with their father's betrothed; let us imagine that the sons are twins, that the throne belongs to the elder, but that the mother has always kept from them which son is older; let us imagine that the mother has finally decided to reveal the secret or, rather, not to reveal it but instead to declare the one who is willing to agree to a certain condition the oldest, and thus put him on the throne; let us imagine that this condition is Rodogune's death. Now we would have what we wanted: both princes undyingly in love with Rodogune; but he who kills his beloved shall rule.

Nice, but could we not complicate the plot further? Could we not make things even more difficult for the good princes? We will try. Let us imagine further that Rodogune learns of Cleopatra's plot; let us go on to imagine that she, in fact, loves one of the princes more than the other, but has not told him, has not told anyone; nor will she, for she has firmly decided that she will choose for her husband neither the prince she loves nor the one to whom the throne might revert, that she will only choose the one who proves himself the most worthy. Rodogune must be avenged, she must take revenge on the princes' mother; Rodogune must declare to them: whichever of you wants me will have to murder his mother!

Bravo! Now that is what I call a real intrigue! These princes are in luck! They will have a lot to do if they want to disentangle themselves! The mother tells them: whichever of you wants to rule will have to kill his beloved! And the beloved says:

whoever wants me has to kill his mother! It goes without saying that these must be very virtuous princes, who love each other from the bottom of their souls, who have great respect for their devil of a mama, and just as much tenderness for their flirting fury of a mistress. For if they are not both very virtuous, then the complication is not nearly as bad as it seems; or it is so bad that is impossible to unravel it. One of them goes and strikes the princess dead in order to have the throne: the story is over. Or the other goes and strikes the mother dead, in order to have the princess: again, the story is done. Or both of them go and strike the beloved dead, and both want the throne: there is no ending here. Or they both strike the mother dead, and both want to have the girl: again, there is no ending. But if they are both genteel and virtuous, then neither will want to strike anyone dead, and so they both stand there prettily, mouths agape, not knowing what they should do, and that is precisely the beauty of it. Admittedly, the play will get a very strange reputation from the fact that its women behave more dreadfully than furious men and its men more effeminately than the feeblest of women: but what harm in that? Rather, this is yet another advantage for the play, insofar as the opposite is so common, so hackneyed! –

But seriously: I do not know if it takes a great deal of effort to make up such fabrications; I have never tried it, and I hope I never have to. But I do know this: such fabrications are very painful to digest.

To be sure, this is not because these are pure fabrications – because there is no trace of them to be found in history. Corneille could have spared himself these concerns. "Perhaps," he says, "one might doubt if the freedom of poetry extends so far that it may concoct a whole story using famous names, as I have done here, where, after the narration in the first act, which lays the foundation for what follows up until the outcomes in the fifth act, nothing occurs that has even the least historical basis. However," he continues, "it seems to me that as long as we retain the outcomes of history, then all of the circumstances leading up to them, all of the preambles to these results are in our power. At least I cannot recall any rule against this, and the practice of the ancients is wholly on my side. For just compare Sophocles' *Electra* to Euripides' *Electra* and see if they have anything more in common than just the result, the final outcomes of their heroine's adventures, to which each arrives via a particular path and idiosyncratic means, so that at least one of them had to be wholly the invention of her author. Or just look at *Iphigenia in Tauris*, which Aristotle points to as a model of a perfect tragedy, and which nonetheless looks very much as if it is nothing more than a fabrication, insofar as it bases itself merely on the supposition that Diana spirited Iphigenia away from the altar on which she was to be sacrificed in a cloud and slipped a deer in her place.[2] Above all, however, Euripides' *Helen* deserves note, where the principle plot, the episodes, the complication, and the resolution are all completely invented, and nothing is taken from history but the names."[3]

To be sure, Corneille had the right to proceed as he saw fit with the facts of history. For example, he could make Rodogune as young as he wanted, and Voltaire is once again very wrong to calculate from the historical record that Rodogune could not have been so young, because she married Démétrius when the princes (who must now be at least twenty) were still children.[4] What is that to the poet? His Rodogune did not even marry Démétrius; she was very young when she wanted to marry the father, and not much older when the sons fell in love with her. Voltaire's need for historical control is insufferable. If instead he would just verify the dates in his own general history of the world![5]

Essay 32

18 August 1767[1]

Corneille could have gone further back in history for examples from the ancients.[2] Many imagine that tragedy was invented in Greece to revive the memory of great and extraordinary events; that therefore its primary purpose was to walk precisely in the footsteps of history, veering neither to the left nor to the right. But they are wrong. For even Thespis* couldn't have cared less about historical accuracy.[3] It is true, he earned a sharp rebuke from Solon for that.[4] But without saying that Solon was more skilled in legislation than poetry, one can avoid the consequences that could be drawn from his disapproval in a different way. In Thespis's hands the art already took liberties that it could not yet fully justify, based on how they were used. Thespis concocted, invented, had the most famous people say and do what he wanted, but it seems he did not understand how to make his fabrications either probable or instructive. Solon noticed only what was untrue in them, without gaining the least impression of what was useful. He inveighed against a poison that, lacking its antidote, easily could have ill effects.

I very much fear that Solon might well have called the great Corneille's fabrications nothing but wretched lies, too. For what is the purpose of all these inventions? Do they make the history that gets saddled with them the least bit more probable?[5] They are not even probable in and of themselves. Corneille boasted that they were very wonderful efforts of his power of invention, and yet he really should have known that it is not the mere act of invention, but rather invention with a purpose, that gives proof of a creative mind.

In history, the poet finds a woman who kills her husband and sons. Such a deed can awaken terror and compassion, and he decides to handle it as tragedy.[6] But history tells him nothing more than mere fact, which is as horrid as it is extraordinary. It provides at most three scenes, which, stripped of any extenuating circumstances, are three improbable scenes. – What is the poet to do?

Depending on how much he deserves this name either the improbability or the insufficient length will seem the greater shortcoming for his play.

If he falls into the first category, then he will be anxious above all to invent a series of causes and effects that make it absolutely necessary for those improbable crimes to have occurred. Dissatisfied with basing their possibility merely on historical authenticity, he will try to construct his characters in such a way as to make the events that set these characters into action arise necessarily from each other; he will try to measure the passions of each character precisely and to develop these passions through

---

* Diogenes Laertius, Bk. I § 59.

gradual steps; he will do all this so that overall we perceive nothing but the most natural, orderly course of events. With every step his characters take, we would have to acknowledge that in the same heat of passion, the same state of affairs, we ourselves would have done the same. Nothing in all this would disconcert us except the imperceptible approach of an end from which our imaginations recoil. Once there, we find ourselves full of the most sincere compassion toward those who are carried away by such a fatal current, and full of terror knowing that a similar current could carry us away to commit deeds that in cold blood we imagine to be completely farfetched. – And if the writer takes this path, if his genius tells him that he will not falter shamefully upon it, then all at once that meager brevity of his plot has also disappeared, and it no longer worries him how he will fill five acts with so few incidents. Now he only worries that five acts will not encompass all of the material that, as he works on it, keeps increasing more and more on its own, now that he has finally figured out its hidden organization and understood how to develop it.

On the other hand, the poet who deserves this name less, who is nothing more than a wit and a good verse writer: he, I say, will object so little to the improbability of his material that, on the contrary, he thinks this is precisely what is astonishing about it, and he would not minimize it at all lest he rob himself of his most certain means for arousing terror and compassion. For he understands so little what this terror and compassion really consist of that he thinks he cannot pile up enough unusual, unexpected, unbelievable, and monstrous things in order to call forth terror and believes he must constantly resort to the most extraordinary and grisly accidents and crimes to awaken compassion. He has thus scarcely flushed from history a Cleopatra, murderess of her husband and sons, than he sees that there is nothing more to do to make a tragedy out of it than to fill in the gaps between the two crimes and to fill them in with things that are at least as repulsive as the crimes themselves. He then kneads all of this – his inventions and the historical material – together into a quite long, quite incomprehensible romantic fiction, and when he has kneaded this together as well as straw and flour might be kneaded together, then he stretches his dough over the wire frame of acts and scenes, has his characters explain and explain, rant and rhyme, and in four, six weeks, depending on whether the rhyming is easy or difficult for him, the miracle is done: it is called a tragedy. It is printed and performed, read and seen, admired or catcalled, retained or forgotten – as kind Fortune will have it. For "& habent sua fata libelli."[7]

Dare I apply this to the great Corneille? Or do I really need to? – According to the mysterious fate that governs literary works as well as people, his *Rodogune* has been admired throughout France, and sometimes throughout Europe, for more than one hundred years as the greatest masterpiece of the greatest tragic playwright. Can one hundred years of admiration be without basis? Where have people kept their eyes, their sensibilities for so long? From 1644 to 1767, was it left exclusively to the Hamburg dramaturg to see spots in the sun, to demote a star to a meteor?

Oh no! In just the previous century an honest Huron sat in the Bastille in Paris.[8] Time grew heavy on his hands, even though he was in Paris, and he studied the French poets out of boredom. This Huron did not like *Rodogune* at all.[9] Later, at the beginning of this century, a pedant somewhere in Italy had his fill of the Greek tragedies and of the works of his countrymen from the sixteenth century, and he too found much to criticize in *Rodogune*.[10] Finally a few years ago even a Frenchman who was otherwise a tremendous admirer of the Corneille name (for, being rich and of a very good heart, he had befriended a poor abandoned granddaughter of this great poet, had her raised under his care, taught her to write pretty verses, collected charity for her, wrote a big, lucrative commentary on her grandfather's works to fund her dowry, etc.) nevertheless declared *Rodogune* to be a very nonsensical poem and wondered himself to death how such a great man as the great Corneille could have written such absurd junk.[11] – The dramaturg has undoubtedly been influenced by one of these, and probably by the last, for after all, it is generally a Frenchman who opens the eyes of foreigners to the mistakes of a Frenchman. Most certainly he echoes this man, or if it is not this one, then at least the Italian, if not the Huron. In any case, he must be repeating the words of one of them. For who could imagine that a German, on his own, would think to – have the audacity to – doubt the excellence of a Frenchman?

I will discuss these predecessors of mine more the next time *Rodogune* is performed.[12] My readers wish to move on, and so do I. For now, just one more word about the translation used for the performance of this play. It was not the old Wolfenbüttel edition by Bressand but rather a brand-new one, in rhymed Alexandrine verse, that was done here and has not yet been published.[13] It need not blush in comparison to the best of this type; it is full of powerful, felicitous passages. However, I know that the translator has too much discretion and taste to undertake such a thankless task again. To translate Corneille well, one must be able to make better verses than he himself did.

Essay 33

21 August 1767[1]

On the thirty-sixth evening (Friday, the 3rd of July), Favart's comedy *Soliman the Second* was performed, also in the presence of His Royal Highness of Denmark.[2]

I do not wish to examine the degree to which history confirms whether Soliman II fell in love with a European slave who was so able to captivate him, so able to bend him to her will, that – against all customs of his kingdom – he felt compelled to unite himself with her officially and declare her empress.[3] It suffices that Marmontel based one of his moral stories on this, in which, however, he made that slave, who was supposedly an Italian, into a Frenchwoman – doubtless because he found it improbable that anyone but a French beauty could achieve such a rare victory over a Sultan.[4]

I really do not know what to say about Marmontel's story. I cannot say that it fails to apply great wit, or lacks all the subtle knowledge of the great world and its vanities and absurdities, or was written without the elegance and grace that characterize this author. From this perspective it is excellent, lovely. But it is supposed to be a moral tale, and I just cannot find where its morality resides. Admittedly, it is not as salacious and offensive as a tale from La Fontaine or Grécourt, but is it moral simply because it is not completely immoral?[5]

A Sultan who yawns in the lap of a lust made disgusting and loathsome to him by daily, unhindered pleasure; who wishes to have his flaccid nerves revived and stimulated by something completely new and special; who is courted in vain by the most subtle sensuality and the most refined tenderness: this sick hedonist is the suffering hero of the story. I call him the suffering: the gourmand has upset his stomach with too many sweets; nothing tastes good to him anymore, until it finally occurs to him to try things that would disgust any healthy stomach, like rotten eggs, rat tails, and caterpillar pie – these taste good to him. The most rare and modest beauty, possessed of the most soulful big blue eyes and the most innocent, sensitive soul, has the Sultan in her power – until she is conquered. Another, more majestic in form, more dazzling in complexion, with florid tirades on her lips and the most lovely play of bewitching tones in her voice, a true muse, only more seductive – is enjoyed and then forgotten. Finally, a female being appears, flighty, careless, wild, witty almost to the point of insolence and merry almost to the point of madness, with a vivid face but not much beauty, more dainty than shapely; this thing, when she first sees the Sultan, blurts out the clumsiest flattery, like a bull at the gate: "Graces au ciel, voici une figure humaine!" (flattery that might be heard, sometimes in a more subtle manner, and sometimes more brazenly, not only by this Sultan but also by many a German prince, nine out of ten of whom, like the Sultan, receive it well without perceiving the insult it actually implies).[6] And the rest of the compliments that follow are just like this initial one – "Vous êtes beaucoup mieux, qu'il n'appartient à un Turc: vous avez même quelque chose d'un François – En vérité ces Turcs sont plaisans – Je me charge seule d'apprendre à vivre à ce Turc – Je ne désespère pas d'en faire quelque jour un François."[7] Yet this being succeeds! She laughs and chides, threatens and mocks, flirts and gripes, until the Sultan not only gives the seraglio a new form to please her but also has to change the law of the kingdom and run the risk of raising the ire of both the clergy and the mob against him if he wants to be just as happy with her as she claims other men in her homeland have been. That was surely worth the trouble!

Marmontel begins his story with the observation that major transformations of a country have often been catalyzed by very insignificant trifles, and he has the Sultan conclude by secretly asking himself: how is it possible that a little upturned nose could overthrow the laws of a kingdom?[8] We are thus almost meant to believe that he only wanted to illustrate through example this observation, that is, this apparent discrepancy between cause and effect. But this lesson would undoubtedly have been too general, and he discloses in his prologue that he had a completely different and much more particular lesson in mind. "I intended," he says, "to show the folly of those who want to use prestige and authority to make a woman complaisant. Thus I used a Sultan and his slave as an example, as the two extremes of domination and dependency."[9] However, Marmontel must surely have lost sight of his purpose while he wrote the play, for almost nothing points toward it. We do not see the least attempt at forcefulness on the part of the Sultan; at the first insolent word the gallant Frenchwoman speaks, he becomes the most diffident, yielding, compliant, obedient, and subservient man, "la meilleure pâte de mari," one scarce to be found in France.[10] Thus, to speak plainly: either there is no moral in this story of Marmontel's, or it is the one I pointed to above when writing of the Sultan's character: after the beetle has swarmed through all the flowers, it ends up lying on the dung heap.

But moral or no moral: for the dramatic writer, it does not matter whether a universal truth can be deduced from his fable or not, so on that account Marmontel's story was neither more nor less suited to be adapted to the stage. Favart did so, and very successfully. I advise all among us who want to enrich our theater from similar stories to compare Favart's achievement with Marmontel's original. If they possess a knack for abstraction, then the most minor changes it suffered (and in part had to suffer) will be instructive, and their sensibility will guide them to some strategy that they could not have discovered through conjecture and which no critic has yet generalized to a rule, even though it deserved to be. For such a strategy would bring more truth and life to their plays than all of the mechanical rules with which jejune critics grapple – the observation of which, in defiance of genius, they would make the sole source of a drama's perfection.

I want to dwell on just one of these changes. But first I must quote the criticism that the French themselves have made regarding this play.* They begin by expressing their doubts about the basis of Marmontel's story. "Soliman the Second," they say, "was one of the great princes of his century; the Turks have no Emperor whose memory is more dear to them than this Soliman. His victories, his talents and his virtues made him an object of veneration even among the enemies over whom he had been victorious: yet what a petty, pitiful role Marmontel gives him to play! According to history, Roxelane was a devious, ambitious woman who was capable of committing the blackest and most audacious deeds to gratify her pride.[11] She used intrigue and false tenderness to bring the Sultan to the point where he raged against his own blood and compromised his legacy with the execution of an innocent son.[12] In Marmontel's story, this Roxelane is a foolish little coquette, the kind found always fluttering about Paris, empty-headed, yet with a heart more good than evil. Are transformations such as these," they ask, "even allowed? Whatever license we may allow a poet or storyteller, should he be permitted to extend that license to the most well-known personages? If he is allowed to change facts at whim, should he be allowed to depict a slutty Lucretia, or a rakish Socrates?"[13]

With all due respect, this goes too far. I do not wish to undertake the defense of M. Marmontel; I have in fact already expressed my opinion that for the writer, characters must be more sacred than facts.† First because, if the characters are precisely observed, the facts, insofar as they are a consequence of the character, cannot turn out much differently on their own; while on the other hand the same facts might be deduced from completely different characters. Second, because what is instructive derives not from the mere facts but rather from the recognition that these characters in these circumstances will and must produce such facts. Anyhow, Marmontel has it completely backwards. It is a fact that there was once a European slave in the seraglio who managed to make herself the legal wife of the emperor. The characters of this slave and this emperor determine the manner in which this fact came to be. Because it could

---

* *Journal Encyclopédique*, January 1762.

† See above in [23].

arise through more than one type of character, then it is of course up to the writer to choose which of these types he wants; whether it is the one that history confirms or some other that is more suited to the moral purpose he joins to his story. However, in the case where he chooses a different character than the historical one, or even chooses one completely opposite to the historical one, he should also refrain from using historical names and preferably attach the known facts to completely unknown persons than impute an unfitting character to a well-known person. The former increases our knowledge, or at least seems to increase it, and is therefore pleasant. The latter contradicts the knowledge we already possess, and is therefore unpleasant. We consider facts to be something incidental, as something that can be common to many people; character, on the other hand, as something essential and unique. We allow the writer to jump about with the former as he likes, as long as he does not make them contradict the characters; in contrast, he can shine a light on the latter but not change them. The smallest change seems to negate their individuality and substitute others in their place, fraudulent persons who usurp strange names and give themselves out to be something that they are not.

Essay 34

25 August 1767[1]

Even so, it seems to me that it is a far more forgivable mistake to deny personages the character that history gives them than to compromise these freely chosen characters either in terms of their intrinsic probability or from the perspective of instructiveness.[2] For the former mistake is fully commensurate with genius; the latter, however, is not.[3] Genius is permitted ignorance of a thousand things that every schoolboy knows; his wealth does not consist in the stockpiled reserves of his memory but rather in that which he engenders from himself, out of his own feelings.*[4] What genius has heard or read, he has either forgotten or only wants to know insofar as it suits his purpose; as a result, he errs, sometimes out of confidence, sometimes from pride, sometimes intentionally, sometimes not, so often and so grossly that other good people like ourselves shake our heads in wonder; we stand astonished and clasp our hands together and cry out: "But how could such a great man not know! – How is it possible that it didn't occur to him? – Did he not think?" Oh, let us be silent. We think we are humiliating him, but from his perspective we make fools of ourselves. Whatever we know better than him only proves that we were more diligent in school than he was, which, unfortunately, we needed to be if we did not want to remain complete idiots.

As far as I am concerned, then, Marmontel's Soliman and Roxelane might have been completely different than the Soliman and Roxelane I learned from history if I had only felt that, even though they are not from this real world, they nevertheless could have belonged to another world where circumstances were coupled to another order, and just as rigorously as they are in this one; a world in which causes and effects

---

* Pindar, *Olympia* II. str. 5, v. 10.

follow another sequence, but still proceed toward the same general effect of the good; in sum, the world of a genius who – if I may be permitted to draw an analogy between the unnamed Creator and his greatest creature – who, I say, in order to emulate the highest Genius in microcosm, transfers, transposes, reduces, and enlarges parts of the present world so as to create his own world, within which he then brings together his own ideas. Because I do not find the latter in Marmontel's work, I think it is right that we not excuse him for the former. Those who cannot or will not protect us from offense must not offend us on purpose. And here Marmontel really did offend, either intentionally or due to his incompetence.

For according to the concept that we are supposed to have of the genius, we are justified in demanding consistency and purpose in all of the characters that the writer develops or creates, if he demands that we regard him as a genius.

Consistency: there must be nothing contradictory in the characters, they must always be uniform, always resemble themselves; they can express themselves more strongly or weakly, according to how circumstances affect them, but none of these circumstances should be powerful enough to change them from black to white. A Turk and a despot must be a Turk and a despot even when he is in love. None of the refinements that a pampered European imagination connects with love must ever occur to the Turk, who only knows sensual love. "I am sick of this caressing machine; there is nothing attractive or flattering in her soft docility. I want difficulties to overcome, and when I have overcome them, I want to be kept in suspense through new difficulties." – A king of France can think this way, but not a Sultan. It is true, if we attribute this way of thinking to a Sultan, then the despot would no longer come into consideration; he relinquishes his despotism in order to enjoy a freer love. But will he therefore suddenly become a tame monkey whom an impudent juggler can make dance as she likes? Marmontel says: "Soliman was too great a man to place the minor affairs of his seraglio on the same footing as important business of state."[5] Very well, but then in the end he also should not have placed important business of state on the same footing as the minor affairs of his seraglio. For the great man does both, that is, he treats trivialities as trivialities and important things as important things. He sought, as Marmontel himself has him declare, free hearts that acquiesce to their enslavement purely out of love for him.[6] He could have found such a heart in Elmire; but does he really know what he wants? The tender Elmire is displaced by a lascivious Délia, until a reckless woman throws a rope around his horns and makes him her slave before he gets to enjoy the ambiguous favor that up to now has always been the death of his desires. Will it not be the same here? I have to laugh at the good Sultan, and yet he deserves my heartfelt compassion. If Elmire and Délia suddenly lose all the qualities that had previously charmed him once he has enjoyed them, what, then, will Roxelane retain for him after that critical moment? Eight days after her coronation, will he still consider it worth having made this sacrifice for her? I fear greatly that on that first morning, as soon as he has wiped the sleep from his eyes, he will already see nothing more in his bride, the Sultana, than her confident cheekiness and her upturned nose. I imagine I hear him calling out: "By Mohammed, what was I thinking?"

I do not deny that the question remains – given all the contradictions that make this Soliman so pitiful and contemptible to us – whether he could be real. There are plenty of people who unite in themselves even more despicable contradictions. However, for precisely that reason, they can never be the object of poetic imitation. They are beneath such imitation, for they lack the quality of instructiveness, unless one were to make their contradictions themselves, that is, their ridiculousness or their unfortunate consequences, instructive – something Marmontel was clearly far from doing with his Soliman. And a character who lacks instructiveness, lacks:

Purpose. – Behaving with purpose is what elevates human beings over lower creatures; inventing and imitating with purpose is what differentiates the genius from minor artists who only invent to invent and imitate to imitate. Such minor artists are content with the diminished pleasure that is associated with the application of their craft; they make this craft their entire purpose, and then demand that we, too, should be content with the equally diminished pleasure that comes from looking at their ingenious yet pointless application of their craft. It is true, the genius starts to learn with the same tiresome imitations; they are his preparatory exercises, and in larger works he also uses such imitations as filler, as moments of rest for our warmer sympathies. It is only when the genius creates and forms his main characters that he connects them with larger, wider purposes: the purpose of teaching us what we must do or not do; the purpose of acquainting us with the intrinsic features of the good and respectable, and of the evil and ridiculous; and the purpose of showing us that the former are, in all their combinations and effects, beautiful and happy even in misfortune, and that the latter, in contrast, ugly and unhappy even when fortunate. In the case of situations where there is no actual emulation, no actual terror for us, there is at least the purpose of engaging our powers of desire and disgust via the kinds of objects that warrant them, and the genius always tries to place these objects in their true light, so that no falsehood misleads us to detest what we should desire and desire what we ought to detest.

So what, of all this, do we find in the characters of Soliman or Roxelane? As I have already said: nothing. But much of the exact opposite is in these characters. They are a couple of people whom we ought to despise: in fact, the one must arouse our disgust, and the other, our indignation. A weakened hedonist and a cunning temptress are depicted with such seductive strokes and delightful colors that it would not surprise me if some husband believed himself justified in growing tired of his virtuous, beautiful, and accommodating wife because she was an Elmire instead of a Roxelane.

If the errors that we adopt are our own errors, then the above-mentioned French critics are correct in blaming Favart for all that is faulty in Marmontel's material.[7] They seem to think that the former has sinned even more than the latter. "Probability," they say, "which may perhaps not matter so much in a story, is absolutely essential in a dramatic piece; and in the current one this has been violated to the extreme. The great Soliman plays a very minor role, and it is unpleasant to view this hero only from such a point of view. The quality of being a Sultan is even more distorted; there is not even the shadow of the absolute power to which all must submit. This power could have been toned down, but it should not have been eliminated entirely. The character of Roxelane pleased because of the way it was played; but when we reflect on it, how does it really look? Is her role in the least bit probable? She talks to the Sultan as if she is talking to a Parisian burgher: she criticizes all of his habits, she contradicts all of his tastes, and she says very harsh and often quite offensive things to him. She might perhaps have been able to say all these things had she done so with more measured expressions. But who can stand to hear the great Soliman bossed around in this manner by a young tramp? He is even supposed to learn the art of ruling from her. The bit of business with the rejected handkerchief is too strong, and the one involving the tossing of the tobacco pipe is absolutely unbearable."[8]

Essay 35

28 August 1767[1]

In all honesty, that last bit of business belonged solely to Favart; Marmontel did not venture it.[2] Moreover, the previous incident is more refined in Marmontel than in Favart. For in Favart, Roxelane gives away the handkerchief that the Sultan had given her. She pretends that Délia deserves it more than she; she appears to reject it – it is an insult.[3] In Marmontel, on the other hand, Roxelane has the Sultan give her the handkerchief and then passes it on to Délia in his name, thereby evading a token of favor that she is not yet willing to accept, and she does so with the most generous and kindhearted air – the Sultan cannot hold anything against her other than that she perceives his sentiments so poorly (or does not want to perceive them better).

Doubtless Favart believed he could make Roxelane's performance even more lively through these embellishments; he saw the tendency to impertinence already in the role, and one more or less could do it no harm, especially if he already had in mind the change he wanted to make with this character at the end. For in spite of the fact that his Roxelane is more reckless in her antics and more brazenly wanton in behavior, he nonetheless made her into a better and more noble character than the one we see in Marmontel's Roxelane. And how is that? Why that?

It is this change that I wanted to address above, and it seems to me that it is so successful and advantageous that it deserved to be noticed by the French, and its creator should have been given credit for it.[4]

Marmontel's Roxelane is really what she seems to be: a foolish, presumptuous little thing who has the good fortune to appeal to the Sultan's taste and who understands the art of increasing that taste through increasingly voracious hunger that she knows not to satisfy until she has reached her goal. Behind Favart's Roxelane, however, there is more: she seems to play the saucy temptress rather than actually to be it and seems to have tested the Sultan through her effrontery rather than to have exploited his weaknesses. For no sooner has she swayed the Sultan to where she wants to have him, no sooner does she see that his love is boundless, than she immediately drops her mask and gives him an explanation that, while seeming somewhat out of the blue, nonetheless shines a light on her previous conduct that reconciles us to her completely. "Now I know you, Sultan; I have probed your soul to its most utmost depths. It is a noble, grand soul, fully open to honorable sentiments. So much virtue enchants me! Now learn to know me. I love you, Soliman; I cannot help but love you! Take back all your rights, take back my freedom, be my Sultan, my hero, my master! You must otherwise think me very vain and unjust. No, do nothing other than what your law allows. There are prejudices one must respect. I want a lover who need not blush on my account. See here in Roxelane nothing but your obedient slave."*,5 This is what she says, and she suddenly becomes completely different to us; the coquette disappears, and a dear girl stands before us, as sensible as she is capricious. Soliman ceases to seem contemptible to us, because this better Roxelane is worthy of his love. Indeed, in that moment, we begin to worry that he might not love her enough, this girl he seemed to love far too much before, and that he might take her at her word – the lover might once again become the despot as soon as his mistress becomes a slave; instead of a fiery confirmation of his decision, he might give her a cold acknowledgment of gratitude for preventing him, in the nick of time, from taking such a dangerous step, and the good child might suddenly lose, through her generosity, everything she had so pains-takingly achieved through willful arrogance. But these fears are in vain, and the play ends to our complete satisfaction.

So what brought Favart to this change? Is it merely impulsive, or did he feel compelled by the particular rules of the genre in which he was working? Why didn't Marmontel also give his story this more satisfactory outcome? Is the opposite of that which is beautiful in the former an error in the latter?

I recall having written elsewhere about the differences between the plot of Aesopian fables and the drama.[6] What is true of the former is true of any moral tale that has the intention of guiding us to intuit a universal moral principle.[7] We are satisfied if this intention is achieved, and it makes no difference to us whether or not that happens by way of a complete story that constitutes a well-rounded whole; the writer can break it off where he wants to, once he reaches his goal. He is not concerned about the interest we take in the fate of the characters he uses to tell the story; he did not intend to interest us but to instruct us. He is concerned only with our minds, not with our hearts, and the latter might be satisfied or not, so long as the former is illuminated. The drama, on the other hand, makes no claim to a single specific lesson flowing out of its story. It is either about the passions kindled and entertained by the course of events and changes of fortunes presented in its plot or about the pleasure afforded by a true and lively depiction of mores and characters. Both of these require a certain completeness of action and a certain satisfying conclusion that we do not miss in the

---

* Sultan, j'ai pénétré ton ame;
   J'en ai démêlé les ressorts.
   Elle est grande, elle est fiere, & la gloire l'enflame,
   Tant de vertus excitent mes transports.
   A ton tour, tu vas me connoître:
   Je t'aime, Soliman; mais tu l'as mérité.
   Reprends tes droits, reprends ma liberté;
   Sois mon Sultan, mon Héros & mon Maître.
   Tu me soupçonnerois d'injuste vanité.
   Va, ne fais rien, que ta loi n'autorise;
   Il est de préjugés qu'on ne doit point trahir,
   Et je veux un Amant, qui n'ai point à rougir:
   Tu vois dans Roxelane une Esclave soumise.

moral tale, because all of our attention is directed to the universal moral principle illuminated by the obvious example of one singular case.

If, then, it is true that Marmontel wanted to use his story to teach that love cannot be forced, that it must be obtained through indulgence and accommodation, not through authority and violence, then he was right to end as he did.[8] The unruly Roxelane is conquered only through yielding; he does not care what we think of her character or the Sultan's, even if we continue to take her for a fool and him for nothing better. Moreover, Marmontel has absolutely no reason to reassure us about the consequences; it can still seem probable to us that the Sultan will soon regret his blind acquiescence – what is that to him? He wanted to show us, in general, the effect acquiescence can have on a woman, so he used one of the wildest women, unconcerned about whether she was worth such acquiescence or not.

But when Favart wanted to bring this story to the theater, he quickly perceived that for the most part the intuition of the moral principle was largely lost as a result of the dramatic form, and that, if it could be completely retained, the pleasure that arose from it was not so great and lively that it would be worth sacrificing a different pleasure that is more intrinsic to the drama. I mean here the pleasure provided by characters that are both clearly imagined and well drawn. Nothing offends us more in this respect than the contradiction we find between their moral worth or worthlessness and the author's treatment of them – that is, when we find that he has either deceived himself, or at least wants to deceive us, by putting what is small up on stilts, giving willful foolishness the veneer of cheerful wisdom, and outfitting vice and absurdity with all of the deceptive charms of fashion, refined behavior, and the sophisticated trappings of persons of quality. The more our first impressions are misled by this, the more severely do we judge; we declare the ugly face that we see so beautifully painted to be even uglier than it really is, and nothing is left to the writer but to choose whether he would rather be considered a preparer of poison or an imbecile. This is how Favart and his characters Soliman and Roxelane would have fared, and Favart understood this. But since he could not change these characters from the beginning without spoiling an abundance of theatrical scenes that he judged to be perfectly suited to the taste of his *parterre*, there was nothing else for him to do but what he did. Now we are glad not to have to taken pleasure in anything that we could not also respect, and at the same time this respect satisfies our curiosity and concern about the future. Since the drama's illusion is much stronger than that of a mere story, we are far more interested in the characters of the former and are not content to see their fate decided merely for the present moment; rather, we want to feel satisfied on their account once and for all.

Essay 36

1 September 1767[1]

As indisputable as it is that, without the happy twist Favart gives to the character of Roxelane at the end, we would have viewed the coronation that follows with mockery and scorn, as nothing other than the ridiculous triumph of a *serva padrona* – and as certain as it is that, absent the change, the Emperor would have seemed nothing but a despicable Pimpinello, and the new Empress nothing but an shrewd ugly Serbinette who, we could predict, would soon treat the poor Sultan, Pimpinello the Second, completely differently – so too does the change itself seem easy and natural, and thus we have to wonder why it has not occurred to many writers, and why therefore so many whimsical and apparently truly funny stories miscarry in the dramatic form.[2]

Take for example the "Widow of Ephesus."[3] This acerbic tale is well known; it is unquestionably the bitterest satire that has ever been written about female recklessness. It has been retold a thousand times since Petronius, and since people have enjoyed even the worst versions, it seemed like the material ought to do well on stage. Houdar de la Motte, among others, made the attempt; but I appeal to more discriminating sensibilities to determine how that attempt turned out.[4] The character of the widow, who provokes a rather enjoyable sardonic smile at the arrogance of marital love, becomes loathsome and awful in the drama. We find here in the drama that the soldier's appeals are not nearly as subtle and pressing and convincing as they seem to us in the story. There we imagine a sensitive little woman whose grief is real, but is undermined by temptation and by her temperament; we see her weakness as the weakness of the whole sex and thus do not feel a particular hatred toward her. We believe that just about any woman would have done what she does, and we even feel obliged to forgive her for coming up with the idea to save her living lover by means of her dead husband's body, because it shows cleverness and presence of mind. Or even more, the cleverness of this idea brings us to surmise that it has probably just been added by the malicious storyteller, who wanted to end his tale on a really nasty note. But in the drama, this presumption cannot arise: what we only hear about in the story, we actually see happen on stage; things we might continue to doubt there are incontrovertibly confirmed by our own perception here. As a mere possibility, the cleverness of the deed delighted us; when it is a reality, we only see its blackness. The idea pleased our minds, but its execution completely shocks our sensibilities. We turn our backs to the stage and concur with Petronius's Lycas (without finding ourselves in the same particular situation as Lycas): "Si justus Imperator fuisset, debuit patrisfamiliae corpus in monimentum referre, mulierem adfigere cruci."[5] And she seems to deserve this punishment so much the more when the writer has employed less art toward her seduction, for in that case we do not damn, in her, the weakness of women in general but rather one extraordinarily reckless, licentious woman in particular. – In short, to bring Petronius's fable successfully to the theater, it would have to keep the same outcome and also not keep it; the widow would have to go as far as she does and also not go so far. – The explanation of this will appear somewhere else![6]

On the thirty-seventh evening (Sunday, the 4th of July), *Nanine* and *The Village Lawyer* were repeated.

On the thirty-eighth evening (Tuesday, the 7th of July), M. de Voltaire's *Mérope* was performed.[7]

Voltaire wrote this tragedy in response to Maffei's *Merope*, presumably in 1737, and presumably while staying at Cirey with his Urania, the Marquise du Châtelet.[8] For by January 1738 the manuscript was already in Paris in the hands of Pater Brumoy, who, as a Jesuit and as the publisher of *Théâtre des Grecs*, was best suited to obtain the most positive advance opinions and use those opinions to shape the expectations of the capital.[9] Brumoy showed it to the author's friends; among others he must have sent it to old Father Tournemine, who, quite flattered to have been consulted by his dear son Voltaire about a tragedy – a matter he little understood – wrote back to Brumoy a little letter full of praises and exaltations, which in turn was later printed in front of each copy of the play itself to instruct and warn any unwelcome critics.[10] In that letter, the play is declared to be one of the most perfect of tragedies, a very model, and from now on we can fully console ourselves over the loss of the play by Euripides with the same subject; or, rather, it is now no longer lost – Voltaire has restored it to us.[11]

As reassured as Voltaire must have been by this, he seems not to have wanted to rush the production, which did not take place until 1743. And he enjoyed all the fruits he could possibly have anticipated from this strategic delay. *Mérope* met with the most exceptional applause, and the *parterre* bestowed an unprecedented honor on the writer.[12] It is true that the public had previously given the great Corneille preferential treatment: his chair on stage was always kept free, even when there was a great crowd, and when he arrived, everyone stood – a distinction that, in France, is shown only to princes of royal blood.[13] When Corneille was in the theater, he was regarded as if he were at home, and when the master of the house appears, what is more appropriate than for his guests to show him their courtesy? But something completely different happened to Voltaire: the *parterre* was curious to know in person the man they had admired so much, and so when the performance ended, they demanded to see him, and shouted, cried out, and made a racket until M. de Voltaire was compelled to step out and allow himself to be ogled and applauded.[14] I do not know which of these two things would have disconcerted me more, the audience's childish curiosity or the writer's vain accommodation. What do people think a writer looks like? Not like other people? And what a weak impression must the work have made, if at that very moment we are not curious about anything other than what the maestro looks like. The true masterpiece, it seems to me, fills us so completely that we forget its creator; we don't regard it as the product of a particular being but of nature in general. Speaking of the sun, Young says that it would have been a sin if heathens hadn't worshiped it.[15] If there is any sense in this hyperbole, it is this: the sun's radiance and splendor are so great and so immense that the primitive man is to be forgiven, because it is only natural that he was unable to imagine the greater radiance and splendor of which the sun is a mere reflection and was so completely lost in admiration of the sun that he did not think about the sun's creator. I suspect the true reason we have so little authoritative knowledge about Homer's life and character is the excellence of his poetry itself. We stand in front of the wide rushing river full of astonishment, without thinking about its source in the mountains. We do not want to know; it is to our advantage to forget that Homer the Smyrnian schoolmaster, Homer the blind beggar, is the very same Homer who so delights us in his works.[16] He brings us among gods and heroes; we would have to be very bored in this company to inquire persistently about the doorman who let us in. The illusion must be very flimsy, and we must perceive relatively little nature and much artifice if we are that curious about the artist. As unflattering, then, as the public's desire to see him in person ought to be to the man of genius in principle (and, really, what does he have over the first marmot that comes around, which the mob is just as eager to have seen?), yet the vanity of French writers seems to have found it agreeable.[17] For as soon as the Parisian *parterre* saw how easily a Voltaire could be lured into this trap, how tame and unctuous such a man could become through dubious flattery, it entertained itself this way more frequently, and seldom was a new play performed after that without its author being immediately called forth, and coming forth very willingly. From Voltaire to Marmontel, and from Marmontel all the way down to Cordier, nearly all had to stand in this pillory.[18] How many hangdog looks must have appeared among them! In the end, the farce went so far that the more serious men in the nation became irritated by it. Wise Pulcinella's clever idea is well known.[19] And just recently a young writer was bold enough to let the *parterre* call for him in vain. He did not appear at all; his play was mediocre, but his conduct all the more courageous and laudable.[20] I would prefer to have done away with such an indecency through my example than to have initiated it with ten *Méropes*.

Essay 37

4 September 1767[1]

I have said that Voltaire's *Mérope* was written in response to Maffei's *Merope*.[2] But response says too little, for the one originates wholly in the other. The story, plot, and morals belong to Maffei: without him Voltaire would have written no *Mérope* at all, or quite certainly a very different one.[3]

To judge the Frenchman's copy correctly, then, we must first get to know the Italian's original; and to properly appreciate the latter's poetic accomplishment, we must first and foremost cast an eye on the historical facts which are the basis of his story.

In the dedication pages of his play, Maffei himself summarizes these facts in the following manner.[4] "That some time after the fall of Troy, when the Heraclids, that is, the descendants of Hercules, reestablished themselves in the Peloponnesus, the area of Messene fell to Cresphontes by lot; that this Cresphontes's wife was named Merope; that, because he showed such favor toward the people, Cresphontes and all of his sons were murdered by powerful men of the state, with the exception of the youngest son, who was being raised by a relative of his mother away from home; that when this youngest son, named Aepytus, was grown, he reclaimed his father's kingdom with the help of the Arcadians and the Dorians and took revenge on his father's murderers – Pausanius tells us all this.[5] That, after Cresphontes and his two sons were killed, Polyphontes, who was also of the race of the Heraclids, seized power; that he also forced Merope to become his wife; that the third son, whom the mother had had removed to safety, later killed the tyrant and recovered the kingdom – Apollodorus relates this.[6] That Merope herself unwittingly sought to kill the escaped son, but that she was prevented from doing so in the nick of time by an old servant who revealed to her that the man she took for her son's murderer was her son himself; that the now-recognized son found an opportunity to slay Polyphontes during a ritual sacrifice – Hyginus reports this, except he gives Aepytus the name Telephon."[7]

It would be surprising if such a story, which has such unusual revelations and reversals of fortune, had not already been exploited by the ancient tragedians.[8] And who says it was not? In his *Poetics*, Aristotle remembers a *Cresphontes* in which Merope recognizes her son just as she is about to kill him, thinking he is the murderer of her son; and Plutarch, in his second discourse on the eating of meat, points without doubt to this very play* when he refers to the stir aroused in the whole theater when Merope raises the axe against her son and to the fear seizing each spectator that the blow will happen before the old servant can arrive.[9] Admittedly, Aristotle mentions this *Cresphontes* without naming the author, but because we find a *Cresphontes* by Euripides cited in Cicero and many other ancient authors, it is unlikely that he would have meant the work of any other poet.[10]

Father Tournemine says in the letter mentioned above: "Aristotle, that wise law-maker of the theater, placed the subject of Merope in the highest rank of subjects for tragedy (*a mis ce sujet au premier rang des sujets tragiques*). Euripides had adapted it, and Aristotle reports that whenever Euripides' *Cresphontes* was presented in the theater of the perceptive Athenians, these people, so accustomed to tragic masterpieces, were exceptionally struck, moved, and entranced."[11] – Pretty phrases, but not much truth! The Father is wrong on both points. With the last thing he says, he has confused Aristotle with Plutarch; with the first he has misunderstood Aristotle.[12] The former is trivial, but it is worth taking the trouble to devote a few words to the latter, since many have misunderstood Aristotle in the same way.

The matter is as follows. In Chapter 14 of his *Poetics*, Aristotle examines what kinds of incidents will arouse terror and compassion.[13] He says that all incidents must happen either between friends, between enemies, or between people who are indifferent to each other. If an enemy kills his enemy, neither the initiation nor the execution of the deed awakens anything more than the general compassion associated with the sight of pain and ruin. And it is the same with persons who are indifferent to one another. Consequently, tragic incidents must occur among friends: a brother must kill his brother, a son his father, a mother her son, or a son his mother – they must kill or want to kill, they must mistreat or want to mistreat the other in some painful way. This can happen with or without knowledge and premeditation; and because the deed must either be carried to completion or not, four categories of incidents emerge that more or less correspond to the aims of tragedy. The first: when the deed is initiated deliberately against a person whose identity is fully known to the perpetrator, but the deed is not completed. The second: when it is initiated with this knowledge, and it is actually completed. The third: when the deed is undertaken and executed without full knowledge, and the perpetrator learns too late the identity of the victim. The fourth: when the deed initiated in ignorance is not successfully executed because the people

---

* Assuming this (and we certainly can make this assumption, because it was neither the practice of the ancients, nor allowed, to steal such distinct situations from each other), the cited passage from Plutarch could probably lead one to a fragment of Euripides that Joshua Barnes has not included, which would be of use to a new editor of the poet's works.

involved recognize each other in time. Aristotle gives preference to the last of these four categories, and because he cites Merope's action in *Cresphontes* as an example of that type, Tournemine and others have taken this to mean that he declares the plot of this drama to be one of the most perfect of tragic plots.

However, just before that Aristotle says that a good tragic plot must not end happily but unhappily.[14] How can these two coexist? It should end unhappily, and yet the incident he favors over all the other tragic incidents, according to the above classification, ends happily. Is it not obvious that the great critic is contradicting himself?

Dacier notes that Victorius was the only one who perceived this difficulty; but because he did not understand what Aristotle was really trying to do throughout the fourteenth chapter, he did not venture the least attempt to resolve it.[15] Dacier says that Aristotle was writing not of plot in general; rather, he wanted to demonstrate the different ways a poet could treat tragic incidents without changing the essentials provided by history and to show which of these ways was the best. For example, if the subject of the play is to be Orestes' murder of Clytemnestra, then, according to Aristotle, four ways of handling this material become apparent: that is, either as an incident of the first, second, third, or fourth category. The poet must consider which is the best and most fitting for his purposes. He cannot treat this murder as an incident belonging to the first category, because according to history it has to happen, and Orestes must do it. It can't belong to the second, because it would be too horrible. It can't belong to the fourth, because once again Clytemnestra would be saved as a result, and she should never be saved. As a result, nothing remains but the third category.

The third! But Aristotle gives preference to the fourth, and not just in individual cases, according to the circumstances, but overall. Honest Dacier often does this: he believes Aristotle to be right not because he is right but because he is Aristotle. In trying to cover up one flaw, he creates another one for Aristotle that is just as compromising. Now, if an adversary has the presence of mind to attack the new flaw instead of the old, then the myth of his old maestro's infallibility can no longer be maintained, which seems to mean much more to him than the truth itself. When so much depends on conforming to history, when the poet is allowed only to moderate, but never completely change, history's generally known facts, won't there be some among these that absolutely must be treated according to the first or second plans? The murder of Clytemnestra ought to be presented in accord with the second, for Orestes committed it with both knowledge and deliberation, but the poet can choose the third because it is more tragic and it does not directly contradict history. Good, so be it. But what about Medea, who murders her children? What other plan can the poet adopt but the second? For she must kill them, and she must do so intentionally; both are well-known from history. What hierarchy can there be among these plans? The one that is most preferable in one case does not even come into consideration in another. Or, to drive Dacier even further into a corner, let us consider not historical events but fictional ones. Let us suppose that Clytemnestra's murder was fictional, and it was up to the poet whether to have it carried out or not, with or without full knowledge. Which plan would he have had to choose to create the most perfect tragedy out of the situation? Dacier himself says: the fourth; for when he prefers the third it is only out of respect for history. The fourth then? The one that ends happily? But the best tragedies, says the very Aristotle who accords the greatest preference to this fourth plan over all the others, are the ones that end unhappily. And that is precisely the contradiction that Dacier wanted to resolve. Did he resolve it, then? On the contrary, he confirmed it.

Essay 38

8 September 1767[1]

I am not the only one who finds Dacier's interpretation unsatisfactory.[2] It was just as inadequate for the German translator of Aristotle's *Poetics*.*[3] He lays out his reasons against it, and although they do not in fact actually refute Dacier's sidestepping, they strike him as sufficiently formidable that he prefers to abandon his author completely rather than hazard another attempt to salvage something that cannot be saved. He concludes: "I leave it to someone with deeper insight to resolve these difficulties. I cannot find a light to elucidate them, and it seems probable to me that our philosopher did not think through this chapter with his usual care."[4]

I confess this does not seem very probable to me. An Aristotle is not readily guilty of such an obvious contradiction.[5] Wherever I might think to have found one in the work of such a man, I would prefer to mistrust my own reason rather than his. I double my attention, I reread the passage ten times and will not believe that he has contradicted himself before I have comprehended, from the whole context of his system, how and why he was misled into this contradiction. If I find nothing that could have misled him into it or that made this contradiction somehow unavoidable, then I am convinced that the contradiction only appears to be so. For otherwise it certainly would have been noticed first by the author, who must have reviewed his material many times, and not by me, the unpracticed reader, who reads it for my own instruction. So I pause, follow the threads of his thoughts back a ways, ponder each word, and continually say to myself: Aristotle can be wrong and was often wrong, but to claim something here and then on the next page claim its complete opposite, that is something Aristotle cannot do. And in the end some explanation will be found.

So without further ado, here is the explanation of which Herr Curtius despaired. I make no claim, however, to the honor of having deeper insight. I will content myself with claiming the honor of more modesty toward a philosopher like Aristotle.

Above everything else, Aristotle recommends a good composition of plot to the tragic poet, and this, above all, is the element that he tries to make easier through many subtle observations.[6] For it is the plot first and foremost that makes a poet a Poet: ten will make do with morals, attitudes, and expressions for every one who is irreproachable and excellent with plot. He defines plot as the imitation of an action, πράξεως; and an action as a linking of incidents, σύνθεσις πραγμάτων.[7] The action is the whole, the incidents are the parts of the whole, and just as the quality of any

---

* Herr Curtius, p. 214.

whole depends on the quality of each of its parts and of their connection to each other, so is the tragic action more or less perfect according to how well its constitutive incidents correspond, individually and collectively, to the purposes of the tragedy. Aristotle classes all of the incidents that could be part of tragic action under three main categories: reversal of fortune, *περιπέτεια*; recognition, *ἀναγνώρισις*; and suffering, *πάθους*.[8] The words themselves say enough about what he understands by the first two terms; under the third term he gathers together everything destructive and painful that could befall the characters: death, wounds, torture, and the like. The first two, reversal of fortune and recognition, are what differentiate the complex plot, *μύθος πεπλεγμένος*, from the simple, *ἁπλοῦς*.[9] They are thus not an essential part of the plot. They only make the action more varied, and thereby more interesting and beautiful, but an action can have its full unity, completeness, and magnitude without them. Without the third, however, no tragic action is conceivable; every tragedy must have forms of suffering, *πάθη*, whether the plot itself is simple or complex, for they speak directly to the purpose of tragedy, the arousal of terror and compassion.[10] By contrast, not every reversal of fortune or recognition but only certain forms of these accomplish the same purpose and help elevate it to a higher degree; others are more of a disadvantage than an advantage. So now, seen from this perspective, when Aristotle looks at the various parts of tragic action that he has classed under these three categories and examines each one, investigating which is the best reversal of fortune, the best recognition, and the best treatment of suffering, then it becomes clear that with regard to the first, the best change in fortune is the one that is most capable of arousing and promoting terror and compassion, which occurs when the change is from better to worse. With regard to the last, that treatment of suffering is best (in the same sense) when the persons threatened by suffering do not know each other but then recognize each other in the very moment their suffering is about to be realized, and as a result the suffering is avoided.

And this is supposed to be contradictory? I do not understand what someone who finds the least contradiction here must be thinking. The philosopher speaks of different parts: why, then, should what he claims about one part necessarily apply to another? Is the potential perfection of the one necessarily the perfection of the other? Or is the perfection of one part also the perfection of the whole? If reversal of fortune and that which Aristotle understands by the word suffering are two different things, as in fact they are, why can one not say completely different things about them? Or is it impossible that a whole might have parts with opposing characteristics? Where does Aristotle say that the best tragedy is nothing but the representation of a change from happiness to unhappiness? Or where does he say that the best tragedy comes down to nothing but the recognition of someone on whom a gruesome, unnatural deed was to have been committed? He says neither the one nor the other of tragedy as a whole, but all of these about a particular part that stands closer or further from the end and that could have more or less influence (or even none at all) on other parts. The reversal of fortune can transpire in the middle of the play, and even if it persists to the end, it still does not constitute the ending itself: an example is the reversal of fortune in *Oedipus*, which finds expression right at the end of the fourth act but to which are added various additional sufferings (*πάθη*) with which the play actually ends. Likewise, the suffering can reach its point of fulfillment in the middle of the play and in that same moment be thwarted by recognition, so that the play is anything but ended as a result of that recognition, as in Euripides' second *Iphigenia*, where (also in the fourth act) Orestes is recognized by his sister just as she is about to sacrifice him.[11] And it can be shown in the example of *Merope* itself how perfectly those most tragic of reversals of fortune can be combined with the most tragic treatment of suffering in one and the same plot.[12] The story certainly has the latter, but what prevents it from also having the first: that is, if, in her eagerness to protect her son from Polyphontes after she has recognized him beneath her dagger, she precipitates either her own or her beloved son's destruction? Why couldn't this play just as well end with the downfall of the mother instead of the tyrant? Why shouldn't the poet be free to drive our compassion to the maximum for such a tender mother, by allowing her to suffer through her own tenderness?

Or why shouldn't he be allowed to take that son, whom he has snatched from the pious vengeance of his mother, and let him nonetheless be defeated by the tyrant's treachery? In both cases, would not such a *Merope* in fact combine the two characteristics of the best tragedy that are found to be so contradictory in the critic's work?[13]

I can readily see what could have brought about the misunderstanding. It is hard to imagine a reversal of fortune from better to worse without thinking of suffering, and it is hard to imagine a recognition that prevents suffering without any change in fortune. Nonetheless, either can exist without the other, not to mention that both also do not necessarily have to affect the same person, and if they do affect the same person, they both need not occur at the same time, but rather one could follow the other or one could be caused by the other. Without considering this, people have only thought about those instances and plots in which either both parts coalesce or one part necessarily excludes the other. That such examples exist is without question. But is the critic then to blame for having drawn up his rules in the most general manner, without having concerned himself with the cases in which his general rules collide, so that one perfection must be sacrificed for another? Does such a collision put him in contradiction with himself? He says: if this part of the plot is to have its perfection, it must have this quality; that one must have another quality; and a third, yet another. But where did he say that all plots must necessarily have all these parts? It suffices for him that there are some plots that could have them all. If your plot does not number among these lucky ones, if it allows you either only the best reversal of fortune or the best treatment of suffering, then consider which of the two you will fare best with and choose. That is all!

Essay 39

11 September 1767[1]

In the end, Aristotle may or may not have contradicted himself, and Tournemine may or may not have understood him correctly: the plot of *Merope* is neither in the first nor second case purely and simply identifiable as a perfect tragic plot.[2] For if Aristotle has contradicted himself, then he has also just claimed the direct opposite, and we must examine first where he was more correct, there or here. If he has not contradicted himself, however – in accord with my explanation – then the good that he finds in it does not apply to the whole plot but rather to only one single part of it. Perhaps Father Tournemine's misuse of his reputation was also merely a Jesuit trick, an artful way of giving us to understand that such a perfect story, reworked by a great poet like Voltaire, would necessarily have to become a masterpiece.

But Tournemine and Tournemine – I fear my readers will ask: "Who is this Tournemine? We don't know any Tournemine." For many may really not know him, and some may ask such a question because they know him all too well, like Montesquieu.*,3

Kindly permit me, then, to substitute M. de Voltaire himself for Father Tournemine. For he, too, seeks to give us the same mistaken idea of Euripides' lost play.[4] He too says that Aristotle, in his immortal *Poetics*, does not hesitate to declare the recognition between Merope and her son to be the most interesting moment of all Greek theater. He also says that Aristotle gave preference to this *coup de théâtre* above all others. And he goes so far as to assure us that Plutarch held this play to be the most moving of all Euripides' plays.†,5 This last is pulled from thin air. For Plutarch does not even once mention by name the play from which he cites the story of Merope; he neither tells us what it is called nor who the author is, never mind declaring it to be the most moving of all Euripides' plays.[6]

Aristotle supposedly does not hesitate to declare that the recognition between Merope and her son was the most interesting moment of all Greek theater! What an expression – does not hesitate to declare! What hyperbole – the most interesting moment of all Greek theater! Should we not conclude from this that Aristotle sifts industriously through all of the interesting moments that a tragedy could have, compares them all, weighs the different examples that he finds from each particular poet against all the others, or at least among the famous poets, and in the end, makes a claim that is as presumptuous as it is certain in favor of this moment from Euripides? Besides, he is only citing an example of a specific kind of interesting moment, and this is not even the only example of this kind. For Aristotle found similar examples in *Iphigenia*, where the sister recognizes the brother, and in the *Helle*, where the son recognizes the mother, in both cases just at the moment when they are about to harm the other.[7]

The second example from *Iphigenia* does in fact come from Euripides, and if, as Dacier surmises, the *Helle* is also a work by this poet, then it would be quite remarkable for Aristotle to have found all three examples of such a happy recognition precisely in the work of the very poet who most frequently employs the unhappy *peripeteia*.[8] And

---

* *Lettres familières.*

† Aristote, dans sa Poétique immortelle, ne balance pas à dire que la reconnaissance de Mérope et de son fils était le moment le plus intéressant de toute la scène grecque. Il donnait à ce coup de théâtre la préférance sur tous les autres. Plutarque dit que les Grecs, ce peuple si sensible, frémissaient de crainte que le vieillard, qui devait arrêter le bras de Mérope, n'arrivât pas assez tôt. Cette pièce, qu'on jouait de son temps, et dont il nous reste très peu de fragments, lui paraissait la plus touchante de toutes les tragédies d'Euripide &c. *Lettre à M. Maffei.*

why remarkable? We have seen that the one does not exclude the other, and although in *Iphigenia* the happy recognition follows on the unhappy *peripeteia*, and the play thus generally ends happily, who knows whether or not an unhappy *peripeteia* might have followed on the happy recognition in the other two, and thereby ended in precisely that manner that earned Euripides the title of being the most tragic of all tragic poets?

With *Merope*, as I have shown, this could have gone two ways; whether or not it really happened cannot be concluded from the few fragments of the *Cresphontes* that are left to us. They contain nothing but moral attitudes and maxims occasionally quoted by later authors and do not throw the least light on the structure of the play.‡,9 From the one bit that appears in Polybius, which is an appeal to the goddess of peace, it seems evident that during the time in which the action takes place, peace had not yet been reestablished in the state of Messene.[10] From a couple of others we could almost conclude that the murder of Cresphontes and his two older sons either made up part of the action or had occurred just before it began, neither of which agrees very well with the recognition of the younger son, who did not come to revenge his father and brothers until many years later. But it is the title itself that gives me the greatest difficulties. If the most significant content is this recognition and revenge of the younger son, why was the play called *Cresphontes*? Cresphontes was the name of the father. The son was, according to some, named Aepytus, and according to others, Telephon; perhaps the first was the correct name and the second the assumed name he bore in foreign lands in order to remain unrecognized and safe from Polyphontes' scrutiny. The father must be long dead when the son retakes possession of the paternal kingdom. Has anyone ever heard of a tragedy being named after a person who does not even appear in it? Corneille and Dacier quickly set this difficulty aside by assuming that the son was also called Cresphontes,§ but with what likelihood?[11] For what reason?

If, however, the discovery that Maffei claims to have made is correct, then we can know the plot of *Cresphontes* with some exactness. He believes he has found it in Hyginus's one hundred eighty-fourth fable.¶,12 For he considers Hyginus's fables in general to be nothing more than the summaries of old tragedies, an opinion shared

---

‡   What Dacier quotes (*Poetique d'Aristote*, Chap. XV. Rem. 23) without remembering where he read it, is in Plutarch's essay "How to profit by one's enemies."

§   *Remarque 22. Sur le Chapitre XV. De la Poet. D'Arist.* Une mere qui va tuer son fils, comme Merope va tuer Cresphonte &c.

¶   – questa scoperta penso io d'aver fatta, nel leggere la Favola 184 d'Igino, la quale a mio credere altro non è, che l'Argomento di quella Tragedia, in cui si rappresenta interamente la condotta di essa. Sovviemmi, che al primo gettar gli occhi, ch'io feci già in quell' Autore, mi apparve subito nella mente, altro non essere le più di quelle Favole, che gli Argomenti delle Tragedie antiche: mi accertai di ciò col confrontarne alcune poche con le Tragedie, che ancora abbiamo; e appunto in questi giorni; [essendomi in questa Città di buoni libri sì ben fornita,] venuta a mano l'ultima edizione d'Igino, mi è stato caro di vedere in un passo addotto, come fu anche il Reinesio di tal sentimento. Una miniera è però questa di Tragici Argomenti, che se fosse stata nota a' Poeti, non avrebbero penato tanto in rinvenir soggetti a lor fantasia: io la scoprirò loro di buona voglia, perchè rendano col loro ingegno alla nostra età ciò, che dal tempo invidioso le fu rapito. Merita dunque, almeno per questo capo, alquanto più di considerazione quell' Operetta, anche tal qual l'abbiamo, che da gli Eruditi non è stato creduto: e quanto al discordar tal volta dagli altri Scrittori delle favolose Storie, questa avvertenza ce ne addita la ragione, non avendole costui narrate secondo la tradizione, ma conforme i Poeti in proprio uso convertendole, le avean ridotte.

by Reinesius before him, and he thus recommends that contemporary poets look in this abandoned shaft for ancient tragic plots rather than inventing new ones for themselves.[13] The advice is not bad and should be followed. And many have followed it, even before Maffei gave it, or without knowing he had given it. Herr Weisse drew the material for his *Thyestes* from this mine, and there is still more down there that awaits a sensible eye.[14] Only it may be that it is not the largest part of Hyginus's work but rather the smallest part that can be used for this purpose. Hyginus's work may, in fact, not have been assembled from summaries of old tragedies at all; it might also have flowed directly or indirectly from the same sources in which the tragedians themselves sought material. Indeed, Hyginus, or whoever made this compilation, seems to have regarded the tragedies as diverted and polluted streams, insofar as in several places, he expressly separates that which had nothing more than the authority of a tragic poet in its favor from the older, more authentic tradition. For example, he tells the story of Ino and the story of Antiopa first according to tradition, and then, in a separate passage, according to Euripides' handling.[15]

Essay 40

15 September 1767[1]

However, I do not mean to imply thereby that, because the name of Euripides does not appear above the one hundred and eighty-fourth fable, it could not have been drawn from his *Cresphontes*.[2] On the contrary, I fully acknowledge that it has the course of action and development of a tragedy, so that even if it isn't one, it could easily become one, one whose plot, in fact, would approach classical simplicity far more than all the new *Meropes*. Judge for yourself: Hyginus's full story, which I only briefly summarized above, is as follows.

Cresphontes was King of Messene and had three sons with his wife, Merope, when Polyphontes raised the rebellion against him in which Cresphontes and his two older sons lost their lives. Polyphontes then usurped both the kingdom and Merope's hand. During the upheaval Merope had found an opportunity to have her third son, named Telephon, sent to a friend in Aetolien for safety. The older Telephon grew, the more anxious Polyphontes became. Polyphontes could expect nothing good from Telephon, and so he promised a great reward to the person who would eliminate him. Telephon heard of this, and because he now felt himself capable of undertaking his revenge, he secretly made his way out of Aetolien, went to Messene, came to the tyrant, said that he had killed Telephon, and demanded the promised reward. Polyphontes took him in as a guest and gave orders to entertain him in his palace until he could question him further. Telephon was brought into the guest room, where he fell asleep from fatigue. In the meantime, the old servant whom mother and son had employed till now for their exchange of messages came in tears to Merope and reported that Telephon was gone from Aetolien, and that no one knew where he had gone. Merope, who knew what the recently arrived stranger boasted of having done, immediately rushed to the guest room with an axe and would have killed him without fail had the old man who followed her there not recognized the son in time and prevented the mother from committing the heinous crime. Now the two made common cause, and Merope pretended to be calm and reconciled to her husband. Polyphontes believed all his wishes had been granted and wanted to show his thanks to the gods through a ritual sacrifice. But when they were all gathered at the altar, Telephon directed the blow, which he had pretended was for slaughtering the sacrificial animal, toward the King; the tyrant fell, and Telephon attained possession of his paternal kingdom.[*,3]

In the sixteenth century two Italian poets, Joh. Bapt. Liviera and Pomponio Torelli, also took the material for their tragedies *Cresphontes* and *Merope* from this fable in Hyginus's collection, and had thus, according to Maffei, followed in Euripides' footsteps without knowing it.[4] But this conviction notwithstanding, Maffei himself was so little interested in making his work into a mere divination of Euripides whereby his *Merope* would resurrect the lost *Cresphontes* that, on the contrary, he deliberately deviated from many of the main features of Euripides' supposed plot and only sought to use, in its full dimension, the one situation that had moved him the most.

Namely, the mother who loved her son with such passion that she wanted to avenge his murder with her own hand gave him the idea to depict maternal tenderness and to animate his play through this one pure and virtuous passion, to the exclusion of all other forms of love. Thus whatever did not completely meet this purpose was changed; in particular, this had to affect the circumstances of Merope's second marriage and the son's foreign upbringing. Merope could not be Polyphontes' wife, for it

---

* In Hyginus's 184th fable, from which the story above is taken, incidents seem to have been mingled together that do not have the least connection to each other. It begins with the fates of Pentheus and Agave and ends with the story of Merope. I cannot fathom how the editor could have left this confusion unannotated; unless it only exists in the edition that I have before me (Joannis Schefferi, Hamburgi 1674). I leave this investigation to someone who has the means for it at hand. Suffice it to say that here, in my edition, the 184th fable ends with the words "quam Licoterses excepit" ["whom Lycotherses received"]. The rest either constitutes another fable, whose opening words have been lost, or – and this seems most probable to me – it belongs with the 137th, so that, both connected, I would read the whole fable of Merope as follows (and we could choose whether we want to make it the 137th or 184th). It goes without saying that in the latter the words "cum qua Polyphontes, occiso Cresphonte, regnum occupavit" ["with whom Polyphontes, after slaying Cresphontes, seized the kingdom"], being an unnecessary repetition, would have to be omitted, along with the "ejus" that follows, which is also already redundant.

MEROPE

Polyphontes, Messeniae rex, Cresphontem Aristomachi filium cum interfecisset, ejus imperium & Meropem uxorem possedit. Filium autem infantem Merope mater, quem ex Cresphonte habebat, absconse ad hospitem in Aetoliam mandavit. Hunc Polyphontes maxima cum industria quaerebat, aurumque pollicebatur, si quis eum necasset. Qui postquam ad puberem aetatem venit, capit consilium, ut exequatur patris & fratrum mortem. Itaque venit ad regem Polyphontem, aurum petitum, dicens se Cresphontis interfecisse filium & Meropis, Telephontem. Interim rex eum jussit in hospitio manere, ut amplius de eo perquireret. Qui cum per lassitudinem obdormisset, senex qui inter matrem & filium internuncius erat, flens ad Meropem venit, negans eum apud hospitem esse, nec comparere. Merope credens eum esse filii sui interfectorem, qui dormiebat, in Chalcidicum cum securi venit, inscia ut filium suum interficeret, quem senex cognovit, & matrem ab scelere retraxit. Merope postquam invenit, occasionem sibi datam esse, ab inimico se ulciscendi, redit cum Polyphonte in gratiam. Rex laetus cum rem divinam faceret, hospes falso simulavit se hostiam percussisse, eumque interfecit, patriumque regnum adeptus est.

seemed to the poet to clash with the conscience of such a pious mother to have surrendered herself to the embraces of a second husband whom she knew to have murdered her first and whose own self-preservation required that he get rid of everyone who could have a firmer claim to the throne. The son must not be raised in complete safety and comfort, with full knowledge of his rank and destiny, by a noble guest and friend of his father's house: for maternal love will naturally cool if not stimulated and exerted by constantly imagining the discomforts and continually new dangers into which its absent object can stumble. He must not come with the express purpose of revenging himself on the tyrant; he must not be held by his mother to be the murderer of her son because he pretends to be so, but rather because a certain chain of coincidences draws this suspicion upon him. For if he knows his mother, then her dilemma is over with the first verbal explanation, and there is not enough space to play out her moving anguish and tender despair.

And given these changes, one can pretty well imagine Maffei's plot. Polyphontes has been ruling for fifteen years, and yet he still does not yet feel himself secure enough on the throne. For the people are still devoted to the house of their previous king and count on its last salvaged offshoot. To pacify the discontented, he comes up with the idea of marrying Merope. He offers her his hand under the pretense of real love. But Merope rejects him and his pretense with too much delicacy; so he then tries to obtain through threats and violence what his deceptions could not accomplish. Just as he is pressuring her most fiercely, a young man seized on the highway for committing a murder is brought before him. Aegisthus, so the youth calls himself, had done nothing but defend his own life against a robber; his appearance reveals so much nobility and innocence, his speech so much truth, that Merope (who also notices a certain shape to his mouth that her husband had) is moved to plead with the King for him, and the King pardons him. Directly on the heels of this, Merope realizes her youngest son is missing; she had entrusted him, after her husband's death, to an old servant named Polydorus, with orders that he be raised as Polydorus's own son. He had secretly left the old man, whom he believed to be his father, to see the world; but now he is nowhere to be found. A mother's heart always suspects the worst: someone has been killed on the highway – what if it were her son? This is what she thinks, and her anxious suspicions are strengthened by different circumstances, by the readiness of the King to pardon him, but primarily by a ring found on Aegisthus and which she is told Aegisthus took from the slain man. This is her husband's signet ring, which she had given Polydorus to bestow on her son when he was grown and ready to learn of his rank. Straightaway she has the youth, for whom she herself had earlier sought favor, bound to a column, with the intention of piercing his heart with her own hand. The youth takes this moment to remember his parents; the word Messene slips out of his mouth; he recalls his father's command to cautiously avoid this place. Merope demands an explanation of this; meanwhile the King comes in and the youth is freed. As close as Merope was to the recognition of her mistake, when she sees how scornful the King is in triumph over her despair, she falls even more deeply into error. Now Aegisthus is unquestionably her son's murderer, and nothing shall protect him from her revenge. As night falls, she learns that he has fallen asleep in a parlor, and she comes with an axe to split open his head. She has raised the axe for the blow when

Polydorus, who had slipped into that same parlor moments earlier and recognized the sleeping Aegisthus, falls into her arms. Aegisthus awakens and flees, and Polydorus reveals to Merope that the presumed murderer of her son is her real son. She wants to follow him and would have easily revealed his identity to the tyrant through her impetuous affection had the old man not held her back. In the early morning, her marriage to the King is supposed to be finalized; she must go to the altar, but she would rather die than give her consent. In the meantime, Polydorus has also taught Aegisthus to know his true identity; Aegisthus rushes to the temple, presses through the crowd, and – the rest is as told by Hyginus.

Essay 41

18 September 1767[1]

The worse things looked in general for the Italian theater at the beginning of this century, the greater was the applause and jubilation with which Maffei's *Merope* was received.[2]

> *Cedite Romani scriptores, cedite Graii,*
> *Nescio quid majus nascitur Oedipode.*[3]

cried Leonardo Adami, who had only seen the first two acts of the play in Rome.[4] During all of Carnival in Venice in 1714 almost no other play but *Merope* was performed; the whole world wanted to see the new tragedy again and again, and even the opera stages found themselves abandoned because of it. It was printed four times in one year; and in the space of sixteen years (from 1714 to 1730) more than thirty editions of it were produced in and out of Italy, in Vienna, Paris, and London. It was translated into French, English, and German, and there were plans to have it printed with all of these translations together.[5] It had already been translated into French twice when M. de Voltaire wanted to do it over again himself, in order to really bring it onto the French stage. But he quickly found that this could not be achieved through an actual translation, the reasons for which he copiously elaborates in the letter to the Marquis that he later published as a preface to his own *Mérope*.[6]

"In the Italian *Merope*," he says, "the tone is far too naïve and bourgeois, and the taste of the French *parterre* is too refined and delicate to be pleased by pure and simple nature. It does not want to see nature except under certain artistic conditions, and these conditions are of course quite different in Paris than in Verona."[7] The whole letter is composed with the greatest *politesse*: Maffei has not erred in the least; all his oversights and shortcomings are attributed to the taste of his nation; these may even be considered beautiful, but beautiful, unfortunately, only for Italy. Surely one cannot criticize more courteously! But this desperate courtesy! Even a Frenchman will find it burdensome when his vanity suffers in the least thereby. Courtesy makes us appear gracious, but not great, and the Frenchman wishes to appear equally great and gracious.

And therefore, what follows M. de Voltaire's gallant dedication? The writing of a certain de la Lindelle, who writes as rudely of the good Maffei as Voltaire has been courteous.[8] This de la Lindelle has a style very much like that of Voltaire; it is too bad that such a good writer has not written more and has remained so unknown, besides.[9] But whether Lindelle is Voltaire or in fact really Lindelle, anyone who wants to see a French Janus-head that smiles in the most flattering way in front and makes the most sneering of faces in back should read both letters in one sitting.[10] I should not wish to have written either, but least of all both. Voltaire stands on this side of the truth out of courtesy, and Lindelle wanders far over to the other side out of a desire to denigrate. The former would have had to be more frank, and the latter more just, to avoid the suspicion that the same writer wanted to bring up again under a pseudonym what he had earlier forgiven under his own name.

Voltaire may give the Marquis as much credit as he pleases for being one of the first Italians who had enough courage and strength to write a tragedy without gallantry, in which the entire intrigue rests on a mother's love and the greatest tenderness springs from the purest of virtues.[11] He may complain as much as he likes that the false delicacy of his nation will not allow him to make use of the easiest and most natural means offered by the circumstances for building the intrigue, or of the unaffected and honest dialogue that the situation itself hands to the characters.[12] The Parisian *parterre* is undoubtedly quite wrong when it refuses to hear of a ring on stage again, ever since Boileau mocked the royal ring in his satires,* and when it consequently forces its playwrights to resort to every other means of recognition, even the most unsuitable, rather than use a ring, which the whole world from time immemorial has associated with a form of recognition, a form of affirmation of a person.[13] The *parterre* is quite wrong when it refuses to allow a young person – who considers himself to be the son of common parents and roams the land alone in search of adventure, and who has just committed a murder – to be taken for a robber, because it predicts that he must be the hero of the play;† and it is wrong to be offended that no one in the play wants to believe that such a man could possibly own a valuable ring, since there is not an ensign in the King's army who does not possess "*de belles Nippes.*"[14] The Parisian *parterre*, I say, is wrong on this and similar counts; but why, in cases where it is certainly not wrong, does Voltaire seem to wish to blame this *parterre* rather than Maffei? If French courtesy toward foreigners consists of agreeing with them even in those cases where they should be ashamed to be correct, then I do not know what is more offensive and rude to a free person than this French courtesy. The blather that Maffei puts into his trusty Polydorus's mouth about merry weddings and magnificent coronations that he has attended in the past, and just at the moment when the interest is at its peak and the spectators' imaginations are occupied by other things entirely: this Nestorian blather – Nestorian and misplaced, to boot – cannot be excused through differences of taste between different cultures and peoples.[15] The taste for this must be the same

---

* Je n'ai pu me servir comme [M. Maffei] d'un anneau, parce que depuis l'*anneau royal* dont Boileau se moque dans ses Satires, cela semblerait trop petit sur notre théâtre.

† Je n'oserais hasarder de faire prendre un héros pour un voleur, quoique la circonstance où il se trouve autorise cette méprise.

everywhere, and the Italian does not have his own taste, but rather none at all, if he does not yawn and become just as irritated by it as the Frenchman. Voltaire says to the Marquis, "In your tragedy you took the liberty of translating and using Virgil's beautiful and moving comparison:

> *Qualis populea moerens Philomela sub umbra*
> *Amissos queritur foetus . . .*[16]

If I were to take such a liberty, I would be sent back to the epic poem. For you cannot believe how strict the master is whom we must try to please – I mean our audience. They demand that in a tragedy it should always be the hero who speaks and never the poet, and they think that in critical incidents, in council gatherings, in a furious passion, or pressing danger, no kings, no ministers should ever make poetical comparisons."[17] But does this audience thus demand something wrong? Doesn't it mean that they care about the truth? Shouldn't every audience demand this and think exactly this way? An audience that judges otherwise does not deserve this name: but does Voltaire have to turn the entire Italian audience into such an audience because he does not have enough candor to tell the poet straight out that he indulges himself more than once and sticks his own head out from behind the curtains? Moreover, even if we overlook the fact that it is very difficult to find a suitable place for extensive comparisons in a tragedy in general, he should have noted that this one from Virgil is totally misused by Maffei. In Virgil, it intensifies compassion and is in fact suited to that purpose; in Maffei, however, it is uttered by the very person who triumphs over the unhappiness that it represents, and, in accord with Polyphontes' sentiments, it would have to arouse more scorn than compassion. Voltaire does not shy away from blaming even more significant errors – some that have an even greater effect on the whole – on the taste of Italians in general rather than on one single poet among them, and believes himself possessed of the finest manners when he offers Maffei the consolation that his whole nation does not understand this any better than he does; that his mistakes are the mistakes of his nation; that, however, the mistakes of a whole nation are not real mistakes, because it does not really matter what is actually good or bad but rather what the nation holds to be good or bad. "How should I have dared," he continues with a deep bow to the Marquis, and at the same time with a trick up his sleeve, "to let mere secondary characters speak with each other as you have? In your play, they serve to prepare the interesting scenes between the main characters; they are the avenues to a beautiful palace; but our impatient audience wants to be inside the palace immediately. We must keep in mind the taste of a people that has sated itself on masterpieces and is therefore quite spoiled."[18] What does this say, other than: "My Monsieur Marquis, your play has many, many cold, boring, useless scenes. But far be it from me to reproach you for it! Heaven forbid! I am a Frenchman, I know the rules, I will never rub something unpleasant under someone else's nose. Doubtless you wrote these cold, boring, useless scenes quite deliberately and with great effort, because they are exactly what your nation needs. I wish that I could get away just as tritely, but unfortunately my nation is so, so very far ahead that I must be even further ahead to satisfy my nation. On that account, I will not presume a great deal more about myself than you; but since my nation, which surpasses your nation so much . . . ." I shall not continue my paraphrase, for otherwise,

> *Desinit in piscem mulier formosa superne*:[19]

courtesy turns into *persiflage* (I use this French word because we Germans know nothing of this matter) and *persiflage* turns into senseless pride.[20]

Essay 42

22 September 1767[1]

It cannot be denied that a good portion of the errors that Voltaire seems to excuse in his predecessor as idiosyncrasies of Italian taste – only so that he can blame them on the Italian nation in general – I say that these and many more and greater errors are in Maffei's *Merope*.[2] In his youth Maffei had a great aptitude for poetry; he wrote verse with great ease in all the different styles of the most famous poets in his land; but this aptitude and ease are no indicators of the true genius required for tragedy. He then applied himself to history, criticism, and the study of the classics, and I am doubtful that these studies are the correct nourishment for the tragic genius. He was immersed in the study of church fathers and ecclesiastical documents, writing against Pfaffe and Basnage when, in response to social pressure, he took up his *Merope* and completed it in less than two months.[3] If this man had written a masterpiece amidst such occupations and in so short a time, either he must have had the most extraordinary mind, or a tragedy generally is a thing of very little account. Yet he was able to achieve what a man of learning and good classical taste can achieve who looks upon such a thing more as recreation than as work that is worthy of him. His structure is more labored and overwrought than felicitous; his characters are taken from the dissections of moralists or from famous examples in books rather than taken from life; his expression conveys more imagination than feeling; and we sense the litterateur and versifier everywhere but seldom the genius and poet.

As a versifier he is too eager in his pursuit of descriptions and similes. He has several excellent, faithful images which, if he were to speak them himself, could not be admired enough, but which, when spoken by his characters, are unbearable and degenerate into the most ludicrous nonsense. For example, it is certainly fitting that Aegisthus describe his fight with the robber whom he killed in elaborate detail, since his defense rests on these circumstances; but nobody would forgive even a cold, garrulous lawyer who spoke on his behalf, let alone Aegisthus himself, for giving the most detailed description of every miniscule phenomenon associated with the fall of a heavy body into the water – how it shoots in; the kind of noise with which it parts the water that then shoots high in the air; and how the river closes back over it – after confessing that he threw the corpse into the river.[*],[4] A person who stands before his judge and must defend his life has more important things in mind, such that he could not be so childishly exact in his story.

As litterateur he has shown too much deference for the simplicity with which ancient Greek customs and behaviors are depicted in Homer and Euripides, which definitely need to be – I will not say, ennobled, but rather – brought closer to our own if they are not to be more damaging than conducive to the tragedy's pathos. In addition, he has too deliberately tried to imitate beautiful passages from the ancients without making a distinction between the kind of work from which he has taken them and the kind of work into which he has brought them. In the epic, Nestor is a talkative, friendly old man; but the Polydorus modeled after him becomes, in the tragedy, a loathsome and sententious old windbag. If Maffei had really wanted to follow Euripides' supposed plan, the litterateur would have written something we would find completely laughable. He would have regarded it as his duty to use all of the little fragments left us from *Cresphontes* and to weave them faithfully into his play.[†],[5] Then, wherever he thought they fit best, he would have set them up as posts to guide and direct the path of his dialogue. What a pedantic constraint! And for what purpose? If it isn't these moral maxims that fill one's gaps, it will be others.

Nevertheless, there are in turn passages where we could wish that the litterateur had forgotten himself less. For example, after the recognition has occurred and Merope has realized that she has twice been in danger of murdering her own son, he has Ismene cry out in astonishment:[6] "What marvelous events, more marvelous than have ever been invented for the stage!"

> *Con così strani avvenimenti uom forse*
> *Non vide mai favoleggiar le scene.*[7]

Maffei did not remember that the story of his play took place in a time when theater had not yet been imagined, in the time before Homer, whose poems scattered the first seeds of drama. I would not hold this carelessness against anyone other than a person who thought it was necessary to excuse himself in the prologue for having

---

[*] Atto I. Sc. III.
   [. . .] in core
   Però mi venne di lanciar nel fiume
   Il morto, o semivivo; e con fatica
   (Ch' inutil' era per riuscire, e vana)
   L'alzai da terra, e in terra rimaneva
   Una pozza di sangue: a mezzo il ponte
   Portailo in fretta, di vermiglia striscia
   Sempre rigando il suol; quinci cadere
   Col capo in giù il lasciai: piombò, e gran tonfo
   S' udì nel profondarsi: in alto salse
   Lo spruzzo, e l'onda sopra lui si chiuse.

[†] Non essendo dunque stato mio pensiero di seguir la Tragedia d'Euripide, non ho cercato per conseguenza di porre nella mia que'sentimenti di essa, che son rimasti qua, e là; avendone tradotti cinque versi Cicerone, e recati tre passi Plutarco, e due versi Gellio, ed alcuni trovandosene ancora, se la memoria non m'inganna, presso Stobeo.

used the name Messene during a time when we know there was no city with this name, because Homer doesn't mention one. A poet may deal with such trivialities as he likes; we only ask that he remain consistent and not scruple over something in one place and brazenly dodge it in another, unless we are to believe that he offends more out of ignorance than out of willful disregard. Anyway, I would not like the cited lines even if they were not anachronistic. The tragic playwright should avoid anything that can remind the spectators of their illusion, for as soon as they are reminded of it, it is gone. Here it certainly seems as if Maffei would like to reinforce the illusion, insofar as he explicitly plants an image of "the theater" outside the theater, but the mere words "stage" and "invented" are already problematic and lead us precisely in the direction from which they were supposed to divert us. The comic playwright, by contrast, is allowed to compare his theatrics with other theatrics in this manner, because it does not demand the same degree of illusion to arouse our laughter as our compassion.

I have already mentioned what a hard time de la Lindelle gives Maffei.[8] According to his reckoning, Maffei made do with what his material had to offer on its own, without applying the least art to it: his dialogue has no verisimilitude, grace, or dignity; it is full of trivial and low matters that would hardly be tolerated in a farce, on Harlequin's turf; the whole thing abounds with inconsistencies and schoolboy mistakes. "In a word," he concludes, "Maffei's work has a very beautiful subject, but it is a very bad play. Everyone in Paris agrees that they could not have withstood its performance, and even in Italy sensible people think very little of it. During his travels, the author has vainly engaged the worst writers to translate his tragedy; he could more easily pay a translator than improve his play."[9]

Just as there are rarely compliments without any lies, so are there also rarely insults without any truth. In many of his points against Maffei, Lindelle is correct, and he may be as polite or rude as he pleases if he is content merely to criticize him. But he wants to trample him underfoot, destroy him, and he sets about it blindly and deceitfully. He is not ashamed to tell outright lies and commit blatant fraud just so he can provoke malicious laughter. Out of three blows he strikes, one misses the mark, and of the other two that graze or hit his opponent, one also unfailingly strikes the person for whom this tilting match is supposed to clear the way: Voltaire himself. Voltaire seems partly to have felt this and is consequently not remiss in defending Maffei, in his answer to Lindelle, on all those points where he believes he must also defend himself. All this correspondence with himself, it seems to me, is missing its most important bit: Maffei's answer. If only M. de Voltaire had shared this with us as well.[10] Or was it not quite what he hoped to coax out through his flattery? Did Maffei in fact presume to clarify instead for him the peculiarities of French taste? To show him why the French *Mérope* would be as little liked in Italy as the Italian one in France? –

Essay 43

25 September 1767[1]

One might well assume such a thing.[2] But I would rather prove what I have said myself than guess what others could have said.

To begin with, Lindelle's criticism can be softened on nearly every point. If Maffei has erred, he certainly has not always erred as clumsily as Lindelle would have us believe. He says, for example, that Aegisthus cries out: "Oh my old father!" when Merope is about to stab him. And that the Queen is so moved by these words, "old father," that she abandons her purpose and conceives the suspicion that Aegisthus might well be her son. Is this not, he adds scornfully, a very well-founded suspicion? For indeed, it is something quite unusual for a young man to have an old father! "Maffei," he continues, "wanted to use this mistake, this lack of art and genius, to improve on another mistake he had made in the first edition of his play. There Aegisthus cries out: 'Ah, Polydorus, my father!' And this Polydorus was the very man to whom Merope had entrusted her son. At the name Polydorus, the Queen would no longer have doubted whether Aegisthus was her son and the play would have been over. Now this mistake has been erased, but a much clumsier one has taken its place."[3] It is true, in the first edition Aegisthus calls his father Polydorus, but in later editions there is no mention of a father at all. The Queen hesitates only upon hearing Polydorus named as the man who had warned Aegisthus not to set foot in the territory of Messene. Moreover, she does not give up her purpose because of this, she merely demands further explanation, and before she can receive that, the king comes in. The king has Aegisthus unbound, and because he sanctions and praises the deed for which Aegisthus was brought in and promises to reward it as a real heroic deed, Merope must fall back on her original suspicion. Can the person Polyphontes wants to reward for having killed her son actually be her son? This conclusion must necessarily seem more important to her than a mere name. And now she regrets that for the sake of a name, one that of course many could bear, she has hesitated in her revenge:

> *Che dubitar? misera, ed io da un nome*
> *Trattener mi lasciai, quasi un tal nome*
> *Altri aver non potesse . . .*[4]

And the tyrant's subsequent remarks can only confirm her opinion that he must have the most reliable and complete information concerning her son's death. Is this then so completely hackneyed? I do not think so. Rather, I must confess that I do not find Maffei's improvement to be very necessary in the first place. Let Aegisthus say that his father's name is Polydorus after all! Whether it was his father or his friend who had that name and warned him against Messene does not matter much. It is enough that Merope, knowing that the tyrant has hunted her son so eagerly for so long, must presume despite any contradictions that the king's belief about him is more likely true than what she could infer from the mere coincidence of a name. Of course, if she knew the tyrant's belief – that Aegisthus is her son's murderer – was based on nothing more than her own suspicion, then that would be something else. But she does not know that; on the contrary, she has every reason to believe that he knows what he is talking about. – It goes without saying that I am not trying to pass off as beautiful something that can only be excused as necessity; the poet could certainly have constructed his plot with more subtlety. However, I do want to say that even in the way he has arranged things, Merope still does not act without sufficient reason, and it is quite possible and probable that Merope could persist in her resolution of revenge and attempt again to execute it at the first opportunity. What I confess that I find offensive is not that she comes a second time to kill her son as the murderer of her son but rather that she is prevented a second time from doing so by mere lucky chance. I would forgive the playwright for not developing Merope along principles of greater probability, because her passion could well sway her toward principles that are less probable. But I cannot forgive him for taking such liberty with coincidence and for being so lavish with the marvelous, like he would be with the most common, ordinary occurrences. That chance would render the mother such a pious service once, that may be; the more we like a surprise, the more likely it is that we will believe it. But that chance would prevent the same hasty act a second time in the same way no longer resembles coincidence; the same surprise that is repeated is no longer a surprise. Its monotony offends, and we are annoyed by the playwright who may know quite well how to be as whimsical as chance, but who is not nearly as diverse.

I will only list two of Lindelle's obvious and intentional falsifications. – "The fourth act," he says, "begins with a cold and unnecessary scene between the tyrant and Merope's confidante; immediately afterward, this confidante encounters the young Aegisthus, I myself know not how, and persuades him to retire in the vestibule so that once he has fallen asleep, the Queen can slay him at her leisure. He really does fall asleep, just as he has promised. Oh lovely! and the Queen comes a second time, axe in hand, to slay the young man, who sleeps expressly for that purpose. This same situation, repeated twice, betrays the most extreme sterility, and this young man's sleeping is so ridiculous that nothing could be more laughable."[5] But is it really true that the confidante persuades him to this sleep? Lindelle lies about that.[*,6] Aegisthus meets the confidante and asks her to reveal to him why the Queen is so furious with him. The confidante answers that she will gladly tell him everything, but important business calls her to be elsewhere right now; he should wait here a bit, she will be back soon. Without question, the confidante intends to deliver him into the Queen's hands; she persuades him to stay but not to sleep, and Aegisthus, who (in accord with his promise) stays, sleeps – not because he promised to sleep, but because he is tired, because it is night, because he does not see where else he will be able to spend the night but here.[†,7] – Lindelle's second lie is of the same sort. "After the old Polydorus

---

* And M. de Voltaire as well. For it is not just that Lindelle says: "ensuite cette suivante rencontre le jeune Egiste, je ne sais comment, et lui persuade de se reposer dans le vestibule, afin que, quand il sera endormi, la reine puisse le tuer tout à son aise," but M. de Voltaire himself also writes: "la confidente [sic] de Mérope engageât le jeune Egiste à dormir sur la scène, afin de donner le tems à la reine de venir l'y assassiner." I need not even say what can be deduced from this concurrence. It is rare for a liar to agree with himself, and when two liars agree with each other, it is surely a stacked deck.

† Atto IV. Sc. II
  EGI.   Ma di tanto furor, di tanto affanno
          Qual' ebbe mai cagion? – –
  ISM.   Il tutto
          Scoprirti io non ricuso; ma egli è d'uopo
          Che qui t'arresti per brev'ora: urgente

prevents her from the murder of her son," he says, "Merope asks him what kind of a reward he wants for it, and the old fool begs her to make him young again."[8] Begs her to make him young again? "The reward for my service," the old man answers, "is this service itself; is that I see you happy. What more could you give me? I need nothing, I ask for nothing. I could wish just one thing for myself, but it is neither in your power nor in the power of any mortal to grant it to me – that the burden of my years which weigh me down would be lightened, etc."[‡,9] Does that mean: lighten this burden of mine? Give me strength and youth again? I am not saying by any means that such a complaint about the discomforts of old age occurs here in the most suitable place, even though they are completely in character for Polydorus. But is every bit of awkwardness necessarily madness? And wouldn't Polydorus and his playwright have to be mad in the truest sense of the word, if the latter actually put in the former's mouth the request that Lindelle brazenly fabricates? He fabricates! Lies! Do such trivialities deserve such hard words? – Trivialities? If they were important enough to Lindelle to lie about, shouldn't they be important enough to a third person to point out that he has lied?

Essay 44

29 September 1767[1]

I now come to the criticism made by Lindelle that applies to Voltaire just as much as Maffei, for whom alone it was meant.[2] I will set aside the two points that Voltaire himself realized would rebound back upon him. – Lindelle had said that in Maffei's play, the signs by which Merope deduced that Aegisthus was her son's murderer were very weak and ignoble. Voltaire answers: "I cannot deny it; I think Maffei has shown more art than myself in the way he has Merope believe that her son is the murderer of her son. He could make use of a ring for this purpose, which I dare not, because

---

	Cura or mi chiama altrove.
EGI.	Io volentieri
	T'attendo quanto vuoi.
ISM.	Ma non partire
	E non far poi, ch'io qua ritorni indarno.
EGI.	Mia fe do in pegno; e dove gir dovrei? –

‡ Atto IV. Sc. VII

MER.	Ma quale, o mio fedel, qual potrò io
	Darti già mai mercè, che i merti agguagli?
POL.	Il mio stesso servir fu premio; ed ora
	M'è, il vederti contenta ampia mercede.
	Che vuoi tu darmi? io nulla bramo: caro
	Sol mi saria ciò, ch' altri dar non puote.
	Che scemato mi fosse il grave incarco
	De gli anni, che mi sta sul capo, e a terra
	Il curva, e preme sì, che parmi un monte –

ever since the royal ring that Boileau mocks in his satires, it would seem very trite in our theater."[3] But did Voltaire then have to choose an old suit of armor instead of a ring? When Narbas took the child with him, what in the world moved him to take his murdered father's armor as well?[4] So that Aegisthus, when grown, could get by with his father's old armor and not have to buy himself a new one? The farsighted old man! Did he also take some old clothes from the mother? Or did this just happen so that one day Aegisthus could be recognized by the armor? Was there really no other armor like it? Was it, perhaps, some kind of family armor that Vulcan himself had made for the great-grandfather?[5] An impenetrable armor? Or at least decorated with beautiful figures and symbols, by which Euricles and Merope could immediately recognize it again after fifteen years?[6] If that is the case, then of course the old man had to take it along, and M. de Voltaire has reason to require of him that even in such bloody confusion, in which another man would only have thought of the child, he could also think of such a useful furnishing! For even if Aegisthus already lost his father's kingdom, at least he did not also have to lose his father's armor, in which he could someday reconquer that kingdom. – Secondly, Lindelle had railed against Maffei's Polyphontes, who wants to marry Merope by hook or by crook. As if Voltaire's Polyphontes did not also want this! Voltaire answers him so: "Neither Maffei nor I have given urgent enough reasons to explain why Polyphontes absolutely must have Merope for his wife. That is perhaps a fault inherent in the source material, but I confess to you that I find such a flaw trivial if it awakens considerable interest."[7] No, the fault is not inherent in the source material. For in this circumstance Maffei had in fact adapted the original material. Why did Voltaire need to adopt this change, if he did not see any advantage in doing so? –

There are a number of points on which Voltaire might similarly have examined himself, but what father sees all his child's faults? The stranger, to whom they are obvious, does not need to have sharper eyes than the father; he only needs not to be the father. Let us suppose, then, that I am this stranger!

Lindelle alleges that Maffei often does not connect his scenes, that he often leaves the stage empty, that his characters often enter and exit without cause; these are all significant defects, which nowadays are no longer tolerated in even the lowest class of poets.[8] – These are significant defects? But that is generally the language of the French critic; I must allow him this if I do not want to start with him from the very beginning. As significant or insignificant as these defects may be, do we want to take Lindelle at his word that they are so rare among the poets of his nation? It is true, they are the ones who pride themselves on being the greatest adherents to the rules, but they are also the ones who either broaden these rules so much that it is hardly worth the effort anymore to set them out as rules, or they observe them in such a heavy-handed and forced way that it offends more to see them observed in this way than not at all.[*][9] In particular Voltaire is a master at making the chains of art so light and loose that he maintains full liberty to move as he wants; and yet he often moves

---

* This was, in part, also our Schlegel's opinion. "To tell the truth," he says in his "Thoughts on the Improvement of the Danish Theater," "the English, who do not boast of any unity of place, observe that unity for the most part much better than the French, who take great pride in observing Aristotle's

so awkwardly and heavily and makes such anxious contortions that one might think each of his limbs had its own ball and chain. It takes great effort for me to look at a work of genius from this perspective, but because it remains fashionable among the common class of critics to look at works from no other perspective than this one, and because this is the perspective from which the admirers of French theater clamor most loudly, I will first inspect it more closely before I join in that clamor.

1   The setting is Messene, in Mérope's palace. From the start, this is not the strict unity of place demanded by a Hédelin, according to the principles and examples of the ancient writers.[10] The setting need not be an entire palace but rather only part of a palace, as it can be seen from one given standpoint. Whether it is an entire palace, or an entire city, or an entire province is fundamentally the same inconsistency. But while we find no explicit mandate in the ancient writers, Corneille did stretch this rule to claim that a single city ought to suffice as unity of place.[11] He had to be this acquiescent if he wanted to justify his best plays in line with this rule. So what was allowed to Corneille must also be right for Voltaire. Thus, I will not object to the fact that the action has to be imagined first in the queen's chamber, then in this or that hall, then in the vestibule, and then in who knows what other place. It is just that he should have observed the same caution with these changes that Corneille recommended: namely, they must not occur in the same act, much less in the same scene. The location where the act begins should remain constant throughout the whole act; to change it completely in the very same scene, even just to broaden or narrow it, is the greatest inconsistency in the world. – The third act of *Mérope* may take place in an open space, under a colonnade, or in a hall that permits a view of Cresphontes' tomb in a recess, the tomb on which the Queen intends to execute Aegisthus with her own hand. Can one imagine anything worse than watching Euricles close off the recess as he leads Aegisthus away in the middle of the fourth scene? How does he close it? Does a curtain fall behind him? If ever the use of a curtain fit what Hédelin says about such curtains in general, it would be this one,[†] especially if we consider the reasons why Aegisthus must be led away so suddenly, why he

---

rules so exactly. That the decor of a scene not be changed is really the least important factor. But when we are given no clear reason why characters find themselves in one place rather than having remained where they were before; or why one character behaves like the owner and resident of a room in which, moments before, another character, also acting like the owner of the house, has conversed with himself or a confidant with equanimity, without any probable justification given for this occurrence; in short, when the characters only come into the indicated room or garden so that they can enter the stage: then the playwright, instead of writing 'The setting is a room in Climene's house,' would have done better simply to put under the list of characters: 'The setting is in the theater.' Or to speak seriously, it would have been far better if the author had followed the custom of the English and changed the scene from one house to another, thereby having the spectator follow his hero rather than putting his hero to the trouble of pleasing the spectator by showing up somewhere he does not belong."

†   On met des rideaux qui se tirent & retirent, pour faire que les Acteurs paroissent & disparoissent selon la necessité du Sujet – ces rideaux ne sont bons qu'à faire des couvertures pour berner ceux qui les on inventez, & ceux qui les approuvent. *Pratique du Théâtre* Liv. II. chap. 6.

must be whisked from our sight through this mechanism, which I will discuss later.[12] – Just such a curtain is raised in the fifth act. The first six scenes play out in a hall of the palace; in the seventh scene, we are suddenly supposed to get an open view into the temple, so that we can see a dead body in a bloody robe. Through what miracle? And was this sight really worth this miracle? It seems that the doors of this temple suddenly open, Mérope bursts through them with the entire populace behind her, and this is how we gain sight of the temple's interior. I understand: this temple was her widowed Royal Majesty's palace chapel, which abutted right against the hall and was connected to it, so that her Highness could always get to her place of devotion without getting her feet wet. But we should not only see them exit by this route but also enter; at the very least we should have seen Aegisthus do so, who, at the end of the fourth scene, has to run and must take the shortest path if eight lines later he is to have completed his deed.

Essay 45

2 October 1767[1]

2   M. de Voltaire has played equally fast and free with the unity of time.[2] Simply consider everything that is going on in his *Mérope* in one day, and tell me how many inconsistencies one has to imagine in the process. Let's take one full, natural day; let's even give it the extension to thirty hours that Corneille is willing to grant.[3] It is true, I see no physical limitations that would prevent all of the events from happening in this time period; but the moral limitations are that much greater. Admittedly, it is not impossible for a man to propose to a woman and marry her within twelve hours, particularly if he can use force to drag her to the altar. But when this happens, do we not need to know that such violent haste is justified by the most compelling and urgent reasons? If, on the contrary, there is no hint of such reasons, by what means, then, should what is merely physically possible become plausible to us? The state intends to elect a king; only Polyphontes and the absent Aegisthus can come into consideration; in order to nullify Aegisthus's claims, Polyphontes intends to marry his mother; on the very day the election is to happen, he makes his proposal; the election proceeds and comes out in his favor; Polyphontes is now king, and we should understand that Aegisthus might now reappear when he will, and the newly elected king could put up with it for a time. But instead, Polyphontes insists on the marriage and insists, moreover, that it be performed that very day, the very same day he offered his hand to Mérope for the first time, the very same day that the people proclaimed him king. Such an old soldier, and such a hot-blooded suitor! But his courtship is nothing but politics. So much the worse that he so badly mistreats the woman he wants to use to his benefit. Mérope had denied him her hand before he was king, when she had to believe that her hand in marriage would be instrumental to helping him to the throne. But now he is king, and became so without basing it on the title of being her husband; let him repeat his proposal, and perhaps she submits; let him give her time to forget the distance that previously existed

between them and to get used to considering him as her equal, and maybe it will take only a little time. If he cannot win her, what is the point of forcing her? Will it remain a secret to her supporters that she has been forced? Will they not feel compelled to hate him for this? Will they not also regard themselves as bound to join in Aegisthus's cause as soon as he appears and, for his sake, to fight for his mother's cause as well? Never mind that, after fifteen long years of diligent seeking, fate has now delivered this Aegisthus himself into the hands of the tyrant and has thereby offered him the means to possess the throne, free of all other claims, a means that is much quicker and much more infallible than the marriage with the mother; no, he should and must be married, today, this evening; the new king will sleep with the old queen this very night, or else! Can we imagine anything more preposterous? In theory, I mean; for it is obviously out of the question that a person with even a spark of sense could behave this way. Now how does it help the playwright, if the particular events of a given act do not need much more time to occur than it takes to perform the act itself, and that this time, together with what must be added in for the intervals, is far from requiring a full circuit of the sun: has he thereby observed the unity of time? He has fulfilled the letter of the law but not its spirit. For what he makes happen in one day can indeed be done in one day, but no reasonable person will do it in one day. It is not enough to observe the physical unity of time; the moral unity must be considered as well, as each and every one of us is sensitive to its violation. In contrast, the violation of the physical unity of time is not always as generally offensive, even though it usually involves an impossibility, because this impossibility can remain unknown to many. If, for example, there is a journey from one place to another in a play, and this journey alone requires more than one day, the error is only noticeable to those who know the distance from the first place to the second. While not every person knows geographical distances, everyone can notice for himself what kind of actions need just one day and what kind should take longer. The playwright who only understands how to observe the physical unity of time through a violation of the moral unity and does not scruple to sacrifice the latter to the former works against his own interests and sacrifices the essential to the coincidental. – Maffei at least enlists a night to help out, and the wedding that Polyphontes suggests to Merope today is not performed until the following morning. In addition, in his play it does not take place on the same day that Polyphontes ascends to the throne; as a result, the events are not as closely condensed; they hurry along, but they are not rushed. Voltaire's Polyphontes is a mayfly of a king who does not deserve to rule a second day because he begins his first day in such a completely inept and ill-advised manner.[4]

3 Lindelle says that Maffei often does not join his scenes together, and the stage remains empty, a mistake that nowadays is no longer tolerated in even the lowest class of poets.[5] "The connecting of scenes," Corneille says, "is a great ornament of a poem, and nothing can better assure us of the continuity of action than the continuity of the performance. But it is only an ornament, and not a rule, for the ancients did not always subject themselves to it, etc."[6] What? Has tragedy among the French become so much more perfected since their great Corneille,

that what he simply regarded as a missing ornament is now an unforgivable mistake? Or have the French, since his time, learned to misunderstand the essentials of tragedy so much further that they give enormous value to things that are, at base, worthless? Until this question is resolved, Corneille should be at least as credible as Lindelle, and that which, according to Corneille, is no outright error in Maffei can be balanced against the less debatable one in Voltaire, which is that he often leaves the stage full for a longer time than he should. When in the first act, for example, Polyphontes comes to the Queen, and she exits at the end of the third scene, what right does Polyphontes have to remain in the Queen's chamber? Is this chamber the place where he should so freely express himself to his confidant? The playwright's need betrays itself all too clearly in the fourth scene, when we learn things that we certainly need to know but in a place where we never would have expected to do so.

4   Maffei often does not give any motivation for the entrances and exits of his characters; just as often, Voltaire gives a false motivation, which really is worse. It is not enough for a person to say why he comes in; we must also perceive from the context that he must come in for that reason. It is not enough for him to say why he exits; we must also see in what follows that he really has left for that purpose. Otherwise, what the playwright puts in the character's mouth is just an excuse and not a cause. For example, when Euricles exits in the third scene of the second act in order to, as he says, gather the Queen's friends, then we ought to hear something afterwards about these friends and this gathering.[7] But because we do not hear anything of the sort, what he says is an immature *Peto veniam exeundi*, with the first best lie that occurs to the boy.[8] He does not leave in order to do what he says but rather so that, a few lines later, he can return with information that the poet could find no other way to share. Voltaire is even clumsier in his handling of the ends of whole acts. At the end of the third, Polyphontes tells Merope that the altar awaits her, that everything is ready for their solemn union; and he exits with a "Venez, Madame."[9] But Madame does not follow him, and instead exits with an exclamation through another wing. Then Polyphontes begins the fourth act, and, rather than expressing his displeasure that the Queen did not follow him into the temple (for he had been mistaken; there was still time before the marriage ceremony), he instead blabbers again with this Erox about things that he should have chitchatted about in the privacy of his own house and his own rooms, rather than here.[10] Now, the fourth act ends exactly like the third. Polyphontes summons the Queen to the temple again, Mérope herself cries out,

>   *Courons tous vers le temple où m'attend mon outrage;*[11]

and says to the sacrificial priests, who are to take her there,

>   *Vous venez à l'autel entraîner la victime.*[12]

Consequently, at the beginning of the fifth act they will surely be in the temple, if not already returned from it? Neither of these; good things take time. Polyphontes has forgotten something and returns one more time and then also sends the Queen away again. Excellent! Between the third and fourth and between the fourth and fifth acts, not only does what should happen not happen, but in fact nothing happens at all, and the third and fourth acts only end so that the fourth and fifth can begin.

Essay 46

6 October 1767[1]

It is one thing to acknowledge the rules; it is another to really observe them.[2] The French do the former; only the ancients seem to have understood the latter.

Unity of action was the first dramatic law among the ancients; the unity of time and unity of place were both only consequences of that first law, which they would not have observed more than absolutely necessary had the incorporation of the chorus not occurred.[3] But because their actions required a crowd of people as witnesses, and because this crowd always remained the same and could neither distance themselves from their homes nor remain outside longer than one normally would out of mere curiosity, the ancients could hardly do otherwise than to limit the location to a single individual spot and the time to one single day. They then submitted to this restriction *bona fide*, but with a flexibility, with an understanding that seven times out of nine they won far more than they lost by doing so. For they let this constraint induce them to simplify the action itself so much and to exclude everything superfluous with such care, that, reduced to its most essential elements, it became nothing other than an ideal of this action, which developed most successfully into precisely the form that demanded the very least addition of circumstances of time and place.

On the other hand, the French – who developed no taste for the true unity of action and who had already been spoiled by the wild intrigues of Spanish plays before they became acquainted with Greek simplicity – saw the unities of time and place not as consequences of unity of action but as absolutely essential requirements in and of themselves to the presentation of an action, which they would also have to make work in their richer and more complicated plots with the same strictness that only the use of the chorus (which they had already completely abolished) could require. But because they discovered how difficult, in fact how often impossible this was, they made a deal with the tyrannical rules that they did not have courage enough to break away from. Instead of a single place, they introduced an uncertain place, in which one might imagine himself now here, now there, as long as all these places were not too far apart and none needed particular scenery, so that the same scenery could serve the one just about as well as the other. Instead of the unity of a day they substituted the unity of duration and allowed a certain period of time to count for a day as long as, however much and sundry might occur, we do not hear of a sunrise or sunset and nobody goes to bed (or at least does not go to bed more than once).

Nobody would have held this against them, for excellent plays can still be written accordingly, and as the proverb goes, drill the wood where it is thinnest. – But then I must at least allow my neighbor to drill there too. I must not always show him the thickest edge or the knottiest part of the board and shout: drill through it there for me!

that's where I usually drill! – Nevertheless, that is how all the French critics cry out, especially when they write of dramatic works from England. What a fuss they make over conformity to the rules, which they have made infinitely easier for themselves! – But it is making me nauseous to keep lingering on these items.

As far as I am concerned, Voltaire's *Mérope* and Maffei's *Merope* could last for eight days and play out in seven locations in Greece! If only they had the refinements that would make me forget these pedantries!

The most strict conformance to the rules cannot offset the smallest mistakes in the characters. It did not escape Lindelle how crudely Maffei's Polyphontes often speaks and acts. He is right to mock the awful maxims Maffei puts into his tyrant's mouth.[4] To eliminate the country's best and most noble; to enthrall the people in all those sensual pleasures that could weaken them and make them effeminate; to let the worst crimes go unpunished under the pretense of compassion and mercy; and so on: if there is a tyrant who adopts this insane manner of governing, will he go so far as to boast of it? This is how one depicts tyrants in a school exercise, but no one to date has ever really spoken of himself in such a way.[*,5] – It is true, Voltaire does not have his Polyphontes declaim in such a cold, lunatic manner, but now and again he has him say things that no man of this type would ever allow to cross his lips. For example:

> . . . *Des Dieux quelquefois la longue patience*
> *Fait sur nous à pas lents descendre la vengeance . . .*[6]

A Polyphontes probably ought to make this observation, but he never does. Still less will he make it in the same moment that he spurs himself to new crimes:

> *Eh bien, encor ce crime! . . .*[7]

---

* Atto III. Sc. II.
  . . . Quando
  Saran da poi sopiti alquanto, e queti
  Gli animi, l'arte del regnar mi giovi.
  Per mute oblique vie n'andranno a Stige
  L'alme più audaci, e generose. A i vizi,
  Per cui vigor si abbatte, ardir si toglie,
  Il freno allargherò. Lunga clemenza
  Con pompa di pietà farò, che splenda
  Su i delinquenti; a i gran delitti invito,
  Onde restino i buoni esposti, e paghi
  Renda gl'iniqui la licenza; ed onde
  Poi fra se distruggendosi, in crudeli
  Gare private il lor furor si stempri.
  Udrai sovente risonar gli editti,
  E raddopiar le leggi, che al sovrano
  Giovan servate, e transgredite. Udrai
  Correr minaccia ognor di guerra esterna;
  Ond' io n'andrò su l'atterrita plebe
  Sempre crescendo i pesi, e peregrine
  Milizie introdurrò.

I have already touched on how carelessly and heedlessly he acts toward Mérope. His behavior toward Aegisthus even less resembles the cunning and decisive man that the playwright depicts for us from the beginning. Aegisthus really should not have been compelled to appear at the sacrifice. What is he supposed to do there? Pledge his allegiance? Before the people? Amidst the cries of his despairing mother? Won't precisely what Polyphontes himself had earlier feared now inevitably happen?[†,8] He has every reason to fear Aegisthus; Aegisthus need only demand his sword back to decide the battle between them at once; and he lets this daredevil Aegisthus come so near to him on the altar, where it's likely that the first thing he'll get his hands on will be a sword? Maffei's Polyphontes is free from this absurdity; he does not know Aegisthus and takes him for his friend. So why wouldn't Aegisthus have been allowed to approach him at the altar? Nobody was watching his movements; the blow had been struck and he was ready for the second before it could occur to anyone to avenge the first.

"When, in Maffei's play, Merope learns that her son was murdered," Lindelle writes, "she wants to rip the murderer's heart from his chest and tear it to pieces with her teeth.[‡,9] In other words, to comport herself like a cannibal and not like a grieving mother; decency ought always to be observed."[10] Quite right, but although the French Mérope is too delicate to bite straightaway into a raw heart, it seems to me she is fundamentally just as much a cannibal as the Italian one. –

Essay 47

9 October 1767[1]

And how is that? – If it is indisputable that we must judge people more by their actions than by their words, and that a rash word uttered in the heat of passion indicates little about a person's moral character, whereas a premeditated action indicates everything, then I am likely right.[2] A Merope who succumbs to the most anxious

---

† Acte I. Sc. 4.
  Si ce fils, tant pleuré, dans Messène est produit,
  De quinze ans de travaux j'ai perdu tout le fruit.
  Crois-moi, ces préjugés de sang et de naissance
  Revivront dans les coeurs, y prendront sa défense.
  Le souvenir du père, et cent rois pour aïeux,
  Cet honneur prétendu d'être issu de nos dieux;
  Les cris, le désespoir d'une mère éplorée,
  Détruiront ma puissance encor mal assurée.
‡ Atto II. Sc. 6
  Quel scelerato in mio poter vorrei,
  Per trarne prima, s'ebbe parte in questo
  Assassinio il Tiranno; io voglio poi
  Con una scure spalancargli il petto,
  Voglio strappargli il cor, voglio co' denti
  Lacerarlo, e sbranarlo.

misery in her uncertainty over the fate of her son, who always prepares for the worst, and in imagining how unhappy her absent son might be, extends her compassion to all unhappy people: this is the beautiful ideal of a mother. A Merope who, in the moment that she learns of the loss of the object of her devotion, sinks to the ground numbed by pain, then suddenly rallies again as soon as she hears that the murderer is in her power, and rants and raves and threatens to perform the most bloody and terrible revenge on him, and would really carry it out if he ever fell into her hands: this is also the same ideal, only in a state of violent action that gains in expression and power what it loses in beauty and emotion. But a Mérope who takes her time for this revenge, prepares for it beforehand, arranges ceremonies for it, and wants herself to be the executioner, not to kill but to torture, not to punish but so that her eyes can feast on punishment: is this still a mother? Yes, perhaps, but a mother as we might imagine one to be among the cannibals; a mother like every she-bear is. – A person may like Mérope's action if he wants; he should just not tell me that he does, if I am not to despise him as much as I loathe him.

Perhaps M. de Voltaire would like to attribute this, as well, to a fault inherent in the source material; perhaps he would like to say, Merope must want to kill Aegisthus with her own hands or the whole *coup de théâtre* so praised by Aristotle, which so enraptured the sensitive Athenians of his times, would fall away.[3] But M. de Voltaire would be wrong once again, and have once again taken Maffei's arbitrary changes for the original subject itself. The original material does indeed demand that Merope should wish to murder Aegisthus with her own hand, but it by no means demands that she must do it with full deliberation. Notably, she does not appear to have done it in such a way in Euripides, if we are permitted to assume Hyginus's fable is an excerpt from his play.[4] The old man comes weeping to the queen and says that her son has left him; she had just heard that a stranger has arrived who boasts of having killed him and that this stranger is sleeping peacefully under her roof; she seizes the very first thing that comes to hand, hurries angrily to the sleeper's room, the old man following her, and the recognition happens in the moment in which the crime should occur. That was very simple and natural, very moving and human! The Athenians trembled for Aegisthus without being allowed to loathe Merope. They trembled for Merope herself, who ran the risk of becoming her son's murderer through the most well-intentioned haste. But Maffei and Voltaire only make me tremble for Aegisthus, because I am so annoyed with their Merope that I almost wish she had completed the deed. If only she had! If she can take time for her revenge, she should have also taken time for investigation. Why is she such a bloodthirsty beast? He killed her son: good, she can do what she wants to the murderer in the first heat of the moment, I forgive her, she is a person and a mother; and I will readily lament and despair with her when she realizes how much she regrets her first rash passion. But Madame, a young man who had interested you so much a moment earlier and in whom you recognized so many signs of honesty and innocence – to want to slaughter him with your own hand as your son's murderer on his father's tomb, to call on the aid of guards and priests, because he is found possessing an old suit of armor that only your son ought to wear – oh, fie, Madame! If I am not much mistaken, they would have booed you off the stage in Athens.

I have already mentioned that the impropriety with which Polyphontes demands marriage after fifteen years with the now much older Merope is not a fault inherent in the source material.[5] For according to Hyginus's fable, Polyphontes had married Merope right after the murder of Cresphontes, and it is easy to believe that even Euripides had adopted this circumstance. And why should he not have? The very same reasons that Voltaire's Euricles gives to coax Mérope to marry the tyrant now, after fifteen years, might have coaxed her to it fifteen years before.[*,6] It was very common among ancient Greek women to overcome their disgust toward the murderers of their husbands and take them as their second husbands when they saw that the children from their first marriage could gain an advantage thereby. I remember having read something similar in the Greek romance by Chariton that was published by d'Orville, in which a mother makes the decision for the sake of her unborn baby in a very moving way.[7] I think the passage deserves to be cited, but I do not have the book to hand. Enough that what Voltaire himself gives Euricles to say would have been sufficient to justify his Mérope's behavior, had he introduced her as Polyphontes' wife. As a result the cold scenes of political love would have been dropped, and I see more than one means by which our interest could have been far better engaged and the situations made much more intriguing because of this circumstance.

But Voltaire absolutely wanted to stay on the trail Maffei had blazed for him, and because it did not even once occur to him that there could be a better one, that this better one was in fact the one that had been trod in ancient times, he contented himself with clearing from its track a couple of minor stones over which he believed his predecessor had nearly stumbled. Would he otherwise have also retained this from Maffei – that Aegisthus, unaware of his true identity, must land completely by chance in Messene, and then, in that very place, and as a result of minor, ambiguous clues,

---

* Acte II. Sc. I

MER: Non, mon fils ne le souffrirait pas.
L'exil, où son enfance a langui condamnée,
Lui serait moins affreux que ce lâche hyménée.
EUR: Il le condamnerait, si, paisible en son rang,
Il n'en croyait ici que les droits de son sang;
Mais si par les malheurs son âme était instruite,
Sur ses vrais intérêts s'il réglait sa conduite,
De ses tristes amis s'il consultait la voix,
Et la nécessité, souveraine des lois,
Il verrait que jamais sa malheureuse mère
Ne lui donna d'amour une marque plus chère.
MER: Ah! que me dites-vous?
EUR: De dure vérités,
Qui m'arrachent mon zèle et vos calamités.
MER: Quoi! Vous me demandez que l'intérêt surmonte
Cette invincible horreur que j'ai pour Polifonte!
Vous, qui me l'avez peint de si noires couleurs!
EUR: Je l'ai peint dangereux, je connais ses fureurs;
Mais il est tout-puissant; mais rien ne lui résiste;
Il est sans héritier, et vous aimez Egiste.

fall under suspicion of being his own murderer? In Euripides, Aegisthus knew exactly who he was and came to Messene with revenge as his express purpose and gave himself out to be the murderer of Aegisthus; he only failed to reveal himself to his mother, whether out of caution or mistrust or some other reason – the poet will certainly not have left him wanting for reasons.[8] Previously I lent Maffei some reasons of my own for all of the changes he made to Euripides' plot.[9] But I am very far from declaring the reasons sufficiently important and the changes sufficiently successful. Rather, I contend that every step he ventured that strayed from the footsteps of the Greeks became a misstep. That Aegisthus does not know who he is, that he comes to Messene by accident and is taken for Aegisthus's murderer "per combinazione d'accidenti" (as Maffei puts it): this does not only give the whole story a very confused, ambiguous, and fanciful character but also profoundly weakens the impact.[10] In Euripides, the spectator knew from Aegisthus himself that he is Aegisthus, and the more certainly he knew that Merope was coming to kill her own son, the necessarily greater must have been the terror that seized him and the more afflicting must have been the compassion he knew he would feel if Merope were not prevented in time from executing the deed.[11] In Maffei and Voltaire, on the other hand, we only suppose that the presumed murderer of the son might well be the son himself, and our greatest terror is saved for the one moment in which it ceases to be terror. The worst thing about it is this: the reasons that lead us to guess that the young stranger is Merope's son are precisely the reasons why Merope herself should guess it and, especially in Voltaire's play, we do not know him in any way, shape, or form better than she herself could. So we either trust these reasons just as much as Merope trusts them, or we trust them more. If we trust them just as much, then, along with her, we take the young man for a liar, and the fate she intends for him cannot move us very much. If we trust them more, then we blame Merope for not paying better attention to them and for allowing herself to be carried away by far shallower reasons. Neither suffices.

Essay 48

13 October 1767[1]

It is true that our surprise is greater when we do not learn with full certainty that Aegisthus is Aegisthus until Merope herself does.[2] But please: the paltry pleasure of surprise! And why does a playwright need to surprise us? He can surprise his characters as much as he likes; we will get our share, even if we have already long foreseen what must hit them wholly unexpectedly. Indeed, our share will be so much the stronger and more vivid, the longer and more certainly we have seen it coming.

On this point I will let the best French critic speak for me.[3] "In complex plays," Diderot says* "the interest is more the effect of the plot than the speeches; in simple plays, on the other hand, it is more the effect of the speeches than the plot. But whose

---

* In his *Discourse on Dramatic Poetry*, after *The Father of the Family*; p. 327 of the trans.

interest is of most concern? That of the characters? Or the audience? The audience members are only witnesses, about whom we know nothing. Then it is the characters we must keep in mind. Without doubt![4] Let them tighten the knot without knowing it – let everything be impenetrable for them; bring them, without their noticing it, closer and closer to the resolution. As long as they are agitated, we spectators will surrender to the same agitation, we will have to feel it as well. – I am far from thinking with the majority of critics who have written about the art of dramatic writing that the resolution must be hidden from the spectator. On the contrary, I thought that it would not be beyond my capacity if I undertook to write a work in which the resolution would be revealed in the very first scene, and the most intense interest would arise out of this very circumstance. – Everything must be clear for the spectator. He is the confidant of every single character – he knows everything that will occur and everything that has already occurred; and there are a hundred moments where one cannot do better than to tell him directly what is going to happen. – Oh, you inventors of general rules, how little you understand the art, and how little you possess of the genius that produced the models on which you established those rules and can violate them at will! – One may find my thoughts to be as paradoxical as one likes; this much I know for certain: that for every single occasion in which it is useful to hide an important incident from the spectator until it comes to pass, there are always ten or more in which his engagement demands the exact opposite. – The poet achieves a brief surprise by means of his secret; think of what prolonged suspense he could have pitched us into had he not made a surprise out of it![5] I can only pity for an instant someone who is hit and struck down in an instant. But what becomes of me if I expect the blow, if I see a violent storm gathering over my own head or someone else's, which hovers there for a length of time? – As far as I am concerned, the characters do not need to know each other, as long as the spectators know all of them. – Indeed, I would almost argue that material needing such concealments is thankless material, and a plot that takes refuge in such concealments is not as good as one that could have dispensed with them. They will never give rise to something dynamic. In that case, we will always have to occupy ourselves with preparations that are either far too obscure or far too obvious. The whole piece will become a web of little artifices by which one can produce nothing more than a brief surprise. If, on the other hand, everything that concerns the characters is known, then I see in this possibility the source of the most powerful emotions. – Why do certain monologues have such a great effect? It is because they confide a character's secret designs to me, and in that instant this confidence fills me with fear or hope. – If the characters' state is unknown, the spectator cannot take a stronger interest in the action than the characters do. But the spectator's interest will double if he has sufficient insight and feels that the actions and speeches would be completely different if the characters knew each other. Only then will I tremble in expectation of what will become of them, when I can compare what they really are to what they do or want to do."[6]

Applying this to Aegisthus, it is clear which of the two plots Diderot would favor: whether the old one in Euripides, in which from the very beginning the spectator knows Aegisthus as well as he knows himself; or the new one by Maffei that Voltaire so blindly adopted, in which Aegisthus is a mystery to both himself and the spectator and consequently makes the whole play a "web of little artifices" that can produce nothing but a brief surprise.[7]

Diderot is also not completely wrong in characterizing as both new and well-established his thoughts about the expendability and insignificance of all vague expectations and sudden surprises intended for the audience. His thoughts are new with respect to their abstraction but very old with respect to the models from which they have been abstracted. His thoughts are new considering that his predecessors only urged the opposite; but neither Aristotle nor Horace were among these predecessors, and nothing slipped from the pens of these two that could have reinforced their successive interpreters in their predilection for that opposite, the positive effects of which they had perceived in neither the majority of ancient plays nor the best of them.

Euripides in particular was so confident that he nearly always showed spectators, in advance, the goal toward which he wanted to lead them. Indeed, I am very inclined, because of this, to undertake a defense of his prologues, which so displease modern critics. "It is not enough," Hédelin says, "that he has one of his main characters tell the audience virtually everything that has happened before the action of the play, in order to make what follows understandable; he also often uses a god for this purpose, whom we must assume knows everything and through whom he makes known not only what has happened but also everything that is going to happen. Consequently, right at the beginning we learn the resolution and the whole catastrophe, and we see each incident coming far in advance. This is, however, a very pronounced mistake completely at odds with the suspense and expectation that should constantly reign in the theater; it destroys all the charms of the play, which are based almost solely on novelty and surprise."[†,8] No: the most tragic of all the tragic poets did not think so little of his art; he knew that it was capable of a much higher perfection, and that satisfying a childish curiosity was the least to which it could aspire.[9] Thus without a qualm he allowed his audience to know as much about the coming action as ever a god could know, obliging himself to generate the emotion he wanted not through what would occur, but through the manner in which it would occur. Therefore nothing really ought to offend the critics here, except for the following: that he has not sought to convey the necessary knowledge of the past and future through a more subtle device, that he used a higher being for this purpose, who has no other role in the action, and that he has this higher being speak directly to the audience, thereby mixing the dramatic genre with the narrative.[10] If, then, they limited their criticism to this alone, what would be their criticism? Is the useful and necessary never welcome unless it comes at us in a furtive way? Are there not things, especially in the future, that only a god can know? And if the audience's engagement depends on such things, is it not better that we learn of them beforehand through the intervention of a god than not at all? And finally, what is really meant by the mixing of genres? In textbooks they are distinguished as precisely as possible from each other; but if a genius with higher purposes allows several of them to flow together in one and the same work, we should forget the textbook and simply ask whether he has achieved these higher purposes.

---

† *Pratique du Théâtre* Lib. III. chap. I.

What does it matter to me if a play by Euripides is neither wholly a narrative nor wholly a drama? Call it a hybrid if you like; it is enough that this hybrid pleases and edifies me more than the rule-bound creations of your proper Racines, or whoever else they might be. Just because the mule is neither a horse nor a donkey, is he any less useful as a pack animal?

Essay 49

16 October 1767[1]

In a nutshell: where Euripides' critics believe they see nothing but a poet who makes his work as easy as possible out of convenience, or ineptitude, or both, and where they believe they find the art of drama in its infancy, I see it as having reached the height of perfection and admire Euripides as a master who essentially adheres to rules exactly as much as necessary and only appears to diverge from those rules because he wants to give his plays an additional beauty that exceeds their bounds.[2]

For it is clear that all of the plays whose prologues are such an irritation are perfectly complete and perfectly understandable without these prologues. For example, delete Mercury's prologue from *Ion*, or Polydorus's from *Hecuba*, and let the first begin with Ion's morning prayers, the second with Hecuba's complaints: are they in the least bit maimed thereby?[3] How would you miss what you have deleted, if it were not there at all? Does the whole not retain the same course, the same coherence? Suppose we admit that, according to your way of thinking, the plays would be even more beautiful if we did not know from the prologue that Ion, whom Creusa wants to have poisoned, is Creusa's son and that Creusa, who wants to drag Ion from the altar to a shameful death, is Ion's mother, and if we did not know that on the very day that Hecuba must surrender her daughter in sacrifice, the unhappy old woman will also learn of the death of her last and only remaining son. For all of this would provide the most splendid surprises, and in addition these surprises would be properly prepared for; you could not say that they broke like lightning out of clear skies, or that they did not follow but simply arose, or that something was suddenly imposed upon you rather than discovered by you. And yet you still quarrel with the poet? You still accuse him of a lack of art? Forgive him one mistake that is rectified with the stroke of a pen. The gardener quietly prunes a rampant shoot without chiding the healthy tree that sprouted it. Assume for a moment – it is true, this means assuming a great deal – that perhaps Euripides could have had just as much insight and taste as you, and that you find it that much more surprising that he still could have made such a gross mistake with such great insight and refined taste; suppose all this with me and regard what you call a mistake from my point of view. Euripides saw just as well as we do that, for example, his *Ion* could exist without the prologue, that on its own it was a play that maintained the suspense and expectation of the audience to the end. But this suspense and expectation were of no importance to him. For if the audience first discovered in the fifth act that Ion is Creusa's son, then, to them, it is not her son but a stranger, an enemy, whom she wants to get rid of in the third act; and it is not Ion's mother against whom Ion wants vengeance in the fourth act but merely an assassin. In that case, where shall terror and compassion come from?[4] The mere conjecture that might be drawn somehow from coincidental circumstances, namely that Ion and Creusa might possibly be more closely related to each other than they think, would not have been sufficient for that purpose. This conjecture had to become certainty, and if the audience could only obtain this certainty from outside, if it was not possible to glean it from one of the characters themselves, was it then not better for the poet to convey it by the only means possible than not at all? Say what you will about this means; it suffices that it helped him achieve his goal, which is why his tragedy is what a tragedy should be; and if you are still indignant that he has sacrificed the form to the substance, then seek out for your learned criticism only plays in which the substance is sacrificed to the form, and you will be rewarded! Go ahead and enjoy Whitehead's *Creusa*, in which no god predicts anything, in which you learn everything from a prattling old confidant who is interrogated by a sly gypsy-woman; go ahead and like it better than Euripides' *Ion*, and I will never envy you![5]

When Aristotle called Euripides the most tragic of all tragic poets, he was not merely looking at the fact that most of his plays have a calamitous catastrophe (although I know that many interpret the Stagirite in this way).[6] This artistic device could have been quickly imitated, and the bungler who did a good job of strangling and murdering and allowed none of his characters to leave the stage sound or alive would be permitted to consider himself just as tragic as Euripides. No question about it, Aristotle had numerous qualities in mind that justified conferring this title on Euripides. Without doubt the aforementioned quality belonged among them, by virtue of which Euripides showed the spectators far in advance all of the misfortune that should surprise his characters, in order to fill the spectators with compassion for characters at a point when the characters themselves are far from believing they warrant compassion. – Socrates was Euripides' teacher and friend, and many seem to hold the opinion that the only thing the poet took from this friendship with the philosopher was the abundance of beautiful moral maxims that he scatters so lavishly throughout his plays.[7] I think he owes much more to this friendship. Without it he might well have been just as rich in sayings, but he might never have been so tragic. Beautiful sentences and morals are, in general, precisely what we hear the least from a philosopher like Socrates: his way of life is the only moral he preaches. But to know humankind and ourselves, to be attentive to our feelings, to determine and love the smoothest and shortest paths of nature in everything, and to judge everything according to its purpose – this is what we learn in his company, this is what Euripides learned from Socrates, and what made him first in his art. Fortunate the poet who has such a friend, – and can consult him any time, day or night! –

Voltaire, too, apparently sensed that it would be good if he introduced Mérope's son to us right at the beginning, if he could set us off immediately knowing that the appealing, unfortunate youth, whom Mérope initially takes under her protection and shortly thereafter wants to execute as the murderer of her Aegisthus, is this very same Aegisthus. But the youth does not know his own identity; moreover, there is nobody else there who knows him better and through whom we could learn who he is. What does the poet do, then? How does he ensure that we know with certainty that Mérope is raising a dagger against her own son even before old Narbas cries out?[8] Oh, he does it very cleverly! Only a Voltaire could have come up with such a device! – As soon as the unknown youth enters, he puts the full name Aegisthus in big, beautiful, distinct letters above his first speech and above each of his subsequent speeches.[9] Now we know it; Mérope has already called her son by this name more than once in the previous scene, and even if she had not, we would only need to look at the list of characters printed in front – there it stands, in great detail! Of course it is a bit ridiculous when the character, above whose speeches we have now read the name Aegisthus over ten times, when asked:

> . . . *Narbas vous est connu?*
> *Le nom d'Egiste au moins jusqu'à vous es venu?*
> *Quel était votre état, votre rang, votre père?*[10]

answers:

> *Mon père est un vieillard accablé de misère;*
> *Policlète est son nom; mais Egiste, Narbas,*
> *Ceux dont vous me parlez, je ne les connais pas.*[11]

Admittedly, it is very odd that we also do not hear any other name for this Aegisthus whose name is not Aegisthus; that, when he tells the queen his father's name is Polycletes, he does not also add that his name is so and so. For he must have a name, and M. de Voltaire surely could have invented one for him, since he has invented so much! Readers who do not know all of the ins and outs of tragedy could easily get confounded by this. They read that a young man has been brought here who has committed a murder on the highway; this young man, they see, is named Aegisthus, but he says that this is not his name, but also does not say what his name is. Oh, they conclude, there is something wrong with that lad, he is a shrewd bandit, young as he is, and innocent as he claims to be. Inexperienced readers are in danger of thinking thus, I say, and yet I believe in all seriousness that it is better for the experienced reader to learn, even in this manner, who the unknown youth is right at the beginning, than not to know at all. But do not tell me that this manner of instructing them is in the least bit more artistic and refined than a prologue in the style of Euripides! –

Essay 50

20 October 1767[1]

In Maffei's play, the young man has his two names, as he should: he is called Aegisthus, as the son of Polydorus, and Cresphontes, as the son of Merope.[2] In the list of characters he is only introduced under the latter name, and Becelli claims for himself no small credit that in his edition of the play the list of *Dramatis personae* does not reveal

Aegisthus's true identity in advance.*,[3] That is to say, the Italians are even greater lovers of surprise than the French. –

But back to Mérope! – Truly, I pity my readers, who expected from these pages a theatrical newspaper that would be as varied and colorful and as entertaining and droll as only a theatrical newspaper can be.[4] But instead of getting the contents of plays produced here, distilled into little funny or moving stories, instead of light biographies of amusing, eccentric, harebrained creatures (as those who give themselves over to the writing of comedies surely must be), instead of entertaining and slightly scandalous anecdotes about actors – and particularly actresses – instead of all these agreeable little tidbits they anticipated, they get long, serious, dry critiques of old familiar plays, labored investigations of what should and should not be in a tragedy, and now and again even explanations of Aristotle. This is what they are supposed to read? As I said, I pity them; they have been terribly misled! – But between you and me: better them than me. And I would be very much misled, if I had to make their expectations my laws. Not that their expectations would be difficult to fulfill; in fact, not at all. Rather, I would find them very easy, if they would only better comport with my purposes.

Meanwhile, I must really try to get away from the subject of Merope. – I really only wanted to prove that Voltaire's *Mérope* was basically nothing but Maffei's *Merope*, and I think I have proved this. Aristotle says that it is not sharing the same subject that makes two plays the same but sharing the same complication and resolution.[5] Thus it is not because Voltaire took up the same story as Maffei but because he treated it in the same way that he is revealed here to be nothing more than Maffei's translator and imitator. Maffei did not merely reproduce Euripides' *Merope;* he made his own *Merope*, for he completely departed from Euripides' plot, and in his resolve to write a play free of romance, in which the entire interest derives from maternal tenderness, he transformed the whole story.[6] Whether it was done well or badly is not the issue here; it suffices that he transformed it. Voltaire, however, borrowed the whole transformed story from Maffei – he borrowed the fact that Merope is not married to Polyphontes; he borrowed the political circumstances that lead the tyrant to believe that he must press for this marriage now, after fifteen years; he borrowed the fact that Merope's son does not know who he is; he borrowed how and why this son leaves his supposed father; he borrowed the incident that brings Aegisthus to Messene as a murderer; he borrowed the misinterpretation that leads to him being taken for his own murderer; he borrowed the vague stirrings of maternal love when Merope first sees Aegisthus; he borrowed both the pretext for why Aegisthus should die in front of Merope by her own hand and the discovery of his accomplices – in short, Voltaire borrowed the entire entanglement from Maffei. And did he not also take the whole resolution from him as well, insofar as he learned from him how to connect the sacrifice at which Polyphontes was to be killed to the main action? Maffei made it into a marriage celebration, and perhaps this is why he had his tyrant insist just then on the

---

* Fin ne i nomi de' Personaggi si è levato quell'errore, comunissimo alle stampe d'ogni Drama, di scoprire il secreto nel premettergli, e per conseguenza di levare il piacere a chi legge, overo ascolta, essendosi messo *Egisto*, dov'era, *Cresfonte sotto nome d'Egisto*.

union with Merope, to make this sacrifice seem more natural. What Maffei invented, Voltaire imitated.

It is true, Voltaire gave a different turn to some of the circumstances he borrowed from Maffei. For example, instead of Polyphontes having already ruled for fifteen years, as he does in Maffei, Voltaire has the unrest in Messene last for the whole fifteen years, with the most improbable anarchy persisting in the state the whole time. Instead of having Aegisthus attacked by a robber on the road, as Maffei does, Voltaire has him assaulted in the temple of Hercules by two unknown men who take offense that he is supplicating Hercules, the God of the temple, to aid the Heraclids, the descendants of that God. Instead of having Aegisthus fall under suspicion because of a ring, Voltaire has this suspicion arise because of a suit of armor, etc. But all these changes concern the most negligible trivialities, nearly all of which are peripheral to the play and have no influence on the economy of the play itself. And yet I would gladly credit these changes to Voltaire as expressions of his creative genius if only I found that he had understood how to follow through on all of the implications of the changes he thought he had to make. I will explain myself using the second of the examples cited above. Maffei has his Aegisthus attacked by a robber who seizes the moment in which he sees him alone on the road, not far from a bridge over the Pamiso; Aegisthus slays the robber and throws the body in the river, out of fear that if the body were to be found on the street, the murderer will be sought and someone will be able to identify Aegisthus as such.[7] Voltaire thought: a robber who wants to pull off a prince's cloak and take his purse is far too common a scene for my refined and noble *parterre*; better to turn this robber into a malcontent who assaults Aegisthus thinking he is a supporter of the Heraclids. And why just one? Better two: that makes Aegisthus's heroic deed even greater, and the one of these two that escapes, if he is made to be the older, can be taken for Narbas later on.[8] Very good, my dear Johann Balhorn; but let us keep going.[9] When Aegisthus has killed one of these malcontents, what does he do next? He also drags the dead body into the water. Also? But how? And why? From the empty highway to the nearby river is fully understandable, but from the temple to the river? Was there no one but them in this temple? Let it be so, that is still not even the grossest absurdity. The "how" could be imagined somehow, but the "why" – absolutely not. Maffei's Aegisthus carries the body to the river because he fears being pursued and recognized otherwise, because he believes that once he has got rid of the body, nothing could reveal his deed, that then his deed would be buried in the river together with the body. But can Voltaire's Aegisthus believe this, too? Never, or the second man could not have been allowed to escape. Will he be satisfied to have escaped with his life? Will he not observe Aegisthus from a distance, no matter how frightened he may be? Will he not pursue him with his shouts, until others arrest him? Will he not accuse him, and bear witness against him? So how does it help the murderer to have carried away the *Corpus delicti*?[10] Here is a witness who can prove it. He should have spared himself this vain effort and instead hurried over the border, the sooner the better. Of course, for the sake of what follows the body had to be thrown in the water; it was just as necessary for Voltaire as it was for Maffei that Merope should not be torn from her misapprehension through viewing it. However, what Aegisthus does for his own best interests in the latter, he does to please the poet in the former. For Voltaire changes the cause without considering that he needs the effect of this cause, which now derives from nothing other than the poet's requirement.

Only one change that Voltaire made to Maffei's plot deserves to be called an improvement: namely, that he eliminates Mérope's repeated attempts to revenge herself on the presumed murderer of her son and instead has Aegisthus's recognition occur in Polyphontes' presence. I recognize the poet in this, and in particular the second scene of the fourth act is superb. I only wish that the general recognition that appears about to ensue on both sides in the fourth scene of the third act could have been handled with more art. For to have Aegisthus led away all of a sudden by Euricles and to have the recess close behind him is very heavy handed.[11] It is not at all better than the hasty escape with which Aegisthus rescues himself in Maffei and which Voltaire has his Lindelle mock so much.[12] Or rather, this escape is more natural by far, if only the poet had brought mother and son together again afterward and had not completely withheld from us the first emotional outburst of their mutual feelings for each other. Perhaps Voltaire would not have divided the recognition at all if he had not needed to extend his material in order to fill up five acts. He complains more than once about "cette longue carriére de cinq actes qui est prodigieusement difficile à remplir sans episodes."[13] – And for now, enough of Mérope!

Essay 51

23 October 1767[1]

On the thirty-ninth evening (Wednesday, the 8th of July), *The Married Philosopher* and *The New Agnes* were presented again.*,[2]

Chevrier says† that Destouches drew his play from a comedy by Campistron, and that if the latter had not written his *Jaloux Désabusé*, we probably would not have a *Married Philosopher.*[3] Campistron's comedy is fairly obscure; I do not know if it has ever been performed at any German theater, and there is no translation of it available. We are thus all the more justified in wanting to know what lies behind Chevrier's claim.

This, in brief, is the plot of Campistron's play: a brother has control of the considerable assets of his sister, and in order not to lose them, he would rather she not marry at all. But the brother's wife has better ideas, or at least different ones, and in order to prevail upon him to take care of his sister, she tries to make him jealous in every possible manner by enthusiastically receiving various young men into her home who come under the pretext of courting her sister-in-law. The ruse succeeds, the husband becomes jealous, and finally, in order to eliminate his wife's excuse for having suitors around, he agrees to his sister's marriage to Clitandre, one of his wife's relatives whom she had charmed by playing the coquette. The husband recognizes that he has

---

* See the fifth and seventh evenings [Essays 10 and 12].

† *L'Observateur des Spectacles* Vol. II, p. 135.

been duped, but he accepts it with equanimity when he realizes that his jealousy was unfounded.

What does this plot have in common with the plot of *The Married Philosopher?* As far as the plot is concerned, nothing at all. But here is a passage from the second act of Campistron's play between the jealous husband, Dorante, and his secretary, Dubois. This will demonstrate what Chevrier meant.

DUBOIS: What is the matter with you?

DORANTE: I am morose, vexed; all of my previous serenity is gone, my joy is at an end. Heaven has sent me a tyrant, an executioner, who will not cease torturing and punishing me –

DUBOIS: And who is this tyrant, this executioner?

DORANTE: My wife.

DUBOIS: Your wife, sir?

DORANTE: Yes, my wife, my wife. – She is driving me to despair.

DUBOIS: You hate her then?

DORANTE: Would God I did! Then I would be at peace. – But I love her, and love her so much – Damned misery!

DUBOIS: You're not jealous, are you?

DORANTE: Madly.

DUBOIS: What? You, sir? You, jealous? You, who, when it came to jealousy, always –

DORANTE: Laughed and mocked. That makes it all the worse for me now. What a peacock I've been to let myself be dragged along with the wretched ways of the *beau monde*! To agree with the braying fools who laugh at the propriety and discipline of our matrimonial ancestors! And I didn't simply agree; it wasn't long before I set the tone. There's not a bit of nonsense I failed to spout in order to demonstrate wit and *savoir vivre*! Marital fidelity, constant love, phooey, how much that reeks of the *petit bourgeois*. The husband who does not let his wife have her way is a bear! If he holds it against her when she flirts with other men, he belongs in a madhouse. This is how I spoke, and I'm the one who should have been sent to the madhouse for saying such things. –

DUBOIS: But why did you speak so?

DORANTE: Do you not hear me? Because I was a peacock, I believed it sounded gallant and wise. – In the meantime, my family wanted to see me married. They suggested a young, innocent girl, and I took her. Things would go well with her, I thought, she would not change my way of thinking very much. I don't love her particularly now, and possessing her ought to make me even more indifferent. But how greatly I deceived myself! She became more beautiful and more charming each day. I saw it and became inflamed, ever more inflamed, and now I am so in love, so in love with her –

DUBOIS: Well, that's what I call being captured!

DORANTE: Now I am so jealous that I am ashamed to admit it even to you. – All of my friends are repugnant to me, and I'm suspicious of them; those whom I could not have around enough before, I'd now rather see going than coming. Why do they come to my house, anyway? What do these idlers want? Why do they so

flatter my wife? One praises her intelligence, the other extols to heaven her pleasing nature. Her heavenly eyes enchant this man, her lovely teeth, this other. They
all find her extremely charming, extremely admirable, and they always end their
damned babble by observing what a fortunate, enviable husband I am.

DUBOIS: Yes, yes, it is true, that's how it goes.

DORANTE: Oh, they go even further with their shameless audacity! She is barely out
of bed, and they are at her *toilette*. That's something you ought to see and hear!
Each competes with the other in demonstrating his attentiveness and wit. One
vulgar notion, nasty bit of mockery, or titillating anecdote follows another, and
all of it with gestures, looks, and flirtations that my wife accepts so genially and
answers so obligingly – that I am fit to be tied! Can you imagine, Dubois? I am
forced to watch as they kiss her hand.

DUBOIS: That is harsh!

DORANTE: And at the same time, I dare not utter a word. For what would the *beau
monde* say? What kind of fool would I make of myself if I were to vent my
displeasure? Children on the street would point their fingers at me. Every day
there'd be a new epigram or disparaging song about me, etc.[4]

This must be the scenario that Chevrier found similar to *The Married Philosopher.* Just
as Campistron's jealous husband is ashamed to admit his jealousy because he previously made fun of this weakness, Destouches's philosopher is ashamed to make his
marriage public because he had earlier mocked all serious love and had declared the
bachelor state as the only respectable way for a free and wise man to live. This shame
they have in common cannot fail to bring them both into similar awkward situations.
So, for example, Campistron's Dorante finds himself in a dilemma when he asks his
wife to get rid of the tiresome visitors and she indicates to him that this is a matter he
must take care of himself; this is almost the same as the dilemma faced by Destouches's
Ariste when he must tell the Marquis that he cannot pin his hopes on Mélite.[5] Similarly, when the jealous Dorante hears his friends mocking jealousy in his presence and
he must agree, he suffers in more or less the same way as the philosopher Ariste, who
feels compelled to say that he is unquestionably far too clever and careful to let himself
be misled into such folly as marriage.

   Nevertheless, I do not see why Destouches needed to have the earlier play at hand,
and it is fully conceivable to me that we could have Destouches's play even if Campistron's were not around. Wildly differing characters can get into similar situations; in
a comedy, because the characters are the main business and the situations exist merely
to get them going and to allow them to express themselves, we must look not to the
situations but to the characters if we want to determine whether a play deserves to
be called an original or a copy. It is the other way around with tragedy, where the
characters are less essential and where the situations are the primary source of terror and compassion.[6] Therefore similar situations produce similar tragedies, but not
similar comedies. In contrast, similar characters produce similar comedies, whereas in
tragedies they hardly come into consideration.

   The playwright's son, who provided the splendid edition of his father's *Oeuvres*
that appeared a few years ago in four quarto volumes, published by the royal press in

Paris, tells an anecdote in the prologue to this edition that particularly pertains to this play.[7] Namely, the playwright had married in England, and for certain reasons had to keep his marriage a secret. One person from his wife's family blurted out the secret earlier than he cared for, and this gave the occasion for *The Married Philosopher*.[8] If this is true – and why should we not believe this from his son? – then the presumed imitation of Campistron is all the more dismissible.

Essay 52

27 October 1767[1]

On the fortieth evening (Thursday, the 9th of July), Schlegel's *The Triumph of the Good Women* was performed.[2]

  This comedy is unquestionably one of the best German originals. It was, as far as I know, the playwright's last comic work, one which both immeasurably surpasses its earlier siblings and demonstrates the maturity of its creator. *The Busy Idler* was his first youthful attempt, and it turned out the way all such youthful attempts turn out.[3] May the spirit of wit forgive these, and refrain from punishing those who found far too much wit in them![4] It contains the coldest and most boring, mundane drivel, which could only occur in the house of a Meissen fur trader. I would not know if it has ever been produced, and I doubt that a performance would be tolerable. *The Mysterious Man* is much better, even if it is in no way equal to the mysterious man that Molière depicted in the passage from which Schlegel claims to have taken the inspiration for this play.*,[5] Molière's mysterious man is a fop with inflated self-regard; Schlegel's mysterious man, on the other hand, is a good honest sheep who wants to play the fox in order not to be eaten by wolves. This is why he has so much in common with the mistrustful character that Cronegk later brought to the stage.[6] But since both characters, or rather both nuances of the same character, can only be found in such small and miserable or misanthropic and ugly souls, they will necessarily awaken more pity or disgust than laughter in our imaginations. *The Mysterious Man* was produced here previously; across the board, people assured me they found it more ridiculous than funny, and given the observation made above, I can believe it.[7]

---

* *Le Misanthrope* Acte II. Sc. 4.
  C'est de la tête aux pieds, un homme tout mystère.
  Qui vous jette, en passant, un coup d'oeil égaré,
  Et sans aucune affaire est toujours affairé.
  Tout ce qu'il vous débite en grimaces abonde.
  A force de façons il assome le monde.
  Sans cesse il a tout bas, pour rompre l'entretien,
  Un secret à vous dire, et ce secret n'est rien.
  De la moindre vétille, il fait une merveille
  Et jusques au bonjour, il dit tout à l'oreille.

On the other hand, *The Triumph of the Good Women* has received eminent acclaim wherever and whenever it has been performed, and it is clear that this approval is based on true merits and that it is not the effect of a surprisingly overpowering production, because so far nobody has retracted his approval after having read the play. He who reads the play first likes it even more when he sees it performed; and he who sees it performed first likes it even more when he reads it. In addition, the strictest critics have singled out this play from his other comedies to the same extent that they have generally preferred those to the usual junk heap of German comedies.

"I read," says one of them, "*The Busy Idler*. The characters seemed drawn perfectly from life: every day we see such idlers, such doting mothers, such shallow-minded visitors, and such stupid fur traders. This is how the German middle class thinks, lives, and acts. The playwright has done his duty, he has depicted us as we are. However, I yawned in boredom. – Then I read *The Triumph of the Good Women*. What a difference! Here I find life in the characters, fire in their actions, true wit in their speeches, and the tone of an elegant manner of living in their intercourse."[8]

The primary flaw that this same critic observed in the play is that the characters are not German. And unfortunately we must concede this. But we are already sufficiently used to foreign – particularly French – customs in our comedies for this to have an especially negative effect on us.

"Nikander," it says, "is a French adventurer who aims at conquests, chases all women, is not seriously inclined toward any of them, tries to topple all peaceful marriages into disunity and to become the seducer of all women and the terror of all men, and who despite all this does not have a bad heart. The prevailing corruption of morals and principles seems to have swept him along. Good lord! A German who would live like this would have to have the most corrupt heart in the world. – Hilaria, Nikander's wife, abandoned four weeks after their wedding, has not seen him in ten years and now comes looking for him on a whim. She dresses as a man, and under the name Philinte follows him into all the houses where he seeks adventure. Philinte is more witty, fickle, and impudent than Nikander. The women are more attracted to Philinte, and whenever he shows up with his brazen but courteous nature, Nikander is left standing there like a dummy. This gives rise to very lively situations. The invention is clever, the double character is drawn well and put successfully into action; but the original for this dandy is certainly no German."

"What I also do not like about this comedy," he continues, "is the character of Agenor. In order to make the triumph of the good women complete, this Agenor is portrayed as a far too ugly husband. He tyrannizes his innocent Juliane in the most unworthy way and genuinely wants to torment her. He is surly every time he appears, mocking of his aggrieved wife's tears, suspicious of her caresses, spiteful enough to give her most innocent words and actions a false turn and construe them to her disadvantage, jealous, hard, insensitive, and, of course, in love with his wife's chambermaid. – Such a man is far too corrupt for us to imagine him capable of speedy improvement. The playwright gives him a supporting role in which the wrinkles of his worthless heart cannot sufficiently unfold. He blusters, and neither Juliane nor the reader really knows what he wants. The playwright also had no room to properly prepare and arrange his development. He had to be satisfied to do so in passing, because the main action is focused upon Nikander and Philinte. Katherine, Juliane's warm-hearted chambermaid whom Agenor pursues, says right at the end of the comedy: 'The quickest conversions are not always the most genuine ones!' At least while this girl is in the house, I would not wish to answer for sincerity.'"[9]

I am glad that the best German comedy has fallen into the hands of the right German critic. And in fact, it was perhaps the first comedy that this man evaluated.

End of the First Volume.

VOLUME II

Essay 53

3 November 1767[1]

On the forty-first evening (Friday, the 10th of July), *Cénie* and *The Man of the Clock* were repeated.*

"*Cénie*," declares Chevrier,† "appears under the name of Mme. Grafigny, but it is a work by the Abbé de Voisenon.[2] It was originally in verse, but because Mme. Grafigny was fifty-four when she first had the notion to play author and had never written a verse in her life, she translated *Cénie* into prose." "Mais l'Auteur," he adds, "y a laissé 81 vers qui y existent dans leur entier."[3] Doubtless that refers to individual lines strewn here and there that have lost their rhyme but retained the meter. Yet if Chevrier had no other proof that the play had been in verse, then we might reasonably find cause to doubt it. In general, French verse comes so close to prose that it seems to require effort to write in a more elevated style without entire verses suddenly emerging that lack nothing but rhyme. And it is precisely from those who make no verses at all that such verses escape most readily, because they have no ear for meter and therefore understand as little how to avoid it as how to observe it.

What other signs are there in *Cénie* to indicate that it did not flow from a woman's pen? "Women, in general," says Rousseau,‡ "do not like any art, know nothing about any, and have no genius. They can succeed in little works which require only quick wit, taste, grace, and sometimes even a bit of philosophy and reasoning. They can acquire science, erudition, talents, and everything which is acquired by dint of work. But that celestial flame which warms and sets fire to the soul, that genius which

---

* See the 23rd and 29th evenings [Essays 20 and 22].
† *Observateur des Spectacles* Vol. I, p. 211.
‡ *à d'Alembert* p. 193.

consumes and devours, that burning eloquence, those sublime transports which carry their raptures to the depths of hearts, will always lack in the writings of women [. . .]."[4]

So are these lacking in *Cénie?* Or, if they are not lacking, then must *Cénie* necessarily be the work of a man? Rousseau himself would not draw this conclusion. Rather, he says that what he must deny to women in general, he would not challenge in any particular woman. ("Ce n'est pas à une femme, mais aux femmes que je refuse les talens des hommes."§)[5] And he says this precisely with respect to *Cénie*, precisely where he cites Grafigny as its author. And it should be noted that Grafigny was not his friend, that she had spoken ill of him, and that he complains about her in that very same passage.[6] All of this notwithstanding, he would rather declare her an exception to his rule than to allude in the least to Chevrier's allegation, which he certainly would have had candor enough to do if he had not been convinced of the opposite.

Chevrier has more such disparaging privy information. This very Abbé, Chevrier wants us to know, worked for Favart.[7] He wrote the comic opera *Annette and Lubin*, not she, the actress, who (he claims) could barely read.[8] His evidence is a popular tune about it that went around in the streets of Paris, and it is certainly true that the street ballads are some of the most credible documents in French history.

Why a man of the cloth would send an amorous light opera into the world under an alias is easy to understand, after all. But why he would not want to own up to *Cénie*, which I would choose over most sermons, is difficult to see. After all, this Abbé already had more than one play performed and published, of which everyone knew him as the author, and which do not come even close to *Cénie*. If he wanted to extend a gallant gesture toward a fifty-four-year-old woman, is it likely that he would have done it with his very best work? –

On the forty-second evening (Monday, the 13th of July), Molière's *The School for Wives* was performed.[9]

Molière had already written his *School for Husbands* when he followed it with *The School for Wives* in 1662.[10] One who does not know these plays would be very mistaken to believe that one delivers a sermon on duty to women and the other preaches similarly to men. They are both witty farces in which a pair of young girls, one of whom has been raised most strictly and the other of whom has grown up in complete simplicity, deceive a pair of old fools; both should have been called *The School for Husbands* if Molière had merely wanted to teach that the dumbest girl is always clever enough to deceive and that coercion and control reap far less reward than lenience and freedom. There is really not much for the female sex to learn from *The School for Wives*, unless Molière meant this title to emphasize the "Marital Maxims" from the second scene of the third act, in which, however, the duties of women are made rather ludicrous.[11]

"The two most successful subjects of tragedy and comedy," Trublet says,¶ "are *The Cid* and *The School for Wives*. But both of these were treated by Corneille and Molière

---

§ Ibid. p. 78.
¶ *Essais de Litt. & de Morale* Vol. IV, p. 295.

before these poets had reached their full force. I have this observation," he adds, "from M. de Fontenelle."[12]

If only Trublet had asked M. de Fontenelle what he means by this. Or, if it were already comprehensible enough to him: if only he had taken a couple of words to make it understandable to his readers, too. For my part, I confess that I do not foresee where Fontenelle wished to go with this riddle. I think he misspoke, or Trublet misheard.

In any case, if, in these men's opinion, the subject of *The School for Wives* is especially successful, and Molière fell somewhat short in his execution, then he could not have taken much pride in the play as a whole. For the subject matter is not original to him but taken partly from a Spanish story found in Scarron under the title *The Useless Precaution* and partly from the playful *The Nights of Straparola*, in which a lover confides each day to one of his friends how far he has come with his beloved, without knowing that this friend is his rival.[13]

"*The School for Wives*," M. de Voltaire says, "was a whole new genre of play, in which everything is simply narrative, although it is such artful narrative that it all seems to be action."[14]

If the novelty consists in this, then it is best that the new genre be abandoned. Narrative remains narrative, regardless how artful, and in the theater we want to see real action. – But is it really true that everything is narrated in the play? Voltaire should not have rehashed this old accusation; or, instead of turning it into apparent praise, he should at least have included the response Molière himself furnished, which is very fitting. Namely, that, by virtue of the play's intrinsic composition, its narratives are really actions; they have everything necessary for comic action, and it is just splitting hairs to deny them this name here.**[15] For the incidents that are related are less significant than the impression these incidents make on the deceived old man when he learns of them. Molière primarily wanted to depict the ridiculousness of this old man, so we must primarily see how he behaves in response to the misfortunes that threaten him; and we would not have seen this as clearly if the poet had let happen before our eyes what he allows to be narrated, and, in return, had allowed to be narrated what he has occur before our eyes. The vexation Arnolphe feels, the constraint he puts upon himself to hide this vexation, the derisive tone he adopts when he believes he has prevented Horace's further progress, the astonishment and mute infuriation we see in him when he realizes that Horace nevertheless pursues his aims with success: these are actions, and much more comic actions than anything that occurs outside the scene.[16] Similarly, we find more action in Agnès's narration of becoming acquainted with Horace than we would if we actually saw them become acquainted on stage.

Therefore, instead of saying of *The School for Wives* that everything in it appears to be action even though it is all only narration, I think it could be more correct to say that everything in it is action even though it all appears to be merely narration.

** In the *Critique of the School for Wives*, in the person of Dorante: "Les recits euxmêmes y sont des actions suivant la constitution du sujet."

Essay 54

6 November 1767[1]

On the forty-third evening (Tuesday, the 14th of July), Nivelle de la Chaussée's *School for Mothers* was repeated, and on the forty-fourth evening (that is, the 15th of July), *The Earl of Essex* was repeated.[*,2]

Since from time immemorial the English have liked to bring *domestica facta* to their stage, one might readily assume that they do not lack for tragedies about this subject.[3] The oldest is by John Banks, under the title *The Unhappy Favourite: or, The Earl of Essex*.[4] It premiered in the theater in 1682 to general acclaim.[5] At the time, the French already had three Essexes: Calprenède's from 1638, Boyer's from 1678, and the younger Corneille's from the same year.[6] However, if the English wanted to deny that the French had once again beaten them to the punch, they might claim Daniel's *Philotas*, a tragedy from 1611 which is believed to have the history and character of the Earl under a different name.[†,7]

Banks seems not to have known any of his French predecessors. He did, however, follow a novel that had the title *The history of the most renowned Queen Elizabeth, and her great favourite, the Earl of Essex*,[‡] in which he found the material sufficiently developed that he only needed to render it in dialogue and give it the external form of a drama.[8] Here is the whole plot, as excerpted by the author of the text cited below. Perhaps my readers will find it worthwhile to compare it with Corneille's play.[9]

"To heighten our Compassion for the unhappy Earl, and justify the Queen's vehement Affection for him, he is represented as possest of all those eminent Qualities which compose a Hero; and to be a faultless Character requires only to have had a greater Command over his Passions. *Burleigh*, first Minister to the Queen, jealous of her Glory, and envious of the Favours heap'd on *Essex*, is continually labouring to render him suspected. Sir *Walter Raleigh*, no less his Enemy, joins his Endeavors for the same End, and both are abetted by the malicious Countess of *Nottingham*, who, having been passionately in Love with *Essex*, and rejected by him, seeks to ruin what she can't enjoy. The Impetuosity of the Earl's Temper gave them but too great an Opportunity, and they accomplish'd their Ends in the following Manner.

A Rebellion breaking out in *Ireland*, headed by *Tyronne*, a very valiant Man, *Essex*, as being Lord-Lieutenant of that Kingdom, and Captain-General of all her Majesty's Forces both by Sea and Land, marched with a powerful Army against him; after some slight Skirmishes, the Earl's Troops being much harassed, and the Enemy posted very advantageously, he yielded to a Parley, which being very private, was represented to the Queen as derogatory to her Honour, and as if the Earl was not free from some clandestine Designs. *Burleigh* and *Raleigh*, with some other Members of both Houses, petition her for Leave to impeach him of High Treason, which she not only refuses, but

* See the 26th and 27th evening [Essay 21].
† Cibber's *Lives of the Engl. Poets.* Vol. I. p. 147.
‡ *The Companion to the Theatre.* Vol. II. p. 99.

is extremely incensed that such a Motion has been made, repeats the former Services the Earl has done the Nation, and reproaches them with Malice, Envy, and Ingratitude: The Earl of *Southampton*, a very sincere Friend of *Essex*, urges every Thing he can in his Behalf, and extols the Queen's Justice in protecting him; so that for that Time his Enemies are put to Silence. [(First Act)]

The Queen, however, not satisfied with his Behavior, sends Orders to him to repair his past Conduct, and not quit *Ireland* till the Rebels are totally subdued, and all Things quieted; but the Earl hearing of the Accusations which had been brought against him, was too impatient to be clear'd; and having engaged *Tyronne* to lay down his Arms, came over in spite of the Queen's positive Command to the contrary. His cruel Foes rejoiced; all his Friends were alarmed at this imprudent Step; the Countess of *Rutland*, to whom he was privately married, trembled for the Consequence; and the Queen herself was beyond Measure afflicted to find that his rash Proceeding now left her no Pretence to espouse his Cause, without manifesting a Tenderness which she was desirous of concealing from the whole World. The Consideration of her Dignity, heighten'd by her native Haughtiness, and the secret Love she bears him, occasion cruel Conflicts in her breast; long she debates within herself, whether she shall obey the Dictates of the *one*, and send the audacious Man to the Tower, or comply with the soft Impulse of the *other*, and admit the beloved Criminal to justify himself before her: The latter, after much Struggling, gets the better, but not without some Restrictions; she resolves to see him, but to receive him in such a Manner as shall leave him no Room to hope she will easily pardon his Offences.

Burleigh, Raleigh, and *Nottingham* are present at this Interview, on the latter of which she leans, and seems busy in Discourse, without once looking on the Earl; and, after suffering him to kneel some Time, quits the Room, sternly commanding all who have Loyalty to follow her, and leave the Traitor to himself. None dare to disobey, even *Southampton* goes, but soon returns, and, with the disconsolate *Rutland*, bewail his Misfortunes. Immediately after *Burleigh* and *Raleigh* are sent to demand his Staff of Offices, which he refuses to resign to any but the Queen herself; and both he and *Southampton* treat those Ministers with Contempt. [(Second Act)]

The Queen being presently informed of this Behavior, is highly incens'd, yet still divided in her Thoughts; she cannot brook the Railings of *Nottingham* against him, and the Praises bestowed on him by the unwary *Rutland* make her yet more uneasy, by the Discovery that [*Rutland*] loves him: She, however, at last, commands he shall be brought into her Presence: he attempts to vindicate his Conduct, but the Reasons he gives seem too weak to convince her Judgment of his Innocence. She pardons him to satisfy the secret Affection she has for him; but deprives him of all his Honours in Consideration of what she thought owing to herself as Queen. Here the Earl is no longer able to restrain the Impetuosity of his Nature, he throws his Staff at her Feet, accompanied with some Expressions, that sound [so much like reproaches that they drive the Queen's anger to utmost fury. She answers him in a manner quite natural for one in a fury, without concern for decorum and majesty, without concern for the consequences: namely, instead of giving an answer, she slaps him. The Earl reaches for his sword; and only the thought that it is his Queen, and not his King, who has hit him, in short, that it is a woman from whom he has this blow, restrains him from actually assaulting her.]¹⁰ *Southampton* conjures him to be more moderate; [Essex] goes on repeating his Services, and accusing *Burleigh, Raleigh*, and even her Majesty, of Injustice. She leaves him in the utmost Rage, and none remain with him but *Southampton*, who in this Exigence will not forsake him. [(Third Act)]

Grown desperate with his Misfortunes, he runs head-long into the City, proclaims his Wrongs, and inveighs against the Ministry. All this is told with Aggravations to the Queen, who orders the two Earls to be seized. They are pursued and taken, and sent close Prisoners to the Tower, there to wait their Trial. [In the meantime the Queen's anger has abated, making room for more favorable thoughts toward Essex. Thus]¹¹ the Queen, in spite of all can be said to her, will needs see *Essex* before he goes, and fearing his Crimes were too flagrant to escape Sentence, in order to save his Life, gives him a Ring, with a solemn Promise, that whenever he sends that, to grant him in Return whatever he shall ask. [But she almost immediately regrets having been so benevolent to him again when she discovers that he is married to Rutland, and discovers this from Rutland herself, when she comes to beg mercy for him]."¹² [(Fourth Act)]

Essay 55

10 November 1767¹

"As she expected, he was found guilty by the Law, and condemned to lose his Head; as was also his Friend *Southampton*.² Her Majesty knew that by her Prerogative she had a Right to pardon him; but then she thought such a Grace would too much betray a Weakness unworthy of a Queen, and waited till he should send the Ring, and beg his Life. Impatient till she knows him secure she sends *Nottingham* to him, who pretending the greatest Compassion for him, is intrusted by him with this precious Pledge of Safety, and with it a Petition to the Queen for Mercy. She [Nottingham] had now all she wish'd in her Possession, and a full Opportunity to revenge the Contempt he had shewn her Charms. [Instead of carrying out his charge, she defames him in the most malicious way and portrays him as proud, spiteful, and firmly resolved not to beg for mercy (instead allowing things to reach an extreme), to such a degree that the Queen can hardly believe her report. But after repeated assurances, and full of anger and despair, she] gives Orders that the Sentence past [sic] on *Essex* shall be immediately executed.³ The malicious *Nottingham*, who now engrosses her Ear, persuades her to pardon the Earl of *Southampton*, not out of any real Pity for that Nobleman, but because she imagines *Essex* will feel the Severity of his own Doom more deeply, in seeing that Mercy which is denied to himself bestowed on his Friend. To imbitter Death the more, she also intreats his unhappy Wife may be permitted to see him as he is conducting [sic] to the Block; to both these the Queen consents, but unhappily for the cruel Adviser, the Earl then gives a Letter to his Wife to be delivered to the Queen, who being at that Time in the Tower, receives it, soon after the Earl is carried off; and finding by it that the Earl had sent the Ring, and beg'd his Life by *Nottingham*, sends to forbid the Execution; but *Burleigh* and *Raleigh*, who were intrusted with the fatal Orders, took so much Care they should not be delayed, that the Earl was dead before the Arrival of this second Message. The Queen is grieved beyond Measure, banishes the treacherous *Nottingham* for ever from her Presence, and is much displeased with all who had shewn themselves Enemies to the unfortunate Earl."

There is enough in this plot summary to deduce that Banks's *Essex* was a play with far more nature, truth, and consistency than can be found in the *Essex* of Corneille.[4] Banks adhered very closely to history, other than shifting several events closer together and giving them a more immediate influence on his hero's final fate. Neither the episode with the slap nor the one with the ring is invented; both are found, as I noted earlier, in the history, only the former occurs much earlier and on a completely different occasion, as can also be presumed about the latter.[5] It is far more conceivable that the Queen would have given the Earl the ring at a time when she was completely satisfied with him, than that she should give him this pledge of her favor only at the moment when he had made himself least worthy of it and at the same time needed it most. This ring should remind her how dear the Earl once was to her when he received it from her, and this memory should then restore all the merit he unhappily stood to lose in her eyes. But what use is this sign, this memory, from one moment to the next? Does she fear herself so unable to control her tender inclinations for a few hours that she must deliberately bind them in such a manner? If she has seriously forgiven him, if his life is really important to her: why all the fighting over nothing? Why could she not let the matter rest with verbal assurances? If she gave the Earl the ring just to pacify him, then it commits her to keep her word to him whether he returns the ring or not. If, however, she gave it in order to be assured, through its return, of the Earl's enduring regret and submission: how can she trust his most deadly enemy with such an important matter? And had not Nottingham proven herself to be so just recently?

Thus the way Banks used the ring does not have an optimal effect. It seems to me that it would be better if the Queen had completely forgotten it, and it had been handed over to her suddenly, but too late, just as she was being persuaded of the Earl's innocence, or at least of his lesser guilt, on other grounds. The gift of the ring should have occurred long before the action of the play, and only the Earl should have known its value; but he would not have wanted to make use of it until he saw that no heed was paid to his explanations, and that the Queen was far too set against him for him to hope to convince her, so that he thus had to try to stir her emotionally. And in the moment she were moved, she would be convinced: the recognition of his innocence and the reminder of her promise to believe him innocent even if he seems guilty should take her suddenly by surprise, but only after it is too late for her to acknowledge the truth and be just.

Banks was much more successful in weaving the slap into his play. – But a slap in a tragedy! How English, how undignified! – Before my fine readers scoff at this too much, I beg them to remember the slap in *The Cid*.[6] The observation M. de Voltaire made about it is remarkable in many respects. "Nowadays," he says, "one would not dare give a hero a smack upside the head. The actors themselves do not know how to go about such a thing; they only pretend to do it. Such a thing is not even allowed in comedies anymore, and this is the only example we have of it on the tragic stage. It is possible that this is one among other reasons that *The Cid* is called a tragicomedy; in the past, nearly all of the plays of Scudéry and Boisrobert were tragicomedies.[7]

In France, it was long thought that people could not endure uninterrupted tragedy without some interjection of the ordinary. The word tragicomedy itself is very old: Plautus uses it to characterize his *Amphitryon* because while Sosia's adventures are comic, Amphitryon himself is quite seriously aggrieved."[8] – What won't that M. de Voltaire write! How he loves to show a little learning, and how he usually goes wrong in the process!

It is not true that the slap in *The Cid* is the only one on the tragic stage. Either Voltaire did not know Banks's *Essex*, or he assumed that only the tragic theater of his nation merited this name. Both bespeak ignorance; only the latter conveys more vanity than ignorance. What he adds with regard to the label tragicomedy is just as incorrect. Tragicomedy is the representation of an important action by noble people that has a happy outcome.[9] That describes *The Cid*, and the slap did not come into consideration whatsoever. Notwithstanding this slap, Corneille later called his play a tragedy, once he had laid aside the prejudice that a tragedy necessarily had to have a catastrophe.[10] It is true that Plautus used the word "Tragicocomoedia," but he used it merely in jest and not to designate a special genre.[11] Moreover, nobody borrowed it from him in this sense until it occurred to sixteenth-century Spanish and Italian poets to give this name to certain of their dramatic monstrosities.*,[12] But even if Plautus had labeled his *Amphitryon* thusly in earnest, it would not have been for the reasons that Voltaire imputed to him. Plautus would not have wanted to call his play a tragicomedy because the part that Sosia plays in the action is comic and the part Amphitryon plays is tragic.[13] His play is completely comic, and we laugh just as much at Amphitryon's quandary as we do at Sosia's. Rather, it is because this comic action mainly occurs among nobler characters than we usually see in comedy. Plautus himself explains this clearly enough:

> *Faciam ut commixta sit Tragico-comoedia:*
> *Nam me perpetuo facere ut sit Comoedia*
> *Reges quo veniant & di, non par arbitror.*
> *Quid igitur? quoniam hic servus quoque partes habet,*
> *Faciam hanc, proinde ut dixi, Tragico-comoediam.*[14]

---

* I do not know who actually used this name first, but I do know this for certain: it was not Garnier. Hédelin said: "Je ne sçai si Garnier fut le premier qui s'en servit, mais il a fait porter ce titre à sa *Bradamante*, ce que depuis plusieurs ont imité." (*Prat. du Th.* liv. II. ch. 10). And the historians of French theater should have let it rest at that. But they turned Hédelin's light supposition into a certainty and congratulated their countryman for such a fine invention. "Voici la premiére Tragi-Comédie, ou pour mieux dire le premier Poëme du Théatre, qui a porté ce titre – Garnier ne connoissoit pas assez le titre – Garnier ne connoissoit pas assez le finesses de l'art qu'il professoit; tenons-lui cependent compte d'avoir le premier, & sans le secours des anciens, ni de ses contemporains, fait entrevoir une idée, qui n'a pas été inutile à beaucoup d'Auteurs du dernier siécle." Garnier's *Bradamante* is from 1582, and I know plenty of much earlier Spanish and Italian plays that bear this title.

Essay 56

13 November 1767[1]

But let's return to that slap. – First of all, a slap received by a man of honor from his equal or from someone of higher rank is considered such an insulting injury that the law cannot provide sufficient reparation.[2] It cannot be punished by a third party; it needs to be revenged by the injured person himself, and in the same particular manner in which it was committed. Whether this is required by true or false honor is not under discussion here. As I said, this is simply the way things are.

And if this is the way things are in the world, why not in the theater as well? If slaps happen in the real world, why not here, too?

"The actors," M. de Voltaire says, "do not know how to go about such a thing."[3] They probably should; but no one likes to be slapped, even if it's under an assumed name. The blow sets them on fire. The character is the recipient, but the actor feels it, and the emotion undoes the dissimulation. The actor loses his composure, his face involuntarily expresses shame and confusion, he should look angry but instead looks silly, and when an actor's own feelings collide with his role, it makes us laugh.

This is not the only situation in which we might regret the abolishment of masks. An actor can undoubtedly keep more composure under a mask; his own person has less opportunity to break out, and if it does, we are much less aware of this outbreak.

But the actor can react to a slap on the face however he wants: the playwright may well work for the actor, but he does not therefore have to avoid everything that the actor finds uncomfortable or difficult. No actor can blush at will, but the playwright may still tell him to do so and may have one actor say that he sees the other blush. The actor does not want to be slapped in the face, he believes it derides him, it confuses him, it causes him pain: very good! If he has not yet developed his art to the degree that such a thing does not confuse him, if he does not love his art enough to put up with a little bit of humiliation for its benefit, then he should deal with the situation as best he can, either by dodging the blow or holding up his hand. In any case, he should not demand that the playwright have more concern for the actor than for the person whom the actor represents. If the real Diego and the real Essex must receive a slap, what argument can their representatives make against it?[4]

But perhaps the spectator does not want to see a blow delivered? Or at the most only to a servant, for whom it is not particularly insulting, for whom it is a chastisement fitting to his station? A hero, however, a slap to a hero! How petty, how indecent! – And if it should be so? If this very impropriety should be, and becomes, the source of the most violent resolutions and the bloodiest revenge? Where no other, more trivial, insult could have had these terrible effects? Should something that can be so tragic in its consequences, that must necessarily be tragic among certain persons, be excluded from tragedy because it also has a place in comedy and farce? Why should that which makes us laugh in one instance not also horrify us in another?

If I wanted to see such slaps banned from a genre of drama, it would be from the comedy. For what kind of consequences can they have there? Sad ones? They are beyond its sphere. Ridiculous ones? They are beneath it, and belong to the farce. None at all? Then it is not worth the effort to have them given at all. Anyone who gives them will convey nothing but common thuggery, and anyone who receives them nothing but servile timidity. The slap thus belongs only in the domain of the two extremes, tragedy and farce; these have in common many suchlike things at which we either scoff or tremble.

And I ask everyone who has seen *The Cid* performed, or has only read it carefully, if he was not overtaken by a shudder when the boastful Gormas dared to hit the dignified old Diego?[5] If he did not feel the most sensitive compassion for the latter and the most bitter indignation toward the former? If all the tragic, bloody consequences that this insulting encounter would necessarily bring in its wake did not immediately spring to mind and fill him with expectation and fear? Given this, should an incident that has all these effects on him not be tragic?

If anyone ever laughed at this blow, it was surely someone in the gallery who was all too familiar with such slaps and deserved one from his neighbor at that very moment.[6] But if the clumsy manner in which the actor comported himself made a spectator smile against his will, that person would quickly bite his lip and immediately try to transport himself back into the illusion which nearly every violent action tends, more or less, to disrupt.

I also wonder what other insult could possibly take the place of a slap? In the case of any other insult, it would be in the king's power to provide satisfaction to the injured party; for any other, the son could refuse to sacrifice the father of his beloved to his own father.[7] For this one offense alone the *Pundonor* accepts neither excuse nor apology, and all conciliatory means are in vain, even those the monarch himself initiates.[8] Corneille has Gormas answer very much in accord with this way of thinking when he responds to the king's suggestion that he placate Diego:

> *Ces satisfactions n'apaisent point une âme:*
> *Qui les reçoit n'a rien, qui les fait se diffame.*
> *Et de tous ces accords l'effet le plus commun,*
> *C'est de déshonorer deux hommes au lieu d'un.*[9]

In France at the time, it had not been long since the edict against dueling was enacted, which these same maxims directly contradicted.[10] Corneille thus received orders to strike all these lines and they were banned from the actor's lips. But every spectator added them from memory and from personal emotion.

In *Essex*, the slap becomes even more critical because it is given by a person who is not bound by the laws of honor. She is a woman and a queen: what can the injured party do with her? He would scoff at a woman ready and able to fight, for a woman can neither offend him nor best him. But this woman is also the sovereign, whose insults are indelible because they are imbued with her dignity and thus acquire a kind of legitimacy. What, then, can seem more natural, than that Essex rebels against this very dignity and rages against the heights that remove the offender beyond the reach of his revenge? I cannot imagine what could otherwise have made his final misbehavior probable. Mere disgrace, mere removal from his posts of honor could not and would not drive him to such an extreme. But beside himself at being treated so slavishly, we see everything that despair drives him to undertake – while not with approval, then at least with pardon. From this perspective, the Queen herself must recognize him as worthy of her forgiveness, and thus we have far more compassion for him than he seems to deserve in history, where what he does here in his initial anger over offended honor happens instead out of self-interest and other base intentions.

History says that the dispute in which Essex received the box on the ear was over the choice of a King of Ireland.[11] When he saw that the Queen was adamant in her opinion, he turned his back on her in a contemptuous manner. In that moment he felt her hand, and his hand reached for his sword. He swore that he neither could nor would suffer such an insult, that he would not tolerate it from her father Henry himself, and he withdrew from court. The letter that he wrote to Chancellor Egerton about this incident was composed with the most noble pride, and he appeared firmly resolved never to come near the Queen again. Nevertheless, we soon find him fully back in her grace and back in action as an ambitious favorite. This reconciliation, if serious, gives us a very bad impression of him, and we don't have a much better one if it was feigned. In that case, he really was a traitor who put up with everything until he believed the right moment had come. In the end, a measly patent on sweet wine that the Queen took from him infuriated him far more than the slap, and he was so blinded by his anger over this reduction of his income that he burst out without thinking.[12] This is how we find him in history, and we despise him. But not in Banks, who makes his rebellion the immediate consequence of the box on the ear and does not attribute to him any traitorous intentions against his queen. His error is the error of a noble passion that he regrets, that he is pardoned for, and that he would not have been punished for were it not for the malevolence of his enemies.

Essay 57

17 November 1767[1]

Banks retained the actual words Essex exclaimed over the slap.[2] Except Banks has Essex refer not only to the one Henry, but to all the world's Henrys, and an Alexander, too.*,[3] His Essex is altogether too much a boaster, and little is lacking to make him just as great a Gascon as the Essex of that Gascon Calprenède.[4] Meanwhile, he bears his misfortune much too timidly, and in no time he is just as groveling toward

---

* Act III.

   – – – By all
The Subtilty, and Woman in your Sex,
I swear, that had you been a Man you durst not,
Nay, your bold Father Harry durst not this
Have done – Why say I him? Not all the Harrys,
Nor Alexander's self, were he alive,
Shou'd boast of such a deed on Essex done
Without revenge. – – –

the Queen as he had previously been impudent. Banks drew too much from life in his depiction of Essex. A character who is so inconsistent is no character and for that very reason unworthy of dramatic imitation. In a historical figure we can assume such self-contradictions indicate deception because we seldom get to know the innermost workings of the heart; but in the drama we become so intimately acquainted with the hero that we know right away whether his cast of mind conforms – or not – with actions we would not have expected of him. Regardless of whether they do or not, in neither case can the tragic poet use such a character properly. Without deception the character disappears; with it, his dignity is gone.

Banks could not fall into this error with Elizabeth. This woman remains completely consistent in history as only few men do. Her tenderness and her secret love for Essex are handled with great propriety; moreover, she remains something of a mystery. His Elizabeth does not complain about coldness and contempt and passion and fate like Corneille's Elizabeth; she does not speak of a poison that consumes her; she does not grouse that the ingrate prefers a Suffolk to her, after she had given him to understand clearly enough that he should sigh for her alone, etc.[5] No such laments pass through her lips. She never speaks as one in love, but she acts like one. We never hear it, but we see how dear to her Essex once was and still is. A few sparks of jealousy betray her; otherwise we would simply take her for nothing but his friend.

The art with which Banks put her sentiments about the Earl into action can be seen in the following scenes from the third act. – The queen believes she is alone and reflects on the unfortunate constraint of her rank, which does not allow her to act according to the true inclination of her heart. While so engaged, she becomes aware of Nottingham, who has followed her.[6] –

THE QUEEN: You here, Nottingham? I thought I was alone.

NOTTINGHAM: Pardon me for being so bold, Queen. And yet my duty orders me to be even bolder. – Something troubles you. I must ask – but first I beg pardon on my knees that I ask it – what is it that troubles you? What is it that hangs so heavy on this noble soul? – Or are you not well?

QUEEN: Rise, I pray you. – I am quite well. – I thank you for your love. – I am only troubled, a little troubled, – because of my people. I have reigned long, and, I fear, too long for them. They begin to grow weary of me. – New crowns are like new garlands, the freshest are the loveliest. My sun is going down; at its midday it warmed too much and people felt too hot; they wish it were already set. – Tell me, what do people say about Essex's coming?

NOT: – About Essex's coming – they do not say the best. But about him – he is known to be such a brave man –

QUEEN: What? Brave? When he has served me thus? – The traitor!

NOT: Indeed, it was not well –

QUEEN: Not well! Not well? – Nothing else?

NOT: It was a bold and heinous deed.

QUEEN: Was it not, Nottingham? – To hold my order in such contempt! He deserved to die for it. Far lesser crimes have cost a hundred nearer favorites their heads.[7]

NOT: Most true. – And yet should Essex come away with a lesser punishment with so much greater guilt? Should he not die?

QUEEN: He should! – He should die, and in the most agonizing torment! – His anguish should be like his treachery, the greatest of all! – And then I will have his head and his limbs stuck on the highest battlements, not under dark gates or on low bridges, so that everyone who passes by sees them and cries out: See there, the proud ungrateful Essex! This Essex, who defied the justice of his Queen! – Well done! No more than he deserved! – What do you say, Nottingham? Do you not agree? – You are silent? Why are you silent? Do you yet wish to plead his cause?

NOT: Because you order it, Queen, I will tell you everything the world says of this proud ungrateful man. –

QUEEN: Do so! – Let me hear: what does the world say of him and me?

NOT: Of you, Queen? – Who is there, who does not speak of you with rapture and wonder? The praise of you that rings out from every tongue is no less sincere than the praise of dead saints. They only wish this one thing, and wish it with the kindest tears, sprung from purest love toward you – this one thing, that you would be pleased to redress their grievances against this Essex, no longer protect such a traitor, no longer keep him from justice and shame, finally deliver him to vengeance –

QUEEN: Who tells me what to do?

NOT: Tells you what to do! – Does one tell heaven what to do, when one beseeches in deepest submission? – And this is how they beseech you against this man, whose character is so bad, so evil, that he does not even see it worth his trouble to play the hypocrite. – How proud! How arrogant! Foolishly, vulgarly proud, proud just like a low lackey in his colorful fur-trimmed livery! – That he is bold, they will admit, but the way a wolf or bear is, blindly, without plan or caution. True courage, which raises a noble soul above fortune and misfortune, is foreign to him. The least affront enrages him, he rants and raves over nothing, everyone should humble themselves before him, he alone wants to shine and stand out everywhere. Lucifer himself, who sowed the first seeds of vice in heaven, was not more covetous and ambitious than he. But just as he tumbled from heaven –

QUEEN: Enough, Nottingham, enough! – You rail yourself quite out of breath. – I do not want to hear any more. – *Aside:* Poison and blisters on her tongue! – Indeed, Nottingham, you should be ashamed to even repeat such base lies of the vilest rabble. And it is not even true that the rabble says this. They do not even think it. But you, you wish they would.

NOT: I am astonished, Queen –

QUEEN: About what?

NOT: You yourself commanded me to speak.

QUEEN: Yes, but had I only noticed how welcome this command was to you! How ready you were for it! Suddenly your face glowed, your eyes flashed; your full heart rejoiced to overflowing, and each word, each gesture had its well-aimed arrow that hit me as well.

NOT: Pardon me, Queen, if I have failed in the expression of my duty. I modeled it after yours.

QUEEN: After mine? – I am his Queen. I have leave to use the thing I have made as I please. – Besides, he has made himself guilty of the most monstrous crimes against my person. He has wronged me, not you. – How could the poor man have wronged you? You have no laws that he has overstepped, no subjects he has aggrieved, no crown he could strive for. What kind of cruel pleasure do you take in hitting a poor drowning man on the head rather than reaching out a hand to save him? –

NOT: I am to blame –

QUEEN: Enough of this! – Your Queen, the world, fate itself are against this man, and yet he seems to you to deserve no pity or excuse? –

NOT: I confess, Queen, –

QUEEN: Go, you are forgiven. – Call Rutland to come right away. –[8]

Essay 58

20 November 1767[1]

Nottingham goes, and soon after Rutland appears.[2] One must recall that Rutland is married to Essex, but the Queen does not know.[3]

QUEEN: How now, dear Rutland? I sent for you. – How are you? For some time you have seemed sad. Why this somber cloud gathered about your lovely eyes? Cheer up, dear Rutland; I will find you a brave husband.

RUTLAND: Generous lady! – I do not deserve to have my Queen look down upon me so graciously.

QUEEN: How can you speak thus? I love you, indeed I love you well. – You shall see from this: just now I had a dispute with Nottingham – that unpleasant woman! – about, in fact, my Lord of Essex.

RUT: Ah!

QUEEN: She angered me quite a bit. I could not stand her sight any longer.

RUT *Aside:* How I startle at that dear name! My face will betray me. I feel it, I am becoming pale – and now I blush again –

QUEEN: You blush at what I say?

RUT: Your surprising, gracious confidence, Queen –

QUEEN: I know you deserve my trust. – Come, Rutland, I will tell you everything. You should advise me. – There is no doubt, dear Rutland, that you will have heard how much the people rail against the poor unhappy man, the crimes they charge him with. But perhaps you do not yet know the worst? He arrived today from Ireland, against my strict commands, and left affairs there in utmost confusion.

RUT: May I tell you, Queen, what I think? – The clamor of the people is not always the voice of truth. Their hate is often so unfounded –

QUEEN: You speak the true thoughts of my soul. – But, dear Rutland, he is nonetheless to blame. – Come here, my dear, let me lean upon your breast. – Oh it is certain, they provoke me too much! No, I will not let myself be brought under their yoke in that way. They forget, that I am their Queen. – Ah, dear, I have long wanted a friend like you, to whom I can pour out my sorrows! –

RUT: Behold my tears, Queen – To see you suffer so, you whom I admire so much! – Oh, if only my good angel would put thoughts in my soul and words on my tongue to charm the storm in your heart and pour balsam on your wounds!

QUEEN: Oh, then you would be my good angel, compassionate Rutland! – Say, is it not a pity, that so brave a man should be a traitor? That such a hero, honored as a god, can stoop so low to gain a petty throne from me?

RUT: That is what he is said to have wanted? Could he have wanted that? No, Queen, certainly not, certainly not! How often have I heard him speak of you! With what devotion, with what admiration, with what delight have I heard him speak of you!

QUEEN: Have you really heard him speak of me?

RUT: And always as a man inspired, who speaks not with cold consideration, but with an inner feeling he cannot master. She is, he said, the goddess of her sex, raised so far above all other women that what we admire most in them, beauty and charm, are in her merely the shadows that offset a greater luster. Every feminine perfection is absorbed by her as the weak shimmer of a star is absorbed into the overflowing brightness of sunlight. Nothing exceeds her goodness; in her person benevolence itself rules this happy isle; her laws are drawn from the eternal codes of heaven and are registered again there by angels. – Oh, he then interrupted himself with a sigh that expressed the entirety of his loyal heart, oh, that she cannot be immortal! I do not wish to survive that terrible moment when God calls back this reflection of himself and instantly spreads darkness and confusion over Britain.

QUEEN: Did he say that, Rutland?

RUT: That, and much more. Always just as fresh and true in your praise, whose inexhaustible source overflowed with the most sincere views of you –

QUEEN: Oh, Rutland, how gladly I believe the testimonials you give of him!

RUT: And yet you can still believe him to be a traitor?

QUEEN: No – but he has still broken the laws. – I shame myself to protect him longer. – I may not even dare to see him.

RUT: Not see him, Queen? Not see him? By the pity that has set up its throne in your soul, I entreat you: you must see him! Shame? Whose? For showing mercy to an unfortunate man? – God has mercy: should Kings insult mercy? – No, Queen, be equal to yourself here. Yes, you will, you will see him, see him at least once –

QUEEN: Him, the man who could so defy my explicit command? Him, the man who dares bring himself audaciously before my eyes? Why did he not stay where I ordered him to stay?

RUT: Do not attribute this to a crime! Lay the blame on the danger he saw himself in. He heard what was proceeding here, how much they sought to belittle him and make him suspect in your eyes. Thus he came, though without permission, with the best intention: with the intention to clear himself and not allow you to be deceived.

QUEEN: Good, then I will see him, and see him straight. – Oh, my Rutland, how dearly I wish to find him just as honest as I know him to be brave!

RUT: Oh nourish this most kind belief! Your royal soul cannot nurture a more righteous one. – Honest! You will certainly find him so. I would swear for him, by all your splendor I would swear for him that he has never ceased to be so. His soul is purer than the sun, which has spots and draws earthly vapors toward itself, and breeds vermin. – You say he is brave, and who does not say this? But a brave man is not capable of baseness. Think how he chastised the rebels, and how dreadful he made you to Spain, who spent the treasures of his Indies against you in vain. His name flew ahead of your fleets and armies, and even before they arrived, often his name had already won the battle.

QUEEN *Aside:* How eloquent she is! – Ha! This passion, this ardency – mere pity does not go so far. – I will hear it straight! – *to her:* And then, Rutland, his form –

RUT: Right, queen, his form. – Never has a form been more in keeping with the inner perfection! – Admit it, you, who yourself are so beautiful, that a more beautiful man has never been seen! A form so worthy, so noble, so bold and commanding! Every limb in such harmony with the others! And the whole with such soft lovely contours! Nature's true model for creating a perfect man! The rare pattern for art, which must search through a hundred subjects for what it finds here all together!

QUEEN *Aside:* I thought so! – I can tolerate no more. – *to her:* What is the matter, Rutland? You are beside yourself. Your words and images come crowding one upon the other. What has thus overcome you? Is it just your Queen, or is it Essex himself that effects this true, or this forced, passion in you? – *Aside:* she is silent; – most certainly, she loves him. – What have I done? What new storm have I roused in my breast? etc.

Here Burleigh and Nottingham appear again to tell the queen that Essex awaits her orders. He is to come before her. "Rutland," the Queen says, "we must defer this subject till another time. – Come hither, Nottingham." This streak of jealousy is excellent. Essex enters, and now comes the scene with the box on the ear. I do not know how it could be prepared with greater understanding or success. At first Essex seems to want to be completely submissive, but when she orders him to defend himself, he becomes more and more heated; he huffs and puffs and brags and blusters. Nevertheless, none of this could have riled the Queen so much had her heart not already been embittered with jealousy. It is really the jealous lover who hits him; she merely employs the hand of the Queen to do so. In general, jealousy loves to hit.

For my part, I would rather have merely imagined these scenes than to have written the whole of Corneille's *Essex*. They are so distinctive, so full of life and truth, that the Frenchman's best effort pales in comparison.

Essay 59

24 November 1767[1]

Note that Banks's style should not be judged from my translation.[2] I have had to depart completely from his mode of expression. It is at once so common and so precious, so abased and so pretentious, and not just differing from character to character but in all aspects, that it could serve as a model of this kind of muddle. I have tried to sneak between the two cliffs as well as possible, but in the process preferred to run aground against the one rather than the other.

I have been more on guard against bombast than against plainness. The majority might perhaps have done exactly the opposite, for many consider bombast and tragedy to be one and the same. Not just many readers, but also many poets themselves. Their heroes should speak like other men? What kind of heroes would those be? *Ampullae & sesquipedalia verba*, sentences and bluster and foot-and-a-half-long words, that is what they consider the true tone of tragedy.[3]

"We have spared no effort," Diderot says,* (note that he speaks primarily of his own countrymen), "to corrupt the drama. We have retained from the Ancients the emphatic versification which was so suitable for languages with strong measures and heavy stresses, for spacious theatres, for a declamation which was scored and accompanied by instruments; and we have abandoned their simplicity of plot and dialogue, and the truth of their tableaux."[4]

Diderot could have added one more reason why we ought not to take the mode of expression of the ancient tragedies as a model. In those plays, all of the characters speak and converse in an open public plaza, in the presence of a curious crowd of people. Thus they nearly always need to speak with caution and respect for their dignity; they cannot simply unload their thoughts and feelings with the first words that come to mind, they must measure and choose them. But we moderns who have abolished the chorus and, for the most part, keep our characters within their four walls, what grounds can we have then for such decorous, fastidious, pretentious speech? No one hears it other than those the characters allow to hear it; nobody speaks but people who are also involved in the action and who are therefore in the heat of passion themselves and have neither the inclination nor the leisure to control their expressions. That was the domain of the chorus, which, as tightly as it might have been woven into the play, nevertheless never took part in the action and always judged the active characters more than it really sympathized with their fates. In any case, it is fruitless to invoke the higher rank of the characters. Noble people have learned to express themselves better than common men, but they do not perpetually put on airs to express themselves better. Least of all in the heat of passion, for which every person has his own eloquence, an eloquence inspired only by nature and learned in no school, which the least educated man can command just as well as the most polished.

There can never be any feeling conveyed with labored, precious, bombastic language. It produces no feeling and cannot bring forth any. Feeling does, however, go hand in hand with the simplest, commonest, plainest words and sayings.

I am fully aware that no queen on the French stage has ever spoken the way I have Banks's Elizabeth speak. In Paris, the humble, intimate tone she uses to converse with her women would not even be seen as appropriate for a good noble countrywoman. "Are you not well? – I am quite well. Rise, I pray you. – I am only

---

* Second Conversation on *The Natural Son*.

troubled, a little troubled. – Tell me then. – Was it not, Nottingham? Do so! Let me hear! – Enough, enough! – You rail yourself out of breath. – Poison and blisters on her tongue! – I have leave to use the thing I have made as I please. – Hitting a poor man on the head. – How are you? Cheer up, dear Rutland, I will find you a brave husband. – How can you speak thus? – You shall see from this. – She angered me quite a bit. I could not stand her sight any longer. – Come here, my dear, let me lean upon your breast. – I thought so! – I can tolerate no more." – The fine critics would say, "Yes, indeed, it is intolerable!" –

Perhaps many of my readers will say this as well. – For unfortunately there are Germans who are more French than the French. I have gathered all of these bits into a heap to please them. I know their manner of criticizing. They very cleverly line up in a row all of the little negligences that insult their tender ears, that were so hard for the poet to find, and which he scattered about here and there to make the dialogue smooth and the speech more truly appear to come from the inspiration of the moment. Then they set to laughing about them. It is all followed with a pitying shrug of the shoulders: "you can hear that the good man does not know the great world, that he has not heard many queens speak; Racine understood this better, but then Racine lived at court."

None of this bothers me. So much the worse for queens if they do not, or are not permitted to, speak this way. I have long believed that the court is hardly the place where a poet can study nature. But when pomp and etiquette make machines out of people, then it is the task of the poet to make people out of these machines again. True queens might speak as affectedly and artificially as they want; his queens must speak naturally. He should just listen studiously to Euripides' *Hecuba* and rest content even if he has not heard another queen speak.[5]

Nothing is more modest and decent than simple nature. Coarseness and smut are as far removed from her as pomposity and bombast are from the sublime.[6] The same feeling that apprehends the boundary there will also detect it here. The most pompous poet is therefore without fail the most vulgar. The two faults are inseparable, and no genre affords more opportunities to lapse into both than tragedy.

In the case of their Banks, the English seem to have taken offense primarily to one of the two. They were less critical of his bombast than of the vulgar speech he gives to such noble, historically dazzling people, and they long wished that his play might be rewritten by a man who had better mastery of tragic expression.[†] And indeed, this eventually happened. Jones and Brooke took it upon themselves at almost the same time.[7] Henry Jones, an Irishman by birth, was a mason by trade and, like old Ben Jonson, traded his trowel for a pen.[8] After he had a volume of poetry published on

---

[†] (*Companion to the Theatre* Vol. II p. 105.) – The Diction is every where very bad, and in some Places so low, that it even becomes unnatural. – And I think there cannot be a greater Proof of the little Encouragement this Age affords to Merit, than that no Gentleman possest of a true Genius and Spirit of Poetry, thinks it worth his Attention to adorn so celebrated a Part of History with that Dignity of Expression befitting Tragedy in general, but more particularly, where the Characters are perhaps the greatest the World ever produced.

subscription that established his reputation as a man of great talent, he brought his *Essex* to the stage in 1753. When this was performed in London, the one by Henry Brooke had already played in Dublin. But Brooke did not have his published until a few years later, and so it can very well be that, as some accuse, he might just as well have used Jones's *Essex* as Banks's. There is also supposed to be an *Essex* by James Ralph in existence.[9] I confess that I have not read any of them and know all three only from the literary journals. A French critic says of Brooke's *Essex* that he combined Banks's fire and pathos with Jones's beautiful poetry. What he adds concerning Rutland's role, and her despair at her husband's execution, is remarkable;[‡] from it we also come to know a side of the Parisian *parterre* that does it little honor.[10]

But I have read a Spanish *Essex* that is far too peculiar not to say something about it in passing.

Essay 60

27 November 1767[1]

It is by an unknown author and carries the title: *To Die for His Lady.*[*,2] I find it in a collection of comedies published by Joseph Padrino in Seville, in which it is the seventy-fourth play.[3] I do not know when it was produced, and I see nothing from which we might glean a date.[4] It is clear that its author neither used the French and English poets who had adapted the same history, nor was used by them. It is completely original. Yet I do not want to preempt the judgment of my readers.

Essex returns from his expedition against the Spanish and wants to deliver his report to the Queen in London. When he arrives, he hears that she is two miles from the city at the country estate of one of her ladies-in-waiting, Blanca. This Blanca is the earl's lover, and while her father was still alive he had had many secret rendezvous with her on this estate. He proceeds there right away and makes use of the key he retained to the garden gate he used to use. It is natural that he would rather show himself to his beloved than to the Queen. As he sneaks through the garden toward her rooms, he becomes aware of a woman on the shadowy bank of an arm of the Thames that winds through the garden. It is a muggy summer evening, and she sits with her bare feet in the water and cools herself off. He stands still, utterly amazed by her beauty, even though she has covered her face with a half-mask so as not to be recognized. (As is customary in such things, this beauty is described at great length, and in particular there are some very cunning things said about the lovely white feet

---

‡ (*Journal Encycl.* Mars 1761.) [Mr. Brooke] a aussi fait tomber en demence la Comtesse de Rutland, au moment que cet illustre [coupable, son] époux, est conduit à l'échafaud; ce moment où cette Comtesse est un objet bien digne de pitié, a produit une trés grande sensation, & a été trouvé admirable à Londres: en France il eut paru ridicule, il auroit été sifflé & l'on auroit envoyé la Comtesse avec l'Auteur aux Petites-Maisons.

* *Dar la vida por su Dama, o el Conde de Sex; de un Ingenio de esta Corte.*

in the clear water. It's not enough that the enraptured Earl sees two crystalline pillars standing in a flowing crystal; in his amazement he does not know whether the water is the crystal-become-liquid of her feet, or if her feet are the crystallization of the water, which has condensed into this form.[†,5] The black half-mask on the white face bewilders him even more: he cannot comprehend to what purpose nature has formed such a divine monster and given it a face that pairs such black basalt with such lustrous ivory; whether this is more to amaze or to mock?[‡])[6] Hardly has the woman dressed herself again when, with a cry of: "Die Tyrant!," she is shot at, and two masked men with drawn swords immediately attack her, because the shot seems not to have hit her. Essex does not consider long before rushing to her aid. He attacks the murderers, and they escape. He wants to go after them, but the lady calls him back and asks him not to put his life in danger. She sees that he is wounded, unknots her sash and gives it to him to bind up his wound. At the same time, she says, this sash should serve to make you known to me at the proper time; now I must depart before any more fuss arises over the shooting. I would not like it if the Queen were to learn of the incident, and for that reason I beg you for your silence. She goes, and Essex remains, completely amazed at this peculiar incident, over which he makes all manner of observation with his servant, Cosme. This Cosme is the comic character in the play; he had stayed in front

---

† Las dos colunas [sic] bellas
  metió dentro del rio; y como al vellas
  ví cristal en el rio desatado,
  y ví cristal en ellas condensado,
  no supe si las aguas que se vian
  eran sus pies que líquidos corrian,
  ó si sus dos colunas [sic] se formaban
  de las aguas que allí se congelaban.

The poet pushes this similarity even further when he wants to describe how the lady, in tasting the water, scoops it up with her hollowed hand and carries it to her mouth. This hand, he says, was so similar to the clear water that the river itself recoiled in terror because it feared she might drink some of her own hand along with the water.

Quiso probar acaso
  el agua, y fuéron cristalino vaso
  sus manos, acercólas á los labios,
  y entónces el arroyo lloró agravios;
  y como tanto en fin se parecia
  á sus manos aquello que bebia,
  temí con sobresalto (y no fué en vano)
  que se bebiera parte de la mano.
‡ Yo que al principio ví, ciego y turbado,
  á una parte nevado,
  y en otra negro el rostro,
  juzgué, mirando tan divino monstro,
  que la naturaleza cuidadosa,
  desigualdad uniendo tan hermosa,
  quiso hacer por asombro ó por ultraje,
  de azabache y marfil un maridage.

of the garden when his master went in and had of course heard the shot but was not permitted to come to his help.[7] Fear guarded the gate and blocked his entrance. Cosme is fearful enough for four;[§] this is common to all the Spanish fools.[8] Essex confesses that he would have fallen in love with the beautiful unknown lady without fail if Blanca had not already taken such full possession of his heart that she left no room for any other passion. But, he says, who might she possibly be? What do you think, Cosme? – Who else could it be, Cosme answers, than the gardener's wife, washing her legs?[¶,9] – One can easily deduce the rest from this sketch. They finally both depart: it has become too late; the house could have been set in turmoil by the shooting; as a result, Essex fears he cannot go to Blanca without being noticed and postpones his visit to another time.

Now the Duke of Alanzon enters, with Flora, Blanca's chambermaid.[10] (The scene is still at the country estate, in one of Blanca's rooms; the previous scene was in the garden. It is the following day.) The king of France had proposed a union with his youngest brother to Elizabeth. This is the Duke of Alanzon. He has come to England under the pretext of a diplomatic mission in order to bring about this union. On the part of both parliament and the Queen everything seems to be going very favorably, but then he catches sight of Blanca and falls in love with her. Now he comes to ask Flora to help him with his love. Flora does not hide from him how little he can expect, but without revealing to him the least hint of Blanca's intimacy with the Earl. She only says that Blanca seeks to marry, and that because she cannot depend upon marriage with a man whose rank is so elevated above her own, she hardly would dare give audience to his love. – (We expect that the Duke will protest the purity of his intentions in response to this assertion: but not a word! The Spanish are not nearly as strict and delicate on this point as the French.) He has written a letter to Blanca that Flora is to deliver. He himself wishes to observe what kind of impression this letter will have on her. He gives Flora a gold chain, and Flora hides him in an adjoining gallery as Blanca enters with Cosme, who tells her of the arrival of his master.

Essex arrives. After Blanca welcomes him most tenderly, and after the Earl reassures her most dearly how much he wishes to show himself worthy of her love, Flora and Cosme must depart, and Blanca remains alone with the Earl. She reminds him how eager and steadfast he was in contending for her love. After she resisted him for three years, she finally yielded herself to him and, under the promise of marriage, made him owner of her honor. ("Te hice dueño de mi honor": the expression says quite a bit

---

§ Ruido de armas en la Quinta,
  y dentro el Conde, qué aguardo,
  que no voy á socorrerle?
  Qué aguardo? lindo recado:
  aguardo á que quiera el miedo
  dexarme entrar: —

  Cosme, que ha tenido un miedo,
  que puede valer por quatro.
¶ La muger del Hortelano,
  que se lavaba las piernas.

in Spanish.)[11] Only the hostility that exists between their two families has prevented them from marrying. Essex denies none of this and adds that after the death of her father and brother, only the expedition against the Spanish that was assigned to him has come between them. Now, however, he has successfully completed it; now he wants to petition the Queen immediately for permission for their marriage. – And then, says Blanca, I can safely entrust all of my secrets to you, my beloved, my fiancé, my friend.**,[12]

Essay 61

1 December 1767[1]

At this point, she begins a long story about the fate of Mary of Scotland.[2] We learn (for Essex himself must doubtless have known all this for a long time) that her father and brother were very devoted to this unhappy queen, that she had refused to participate in the oppression of the innocent, that Elizabeth imprisoned her for this and then secretly had her executed in prison. No wonder Blanca hates Elizabeth and is firmly resolved to seek revenge. It is true that, later, Elizabeth received her among her ladies-in-waiting and deemed her worthy of her complete confidence. But Blanca is unforgiving. It was in vain that the Queen recently chose Blanca's country estate over all others to enjoy the season for a few days in peace and quiet. – Blanca wanted to use this very advantage to bring about her ruin. She had written to her uncle, who, fearing that what happened to his brother, her father, might happen to him, had fled to Scotland, where he lived in hiding. The uncle had come, and in brief, the uncle was the one who wanted to murder the Queen in the garden. Now Essex knows who the person is whose life he saved, and we do, too. But Blanca does not know that it is Essex who will thwart her plot. Rather, she counts on the infinite love Essex has pledged to her and ventures not just to make him into an accomplice but to transfer wholly onto him the successful execution of her revenge. He is to write immediately to her uncle, who has fled back to Scotland again, and make common cause with him. The she-tyrant must die, her name is universally hated, her death would be a great service to the country, and no one deserves better than Essex to provide the country such a service.

Essex is completely taken aback by this proposal. Blanca, his dear Blanca, could ask him to commit such treachery? How very ashamed he is, in this moment, of his love! But what should he do? Should he do the proper thing and convey his indignation? Would she then be any less likely to cling to her disgraceful stance? Should he inform the Queen of the matter? That is impossible: Blanca, who is still his dear Blanca, is in danger. Should he try to dissuade her from her decision through pleas and petitions? He would have to be ignorant of what a vengeful creature an injured woman is and

---

** [. . .] bien podré seguramente
revelarte intentos mios
como á galan, como á dueño,
como á esposo, y como á amigo.

how little she allows herself to be softened by entreaties or frightened off by danger. How readily might his dissuasion, his anger bring her into despair, so that she revealed herself to another who would not be so scrupulous and would dare anything out of love for her?*,3 – Having considered this quickly, he resolves to dissimulate in order to trap Roberto (this is Blanca's uncle) along with all of his followers.

Blanca becomes impatient when Essex does not answer her immediately. "Earl," she says, "if you must consult with yourself so long, then you do not love me. Even to doubt is a crime. Ingrate!"†,4 – "Be calm, Blanca!" Essex replies: "I have made a decision." – "To do what?" – "I will give it to you in writing right away."

The Earl sits down to write to her; meanwhile the Duke approaches from the gallery.5 He is curious to see who converses so long with Blanca and is astonished to behold the Earl of Essex. But he is even more shocked by what he hears next. Essex has written to Roberto and reads Blanca the content of his letter, which he intends to send off with Cosme immediately.6 Roberto should come with his friends to London, separately; Essex will support him with his people; Essex has the people's favor;

---

* Hay tal traicion! vive el Cielo,
   que de amarla estoy corrido.
   Blanca, que es mi dulce dueño,
   Blanca, á quien quiero, y estimo,
   me propone tal traicion!
   Qué haré? porque si ofendido,
   respondiendo, como es justo,
   contra su traicion me irrito,
   no por eso he de evitar
   su resuelto desatino.
   Pues darle cuenta á la Reyna
   es imposible, pues quiso
   mi suerte, que tenga parte
   Blanca en aqueste delito.
   Pues si procuro con ruegos
   disuadirla, es desvarío,
   que es una muger resuelta
   animal tan vengativo,
   que no se dobla á los ruegos,
   ántes con afecto impio,
   en el mismo rendimiento
   suelen aguzar los filos:
   y quizá desesperada
   de mi enojo ó mi desvío,
   se declarará con otro
   ménos leal, ménos fino,
   que quizá por ella intente
   lo que yo hacer no he querido.
† Si estás consultando, Conde,
   allá dentro de ti mismo
   lo que has de hacer, no me quieres,
   ya el dudarlo fué delito:
   vive Dios, que eres ingrato.

nothing will be easier than to seize the Queen; she is as good as dead. – "First I would have to die!" cries the Duke suddenly, coming toward them. Blanca and the Earl are taken aback by this sudden appearance, and the latter's shock is not without jealousy. He believes that Blanca had hidden the Duke in her rooms. The Duke vindicates Blanca and avouches that she knew nothing of his presence; he had found the gallery open and had gone in on his own to look at the paintings there.[‡,7]

‡ [DUQ.] [P]or vida del Rey mi hermano,
   y por lo que mas estimo,
   de la Reyna mi señora,
   y por: – pero ya lo digo,
   que en mí es el mayor empeño
   de la verdad el decirlo,
   que no tiene Blanca parte
   de estar yo aquí: –
   [. . . .]
   y estad muy agradecido
   á Blanca de que yo os dé,
   no satisfaccion, aviso
   de esta verdad, porque á vos,
   hombre como yo: –
   COND. Imagino
   que no me conoceis bien.
   DUQ. No os habia conocido
   hasta aquí; mas ya os conozco,
   pues ya tan otro os he visto,
   que os reconozco traidor.
   COND. Quien dixere: –
   DUQ. Yo lo digo:
   no pronuncies algo, Conde,
   que ya no puedo sufriros.
   COND. Qualquier cosa que yo intente: –
   DUQ. Mirad que estoy persuadido,
   que hace la traicion cobardes;
   y así, quando os he cogido
   en un lance, que me da
   de que sois cobarde indicios,
   no he de aprovecharme de esto,
   y así os perdona mi brio
   este rato que teneis
   el valor desminuido,
   que á estar todo vos entero,
   supiera daros castigo.
   COND. Yo soy el Conde de Sex,
   y nadie se me ha atrevido
   sino el hermano del Rey
   de Francia.
   DUQ. Yo tengo brio,
   para que sin ser quien soy,
   pueda mi valor invicto
   castigar, no digo yo
   solo á vos, mas á vos mismo,

THE DUKE: On my brother's life, on the life of the Queen, which is even more dear to me, on – but enough for me to say to you: Blanca is innocent. And, milord, you have only her to thank for this declaration. You do not warrant any consideration here. For people like me make of people like you –

THE EARL: Prince, doubtless you do not really know who I am?

THE DUKE: True, I did not really know you. But I know you now. I thought you were a completely different man, and I find you are a traitor.

THE EARL: Who dares say that?

THE DUKE: I do! – Not another word! I will not hear another word, Earl!

THE EARL: My intention may also have been –

THE DUKE: Look: I am convinced that a traitor has no heart. I encounter you as a traitor: I must take you for a man without a heart. But I do not permit myself to make use of this advantage over you. My honor pardons you because you have forfeited yours. If you were as blameless as I once thought you were, I would know how to chastise you.

THE EARL: I am the Earl of Essex. No one has yet dared treat me thusly except the brother of the King of France.

THE DUKE: If I were not who I am; if you only were, what you are not, a man of honor: then you would really feel who you are dealing with. You, the Earl of Essex? If you are this famous warrior, how could you want to wipe out so many great deeds through one that is so unworthy?

Essay 62

4 December 1767[1]

The Duke now proceeds to reproach him for his wrongdoing in a somewhat milder tone.[2] He advises him to think better of it; he will forget what he has heard; he is reassured that Blanca does not agree with the Earl and that she herself would have said the same thing to him had he, the Duke, not beat her to it.[3] He finally ends: "Once again, Earl, examine your conscience! Distance yourself from such a disgraceful plan! Be yourself again! And if you do not follow my advice, remember that you have a head, and London has an executioner!"[*,4] – With this the Duke departs. Essex is left

---

    siendo leal, que es lo mas
    con que queda encarecido.
    Y pues sois tan gran Soldado,
    no echeis á perder os pido,
    tantas heroycas [sic] hazañas
    con un hecho tan indigno.
* Miradlo mejor: dexad
    un intento tan indigno,
    corresponded á quien sois,
    y sino bastan avisos,
    mirad, que hay verdugo en Lóndres
    y en vos cabeza: harto os digo.

in the most extreme confusion: it pains him to know himself taken for a traitor, but at the same time he dare not defend himself to the Duke at this time; he must be patient and wait until the outcome demonstrates that he was most loyal to his Queen in the very moment when he seemed to be least so.[†,5] He speaks to himself thusly; to Blanca, however, he says that he will send the letter to her uncle right away, and exits. Blanca also leaves, after cursing her unlucky stars but then consoling herself that it is no one worse than the Duke who knows of the Earl's plot.

The Queen appears with her chancellor, to whom she has confided what happened to her in the garden. She orders that her guards occupy all points of access; tomorrow she will return to London. The chancellor thinks they should have the assassins pursued and make a public proclamation promising a handsome reward to the person who informs against them, even if he himself is one of the conspirators. "For since there were two who committed the attack," he says, "one of them might easily be just as faithless a friend as he is a faithless subject."[‡,6] – But the Queen rejects this advice; she thinks it is much better to suppress the whole incident and not to let it be known at all that there are people who would have the audacity to commit such a deed. "We must," she says, "make the world believe that kings are so well guarded that it is impossible for traitors to come near them. Extraordinary crimes are better concealed than punished. For the example of the punishment is inseparable from the example of the sin, and the latter can incite just as much as the former can discourage."[§,7]

Meanwhile, Essex is announced and let in. The report he gives of the happy success of his expedition is brief. The Queen says to him, in a very obliging manner: "Just seeing you again gives me enough knowledge about the outcome of the war."[¶,8] She does not want to hear any further details before she has rewarded his service, and she

---

† [...] no he de responder al Duque
hasta que el suceso mismo
muestre como fuéron falsos
de mi traicion los indicios,
y que soy mas leal, quando
mas traidor he parecido.

‡ [. . .] y pues son dos los culpados
podrá ser que alguno de ellos
entregue al otro, que es llano,
que será traidor amigo,
quien fué desleal vasallo.

§ [. . .] y es gran materia de estado
dar á entender que los Reyes
están en sí tan guardados,
que aunque la traicion los busque,
nunca ha de poder hallarlos;
y así, el secreto averigüe [sic]
enormes delitos, quanto
mas, que castigo y escarmiento
es ilacion el pecado.

¶ [. . .] que ya solo con miraros
sé el suceso de la guerra.

orders the chancellor to immediately issue the Earl a patent as Admiral of England. The chancellor goes; the Queen and Essex are alone; the conversation becomes more intimate; Essex is wearing the sash; the Queen notices it, and Essex would have deduced from this comment alone that it came from her, had he not deduced this already from what Blanca said. The Queen has long loved the Earl in secret, and now she even owes him her life.**,9 It costs her every effort to hide her inclinations. She asks various questions to draw him out and hear whether his heart is already taken and whether he guesses whose life he saved in the garden. Through his answers he gives her to understand that he has, and, at the same time, that he feels more for this person than he might have the audacity to reveal. The Queen is on the brink of revealing herself to him; but her pride wins out over her love. The Earl must struggle with his pride just as much: he cannot free himself of the thought that the Queen loves him, even though he recognizes the presumptuousness of this thought. (It's obvious that this scene would have to consist primarily of speeches that each gives as asides.) She orders him to go and then orders him to wait until the chancellor brings him the patent. He brings it, she presents it to him, he gives his thanks, and the asides begin again with renewed passion:

QUEEN: Foolish love! –
ESSEX: Vain madness! –
QUEEN: How blind! –
ESSEX: How audacious! –
QUEEN: You wish me to sink so low? –
ESSEX: You want me to climb so high? –
QUEEN: Remember, I am the Queen! –
ESSEX: Remember, I am a subject! –
QUEEN: You plunge me into the abyss, –
ESSEX: You raise me up to the sun, –
QUEEN: Without paying heed to my majesty.
ESSEX: Without considering my lowliness.
QUEEN: But, because you have conquered my heart: –
ESSEX: But, because you have conquered my soul: –
QUEEN: Die there, never to be spoken!
ESSEX: Die there, and never cross my lips!††,10

** [. . .] no bastaba, amor tirano,
una inclinacion tan fuerte,
sin que te hayas ayudado
del deberle yo la vida?
†† REYN: Loco amor –
COND: Necio imposible –
REYN: Que ciego –
COND: Que temerario –
REYN: Me abates á tal baxezar –
COND: Me quieres subir tan alto –
REYN: Advierte, que soy la Reyna.

(Is that not a peculiar type of conversation? They speak to each other, and also do not speak to each other. The one hears what the other does not say and responds to what he has not heard. Rather than taking the words out of each other's mouths, they take them from each other's souls. However, it should not be said that one must be a Spaniard to have a taste for such unnatural affectations. Around thirty years ago we Germans still had just as much a taste for it; our "state and hero plays," which were patterned in every respect after the Spanish model, teemed with them.)[11]

After the Queen has granted leave to Essex and ordered him to attend on her again soon, they exit separately, and this concludes the first act. – Spanish plays, as we know, have only three acts, which they call *Jornadas*, days. Their oldest plays had four: they crawled, Lope de Vega said, on all fours, like infants, for they really were still the infants of comedies.[12] Virués was the first to reduce the four acts to three, and Lope followed him in this, although he had also already written the first plays of his youth, or rather his childhood, in four acts.[13] We learn this from a passage in the latter's *The New Art of Writing Plays*,[‡‡,14] which I find contradicts a passage from Cervantes,[§§,15] in which he claims the fame of reducing Spanish plays from the five acts they previously consisted of to three. The Spanish literary critic can determine the outcome of this conflict; I do not wish to dwell on it.

Essay 63

8 December 1767[1]

The Queen has returned from the country estate; Essex has as well.[2] As soon as he arrives in London, he rushes to the court so as not to waste a moment. He and Cosme open the second act, which takes place in the royal palace.[3] On the Earl's orders,

---

COND: Advierte, que soy vasallo.
REYN: Pues me humillas al abismo –
COND: Pues me acercas á los rayos –
REYN: Sin reparar mi grandeza –
COND: Sin mirar mi humilde estado –
REYN: Ya que te admito acá dentro –
COND: Ya que en mí te vas entrando –
REYN: Muere entre el pecho y la voz.
COND: Muere entre el alma, y los labios.

‡‡ *Arte nuevo de hazer Comedias* which is located after Lope's *Rimas*.
El capitán Virúes, insigne ingenio,
puso en tres actos la comedia, que antes
andava en cuatro, como pies de niño,
que eran entonces niñas las comedias;
y yo las escriví, de onze, y doze años,
de a cuatro actos, y de a cuatro pliegos,
porque cada acto un pligo contenía [. . . .]

§§ In the prologue to his plays, [Cervantes writes,] "Donde me atreví à reducir las Comedias à tres Jornadas, de cinco que tenian."

Cosme has furnished himself with pistols; the Earl has secret enemies; he worries about being attacked when he leaves the palace late at night. He tells Cosme to take the pistols to Blanca's room in the meanwhile and have Flora keep them.[4] At the same time, he unties the sash because he wants to go to Blanca. Blanca is jealous, the sash could give her ideas, she could want to have it, and he would have to deny it to her. While he is handing it to Cosme for safekeeping, Blanca comes in. Cosme wants to hide it quickly, but he cannot do it quickly enough to keep Blanca from noticing it. Blanca takes the Earl with her to the Queen, and as he goes, Essex cautions Cosme to keep absolutely mum about the sash and not show it to anyone.

Among his other good qualities, Cosme has this one: he is an arch-chatterbox. He cannot keep a secret for an hour, he is afraid of getting an ulcer from it; and the Earl's prohibition has reminded him just in time that he has exposed himself to this danger for the last thirty-six hours.[*,5] He gives the pistols to Flora and has opened his mouth to tell her the whole story of the masked lady and the sash when he reconsiders: the first person with whom he shares his secret should be much more worthy. It would not be proper if Flora could boast that she had deflowered him of it.[†,6] (I am trying to insert a hint of the great range of Spanish humor.)

Cosme need not wait long for this more worthy person. Blanca is so tormented by her curiosity that she disengages herself from the Earl as soon as possible to find out what Cosme had earlier tried to hide from her so hastily. She thus returns immediately, and after she first asks why he has not already left for Scotland, where the Earl was to send him, and he answers that he will depart at the break of dawn; she demands to know what he is keeping hidden? She presses him; but Cosme does not let himself be pressed for long. He tells her everything he knows about the sash, and Blanca takes it from him. The way he divests himself of his secret is extremely disgusting. His stomach will no longer keep it down; he feels a rising and a churning in his belly; he sticks his finger down his throat; he vomits; and to get a better taste in his mouth again, he rushes out to chew a quince or an olive.[‡,7] Blanca cannot fully make sense of his confusing prattle, but she does understand this much: that the sash was a gift

---

*– yo no me acordaba
　　de decirlo, y lo callaba,
　　y como me lo encargó,
　　ya por decirlo rebiento,
　　que tengo tal propiedad,
　　que en un hora ó la mitad,
　　se me hace postema un cuento.

†　Allá va, Flora: mas no,
　　será á persona mas grave;
　　no es bien que Flora se alabe,
　　que el cuento me desfloró.

‡　[. . . .] ya se me viene á la boca
　　la purga. [. . .]
　　Qué regüeldos tan reveses
　　me vienen! terrible aprieto! [. . . .]
　　mi estómago no lo lleva.
　　Protesto: – qué gran trabajo!

from a lady with whom Essex could fall in love if he were not already in love. "For he is, after all, just a man," she says. "And woe to her who has entrusted her honor to a man! Even the best is still bad!"§.8 – To preempt his unfaithfulness, she determines to marry him, the sooner the better.

The Queen enters and is extremely downhearted. Blanca asks if she should call the other ladies-in-waiting, but the Queen prefers to be alone; only Irene should come and sing outside the room.[9] Blanca exits on one side, and the Earl enters from the other.

Essex loves Blanca, but he is ambitious enough to want to be the Queen's lover as well. He reproaches himself for this ambition, he punishes himself for it, his heart belongs to Blanca, self-serving intentions must not rob her of it, false-hearted expediency must not conquer true feelings.¶.10 Thus when he becomes aware of the Queen, he wants to depart; and when the Queen sees him, she also wants to avoid him. But they both stay. Meanwhile, Irene begins to sing outside the room. She sings a *redondilla*, a short song four lines long, whose meaning is: "If my lovestruck lamentations come to your attention, then oh, let the pity they deserve overpower the displeasure you feel that it is I who convey them."[11] The Queen likes the song, and Essex finds it easy to declare his love through it in an oblique manner. He says that he has glossed it and asks permission to tell her his gloss.**.12 In this gloss, he describes himself as the most tender

---

    meto los dedos. [. . .]
    Y pues la purga he trocado,
    y el secreto he vomitado
    desde el principio hasta el fin,
    y sin dexar cosa alguna,
    tal asco me dió al decillo,
    voy á probar de un membrillo,
    ó á morder de una aceytuna.

§   Es hombre en fin: y ay de aquella,
    que á un hombre fió su honor,
    siendo tan malo el mejor.

¶   [. . . .] abate, abate las alas,
    no subas tanto, busquemos
    mas proporcionada esfera
    á tan limitado vuelo.
    Blanca me quiere, y á Blanca
    adoro yo: ya en mi dueño:
    pues cómo de amor tan noble
    por una ambicion me alejo?
    No conveniencia bastarda
    venza un legítimo afecto[.]

** The Spanish have a form of poetry that they call *glosas*. They take one or several lines as the text, so to speak, and explain or rewrite this text in such a way that the lines themselves are once again interwoven into this explanation or revision. They call the text *mote* ["motto"] or *letra*, and they call each particular exposition *glosa*, which is then also the name of the whole poem. Here, the poet has Essex make Irene's song into a *mote* consisting of four lines, each of which he rewrites into its own individual stanza, which he then ends with the line he has rewritten. The whole looks like this:

MOTE.
Si acaso mis desvaríos
llegaren á tus umbrales,

lover, who is forbidden by his reverence from revealing himself to the object of his love. The Queen praises his poetry, but she disapproves of his manner of loving. "A love that is silenced cannot be great," she says among other things, "for love only grows through being requited, and by remaining silent, one deliberately forfeits requited love."[13]

---

la lástima de ser males
quite el horror de ser mios.

GLOSA.
Aunque el dolor me provoca
decir mis quejas no puedo,
que es mi osadía tan poca,
que entre el respeto y el miedo
se me mueren en la boca:
Y así, no llegan tan mios
mis males á tus orejas,
perdiendo en la voz los brios,
si acaso digo mis quejas,
si acaso mis desvaríos.
El ser tan mal explicados
sea su mayor indicio,
que trocando en mis cuidados
el silencio, y voz su oficio,
quedarán mas ponderados:
Desde hoy por estas señales
sean de ti conocidos,
que sin duda son mis males,
si algunos mal repetidos
llegaren á tus umbrales.
Mas, ay Dios! que mis cuidados,
de tu crueldad conocidos,
aunque mas acreditados,
serán ménos admitidos,
que con los otros mezclados!
Porque no sabiendo á quales
mas tu ingratitud se deba,
viéndolos todos iguales,
fuerza es que en comun te mueva
la lástima de ser males.
En mí este efecto violento
tu hermoso desden le causa:
tuyo y mio es mi tormento;
tuyo, porque eres la causa;
mio, porque yo lo siento:
Sepan, Laura, tus desvíos,
que mis males son tan suyos,
y en mis cuerdos desvaríos,
esto que tienen de tuyos,
quite el horror de ser mios.

All *glosas* do not have to be as symmetrical as this one. One has full freedom to make the stanzas that conclude with the lines of the *mote* as uneven as one wants. One does not even need to weave in all the lines; one can limit oneself to just one, and repeat this more than one time. Incidentally, these *glosas* belong to the older genres of Spanish poetry that pretty much fell out of fashion after Boscán and Garcilaso.

Essay 64

11 December 1767[1]

The Earl rejoins that the most perfect love is one that expects no reward, and requited love is a reward.[2] His silence itself makes his happiness: for as long as he keeps his love quiet, it remains unrejected and he can allow himself to be deceived by the sweet notion that it might be accepted. The unfortunate man may be happy as long as he does not know how unfortunate he is.[*,3] The Queen refutes this sophistry as a person who herself has a stake in Essex no longer adhering to it, and Essex, made bold by this rebuttal, is about to dare make the profession that the Queen claims a lover absolutely must venture, when Blanca enters to announce the Duke. Blanca's appearance brings about one of the most singular *coups de théâtre*.[4] For Blanca is wearing the sash she took from Cosme, which the Queen notices, but Essex does not.[†,5]

* [. . . .] el mas verdadero amor,
  es el que en sí mismo quieto
  descansa, sin atender
  á mas paga, ó mas intento:
  la correspondencia es paga,
  y tener por blanco el precio,
  es querer por grangería;
  [. . . .]
  Dentro está del silencio, y del respeto
  mi amor, y así mi dicha está segura,
  presumiendo tal vez (dulce locura!)
  que es admitído del mayor sugeto.
  Dexándome engañar de este concepto,
  dura mi bien, porque mi engaño dura;
  necia será la lengua, si aventura
  un bien, que está seguro en el secreto.
  [. . .]
  que es feliz, quien no siendo venturoso,
  nunca llega á saber que es desdichado.
† [CON]: Por no morir de mal, quando
  puedo morir del remedio:
  digo, pues (ea, osadía,
  ella me alentó, qué temo?)
  que será bien, que tu Alteza –
  Sale Blanca con la banda puesta.
  BL: Señora, el Duque –
  CON: A mal tiempo
  viene Blanca.
  BL: Está aguardando
  en la antecámara.
  REYN: Ay, Cielo!
  BL: Para entrar –
  REYN: Qué es lo que miro!
  BL: Licencia.
  REYN: Decid (qué veo!)
  decid que espere (estoy loca!)

ESSEX: Then ventured it will be! – Be bold! She herself encourages me. Why do I want to die of the disease, when I can die of the remedy? What am I still afraid of? – Queen, in that case –

BLANCA: The Duke, your Majesty –

ESSEX: Blanca could not come at a more inconvenient moment.

BLANCA: Attends in the antechamber –

QUEEN: Ah! Heaven!

BLANCA: For permission –

QUEEN: What do I see?

BLANCA: To enter.

QUEEN: Tell him – What do I see? – Tell him he should wait. – I am going mad! – Go, tell him.

BLANCA: I obey.

QUEEN: Wait! Come here! Closer! –

BLANCA: What does your Majesty command? –

QUEEN: Oh, certainly! – Tell him – There is no doubt! – Go, entertain him for a moment – Woe is me! – Until I myself come out to him. Go, leave me!

BLANCA: What is this? – I am going.

ESSEX: Blanca is gone. I can continue now –

QUEEN: Ha, jealousy!

ESSEX: – to declare myself. – What I dare do, I dare by dint of your own persuasion.

QUEEN: My gift in strange hands! By god! – But I must be ashamed of myself to let a passion get so much the better of me!

---

decid, andad.
BL: Ya obedezco.
REYN: Vení acá, volved.
BL: Qué manda
vuestra Alteza?
REYN: El daño es cierto.
Decidle (no hay que dudar)
entretenedle un momento
(ay de mí!) miéntras yo salgo,
y dexadme.
BL: Qué es aquesto?
ya voy. *Vase.*
CON: Ya Blanca se fué;
quiero pues volver –
REYN: Ha zelos!
CON: A declararme atrevido,
pues si me atrevo, me atrevo
en fe de sus pretensiones.
REYN: Mi prenda en poder ageno!
vive Dios – Pero es vergüenza,
que pueda tanto un afecto
en mí.
CON: Segun lo que dixo
vuestra Alteza aquí, y supuesto

ESSEX: If then, therefore – as your Majesty said, and as I must concede – the happiness that one purchases through fear – costs dearly – even if one dies more nobly – then I, too, will –

QUEEN: Why are you saying this, Earl?

ESSEX: Because I hope that when I – Why am I still afraid? – if I professed my love to your Majesty – that some Love –

QUEEN: What are you saying here, Earl? You direct this to me? What? Fool! Madman! Do you recognize me? Do you know who I am? And who you are? I think you have lost your mind. [. . .]

And thus Her Majesty goes on reprimanding the poor Earl, and in such fine form! She asks him, does he not know how far heaven is raised above human audacities? Does he not know that the storm winds that seek to penetrate Olympus must roar back when they reach the halfway point? Does he not know that the vapors that rise toward the sun are dispersed by its rays? – The one who believes himself fallen from heaven is Essex. He withdraws, ashamed, and begs for forgiveness. The Queen commands him to stay out of her sight, never to enter her palace again, and to consider himself lucky that she has left him the head in which such vain thoughts were spawned.‡,6 He departs, and the Queen, after letting us know how little her heart corresponds with her speech, also exits.

Blanca and the Duke come in her place to fill the stage. Blanca has freely confessed to the Duke on what terms she and the Earl stand: that he must become her husband or her honor is lost. The Duke makes the decision that he must make; he will free himself of his love, and to repay her trust he promises to support her cause with the Queen when she decides to reveal her relationship with the Earl.

The Queen soon comes back, deep in thought. She is conflicted over whether the Earl is really as guilty as he seems. Perhaps it was another sash that was just very similar to hers. – The Duke comes to her. He says that he is come to ask a favor that Blanca asks for as well. Blanca will explain in more detail, he will leave them alone together, and so he leaves them.

---

que cuesta cara la dicha
que se compra con el miedo,
quiero morir noblemente.
REYN: Por qué lo [decis]?
CON: Qué espero?
si á vuestra Alteza (qué dudo?)
le declarase mi afecto
algun amor –
REYN: Qué decis?
Á mí? Cómo, loco, necio –
Conoceisme? Quién soy yo?
Decid, quién soy? que sospecho
que se os huyó la memoria. [. . .]
‡ [. . . .] No me veais,
y agradecedme que os dexo
cabeza, en que se engendráron
tan livianos pensamientos.

The Queen becomes curious; Blanca becomes confused. Finally Blanca decides to talk. She no longer wants to depend on a man's capricious resolve; she no longer wishes to leave to the discretion of his integrity what she can obtain through force. She begs Elizabeth for her compassion: Elizabeth, the woman, not the Queen. For because she must confess a weakness of her sex, she seeks in her not the Queen, but only the woman.[§,7]

Essay 65

15 December 1767[1]

You? Tell me a weakness? asks the Queen.[2]

BLANCA: Flatteries, sighs, caresses, and especially tears are capable of undermining
    even the purest virtue. How dearly this experience cost me! The Earl –
QUEEN: The Earl? Which Earl?
BLANCA: Essex.
QUEEN: What do I hear?
BLANCA: His seductive tenderness –
QUEEN: The Earl of Essex?
BLANCA: He himself, your highness. –
QUEEN *aside*: I'm dying! – Well? Keep going!
BLANCA: I tremble. – No, I do not dare –

The Queen encourages her and bit by bit draws more out of her than Blanca needs to say, and far more than she herself wishes to hear. She hears where and how the

§ Ya estoy resuelta,
    no á la voluntad mudable
    de un hombre esté yo sujeta,
    que aunque no sé que me olvide,
    es necedad, que yo quiera
    dexar á su cortesía
    lo que puede hacer la fuerza.
    Gran Isabela, escuchadme,
    y al escucharme tu Alteza,
    ponga, aun mas que la atencion,
    la piedad con las orejas.
    Isabela os he llamado
    en esta ocasion, no Reyna,
    que quando vengo á deciros
    del honor una flaqueza,
    que he hecho como muger,
    porque menor os parezca,
    no Reyna, muger os busco,
    solo muger os quisiera.

Earl has been successful,*,3 and when she also finally hears that he has promised marriage to Blanca and that she is pressing for the fulfillment of this promise, the storm that has long been held back breaks forth. She derides the gullible girl in the sharpest possible way and absolutely forbids her to think further of the Earl. Blanca guesses without much trouble that this intensity on the part of the Queen must be jealousy and indicates so to her.

QUEEN: Jealousy? – No; only your conduct disgusts me. – And supposing – yes, supposing I loved the Earl. If I – I loved him, and another were so presumptuous, so foolish, to love him alongside me – what am I saying, to love – just to look at him – what am I saying, to look? – to just let a thought of him come into her head: should this not cost this other person her life? – You see how much a merely supposed, fictionalized jealousy enrages me; judge from that what I would do with a real one. Now I only feign jealousy; beware of really making me so!†,4

With this threat, the Queen exits and leaves Blanca in the most extreme despair. This adds a last straw to the injuries Blanca already had to bear. The Queen has taken her father, her brother, and her estate, and now she wants to take the Earl from her as well. The revenge was already determined, but why should Blanca wait until another executes it for her? She will carry it out herself, this evening. As the Queen's chambermaid, she must help her undress; she is alone with her then and will not lack for an opportunity. – She sees the Queen return with the Chancellor and goes to prepare herself for her undertaking.

The Chancellor has various documents, which the Queen orders him to put on a table; she will look through them before she goes to sleep. The Chancellor praises the exceptional vigilance she applies to her government business; the Queen declares that it is her duty and dismisses him. Now she is alone and sits down with the papers. She wants to free herself from her lovesick suffering and focus her attention on more proper concerns. But the first paper she takes up is a petition from Earl Felix. An Earl! "Must, then," she says, "the very first thing that presents itself to me be from an Earl!" This stroke is excellent. Suddenly, she is once again preoccupied heart and soul with the same Earl about whom she did not want to think. His love for Blanca is a thorn

---

* BLANCA: [. . . .] le llamé una noche obscura.
  REYNA: Y vino á verte?
  BLANCA: Pluguiera
  á Dios, que no fuera tanta
  mi desdicha y su fineza.
  Vino mas galan que nunca,
  y yo, que dos veces ciega
  por mi mal, estaba entónces
  del amor y las tinieblas: –
† REYNA: [. . . .] Este es el zelo, Blanca.
  BLANCA: Añadiéndole una letra.
  REYNA: Qué decís?

in her heart that makes life a burden for her. Until death frees her from this torment, she will seek relief from death's brother, and so she falls asleep.

Meanwhile, Blanca enters, with one of the Earl's pistols, which she found in her room. (The playwright had not brought them in at the beginning of the act for nothing). She finds the Queen alone and asleep: could she have wished for a more convenient moment? But a moment ago, the Earl had looked for Blanca and not found her in her room. Doubtless you guess what happens next. He comes to look for her here and comes just in time to seize the murderous Blanca and wrench from her the pistol that she already had cocked and pointed at the Queen. But whilst he struggles with her, the shot goes off; the Queen wakes up and everyone in the palace comes running.

QUEEN *waking up*: Ha! What is that?
CHANCELLOR: Let's go, let's go! What was that sound of a shot, in the Queen's room? What is happening here?
ESSEX *with the pistol in his hand*: Horrible coincidence!
QUEEN: What is this, Earl?
ESSEX: What should I do?
QUEEN: Blanca, what is this?
BLANCA: My death is assured!

BLANCA: Señora, que
si acaso posible fuera,
á no ser vos la que dice
esas palabras, dixera,
que de zelos: –
REYNA: Qué son zelos?
no son zelos, es ofensa
que me estais haciendo vos.
Supongamos que quisiera
al Conde en esta ocasion:
pues si yo al Conde quisiera,
y alguna, atrevida, loca,
presumida, descompuesta,
le quisiera: – qué es querer?
le mirara, que le viera: –
qué es verle? no sé qué diga,
no hay cosa que ménos sea: [. . . .]
no la quitara la vida,
la sangre no la bebiera, [. . . .]
los zelos, aunque fingidos,
me arrebatáron la lengua,
y despertáron mi enojo. [. . . .]
Mirad que no me deis zelos,
que si fingido se altera
tanto mi enojo, ved vos,
si fuera verdad, qué hiciera. [. . . .]
escarmentad en las burlas,
no me deis zelos de veras. *Vase.*

ESSEX: Can there be worse confusion?

CHANCELLOR: What? The Earl a traitor?

ESSEX *aside*: What should I do? If I stay silent, the crime falls on me. If I tell the truth, I will be the worthless denouncer of my beloved, my Blanca, my dearest Blanca.

QUEEN: Are you the traitor, Earl? Are you, Blanca? Which of you was my savior? Which my murderer? It seems to me that in my sleep I heard both of you call: Traitoress! Traitor! And yet only one of you can deserve this name. If one of you sought my life, then I am indebted to the other for it. To whom am I indebted, Earl? Who sought it, Blanca? You are silent? – All right, be silent! I will remain in this uncertainty; I will not know who is innocent in order not to know who is guilty. Perhaps it would pain me just as much to discover who my protector is as my enemy. I will gladly forgive Blanca her treachery, I will thank her for it, if only the Earl was innocent in return.[‡,5]

But the Chancellor says: while the Queen may want to let the matter rest, he cannot; the crime is too great; his office requires that he get to the bottom of it, particularly because all appearances speak against the Earl.

QUEEN: The Chancellor is right: we must investigate. – Earl –

ESSEX: Queen! –

QUEEN: Confess the truth. – *aside*: But how much my love fears to hear it! – Was it Blanca?

ESSEX: Unhappy me!

QUEEN: Was it Blanca who wanted to kill me?

ESSEX: No, your Highness, it was not Blanca.

QUEEN: It was you, then?

ESSEX: Dreadful fate! – I do not know.

QUEEN: You do not know? – And how did this murderous weapon come into your hand?

---

‡ REYN: Conde, vos traidor? vos, Blanca?
  el juicio está indiferente:
  quál me libra? quál me mata?
  Conde, Blanca, respondedme:
  tú á la Reyna? tú á la Reyna?
  oí, aunque confusamente:
  ah, traidora! dixo el Conde:
  Blanca dixo: traidor eres.
  Estas razones de entrambos
  á entrambas cosas convienen;
  uno de los dos me libra,
  otro de los dos me ofende.
  Conde, quál me daba vida?
  Blanca, quál me daba muerte?
  decidme: no lo digais,

The Earl is silent, and the Queen orders him to be taken to the tower. Blanca should remain under guard in her room until the matter becomes more clear. They are led away, and the second act ends.

Essay 66

18 December 1767[1]

The third act begins with a long monologue by the Queen, who summons all the ingenuity of love to find the Earl innocent.[2] No "perhaps" is spared in trying to avoid believing that he could be either her murderer or Blanca's lover. She goes to extremes in particular with her suppositions against Blanca; she dwells on this point at length, and not quite as tenderly and properly as we might wish, or as she would on our own stage.[*,3]

The Duke and Chancellor enter: the former, to express his joy over the successful preservation of her life; the latter, to present to her a new piece of evidence that speaks against Essex. His name is on the pistol that was taken from his hand, it belongs to him, and the person to whom it belongs undoubtedly also planned to use it.

Yet nothing seems to damn Essex more incontrovertibly than what follows next. Cosme intended to leave for Scotland at dawn with the aforementioned letter and was restrained.[4] His trip looks very much like flight, and such a flight leads to the supposition that he could have taken part in his master's crime. He is thus brought before the Chancellor, and the Queen orders that he be interrogated in her presence. You can readily guess the tone Cosme uses to defend himself. He knows nothing, and when he is asked where he intended to go, he does not hesitate to tell the truth. He shows the letter that the Earl ordered him to deliver to another Earl in Scotland, and we know what that letter contains. It is read aloud, and Cosme is more than a little shocked when he hears what its purpose was. But he is even more astonished by the letter's end, where the message-bearer is named a confidant to whom Roberto can safely give his answer.[5] "What do I hear?" Cosme exclaims. "I, a confidant? Heaven

---

que neutral mi valor quiere,
por no saber el traidor,
no saber el inocente.
Mejor es quedar confusa,
en duda mi juicio quede,
porque quando mire á alguno,
y de la traicion me acuerde,
á pensar que es el traidor,
que es el leal tambien piense.
Yo le agradeciera á Blanca,
que ella la traidora fuese,
solo á trueque de que el Conde
fuera el que estaba inocente.
* No pudo ser que mintiera
  Blanca en lo que me contó
  de gozarla el Conde? no,

forbid! I am no confidant, I never have been one, and never will be either. – Do I look like a confidant? I would like to know what my master saw in me to take me for one. I, a confidant? I, for whom the least secret is a burden? I know, for example, that Blanca and my master love each other and that they are secretly married to each other. This has burdened my heart for a long time, and now I will say it just so that you, good gentlemen, see precisely what kind of confidant I am. It is a shame that it is not actually something important; I would tell that just as well."[†,6] This news pains the Queen no less than the realization of the Earl's treachery revealed by the misfortunate letter. The Duke believes he must now break his silence and no longer hide from the Queen what he accidentally overheard in Blanca's room. The Chancellor insists upon punishment for the traitor, and as soon as the Queen is alone, both injured majesty and wounded love provoke her to condemn the Earl to death.

Now the poet brings us to the Earl, in prison. The Chancellor comes and informs him that the Parliament has declared him guilty and sentenced him to death, a sentence that is to be executed the next morning. The Earl protests his innocence.

CHANCELLOR: Your innocence, Milord, I would gladly believe; but there is so much evidence against you! – Did you not write the letter to Roberto? Is that not your signature?

---

que Blanca no lo fingiera:
No pudo haberla gozado
sin estar enamorado?
y quando tierno y rendido
entónces la haya querido,
no puede haberla olvidado?
No le viéron mis antojos
entre acogimientos sabios,
muy callando con los labios,
muy bachiller con los ojos,
quando al decir sus enojos
yo su despecho reñí?
† Qué escucho? señores mios,
dos mil demonios me lleven
si yo confidente soy,
si lo he sido, ó si lo fuere,
ni tengo intencion de serlo.
[. . . .] Tengo yo
cara de ser confidente?
Yo no sé qué ha visto en mí
mi amo, para tenerme
en esta opinion, y á fe,
que me holgara de que fuese
cosa de mas importancia
un secretillo muy leve,
que rabio ya por decirlo:
que es, que el Conde á Blanca quiere,
que están casados los dos
en secreto [. . .]

ESSEX: I admit it is.

CHANCELLOR: Did the Duke of Alanzon not expressly hear you, in Blanca's room, plot the Queen's death?

ESSEX: He did indeed hear what he heard.

CHANCELLOR: Did the Queen not see a pistol in your hand when she woke? Does the pistol with your name engraved on it not belong to you?

ESSEX: I cannot deny it.

CHANCELLOR: Then you are guilty.

ESSEX: That, I deny.

CHANCELLOR: Well then, how did you come to write the letter to Roberto?

ESSEX: I do not know.

CHANCELLOR: How did it come to be that the Duke heard the traitorous resolution from your very own mouth?

ESSEX: Because heaven wanted it so.

CHANCELLOR: How did it come to pass that the murderous weapon was found in your hands?

ESSEX: Because I am very unfortunate.

CHANCELLOR: If this is all misfortune and not guilt, then truly, friend, fate is playing a cruel trick on you. You will have to pay for it with your head.

ESSEX: This is terrible.[‡,7]

---

‡ COND: Solo el descargo que tengo
es el de estar inocente.
SEN: Aunque yo quiera creerlo,
no me dexan los indicios;
y advertid, que ya no es tiempo
de dilacion, que mañana
habeis de morir.
COND: Yo muero
inocente.
SEN: Pues decid,
no escribisteis á Roberto
esta carta? Aquesta firma
no es la vuestra?
COND: No lo niego.
SEN: El gran Duque de Alanzon
no os oyó en el aposento
de Blanca trazar la muerte
de la Reyna?
COND: Aqueso es cierto.
SEN: Quando despertó la Reyna,
no os halló, Conde, á vos mesmo
con la pistola en la mano?
Y la pistola, pues vemos,
vuestro nombre allí grabado,
no es vuestra?
COND: Yo os lo concedo.
SEN: Luego vos estais culpado?
COND: Eso solamento niego.

"Does your Honor happen to know," asks Cosme, who is present, "whether they are planning to hang me as well?" The Chancellor answers no, because his master has vindicated him sufficiently. The Earl beseeches the Chancellor to allow him to speak to Blanca one more time before his death. The Chancellor regrets that, as judge, he must deny him this request, because it has been decided to have his execution occur as secretly as possible, out of fear of the many co-conspirators he might have among not only the nobility but also the populace. He urges him to prepare himself for death and leaves. The Earl only wished to speak to Blanca one more time in order to exhort her to abandon her plan. Because he may not do so verbally, he will do it in writing. Love and honor oblige him to sacrifice his life for her; he will implore her not to let this sacrifice, which is on every lover's lips but has only become reality for him, be in vain. It is night; he sits down to write and orders Cosme to deliver to Blanca, immediately after his death, the letter that he will give him later. Cosme leaves in order to catch up on his sleep first.

Essay 67

22 December 1767[1]

A scene now follows that one hardly would have expected.[2] Everything is peaceful and calm, when all of a sudden, the very lady whose life Essex saved in the first act, wearing the same clothing and half mask on her face, comes to the Earl in prison carrying a light in her hand. It is the Queen. "The Earl," she says to herself as she enters, "preserved my life; I am indebted to him for it. The Earl wanted to take my life; that clamors for revenge. Justice has been satisfied by way of his conviction;

SEN: Pues cómo escribisteis, Conde,
la carta al traidor Roberto?
COND: No lo sé.
SEN: Pues cómo el Duque,
que escuchó vuestros intentos,
os convence en la traicion?
COND: Porque así lo quiso el Cielo.
SEN: Cómo, hallado en vuestra mano,
os culpa el vil instrumento?
COND: Porque tengo poca dicha [. . .]
SEN: Pues sabed, que si es desdicha
y no culpa, en tanto aprieto
os pone vuestra fortuna,
Conde amigo, que supuesto
que no dais otro descargo,
en fe de indicios tan ciertos,
mañana vuestra cabeza
ha de pagar: –
[COSME: Malo es esto.]

now gratitude and love must also be satisfied!"*,3 As she comes close, she notices that the Earl is writing. "Doubtless," she says, "to Blanca! What harm is that? I come out of love, out of the most passionate, unselfish love; now is no time for jealousy! – Earl!" – The Earl hears himself called, looks behind him, and springs to his feet in astonishment. "What do I see!" – "No dream," declares the Queen, "but the truth. Hurry and convince yourself of it, and do not waste our precious moments in doubt. – You do remember me? I am the one whose life you rescued. I hear that you are to die tomorrow, and I come to clear my debt to you and give you life for life. I have managed to get the key to the prison. Do not ask me how. Here it is: take it, it will open the gate into the park for you. Escape, Earl, and preserve a life that is so dear to me." –

ESSEX: Dear to you, Madame?
QUEEN: Would I have otherwise risked as much as I do now?
ESSEX: How clever is the fate that hounds me! It finds a way to make me unfortunate through my good fortune itself. I seem fortunate, because the person who wants my death is the one who comes to free me; but I am that much more unfortunate, because the person who offers me freedom wants my death –†,4

The Queen understands from this that Essex knows who she is. He refuses outright the favor she has offered him, but he asks her to exchange it for another.

QUEEN: With what?
ESSEX: With one that I know is in your power to grant, – with the favor of letting me see the face of my Queen. It is the only thing I desire as repayment for what I did for you. By the life I saved for you, I beseech you, Madame, to grant me this favor.
QUEEN *to herself*: What should I do? Perhaps, if he sees me, he will clear himself! I only wish.
ESSEX: Do not delay my happiness, Madame.

---

* El Conde me dió la vida,
   y así obligada me veo:
   el Conde me daba muerte,
   y así ofendida me quejo;
   pues ya que con la sentencia
   esta parte he satisfecho,
   pues cumplí con la justicia,
   con el amor cumplir quiero.
† Ingeniosa mi fortuna,
   halló en la dicha mas nuevo
   modo de hacerme infeliz,
   pues quando dichoso veo,
   que me libra quien me mata,
   tambien desdichado advierto
   que me mata quien me libra.

QUEEN: If this is what you absolutely want, Earl, so be it; but first take this key – your life depends on it. What I may do for you now, I may perhaps not be able to do later. Take it; I wish to know you safe.‡,5

ESSEX *taking the key*: I recognize this precaution with gratitude. – And now, Madame, – I burn to read my fate on the face of the Queen, or on yours.

QUEEN: Earl, although both are the same, nevertheless what you see here belongs to me alone; for what you now see (*as she removes the mask*) is the Queen. The one to whom you first spoke is no more.

ESSEX: Now I die content! To be sure, it is the privilege of the royal visage that it must pardon every guilty man who beholds it, and this benefit of the law must also assist me. Yet I will seek refuge not through this, but rather through myself. I will venture to remind my Queen of the services I rendered to her and the nation –§,6

QUEEN: I have already reminded myself of these. But your crime, Earl, is greater than your services.

ESSEX: And I can promise myself nothing from the Queen's benevolence?

QUEEN: Nothing.

ESSEX: If the Queen is so strict, then I call upon the lady whose life I saved. She will surely deal with me more kindly?

QUEEN: She has already done more than she ought; she opened the path for you to escape justice.

ESSEX: And I have not deserved more from you, from you, who owe me your life?

QUEEN: You have already heard, I am not that lady. But suppose I were: am I not giving back to you just as much as I received from you?

---

‡ Pues si esto ha de ser, primero
  tomad, Conde, aquesta llave,
  que si ha de ser instrumento
  de vuestra vida, quizá
  con otra, quitada el velo,
  seré, que no pueda entónces
  hacer lo que ahora puedo;
  y como á daros la vida
  me empeñé, por lo que os debo,
  por si no puedo despues,
  de esta suerte me prevengo.

§ Ya moriré consolado,
  aunque, si por privilegio,
  en viendo la cara al Rey,
  queda perdonado el reo:
  yo de este indulto, señora,
  vida por ley me prometo;
  esto es en comun, que es
  lo que á todos da el Derecho;
  pero si en particular
  merecer el perdon puedo,
  oid, veréis que me ayuda
  mayor indulto en mis hechos;
  mis hazañas.

ESSEX: How so? Surely not by giving me the key?

QUEEN: Absolutely by doing so.

ESSEX: The path that this key can open for me is less a path to life than a path to infamy. The means to my freedom must not appear to presume fear on my part. The Queen thinks to pay me off with this key for the kingdom that I fought for and won, for the blood I spilled for her, for the life I preserved for her; for all that, this miserable key?[¶,7] I will owe my life to a more respectable means, or die. *As he goes to the window.*

QUEEN: Where are you going?

ESSEX: Worthless instrument for my life and my dishonor! If all of my hopes rest on you, then let the tide take all my hopes to its deepest abyss! *He opens the window and throws the key through the bars into the canal.* My life would be bought at too dear a price through flight.[**,8]

QUEEN: What have you done, Earl? – You have made a grave mistake.

ESSEX: When I die, I will at least be able to say out loud that I leave behind an ungrateful Queen. – If she does not want this accusation, then she should think of another means to rescue me. I have taken this ignoble one from her. I appeal once again to my service; it is up to her either to reward it or to immortalize that service as a monument to her ingratitude.

QUEEN: I must take the latter risk. – For in truth, I could not do more for you without damage to my honor.

ESSEX: Then I must die?

QUEEN: With certainty. The woman wanted to save you; the Queen must let the law take its course. In the morning you must die, and it is already morning. You have my full compassion; my heart breaks with sorrow, but it is simply the fate of kings

---

¶ Luego esta, que así camino
   abrirá á mi vida abriendo,
   tambien la abrirá á mi infamia?
   luego esta, que instrumento
   de mi libertad es, tambien
   lo habrá de ser de mi miedo?
   Esta, que solo me sirve
   de huir, es el desempeño
   de Reynos que os he ganado,
   de servicios que os he hecho?
   Y en fin, de esa vida, de esa,
   que teneis hoy por mi esfuerzo,
   en esta se cifra tanto?

** Vil instrumento
   de mi vida y de mi infamia,
   por esta reja cayendo
   del Parque, que bate el rio
   entre sus cristales, quiero,
   si sois mi esperanza, hundiros:
   caed al humilde centro,
   donde el Támesis sepulte
   mi esperanza y mi remedio.

that they are far less able to act according to their feelings than other people. – Earl, I leave you to your fate!⁹

Essay 68

25 December 1767¹

A few more words exchanged in parting, a few more proclamations in the silence, and then both Earl and Queen exit, each in a different direction.² One must imagine that in leaving, Essex gave Cosme the letter he wrote to Blanca. For a moment later, Cosme comes in with it and says that his master is being led to his death; once that is over, he will deliver the letter as promised. As he looks at it, however, his curiosity is piqued. "What could this letter contain? A proposal of marriage? That would be coming a bit too late. The transcript of his judgment? He will not have sent that to the person it has widowed. His will? This, too, is unlikely. Well, then: what?" He becomes more and more curious; at the same time, he recalls how ignorance of what was in a letter from his master nearly cost him his life once before. "Didn't I just barely escape becoming a confidant because of it? The devil take this complicity! No, that must not happen to me again!" In short, Cosme decides to break open the letter. Of course, its content shocks him. He believes he cannot be rid quickly enough of a note that contains such important and dangerous things; he trembles at the mere thought that someone could find it in his hands before he has turned it over voluntarily, so he rushes to bring it to the Queen straightaway.

Just then, the Queen comes out with the Chancellor. Cosme wants to let her finish with the Chancellor first and so he steps aside. The Queen issues the last orders for the Earl's execution to the Chancellor: it should take place immediately and in total secrecy; the people should learn nothing of it until the beheaded corpse hails them to loyalty and obedience with its silent tongue.*,³ The Chancellor is to bring the head into the hall and lay it under a rug with the bloody axe; afterwards he is to gather the nobles of the realm in order to show them at once both crime and punishment; this would serve both to remind them of their duty and to impress upon them that their Queen is prepared to be as severe as she might wish to be merciful; and this all, as the playwright has her say, is according to the customs and conventions of the land.†,⁴

---

* hasta que el tronco cadáver
le sirva de muda lengua.

† Y así, al salon de Palacio
haréis que llamados vengan
los Grandes, y los Milordes,
y para que allí le vean,
debaxo de una cortina
haréis poner la cabeza
con el sangriento cuchillo,
que amenaza junto á ella,
por símbolo de justicia,
costumbre de Inglaterra;

The Chancellor leaves with this order, and Cosme approaches the Queen. "My master," he says, "gave me this letter to deliver after his death to Blanca. I opened it, I myself do not know why, and because I find things in it that your Majesty must know and that could perhaps assist the Earl, I bring it to your Majesty and not to Blanca." The Queen takes the letter and reads: "Blanca, I approach my final moments; they will not allow me to speak with you; therefore receive my embrace in writing. But first, come to know me: I was never the traitor I might perhaps have seemed to you. I promised to help you with the matter in question only in order the more emphatically to serve the Queen and lure Roberto and his accomplices to London. Judge how great my love is, that nevertheless I will rather die myself than put your life in danger. And now the warning: abandon the plans to which Roberto incites you; you no longer have me, and you will not readily find one again who loves you so much that he will die the death of a traitor for you."[‡,5] –

"Man, what have you brought me here?" the distraught Queen calls out. "Well?" says Cosme, "am I still a confidant?" – "Hurry, fly to save your master! Tell the Chancellor to stop! – You there, guards! Bring him to me this instant – the Earl – hurry!" – And at that moment he is brought in: that is, his corpse. As great as the joy was that suddenly overcame the Queen upon knowing her Earl innocent, just as great are her pain and anger upon seeing him executed. She curses the hastiness with which her orders were executed; and may Blanca tremble! –

Thus concludes this play, with which perhaps I have held up my readers too long. And perhaps not. We are so little acquainted with the dramatic works of the Spanish; I

---

　　y en estando todos juntos,
　　mostrándome justiciera,
　　exhortándolos primero
　　con amor á la obediencia,
　　les mostraré luego al Conde,
　　para que todos entiendan,
　　que en mí hay rigor que los rinda,
　　si hay piedad que los atreva.
‡ Blanca en el último trance,
　　porque hablarte no me dexan,
　　he de escribirte un consejo,
　　y tambien una advertencia.
　　La advertencia es, que yo nunca
　　fuí traidor, que la promesa
　　de ayudarte en lo que sabes,
　　fué por servir á la Reyna,
　　cogiendo á Roberto en Lóndres,
　　y á los que seguirle intentan:
　　para aquesto fué la carta,
　　esto he querido que sepas,
　　porque adviertas el prodigio
　　de mi amor, que así se dexa
　　morir por guardar tu vida.
　　Esta ha sido la advertencia;
　　(válgame Dios!) el consejo

know of not a single one that has been translated or even excerpted for us. For though Agustín de Montiano y Luyando's *Virginia* is written in Spanish, it is no Spanish play.[6] It is merely an attempt in the correct French manner, proper but cool. I gladly confess that I no longer think nearly as favorably of it as I must have previously.[§,7] Since the same author's second play did not turn out better, since the more recent playwrights of that nation who wanted to tread this same path have not been more successful, then they should not hold it against me if I still prefer to turn to their old Lope and Calderón instead of them.[8]

The authentic Spanish plays are wholly consistent with this *Essex* – of course, with more or less all the same strengths and weaknesses. The weaknesses are obvious; one might, however, question me about the strengths. – A completely singular story, a very clever complication, many unusual and new theatrical tricks, the most economical situations, for the most part very well-designed characters that are maintained to the end, and, not infrequently, much dignity and power of expression. –

These are certainly strengths; I do not say that they are the greatest. I do not deny that in part they can very easily slip into the romantic, quixotic, and unnatural, and that among the Spanish they are rarely free of such exaggeration. But take the mechanical regularity from most French plays, and tell me if there is much left over in them other than strengths of this sort? What else do they still have in them that is good other than complication, and theatrical tricks, and situations?

Decorum, one will say.[9] – Well, yes: decorum. All of their complications are more decorous, and more monotonous; all of their theatrical tricks are more decorous, and more hackneyed; all of their situations are more decorous, and more forced. That is what comes of decorum!

But Cosme, this Spanish Hanswurst; this monstrous union of the most vulgar buffoonery and the most portentous seriousness; this mixture of the comic and the tragic for which the Spanish theater is so notorious?[10] I am a long way from defending this combination. If indeed it merely conflicted with decorum – you understand, of course, which decorum I mean here – if this combination had no other faults than that it insulted the reverence nobility demands, than that it went directly against the manners, the etiquette, the ceremonies, and all the other sleights of hand through which they want to convince the greater number of people that there is a smaller number who are made of far better stuff, then the silliest change from low to high, from absurdity to seriousness, and from black to white would be more welcome to me than the cold uniformity through which the good tone, the fine world, the courtly

---

es, que desistas la empresa
á que Roberto te incita,
mira que sin mí te quedas,
y no ha de haber cada dia
quien, por mucho que te quiera,
por conservarte la vida,
por traidor la suya pierda. –
§ *Theatralische Bibliothek*

manners, and whatever else you might call similar miseries unfailingly lulls me to sleep. But whole other matters come into consideration here.

Essay 69

29 December 1767[1]

Although Lope de Vega is considered the creator of Spanish theater, he was not the one who introduced this hybrid tone.[2] The people were already so accustomed to it that he had to conform against his will. In his didactic poem, *The New Art of Writing Plays*, which I already mentioned above, he complains about it at length.[3] Because he saw that it was not possible to please his contemporaries by working within the rules and models of the ancients, he tried at least to set some limits to the irregularity; this was the aim of his poem. Despite the wild and barbaric taste of his nation, he thought it ought still to have its principles, and it would be better to act according to these with a consistent uniformity than to none at all. Plays that do not observe the classical rules can still observe rules and must observe these if they want to please. He wanted to establish rules that were derived from the national taste, and the combination of the serious and the ridiculous was the first.

"You may even let kings" he says, "appear in your plays. I am aware that our wise king (Philip the Second) did not approve of this, either because he perceived that it went against the rules or because he believed it contradicted the majesty of a king to be mixed with the vulgar mob. I freely admit that this is a turning back to Old Comedy, which even brought gods on stage, as we see in Plautus's *Amphitryon*, among others.[4] I also know well enough that Plutarch, speaking of Menander, does not praise the Old Comedy very highly.[5] Thus it is rather difficult for me to defend our fashion. But since we in Spain diverge so far from art, the scholars will have to be silent on this. It is true that comedy mixed with tragedy, Seneca melted together with Terence, produces a monstrosity comparable to Pasiphae's minotaur.[6] But this back and forth actually delights; people simply do not want to see plays other than those that are half serious and half funny. Nature itself teaches us this variety, from which it derives a part of its beauty."*,[7]

---

* Elíjasse el sujeto, y no se mire
(perdonen los preceptos) si es de reyes,
aunque por esto entiendo que el prudente
Filipo, rey de España y señor nuestro,
en viendo un rey en ellos se enfadava:
o fuesse el ver que al arte contradize,
o que la autoridad real no deve
andar fingida entre la humilde plebe.
Esto es bolver a la comedia antigua,
donde vemos que Plauto puso dioses,
como en su *Anfitrión* lo muestra Júpiter.
Sabe Dios que me pesa de aprovarlo,

The final words are the reason I quote this passage. Is it true that nature itself serves as a model for this mixture of the common and the elevated, the farcical and the serious, the funny and the sad? It seems so. But if this is true, then Lope has accomplished more than he intended: he did not merely justify the errors of his stage, but he actually proved that this particular error is not one, since an imitation of nature cannot be an error.

One of our more modern writers says:[8] "It is said of Shakespeare – who of all the poets since Homer understood men, from kings to beggars and from Julius Caesar to Jack Falstaff, better than any and saw through them with a kind of unfathomable intuition – that his plays have no plot, or rather that they have only very faulty, irregular, and badly concocted plots; that the comic and tragic are promiscuously mixed together in them in the most peculiar manner; and that often the same character who has brought us to tears through natural, stirring expression will, just a few moments later, by some odd conceit or baroque expression of emotion, either bring us to the point of laughter or at least cool us down such that it becomes challenging for him to return us to our former state. – People criticize him for this and do not pause to consider that his plays are natural representations of human life for this very reason."[9]

"The life of most people and (if I do say so) the course of life of the great bodies politic themselves (insofar as we consider them to be moral agents) resembles the *Haupt- und Staatsaktionen* of the old gothic taste in so many respects that one might imagine the authors of those plays were far more intelligent than we commonly think, and, while they had no hidden purpose of making a mockery of human life, they at least might have wanted to imitate nature as faithfully as the Greeks set themselves to refining it.[10] Not to mention here the coincidental similarity, that in these plays, as in life, the most important roles are very often played by the worst actors – what can be more similar to each other than both types of *Haupt- und Staatsaktionen* tend to be, not only in their design but also in the division and disposition of their scenes, and in their complications and developments? How rarely do the authors of either ask themselves why they have made this or that one way and not another? How often do they surprise us with incidents for which we are not in the least prepared? How often do we see people coming and going without being able to compass why they came or why they disappeared again? How much is left to chance in both? How often do we see the

---

porque Plutarco, hablando de Menandro,
no siente bien de la comedia antigua.
Mas pues del arte vamos tan remotos,
y en España le hazemos mil agravios,
cierren los doctos esta vez los labios.
Lo trágico y lo cómico mezclado,
y Terencio con Séneca, aunque sea
como otro Minotauro de Pasife,
harán grave una parte, otra ridícula;
que aquesta variedad deleita mucho.
Buen exemplo nos da naturaleza,
que por tal variedad tiene belleza.

greatest effects produced by the most petty causes? How often are serious and important matters handled in a careless manner, and the most meaningless matters treated
with ridiculous gravity? And in both cases, when everything is finally so deplorably
muddled and jumbled together that we begin to despair of the possibility of a resolution: how happy are we to see the knot – not so much unraveled, to be sure – but
sliced through, either by some god jumping down out of paper clouds amidst thunder
and lightning or through some brazen stroke of a dagger.[11] It all boils down to the
same thing, that one way or another the play comes to an end, and the spectators can
applaud or hiss as they want or – dare. Besides, everyone knows what an important
person the noble Hanswurst represents in the comic tragedies we are talking about,
who seems determined to keep his place on stage in the capital of the German Empire,
presumably as an eternal memorial of our ancestors' taste.[12] Would to God this figure only showed up in the theater! But, throughout history, how many great scenes
have we not seen conducted on the stage of the world with – or, what is even worse,
by – a Hanswurst? How often have the greatest men, men born to be the protective
spirits of a throne and the benefactors of whole nations and eras, been forced to see
all their wisdom and valor thwarted by some whimsical prank by a Hanswurst or by
those people who, even if they do not wear his jacket and yellow hose, still embody
his character? How often does the complication in both types of tragicomedy arise
merely from some stupid, mischievous piece of work on Hanswurst's part that spoils
the plans of sensible people before they can suspect anything?" –[13]

If, in this comparison of the great and small, the original and imitated heroic
farce –[14] (which I copied with pleasure from a work that undoubtedly belongs among
the best of our century, but which seems to have been written way too soon for the
German public. In France and England it would have caused the greatest sensation,
and the name of its author would be on every tongue. But here? We have it, and
that is enough. Our greats learn first of all to chew on the ***, and admittedly the
juice from a French novel is much sweeter and easier to digest.[15] When their teeth
have become sharper and their stomachs stronger, when they have, in the meantime,
learned German, then they will finally discover – *Agathon*. This is the work of which
I speak, which I admire so much that I would rather say so here, though it may not be
the most suitable place, than not say anything at all, because I am stunned by the total
silence of our critics with respect to it, or the cold and indifferent tone they use if
they do speak of it. It is the first and only novel for the thinking man, the first novel of
classical taste. Novel? We only give it this label in the hope that it will thereby gain a
few more readers. Those few it might lose on this account are not important anyway.)

Essay 70

1 January 1768[1]

If the sardonic tone did not stand out so much in this comparison, we might consider
it the best defense of the comical tragic – or tragical comic – drama (I once saw it
called a "mixed play" on a title page) and the most careful elaboration of Lope's

ideas.[2] But at the same time it would also contradict those ideas. For it would show that purposely using nature to justify the combination of solemn seriousness with farcical merriment might as well justify any dramatic monstrosity that lacks plot, coherence, and common sense. Consequently, the imitation of nature should not be a principle of art; if it remains one, then by means of the principle itself, art would cease to be art.[3] Or at least it could never be more than, for example, the art of imitating the colorful veins of marble in plaster: the lines can take whatever course they may, they can never be so idiosyncratic that they could not still seem natural; the only lines that do not seem natural are those that give evidence of too much symmetry, too much ratio and proportion, and too much of that which constitutes the art in every other art. By this definition, what is most artful is the worst, and what is wildest is the best.

In the role of critic, our author might speak completely differently.[4] That which the novelist in him seems to support so profoundly would without a doubt be condemned by the critic as a monstrosity of barbaric taste, or at minimum as the first attempts by an uncivilized people at a revival of art, an art mostly shaped by the confluence of random external causes or coincidence, in which judgment or analysis have played little or no part. He would hardly say that the first creators of the mixed play (since the term is there, why should I not use it?) "wanted to imitate nature as faithfully as the Greeks set themselves to refining it."[5]

The words "faithfully" and "refining," as applied to imitation and to nature as the object of imitation, are subject to many misinterpretations. There are people who believe that nature cannot be imitated too faithfully: even those things that displease us in nature will please us in their faithful imitation, by virtue of the imitation itself. There are others who hold the refinement of nature to be farcical: a nature that wants to be more beautiful than nature is for that very reason not nature. Both declare themselves admirers of nature just as it is; the former find nothing to avoid in it, and the latter see nothing to add. It necessarily follows that the former would enjoy the gothic mixed play, just as the latter would not enjoy the masterpieces of the ancients.[6]

But if this were not the case? If the former, as admiring as they are of the most ordinary and quotidian nature, nevertheless declared themselves against the mixing of the farcical and the interesting? And if the latter, egregious as they hold everything that seeks to be better and more beautiful than nature, nevertheless meander through the whole of Greek theater without taking the least offense on that account? How would we explain this contradiction?

We would have to go back and retract what we first claimed about both types. But how would we retract without creating further confusion? The similarity of such *Haupt- und Staatsaktionen* (and the quality of these plays is what we are arguing about) to human life, to the common course of the world, is still so right![7]

I want to bandy about a few thoughts, which, if they themselves are not rigorous enough, could still prompt more rigorous ones. – The main idea is this one: it is true, and at the same time not true, that the comic tragedy of gothic invention faithfully imitates nature. It imitates nature faithfully only in one half and completely neglects the other half: it imitates what is visible in nature without paying the least attention to the nature of our feelings and thoughts.

In nature, everything is bound together; everything interconnects, everything is interchangeable with everything else, everything changes from one thing to another. But in this infinite variety, nature is simply a performance for an infinite spirit. For finite spirits to take their share of pleasure in it, they must learn to give it boundaries that it does not have; they must develop the capacity to isolate elements and direct their attention at will.

We exercise this capacity in every moment of our lives; without it there would be no life for us at all. In the face of too many and varied feelings, we would feel nothing, we would be continually in thrall to present impressions, we would dream without knowing what we dreamed.

The purpose of art is to use the realm of beauty to elevate us out of the flood of detached impressions and to facilitate the fixing of our attention. Everything we might isolate (or wish to be able to isolate) in our thoughts about an object of nature or a combination of different objects, whether in time or space, is in fact actually isolated by art; it manifests this object or combination of objects with a vividness limited only by the feelings it seeks to arouse.

When we witness an important and moving event, and then another, wholly insignificant matter intrudes, we try as much as possible to avoid the distraction that the latter poses for us. We distance ourselves from it, and we must be offended to confront in art what we try to ignore in nature.

Only if this very same occasion takes on all shades of interest as it progresses, and one thing does not merely follow on the other but rather emerges from it by necessity, if seriousness generates laughter, or sadness generates joy (or vice versa) so directly that separating out the one from the other becomes impossible: only then we do not expect art to separate them, and art is even able to take advantage of this impossibility.

But enough of this, you see where I am heading. –

On the forty-fifth evening (Friday, the 17th of July), Romanus's *The Brothers* and Saint-Foix's *The Oracle* were performed.[8]

The first play can count as a German original, even though it is taken for the most part from Terence's *The Brothers*.[9] It has been said that Molière also dipped from this source, notably for his *School for Husbands*.[10] M. de Voltaire makes comments about this allegation, and I so love to quote M. de Voltaire's comments![11] There is always something to learn, even from his most trivial ones; if not always from what he says, at least from what he should have said. "Primus sapientiae gradus est, falsa intelligere" (I cannot bring to mind at the moment where this little saying is from), and I know of no writer in the world better than M. de Voltaire to test whether this first step of wisdom has been reached; and for that, I can also think of no other who could be of less help to us in scaling the second step: "secundus, vera cognoscere."[12] It seems to me that a critical writer ought best to organize his method according to this saying. First he should look for someone with whom he can argue; in this manner he will gradually get into the subject matter, and the rest will sort itself out.[13] In the present work, I candidly confess, I have primarily chosen French writers for that purpose, and among these M. de Voltaire in particular. So now, after a little bow, let's get to it! Anyone to whom this method seems perhaps more malicious than rigorous should know that the rigorous Aristotle himself nearly always made use of it. "Solet Aristoteles," says one of his interpreters, whose work happens to be to hand, "quaerere pugnam in suis libris. Atque hoc facit non temere, & casu, sed certa ratione atque consilio: nam labefactatis aliorum opinionibus," etc.[14] Oh, what a pedant! M. de Voltaire would cry out. – I am guilty merely for lack of confidence in myself.

"Terence's *The Brothers*," M. de Voltaire says, "could at most have given the idea for *The School for Husbands*. In *The Brothers*, there are two older men of different dispositions who raise their sons differently; in *The School for Husbands*, there are two guardians as well, one very strict and one very indulgent: this is the only similarity. In *The Brothers*, there is almost no intrigue at all; by contrast, the intrigue in *The School for Husbands* is subtle, entertaining, and comical. One of Terence's women, who actually should play the most interesting role, only appears on the stage to give birth. Molière's Isabelle is nearly always on stage, is always full of wit and charm, and even plays tricks on her guardian with a certain propriety. In *The Brothers*, the denouement is very improbable: it goes against nature that an old man who has been angry and strict and tight-fisted for sixty years should suddenly become lighthearted and polite and generous. The denouement of *School for Husbands*, however, is the best in all Molière's work: probable, natural, pulled from the intrigue itself, and – surely not least important – extremely funny."[15]

Essay 71

5 January 1768[1]

It would not seem that M. de Voltaire has reread much Terence since he left school with the Jesuits.[2] He speaks of it as an old dream; something of it still floats about in his memory, and he just blithely writes that down, without caring if it has any rhyme or reason. I will not credit his remark that the play's Pamphila "only appears on the stage to give birth."[3] She does not appear on the stage at all, she does not give birth on stage; we only hear her voice from the house; and, moreover, it is entirely unclear why she should play the most interesting role.[4] Not everything of interest to the French was of interest to the Greeks and Romans. In those days, a good girl who had gotten in over her head with her lover and was in danger of being left by him was very unsuitable for a leading role. –

The truly coarse mistake that M. de Voltaire makes concerns the development and the character of Demea. Demea is the surly, strict father, and he is to suddenly change his character entirely. With all due respect to M. de Voltaire, that is not true. Demea maintains his character until the end. Donatus says: "Servatur autem per totam fabulam mitis Micio, saevus Demea, Leno avarus" etc.[5] "Of what concern is Donatus to me?" M. de Voltaire might say. As he pleases, so long as we Germans may be permitted to believe that Donatus read Terence more diligently and understood him better than Voltaire. Yet we are not talking about a lost play, after all: it is still there; one can simply read it.

After Micio tries to placate Demea through the most compelling arguments, he begs him to be free of vexation just for today, to be merry just for today. Finally he gets him to that point, too: today, Demea will let things go, but tomorrow, in the early dawn, his son must go back to the country with him, and there he will not be so lenient; there he will take up with his son exactly where he left off today. He will take along the "music girl" his cousin bought for his son, too, for she is after all a slave, and one that did not cost him anything.[6] She will not have much singing to do, though; she will cook and bake. In the scene that follows, the fourth scene of the fifth act, where Demea is alone, it seems indeed, if one only takes his words at face value, that he wants to give up his old way of thinking and begin to act in line with Micio's principles.[*,7] Yet what follows shows that all of this must be understood in terms of the restraint he is showing today. For later, he even knows how to use this restraint so that it turns into the most punctilious and malicious mockery of his agreeable brother. He pretends to be merry in order to lure the others into genuine extravagance and folly, he makes the bitterest accusations in the most obliging tone, he does not become generous but rather plays the spendthrift, and all for no other purpose than to make everything he calls wasteful seem ridiculous. This is made incontrovertibly clear from the answer he gives to Micio, who has been deceived by appearances and believes him really changed.[†,8] "Hic ostendit Terentius," Donatus says, "magis Demeam simulasse mutatos mores, quam mutavisse."[9]

I would hope, moreover, that M. de Voltaire does not mean that this dissimulation itself runs counter to the character of Demea, who previously has done nothing but chide and scold, because dissimulation demands more composure and coolness than one might believe Demea capable of. In this, too, Terence is blameless, and he has motivated everything so excellently, observed nature and truth at every step so precisely, and taken care to give such subtle shadings to even the smallest transitions that one cannot cease admiring him.

Yet to get behind all of Terence's subtleties, we require the gift of imagining the actor's playing, for the old poets did not include it. Declamation had its own artists, and for the rest they could doubtless depend on the insight of the players, who made a very serious study of their business. Not infrequently the poets themselves were among the players; they said how they wanted it played. And because they generally did not let their plays circulate before they had been performed, before people had seen and heard them, they could all the more easily avoid interrupting the written dialogue with insertions in which the descriptive poet seems in some way to mix in

---

* DEM: [. . .] nam ego vitam duram quam vixi usque adhuc
  prope iam excurso spatio omitto.
† MIC: quid istuc? quae res tam repente mores mutavit tuos?
  quod prolubium? quae istaec subitast largitas?
  DEM: dicam tibi:
  ut id ostenderem, quod te isti facilem et festivom putant,
  id non fieri ex vera vita neque adeo ex aequo et bono
  sed ex assentando, indulgendo et largiendo, Micio.
  nunc adeo si ob eam rem vobis mea vita invisa, Aeschine, est,
  quia non iusta iniusta prorsus omnia omnino obsequor,
  missos facio, effundite, emite, facite quod vobis lubet.

among the characters. If one imagines, however, that in order to spare themselves these insertions, the old poets tried to indicate in the speeches themselves every movement, every gesture, every facial expression, and every particular change in the voice to be observed with each speech, then one will be mistaken. In Terence alone countless passages occur in which there is not the least trace of such an indication and where nevertheless the true understanding can only be met through guessing the true action; indeed, in many places the words seem to say precisely the opposite of what the actor must express through them.

Such passages occur in the very scene in which Demea's supposed change of mind occurs, which I want to quote because to a certain extent the misunderstandings that I am arguing about rest on them. – Demea now knows everything, he has seen with his own eyes that it is his pious and reputable son for whom the "music girl" was abducted, and he breaks into the most uncontrolled tantrum. He laments to heaven and earth and the sea, and then he comes face to face with Micio.

DEMEA: Ha! There he is, the one who has ruined both of them – my sons, he has destroyed both of them!

MICIO: Oh, control yourself, and pull yourself together!

DEMEA: All right, I am controlling myself, I am myself again, no more harsh words will escape my lips. Let's just stay with the facts. Did we not agree, was it not you yourself who first suggested, that each of us should only concern himself with his own? Answer.‡ etc.[10]

Anyone who attends only to the words here and who is not as keen an observer as the poet was can easily believe that Demea spends his rage too quickly and strikes this more peaceful tone too quickly. After a little consideration, in fact, it will perhaps occur to him that the former emotion, if it has come to its extreme, must necessarily subside again; that Demea, upon hearing his brother's reprimand, can only be ashamed of his blustering fury. And that is all very well, but it is, however, not yet correct. We can learn this from Donatus, who has two excellent comments here. "Videtur," he says, "paulo citius destomachatus, quam res etiam incertae poscebant. Sed & hoc morale: nam juste irati, omissa saevitia ad ratiocinationes saepe festinant."[11] When an angry man believes himself to be obviously in the right, when he imagines that nothing can be said to challenge his grievances, then reprimands are precisely the last thing that will stop him; rather he will rush to prove

---

‡ DEM: eccum adest
  communis corruptela nostrum liberum.
  MIC: tandem reprime iracundiam atque ad te redi.
  DEM: repressi, redii. mitto maledicta omnia:
  rem ipsam putemus. dictum hoc inter nos fuit
  (ex te adeost ortum) ne tu curares meum
  neve ego tuom? responde. –

his point, in order to humiliate his opponent through crystal clear persuasion. Yet because he cannot immediately govern the surging of his boiling blood, because the anger that wants to convince is still nothing other than anger, Donatus makes his second comment: "non quid dicatur, sed quo gestu dicatur, specta; & videbis neque adhuc repressisse iracundiam, neque ad se rediisse Demeam."[12] Demea does indeed say, "I am controlling myself, I am myself again"; but face and gesture and voice sufficiently betray that he is not yet himself again. He besieges Micio with one question after another, and Micio needs all his calmness and good humor just to get a word in.

Essay 72

8 January 1768[1]

When Micio finally does manage to get a word in edgewise, he does get through to Demea, but by no means convinces him.[2] Micio robs him of all pretense for being angry over his children's manner of living, and yet Demea starts grousing all over again. Micio simply has to break off and be satisfied that, at least for today, he will have peace from the peevish humor that he cannot change. The tacks Terence has him take in the process are masterful.*,[3]

DEMEA: Now be careful, Micio, where all your pretty principles and dear leniencies will lead.

MICIO: Hush! It'll be better than you think. – And now, enough of all that! For today, do me a favor. Come on, cheer up.

DEMEA: But just for today! I have to do what I must do. – Tomorrow, at the crack of dawn, I am going back to the village, and the boy is coming with me.

MICIO: Even before the crack of dawn, I'd imagine. Just be merry for today!

DEMEA: That singer-girl must come with us, too.

MICIO: Excellent! Then your son will certainly not wish to run away. Just hold onto her tightly.

DEMEA: I'll take care of that! She'll be covered in flour and coal dust and smoke from the mill and the oven. And she'll harvest corn for me in the midday sun until she's as dry and black as an extinguished torch.

MICIO: I like that! Now you're on the right path! – And then, if I were you, I'd make my son sleep with her, whether he wanted to or not.

DEMEA: Are you making fun of me? – With such a disposition, truly, you can afford to be light hearted. Unfortunately, I feel it –

---

* DEM: ne nimium modo
  bonae tuae istae nos rationes, Micio,
  et tuos iste animus aequos subvortat.

MICIO: You're starting up again?
DEMEA: No, no, I'm done.[4]

With regard to Demea's "Are you making fun of me?" Donatus remarks: "Hoc verbum vultu Demeae sic profertur, ut subrisisse videatur invitus. Sed rursus *ego sentio*,
amare severeque dicit."[5] Incomparable! Demea, who was completely serious in wanting to keep and use the music girl not as a music girl but as a common slave, must
laugh at Micio's joke. Micio himself does not need to laugh; the more seriously he
presents himself, the better. Then Demea can say: "Are you making fun of me?" and
force himself to bite back his own laughter. And he does soon bite it back, for he says
the "Unfortunately, I feel it" in an angry and bitter tone. But as involuntary and brief
as the laughter may be, it nonetheless has a great effect. For you have only really won
over a man like Demea when you can make him laugh. The more rarely he experiences such a beneficial convulsion, the longer it affects him; and after he has long
erased every trace of it from his face, it continues to persist without him even knowing
it and has a certain influence on his subsequent conduct. –

But who would have looked for such subtle knowledge from a grammarian? The
ancient grammarians were not what we think of when we hear that name today. They
were people of great insight: their province was the entire broad field of criticism.
What has come down to us of their interpretations of classical writings therefore
deserve to be studied not only because of the language. However, we have to know
how to discern the more recent interpolations. The fact, however, that this Donatus

---

MIC: tace!
non fiet. mitte iam istaec, da te hodie mihi,
exporge frontem.
DEM: scilicet ita tempu' fert.
faciundumst. ceterum ego rus cras cum filio
cum primo luci ibo hinc.
MIC: de nocte censeo
hodie modo hilarum fac te.
DEM: et istam psaltriam
una illuc mecum hinc abstraham.
MIC: pugnaveris.
eo pacto prorsum illi alligaris filium.
modo facito ut illam serves.
DEM: ego istuc videro,
atque ibi favillae plena, fumi ac pollinis
coquendo sit faxo et molendo. praeter haec
meridie ipso faciam ut stipulam colligat.
tam excoctam reddam atque atram quam carbost.
MIC: placet.
nunc mihi videre sapere. atque equidem filium
tum, etiam si nolit, cogam ut cum illa una cubet.
DEM: derides? fortunatu's qui isto animo sies.
ego sentio –
MIC: ah! pergisne?
DEM: iam iam desino.

(Aelius) is so splendidly rich in observations that can cultivate our taste and that he can reveal the hidden merits of his author better than any other comes perhaps less from his own great gifts than from the talent of his author. In Donatus's time the Roman theater had not yet completely declined; Terence's plays were still performed, doubtless still with many of the traditions that came down from times when better Roman tastes prevailed.[6] He needed only to note what he saw and heard; he needed only attentiveness and fidelity in order to convey subtleties that posterity gave him credit for but that he himself could hardly have unearthed. As a result, I know of no work from which a budding actor could learn more than this commentary on Terence by Donatus, and until Latin is more common among our actors, I would very much wish that someone would provide them a good translation of it. It goes without saying, the poet must be present and everything from the commentary that appertains only to the explanation of words should be omitted. Madame Dacier used Donatus badly in this regard, and her translation is watery and stiff.[7] We have a more recent German translation that is more or less correct, but completely misses the mark in terms of comedic language,[†,8] and Donatus is not put to any better use there than by Mme. Dacier. What I propose has not yet been done; but who should do it? Those who could not do better can also not do this; and those who could do something better have no interest in doing it.

Now finally to come from Terence to our imitator.[9] – It is peculiar indeed that Herr Romanus seems to have had the same mistaken ideas as Voltaire. He too believed that the character of Demea undergoes a complete change in the end; at least, this is what happens to the character of his Lysimon.[10] "Oh children," he has him cry out, "be quiet already! You overwhelm me with tenderness. Son, brother, nephew, servant, all praise me, just because I appear for once to be a little bit friendly. Am I then, or am I not? I'm becoming right young again, brother! It's nice to be loved. I do want to remain like this. I do not know when I last had such a pleasant hour." And Frontin says: "Our old man will surely die soon.[‡] The change is far too sudden."[11] Yes indeed, but the aphorism (and the common belief) about unexpected transformations foreboding an approaching death really shouldn't justify something here in all seriousness, should it?[12]

Essay 73

12 January 1768[1]

In Terence, Demea's final speech has a completely different tone.[2] "If this is what you like, then do what you want. I'm not going to worry about anything anymore!" He is not the one who will acquiesce to the others' ways in the future, but rather they who

---

† Halle 1753. For the sake of novelty permit me to quote from this version the same passage that I have just translated above. What flowed from my pen is very different from what it should be, but you will still be able to generally discern what constitutes the achievement that I have to deny to this translation.

‡ Without a doubt, this is how it ought to read, rather than: "die impossibly soon." For the sake of our actors, it is important to make note of such printing errors.

promise to yield to his. – But how is it, one might ask, that Lysimon's final scenes in our German *Brothers* are always received so well in performance?[3] Lysimon's continually falling back into his old character makes these scenes comical; but it also would have had to be so in the former. – I will spare any further discussion until a second performance of the play.[4]

Saint-Foix's *The Oracle*, which concluded this evening, is well known and much loved.[5]

On the forty-sixth evening (Monday, the 20th of July), *Miss Sara* was repeated,* and on the forty-seventh, the next day, *Nanine* was repeated.† Marivaux's one-act play *The Unforeseen Denouement* followed *Nanine*.[6]

Or, as it would better and more literally be called: the unforeseen development. For this is one of those titles that does not so much indicate the subject but rather from the very beginning is meant to obviate certain objections that the writer foresees against his material or its treatment. A father wants to marry his daughter to a young man she has never seen. She is already half-committed to another, but this has been going on so long that it is no longer so compelling. Nevertheless, she would still much rather have him than a complete stranger, and at his instigation even plays the role of a madwoman to scare the new suitor off. The new suitor comes, but luckily he is such a handsome, likable man that she soon forgets her deception and comes to an agreement with him in no time. Give the play a different title, and all of the readers and spectators will cry out: that is very unexpected! To take a complication that has been so carefully knotted over ten scenes and then in one scene not merely to untie it but to suddenly hack it to pieces! Here, however, this flaw is announced in the title itself, and thereby to a certain extent justified. For, if such a case really happened once, why shouldn't it be represented? Indeed, it resembled a comedy in reality; should it then, for that very reason, be that much less suited to comedy? – Strictly speaking, absolutely: the incidents that are called real comedy in everyday life are not the same as those realistic incidents found in comedy; and that is the crux of the matter.

But denouement and development: don't these two words come to the same thing? Not completely. The denouement is that Miss Argante marries Erast and not Dorante, and this is adequately prepared. For her love toward Dorante is so tepid and fickle; she loves him because for the last four years she has not seen anyone but him. Sometimes she loves him more, sometimes less, sometimes not at all; it all depends: if she has not seen him for a long time, then he seems lovable enough to her, but if she sees him every day, he bores her, and, in particular, from time to time a face catches her attention, in comparison to which she finds Dorante's face so bleak, so unattractive, so disgusting! What more is needed, then, to take her completely away from him than that Erast, whom her father intends for her, has such a face? The fact that she takes him is so little unexpected that it would rather be much more unexpected if she were to stay with Dorante. Development, on the other hand, is a more relative word; an

---

* See the 11th evening [Essay 13].
† See the 27th, 33rd, and 37th evenings [Essays 21, 28, and 33].

unexpected development involves a complication that has no consequences and from which the writer suddenly jumps without worrying about the dilemmas in which he has left some of his characters. And so it is here: Peter will take care of Dorante; the writer leaves him to it.[7]

On the forty-eighth evening (Wednesday, July 22nd), Herr Weisse's tragedy *Richard the Third* was performed, with *Duke Michael* at the conclusion.[8]

This play is, beyond dispute, one of our most significant originals. It is rich enough in great merits to show that it was not beyond the power of the writer to avoid the errors with which they are interwoven, had he only trusted that power.

Shakespeare had already brought the life and death of Richard III to the stage, but Herr Weisse did not remember this until his work was already finished.[9] "If I should lose much in the comparison," he says, "at least it will be found that I have not committed plagiarism. But perhaps it would have been a merit to have plagiarized Shakespeare."[10]

Granted, one could plagiarize him. But what is said of Homer – that it would be easier to steal the club from Hercules than a verse from him – could be said of Shakespeare just as well.[11] There is a stamp impressed even on the least of his beauties that immediately calls out to the whole world: I am Shakespeare's! And woe to any other gem that has the nerve to put itself beside it!

Shakespeare wants to be studied, not plundered. If we have genius, Shakespeare must be to us what the *camera obscura* is to the landscape painter: he studiously looks into it in order to learn how nature projects itself onto a flat surface in all cases, but he does not borrow anything from it.[12]

I really do not know of any single scene, or indeed any single speech, in the whole of Shakespeare's play that Herr Weisse could have used as it is there. Even the smallest parts of Shakespeare are tailored to the great dimensions of the history play, and this type of play relates to the tragedy of French taste in much the same way that an expansive fresco relates to a miniature painting for a ring. What can be taken from the former to use in the latter other than perhaps a face, a single figure, at most a small group, which one would then have to make into its own whole? In the same way, Shakespeare's individual thoughts would have to become whole scenes, and individual scenes whole acts. For if you want to properly use the sleeve from a giant's frock to clothe a dwarf, you must not merely make him a sleeve from it but a whole coat.

But even if an author does this, he can rest easy about the charge of plagiarism. Most people will not recognize the flock from which the threads were spun. The few who understand art will not betray the *maestro*; they know that a nugget of gold can be so artfully worked that the value of the form far exceeds the value of the material.

For my part, I truly regret that Shakespeare's *Richard* occurred to our writer so late. He could have known it and still remained just as original as he is; he could have used it without any evidence of a single borrowed thought.

If the same thing had happened to me, I would at least have afterwards used Shakespeare's work as a mirror for wiping from my own work all of the blemishes that my eye had not been able to recognize in it directly. – But how do I know that Herr Weisse did not do this? And why should he not have done it?

Can it not just as well be that those things I consider blemishes, he does not? And is it not very probable that he is more correct than I? I am convinced that the eye of the artist is, for the most part, much more perceptive than the most sharp-eyed of his observers. Of twenty accusations that these latter make against him, he will remember having made and answered nineteen himself as he worked.

Nevertheless, he will not be annoyed to hear from others, too. For he likes it when someone judges his work, be it insipid or thorough, unjust or just, malicious or benign; it's all the same to him, and even the most insipid, unjust, and malicious judgment is preferable to cold admiration.[13] He will know how to put the former to use to his benefit in one way or another, but what can he do with the latter? He would not like to look down his nose at the good honest people who consider him something special, and yet he must shrug his shoulders at them. He is not vain, but he is generally proud, and out of pride he would ten times rather take unearned criticism than unearned praise. –

One can imagine what criticism I want to prepare with this. – Far less of the author and primarily of one or two fellow critics. I do not know where I recently saw printed that I had praised my friend's *Amalia* at the expense of his other comedies.[‡,14] – At the expense? Then surely only the earlier ones? I do believe, my dear sir, that one ought never criticize your older works thusly. Heaven protect you from the insidious compliment that the last is always the best! –

Essay 74

15 January 1768[1]

To the matter. – I would primarily wish for the writer's explanation of Richard's character.[2]

Aristotle would have rejected him out of hand; I could readily get past Aristotle's authority, if I could only just as readily get past his argument.

He assumes that tragedy should arouse compassion and terror, and from that he deduces that its hero should not be either totally virtuous or completely villainous, for the goal will not be reached by the misfortune of either the one or the other.[3]

If I grant this, then *Richard the Third* is a tragedy that misses its aim. If I do not grant this, then I no longer know what a tragedy is.

For as Herr Weisse has depicted him, Richard III is undoubtedly the greatest, most abominable monster the stage has ever borne. I say, the stage; I doubt the earth has ever really borne such a monster.

What kind of compassion can the downfall of this monster awaken? And yet, that is not what he is intended to do; that was not the writer's aim; instead there are other characters in his work whom he has crafted to be the object of our compassion.

---

‡ Just now I remembered: in Herr Schmid's *Supplements to his Theory of Poetry*, p. 45.

But terror? – Should this villain, who fills the void between himself and the throne with corpses, indeed the corpses of those who should have been dearest in the world to him, should this bloodthirsty devil, who boasts of his thirst for blood and is tickled by his crimes, not awaken the most extreme terror?

Certainly he awakens terror, if by terror is meant astonishment at inconceivable crimes, horror over acts of evil that exceed our comprehension, and the shudder that overcomes us at seeing deliberate atrocities committed with pleasure. Of this kind of terror, *Richard the Third* gave me my fair share.

But this kind of terror is so far from being one of the objectives of tragedy that the ancient poets rather tried to diminish it when their characters had to commit some great crime. They often preferred to put the blame on fate, make the crime preordained by a vengeful god, and transform a person of free will into a machine rather than allow us to dwell on the awful idea that people might naturally be capable of such depravity.

The French give Crébillon the nickname "the Terrible."[4] I very much fear this is more on account of this sort of terror, which should not be in tragedy, than for the true type that the philosopher counts as essential to tragedy.[5]

And this should not even have been called terror. The word Aristotle uses means fear; tragedy should arouse compassion and fear, he says, not compassion and terror.[6] It is true, terror is a type of fear; it is a sudden, surprising fear. But this very suddenness, this surprise, which is included in the idea of terror, shows clearly that those who substituted the word terror for the word fear did not at all comprehend what kind of fear Aristotle meant. – I will not cross this path again soon; allow me, therefore, a brief digression.

"Compassion," Aristotle says, "requires someone who suffers undeservedly, and fear requires someone like ourselves. The villain is neither the former nor the latter; consequently, his misfortune cannot awaken either the one or the other."*

This fear, I say, is called terror by modern interpreters and translators, and with this change of words they succeed in making the world's strangest bargain with the philosopher.

One of this crowd says,†,[7] "People have not been able to come to agreement over the explanation of terror, and in every respect it contains one aspect too many, which both keeps it from being universal and limits it. If, with his inclusion of 'like ourselves,' Aristotle understood merely the similarity of humanity, namely that the spectator and the personage onstage are both people, even supposing that their character, worth, and rank were vastly different, then this addition would be superfluous, for it is self-evident. If, however, he thought that only virtuous people or those who had some inherent but forgivable fault could arouse terror, then he was wrong, for reason and experience are against him. Terror indisputably originates from a feeling of humanity: every person is subject to it, and every person shudders at the adverse misfortune

---

* In the 13th chapter of *The Poetics*.
† Herr S. in the prologue to his *Comic Theater*, p. 35.

of others because of it. It is indeed possible that it might occur to someone to deny this feeling; but this would be a wholesale denial of his natural sentiments and thus a blatant affectation based on corrupted principles rather than a real refutation. – Now then, even if an adverse accident unexpectedly befalls an immoral person to whom we have just turned our attention, we lose sight of the immorality and only see the human being. The sight of human misery in general makes us sad, and the sudden sad feeling that we then experience is terror."

Completely correct, only not in the right place! For what does this say against Aristotle? Nothing. Aristotle is not thinking of this terror when he speaks of the fear into which only the misfortune of those like ourselves could set us. This terror that seizes us at the sudden sight of the suffering in store for another is a compassionate terror, and thus understood under the concept of compassion. Aristotle would not say compassion and fear if by fear he meant nothing more than a mere modification of compassion.

"Compassion," says the author of the *Letters on Sentiments*,‡,8 "is a mixed sentiment composed of the love for an object and displeasure over its misfortune. The movements by which compassion reveals itself can be distinguished from the simple symptoms of both love and displeasure, for compassion is a phenomenon. But how varied this phenomenon can become! Change only the specificity of time in the commiserated misfortune, and compassion will reveal itself through completely different signs. For Electra, crying over the urn of her brother, we feel a compassionate sorrow, because she regards the misfortune as over and bewails what she has lost.[9] What we feel over Philoctetes' pain is likewise compassion, but of a somewhat different nature, for the torment that this virtuous man must endure is present and overcomes him before our eyes.[10] When Oedipus, however, is horrified at the sudden revelation of the great secret; when Monime is alarmed at seeing the jealous Mithridates grow pale; when the virtuous Desdemona becomes afraid at hearing the otherwise so tender Othello speak so threateningly to her: what do we feel then?[11] Compassion, every time! But compassionate horror, compassionate fear, compassionate terror. The movements are different, but the essence of the feeling is the same in all these cases. For just as every love is bound up with the readiness to put ourselves in the place of the beloved, so must we share every form of suffering with the beloved person, which we very deliberately call compassion. Why, then, should it not be possible for fear, terror, anger, jealousy, the desire for revenge, and in general all sorts of unpleasant feelings, even envy, to originate in compassion? – One sees from this how very unsuitably the majority of critics divide the tragic passions into terror and compassion. Terror and compassion! Is theatrical terror then not compassion? For whom does the spectator start in fear, when Mérope draws the dagger against her own son?[12] Certainly not for himself, but for Aegisthus, whose preservation we very much desire, and for the misguided queen, who believes him to be her son's murderer. But if we only want to call compassion our displeasure over the present misery of another, then we will have to distinguish from compassion proper not just terror, but also all of the other passions communicated to us by someone else."

‡ *Philosophical Writings* by Herr Moses Mendelssohn, part 2, p. 4.

Essay 75

19 January 1768[1]

These thoughts are so correct, so clear, and so enlightening that you would think everyone could have and must have had them.[2] Nevertheless, I do not want to subsume the insightful observations of the modern philosopher under those of the ancient philosopher; I know very well the former's contributions on the subject of mixed emotions, the true theory of which we owe to him alone. But Aristotle still may have sensed, to some extent, what the modern philosopher dissected so excellently; at the very least it is undeniable that either Aristotle must have thought that tragedy could and should awaken nothing but compassion proper – that is, nothing but displeasure over the present misfortune of another – which is highly unlikely; or he understood the word compassion to encompass all of the passions in general that we might share with another.

For it is certainly not Aristotle who classified the tragic passions as compassion and terror, a notion that has been justifiably criticized. He was misunderstood and mistranslated. He speaks of compassion and fear, not of compassion and terror; and his fear is absolutely not the fear that another's impending misfortune awakens in us for the other person, but rather it is the fear for ourselves that stems from our similarity with the suffering person. It is the fear that the misfortunes we see hanging over that person could befall us ourselves; it is the fear that we ourselves could become the pitied object. In short: this fear is compassion directed at ourselves.

Aristotle always needs to be explained through his own writing. I advise that anyone who wishes to provide us with a new commentary on his *Poetics* that will surpass Dacier's should first and foremost read the philosopher's work from beginning to end.[3] He will find insights into the *Poetics* where he least expected; in particular he must study the books of *Rhetoric* and *Morals*.[4] One would think indeed that the academics who have the writings of Aristotle at their fingertips must have long ago discovered these insights. But among all his works, the *Poetics* was the one to which they paid the least attention. For that matter, they also lacked other knowledge, without which these insights remained unproductive: they knew neither the theater nor its masterpieces.

The authentic explanation of this fear that Aristotle links to tragic compassion can be found in the fifth and eighth chapters of the second book of his *Rhetoric*. It was not at all difficult to recall these chapters; nevertheless, not one of his interpreters seems to have remembered them, or at least no one has taken advantage of what they offer. For even those who understood without reading them that this fear was not compassionate terror still could have learned an important piece from them, namely: the reason why the Stagirite associated compassion with fear, and only fear, and why not with some other passion or with several passions.[5] They know nothing of this reason, and I would love to hear what answer they would spontaneously come up with if you were to ask them, for example, why tragedy cannot and may not arouse compassion and admiration just as well as compassion and fear?

It all depends on Aristotle's conception of compassion. Namely, he believed that a misfortune that becomes the object of our compassion must be so constituted that we might fear it could happen to us or to one of our own. Without this fear, there can be no compassion. For neither the man so beaten down by misfortune that he feels he has nothing left to fear nor the man who thinks himself so perfectly happy that he cannot even imagine how misfortune could befall him – neither the desperate man nor the over-confident man – tends to have compassion for others. Aristotle thus explains what is to be feared and what is deserving of compassion each through the other. He says that we fear everything that would awaken our compassion if it happened to another person,*,6 and we feel compassion for everything affecting another person that would frighten us if it threatened us ourselves. It is not enough, then, that the misfortunate person for whom we are to feel compassion does not deserve his misfortune, whether or not he has brought it upon himself through some weakness. His tormented innocence, or rather his too severely bedeviled guilt, would be lost on us, could not arouse our compassion, if we did not believe in the possibility that his sufferings could also befall us. But this possibility can arise and indeed become a probability as long as the writer does not make him worse than we usually tend to be, when he has him think and behave exactly as we would have thought and behaved in his circumstances (or at least as we believe we would have thought and behaved); in short, when the writer depicts him as cut from the same cloth as we are.7 Out of this similarity would arise the fear that just as we ourselves feel that we resemble him, so our fate could quite easily resemble his; and it is this fear that gives rise to compassion.

This is what Aristotle thought about compassion, and only from this perspective does it become clear why, in his explanation of tragedy, he only named fear alongside compassion. Not because this fear was a special feeling, independent of compassion, which could be aroused with or without compassion, just as compassion could be aroused with or without fear (which was Corneille's misinterpretation): but, according to his explanation of compassion, it necessarily includes fear; because nothing can arouse our compassion other than that which simultaneously awakens our fear.

Corneille had already written all his plays when he started commenting on Aristotle's *Poetics*.†,8 He had devoted fifty years to the theater, and after that experience he undoubtedly could have given us marvelous insights into the old dramatic codex if only he had consulted it more diligently while working on his commentaries. However, he only seems to have done so, if at all, in reference to the mechanical rules of the art. He did not trouble himself with its more essential points, and when he found in the end that he had violated its rules, despite claiming not to have done so, he tried

---

* δ'ἁπλῶς εἰπεῖν, φοβερά ἐστιν ὅσα ἐφ' ἑτέρων γιγνόμενα ἢ μέλλοντα ἐλεεινά ἐστιν. I do not know what Aemilius Portus was thinking (in his edition of the *Rhetoric*, Spirae 1598) in translating this: "Denique ut simpliciter loquar, formidabilia sunt, quaecunque simulac in aliorum potestatem venerunt, vel ventura sunt, miseranda sunt." It should simply read, "quaecunque simulac aliis evenerunt, vel eventura sunt."

† "Je hasarderai quelque chose sur cinquante ans de travail pour la scène," he says in his essay on the drama. His first play, *Mélite*, was in 1625, and his last, *Surena*, in 1675, which makes exactly fifty years; therefore it is certain that in his interpretations of Aristotle he could and did have an eye on all his plays.

to absolve himself through exegesis and had his presumptive master say things that plainly never occurred to him.

Corneille had brought martyrs on the stage and portrayed them as the most perfectly virtuous persons; he had produced the most despicable monsters in the characters of Prusias, Phocas, and Cleopatra.[9] Aristotle declares of both types that they would be unsuited to tragedy because neither could awaken either compassion or fear. What does Corneille answer to this? How does he manage it so that neither his reputation nor Aristotle's might suffer because of this contradiction? "Oh," he says, "it is easy to reconcile ourselves with Aristotle.[‡] We can simply assume that he did not wish to assert that both of these means, both fear and compassion, were necessary at the same time to prompt the cleansing of the passions that he makes the main purpose of tragedy; according to his opinion, just one would be sufficient. [. . .] We can support this explanation," he continues, "from his own writing, if we properly weigh the reasons he gives for excluding those incidents that he disapproves in tragedy. He never says: this or that does not belong in tragedy because it merely awakens compassion and not fear, or this is unbearable because it only awakens fear without arousing compassion. No; rather, he rejects them because, as he says, they bring neither compassion nor fear into effect, and thereby signifies to us that he does not like them because both the one and the other are lacking and that he would not withhold his approval if they just put one of the two into effect."[10]

Essay 76

22 January 1768[1]

But that is fundamentally wrong![2] – I cannot fathom how Dacier, who was otherwise rather attentive to the contortions with which Corneille sought to make Aristotle's text serve his own ends, could overlook this biggest one of all.[3] Yet how could he not overlook it, since it never occurred to him to consult the philosopher's explanation of compassion? – As I said, what Corneille imagines here is fundamentally wrong. Aristotle cannot have meant that, or we would have to believe that he could forget his own explanation, we would have to believe that he could contradict himself in the most flagrant manner. If, according to his theory, no other person's misfortune can arouse our compassion if we do not fear that misfortune for ourselves, then he could not be satisfied with any tragic plot that only aroused compassion and not fear, for he considered the matter itself to be impossible. Such plots did not exist for him; on the contrary, he believed that as soon as they were capable of awakening our compassion, they must also awaken the fear for ourselves – or rather, it is only by means of this fear that they awaken compassion. Still less could he imagine the plot of a tragedy that could arouse fear for ourselves without simultaneously awakening our compassion, for he was convinced that everything that arouses fear in us for ourselves must also

---

‡ Il est aisé de nous accommoder avec Aristote &c.

awaken our compassion, as soon as we see others threatened or harmed by it. This is precisely the case with tragedy, in which we see all the misfortune we fear happening to others and not to ourselves.

It is true that when Aristotle speaks of plots that are unsuitable for tragedy, he often employs the expression that they awaken neither compassion nor fear. But so much the worse for Corneille if he allows himself to be misled by this neither/nor. These disjunctive particles do not always involve what he has them involve. For if we use them to deny two or more things to an object, then the ability of the object to continue to exist if it is missing one or the other of these things depends on whether these things can be separated from each other as easily in nature as we separate them in the abstract, through symbolic expression. For example, if we say of a woman that she is neither beautiful nor witty, to be sure we mean that we would be satisfied if she were just one or the other, for wit and beauty are not just separable in thought but really are separate. But when we say that a person believes in neither heaven nor hell, do we then mean to say that we would be satisfied if he only believed in one of the two, if he believed in heaven but not hell, or hell but not heaven? Surely not, for the person who believes in the one must necessarily believe in the other; heaven and hell, punishment and reward, are relative – if you have the one, you also have the other. Or, to take my example from a related art: when we say "this painting is no good because it has neither line nor color," do we mean to say that a good painting could make do with just one of the two? – This is so clear!

But what if the explanation Aristotle gives of compassion were wrong? What if we could feel compassion for misfortunes and accidents that we do not need be afraid of for ourselves in any way?

It is true: our fear is not necessary to feel displeasure over the physical misfortune of the object of our love. This displeasure emerges merely from our perception of the object's imperfection, just as our love comes from our perception of its perfection, and out of the confluence of this pleasure and displeasure springs the mixed sensation we call compassion.[4]

Even so, I do not believe I must necessarily abandon Aristotle's point.

For even if we can feel compassion for others without fear for ourselves, it is still indisputable that when fear is added to it, our compassion is much stronger and more vivid and tantalizing than it is without it. And what prevents us from believing that it is only through adding in fear for ourselves that our mixed sensation at the physical misfortune of a beloved object matures to the degree to which it deserves to be called an affect?[5]

This is precisely what Aristotle believed. He does not regard compassion in terms of its primitive stirrings but rather simply as affect. Without misconceiving the former, he merely denies to the spark the name of flame. Those compassionate stirrings that lack fear for ourselves he terms "philanthropy," and he only gives the name compassion to the stronger feelings of this type that are combined with fear for ourselves. Thus he does indeed claim that the misfortune of a villain cannot arouse either our compassion or our fear; but he does not necessarily deny him all ability to stir us. Even the villain is still a person, still a being who retains enough perfections amidst all his moral imperfections to make us prefer not to see his ruin and destruction and to feel, in the face of these, something akin to compassion, the elements of compassion, so to speak. But, as noted above, he does not call this compassion-like feeling compassion but rather philanthropy. He says, "We must never allow any villain to pass from adversity to prosperity, for this is the most untragic of all. It has none of all the things it ought to have; it awakens neither philanthropy, nor compassion, nor fear. Moreover, it must not be a complete and total villain who falls from prosperity into adversity, because such an occurrence may awaken philanthropy but neither compassion nor fear."[6] I know of nothing that is bleaker and more tasteless than the common translation of this word philanthropy. Namely, they translate its adjective into Latin with "hominibus gratum"; into French with "ce que peut faire quelque plaisir"; and into German with "what can give pleasure" [*was Vergnügen machen kann*].[7] Only Goulston, as far as I can see, seems not to have misunderstood the philosopher's sense, insofar as he translates φιλανθρωπον with "quod humanitatis sensu tangat."[8] For certainly this philanthropy, which even the misfortune of a villain can awaken, is not to be understood as our joy at his deserved punishment, but rather the feeling of human sympathy that wells up in us for him at the moment of his suffering, despite our understanding that his suffering is fully deserved. Herr Curtius limits these compassionate stirrings for a misfortunate villain to a certain type of misfortune that befalls him: "Those accidents happening to a vice-ridden person that excite in us neither terror nor compassion must be the consequences of his vice," he says, "for if they happen to him by accident, or blamelessly, he retains in the spectator's heart the privileges of humanity, whereby we extend our compassion even to a villain who suffers innocently."[9] But he seems not to have considered this enough. For even when the misfortune that befalls a villain is a direct consequence of his crime, we cannot help but suffer with him at the sight of his misfortune.

"Look at the masses of people who crowd around a condemned man," says the author of the *Letters on Sentiments*.[10] "They have heard of all of the atrocities the depraved has committed; they have abhorred his conduct and perhaps even the man himself. Now he is dragged, maimed and unconscious, onto the dreadful gallows. People work their way through the throng, stand on tiptoe, climb on roofs in order to see the lines of death disfigure his face. His sentence is pronounced; the hangman approaches; one moment will decide his fate. With what longing do all hearts now wish that he would be pardoned! Him? The object of their hatred, whom they themselves would have condemned to death just a moment before? By what means has a ray of love for another human being now stirred in them? Is it not the approach of the punishment, the sight of the most dreadful physical misfortune that somehow reconciles us even with a heinous criminal and earns him our love? Without love we could not possibly have compassion for his fate."

And it is this love, I say, that we can never completely lose toward others; it smolders unceasingly, hiding itself under the ashes of other, stronger feelings, awaiting only a favorable gust of misfortune and pain and ruin to fan it into a flame of compassion. It is this love that Aristotle means by the term philanthropy. We are correct when we call it compassion. But Aristotle was also not wrong in giving it its own name, in order to differentiate it, as I've said, from the highest degree of compassionate feelings, which become an affect through the addition of a believable fear for ourselves.

Essay 77

26 January 1768[1]

I will add one more interjection here.[2] If Aristotle had this concept of compassion's affect as being necessarily combined with fear for ourselves, why did he need to make a special mention of fear? The word compassion already includes it, and it would have been enough if he had merely said: tragedy should prompt the purification of our passions by exciting our compassion. The addition of fear does not say anything more and only makes what he should say ambiguous and uncertain.

I answer: if Aristotle had only wanted to teach us which passions can and should be awakened by tragedy, he certainly would have been able to omit the addition of fear and doubtlessly would have omitted it; for no philosopher was ever more sparing with words than he. But he wanted to teach us at the same time which passions should be purified by means of those awakened in tragedy, and for this purpose he had to think about fear in particular. For although, according to him, compassion's affect cannot exist – either in the theater or out of it – without fear for ourselves, although fear is a necessary ingredient of compassion, the reverse is not also true. Compassion for others is not an ingredient of fear for ourselves. The moment that tragedy is over, our compassion ceases, and nothing remains of all the emotions we have felt except the believable fear for ourselves that the pitied misfortune has allowed us to create. We take this with us; and in the same way that, as an ingredient of compassion, it helps purify compassion, it now also helps to purify itself as an independent passion in and of itself. Consequently, in order to indicate that fear can and really does work in this way, Aristotle found it necessary to highlight it in particular.

It is indisputable that Aristotle did not want to provide any kind of strict, logical definition of tragedy. For he did not confine himself to its essential features but also included several incidental ones, because the customs of his time had made them necessary. If we put these aside and distill the remaining features, we are left with a perfectly precise definition: namely, that tragedy is, in brief, a poem that arouses compassion. According to its genus, it is the imitation of an action, just like the epic and the comedy; but according to its genre, it is the imitation of an action deserving of compassion. All of its rules can be perfectly deduced from these two concepts, and even its dramatic form may be determined by them.

One might perhaps doubt that last statement. At least, I cannot name a single critic who has even thought to attempt it. They all assume the dramatic form of tragedy as something already established, which simply is the way it is, and which we leave this way because it is good. Aristotle alone got to the root of the matter, but in his definition he implied it rather than pointing it out clearly. "Tragedy," he says, "is the imitation of an action that, through compassion and fear (and not through narration), effects the purification of these and similar passions." This is how he expresses it, word for word.[3] Who would not be vexed by the peculiar opposition here, "through compassion and fear (and not through narration)"? Compassion and fear are the means used by tragedy to achieve its purpose; narration can only refer to the manner in which these means are employed or not employed. Does it not seem that Aristotle has taken a leap here? Does it not seem that the proper antithesis to narrative, that is, dramatic form, is clearly missing? But what do the translators do with this gap? One circumvents it quite carefully; the other fills it, but only with words. All of them see nothing more in it than a careless statement to which they do not consider themselves bound to adhere as long as they convey the philosopher's meaning. Dacier translates: "d'une action – qui, sans le secours de la narration, par le moyen de la compassion & de la terreur" and so on.[4] And Curtius: "of an action, which not through narrative but (through the representation of the action itself) by means of terror and pity purifies us of the faults of the represented passions."[5] Oh, very correct! Both say what Aristotle wants to say, only they do not say it how he says it. Yet much depends on this "how," for it is not merely a careless utterance. In short, the matter stands thusly: Aristotle noted that compassion necessarily demands the presence of a misfortune; that misfortunes occurring long ago or looming in the distant future either cannot awaken in us any compassion at all, or only a much weaker compassion than a present misfortune does. Consequently, it is necessary to represent the action by which we want to arouse compassion not as having already occurred – that is, not in the narrative form – but rather as currently occurring – that is, in the dramatic form. And this fact – that our compassion is hardly, or not at all, aroused by narration but rather almost solely by the sight of what is occurring in the moment – is what justifies him in substituting the feature itself for the form in his definition, because the feature is only capable of this one form. If he had thought it possible that our compassion could be aroused through narration as well, then it would have been a very mistaken omission indeed if he had said "not by means of narration, but by means of compassion and fear." But because he was convinced that compassion and fear could only be aroused by a representation through the dramatic form, he could allow himself this leap for the sake of brevity. – For this, I refer my reader to the above-mentioned ninth chapter of the second book of his *Rhetoric*.[*,6]

Regarding the moral purpose Aristotle gives to tragedy, and which he believed he needed to include in its definition: it is well known how much this has been argued over, especially in recent times.[7] But I venture to argue that all who have declared their opposition have not understood Aristotle. They foisted all their own thoughts on him before they knew for certain what his were. They argue over fanciful ideas that they themselves have thought up and imagine how incontrovertibly they refute the philosopher while really they merely dismantle their own fantasies. I cannot enter into a closer discussion of this matter here. But just so that I do not appear to be speaking without any proof at all, I will make two observations:

1   They have Aristotle say, "tragedy should purify us of the flaws of the represented passions by means of terror and compassion."[8] Of the represented passions? So, if the hero encounters calamity on account of curiosity, ambition, love, or anger, then is it our curiosity, ambition, love, or anger that is purified by tragedy?[9] Aristotle never thought anything of the kind. And so the gentlemen enjoy arguing;

---

* ἐπεὶ δ᾽ ἐγγὺς φαινόμενα τὰ πάθη ἐλεεινά ἐστιν, τὰ δὲ μυριοστὸν ἔτος γενόμενα ἢ ἐσόμενα οὔτε ἐλπίζοντες οὔτε μεμνημένοι ἢ ὅλως οὐκ ἐλεοῦσιν ἢ οὐχ ὁμοίως, ἀνάγκη τοὺς συναπεργαζομένους σχήμασι καὶ φωναῖς καὶ ἐσθῆσι καὶ ὅλως ὑποκρίσει ἐλεεινοτέρους εἶναι [*Rhetoric* 2.8.14 – Ed.]

their imagination transforms windmills into giants; they tilt at them in the certain hope of victory and give no mind to any Sancho with nothing more than common sense who, from atop his more circumspect steed, calls after them not to be too hasty and to at least just open their eyes first.[10] *Τῶν τοιούτων παθημάτων*, Aristotle says, and that does not mean "the represented passions"; they should have rendered it with "these and similar ones" or "the passions awakened."[11] The *τοιούτων* refers solely to the preceding compassion and fear; tragedy should arouse our compassion and our fear only to purify these and similar passions, but not all passions without distinction. He says, however, *τοιούτων* and not *τούτων*; he says "these and similar ones" and not just "these" in order to indicate that by the term compassion he understands not merely the so-called compassion proper but rather all philanthropical feelings in general, just as by the term fear he understands not merely displeasure at a misfortune that threatens us but also all displeasures related to it, including displeasure at present and past misfortunes, sadness, and grief.[12] The compassion and fear that tragedy awakens should purify compassion and fear in this widest sense, but it should only purify these passions and no others. Of course, useful lessons and examples can be found in tragedy that serve to purify other passions as well, but these are not tragedy's purpose; tragedy has these in common with the epic and comedy insofar as it is a poem, an imitation of an action in general, but not insofar as it is a tragedy, the imitation of an action worthy of compassion in particular. All genres of poetry should better us; it is lamentable enough if one must prove this, and even more lamentable if there are writers who doubt it. However, all genres cannot improve everything, or at least not all things equally well; and what each can improve to the greatest degree of perfection, and better than any other genre – that alone is its real purpose.

Essay 78

29 January 1768[1]

2   Because Aristotle's opponents did not take into consideration which emotions he actually wanted to have purified in us through compassion and fear in tragedy, it was natural that they must also be wrong about purification itself.[2] At the end of his *Politics*, where Aristotle speaks of the purification of the emotions through music, he promises to engage this purification at greater length in his *Poetics*.[3] "Because, however," Corneille says, "there is nothing at all of this material there, most of his interpreters have arrived at the conclusion that it has come to us incomplete."[4] Nothing at all? For my part, I think that even in what remains to us of his *Poetics*, whether it is much or little, we can find everything on the subject that he considered necessary to say to one who was not altogether unfamiliar with his philosophy. Corneille himself noticed a passage that, in his opinion, could illuminate for us the manner by which purification occurs in tragedy, namely the one in which Aristotle says: "compassion requires someone who suffers undeservedly, and fear requires someone like ourselves."[5] This passage is very

important indeed, only Corneille made a wrong use of it and could hardly have done otherwise, because his mind was stuck on the purification of the emotions in general. "Compassion for a misfortune that we see befall someone like ourselves," he says, "awakens in us the fear that a similar misfortune could befall us. This fear awakens the desire to avoid it, and this desire awakens an attempt to purify, moderate, improve, or totally eradicate the emotion that draws the person whom we pity into misfortune before our very eyes; for reason tells us that, to avoid the effect, one must cut off the cause."[6] But this reasoning, which turns fear into a mere instrument through which compassion effects the purification of emotions, is false and cannot possibly be Aristotle's intention.[7] According to this, tragedy could purify all of the emotions except the two that Aristotle explicitly wants to see purified. It could purify our anger, our curiosity, our envy, our ambition, our hatred, and our love, whichever of these emotions it is that draws the person with whom we commiserate into misfortune. It would only leave our compassion and fear unpurified. For compassion and fear are the emotions that we, and not the characters, feel in tragedy; they are the emotions by means of which the characters move us but not the ones that draw them into misfortune. There could be a play in which they are both; I am well aware of that. But I have not encountered such a play, one in which, namely, the object of our compassion plunges into misfortune though misconceived compassion or fear. Yet this play would be the only one in which what Corneille thinks Aristotle wants to happen in all tragedies actually occurs, and even there it would not happen in the manner demanded by Aristotle. This unique play would be, so to speak, the point at which two inclined straight lines intersect, never to encounter each other again in all eternity. – Even Dacier would not mistake Aristotle's meaning so badly.[8] He was obliged to be more attentive to the words of his author, and these convey quite positively that our compassion and our fear are to be purified by the compassion and fear of tragedy. But because he undoubtedly believed that the benefit of tragedy would be very small if it were limited just to this, he allowed himself to be led astray by Corneille's explanation and additionally assigned to tragedy the similar purification of all the other emotions. And when for his part Corneille denied this and showed through examples that this was more of a beautiful idea than a thing that could generally be achieved in reality, Dacier had to engage with these examples himself and found himself in such a corner that he had to make the most violent twists and turns to extricate himself and his Aristotle from the situation. I say: his Aristotle, for the real one is far from needing such twists and turns. The latter, to repeat it over and over again, thought of no other emotions to be purified by compassion and fear in tragedy other than our compassion and our fear themselves, and it made no difference to him whether tragedy contributed much or little to the purification of the other emotions. Dacier should have stopped at this purification, too; but admittedly he then also would have had to assign a more complete conception to it. "It is not difficult to explain," he says, "how tragedy arouses compassion and fear in order to purify compassion and fear. It excites them by putting before our eyes the misfortune into which a person like ourselves has fallen through unintentional errors, and it purifies them by familiarizing us with this misfortune and thereby teaching us neither to fear it too much nor to be too affected by it when we meet with the same misfortune in reality. – It prepares people to endure the most challenging accidents with courage and disposes the most miserable to consider themselves happy when they compare their own woes to the much greater ones represented in tragedy. For in what condition can a person find himself that, at the sight of an Oedipus, a Philoctetes, or an Orestes, he would not be obliged to recognize that all of the evils he must endure cannot even begin to compare with those that these men must endure?"[9] Now this is true; this explanation cannot have caused Dacier much head-scratching. For he found it almost word for word in the Stoic, who always had half an eye inclined toward apathy.[10] Without registering here the objection that the feeling of our own suffering does not leave room for much compassion along with it and that, as a result, there can be no purification or mitigation of suffering via compassion for a sufferer whose compassion cannot be aroused, I will allow for the validity of everything he says. Only I must ask: how much has he really said thereby? Did he say anything more than that compassion purifies our fear? Certainly not: and that would scarcely be a quarter of Aristotle's claim. For when Aristotle claims that tragedy excites compassion and fear in order to purify compassion and fear, who does not see that this says much more than Dacier thought worth explaining? According to the various combinations of the concepts presented here, anyone who wants to fully exhaust Aristotle's meaning must show, bit by bit: (1) how tragic compassion can, and really does, purify our compassion; (2) how tragic fear can and does purify our fear; (3) how tragic compassion can and does purify our fear; and (4) how tragic fear can and does purify our compassion. Dacier, however, confined himself to just the third point and moreover did this quite badly, elucidating it only halfway to boot. For anyone who strives after a correct and complete understanding of the Aristotelian purification of the emotions will find that each of these four points above actually consists of two things. Since, in brief, this purification rests in nothing else but the transformation of emotions into virtuous dispositions and, according to our philosopher, every virtue is situated between two extremes, then, if tragedy is to transform our compassion into virtue, it must be able to purify us of both extremes of compassion. The same is to be understood of fear. With regard to compassion, tragic compassion must not only purify the soul of one who feels too much compassion but also of one who feels too little. With regard to fear, tragic fear must not only purify the soul of one who fears no misfortune whatsoever but also of one who is afraid of every misfortune, no matter how distant and improbable. Likewise, regarding fear, tragic compassion must navigate between too much and too little, and, vice versa, tragic fear with regard to compassion. But as I said, Dacier has only shown how tragic compassion moderates our excessive fear, and not at all how it remedies the complete lack of fear or raises it to a healthier degree in those who feel too little of it; never mind that he should also have shown the rest. Those who came after him have not made up for what he omitted in the least; however, to settle the conflict – in their opinion – over the benefits of tragedy once and for all, they have pulled in things that belong to poetry in general but not specifically to tragedy as tragedy: for example, that it nourishes and strengthens human propensities, that it should activate the love of virtue and hatred of vice, and so on.*,[11] My dear reader! What poem should not do this? But if every poem is to do this, then this cannot be the distinctive characteristic of tragedy; it cannot be what we are looking for.

Essay 79

2 February 1768[1]

And now to come back to our Richard.[2] – Richard awakens just as little terror as he does compassion: neither terror in the misused sense of the term to mean the sudden surprise of compassion, nor in Aristotle's actual sense, as the salutary fear that we might meet with a similar misfortune.[3] For if he aroused this fear, he would also arouse compassion, just as surely as, conversely, he would arouse fear if we found him even the least bit deserving of our compassion. But he is such a despicable scoundrel, such a devil in the flesh, in whom we find not even one single streak of similarity to ourselves, that I think we could see him delivered to the tortures of hell before our very eyes without feeling in the least for him and without the least fear that such punishments await us, too, if they are consequences of such crimes only. And what, in the end, is the misfortune, the punishment that befalls him? After we are forced to witness so many misdeeds, we hear that he has died with sword in hand. When the Queen is told this, the writer has her say:

> This is something! –

I have never been able to keep myself from muttering under my breath: no, that is absolutely nothing! How many a good king has died thus, defending his crown against a powerful rebel? Richard dies like an honorable man, on the field of battle. Should such a death make up for the displeasure I have felt throughout the play at the triumph of his wicked deeds? (I believe the Greek language is the only one that has a special word to express this displeasure at the happiness of a villain: νέμεσις, νεμεσᾶν.†)[4] His death itself, which ought at least to satisfy my love of justice, further provokes my indignation. "You got off cheaply!" I think. But it is good that there is a justice other than the poetic type!

You will probably say: well then! Let us leave off Richard; the play is titled after him but he is not therefore its hero; he is not the character through which the aim of tragedy is achieved; he has only to be the means of arousing our compassion for others. The Queen, Elizabeth, and the princes: do they not arouse compassion? –

To sidestep all debate: yes. But what is this strange, bitter feeling that mixes itself in with my compassion for these persons? That makes me wish I could spare myself

---

* Curtius, in his "Essay on the Purpose of Tragedy," appended to Aristotle's *Poetics.*
† Aristotle, *Rhetoric* Bk. II. Ch. 9.

this compassion? I do not otherwise wish this when I feel tragic compassion: I usually linger with it willingly and am grateful to the writer for such sweet anguish.

Aristotle said it well, and he nails it on the head! He speaks of a μιαρόν, of something abominable that is present at the misfortune of completely good and innocent people.[5] And are not the Queen, Elisabeth, and the princes just such people? What have they done? How have they brought it upon themselves to be in the claws of this beast? Is it their fault that they have a better right to the throne than he? Especially the little mewling victims, who can hardly tell left from right! Who will deny that they deserve our unmitigated sorrow? But is this sorrow that makes me shiver at the thought of the fate of these people, to which is joined a muttering against Providence and which is haunted by despair, is this sorrow – I will not ask if it is compassion? – Call it what you may – But is this what an imitative art ought to awaken?

Do not say: the history awakens it, it is based on something that really happened. – That really happened? If so: then it will have its good reason in the eternal, infinite connectedness of all things. In that connectedness, everything that appears as blind fate and cruelty in the few parts selected by the poet is wise and good. The poet ought to make a totality from these few parts, one that fully completes itself, in which each thing is fully explained by another and in which no difficulty suddenly arises for which a solution cannot be found within his plan but rather must be sought outside of it, in the general plan of things.[6] The totality made by this mortal creator should be a silhouette of the totality made by the immortal creator; it should accustom us to the thought that just as everything is resolved for the best in the latter, so will it be in the former. And then he forgets this most noble purpose so greatly that he weaves the incomprehensible ways of Providence into his little circle and deliberately awakens our shudder of fear over them? – Oh, spare us this, you who have our hearts in your power! What is the purpose of these sad feelings? To teach us submission? Only cold reason can teach us that, and if the lesson of reason is to take root in us, if we are to maintain confidence and cheerfulness of spirit in our submission, then it is absolutely necessary that we be reminded as little as possible of confounding examples of such undeserved and terrible fates. Away with them from the stage! Away with them, if only it were possible, from all books! –

If, however, there is not a single character in *Richard* possessing the requisite qualities necessary in order for the play really to be what it is called: how has it nevertheless become the interesting play our public considers it to be? If it does not arouse compassion and fear, what then is its effect? For it must, and does, have some effect, and if it does have an effect, does it matter what kind of effect it has? If it engages the spectators, if they enjoy it, what more do we want? Must they of necessity only be engaged and amused according to Aristotle's rules?

That does not sound so wrong, but it can be answered thusly. In general, if *Richard* is no tragedy, it still remains a dramatic poem; and if it lacks the beauties of tragedy, it could still have other beauties: poetry of expression, images, tirades, bold attitudes, fiery and captivating dialogue, auspicious occasions for the actor to exercise the greatest range and variation in his voice and show all his strengths in pantomime, etc.

Richard has many of these beauties, and still others that come nearer to the real beauties of tragedy.

Richard is a loathsome villain, but even the engagement of our loathing is not completely without its pleasures, especially in imitation.

The enormity of the crimes also has a share in the emotions that greatness and boldness awaken in us.

Everything Richard does is an abomination, but all of these abominations serve some purpose. Richard has a plan, and whenever we perceive a plan, our curiosity is piqued; we willingly wait to see whether and how it will be executed. We love anything with a purpose so much that it affords us pleasure regardless of the morality of that purpose.

We wanted Richard to achieve his purpose, and we also wanted him not to achieve it. Its achievement spares us displeasure over means employed completely in vain; if he does not achieve it, then too much blood has been shed for naught, and once it has been shed, we do not like finding it spilled just to pass the time. On the other hand, an achievement of his aims would be a celebration of evil, and that is the worst thing we could hear. The purpose interests us as something to be achieved; but if it were to succeed, we would see nothing but its horror, and we would wish that it had not succeeded. We anticipate this wish, and shudder at the achievement of his aim.

We love the good characters in the play – such a tender, ardent mother, siblings who live for each other so fully – such beings always please us, they always arouse the sweetest and most sympathetic feelings wherever we find them. To see them suffer in complete innocence is bitter, indeed; to be sure, it is not very beneficial for our peace of mind or for our betterment; but it is a feeling, nonetheless.

And thus the play engages us throughout and pleases us through this engagement of our mental faculties. That is true, but the conclusion drawn from this is not true, namely: that we can also be satisfied with it.

A writer can have done much, and yet not have achieved anything thereby. It is not enough that his work affects us; it must also have effects that belong to it, by virtue of its genre.[7] It must have these, above all, and no others could in any way make up for their lack, especially when the genre is of such importance and difficulty and value that all trouble and effort were pointless if it aimed to produce no effects other than those that could just as readily be attained via a genre that had fewer, less demanding standards. One does not need to set a machine in motion to lift a bundle of straw; I need not detonate with a mine what I can knock over with my foot; I do not have to build a bonfire to burn a mosquito.

Essay 80

5 February 1768[1]

Why bother with the laborious work of dramatic form?[2] Why build a theater, costume men and women, rack one's memories, invite the whole city to one place, if I do not want to produce anything more with my work and its performance than some of the feelings that could be produced by a good story, read by anyone curled up at home?

The dramatic form is the only one that allows compassion and fear to be aroused, or at least these emotions cannot be aroused to such a high degree in any other form; and yet people will prefer to arouse all other emotions than these, they will prefer to use it for every purpose other than the one to which it is so eminently suited.[3]

The audience makes do. – That is good, and also not good. For one does not yearn much for the table at which one always merely makes do.

It is well known how keen the Greeks and Romans were about dramas, especially the former about tragic drama. By contrast, how indifferent and cold is our public toward the theater! Where does this difference come from, if not from the fact that the Greeks felt so inspired by such strong and extraordinary feelings at their theater that they could not wait for the moment to experience them again and again; whereas our theater makes such weak impressions upon us that we rarely consider it worth the time and money to experience them? We go to the theater – almost all of us, almost always – out of curiosity or boredom, because everybody else goes or to find company, or out of a desire to see and be seen; only a few, and these only rarely, go with another purpose.

I say we, our public, our stage, but I do not just mean us Germans. We Germans admit openly enough that we still do not have a theater.[4] I do not actually know what is meant by many of our critics who agree with this admission and who are great admirers of French theater. But I do know what I think when I say it. I think, namely, that it is not just we Germans alone but also those who boast of having had a theater for hundreds of years, who brag of having the best theater in all Europe – even the French do not yet have a theater.

Certainly not a tragic one! For even the impressions that the French tragedies produce are so flat and cold! – Listen to what a Frenchman himself has to say about them.

"Among the outstanding beauties of our theater," says M. de Voltaire, "there was a hidden fault that had gone unnoticed because the audience could not on its own have any higher ideas than those which it had been taught by the great masters by way of their models. Only Saint-Évremond picked up on this fault: he said, namely, that our plays do not make enough of an impression, that what ought to awaken compassion arouses tenderness at best, that superficial emotion takes the place of deep agitation and amazement that of terror; in short, that our sentiments did not go deep enough.[5] It cannot be denied: Saint-Évremond laid his finger directly on the secret wound of French theater. One may say as much as one likes that Saint-Évremond was the author of the awful comedy *Sir Politick Wouldbe*, and another, equally awful one, called *The Operas*; that his little social verses are the shallowest and commonest that we have of the genre; that he was nothing but a cheap phrase-turner: but a person can lack all spark of genius and still possess much wit and taste.[6] Unquestionably his taste was very refined, as he discovered the exact reason why most of our plays are so dull and cold. We have always lacked a certain degree of warmth; we had everything else."[7]

That is: we had everything, only not what we should have had; our tragedies were excellent, except that they were not tragedies. And why were they not?

"This coldness," he continues, "this monotonous dullness arose in part from the petty spirit of gallantry that prevailed among our courtiers and ladies, which transformed tragedy into a series of besotted conversations in the style of *Cyrus* and *Clélie*.[8]

Those plays that stood out somewhat consisted of long political speeches of the sort that ruined *Sertorius* and made *Othon* so cold and *Suréna* and *Attila* so bad.[9] But there was also another factor that kept back the high pathos from our scenes and prevented the action from becoming truly tragic, and this was the small, badly constructed theater with its paltry decorations.[10] – What could be done on a couple dozen boards, packed with spectators to boot? What pomp and apparatus could be used there to captivate, enthrall, and deceive the spectator's eye? What great tragic action could be performed there? What freedom could the poet's imagination have there? The plays were supposed to consist of lengthy declamations, and as a result they became more conversations than plays. Every actor wanted to shine in a long monologue, and a play that had none was rejected. – All theatrical action disappeared from the form, along with all of the great expressions of passion, all the powerful pictures of human misery, and all of the terrifying traits that penetrated to the innermost soul; instead of being torn apart, the heart was scarcely touched."[11]

The first reason is quite correct. Gallantry and politics always leave us cold, and no writer in the world has ever succeeded in arousing compassion and fear through them. The former leave us hearing nothing but the fool or the schoolmaster, and the latter require us to hear nothing but human beings.

But the second reason? – Could it be possible that the lack of a spacious theater and good decorations had such influence on the poet's genius? Is it true that every tragic action requires pomp and stage apparatus? Or should the poet instead not compose his play such that it produces its full effect even without these things?

According to Aristotle, he should certainly do this. "Fear and compassion," the philosopher says, "can be aroused through spectacle, but they can also originate from the combination of events themselves; this latter is preferred and is the choice of the better poet. For the plot must be so constructed that, even unseen, anyone who simply listens to its course of events will be moved to compassion and fear at what takes place, just like the story of Oedipus, which one need only hear to be brought to compassion and fear. Achieving this aim by means of spectacle requires less art and is the business of those who undertake the production of the play."[12]

Anyone who has seen the plays of Shakespeare will have had the peculiar experience of witnessing how superfluous theatrical decorations are in general. Which plays could possibly need the assistance of scenery and the whole art of decoration more than these, with their constant interruption and change of place? Yet there was a time when the stages on which they were played consisted of nothing but a curtain of poor rough material which, when raised, revealed bare walls, at most hung with mats or tapestries; there was nothing there but imagination to come to the aid of the spectator's understanding and the actor's performance. Nevertheless, it is said that in those days Shakespeare's plays were more intelligible without any scenery than they later were with it.*[13]

---

* (Cibber's *Lives of the Poets of Great Britain and Ireland* Vol. II, p. 78–79). – Some have insinuated, that fine scenes proved the ruin of acting. – In the reign of Charles I. there was nothing more than a curtain of very coarse stuff, upon the drawing up of which, the stage appeared either with bare walls on the

If, then, the poet need not worry at all about the decorations; if the decorations, even where they appear necessary, can be omitted without any particular disadvantage to his play, why should it be the fault of the narrow, badly constructed theaters that the French poets did not give us plays that are more moving? It is not: the fault is their own.

And experience proves this. For now, the French have a more beautiful and more spacious stage; they no longer tolerate any spectators on it; the wings are empty; the decorator has free rein and can paint and build anything the poet demands[14] – but then where are they, those warmer plays that they have written since? Does M. de Voltaire flatter himself that his *Sémiramis* is such a play? It has pomp and apparatus enough, and a ghost to boot, and yet I can think of no colder play than his *Sémiramis*.[15]

Essay 81

9 February 1768[1]

Do I want to say by this that no Frenchman is capable of writing a truly moving tragic work?[2] That the volatile spirit of that nation is not equal to the task? – I would be ashamed of myself if such a thought even occurred to me. Germany has not yet made itself foolish with its own Bouhours, and I, for my part, would not have the least inclination to play that part.[3] For I am quite convinced that no nation in the world possesses exclusive rights to any intellectual gift over other nations. Of course, we say: the thoughtful Englishman, the witty Frenchman. But who made this distinction? Certainly not nature, which distributes everything equally amongst all. There are just as many witty Englishmen as there are witty Frenchmen, and just as many thoughtful Frenchmen as thoughtful Englishmen, while the bulk of the populace is neither.

So what is my point? I merely want to say that the French do not yet have what they certainly could have: true tragedy. And why do they not yet have it? – If M. de Voltaire had wanted to hit upon the reason, he would have had to know himself better.

I believe they do not have it yet because they think they have already had it for a long time. And they are certainly strengthened in this belief by something they have preeminently above all other nations, but which is no gift of nature: namely, their vanity.

As it goes with nations, so it goes with individual people. – Gottsched (it will be readily understood why I alight upon him at this point) was held to be a poet in his youth, because in those days people did not yet know the difference between a versifier and a poet. Philosophy and criticism gradually brought this difference to light, and if Gottsched had been willing to keep pace with the century, if he had developed

---

sides, coarsly [sic] matted, or covered with tapestry; so that for the place originally represented, and all the successive changes, in which the poets of those times freely indulged themselves, there was nothing to help the spectator's understanding, or to assist the actor's performance, but bare imagination. – The spirit and judgment of the actors supplied all deficiencies, and made as some would insinuate, plays more intelligible without scenes, than they afterwards were with them.

and refined his insights and taste along with the insights and the taste of his era, then perhaps he might have really grown from versifier to poet. But because he had heard himself called the greatest poet so often, because his vanity had convinced him he was one, this did not happen. He could not possibly acquire what he believed he already possessed, and the older he got, the more stubborn and shameless he was in asserting his claim to this imaginary prize.

It seems to me that the same thing happened to the French. No sooner had Corneille rescued their theater a little from its state of barbarity than they believed it close to perfection. It seemed to them that Racine gave it the finishing touch, and after that it was no longer a question (which, indeed, it had never been) of whether a tragic poet could be more lofty, more moving than Corneille and Racine. Rather, it was accepted that this was impossible, and all the poets who followed would dedicate themselves only to emulating one or the other as much as possible. For a hundred years they have deluded themselves and to some degree their neighbors; now let someone come and tell them this, and see what they say!

Of the two, however, it is Corneille who has caused the most harm and had the most ruinous influence on their tragic poets. For Racine only misled through his examples; Corneille, on the other hand, through both his examples and his teachings.

These latter, in particular, accepted as oracles by the whole nation (excepting one or two pedants, a Hédelin, a Dacier, who often did not know themselves what they wanted) and followed by all subsequent poets, have – I will venture to prove this bit by bit – been able to produce nothing other than the most callow, watered down, untragical stuff.[4]

Aristotle's rules are all calculated to produce the highest effects of tragedy. But what does Corneille do with them? First, he presents them falsely and cockeyed; and then, because he still finds them far too stringent, he seeks in one after the other, "quelque moderation, quelque favorable interpretation"; he weakens and mutilates, misinterprets and thwarts each one – and why?[5] "Pour n'être pas obligés de condamner beaucoup de poemes que nous avons vû réussir sur nos théâtres": so as not to have to condemn many plays that found success on our stages. A fine reason!

I will quickly touch on the main points. I have already noted some of them, but for the sake of coherence I must repeat them again here.

1   Aristotle says: tragedy should arouse compassion and fear. – Corneille says: oh yes, but as the case may be; it is not always really necessary to have both simultaneously, we are also satisfied with one at a time, now compassion without fear, and now fear without compassion. For otherwise where would I be? – I, the great Corneille, and my Rodrigue and my Chimène?[6] These good children arouse compassion, very great compassion indeed, but hardly any fear. And on the other hand: where would I be with my Cleopatra, my Prusias, my Phocas?[7] Who can have compassion for these wretches? But they do arouse fear. – This is what Corneille thought, and the French followed his thought.

2   Aristotle says: tragedy should arouse compassion and fear; both, understood, through one and the same person. – Corneille says: if that works, very good. But it is not absolutely necessary, and one can just as well employ different persons

to produce these two feelings, as I have done in my *Rodogune*.[8] – This is what Corneille did, and the French imitate him.

3   Aristotle says: by means of the compassion and fear awakened in tragedy, our compassion and fear and all that belongs to them should be purified. – Corneille knows absolutely nothing of this and imagines that Aristotle wanted to say that tragedy awakens our compassion to excite our fear, in order to purify, through fear, those passions in us that caused the misfortune of the character with whom we commiserate.[9] I will not discuss the value of this intention; suffice it to say that this is not Aristotelian, and that because Corneille gave his tragedies a completely different purpose, they also necessarily had to become completely different works from those that Aristotle used to abstract his purpose; they had to become tragedies that were not true tragedies. And this is what became not just of his tragedies but of all French tragedies, because all of their authors had Corneille's purpose instead of Aristotle's firmly in mind. I have already said that Dacier wanted to combine these two purposes, but also that through this combining, the first [Aristotle's purpose] is weakened and keeps tragedy from having its greatest effect.[10] In addition, as I have shown, Dacier had only a very incomplete understanding of the first of these purposes, and thus it was no wonder he imagined that French tragedies of his time had fulfilled the former purpose rather than the latter. "Our tragedy," he says, "is rather successful in the former of these, in exciting and purifying compassion and fear. But it only very rarely succeeds in the latter, which is nevertheless the more important, and purifies the other passions but little – or, because it usually contains nothing but love intrigues, if it does purify a passion, it is only that of love, from which it becomes clear that it has a very minor benefit."*[11] But just the opposite! There are rather more French tragedies that achieve the second purpose than the first. I know of several French plays that quite correctly shine light on the unfortunate consequences of some passion, from which we can draw many good lessons with regard to that passion. But I know of no play that arouses my compassion to the degree to which tragedy ought to arouse it and to which I know for certain tragedy can arouse it from my experience of many Greek and English plays. Various French tragedies are very refined, very instructive works that I consider worthy of all sorts of praise: it's just that they are not tragedies. Their authors cannot have been anything but intelligent men; some of them are not undeserving of higher rank among poets: it's just that they are not tragic poets. Their Corneille and Racine, their Crébillon and Voltaire have little or nothing of that which makes Sophocles a Sophocles, Euripides a Euripides, and Shakespeare a Shakespeare.[12] The latter are seldom at variance with Aristotle's essential demands; the former, however, much more often. And now to continue –

---

* (*La Poëtique d'Aristote* Ch. VI, Rem. 8) "Nôtre Tragedie peut réussir assez dans la premiere partie, c'est-à-dire, qu'elle peut exciter & purger la terreur & la compassion. Mais elle parvient rarement à la derniere, qui est pourtant la plus utile, elle purge peu les autres passions, ou comme elle roule ordinairement sur des intrigues d'amour, si elle en purgeoit quelqu'une, ce seroit celle-là seule, & par là il est aisé de voir qu'elle ne fait que peu de fruit."

Essay 82

12 February 1768[1]

4   Aristotle says: one must not allow a completely good man without any faults to meet with misfortune in tragedy, for such a thing would be abominable.[2] – "Quite right," says Corneille, "such an outcome awakens more indignation and hatred against him who causes the suffering than compassion for the one whom it befalls. This first feeling, which should not be the essential effect of tragedy, would, if not handled very subtly, stifle that which actually ought to be evoked. The spectator would leave dissatisfied, because far too much anger would be mixed in with his compassion – a compassion he would have appreciated had it been the only thing he took away."[3] But – Corneille follows up, for he must always follow with a but – but if this reason disappears, if the poet contrives things so that the virtuous person who suffers awakens more compassion for himself than indignation against the one who made him suffer: what then? – "Oh, well then," Corneille says, "I maintain that no objection whatsoever should be made against portraying even the most virtuous of men in misfortune."*[4] – I do not understand how anyone can babble such nonsense against the philosopher and give the appearance of understanding him while having him say things he never thought. Aristotle says that the completely unmerited misfortune of a virtuous man is no subject for a tragedy, because it is abominable. Corneille changes this "because," this reason, into an "insofar," a mere condition under which it ceases to be tragic. Aristotle says: it is altogether abominable, and for that very reason untragical. But Corneille says: it is untragical insofar as it is abominable. Aristotle finds the abomination in the type of misfortune itself; Corneille, on the other hand, ascribes it to the displeasure it provokes against its originator. He does not see, or does not want to see, that this abomination is something quite different from displeasure, that even when the latter disappears completely, the former can still be present in full measure. Enough that many of his plays, which he purports to have written by hardly violating Aristotle's rules, only appear to be justified by this *quid pro quo* to begin with, but he is also presumptuous enough to imagine that if Aristotle had known these plays, he would have conformed his doctrines to them more closely and abstracted from them various methods by which the misfortune of a virtuous man could become a tragic subject. "En voici," he says, "deux ou trois manières, que peut-être Aristote n'a su prévoir, parcequ'on n'en voyait pas d'exemples sur les théâtres de son temps."[5] And from whom come these examples? From whom else, other than he himself? And what are these two or three methods? We will see very quickly. – "The first," he says, "is when a very virtuous person is persecuted by a very vicious person and escapes the danger in such a way that the vicious person himself is ensnared in it, as happens in *Rodogune* and in *Héraclius*, where it would have been completely

---

* "J'estime qu'il ne faut point faire de difficulté d'exposer sur la scène des hommes très vertueux."

unbearable had Antiochus and Rodogune perished in the first play, and Héraclius, Pulchérie, and Martian in the second, but Cleopatra and Phocas had triumphed.[6] The misfortune of the first of these awakens a compassion which is not stifled by the revulsion we feel toward their persecutors, because we continually hope that some fortunate circumstance will transpire to save them from defeat."[7] Corneille may try all he wants to make us believe that Aristotle did not know this method! He knew it so well that, where he did not reject it out of hand, he at least expressly declared it more suited to comedy than to tragedy. How is it possible that Corneille had forgotten this? But this is what happens to everyone who begins by making their cause the cause of truth. Moreover, for all intents and purposes, this method does not apply at all to the case in point. In this case, the virtuous person does not become unhappy but is rather on the path to misfortune, which can readily arouse compassionate concern for him without being abominable. – Now for the second method! "It can also happen," Corneille says, "that a very virtuous man is persecuted and perishes at the orders of another who is not vicious enough to warrant much displeasure from us, in that he shows more weakness than wickedness in his persecution of the virtuous man. When Felix lets his son-in-law Polyeucte perish, it is not due to an angry zeal against Christians, which would make him detestable to us, but merely to a servile timidity that keeps Felix from saving him in the presence of Severus, whose hatred and revenge he fears.[8] We feel a certain aversion for him and disapprove of his conduct, but this aversion does not outweigh the compassion we feel for Polyeucte, and it also does not prevent his miraculous conversion from fully reconciling him again with the audience at the end of the play."[9] I think there have probably been tragic bunglers at all times, even in Athens. Why, then, should Aristotle not have had a similarly constructed play, so that he might be just as enlightened as Corneille? What a farce! Timid, wavering, indecisive characters like Felix are just one more mistake in such plays and make them even more cold and repulsive on the one hand without making them any less abominable on the other. For, as I have said above, abomination rests not in the displeasure or aversion that they awaken but rather in the misfortune itself that befalls those who are innocent; that it strikes the innocent at random, regardless of whether their persecutors are evil or weak or attack them with or without premeditation. The thought that there could be people who meet with misfortune through no fault of their own is in and of itself abominable. The pagans tried to keep this abominable thought as far from them as possible; and we want to maintain it? We want to enjoy plays that confirm it? We, whom religion and reason should have convinced that it is as incorrect as it is blasphemous? – The same would certainly apply to the third method, if Corneille himself had not forgotten to specify what it was.

5   Corneille also contributes his own refinements of what Aristotle says about the unsuitability of making a completely vicious person, whose misfortune can awaken neither compassion nor fear, into a tragic hero.[10] He admits that, to be sure, such a man cannot awaken compassion, but he can certainly awaken fear. For even if none of the spectators believe themselves capable of his vices, and

consequently have no need to fear his same misfortune in its entirety, nonetheless each could harbor some imperfection similar to those vices and learn to be on guard against them through fear of its proportionate, but no less unfortunate, consequences. But this is based on the false conception Corneille had of fear and of the purification of the emotions to be awakened in tragedy, and it contradicts itself. For I have already shown that the arousal of compassion is inseparable from the arousal of fear, and if it were possible for the villain to arouse our fear, he would also necessarily have to arouse our compassion.[11] Since he cannot do the latter, as Corneille himself admits, he also cannot do the former, and so this villain cannot help to achieve the purpose of tragedy. Aristotle even considers him less suited to this purpose than the completely virtuous man, saying explicitly that if one cannot have a hero of the middle type, one ought rather to choose a better man than a worse one. The reason is clear: a person can be very, very good and yet still have more than one weakness, still make more than one mistake by which he is plunged into an unforeseen misfortune that fills us with compassion and melancholy, without being in the least abominable, because it is the natural consequence of his error. – What Dubos[†] says of the use of vicious persons in tragedy is not what Corneille means.[12] Dubos only wishes to allow them in secondary roles, merely as tools to make the main characters less culpable; merely as foils. Corneille, however, wants to let them form the main interest, as in *Rodogune*, and this is precisely what is at odds with the purpose of tragedy. Dubos also very correctly observes that the misfortune of these secondary villains makes no impression on us. In *Britannicus* we hardly notice the death of Narcissus, he says.[13] But for that very reason the poet should avoid these characters as much as possible. If their misfortune does not directly serve the purpose of tragedy, if they are merely the means through which the poet could better achieve its purpose through other characters, then it goes without saying that the play would be even better if it produced the same effect without them. The simpler a machine is, the fewer springs and wheels and weights it has, the more perfect it is.

Essay 83

16 February 1768[1]

6   And finally: the misinterpretation of the first and most essential quality Aristotle requires regarding the moral behavior of tragic characters.[2] Their morals should be good. – "Good?" Corneille asks, "If good here is supposed to mean virtuous, then things look bad for the majority of both old and new tragedies, which abound in wicked and vicious characters, or at least characters tainted with some weakness that does not sit well with virtue."[3] He is particularly anxious about his Cleopatra in *Rodogune*. Corneille absolutely does not want to consider Aristotle's

---

† *Réflexions Critiques* Tome I, Sect. XV.

proscribed goodness as moral goodness; it must be a different type of goodness, equally compatible with the morally bad and the morally good. Nevertheless, Aristotle unequivocally does mean moral goodness, only he distinguishes between virtuous persons and persons who demonstrate virtuous moral behavior under certain circumstances. In short, Corneille attaches a completely false idea to moral behavior, and he has not understood at all what *proairesis* is, through which alone, according to our philosopher, free actions become good or bad behavior.[4] I cannot plunge into an extensive proof now; such a proof can only be made with sufficient clarity by means of the context, by means of the syllogistic sequence of all the ideas of the Greek critic. I will thus save it for another occasion, since now it is only necessary to show what an unfortunate detour Corneille took when he wandered down the wrong path. It led to the following conclusion: that Aristotle considered moral good to be found in the brilliant and elevated character of an inclination, whether virtuous or criminal, that is either inherent in or can be attributed to the person one portrays: "le caractère brillant et élevé d'une habitude vertueuse ou criminelle, selon qu'elle est propre et convenable à la personne qu'on introduit."[5] He says, "Cleopatra, in *Rodogune*, is wicked in the extreme; she shies away from no act of murder if it can help her maintain possession of the throne that she values most in the world; her lust for power really is that fierce. But all her crimes are aligned with a certain greatness of soul that has something so noble that, even as we condemn her actions, we still have to admire the source from which they spring. I dare say the same thing about *The Liar*.[6] Lying is unquestionably an immoral habit, but Dorante is so quick-witted and animated when he delivers his lies that this imperfection suits him quite well, and the spectators are bound to acknowledge that the talent of lying like this is a vice no fool is capable of."[7] – Truly, Corneille could not have had a more pernicious idea! Follow it to its execution, and there's the end to all truth, all illusion, and all moral benefit of tragedy! For virtue, which is always modest and simple, will be rendered vain and romantic through this brilliance, while vice will be coated with a varnish that dazzles us from all sides, regardless of the standpoint from which we view it. What foolishness, to hide the inner ugliness of a vice and hope that its dire consequences alone will terrify! Consequences are unpredictable, and experience teaches that they can just as easily be positive as negative. This brings us back to the purification of the emotions as Corneille understood them. The way I imagine it, the way Aristotle taught it, has absolutely nothing to do with this deceptive brilliance. The false allure that is here applied to vice makes me discern perfections where there are none; it makes me feel compassion where I should not. – Dacier, it is true, has already contradicted this explanation, but for even less cogent reasons, and the explanation he adopted in its place with Père le Bossu is nearly just as detrimental, at the very least to the poetical perfection of the play.[8] He says, namely, that "morals should be good" means nothing more than that they should be well expressed, "qu'elles soient bien marquées."[9] This is certainly a rule that, correctly understood and in its proper place, deserves the dramatic poet's full attention. If only the French examples did not reveal that they took "well expressed" to mean *strongly expressed*. They overloaded the expression, they put pressure on pressure, until characterized persons became personified characters and vicious or virtuous human beings became bare skeletons of vices and virtues. –

I will break off from this material here. Whoever is equal to the task can make the application to *Richard* himself.[10]

I probably do not need to say anything about *Duke Michael*, which followed *Richard*.[11] What theater has not produced it, and who has not seen or read it? Krüger, however, can hardly take credit for it; it was taken wholly from a story in the *Bremen Contributions*.[12] The many good satirical strokes it contains belong to that writer, as well as the whole course of the plot. Nothing but the dramatic form belongs to Krüger. Yet with Krüger's passing, our stage lost much indeed.[13] He had talent for low comedy, as his *Candidates* proved.[14] But where he tries to be moving and noble, he is chilly and affected. Herr Löwen collected his works, from which, however, his *Clergymen in the Country* is missing.[15] That play was Krüger's first attempt at drama, while he was still studying in Berlin at the Graue Kloster.[16]

On the forty-ninth evening (Thursday, July 23rd), M. de Voltaire's comedy *The Woman Who Is Right* was performed, and L'Affichard's *Is he a member of the family?** was repeated to conclude the evening.[17]

The Woman Who Is Right is one of the plays M. de Voltaire wrote for his private theater.[18] It was certainly good enough for that. It played in Carouge in 1758, but as far as I know, not yet in Paris.[19] It isn't as if there haven't been worse plays performed there since; the Marins and Le Brets have taken care of that.[20] It is rather because – actually, I have no idea. For I, at least, would much prefer to see a great man in his pajamas and nightcap than a bungler in his Sunday best.

The play does not have much in the way of characters or interest, but it has several situations that are comical enough.[21] The comedy, it must be said, is of the most common sort, based on nothing but incognito, misrecognitions, and misunderstandings. But the laughers are not bothered, our German laughers least of all, so long as the strangeness of the customs and the wretched translation do not make the *mot pour rire* incomprehensible.[22]

On the fiftieth evening (Friday, the 24th of July), Gresset's *Sidney* was repeated. The evening ended with *The Seeing Blindman*.[23]

This brief play is by Le Grand, and also not by him. He borrowed the title and intrigue and everything else from an old play by de Brosse.[24] An officer, getting on in years, wants to marry a young widow he is in love with when he receives orders to report to the army. He takes leave of his betrothed with mutual assurances of the most heartfelt tenderness. But no sooner is he gone than the widow accepts the attentions of the son of this officer. His daughter likewise takes advantage of her father's absence and receives into her house a young man whom she loves. This double intrigue is

---

* See the 17th evening [Essay 17].

reported to the father who, in order to convince himself of it, has someone write to them that he has lost his sight. The ruse succeeds; he returns to Paris and, with the help of a servant who knows of the deception, he sees everything that is happening in his house. It is easy to guess what happens: since the officer can no longer have any doubts of the widow's fickleness, he allows his son to marry her, and he gives his daughter the same permission to marry her lover. The scenes between the widow and the officer's son in the older man's presence contain a lot of comedy: the widow asserts that she is deeply affected by his misfortune but that she loves him no less for it, and at the same time she winks at his son, her lover, and demonstrates her tenderness to him through other gestures. That is the plot of the old play by de Brosse and also the plot of the new play by Le Grand, except that in the latter the intrigue with the daughter has been left off in order to bring the former's five acts more easily into one. The father has become an uncle, and there are some other similar small changes besides. In the end, it doesn't matter where it originated; all that matters is that it pleases greatly. The translation is in verse and is perhaps one of the best we have; at any rate, it is very fluid and has many funny lines.[25]

Essay 84

19 February 1768[1]

On the fifty-first evening (Monday, the 27th of July), M. Diderot's *The Father of the Family* was performed.[2]

As this excellent play (which the French find only so-so – it only managed with great effort to appear once or twice in the Parisian theaters) will, to all appearances, survive long, very long – and why not forever? – in our theater, as it cannot be performed here enough; I hope to have sufficient space and opportunity to dig out everything I have noted from time to time, not only about the play itself, but also about the author's entire dramatic system.[3]

I will reach quite far back. – The conversations appended to *The Natural Son*, which he published in 1757, were not the first place where Diderot expressed his dissatisfaction with his nation's theater.[4] Several years earlier, he observed that he did not share the grand conception of French theater with which his countrymen deceived themselves and with which by extension Europe allowed itself to be deceived. But he did this in a book in which, it must be said, people did not seek such things, in a book so dominated by a satiric tone that even what was sound and reasonable in it appeared to most readers to be nothing but farce and mockery. Doubtless Diderot had his reasons for preferring to publish his real opinions initially in such a book; a clever man often first says with a laugh what he wants to repeat later in earnest.

This book is called *Les bijoux indiscrets*, and now Diderot wishes he had never written it.[5] He is quite right in wishing this, too; but he did write it, and he must have written it if he does not want to be a plagiarist.[6] It is also certain that this book could only have been written by the sort of young man who would later be ashamed of having written it.

It is probably for the best if only the fewest among my readers know this book. I will be very careful not to make it better known to them than serves my business here. −

An emperor − I know not where, or which − made certain jewels blab so much ugly drivel by means of a certain magic ring, that his favorite did not wish to hear any more of it.[7] She would have liked to disown the whole of her sex; at the very least, she resolved to limit her company only to that of the Sultan himself and a couple of clever men. These were Selim and Ricaric: Selim, a courtier, and Ricaric, a member of the imperial academy, a man who had studied the classics and admired them greatly without being a pedant.[8] At one point the favorite entertains herself with these two, and the conversation lights on the miserable tone of academic speeches, a topic that irritates no one more than the Sultan because it annoys him to always hear himself praised at the expense of his father and forefathers and because he foresees that the academy will one day likewise sacrifice his fame to the fame of his successors. Selim, as a courtier, agrees with everything the Sultan says, and thus the conversation about theater begins, which I share with my readers in full.[9]

"I believe, my lord, you are mistaken," said Ricaric to Selim. "The academy is still the sanctuary of good taste, and its finest days have boasted neither philosophers nor poets whom we cannot match with those from our time. Our theater was, and still is, considered the best theater in all of Africa. What a work is the *Tamerlane* of Tuxigraphe![10] It combines Eurisope's pathos with Azophe's sublimity.[11] It is pure antiquity!"

"I saw the first performance of *Tamerlane*," said the favorite, "and similarly found the play's threads drawn very properly, its dialogue very elegant, and the propriety very well observed."

"What a difference," interrupted Ricaric, "between an author like Tuxigraphe, nourished through reading the ancients, and the majority of our moderns!"

"But these moderns," said Selim, "whom you attack so vigorously here, are not nearly as despicable as you pretend. Or what? Do you find no genius, no invention, no passion, no character, no details, no tirades there? What do I care about rules if I am given to feel pleasure? Indeed, it is not the observations of the wise Almudir and the learned Abdaldok, nor the poetics of the erudite Facardin, none of which I have read, which make me admire the plays of Aboulcazem, Muhardar, Albaboukre, and so many other Saracens! Is there any rule other than the imitation of nature? And have we not the same eyes that they used to study her?"

"Nature," answered Ricaric, "shows us a different form every moment. They are all true, but they are not all equally beautiful. We must learn how to choose from these works, which you seem not to esteem very highly. They are the collected experiences of their authors and their predecessors. No matter how intelligent we may be, we still only acquire our insights one after the other, and a single person flatters himself to think he alone could observe, in the short space of his life, everything that had been discovered in the centuries that preceded him. Otherwise it could be said that a science owed its origin, its progress, and its perfection to one single mind, which, of course, counters all experience."

"My good sir," Selim answered him, "nothing follows from that except that the moderns, who can benefit from all of the treasures that have been collected to date, must be richer than the ancients; or if you do not like that comparison – that having climbed on the shoulders of these giants, they must be able to see much further than the giants themselves. What, indeed, is their physics, their astronomy, their navigation, their mechanics, their mathematics in comparison to ours? Why then should we not be equally superior to them in eloquence and poetry?"

"Selim," the Sultan's favorite responded, "the difference is great, and Ricaric can explain the reasons for it another time. He may tell you why our tragedies are worse than those of the ancients, but I can easily prove to you myself that they are so. I will not," she continued, "accuse you of not having read the ancients. You have pursued too much refined knowledge for the theater of the ancients to be unknown to you. Now put aside certain ideas that relate to their customs, their morals, and their religion, and that only offend you because circumstances have changed; and now tell me whether their subjects are not still noble, well-chosen, and interesting? Does the action not develop, as it were, on its own? Does not the simple dialogue come very near to nature? Are the resolutions the least bit forced? Is the interest divided, the action overloaded with episodes? Transport yourself in thought to the island of Alindala, examine everything that happened there, listen to everything said there from the moment the young Ibrahim and the devious Forfanti landed on it, approach the cave of the unhappy Polipsile, do not lose a single word of his complaints, and tell me if the slightest thing occurs that could disturb your illusion?[12] Name for me one single modern play that could withstand the same test and can lay claim to the same degree of perfection, and you will have won."

"By Brahma!" the Sultan cried out, yawning, "Madame has made us an excellent academic lecture."

"I do not understand the rules," the favorite continued, "and even less the scholarly words in which they have been couched. But I know that only the true can please and move us. I also know that the perfection of a play consists of such an exact imitation of an action that a spectator, continually deceived, believes he is present at the action itself. Is there anything even the least bit similar to this in the tragedies you praise so highly?"

Essay 85

23 February 1768[1]

"Will you praise their course of events?[2] Those are generally so busy and complicated that it would be a miracle if so many things really happened in such a short time. The ruin or preservation of a kingdom, the marriage of a princess, the fall of a prince, all this happens as quickly as a turn of the hand. Is a conspiracy involved? It is conceived in the first act, pulled together in the second, all the measures are taken, all obstacles removed, and the conspirators are ready for action in the third; and in the next act there will be a revolt, an encounter, perhaps even a pitched battle. And you will call all this well-conducted, interesting, fiery, realistic? I can forgive you, least of all, such an opinion, you who know how much it often costs to carry off the most miserable intrigue and how much time is absorbed by preambles, discussions, and consultations in even the smallest political affair."

"It is true, Madame," Selim answered, "our plays are a little exaggerated, but that is a necessary evil; we would be left cold without the help of the episodes."

"So in a nutshell: in order to lend fire and spirit to the imitation of an action, one must represent the action neither as it is, nor as it should be. Can anything more ridiculous be imagined? Hardly, unless it were to have the violin play a lively tune or a jaunty sonata just when the spectators should feel concern for the prince who is on the point of losing his beloved, his throne, and his life."

"Madame," said Mongogul, "you are perfectly right; they ought rather to play sad arias, and I will go order some played for you right now." At this he got up and left, and Selim, Ricaric, and the favorite continued the conversation among themselves.

"At the very least, Madame," replied Selim, "you will not deny that if the episodes draw us out of the illusion, the dialogue pulls us back in again. I do not know of anyone who understands this better than our tragic writers."

"Then no one understands it at all," Mirzoza answered. "The artificial language, the wit, and the playfulness that predominate in them are thousands and thousands of miles away from nature. The author tries to conceal himself in vain; he never escapes my sight, and I see him constantly behind his characters. Cinna, Sertorius, Maximus, and Aemilia serve constantly as Corneille's mouthpieces.[3] In the plays of our ancient Saracen authors, people do not speak to each other that way. M. Ricaric can translate some passages from them for you if you like, and you will hear the pure nature expressed by their words. I would love to say to the moderns: 'My good sirs, instead of giving your characters wit for all occasions, try rather to put them into circumstances that inspire some wit in them.'"

"To judge by what Madame has said about the conduct and dialogue of our dramatic plays, it does not seem," Selim said, "that she will grant much mercy to the resolutions."

"No, certainly not," the favorite rejoined, "there are a hundred bad ones for every good one. One is not sufficiently led up to, another comes about miraculously. If the author does not know what he should do with a character that he has dragged from scene to scene for five long acts, he quickly finishes him off with a good stab of the dagger, everyone starts to cry, and I, I laugh like a madwoman. And then, has anyone ever spoken the way we declaim? Do princes and kings tend to walk differently than any other man who is able to walk well? Have they ever gesticulated like people who are crazy or possessed? And when princesses speak, do they speak in such a shrill tone? People universally assume that we have brought tragedy to a high degree of perfection, and I, for my part, think there is little doubt that among all the genres of literature to which the Africans have applied themselves in recent centuries, this is the one that has remained the most imperfect."

The favorite was at just this point in her diatribe against our theatrical works when Mongogul returned. "Madame," he said, "you will do me a service by continuing. You see, I do understand how to cut short a poetical subject if I find it too long."

"Let us assume for a moment," the favorite continued, "someone were to come fresh from Angote who has never in his life heard anything about the theater but who lacks neither understanding nor worldliness, who has some knowledge of how things go at court, who is not completely unacquainted with the intrigues of the courtiers, the jealousy of the ministers, and the gossip of women, and to whom I said in confidence: 'My friend, there are terrible undertakings in the seraglio. The prince, who is displeased with his son because he suspects him of being in love with Manimonbanda, is a man I consider capable of wreaking the most gruesome revenge on both of them. Based on everything we know, this situation will have very dismal consequences. If you wish, I will arrange it so that you can be witness to all that occurs.' He accepts my offer, and I lead him into a box screened by latticework, from which he sees the theater, which he takes to be the Sultan's palace. Do you really think that, notwithstanding all the seriousness I try to maintain, this stranger's deception could last a moment? Or rather, must you not admit that, on seeing the actors' stiff walking, their marvelous clothing, their extravagant gestures, the odd emphasis of their rhymed and measured speech, and a thousand other striking inconsistencies, he would laugh in my face from the very first scene and straightaway say that either I was trying to put one over on him or the prince and his whole court must have lost their minds?"

"I confess," said Selim, "that this assumed case embarrasses me; but may I suggest that we go to the theater certain that we will be present at the imitation of an action and not at the action itself."

"Should, then, this conviction keep the action from being represented in the most natural way possible?" rejoined Mirzoza. –

At this point the conversation moves gradually to other things that do not concern us. Let's turn again to see what we have read. Nothing but pure Diderot! Yet all these truths fell on deaf ears at the time. They did not arouse any feeling among the French public until they were repeated with full didactic assiduity and accompanied by examples in which the author took care to remove some of the criticized shortcomings and better clarified the path of nature and illusion. Now envy awakened criticism. Now it was clear why Diderot did not find his nation's theater at the peak of perfection, where we should absolutely believe it to be, and why he found so many faults in its lauded masterpieces: only and solely to make room for his own plays. He had to decry the method of his predecessors because he perceived that he would remain infinitely below them if he followed the same method. He had to be a miserable charlatan who condemned all foreign elixirs so that no one bought any but his own. And thus did the Palissots attack his plays.[4]

To be sure, he had also given them several openings in his play *The Natural Son*.[5] This first attempt is far from equal to *The Father of the Family*.[6] Overly uniform characters that are also too romantic and sentimental, stiff and flamboyant dialogue, a pedantic jingling of newfangled philosophical sentences: all of this made easy sport for the critics. In particular, the solemn Theresa (or Constance, as she was called in the original), who even goes courting philosophically, who speaks so wisely of the virtuous children she intends to have with a man who does not like her, drew laughter down upon her.[7] One cannot deny, moreover, that the form Diderot gave to the appended "Conversations" and the tone he adopted there were a bit vain and pompous; that several comments presented there as completely new discoveries were, in fact, not new and not the author's own; and that other comments did not actually possess the soundness they seemed to have in their dazzling delivery.[8]

Essay 86

26 February 1768[1]

For example, Diderot claimed* that in human nature there are at most only a dozen truly comic, boldly delineated characters, and that the small differences in men's characters cannot be handled as successfully as the pure, unmixed characters.[2] He thus suggested bringing social groups rather than characters to the stage and wanted to make the treatment of the former the particular business of serious comedy.[3] "Until now," he says, "character has been the main object of comedy, and social standing has been accidental; but social standing really should be the main focus, and character accidental. The whole plot used to arise out of character; in general, the circumstances under which character best expressed itself were sought, and these circumstances were linked together. Going forward, a man's social standing, with its duties, its advantages, and its inconveniences, must serve as the foundation for the work. To me, this source appears far more fruitful, more extensive, and more beneficial than the source of character. If the character were even a bit too exaggerated, the spectator could say to himself: that is not me. But he cannot possibly deny that the social standing portrayed is his own; he cannot possibly mistake his own duties. He must necessarily apply what he hears to himself."[4]

Palissot's objection† to this is not baseless.[5] He denies that nature has such a paucity of original characters that comic writers could have exhausted the supply. Molière still envisioned sufficient numbers of new characters and believed he had treated scarcely the smallest part of those that he could have treated. The passage in which he sketches out many of them in rapid succession is as extraordinary as it is instructive, insofar as it allows us to suppose that *The Misanthrope* would hardly have remained his *non plus ultra* of high comedy had he lived longer.‡,[6] Palissot himself is not unsuccessful in adding a few new characters from his own observation: the dumb patron, with his groveling clients; the man in the wrong place; the malicious man, whose elaborate attacks are thwarted by the naïveté of a trusting and upright man; the false philosopher;

---

* See the "Conversations" appended to *The Natural Son*.

† *Petites Lettres sur de grands Philosophes*, Lettre II.

‡ (*Impromptu de Versailles* Sc. 4). "Eh! mon pauvre Marquis, nous lui (à Molière) en fournirons toujours assez, et nous ne prenons guère le chemin de nous rendre sages pour tout ce qu'il fait et tout ce qu'il dit. [. . .] Crois-tu qu'il ait épuisé dans ses comédies tout le ridicule des hommes? et, sans sortir de la Cour, n'a-t-il pas encore vingt caractères de gens où il n'a point touché? N'a-t-il pas, par exemple, ceux qui se font les plus grandes amitiés du monde, et qui, le dos tourné, font galanterie de se déchirer l'un l'autre? N'a-t-il pas ces adulateurs à outrance, ces flatteurs insipides, qui n'assaisonnent d'aucun sel les louanges qu'ils donnent, et dont toutes les flatteries ont une douceur fade qui fait mal au cœur à ceux qui les écoutent? N'a-t-il pas ces lâches courtisans de la faveur, ces perfides adorateurs de la fortune, qui vous encensent dans la prospérité et vous accablent dans la disgrâce? N'a-t-il pas ceux qui sont toujours mécontents de la Cour, ces suivants inutiles, ces incommodes assidus, ces gens, dis-je, qui pour services ne peuvent compter que des importunités, et qui veulent que l'on les récompense d'avoir obsédé le Prince dix ans durant? N'a-t-il pas ceux qui caressent également tout le monde, qui promènent leurs civilités à droit et à gauche, et courent à tous ceux qu'ils voient avec les mêmes embrassades et les mêmes protestations d'amitié? [. . .] Va, va, Marquis, Molière aura toujours plus de sujets qu'il n'en voudra, et tout ce qu'il a touché jusqu'ici n'est rien que bagatelle au prix de ce qui reste."

the eccentric man, whom Destouches is said to have missed; the hypocrite of social virtues, because religious hypocrites are somewhat out of fashion.[7] – These are truly uncommon views that infinitely extend a far-reaching vision. There is harvest enough here for the few reapers who dare take it on!

And even if, Palissot says, there really are so few comic characters, and all these few really have been worked into plays, would social position remedy this dilemma? Let us choose one; for example, the position of the judge. Will I not have to give the judge some stamp of character? Will he not need to be sad or merry, serious or lighthearted, affable or blustery? Won't it be this character alone that lifts him out of the category of metaphysical abstraction and makes him into a real person? Consequently, won't the foundation of the plot and moral of the play still rest on character? Consequently, won't the social position once again be merely coincidental?

To be sure, Diderot could respond to this: Yes, the person that I invest with social position must also have his individual moral character; but I want to ensure that it does not clash, but rather harmonizes as well as possible, with the duties and relationships of his social standing. Thus, if this person is a judge, then it is not up to me whether I want to make him serious or lighthearted, affable or blustery; he must necessarily be serious and affable to the degree required by the business at hand.

I say Diderot could answer so, but at the same time he would have approached another precipice: namely, the precipice of the perfect character. Characters based on his social positions would never do anything other than what they must do according to duty and conscience; they would do everything according to the book. Do we expect that in comedy? Could such representations be sufficiently appealing? Will the benefits we might hope to gain from them be sufficiently great to justify the trouble of establishing a new genre and writing a poetics for it?[8]

It seems to me that in general Diderot has not sufficiently reconnoitered the precipice of the perfect character.[9] In his plays he steers pretty much directly toward it, and in his critical navigation charts there is absolutely no caution against it. On the contrary, there are things there that advise steering right to it. We need only remember what he says about the contrast between the characters in Terence's *The Brothers*.[§,10] "The two contrasting fathers in it are drawn with such similar intensity, that it would defy the most subtle critic to tell whether Micio or Demea is the main character.[11] If he makes his judgment before the last scene, he might easily be amazed that the character he has considered a reasonable man through a full five acts is nothing but a fool and that the one he considered a fool could very well be the reasonable man. One could almost say, at the beginning of the fifth act, that the difficulty of the contrast forced the author to abandon his purpose and reverse the whole interest of the play. But what is the result? It is that we no longer know whom we should be interested in. From the beginning, we have been for Micio and against Demea, and at the end we are for neither of them. We ought almost to demand a third father, who occupied the middle between these two characters and demonstrated both their faults."[12]

Not I! I reject him, this third father, whether he be in the same play or by himself. Where is there a father who does not believe he knows how a father should be? We all

§ In *On Dramatic Poetry*, appended to *The Father of the Family*.

believe ourselves to be on the right path; we only ask to be warned about the wrong paths on either side from time to time.

Diderot is correct: it is better if the characters are merely different rather than being contrasted. Contrasted characters are less natural and augment the romantic tone that is all too common in dramatic events. For every social group in real life where the contrast between characters manifests itself as prominently as the comic writer requires, there are always a thousand in which those characters are only different. Very correct! But isn't a character who always sticks exactly to that path prescribed to him by reason and virtue a much rarer phenomenon? For every twenty social groups in real life, we will sooner find ten with fathers who take completely contradictory paths in the upbringing of their children than one that could boast a true father. In addition, this true father is always the same, always singular, while the variations on him are infinite. Consequently, plays that feature the true father will not only be more unnatural individually but will also be collectively more uniform than those that introduce fathers with different principles. It also goes without saying that the characters who seem merely different in peaceful society begin to polarize as soon as a conflicting interest sets them in motion. Indeed, it is natural that they should then try to make themselves even more different from each other than they really are. The lively man becomes fire and flame against the man who strikes him as too tepid, and the tepid man becomes as cold as ice in order to provoke the other to as many rash acts as might serve his purposes.

Essays 87 and 88

4 March 1768[1]

Similarly, other observations made by Palissot are, if not completely correct, also not wholly incorrect.[2] He sees the ring he wants to spear with his lance clearly enough, but in the heat of the attack, the lance goes off course and he misses his mark.

Thus, he says of *The Natural Son* (among other things): "What a curious title! The natural son! Why is the play called this? What influence does Dorval's birth have? What event does it prompt? For what situation does it provide an opportunity? What gap does it fill? What can the author's purpose have been? To reheat a couple of observations over the prejudice against illegitimate birth? What reasonable human being does not already know how unjust such a prejudice is?"[3]

If Diderot were to answer to this: This circumstance was absolutely necessary to the complication of my plot; without it, it would have been far more improbable that Dorval did not know his sister and that his sister did not know she had a brother.[4] It was within my discretion to take my title from this, and I could have taken my title from an even more trivial circumstance. – If Diderot were to give this answer, I say, would Palissot not be more or less rebutted?

Having said that, the character of the natural son is open to a completely different criticism, which Palissot could have used to attack the writer far more sharply. Namely this: that the circumstance of illegitimate birth and the consequent abandonment and isolation from society that Dorval experienced for so many years is far too idiosyncratic and particular a circumstance, with far too much influence on the formation of his character, for it to have the general applicability that, according to Diderot's own theory, a comic character must have. – The opportunity tempts me to a digression on this theory; and how can I resist this type of temptation in a text of this kind?[5]

"The comic genre," says Diderot,[*] "has types, and the tragic one has individuals. I will explain. The hero of a tragedy is such and such a man: he is Regulus, or Brutus, or Cato and none other. The primary character of a comedy, on the other hand, must represent a large number of people. If one were to give him, by chance, such a unique physiognomy that he only resembled a single individual, then comedy would regress back into its infancy. – It seems to me that Terence once made this mistake. His *Heauton Timorumenos* is a father who grieves over the violent resolution to which he drove his son through excessive severity, and who now punishes himself on that account by feeding and clothing himself miserably, avoiding all society, dismissing his servants, and cultivating his fields with his own hands.[6] It can quite surely be said that there is no such father. The largest city could scarcely provide a single example in a hundred years of such unusual grief."[7]

First, the instance of the *Heauton Timorumenos*. If this character is really to be criticized, then the criticism should fall on Menander rather than Terence. Menander created the character and, to all appearances, gave him a much more extensive role to play in his work than in Terence's version, where his sphere had to be significantly restricted because of the doubled intrigue.[†,8] But the fact that it originated in Menander would alone have discouraged me, at least, from damning Terence on its account. To be sure, "ὦ Μένανδρε καὶ βίε, πότερος ἄρ ὑμῶν πότερον ἐμιμήσατο" is more frigid than witty, but would it have been said at all about a poet who was capable of depicting characters of which the largest city could scarcely provide a single example in a whole century?[9] Indeed, it is likely that in a hundred plus plays,

---

* "Conversations."

† [In the following, we have provided translations in square brackets for the quoted Latin phrases so that the reader can follow Lessing's long footnote. Our translations are indicated by "Tr." Page numbers in parens indicate quotations taken from John Barsby's translation of the prologue to *Heauton Timorumenos* in *Terence* I: 181–3. – Tr.]

That is, if the sixth line of the Prologue,

   duplex quae ex argumento facta est simplici. ["a double play based on a single plot" (181)]

was really written thusly by the poet and is not to be understood differently than Dacier and Colman, Terence's later English translator, explain it. "Terence only meant to say, that he had doubled the characters; instead of one old man, one young gallant, one mistress, as in Menander, he had two old men &c. He therefore adds very properly: *novam esse ostendi*, ["I have revealed to you that it is a new play" (181)] – which certainly could not have been implied, had the characters been the same in the Greek poet." Adrian Barlandus, as well, and even the old *Glossa interlinealis* of Ascensius did not understand the "duplex" otherwise. The latter says "propter senes & juvenes" ["because of the old men and the young men" – Tr.]; and the former writes "nam in hac latina senes duo, adolescentes item duo sunt" ["for in the Latin version of this play there are two old men and two young men." – Tr.]. And yet I cannot get my mind around this interpretation, because I do not see what remains of the play if you take away the characters by way of whom Terence is said to have doubled the old man, the male lover, and the female beloved. It is inconceivable to me how Menander could have handled this subject without Chremes and Clitipho; they are both woven in so expertly that I can imagine neither the complication nor the resolution without them. I will not even mention another explanation, by which Julius Scaliger made one such character could have escaped him. The most fertile brain can write itself dry, and when the power of imagination cannot recall any more real objects for imitation, it composes them on its own, the majority of which, of course, become caricatures. Diderot claims to have observed that Horace, who had an especially fastidious taste, saw this error we are talking about and criticized it subtly in passing.[10]

---

himself ridiculous. Moreover, the one Eugraphius gave, which was taken up by Faerno, is completely ham-fisted. The critics, in their confusion, have tried sometimes changing the "duplex," sometimes the "simplici" in the line, which the manuscripts justify to some extent. Several have read:

duplex quae ex argumento facta est duplici. ["a double play crafted from a double plot" – Tr.]

Others:

simplex quae ex argumento facta est duplici. ["a single play crafted from a double plot" – Tr.]

What is left but that someone should now read:

simplex quae ex argumento facta est simplici? ["a single play crafted from a single plot" – Tr.]

And in all seriousness: that is the way I would most prefer to read it. Look at the passage in context, and consider my reasons.

ex integra Graeca integram comoediam
hodie sum acturus Heautontimorumenon:
simplex quae ex argumento facta es simplici.
["Today I am about to perform a complete comedy from a complete Greek play, 'The Self-Tormentor,' which has been crafted as a single play from a single plot" – Tr.]

The accusations against Terence made by his envious colleagues in the theater are well known:

multas contaminasse graecas, dum facit
paucas latinas –
["contaminated many Greek plays while creating few Latin ones" (181)]

Namely, he often fused two plays into one and made one Latin comedy out of two Greek ones. In such manner he put together his *Andria* out of Menander's *Andria* and *Perinthia*, his *Eunuchus* from the very same writer's *Eunuchus* and *Colax*, his *Brothers* from Menander's *Brothers* and a play by Diphilus. He justifies himself against these accusations in the Prologue to *Heauton Timorumenos*. He concedes the matter itself, but he claims to have done nothing other than what good poets before him had done.

[. . .] id esse factum hic non negat
neque se pigere, & delinde factum iri autumat.
habet bonorum exemplum: quo exemplo sibi
licere id facere, quod illi fecerunt, putat.
["He does not deny that this is so; he does not regret it and he declares that he will do the same again. He has good writers as a precedent, and he reckons that with them as a precedent he is permitted to do what they did." (181; 183)]

I have done it, he says, and I think that I will do it again, and often. But that refers to earlier plays, and not the present one, the *Heauton Timorumenos*. For this latter was not taken from two Greek plays but rather from a single one with the same name. And that, I think, is what he wants to say in the disputed line, as I propose to read it:

simplex quae ex argumento facta est simplici.

Terence wants to say, my play is just as simple as Menander's play; I have inserted nothing from other plays; as long as it is, it is taken from the Greek play, and the Greek play is completely included in my Latin one; consequently I give

ex integra Graeca integram comoediam. ["a complete comedy from a complete Greek play" – Tr.]

271

The passage is said to be in the second Satire of the first volume, where Horace sets out to demonstrate "that fools tend to fall from one extreme into its opposite. Fufidius," he says, "fears being considered a spendthrift. Do you know what he does? He lends monthly at five percent and takes payment in advance. The more the other man needs money, the more he demands. He knows the names of all the young people from good families who are entering society and who have strict fathers to lament. But perhaps you think that this person now spends in a way that matches his income? You'd be very wrong! He is his own worst enemy, and the father in the play who punishes himself because his son has run away cannot torment himself worse: *non se pejus cruciaverit*."[11] – This *worse*, this *pejus*, has, according to Diderot, a double meaning. On the one hand it applies to Fufidius, and on the other, to Terence. Such passing shots, he claims, are completely in character for Horace.

This last claim may be true without its being applied to the passage under discussion. For here, it seems to me, this passing shot would be at odds with the main point. Fufidius is not such a great fool, if there are more such fools like him. If the father in Terence torments himself so absurdly, if he has as little reason to torment himself as Fufidius does, then they are equally ridiculous, and Fufidius is less singular and absurd. It is only if Fufidius is just as severe and harsh with himself for no reason as the father

---

The meaning Faerno found given for the word "integra" in an old glossary, that it is tantamount to "a nullo tacta" ["touched by no one" – Tr.], is obviously wrong here, because it would only apply to the first "integra" but in no way the second "integram." – And so I believe that my assumption and interpretation deserve a hearing! Only we will bump up against the line that follows right after:

> *novam esse ostendi, & quae esset* – ["I have revealed to you that it is a new play and given you its name" (181)]

It will be said: if Terence acknowledges that he has taken the whole play from one single play by Menander, how can he pretend to have proven through this same acknowledgment that his play is new, "novam esse"? – I can alleviate this difficulty very easily through an explanation of these very words; in fact, an explanation which I venture to maintain is absolutely the only true one, even though it belongs to me alone, and no other interpreter, as far as I know, has even come close to it. I say, namely, that the words

> *Novam esse ostendi, & quae esset* –

by no means refer to what Terence has the prologue speaker say in the previous lines. Rather, "apud Aediles" ["to the Aediles" – Tr.] must be understood; "novus" does not mean here what flowed from Terence's own mind, but rather simply what had not yet existed in Latin. He wants to say: I have proven to the Aediles, who purchased it from me, that my play is a new play, that is, it is a play that has not yet appeared in Latin, which I myself translated from Greek. To readily agree with me on this point, one need only remember the dispute he had with the Aediles over his *Eunuchus*. He had sold it to them as a new play, translated by him from Greek, but his adversary, Lavinius, wanted to convince the Aediles that he had not taken it from Greek but rather from two old plays by Naevius and Plautus. To be sure, *Eunuchus* had much in common with these plays, but still Lavinius's allegation was false, for Terence had only drawn from the very same Greek source that, unbeknownst to him, Naevius and Plautus had already used before him. Consequently, in order to forestall aspersions against his *Heauton Timorumenos*: what was more natural than for him to have shown the Aediles the Greek original and instructed them about its contents? Indeed, the Aediles themselves could easily have demanded it of him. And that is what

> *Novam esse ostendi, & quae esset*

refers to.

in Terence is with reason, if the former does out of filthy greed what the latter does out of regret and sorrow, only then will the former become infinitely more ridiculous and despicable to us than the latter is compelling.

And to be sure, every great sorrow is of the same type as this father's sorrow; one that cannot forget itself, that torments itself. It goes against all experience to say that an example of such sorrow is scarce to be found in a century; on the contrary, every sorrow acts somewhat the same way, more or less, with this or that variation. Cicero had observed the nature of sorrow more precisely, and consequently he saw in the behavior of the Heauton Timorumenos nothing more than what all grievers do, not merely when carried away by emotion but also when they think they must grimly carry on.‡ "Haec omnia recta, vera, debita putantes, faciunt in dolore: maximeque declaratur, hoc quasi officii iudicio fieri, quod si qui forte, cum se in luctu esse vellent, aliquid fecerunt humanius, aut si hilarius locuti essent, revocant se rursus ad moesti-tiam, peccatique se insimulant, quod dolere intermiserint: pueros vero matres & mag-istri castigare etiam solent, nec verbis solum, sed etiam verberibus, si quid in domestico luctu hilarius ab iis factum est, aut dictum: plorare cogunt. [. . .] Quid ille Terentianus ipse se puniens?" etc.[12]

But Menedemus, the self-tormentor in Terence's play, is not only severe with himself out of sorrow; rather, the primary reason and purpose for denying himself even the smallest expenditure is in order to save that much more for his absent son, and thereby to assure a more comfortable life in the future for the one upon whom he has forced such discomfort in the present. Is there anything here that a hundred fathers would not do? If Diderot is implying that what is singular and unusual in this is that Menedemus himself hoes, digs, and cultivates, then in his haste he was clearly thinking more about our modern customs than ancient ones. True, a rich father today would not so easily do this, for only the minority would know how. But the wealthiest and most prominent Romans and Greeks were more familiar with all agricultural work and were not ashamed to set their hands to it.

Yet let us say that everything is exactly as Diderot says! Let the character of the self-tormentor be − on account of his singularity, on account of this trait that nearly only pertains to him alone − as unsuited for a comic character as he likes. Did Diderot not make the exact same mistake? For what could be more singular than the character of his Dorval?[13] What character has a more idiosyncratic trait than the character of this natural son? "Right after my birth," he has him say, "I was abandoned to a place that can be called the border between solitude and society; and when I opened my eyes to look for the ties that bound me to humanity, I could scarce see any traces of them. For thirty years I wandered about among mankind, lonely, unacknowledged, neglected, without feeling the tenderness of any other human being or having met another person who sought mine in return."[14] It is easy to believe that an illegitimate child can seek his parents in vain, that he can look in vain for people to whom he is bound by closer ties of blood − this is something that happens to nine out of ten. But that he could wander the world for thirty years without feeling the tenderness of any other human being, or meeting another person who sought his: that, I would almost say, is simply impossible.

‡ *Tusc. Quaest.* Bk. III, sect. 27.

Or if it were possible, what abundance of very particular circumstances must have come together from both sides, from the side of the world and the side of this person so long isolated from the world, in order to make this sad possibility a reality? Many centuries will elapse before the possibility will become real again. Heaven forbid that I ever imagine the human species in any other way! Otherwise, I would rather wish to have been born a bear than a human. No – no person can be forsaken so long among other people. No matter where he has been tossed, as long as he falls among humans, he falls among creatures who, before he has even had time to see where he is, stand ready on all sides to link themselves to him. If not prominent, then lowly people; if not happy, then unhappy people! But they are people nonetheless. Just as a drop need only disturb the surface of water in order to be taken up by it and absorbed completely into it, whatever the water may be called, puddle or spring, river or lake, strait or ocean.

Nevertheless, this thirty-year isolation among men is to have formed Dorval's character. Now, what character can look similar to him? Who can recognize himself in him? Even recognize himself the least bit?

Yet I find Diderot has tried to secure himself a way out. In what follows the passage quoted above, he says: "In the serious genre the characters are often just as universal as in the comic genre, but they will always be less individual than in the tragic."[15] He would therefore answer: the character of Dorval is no comic character, he is a character that fits the requirements of serious drama.[16] Just as the latter should fill the space between comedy and tragedy, so must its characters occupy the middle between comic and tragic characters. They need not be so universal as the former as long as they are not so completely individual as the latter, and the character of Dorval might very well be of this type.

Thus we are happily back to the point from which we departed. We wanted to investigate whether it was true that tragedies have individuals but comedies have types; that is, whether it is true that the characters of a comedy must simultaneously encompass and represent a large number of people, whereas the hero of a tragedy should only be this or that person, only Regulus, or Brutus, or Cato. If this is true, then what Diderot says of the characters of the middle genre, which he calls serious comedy, presents no difficulties, and the character of his Dorval would deserve no criticism. If, on the other hand, it is not true, then this, too, falls away, and there can be no justification for the character of the natural son based on such an unfounded division.

Essay 89

8 March 1768[1]

First I must note that Diderot left his assertion without any proof.[2] He must have regarded it as a truth that no man could or would call into question, a truth whose reason was clear the moment one thought about it. And should he have found this reason in the real names of the tragic characters? Because these are called Achilles and Alexander and Cato and Augustus, and because Achilles, Alexander, Cato, and Augustus were real, individual persons, ought he to have deduced from this that everything the poet has them say and do in the tragedy must also only belong to these unique persons with these names, and no one else in the world? It almost seems so.

But Aristotle had already refuted this mistake two thousand years ago; and based on the opposition of both history and poetry to reality, he established the essential difference between the two genres, along with the greater benefit of the latter over the former. He did it, moreover, in such an illuminating manner that I need only quote his words to awaken no small amazement over how Diderot could fail to be of the same mind.

Aristotle says,* after he has established the essential characteristics of the poetic plot: "From this it is clearly evident that the function of the poet is not to relate what has happened but rather to relate the essence of the event and what was possible according to probability or necessity. For the history writer and the poet do not differentiate themselves through verse or prose, insofar as one could render the books of Herodotus in verse and they will become no less a history in metered writing than they were in unmetered writing.[3] Rather they differentiate themselves in the fact that the former relates what has happened but the latter relates the essence of what has happened. For this reason, then, poetry is more philosophical and useful than history. Poetry engages the universal and history the particular. The universal is how such or such a man would speak or act according to probability or necessity; this is what poetry tries to do by assigning names. The particular, on the other hand, is what Alcibiades did or suffered.[4] In comedy this has already demonstrated itself quite transparently, for when the plot is constructed according to probability, typical names are consequently assigned, unlike in the iambic poets, who stay with particular individuals. In tragedy, however, they keep to real names, because the possible is believable, and we will not believe that something is possible if it has never happened; conversely, something that has happened must obviously be possible, because it would not have happened if it were not possible. And yet among the tragedies there are some that have only one or two well-known names, the rest being fictitious; and some have no known names at all, as in Agathon's *Flower*.[5] For in this play the actions and names are equally fictitious, and yet it pleases no less for that."[6]

There are several things in this passage, which I have quoted according to my own translation and in which I have remained as close to the exact words as possible, that have either been misconstrued or completely misunderstood by the commentators I could consult. I have to take into consideration those that belong to the matter at hand here.

It is incontrovertible that Aristotle simply did not differentiate between the characters in tragedy and comedy with regard to their universality. Both the one and the other, and even including characters in the epic, that is, all characters in poetic representation without any exception, ought to speak and act not the way only they could but rather the way any essentially similar person would and must speak or act under the same circumstances. The sole reason why poetry is more philosophical and consequently more instructive than history rests on this καθόλου, on this universality.[7] And if it is true, as Diderot says, that the comic poet who gives his characters

---

* *Poetics*, Ch. 9.

such singular physiognomies that no other individual in the world resembled them would send comedy back to its infancy and pervert it into satire, then it is equally true that the tragic poet who only represents this or that particular person, only Caesar or Cato, with all the idiosyncrasies we know of them, and who fails to show how all these idiosyncrasies connect with the character type of Caesar and Cato, a character type that can be held in common with others – this, I say, would weaken tragedy and debase it to history.[8]

But Aristotle also says that poetry aims at this universality of the characters with the names it assigns to them (*οὗ στοχάζεται ἡ ποίησις ὀνόματα ἐπιτιθεμένη*), which has demonstrated itself clearly and particularly in comedy.[9] And it is this that Aristotle's commentators have contented themselves with repeating, but without elucidating in the least. However, several have expressed themselves on this in such a way that we can clearly see they must either have thought nothing of it at all or something completely wrong. The question is: when poetry assigns names to its characters, how does it serve the universality of these characters? And how has this, its concern for the universality of characters, particularly in comedy, long been apparent?

Dacier translates the words "*ἔστιν δὲ καθόλου μέν, τῷ ποίῳ τὰ ποῖα ἄττα συμβαίνει λέγειν ἢ πράττειν κατὰ τὸ εἰκὸς ἢ τὸ ἀναγκαῖον, οὗ στοχάζεται ἡ ποίησις ὀνόματα ἐπιτιθεμένη*" with: "[u]ne chose generale, c'est ce que tout homme d'un tel ou d'un tel caractére, a dû dire, ou faire vraisemblablement ou nécessairement, ce qui est le but de la poësie, lors même, qu'elle impose les noms à ses personnages."[10] Herr Curtius translates them exactly the same way: "The universal is that which anyone, because of his specific character, says or does according to probability or necessity. This universality is the ultimate goal of poetry, even if it attributes specific names to the characters."[11] These two are in agreement, as well, in their commentaries on these words: the one says exactly what the other does. Both explain what the universal is, and both say that this universality is the purpose of poetry; but neither says a word about how poetry serves this universality with respect to the assignation of names. Rather, through their *lors même* and "even if" the Frenchman and the German show clearly that they had nothing to say about it, indeed that they did not understand what Aristotle wanted to say.[12] For this *lors même*, this "even if," means nothing more in their translations than "although," and consequently they have Aristotle merely say that *notwithstanding* its attribution of names of individual persons to its characters, poetry nevertheless does not aim at the singularity of these persons but rather at their universality. Dacier's words, which I will quote in the footnote, demonstrate this clearly.[†,13] Now it is true that the sense here is actually not false, but it also does not exhaust Aristotle's meaning. It is not enough that poetry can aim at the universal

---

† "Aristote prévient icy une objection, qu'on pourvoit luy faire, sur la définition, qu'il vient de donner, d'une chose generale; car les ignorans n'auroient pas manqué de luy dire, qu'Homere, par exemple, n'a point en véüe d'écrire une action generale & universelle, mais une action particuliere, puisqu'il raconte ce qu'ont fait de certains hommes, comme Achille, Agamemnon, Ulysse, &c. & que par consequent, il n'y aucune difference entre Homere & un Historien, qui auroit écrit les actions d'Achille. Ce Philosophe va au devant de cette objection, en faisant voir que les Poëtes, c'est-à-dire, les Auteurs d'une Tragedie ou d'un Poëme Epique, lors même qu'ils imposent les noms à leurs personnages, ne pensent en aucune maniére à les faire parler véritablement, ce qu'ils seroient obligez de faire, s'ils écrivoient les

notwithstanding the names taken from individual persons; Aristotle says that it aims at the universal with these names themselves: *οὗ στοχάζεται.*[14] I should certainly think that the two were not the same. If, however, they are not the same, then we necessarily light upon the question: how does poetry aspire to this? And the commentators give no answer to this question.

Essay 90

11 March 1768[1]

In answer to how it aspires to this, Aristotle says it has been demonstrated clearly by comedy:[2] *ἐπὶ μὲν οὖν τῆς κωμῳδίας ἤδη τοῦτο δῆλον γέγονεν: συστήσαντες γὰρ τὸν μῦθον διὰ τῶν εἰκότων οὕτω τὰ τυχόντα ὀνόματα ἐπιτιθέασι, καὶ οὐχ ὥσπερ οἱ ἰαμβοποιοὶ περὶ τῶν καθ' ἕκαστον ποιοῦσιν.*[3] I must also quote the translations of this by Dacier and Curtius. Dacier says: "C'est ce qui est déja rendu sensible dans las comedie, car les Poëtes comiques, aprés avoir dressé leur sujet sur la vray-semblance [sic], imposent aprés cela à leurs personnages tels noms qu'il leur plaît, & n'imitent pas les Poëtes satyriques, qui ne s'attachent qu'aux chose particulieres."[4] And Curtius: "In the comedy this has long been visible. For when the writers of comedy conceived the plot of the story according to probability, they attributed arbitrary names to the characters and did not have something particular in mind like the iambic poets did."[5] What do we find in these translations that corresponds to what concerns Aristotle most? Both have him saying only that the comic writers did not do the same as the iambic (that is, satiric) poets in keeping to the individual but rather tended to the universal with their characters, to whom they gave *arbitrary* names: "tels noms qu'il leur plaît."[6] Granted, now, that *τὰ τυχόντα ὀνόματα* could mean such names, where have both translators left the *οὕτω*?[7] Did this *οὕτω* mean absolutely nothing to them? And yet it says everything here: for according to this *οὕτω* the comic writers did not only give arbitrary names to their characters, but they gave them these arbitrary names "so": *οὕτω* [thusly]. And how "so"? "So," that they aimed at universality with these very names: *οὗ στοχάζεται ἡ ποίησις ὀνόματα ἐπιτιθεμένη.*[8] And how did that happen? Find me one word about it in the commentaries by Dacier and Curtius!

Without any further beating about the bush, it happened like this. Comedy gave names to its characters that expressed the essence of these characters by means of their

---

actions particulieres & véritables d'un certain homme nommé Achille, ou Edipe, mais qu'ils se proposent de les faire parler & agir necessairement ou vray-semblablement; c'est-à-dire, de leur faire dire, & faire tout ce que des hommes de ce même caractére doivent faire & dire en cet état, ou par necessité, ou au moins selon les regles de la vray-semblance; ce qui prouve incontestablement que ce sont des actions generales & universelles." Herr Curtius does not say anything different in his commentary, only he wants to show the universal and the particular through examples that do not exactly prove that he has gotten to the heart of the matter. For according to them, it would only be personified characters that the poet has speak and act, whereas it should in fact be characterized persons.

grammatical derivation and composition, or some other meaning. In short, it gave them telling names, names one needed only to hear in order to know instantly what kind of person it was who bore the name. I will quote a passage from Donatus on this here:[9] "Nomina personarum," he says with regard to the first line of the first act of *The Brothers*, "in comoediis duntaxat, habere debent rationem & etymologiam. Etenim absurdum est, comicum aperte argumentum confingere: vel nomen personae incongruum dare vel officium quod sit a nomine diversum.*,[10] Hinc servus fidelis *Parmeno*: infidelis vel *Syrus* vel *Geta*; miles *Thraso* vel *Polemon*: juvens *Pamphilus*: matrona *Myrrhina*, & puer ab odore *Storax*: vel a ludo & a gesticulatione *Circus*: & item similia. In quibus summum Poetae visum est, si quid et contrario repugnans contrarium diversumque protulerit, nisi per ἀντίφρασιν nomen imposuerit joculariter, ut *Misargyrides* in Plauto diciter trapezita."[11] Anyone who wishes to be convinced of this through further examples need only look at the names in Plautus and Terence. Because their plays have all been taken from the Greek, the names of their characters are also of Greek origin and always refer, etymologically, to the social status, way of thinking, or some other thing that these characters could have in common with many others, even if we cannot still always specify such etymologies with clarity and certainty.

I am not going to dwell on such a well-known matter; but I do wonder how Aristotle's interpreters could have failed to remember it, when Aristotle so undeniably points it out. For what can be more true, more clear, than what the philosopher says of the consideration poetry has for universality in issuing names? What can be more undeniable, than that ἐπὶ μὲν τῆς κωμῳδίας ἤδη τοῦτο δῆλον γέγονεν; that this consideration has apparently long been demonstrated, especially in comedy?[12] From its first origins, that is, as soon as the iambic poets rose from the particular to the universal, as soon as instructive comedy grew out of libelous satire, they tried to indicate universality through the names themselves. The boastful cowardly soldier was not named for this or that leader from this or that clan; he was called Pyrgopolinices, Captain *Battering-ram*.[13] The miserable parasite who was eager to please him was not named after some poor fellow in the city; he was called Artotrogus, *Crumbcarrier*.[14] The youth who plunged his father into debt through his expenditures, particularly on horses, was not named for the son of this or that upright citizen; he was called Pheidippides, Squire *Sparesteed*.[15]

It could be objected that such signifying names might only have been an invention of Greek New Comedy, whose poets were strictly forbidden to make use of real names, and

---

* This could easily be misunderstood. That is, if one wanted to understand it as if Donatus also held "comicum aperte argumentum confingere" ["to openly invent a comedic plot"] to be absurd. Of course, that is not at all Donatus's meaning. Rather, he intends to say that, because the comic writer manifestly invents his subject, it would be absurd if he nonetheless attributed unsuitable names to his characters, or occupations that conflicted with their names. For certainly, since the subject is completely the poet's, it is wholly and singularly up to him what kind of names he gives his characters, or what kind of social standing or occupation he wants to connect with these names. Therefore, perhaps Donatus ought not to have expressed himself so ambivalently, and by changing a single syllable, this hindrance is avoided. Namely, it should either read: "Absurdum est, comicum aperte argumentum confingentem vel nomen personae" etc; or even "aperte argumentum confingere & nomen personae" etc.

that Aristotle did not know these New Comedies and therefore could not have taken them into consideration for his rules.[16] Hurd claims this latter,[†,17] but this is just as false as the claim that the older Greek comedies only made use of real names. Even in those plays whose primary, sole purpose was to make a certain well-known person ridiculous and hated, nearly all the names except for that of this one real person were made up, and made up in such a way as to correspond with their social standing and character.

Essay 91

15 March 1768[1]

Indeed, it could be said that the real names themselves often tended more to the universal than to the particular.[2] With the name Socrates, Aristophanes intended to make ridiculous and suspect not just the individual Socrates, but all Sophists who meddle in the upbringing of young people.[3] The dangerous Sophist in general was his subject, and he only called him Socrates because Socrates was decried as such. Hence a number of traits that did not apply to *the* Socrates, so that Socrates himself could confidently stand up in the theater and offer himself for comparison.[4] But the essence of comedy is very much misunderstood if these nonmatching traits are declared to be

---

† Hurd, in his "Dissertation on the Provinces of the Drama": "From the account of comedy, here given, it may appear, that the idea of this drama is much enlarged beyond what it was in Aristotle's time; who defines it to be an imitation of light and trivial actions, provoking ridicule. His notion was taken from the state and practice of the Athenian stage; that is from the old or middle comedy, which answer to this description. The great revolution, which the introduction of the new comedy made in the drama, did not happen till afterwards" [Hurd, "Dissertation" 201]. But Hurd merely assumes this so that his explanation of comedy does not appear to conflict with Aristotle's so directly. Aristotle did indeed live to see the New Comedy, and he recalls it specifically in the *Nicomachean Ethics*, where he deals with decent and indecent jokes (Bk. IV, ch. 14). *ἴδοι δ᾽ ἄν τις καὶ ἐκ τῶν κωμῳδιῶν τῶν παλαιῶν καὶ τῶν καινῶν· τοῖς μὲν γὰρ ἦν γελοῖον ἡ αἰσχρολογία, τοῖς δὲ μᾶλλον ἡ ὑπόνοια.* ["The difference may be seen by comparing the old and the new comedies; the earlier dramatists found their fun in obscenity, the moderns prefer innuendo, which marks a great advance in decorum." Tr. by H. Rackham, *Nicomachean Ethics* 4.8.6.] One could, of course, say that we are to understand *Middle* here for *New*, for since there were no New Comedies yet, the Middle ones must have been called new. One could add that Aristotle died in the same Olympiad in which Menander premiered his first play; in fact, it was the year before (Eusebius in *Chronico ad Olymp.* CXIV. 4). But one would be wrong to reckon the beginning of New Comedy from Menander; Menander was the first writer of this epoch in terms of poetic merit, but not in terms of time. Philemon, who also belongs to that era, wrote much earlier, and the transition from the Middle to New Comedy was so imperceptible that Aristotle cannot possibly have lacked for examples of it. Aristophanes himself had already provided such an example; his *Cocalus* was so constituted that Philemon could appropriate it with few changes. It says in the *Life of Aristophanes*: "*Κώκαλον ἐν ῳ εἰσάγει φθοραν καὶ ἀναγνωρισμὸν καὶ τἄλλα πάντα ἁ ἐζήλωσε Μένανδρος.*" Thus, since Aristophanes provided examples of all the various modifications of comedy, Aristotle could also build his definition of comedy on all of them. That is what he did, and comedy did not develop further to a point beyond which this explanation became too narrow. If Hurd had only understood this correctly, he would not have found it necessary to take refuge in Aristotle's supposed lack of experience in order to remove all conflict between his own ideas of comedy (which were of course in and of themselves correct) and Aristotle's.

nothing but malicious slanders and not recognized for what they really are: a broadening of the individual character, an elevation of the personal to the universal!

Here several things might be said about the use of real names in Greek comedy in general that have not yet been as precisely explained by scholars as they really deserved to be. It might be noted that this use was not at all common in Old Greek Comedy;[*,5] that only this or that poet occasionally ventured it;[†,6] and that, consequently, it cannot be seen as a differentiating feature of that epoch of comedy.[‡,7] It might be shown

---

* If, according to Aristotle, the scheme of comedy was taken from Homer's *Margites*, οὐ ψόγον ἀλλὰ τὸ γελοῖον δραματοποιήσας ["by dramatizing the ludicrous instead of writing personal satire" – Tr. Butcher, *Poetics* (Part IV)], then to all appearances the invented names will have been introduced from the very beginning. For Margites was likely not the real name of a specific person, insofar as Μαργίτης was more likely derived from μάργης than μάργης originated from Μαργίτης. We also find – for example, from Pherecrates – that several of the poets of Old Comedy expressly claim that they avoid all bawdiness, which would not have been possible with the use of real names.

† Personal and explicit satire was so little an essential feature of Old Comedy, that we easily identify the first of their poets to venture it. It was Cratinus, who first τῳ χαριεντι της κωμωδιας το ὠφελιμον προσεθηκε, τους κακως πραττοντας διαβαλλων, και ὡσπερ δημοσια μαστιγι τη κωμωδια κολαζων ["to the fun of comedy added a usefulness by attacking those who behaved badly and punishing them by using comedy as a sort of public whip" – Tr. Ian C. Storey, *Fragments of Old Comedy* 260–1]. And even he only dared at first to do this with profligate commoners from whom he had nothing to fear. Aristophanes jealously claimed the honor of having been the first to venture this with the great men of the state (*Eir.* [*Peace*] v. 750):

οὐκ ἰδιώτας ἀνθρωπίσκους κωμῳδῶν οὐδὲ γυναῖκας,
ἀλλ᾽ Ἡρακλέους ὀργήν τιν᾽ ἔχων τοῖσι μεγίστοις ἐπεχείρει
["Moreover it's not obscure private persons or women that he stages in his comedies; but, bold as Heracles, it's the very greatest whom he attacks" – Tr. Anonymous, *Peace* 699]

Indeed, he would have preferred to consider this boldness his personal privilege. He was extremely resentful when he saw that so many other poets, whom he disdained, followed his lead in this.

‡ Which nevertheless nearly always happens. In fact, they go even further and want to maintain that real events were connected to those real names that the writer had no part in inventing. Even Dacier says: "Aristote n'a pû vouloir dire qu'Epicharmus & Phormys inventerent les sujets de leurs pieces, puisque l'un & l'autre ont été des Poëtes de la vieille Comedie, où il n'y avoit rien de feint, & que ces avantures feintes, ne commencerent à être mises sur le theatre, que du temps d'Alexandre le Grand, c'est-à-dire, dans la nouvelle Comedie." (*Remarque sur le Chap. V. de la Poetique d'Aristote*). We might be justified in thinking that only someone who never even took a peek at Aristophanes' plays could say such a thing. The arguments and plots of the Old Greek Comedies were just as invented as the arguments and plots of the New could ever be. Not a single one of Aristophanes' extant plays presents an event that really happened; and just because they allude, in part, to real events, it still cannot be said that the poet did not invent them. When Aristotle takes as a given ὅτι τὸν ποιητὴν μᾶλλον τῶν μύθων εἶναι δεῖ ποιητὴν ἢ τῶν μέτρων ["that the poet . . . should be the maker of plots rather than of verses" – Tr. Butcher, *Poetics* (Part. IX)], would he not have had to completely exclude the authors of Old Greek Comedy from the category of poet if he had believed that they had not invented the arguments of their plays? But just as, according to him, borrowing names and circumstances from actual history can be consistent with poetic invention in tragedy, so, according to him, it must also be possible in comedy. It cannot possibly have been in keeping with his ideas that, by using real names and alluding to real events, comedy would fall back into the iambic obsession with satire; rather, he must have believed that to καθόλου ποιεῖν λόγους καὶ μύθους ["generalize his themes and plots" – Tr. Butcher, *Poetics* (Part V)] was quite compatible with it. He concedes this to the oldest comic poets, Epicharmus, Phormis, and Crates, and would certainly not have denied it to Aristophanes even though he knew how much he had explicitly mocked not only Cleon and Hyperbolus but also Pericles and Socrates.

that, when it was finally expressly prohibited by law, there were still certain people either explicitly excluded from the protection of this law or implicitly assumed to be so.[8] Even in Menander's plays there were still plenty of people named and made ridiculous through use of their real names.[§,9] But I must not drift from one digression into another.

I want only to make the application to real names in tragedy. Just as Aristophanes' Socrates did not and was not intended to represent the individual man of that name; just as this personified model of vain and dangerous book-learning only received the name Socrates because Socrates was in part known to be such a deceiver and seducer, and in part ought to have been better known as such; just as the mere concept of social standing and character that people connected with the name Socrates, and ought to have more closely connected with it, determined the poet's choice of the name: in just this same way, the very concept of character that we commonly associate with the names Regulus, Cato, or Brutus is the reason the tragic writer attributes these names to his characters. He puts a Regulus or Brutus on stage not to make us familiar with the real adventures of these men, not to revive their memory, but rather to entertain us with the kinds of adventures that men of their character in general could and might encounter. Now it is indeed true that we have abstracted their characters from the real events in their lives, but it does not follow that their characters must lead us back to their adventures. Often they can bring us much more quickly and naturally to completely other adventures that have nothing more in common with those real ones than that they have flowed together out of a single source, but by untraceable detours and over tracks of land that have muddied their purity. In such a case, the poet will certainly give preference to the invented over the real, but still give the character the real name. And this is for two reasons: first, because we are already accustomed, upon hearing these names, to think of the character as it appears in its general form; and second, because real events seem to attach to real names, and everything that has once occurred is more believable than something that has not occurred. The first of these reasons flows from the overall connection among Aristotelian concepts; it is foundational, and Aristotle did not need to dwell on it any more laboriously. But he did need to dwell on the second, as a reason that came from elsewhere. But this latter matter falls outside my topic here, and in general the commentators have misunderstood the second reason less than the first.

Now to come back to Diderot's claim.[10] If I may be permitted to believe that I have correctly explained Aristotle's theory, then I may also be permitted to believe I have proved, through my explanation, that the matter cannot possibly be other than what Aristotle theorizes. The characters in tragedy must be just as universal as the characters in comedy. The difference Diderot asserts is wrong, or else Diderot must

---

§ The strictness with which Plato wanted to forbid ridiculing someone in comedy in his Republic (μήτε ἄνευ θυμοῦ, μηδαμῶς μηδένα τῶν πολιτῶν κωμῳδεῖν) ["A composer of a comedy or of any iambic or lyric song shall be strictly forbidden to ridicule any of the citizens either by word or by mimicry, whether with or without passion"; Plato, *Laws* 11.935e] was never enforced in the real Republic. I do not wish to allege that in Menander's plays many a cynical philosopher or courtesan was called out by name: it could be answered that this scum of humanity did not belong among the citizenry. But Ctesippus, the son of Chabrias, was certainly an Athenian citizen, as good as any other, and we can see what Menander said of him (*Menandri* p. 137, Edit. Cl.).

comprehend something completely different under the idea of universality of a character than Aristotle did.

Essay 92

18 March 1768[1]

And why could this last not be true?[2] In fact, I find another, no less admirable critic, who expresses himself nearly the same as Diderot, seems to contradict Aristotle just as unequivocally, and yet nevertheless fundamentally contradicts him so little that I have to recognize him, among all critics, as the one who has shed the most light on this subject.

This would be the English commentator on Horace's *Art of Poetry*, Hurd, who belongs to the class of writers who remain unknown to us until they are translated.[3] I do not wish to praise him here in order to precipitate a hasty introduction. If the German who is up to the task has not yet been found, then perhaps there are not many readers among us for whom it is of great concern. The diligent man, full of good intentions, should not be overhasty with it, and what I say here about a still untranslated good book is not meant to be taken as a hint for the quill he always has at the ready.[4]

Hurd appended a *Dissertation on the Provinces of Drama* to his commentary.[5] He believed he had observed that previously only the general laws of this form of poetry had been taken into consideration, without establishing the boundaries of its various genres.[6] Nevertheless, this would be required in order to reach a fair verdict on the merits of each particular type. Consequently, after he established the purpose of drama in general, and of its three genres in particular – tragedy, comedy, and farce – he gathered from these general and particular purposes both those qualities they have in common and those that differentiate them from each other.

Among the latter, he counts this difference with regard to tragedy and comedy: that real incidents are more suitable to tragedy, whereas fictitious incidents are more suitable to comedy. He continues thusly: "The same genius in the two dramas is observable, in their draught of *characters*. Comedy makes all its characters *general*; Tragedy, *particular*. The *Avare* of Molière is not so properly the picture of a *covetous man*, as of *covetousness* itself.[7] Racine's *Nero*, on the other hand, is not a picture of *cruelty*, but of a *cruel man*."[8]

Hurd seems to conclude that if tragedy requires a reference to a true event, then its characters must also be real, that is, constructed as really existing individuals. If, on the other hand, comedy can be satisfied with fictitious incidents, if it prefers probable incidents that allow its characters to be displayed in their full range, rather than true ones that do not allow them such a broad scope, then its characters also can and must be even more general than they exist in nature. This is all the more so given that generality itself acquires a type of existence in our imagination that relates exactly the same way to the real existence of the individual as the probable does to the true.

I do not want to examine here whether this manner of deducing is not merely circular; I will merely assume the conclusion, just as it is, just as it seems to contradict Aristotle's theory completely. Yet, as I said, it merely seems to, which becomes clear from Hurd's further explanation.

"Yet here," he continues, "it will be proper to guard against two mistakes, which the principles now delivered may be thought to countenance.[9]

The *first* is with regard to *tragic* characters, which I say are *particular*. My meaning is, they are *more* particular than those of comedy. That is, the *end* of tragedy does not require or permit the poet to draw together so many of those characteristic circumstances which shew the manners, as Comedy. For, in the former of these dramas, no more of *character* is shewn, than what the course of the action necessarily calls forth. Whereas, all or most of the features, by which is it usually distinguished, are sought out and industriously displayed in the *latter*.

The case is much the same as in *portrait painting*; where, if a great master be required to draw a *particular face*, he gives the very lineaments he finds in it; yet so far resembling to what he observes of the same turn in other faces, as not to affect any minute circumstance of peculiarity. But if the same artist were to design a *head* in general, he would assemble together all the customary traits and features, any where observable through the species, which should best express the idea, whatever it was, he had conceived in his own mind and wanted to exhibit in the picture.

There is much the same difference between the two sorts of *dramatic* portraits. Whence it appears that in calling the tragic character *particular*, I suppose it only *less representative* of the kind than the comic; not that the draught of so much character as it is concerned to represent should not be *general*: the contrary of which I have asserted and explained at large elsewhere.[*]

Next, I have said, the characters of just comedy are *general*. And this I explain by the instance of the *Avare* of Molière, which conforms more to the idea of *avarice*, than to that of the real *avaricious man*. But here again, the reader will not understand me, as saying this in the strict sense of the words. I even think Molière faulty in the instance given; though, with some necessary explanation, it may well enough serve to express my meaning.

The view of the comic scene being to delineate characters, this end, I suppose, will be attained most perfectly, by making those characters as *universal* as possible. For thus the person shewn in the drama being the representative of all characters of the same kind, furnishes in the highest degree the entertainment of *humor*. But then this universality must be such as agrees not to our idea of the *possible* effects of the character as conceived in the abstract, but to the *actual* exertion of its powers; which experience justifies, and common life allows. Molière, and before him Plautus, had offended in this; that for a picture of the *avaricious man*, they presented us with a fantastic unpleasing draught of the *passion*

---

[*] In his notes on these verses of Horace's *Art of Poetry*: "Respicere exemplar vitae morumque jubebo Doctum imitatorem, & veras hinc ducere voces," where Hurd demonstrates that the *truth* demanded by Horace here "means such an expression, as conforms to the general nature of things; *falsehood*, that, which, however suitable to the particular instance in view, doth not yet correspond to such *general nature*." [Hurd, "Notes on the Art of Poetry" 252 – Ed.]

of avarice.[10] I call this a *fantastic* draught, because it hath no archetype in nature. And it is, farther, an *unpleasing* one, for, being the delineation of a *simple passion unmixed*, it wanted all those

> – lights and shades, whose well accorded strife
> gives all the strength and colour of our life.[11]

These *lights* and *shades* (as the poet finely calls the intermixture of many passions, which, with the *leading* or principal one, form the human character) must be blended together in every picture of dramatic manners; because the avowed business of the drama is to image real life. Yet the draught of the *leading* passion must be as general as this *strife* in nature permits, in order to express the intended character more perfectly."[12]

Essay 93

22 March 1768[1]

"All which again is easily illustrated in the instance of painting.[2] In *portraits of character*, as we may call those that give a picture of *manners*, the artist, if he be of real ability, will not go to work on the possibility of an abstract idea. All he intends, is to shew that some one quality *predominates*: and this he images strongly, and by such signatures as are most conspicuous in the operation of the *leading passion*. And when he hath done this, we may, in common speech or in compliment, if we please, to his art, say of such a portrait that it images to us not the *man* but the *passion*; just as the ancients observed of the famous statue of Apollodorus by Silarion, that it expressed not the angry *Apollodorus*, but his passion of *anger.**,[3] But by this must be understood only that he has well expressed the leading parts of the designed character. For the rest he treats his *subjects* as he would any other; that is, he represents the *concomitant affections*, or considers merely that general symmetry and proportion which are expected in a human figure. And this is to copy nature, which affords no specimen of a man turned all into a single passion. No metamorphosis could be more strange or incredible. Yet portraits of this vicious taste are the admiration of common starers, who, if they find a picture of a *miser* for instance (as there is no commoner subject of moral portraits) in a collection, where every muscle is strained, and feature hardened into the expression of this idea, never fail to profess their wonder and approbation of it. – On this idea of excellence, Le Brun's book of the PASSIONS must be said to contain a set of the justest *moral portraits*:[4] And the CHARACTERS of Theophrastus might be recommended, in a *dramatic* view, as preferable to those of Terence.[5]

The virtuosi in the fine arts would certainly laugh at the former of these judgments. But the latter, I suspect, will not be thought so extraordinary. At least if one may guess from the practice of some of our best comic writers, and the success which

---

* "Non hominem ex aere fecit, sed iracundiam." *Plinius libr.* 34.8.

such plays have commonly met with. It were easy to instance in almost all plays of character. But if the reader would see the extravagance of building manners on abstract ideas in its full light, he needs only turn to B. Jonson's *Every man out of his humour*,†,6 which under the name of a *play of character* is in fact, an unnatural, and as the

---

† B. Jonson has two comedies that have "humour" in the title: one is *Every Man in his Humour*, and the other *Every Man out of his Humour*. The word "humour" gained popularity in his time and was misused in the most absurd ways. He noted both this misuse and the actual meaning of the word in the following passage:

> As when some one peculiar quality
> Doth so possess a man, that it doth draw
> All his affects, his spirits, and his powers,
> In their constructions, all to run one way,
> This may be truly said to be a humour
> But that a rook, by wearing a py'd feather,
> The cable hatband, or the three-piled ruff,
> A yard of shoe-tye, or the Switzer's knot
> On his French garters, should affect a humour!
> O, it is more than most ridiculous.

Both of Jonson's plays are thus very important documents in the history of humours, the second even more than the first. Humour, which we now associate so predominantly with the British, was at that time mostly an affectation among them, and Jonson depicted humour primarily to ridicule this affectation. To be precise: only this affected humour should be the object of the comedy, never the real. For the desire to distinguish oneself from others and make oneself noticeable through some idiosyncrasy is a universal human weakness that, depending on the quality of the means it chooses, can become absurd or even punishable. Those things, however, through which either nature itself or a persistent habit that has become natural differentiates an individual person from all others, are far too special to comport with the general philosophical purpose of drama. The glut of humour in many English plays may thus very well be what makes them unique, but not what makes them better. It is certain that there is no trace of humour to be found in the drama of antiquity. The ancient dramatic poets knew the trick of individualizing their characters even without humour; indeed, the ancient poets in general did. To be sure, the ancient historians and rhetoricians display humour now and then, namely when historical truth or the explanation of a certain fact requires this precise depiction $\kappa\alpha\theta$' $\check{\epsilon}\kappa\alpha\sigma\tau o\nu$. I have diligently collected sufficient examples of it, which I would also like to categorize merely for the purpose of rectifying an error that has become somewhat common. Namely, currently we translate – almost universally – "humour" with "mood" [*Laune* – Tr.]; and I believe I am the first to have translated it thus. I was very wrong in so doing, and I wish I had not been followed in this. For I think I can prove incontrovertibly that "humour" and "mood" are completely different things, indeed things that from a certain understanding are directly opposite. Mood can become a humour, but humour is, with this one case excepted, never a mood. I should have better researched and more precisely considered the roots of our German word and its usual usage. I concluded too hastily that because "mood" expresses the French "humeur" it could also express the English "humour"; but the French themselves cannot translate "humour" with "humeur." – Of the two plays by Jonson cited, the first, *Every Man in His Humour*, exhibits the mistake Hurd finds to blame here to a lesser degree. The humour demonstrated by the characters is neither so individual nor so exaggerated that it could not be compatible with nature; in addition, they are also more or less appropriately united in a common plot. In contrast, in the second, *Every Man Out of His Humour*, there is hardly any plot. A bunch of the most marvelous fools appear one after the other, we know neither how nor why, and their dialogue is constantly interrupted by a couple of friends of the author who are called "Grex" and who make observations about the characters of the personages and about the skill of the writer in handling them. The "out of his humour" indicates that all of the personages get into circumstances in which they become tired and weary of their humour.

painters call it, *hard* delineation of a group of *simply existing passions*, wholly chimerical, and unlike to any thing we observe in the commerce of real life. Yet this comedy has always had its admirers. And *Randolph*, in particular, was so taken with the design, that he seems to have formed his *muse's looking-glass* in express imitation of it.[7]

Shakespeare, we may observe, is in this as in all the other more essential beauties of the drama, a perfect model. If the discerning reader peruse attentively his comedies with this view, he will find his *best-marked* characters discoursing through a great deal of their *parts*, just like any other, and only expressing their essential and leading qualities occasionally, and as circumstances concur to give an easy exposition to them. This singular excellence of his comedy, was the effect of his copying faithfully after nature, and of the force and vivacity of his genius, which made him attentive to what the progress of the scene successively presented to him: whilst *imitation* and *inferior talents* occasion little writers to wind themselves up into the habit of attending perpetually to their main view, and a solicitude to keep their favourite characters in constant play and agitation. Though in this illiberal exercise of their wit, they may be said to use the *persons of their drama* as a certain facetious sort do their *acquaintance*, whom they urge and tease with their civilities, not to give them a reasonable share in the conversation, but to force them to play *tricks* for the diversion of the company."

Essay 94

25 March 1768[1]

So much for Hurd's ideas about the universality of comic characters and the limits of this universality.[2] – Yet it will be necessary to quote the second passage, where he claims to have explained how tragic characters, although they are only particular, nevertheless obtain a universality, before we can draw a general conclusion whether and how Hurd agrees with Diderot, and both with Aristotle.

"*Truth* in poetry," he says,[3] "means such an expression, as conforms to the general nature of things; *falsehood*, that, which however suitable to the particular instance in view, doth yet not correspond to such *general nature*. To attain to this *truth* of expression in dramatic poetry two things are prescribed:*[4] 1. A diligent study of the Socratic philosophy; and 2. A masterly knowledge and comprehension of human life. The *first*, because it is the peculiar distinction of this school *ad veritatem vitae propius accedere*.†[5] And the *latter*, as rendering the imitation more universally striking. This will be understood by reflecting that *truth* may be followed too closely in works of imitation, as is evident in two respects. For, 1. the artist, when he would give a Copy of nature, may confine himself too scrupulously to the exhibition of *particulars*, and so fail of representing the general idea of the *kind*. Or, 2. in applying himself to give the *general* idea, he may collect it from an enlarged view of *real* life, whereas it were still better taken from the nobler conception of it as subsisting only in the *mind*. This last is the kind of censure we pass

---

* *De arte poet.* v. 310, 317, 318.
† *Cic. de Orat.* I. 51.

upon the *Flemish* school of painting, which takes its model from real nature, and not, as the *Italian*, from the contemplative idea of beauty.‡,6 The *former* corresponds to that other fault objected also to the Flemish masters, which consists in their copying from particular odd and grotesque nature in contradistinction to general and graceful nature.

We see then that in deviating from particular and partial, the poet more faithfully imitates *universal*, truth. And thus an answer occurs to that refined argument, which Plato invented and urged, with much seeming complacency, against poetry. It is, that *poetical imitation is at a great distance from truth*. 'Poetical expression, says the Philosopher, is the copy of the poet's own conceptions; the poet's conception, of things; and things, of the standing archetype, as existing in the divine mind. Thus the poet's expression is a copy at third hand, from the primary, original truth.'§,7 Now the diligent study of this rule of the poet obviates this reasoning at once. For, by abstracting from existences all that peculiarly respects and discriminates the *individual*, the poet's conception, as it were neglecting the intermediate particular objects, catches, as far as may be, and reflects the divine archetypal idea, and so becomes itself the copy or image of truth. Hence too we are taught the force of that unusual encomium on poetry by the great critic, *that it is something more severe and philosophical than history*, φιλοσοφώτερον καὶ σπονδαιοτερόν ποιησις ἐςιν.8 The reason follows, which is now very intelligible: ἡ μὲν γὰρ ποίησις μᾶλλον τὰ καθόλου, ἡ δ᾽ ἱστορία τὰ καθ᾽ ἕκαστον λέγει.¶,9 And this will further explain an essential difference, as we are told, between the two great rivals of the Greek stage. Sophocles, in return to such as objected a want of truth in his characters, used to plead, *that he drew men such as they ought to be, Euripides such as they were*. Σοφοκλῆς ἔφη αὐτὸς μὲν οἵους δεῖ ποιεῖν, Εὐριπίδην δὲ οἷοι εἰσίν.**,10 The meaning of which is, Sophocles, from his more extended commerce with mankind, had enlarged and widened the narrow, partial conception, arising from the contemplation of *particular* characters, into a complete comprehension of the *kind*. Whereas the philosophic Euripides, having been mostly conversant in the academy, when he came to look into life, keeping his eye too intent on single, really existing personages, sunk the *kind* in the *individual*; and so painted his characters naturally indeed, and *truly*, with regard to the objects in view, but sometimes without that general and universally striking likeness, which is demanded to the full exhibition of poetical truth.††,11

---

‡ In conformity with the *Antique*. "Nec enim Phidias, cum faceret Jovis formam aut Minervae, contemplabatur aliquem e quo similitudinem duceret: sed ipsius in mente incidebat species pulchritudinis eximia quaedam, quam intuens in eaque defixus ad illius similitudinem artem et manum dirigebat" (Cic. *Orat.* 2).

§ Plato, *de Rep.* L. X.

¶ *Poetics* Ch. 9.

** Ibid., Ch. 25.

†† This explanation is far preferable to the one Dacier gives on this passage in Aristotle. According to the words of the translation, Dacier seems indeed to say just what Hurd says: "que Sophocle faisoit ses Heros, comme ils devoient être, & qu'Euripide les faisoit comme ils étoient" [Aristotle and Dacier 433 – Ed.]. But in fact he connects a completely different idea with it. Hurd understands the *as they should be* to mean the general and abstract idea of kind according to which the poet ought to depict his characters, rather than according to their individual differences. Dacier, however, understands it to mean a higher moral perfection that a human being is capable of achieving, even though he only rarely does; and this, he says, is what Sophocles usually attributed to his characters: "Sophocle tâchoit

But here an objection meets us, which must not be overlooked. It will be said, 'that philosophic speculations are more likely to render men's views *abstract* and *general* than to confine them to *individuals*. This latter is a fault arising from the *small number* of objects men happen to contemplate: and may be removed not only by taking a view of many *particulars*, which is knowledge of the world; but also by reflecting on the *general nature* of men, as it appears in good books of morality. For the writers of such books form their *general* notion of human nature from an extensive experience (either their own, or that of others) without which their writings are of no value.' The answer, I think, is this. *By reflecting on the general nature of man* the philosopher learns, what is the tenor of action arising from the predominancy of certain qualities or properties: *i.e.* in general, what that conduct is, which the imputed character requires. But to perceive clearly and certainly, how far, and with what degree of strength this or that character will, on particular occasions, most probably shew itself, this is the fruit only of a knowledge of the world. Instances of a want of this knowledge cannot be supposed frequent in such a writer, as Euripides; nor, when they occur, so glaring as to strike a common reader. They are niceties, which can only be discerned by the true critic; and even to *him*, at this distance of time, from an ignorance of the Greek manners, that may possibly appear a fault, which is a real beauty. It would be therefore dangerous to think of pointing out the places, which Aristotle might believe liable to this censure in Euripides. I will however presume to mention one, which, if not justly criticized, will, at least, serve to illustrate my meaning."[12]

Essay 95

29 March 1768[1]

"The story of his *Electra* is well known.[2] The poet had to paint, in the character of this princess, a virtuous, but fierce, resentful woman; stung by a sense of personal ill treatment; and instigated to the revenge of a father's death, by still stronger motives.[3] A disposition of this warm temperament, it might be concluded by the philosopher in his closet, would be prompt to shew itself. *Electra* would, on any proper occasion, be ready to avow her resentment, as well as to forward the execution of her purpose. But to what lengths would this *resentment* go? *i.e.* what degree of fierceness might *Electra* express, without affording occasion to a person widely skilled in mankind, and the operation of the passions, to say, 'this is improbable?' Here abstract theories will be of little service. Even a moderate acquaintance with real life will be unable to direct us. Many individuals may have fallen under observation, that will justify the poet in carrying the expression of

---

de rendre ses imitations parfaites, en suivant toûjours bien plus ce qu'une belle Nature étoit capable de faire, que ce qu'elle faisoit" [Aristotle and Dacier 433 – Ed.]. Except this higher moral perfection does not belong to that general concept; it pertains to the individual but not the species, and the poet who attributes it to his characters is depicting the exact opposite, more in the manner of Euripides than Sophocles. The further explanation of this deserves more than a note.

such a *resentment* to any extreme. History would, perhaps, furnish examples, in which a virtuous resentment hath been carried even farther than is here represented by the poet. What way then of determining the precise bounds and limits of it? Only by observing in numerous instances, *i.e.* from a large extensive knowledge of practical life, how far it usually, in such characters, and under such circumstances, prevails. Hence a difference of representation will arise in proportion to the extent of that *knowledge.* Let us now see, how the character before us, hath, in fact, been managed by Euripides.

In that fine scene, which passes between Electra and Orestes, whom as yet she suspects not to be her brother, the conversation very naturally turns upon Electra's distresses, and the author of them, Clytemnestra, as well as on her hopes of deliverance from them by the means of Orestes.[4] The dialogue upon this proceeds:

OR. What then of Orestes, were he to return to this Argos?
EL. Ah! wherefore that question, when there is no prospect of his return at all?
OR. But supposing he should return, how would he go about to revenge the death of his father?
EL. In the same way, in which that father suffered from the daring attempts of his enemies.
OR. And could you then dare to undertake with him the murder of your mother?
EL. Yes, with that very steel, with which she murdered my father.
OR. And am I at liberty to relate this to your brother, as your fixed resolution?
EL. I desire only to live, till I have murdered my mother.

The Greek is still stronger:

Θανοιμι, μητρος ἁιμ᾽ἐπισφαζασ᾽ἐμης.
May I die, as soon as I have murdered my mother!

Now that this last sentence is absolutely unnatural, will not be pretended. There have been doubtless many examples, under the like circumstances, of an expression of revenge carried thus far. Yet, I think, we can hardly help being a little shocked at the fierceness of *this* expression. At least *Sophocles* has not thought fit to carry it to that extreme. In him, *Electra* contents herself with saying to *Orestes*, on a similar occasion: 'The conduct of this affair now rests upon you. Only let me observe this to you, that, had I been left alone, I would not have failed in one of these two purposes, either to deliver myself gloriously, or to perish gloriously.'

Whether this representation of Sophocles be not more agreeable to *truth*, as collected from wide observation, *i.e.* from human nature at large, than that of Euripides, the capable reader will judge. If it be, the reason I suppose to have been, *that Sophocles painted his characters, such, as, from attending to numerous instances of the same kind, he would conclude they ought to be; Euripides, such, as a narrower sphere of observation had persuaded him they were.*[5]

Excellent! Regardless of my purpose in citing these long passages from Hurd, they contain so many fine observations that the reader will not demand an apology for their insertion. I only worry that because of it, he may have lost sight of my purpose

itself. It was this: to show that Hurd, like Diderot, assigns particular characters to tragedy and universal ones only to comedy, and nevertheless he did not want to contradict
Aristotle, who required universality of all poetic characters and consequently also
of the tragic ones.[6] Hurd explains himself thusly: the tragic character would indeed
have to be particular, or less general than the comic character; that is, it would have
to make the kind to which it belongs less obvious. Nevertheless, that small part of
the character that is worth showing must be drawn according to the universality that
Aristotle requires.[*]

And now we might pose the question of whether Diderot also wanted to be
understood in the same way. – Why not, if it were important to him never to find
himself in contradiction with Aristotle? It is of concern to me that two intelligent
minds do not say yes and no about the same matter, so I might be allowed to foist this
interpretation on him, to lend him this way out.

But rather let me speak briefly of this way out itself! – It seems to me it both is, and
is not, a way out. For the word *general* is taken to have two very different meanings.
The one which Hurd and Diderot deny to the tragic character is not the same as the
one affirmed for it by Hurd. Certainly the way out is based on this; but how, if the
one absolutely excludes the other?

In the first meaning, a *general* character is one in which what has been observed in
several or all individuals is pulled together; it is called, in a word, a *composite* character,
more the personified idea of a character than a characterized person. In the second
meaning, however, a *general* character is one in which a certain average or a certain
mean proportion has been taken from what has been observed in several or all individuals; it is called, in a word, a *common* character, of course not insofar as the character
itself is common but only insofar as it is common to a certain degree and measure.

Hurd is completely correct in explaining Aristotle's $\kappa\alpha\theta o\lambda ov$ as generality in
the second sense.[7] But then when Aristotle demands this generality both of the
comic character as well as the tragic, how is it possible that the same character
can at the same time also have generality in the first sense? How is it possible for
it to be simultaneously *composite* and *common*? And even granted such a character
were not a composite nearly to the degree of the characters in the Jonson play
that Hurd criticizes, granted that it would still bring to mind an individual and
that there were examples of its expression just as strongly and consistently in other
human beings: would it nevertheless not still be far more *uncommon* than Aristotle's
generality permits?[8]

That is the difficulty! – I remind my readers here that these pages are intended to
contain anything but a dramatic system. I am under no obligation to resolve all the
difficulties I pose. My thoughts might seem to become more and more disconnected,
they may even seem to contradict: they need only be thoughts that provide my readers material to think for themselves. Here I want nothing more than to disseminate
Fermenta cognitionis.[9]

---

* In calling the tragic character *particular*, I suppose it only *less representative* of the kind than the comic;
not that the draught of so much character as it is concerned to represent should not be *general*. [Hurd,
"Dissertation on the Provinces of Drama" 184 – Ed.]

Essay 96

1 April 1768[1]

On the fifty-second evening (Tuesday, the 28th of July), Herr Romanus's *The Brothers* was repeated.[2]

Or should I rather say, *The Brothers* of Herr Romanus? Namely, because of a comment made by Donatus on Terence's *Brothers*: "Hanc dicunt fabulam secundo loco actam, etiam tum rudi nomine poetae; itaque sic pronunciatam, Adelphoi Terenti, non Terenti Adelphoi, quod adhuc magis de fabulae nomine poeta, quam de poetae nomine fabula commendabatur."[3] Herr Romanus published his comedies without his name on them, and yet his name became known because of them. Even today, those plays of his that have retained their place in our theater spread his name to provinces of Germany where it would never have been heard without them. But what adverse fate discouraged this man, too, from continuing his work for the theater until his plays had ceased to recommend his name and his name would have recommended his plays instead?

The majority of what we Germans as yet have in the area of literature are attempts by young people.[4] Indeed, it is practically a universal prejudice among us that it is only fitting for young people to work in this field. It is said that men have more serious studies or more important business visited upon them by the church or state.[5] Verse and comedy are leisure activities; at best they are seen as somewhat useful etudes that a person might occupy himself with prior to his twenty-fifth year, at most. As soon as we approach the age of manhood, we are to devote all our energies to a useful profession; and if this profession leaves us some time to write, we should write only what compliments our dignity and our professional rank: a handsome compendium of the higher faculties, a solid chronicle of the beloved hometown, an edifying sermon, or the like.

From this it also follows that our literature has a youthful, nay even childish, aspect when compared not merely to the literature of antiquity, but to that of nearly all modern civilized nations, and it will continue so for a long, long time. It is not lacking in blood and life or color and passion, but it is very much lacking in vigor and nerve, pith and bones. Our literature still has so few works that a thinking man will gladly take up when he wants to rest and restore himself by ruminating beyond the monotonous, tedious compass of his daily business! What kind of nourishment can such a man find, for example, in our extremely trivial comedies? Puns, proverbs, the kind of little jokes one hears on the streets every day: such stuff may indeed cause laughter in the *parterre*, which enjoys itself as well as it can; but anyone who wants more than a belly laugh out of it, anyone who wants to laugh with his reason as well, will go there once and never return.

He who has nothing can give nothing. A young man just entering the world for the first time himself cannot possibly know the world and depict it. The greatest comic genius appears hollow and empty in his youthful works; even Menander's first plays, says Plutarch,* are not to be compared with his later and final plays.[6] But from these, he adds, we can deduce what he would have achieved had he lived longer. And

---

* *Επιτ. της συγκρισεως Αρις. και Μεναν.* p. 1588. Ed. Henr. Stephani.

how young do we think Menander was when he died? How many comedies do we think he wrote? No fewer than a hundred and five, and no younger than twenty-five.

None among all our deceased comic writers worth talking about reached that age; none of those currently living are yet so old; and none from either group has written a quarter as many plays. And therefore criticism should not find the same things to say about them as it did about Menander? – But it should just take the risk and speak!

And it is not only the authors who hear that criticism with displeasure. We now have, thanks be to heaven, a species of critics whose best criticism consists of making all criticism suspect.[7] "Genius! Genius!" they scream. "The genius defies all rules! What the genius creates is the rule!"[8] Thus they flatter the genius; I think it is so that we will take them all for geniuses, too. Yet they too clearly betray the fact that they do not feel even the least spark of it in themselves when they add, in the very same breath, that "rules oppress the genius!" – as if genius allowed itself to be oppressed by anything in the world! Much less by something that, as they themselves admit, is derived from genius itself. Not every critic is a genius, but every genius is a born critic. He has internalized a sample of all rules. He understands and keeps and follows only those that express his feeling in words. And this feeling of his, expressed in words, should be able to limit his activity? Rationalize with him about it as much as you want; he will only understand you insofar as he intuitively recognizes your general axioms in a unique context at a given moment, and only the memory of this unique case will remain for him, which can have no stronger or weaker effect on his powers as he works than can the memory of a felicitous example or of one of his own happy experiences. Thus to claim that rules and criticism can oppress genius is to claim, in different words, that example and practice can do the same; it means limiting genius not only to itself but even solely to its first attempt.

These wise gentlemen are no better at knowing what they want when they whine so comically over the unfavorable impression criticism makes on the adoring public. They would rather like to convince us that no person will find a butterfly colorful and beautiful anymore once the evil magnifying glass allows them to see that its colors are only dust.

"Our theater," they say, "is still at far too tender an age to be able to withstand the monarchical scepter of criticism. – It is almost more crucial to demonstrate the means by which the ideal can be achieved than to show how distant we remain from that ideal. – The theater must be reformed through examples, not through rules. – It is easier to reason than to invent on one's own."[9]

Does this amount to cloaking thoughts in words, or does it not rather amount to seeking thoughts for the words and failing to grasp any? – And who are these people who speak so much of examples and inventing on one's own? What kind of examples have they given? What have they themselves invented? – Clever minds! When they are presented with examples to judge, they prefer rules, and when they are to judge rules, they prefer to have examples. Instead of proving that a criticism is wrong, they prove that it is too severe and think they have dismissed it. Instead of disproving a line of reasoning, they note that inventing is more difficult than reasoning and think they have rebutted!

Anyone who reasons correctly also invents, and anyone who wants to invent must be able to reason. Only those who have no disposition to either believe that the one can be separated from the other.[10]

But why do I bother with these prattlers? I will go my own way, unconcerned about what the crickets chirp along the way. Taking even one step off the path to stomp on them is already too much. Their summer ends soon enough!

Thus, without further introduction, to the comments about Herr Romanus's *The Brothers* I promised on the occasion of its first performance![†] The most notable of these relate to the changes he thought necessary to make to Terence's plot in order to make it conform more closely to our own customs.

What is to be said in general about the necessity of these changes? If we have so little difficulty seeing Roman or Greek customs depicted in tragedy, why not also in comedy? Whence comes the rule, if it is a rule, of setting the scene of the former in a distant land, among a strange people, but the latter here in our native land?[11] Whence comes the obligation we impose upon the writer to depict as precisely as possible the customs of the people among whom he sets his action in the former, when we only demand the depiction of our own customs in the latter? "This appears, at first sight, whimsical and capricious," Pope says at one point, "but [it] has its foundation in nature. What we chiefly seek in comedy is a true image of life and *manners*; but we are not easily brought to think we have it given us, when dressed in foreign modes and fashions. And yet a good writer must follow his scene and observe decorum. On the contrary, 'tis the action in tragedy which most engages our attention. But to fit a domestic occurrence for the stage, we must take greater liberties with the action than a well-known story will allow."[12]

Essay 97

5 April 1768[1]

Strictly speaking, this resolution may not be satisfying in all plays.[2] Granted that foreign customs do not meet the aims of comedy as well as native customs, the question remains whether native customs do not also have a better relation to the aims of tragedy than foreign ones. This question cannot be answered merely by pointing to the difficulty of making a native incident suitable for the stage without noticeable and offensive changes. Certainly native customs require native incidents; if, however, tragedy achieves its aim most easily and surely by use of the former, then it surely must be better to overcome all the difficulties posed by the treatment of the latter than to fall short with regard to the most essential element, which is, unquestionably, its aim. Moreover, not all native incidents require such noticeable and offensive changes, and there is no obligation to work with those that do require them. Aristotle has already observed that there could be, and are, episodes that have come to pass exactly as the

[†] Essay 73, 234.

poet requires.[3] As those are very rare, however, he also concluded that the poet should be less worried about the minority of his audience that might have knowledge of the true circumstances than about falling short in the fulfillment of his duty.

The advantage that native customs have in comedy rests on our intimate acquaintance with them. The writer does not need to first make them known to us; he is relieved of all the necessary descriptions and hints pertaining to them; he can have his characters behave according to their customs right away without first having to give a tiresome description of the customs themselves. Native customs thus lighten his work and promote the illusion for his audience.

Now why should the tragic poet forgo this important double advantage? He, too, has reason to lighten his work as much as possible and not to waste his energy on secondary aims but to spare it wholly for the primary aim. For him, too, everything depends on the audience's illusion. – It could be answered here that tragedy does not have great need of customs, that it could be completely freed of them. But by this reasoning, it needs no foreign customs either; and it will always be better if the few customs it wishes to have and show are taken from native rather than foreign ones.

The Greeks, at any rate, never took anything but their own customs as a basis, not only in comedies but also in tragedies. In fact, they preferred to lend foreign peoples, from whose history they borrowed the material for their tragedies from time to time, their own Greek customs rather than weakening the effects of the stage through incomprehensible barbaric customs. They gave little or no importance to the illusion of historical fidelity, which is so anxiously recommended to our tragic writers. The most notable proof of this could be Aeschylus's *Persians*, and the reason why they felt themselves so little bound by historical fidelity is easy to infer from the aim of tragedy.[4]

But I am focusing too much on the very aspect of the problem that least concerns me here. Indeed, in claiming that native customs would also be more advantageous than foreign ones in tragedy, I am already taking for granted that they are so in comedy. And if they are, as at least I believe they are, then in general I cannot but approve of the changes that Herr Romanus made to Terence's play with respect to them.

He was right to rework a plot so tightly interwoven with customs that were peculiarly Greek and Roman. An example draws its power only from its internal probability, which each person judges according to his own sense of the familiar. All application disappears if we first must struggle to imagine ourselves in foreign circumstances. But such a reworking is no easy matter. The more perfect the plot, the less even the smallest part can be changed without destroying the whole. And fatal! – if one settles for mere patchwork instead of recreating in the real sense of the word.

The play is called *The Brothers*, and in Terence this was for two reasons.[5] Not only are the two old men, Micio and Demea, brothers; the two young ones, Aeschinus and Ctesipho, are as well. Demea is the father of these two; Micio has adopted one of them, Aeschinus, as his own son. Now, I do not understand why our author did not like this adoption. I do know that adoption still remains customary among us today, and fully on the same terms as it was among the Romans. Nevertheless, he departed from it: in his play there are only the two older brothers, and each has a son by birth that he raises according to his own methods. "But so much better!" you will probably say. For now the two old men are both also real fathers, and the play is really a "school for fathers," that is, for such fathers on whom nature has imposed paternal duties and not for those who have voluntarily undertaken those duties but fail to submit themselves further than serves their own comfort.[6]

Pater esse disce ab illis, qui vere *sciunt!*[7]

Very well! Only it is too bad that, as a result of the dissolution of this single knot – which in Terence binds Aeschinus and Ctesipho to each other and both to Demea, their father – the entire machine falls apart; and instead of a single, general interest we have two completely different ones that are held together merely by virtue of the writer's dexterity, and in no way by their own nature!

For if Aeschinus is not Micio's adopted son, but his son by birth, then why should Demea care so much about him? My brother's son does not concern me nearly as much as my own. If I discover that someone spoils my own son, even with the best intentions in the world, I would be right to confront this well-meaning corrupter with the same vehemence that Demea shows in confronting Micio in Terence's play. But if it is not my son, if it is the corruptor's own son, what more can I do, what more may I do, than warn this corruptor? And, if he is my brother, do so often and earnestly? Our author removes Demea from the relationship he has in Terence but leaves him the same storminess that only that relationship could justify. In fact, in his play Demea curses and rages with even more vexation than in Terence's. He wants to get really angry because "he must suffer dishonor and disgrace because of his brother's son."[8] But if his brother were to answer: "You are not very smart, my dear brother, if you think you could be exposed to dishonor and disgrace by my child. If my son is and remains a scoundrel, the misfortune as well as the disgrace remain mine alone. You may mean well with your zeal, but it goes too far, it offends me. If you are going to keep irritating me in this manner, then stay away from my house! etc." If, as I say, Micio were to give this answer, would the comedy not suddenly be over? Is it possible that Micio would not answer in this way? In fact, would he not actually have to answer this way?

How much more suitable is Demea's zealousness in Terence's play. This Aeschinus, whom he believes is leading such a debauched life, is still his son, even though his brother has adopted him as his own child. And nevertheless, the Roman Micio asserts his rights far more than the German Micio. He says, you have given your son over to me, take care of the one remaining to you:

[. . .] *nam ambos curare; propemodum*
reposcere illum est, quem dedisti [. . .][9]

This veiled threat, to give the son back, is also what silences him, and yet Micio cannot wish that it should stifle all his paternal feelings. It must certainly irritate Micio that, in what follows, Demea does not stop constantly rebuking him; but he also cannot blame the father for not wanting to let his son be ruined completely. In short, Terence's Demea is a man who is concerned for the well-being of the person nature charged him to care for; he doubtlessly goes about it in the wrong manner, but this manner does not diminish the reason. Our author's Demea, on the other hand, is a troublesome quarreler who believes kinship justifies all manner of incivilities that Micio would in no way have to tolerate from a mere brother.

Essay 98

8 April 1768[1]

The elimination of the doubled pairs of brothers also renders the relationship between the two young men cockeyed and false.[2] I hold it against the German Aeschinus that he "often believed he had to participate in Ctesipho's foolishness in order to wrest him, as his cousin, from public disgrace and danger."[*,3] What? His cousin? And is it really appropriate for his real father to respond: "I approve of the care and prudence you have shown in this, and I will not prohibit you going forward"?[4] What does the father not prohibit his son to do? To take part in the follies of a rowdy cousin? In fact, he should forbid him from doing that. He really ought to say to him: "Try to keep your cousin away from committing foolishness as much as possible. But if you find that he absolutely insists on it, then distance yourself from him, for your good name must be more precious to you than his is."

We only forgive a blood brother for going any further in this. Only with real brothers does it give us joy when one boasts of the other:

> [. . .] *Illius opera nunc vivo! Festivum caput,*
> *qui omnia sibi post putarit esse prae meo commodo:*
> *maledicta, famam, meum amorem & peccatum in se transtulit.*[5]

For we do not wish to see wisdom set any limits on brotherly love. Of course, it is true that our author knew how to spare his Aeschinus the foolishness that Terence's Aeschinus commits on behalf of his brother. He transformed a violent abduction into a little scuffle, in which his well-bred youth played no part other than wanting to prevent it. But nonetheless, he has this well-bred youth do far too much for a poorly raised cousin. Is it really likely he would ever allow his cousin to bring a little creature like Citalise into his house?[6] Into his father's house? Under the eyes of his virtuous beloved? It is not because of the seductive Damis,[†] that plague of young people, that the German Aeschinus allows his debauched cousin the use of his house; it simply serves the convenience of the writer.[7]

How perfectly this all is connected in Terence's play! How correctly and necessarily he motivates even the most trivial detail! Aeschinus takes by force, from the house of a slave trader, a girl his brother is in love with. But he does it less to accommodate his brother's desires than to prevent a greater evil. The slave trader wants to send the girl

---

[*] Act I, Sc. 3, p. 18.
[†] p. 30.

to a foreign market right away, and the brother wants to follow her; he would rather leave his fatherland than lose sight of the object of his love.‡·8 Aeschinus learns of this resolution in the nick of time. What should he do? He quickly seizes the girl and brings her into his uncle's house, in order to reveal the whole business to this good man. For the girl has been taken but her owner must still be paid. Micio pays without hesitation and rejoices – not over what the young men have done, but rather over the brotherly love he sees as the reason for their action and over the trust they have placed in him. The chief part is done; why should he not throw in a little something to give them a perfectly enjoyable day?

> [. . .] *argentum annumeravit ilico.*
> *dedit praeterea in sumptum dimidium minae.*9

He has bought the girl for Ctesipho; why shouldn't he allow him to enjoy himself with her in his house? According to the ancient customs, there is nothing here that contradicts virtue and respectability whatsoever.

But not so in our *Brothers*! The benevolent father's house is abused in the most unseemly manner. First, without his knowledge, but in the end, even with his consent. Citalise is a far more disreputable person than the *psaltria* in Terence, and our Ctesipho actually wants to marry her.10 If this is what the Terentian Ctesipho had planned with his *psaltria*, the Terentian Micio would have conducted himself very differently in the affair. He would have shown Citalise the door and would have come to an agreement with the father on the most powerful means to keep such a wantonly emancipated boy in check.

In general, the German Ctesipho is depicted as far too corrupt from the very beginning, and here, too, our author has departed from his model. The passage where he converses with his cousin about his father always makes me shudder.§·11

LEANDER: But how does that accord with the respect and love you owe your father?

LYCAST: Respect? Love? Hm! He had better not ask those of me.

LEANDER: He should not ask them of you?

LYCAST: No, certainly not. I am not fond of my father. I would be lying if I said so.

LEANDER: Callous son! You are not thinking through what you are saying. Not to love the one who gave you life! You may say such things now, while he is still alive. But once you have lost him, then I will ask you again.

LYCAST: Hm! I don't exactly know what would happen then. In any case, I would probably still not actually be wrong. For I think he would not do any better. He says to me nearly every day: "If I were only rid of you! If you were only gone!" You call that love? Can you ask me to love him back?

---

‡ Act 2, Sc. 4.
  AES: hoc mihi dolet, nos paene sero scisse et paene in eum locum
  redisse ut, si omnes cuperent, nil tibi possent auxiliarier.
  CTE: pudebat.
  AES: ah! stultitiast istaec, non pudor. tam ob parvulam
  rem paene e patria! turpe dictu. deos quaeso ut istaec prohibeant.
§ Act 1, Sc. 6.

Even the strictest discipline would not tempt a child to such unnatural attitudes. The heart that, for whatever reason, is capable of such attitudes deserves to be treated like a slave. If we are to take the part of the debauched son against the strict father, then his excesses must not reveal a heart that is fundamentally wicked; they must be nothing but excesses of temperament, youthful indiscretions, follies of caprice and willfulness. Terence and Menander depicted their Ctesipho according to this principle.[12] No matter how strictly his father treats him, not a single malicious word against his father escapes his lips. And he makes up for the single instance that could be seen as such in the most excellent manner. He would like to enjoy his lover in peace for at least a couple of days; he rejoices that his father is back at work in the country and hopes that he tires himself out, that he tires himself so much that he will not be able to get out of bed for three whole days. A rash wish! But we see what he adds:

> [. . .] *utinam quidem!*
> *quod cum salute ejus fiat, ita se defetigarit velim*
> *ut triduo hoc perpetuo prorsum e lecto nequeat surgere.*[13]

Quod cum salute ejus fiat! As long as he doesn't come to any harm! – So right! So right, kind young man! Always go where joy and love call you. For you, we gladly turn a blind eye! The wickedness you commit will not be very wicked! You have a stricter overseer in yourself than your father ever was! – And there are several lines of this type in the scene from which this passage is taken. The German Ctesipho is a cunning knave, comfortable with lies and deceit; the Roman, on the other hand, is thrown into utter confusion by a small subterfuge he could use to justify his absence to his father:

CTE: rogitabit me: ubi fuerim? quem ego hodie toto non vidi die.
    quid dicam?
SYR: nilne in mentemst?
CTE: numquam quicquam.
SYR: tanto nequior.
    cliens, amicus, hospes nemost vobis?
CTE: sunt. quid postea?
SYR: hisce opera ut data sit?
CTE: quae non data sit? non potest fieri.[14]

That naïve, truthful "quae non data sit!" The good young man seeks an excuse, and the mischievous servant proposes that he lie. A lie! No, that can't be done: "non potest fieri!"

Essay 99

12 April 1768[1]

Consequently, Terence did not have to depict his Ctesipho as ashamed at the end of the play and thereby on the path to improvement.[2] But this is exactly what our author had to do. I only fear that the spectator cannot take the groveling repentance and the fearful submission of such a reckless delinquent seriously. And likewise, his father's change of heart. Both of these reversals are so little grounded in their characters that we feel a bit too keenly the writer's need to find an end to his play and his difficulty in finding a better way to end it. – I have no idea where so many comic writers have derived the rule that at the end of the play the wicked must necessarily either be punished or improve themselves. This rule might be more pertinent to tragedy: there, it can reconcile us with fate and turn discontent into compassion. But I think that in comedy, it not only fails to help but rather spoils a great deal. At the very least, it makes the outcome awkward, cold, and dull. If the various characters I assemble in a play just bring that play to an end, why should they not remain as they were? But of course the action must consist of something more than simply a collision of characters. Such an action can only end with some of these characters giving in and changing; and a play that has little or nothing more than this does not approach its end so much as gradually drift off. If, on the other hand, that collision persists with the same intensity even as the plot approaches its end, then it is easy to see that the ending can be just as lively and entertaining as the middle was. And that is precisely the difference between Terence's final act and the final act of our author. As soon as we hear, in the latter, that the strict father has discovered the truth, we can count the rest on our fingers, for this is, after all, the fifth act. At first he will rant and rave; then he will allow himself to be placated, recognize his wrongs, and want to change so that he will never again be able to provide material for such a comedy. Likewise, the wayward son will come, apologize, promise to improve – in short, everything will be hunky-dory. In contrast, I would like to see the person who can predict all of the twists and turns in Terence's fifth act! The intrigue is long over, but the continuing play among the characters lets us hardly see that the end is near. No one changes, but each reins in the other just enough to keep him safe from the disadvantages of excess. Through the stingy Demea's maneuvering, the free-spending Micio is brought to a point where he himself recognizes the extravagance of his conduct, and asks:

Quod proluvium? quae istaec subita est largitas?[3]

Just as, vice versa, the strict Demea is led by the accommodating Micio to finally recognize that it is not enough always to criticize and punish, but it is also good "obsecundare in loco."[4]

I want to bring up just one more small matter by which our author, once again to his own disadvantage, has distanced himself from his model.

Terence himself says that he took an episode from a play by Diphilus and brought it into Menander's *Brothers*, and thus put *his* play together.[5] This episode is the violent abduction of the *psaltria* by Aeschinus, and Diphilus's play was called *The Dying Companions.*[6]

Synapothnescontes Diphili comoedia est [. . .]
in Graeca adulescens est qui lenoni eripit
meretricem in prima fabula [. . .]

[. . .] eumhic locum sumpsit sibi
in Adelphos [. . .][7]

Judging from these two circumstances, Diphilus wanted to present a pair of lovers who were firmly resolved to die with each other rather than allow themselves to be parted; and who knows what might have happened if a friend had not intervened and abducted the girl for her lover? Terence toned down the decision to die together by making it simply a decision on the part of the lover to follow the girl, abandoning father and fatherland for her. Donatus says this expressly: "Menander mori illum voluisse fingit, Terentius fugere."[8] But shouldn't it say *Diphilus* instead of *Menander* in Donatus's comment? Most certainly, as Peter Nannius has already noted.*·[9] For the poet, as we have seen, says himself that he has borrowed this whole episode of the abduction not from Menander but from Diphilus, and Diphilus's play even speaks of dying in his title.

Meanwhile, of course, in place of this abduction borrowed from Diphilus, there must have been some other intrigue that Aeschinus similarly took part in on behalf of Ctesipho and through which he aroused the very suspicion in his beloved that in the end successfully hastened their union. What this consisted of is hard to guess. Whatever it was, it most certainly would have taken place just before the beginning of the play, just like the abduction Terence uses for the same purpose. For this must have been what everyone was talking about as Demea came into the city; this, too, must have been the instigation and matter over which Demea begins the argument with his brother right at the beginning, and in which both of their dispositions are developed so splendidly:

[. . .] nam illa quae antehac facta sunt
omitto: modo quid dissignavit? [. . .]
fores effregit atque in aedis irruit
alienas [. . .]
[. . .] clamant omnes indignissume
factum esse. hoc advenienti quot mihi, Micio,
dixere! in orest omni populo, denique.[10]

Now I have already said that our author changed this violent abduction into a little scuffle. He may have had his good reasons for doing so – if only he had not had this scuffle itself happen so late. In and of itself, this should have been and must have been what infuriates the strict father. In this play, however, he is enraged already before the scuffle even happens, and we have no idea why. He comes on stage and quarrels without the least cause. He does say: "Everyone is talking about the bad conduct of your

---

* *Sylloge v. Miscell. cap. 10*: "Videat quaeso accuratus lector, num pro Menandro legendum sit Diphilus. Certe vel tota Comoedia, vel pars istius argumenti, quod hic tractatur, ad verbum e Diphilo translata est. – Ita cum Diphili comoedia a commoriendo nomen habeat, & ibi dicatur adolescens mori voluisse, quod Terentius in fugere mutavit: omnino adducor, eam imitationem a Diphilo, non a Menandro mutuatam esse, & ex eo commoriendi cum puella studio Synapothnescontes nomen fabulae inditum esse."

son; I barely set foot in the city and I get a ghastly surprise."[11] But just what all these people are talking about, what this shock he has gotten consists of, and why he has expressly come to quarrel with his brother – we do not hear any of this, and we cannot divine it from the play, either. In short, our author could certainly have changed the circumstance that gets Demea up in arms, but he should not have moved it! At the very least, if he did want to move it, then in the first act he should have had Demea gradually express his dissatisfaction over his brother's method of raising his son and not have him explode with it all at once.

If only those plays by Menander that Terence used had come down to us! I can think of nothing that would be more instructive than a comparison of these Greek originals with their Latin copies.

For it is certain that Terence was no slavish translator. Even where he retained in their totality all the threads of Menander's play, he still allowed himself some small additions, some amplifications or attenuations of this or that feature; Donatus indicates various instances of this in his *Scholia*.[12] It is only a shame that Donatus always writes of these so succinctly and often so opaquely (because in his time Menander's plays themselves were still in everyone's hands), so that it becomes difficult to say anything authoritative about the value or worthlessness of such Terentian refinements. A noteworthy example of this can be found in *The Brothers*.

Essay 100

15 April 1768[1]

As we have observed, in the fifth act Demea wants to teach Micio a lesson in his own manner.[2] He pretends to be fun-loving so that the others frolic in real excesses and follies; he plays the spendthrift, but with his brother's purse, not his own; and he would like to ruin him in a single blow, just to have the vicious pleasure of being able to say at the end: "Now look what your generosity has gotten you!" As long as the honest Micio only spends his own fortune, we can be somewhat amused by the malicious fun. But then the traitor gets the idea of setting up our good old confirmed bachelor with a decrepit old biddy. Just the thought makes us laugh at first, but when we finally see that it is serious, that Micio is really getting caught in a noose that he could have avoided with a single serious turn – in truth, we hardly know anymore who piques us more, Demea or Micio.*[3]

DEMEA: Yes indeed, this is my will. From now on, these good people belong to our family; we must help them, join with them in every way.
AESCHINUS: Please, father.
MICIO: I am not at all opposed to that.
DEMEA: There is no better thing for us to do. – First of all, she is his wife's mother –

---

* Act 5, Sc. 8 [Terence, *Adelphi/The Brothers* 2: 356–60 – Ed.]
   DEM: Ego vero iubeo et hac re et aliis omnibus

MICIO: Yes, so what?

DEMEA: She's honest, respectable –

MICIO: So I hear.

DEMEA: She's also getting on in years.

MICIO: That's true.

---

quam maxume unam facere nos hanc familiam,
colere, adiuvare, adiungere.
AES: ita quaeso, pater.
MIC: haud aliter censeo.
DEM: immo hercle ita nobis decet.
primum huius uxorist mater.
MIC: est. quid postea?
DEM: proba et modesta.
MIC: ita aiunt.
DEM: natu grandior.
MIC: scio.
DEM: parere iamdiu haec per annos non potest,
nec qui eam respiciat quisquamst. solast.
MIC: quam hic rem agit?
DEM: hanc te aequomst ducere, et te operam ut fiat dare.
MIC: me ducere autem?
DEM: te.
MIC: me?
DEM: te. inquam.
MIC: ineptis.
DEM: si tu sis homo,
hic faciat.
AES: mi pater!
MIC: quid tu autem huic, asine, auscultas?
DEM: nil agis.
fieri aliter non potest.
MIC: deliras.
AES: sine te exorem, mi pater.
MIC: insanis, aufer!
DEM: age, da veniam filio.
MIC: satin sanus es?
ego novos maritus anno demum quinto et sexagensumo
fiam atque anum decrepitam ducam? idne estis auctores mihi?
AES: fac. promisi ego illis.
MIC: promisti autem? de te largitor, puer.
DEM: age, quid si quid te maius oret?
MIC: quasi non hoc sit maxumum.
DEM: da veniam.
AES: ne gravare.
DEM: fac, promitte.
MIC: non omittitis?
AES: non, nisi te exorem.
MIC: vis est haec quidem.
DEM: age prolixe, Micio.
MIC: etsi hoc mihi pravom, ineptum absurdum atque alienum a vita mea
videtur, si vos tanto opere istuc voltis, fiat.

DEMEA: She's long past the age where she can have any more children. And there's
nobody looking after her, she's completely alone.

MICIO: What is he getting at?

DEMEA: The right thing for you to do, brother, is marry her. And you (*to Aeschinus*)
must get him to do it.

MICIO: Me? Marry her?

DEMEA: You!

MICIO: Me?

DEMEA: You! As I said, you!

MICIO: You are out of your mind.

DEMEA *to Aeschinus*: Now show what you can do. He must!

AESCHINUS: Father –

MICIO: What? – And you, you coxcomb, are with him on this?

DEMEA: It's no use protesting. It can't be otherwise.

MICIO: You're out of your mind.

AESCHINUS: Let yourself be persuaded, father.

MICIO: Have you gone mad? Get out of here!

AESCHINUS: Come on, make your son happy!

MICIO: Have you completely lost your mind? Me, marry at sixty-five? And marry a
decrepit old woman to boot? You're expecting me to go through with this?

AESCHINUS: Do it, I promised them.

MICIO: You promised them, did you? – Promise what you want on your own behalf,
laddie.

DEMEA: Well! And if he were asking you for something even more important?

MICIO: As if there could be something more important than this?

DEMEA: So agree with him, then.

AESCHINUS: Don't oppose us!

DEMEA: Come on, promise!

MICIO: How long can this go on?

AESCHINUS: Until you say yes.

MICIO: But this means you're forcing me!

DEMEA: Go beyond your duty, good Micio.

MICIO: Well, then – even though I find this very unjust and vulgar, and even though
it goes against both my reason and my way of life – since you both insist on it
so much, so be it!

"No," says the critic, "that is too much!"[4] The Poet's conduct here is justly liable to
censure: the only consideration that can be urged in his defence is, that he meant to
shew the inconveniences arising from too unbounded a good-nature. But Micio has
all along been represented so agreeable, and possessed of so much judgment, good
sense, and knowledge of the world, that this last piece of extravagance must shock
probability, and offend the delicacy of the spectator. Thus, as already noted: the poet
is to be censured, he is by all means to be censured!"[5]

But which poet? Terence, or Menander? Or both? – Colman, the recent English
translator of Terence, wants to shove the majority of the blame onto Menander,

believing he can prove by way of one of Donatus's comments that Terence very much tempered the inconsistency of his original, at least in this scene.[6] Donatus says: "Apud Menandrum senex de nuptiis non gravatur. Ergo Terentius *ευρητικως*."[7]

"It is surprising," Colman declares, "that none of the criticks [sic] on this passage have taken notice of this observation of Donatus, especially as our loss of Menander makes it rather curious. It is plain that Terence in the plan of this last act followed Menander: and in the present circumstance though he has adopted the absurdity of marrying Micio to the old lady, yet we learn from Donatus that he rather improved on his original by making Micio express a repugnance to such a match, which it seems he did not in the play of Menander."[8]

We cannot exclude the possibility that, for once, a Roman poet could have done something better than a Greek one. But the fact that it is possible does not incline me to want to believe it.

Colman also claims that Donatus's words "Apud Menandrum senex de nuptiis non gravatur" mean "in Menander's play the old man does not protest against the marriage." But how, when they do not mean that? When they would better be translated: "in Menander's play the old man does not find the thought of marriage so burdensome?" "Nuptias gravari" would indeed certainly mean the former, but would "de nuptiis gravari" as well? In the first figure of speech "gravari" is used, so to speak, as a deponent verb;[9] in the second, however, it is really much more a passive verb, and as such not only tolerates my interpretation but perhaps cannot tolerate any other but mine.[10]

If this were so: how would things then stand with Terence? He would not have improved his original but rather made it worse; he would not have tempered all the absurdity over Micio's betrothal through the refusal but would himself have invented it. "Terentius *ευρητικως*!"[11] It's just that creative efforts by imitators fall so short!

Essays 101, 102, 103, and 104

19 April 1768[1]

One hundred and first through one hundred and fourth? – I had intended for the year's run of these pages to consist of just a hundred essays. To be sure, fifty-two weeks and two essays a week come out to a hundred and four. But why should the weekly journalist alone among all wage-workers get no holidays? And just four in a year, that's hardly any!

But Dodsley and Company have explicitly promised the public, in my name, a hundred and four essays.[2] I must not make these good people liars.

The only question is: how do I best begin? – The material is already cut; I'll have to either patch it or stretch it. – But that sounds so amateurish. I have an idea that should have occurred to me right away: it is the actor's custom of having a small afterpiece that follows the main performance. The afterpiece can be about anything at all, and it does not have to have any connection with what preceded it. – Such an afterpiece, then, shall fill the pages I wanted to spare myself.

First a word about myself! For why shouldn't an afterpiece be permitted a prologue, starting with a "poeta cum primum animum ad scribendum appulit"?[3]

When, some time ago, a few good people here had the idea of trying to see whether something more could be done for the German theater than could happen under the direction of a so-called principal, they thought of me – I have no idea why – and allowed themselves to dream that I could somehow be useful to this undertaking.[4] – I was just standing idly by in the marketplace; no one wanted to hire me, doubtless because no one knew what to do with me, except these friends![5] – Thus far, no occupation has really held much interest for me. I have never asked for or even offered my services for anything; but at the same time I have never rejected out of hand anything for which I am believed to be well-matched.

Did I want to contribute to the improvement of the theater here? That was easily answered. My only reservations were whether I could and how I might best do so.

I am neither an actor nor a playwright.

It is true I am sometimes accorded the honor of being identified as the latter. But only because I am misjudged. One ought not to draw such a generous conclusion from the few attempts at drama I have ventured. Not everyone who takes up a brush and spreads a bunch of color around is a painter. The oldest attempts were written at that time of life in which we so willingly mistake delight and prolific ease for genius. All that is tolerable in my more recent attempts is due, I am well aware, to criticism alone. I do not feel in myself the living spring that works its way up by virtue of its own energy and bursts forth, under its own force, in such rich, fresh, and pure streams.[6] I have to force everything up and out of myself with the use of pumps and pipes. I would be very poor, cold, and shortsighted had I not to some extent learned how to unobtrusively borrow foreign treasures, warm myself at foreign fires, and strengthen my eyes through the glasses of art. As such, I was always ashamed or upset when I read or heard something against criticism. It was said to stifle genius, and yet I flattered myself that I had obtained from it something that comes very near to genius. I am a lame man who cannot possibly be edified by an invective against crutches.[7]

Yet, of course, just as crutches can help a lame man move from one place to another but cannot turn him into a runner, so it is with criticism. If, with its help, I can bring something into being that is better than what someone with my talents would do without criticism, yet nonetheless it costs me too much time; I must be free of other business and uninterrupted by external distractions, I must have all my reading at the ready, and I must, at every step, be able to calmly rifle through all of the observations I have ever made regarding customs and passions. As such, no one in the world could be less suited than I to labor to entertain the theater with novelty.

I must therefore take a pass at doing for the German theater what Goldoni did for the Italian in enriching it with thirteen new plays in one year.[8] Indeed, I would take a pass at it even if I could do it. I am more distrustful of first thoughts than even de la Casa or the old Shandy ever were.[9] For even if I do not take them to be the temptations of the evil one,*[,10] whether we take that literally or allegorically, I still believe that first

---

* "An opinion *John de la Casa*, archbishop of Benevento, was afflicted with – which opinion was, – that whenever a Christian was writing a book (not for his private amusement, but) where his intent and purpose was bona fide, to print and publish it to the world, his first thoughts were always the temptations of the evil one. – My father was hugely pleased with this theory of John de la Casa; and (had it not cramped him a little in his creed) I believe would have given ten of the best acres in the Shandy

thoughts are the first, and that the best does not always tend to float on the top of every soup. My first thoughts are surely not a jot better than the average man's; and the wise thing for the average man to do with those first thoughts is to keep them under wraps.

At last someone hit upon the idea of using me for the very thing that makes me such a slow, or – as it seems to my more energetic friends – lazy worker: criticism. And thus originated the idea for this journal.

I liked this idea. It reminded me of the *didaskalia* of the Greeks, that is, of the short reports, which even Aristotle thought worthwhile to write, about the plays of the Greek stage. It reminded me of how I once long ago laughed to myself at the highly learned Casaubon, who, out of deep respect for concrete knowledge, imagined that Aristotle primarily wrote his *didaskalia* in order to rectify the chronology.[†,11] – Truly, it would have been an eternal disgrace to Aristotle if he had concerned himself more with the poetic value of the plays, with their influence on morals, and with the education of taste than with the year of the Olympiad, the Olympiad itself, and the names of the Archons under whom those plays were first performed![12]

I had the intention of calling this journal the "Hamburg Didaskalia." But this title sounded too foreign to me, and now I am very glad that I preferred the present one. What I wanted to include or not include in a Dramaturgy was up to me; at least Lione Allacci had nothing to dictate to me on the subject.[13] But the scholars claim to know what a *didaskalia* ought to look like, even if it is only from Terence's extant *Didascaliae*, which Casaubon called "brevitur & eleganter scriptas."[14] I had no desire to write my Didaskalia either so briefly or elegantly, and our present-day Casaubons would certainly have shaken their heads when they discovered how seldom I commemorated some chronological incident that could, one day in the future, shed light on some historical fact when millions of other books had been lost. In which year of the reign of Louis XIV or Louis XV, and whether in Paris or at Versailles, and whether in the presence of blood royalty or not, this or that French masterpiece was first performed – they would have searched for this in my work and, to their great astonishment, not have found it.

I explained in my Notice what these pages were rather to be; my readers will know what they have actually become. Not exactly what I promised to make them: something else, but yet, I think, nothing worse.

"It will follow every step here that is relevant to the art of both the writer and the actor."[15]

I very quickly grew weary of the last part. We have actors, but no art of acting.[16] If there ever were such an art, it is gone; we have lost it; it must be entirely reinvented.

---

estate, to have been the broacher of it; – but as he could not have the honour of it in the literal sense of the doctrine, he took up with the allegory of it. Prejudice of education, he would say, is the devil &c." (*Life and Op. of Tristram Shandy* Vol. V. p. 74).

† (*Animadv. in Athenaeum* Libr. VI. cap. 7) "Διδασκαλια accipitur pro eo scripto, quo explicatur ubi, quando, quomodo & quo eventu fabula aliqua fuerit acta. – Quantum critici hac diligentia veteres chronologos adjuverint, soli aestimabunt illi, qui norunt quam infirma & tenula praesidia habuerint, qui ad ineundam fugacis temporis rationem primi animum appulerunt. Ego non dubito, eo potissimum spectasse Aristotelem, cum Διδασκαλιας suas componeret."

There is plenty of general commentary on the subject in many languages; but specific, universally acknowledged rules that are clearly and precisely formulated and by which the criticism or praise of an actor in any particular case may be justified? Of these I can think of perhaps two or three. That is why all arguments on this subject seem dithering and ambivalent; that is why it is really not surprising that the actor with a successful career may find himself injured from all sides. He will believe himself criticized too much and never praised enough; all too often, he will not even know for certain whether someone intends to criticize or praise him. It has long been noted overall that the sensitivity of artists with regard to criticism increases in exact proportion to the decrease in the certainty and clarity and number of principles of their art. – So much for my excuses, on my own account and on account of those without whom I would not have to excuse myself.

But the first part of my promise? With regard to that, admittedly, the "here" has not much come into consideration – and how could it have? The gates had hardly opened, and people already wanted to see the competitors at their goal, a goal that continually got set farther and farther away.[17] When the public asks: "so what has really taken place?" and answers itself with a sarcastic, "nothing," then I ask in reply: "and what has the public done, then, to make it possible for something to happen?" Also nothing, and in fact, something even worse than nothing. The public not only did not encourage the work, it didn't even allow it to run its natural course. – And about the well-intentioned idea of creating a national theater for the Germans, when we Germans are not yet a nation! I am not talking about our political constitution but rather simply about our moral character. You could almost say this consists of: not wanting to have one of our own at all. We remain the sworn imitators of everything foreign and in particular the subservient admirers of the never sufficiently admired French. Everything that comes to us from that side of the Rhine is beautiful, charming, lovely, divine; we would rather deny our sight and hearing than find it otherwise; we would rather be persuaded to take clumsiness for spontaneity, insolence for grace, grimaces for expression, a jingle of rhyme for poetry, and howling for music than have the least doubt about the share of superiority in everything that is good and beautiful and noble and proper that this amiable nation, this first among all nations in the world (as it likes to call itself so very modestly), has received from a just Fate –

But this platitude is so trite, and its closer application could so easily become bitter, that I would rather cease now.

Thus, instead of tracing here the steps that the art of playwriting actually could have taken, I was compelled to dwell on those it would preliminarily have to take in order to be able to run its course with bigger and faster steps in the end. They were steps a lost man had to retrace in order to return to the right path and refocus upon his goal.

Everyone has the right to boast of his diligence: I believe I have studied the art of dramatic writing, studied it more than twenty who practice it. Moreover, I have practiced it as much as is needed to be permitted to have a judgment in the matter, for I know very well that, just as it is with the painter who does not like to be criticized by anyone who has no idea how to use a brush, so it is with the writer, too. I have at least made an attempt at what he must carry out and, though I cannot do it, I can still make a judgment about whether or not it can be done at all. I demand just a voice in this company, where so many who claim one would be more silent than fish if they had not learned to parrot what this or that foreigner had said.

But a person can study – and indeed study himself deeply – into error. What reassures me that this has not happened to me, that I do not misunderstand the essence of the art of playwriting, is that I understand it exactly as Aristotle abstracted it from countless masterpieces of the Greek stage. I have my own thoughts about the origin and foundation of this philosopher's *Poetics* that I could not express here without going on too long. Nevertheless, I do not hesitate to admit (even if I should be ridiculed for it in these enlightened times!) that I consider it to be just as infallible a work as Euclid's *Elements*.[18] Its principles are just as true and certain, if not as easy to comprehend, and as a result they are more susceptible to chicanery than anything contained in that latter work. In particular, with regard to tragedy, which is the subject by Aristotle that time has best preserved for us, I venture to prove incontrovertibly that we cannot distance ourselves the least bit from Aristotle's guiding principles without distancing ourselves just as much from perfection.

Armed with this conviction, I set out to assess some of the most famous examples of French theater in detail. For this theater was supposedly formed entirely according to Aristotle's rules; and in particular, this theater wanted to convince us Germans that it was only through observance of these rules that it attained that height of perfection from which it looks so far down on the theater of all other modern nations. And we have long believed this so firmly that, among our writers, imitating the French and writing according to the rules of antiquity have become one and the same thing.

Nevertheless, the prejudice could not hold up forever against our instincts. Happily, these were awakened from their slumber by some English plays, and we finally discovered that tragedy was capable of a completely different effect than the one Corneille and Racine wanted to assign it. But blinded by this sudden ray of truth, we rebounded against the edge of another precipice. Certain rules that had been made so familiar to us by the French plays were too obviously lacking in the English ones. What conclusion was drawn from this? This: that even without these rules, the aim of tragedy could be achieved, that in fact these rules could likely be at fault if one did not quite achieve that aim.

And that could have sufficed! – But people started mixing up *these* rules with *all* rules and declared that stipulating what genius should and should not do was simply pedantry. In short, we were at the point of willfully forfeiting all knowledge from past times and demanding that each writer reinvent the art for himself from scratch.

I would be all too vain in crediting myself with having done some good for our theater if I were to believe I had hit upon the only means for inhibiting this fermentation of taste.[19] I can at least flatter myself that I have worked toward that, insofar as nothing was more important to me than challenging the French theater's obsession with rules. No other nation has more misunderstood the rules of ancient drama than the French. They mistook as essential some of Aristotle's passing observations regarding the most fitting external constitution of the drama, and thereby they so enfeebled what was essential through various restrictions and interpretations that nothing could develop other than works that remained distant from the highest effect, which was the basis on which the philosopher had devised his rules.

I will dare to say something here that you can take as you like! – Name me one play by the great Corneille that I could not do better. How much do you want to bet? –

But no, I do not want anyone to take this for boasting. So take careful note of what I add: I will do it better for certain – and yet still be no Corneille – and yet still not have written a masterpiece. I will do it better for certain – and yet pride myself little on it. I will have done nothing more than anyone else can do – anyone who has as much faith in Aristotle as I do.

A barrel for our critical whales![20] I rejoice in advance over how splendidly they will play with it. It has been thrown out just for them alone, in particular for the little whale in Halle's briny waters.[21]

And with this segue – it need not be any more clever – I shall allow the serious tone of the prologue to dissolve into that of the afterpiece for which I reserved these last pages. And who else could have reminded me that it was time to begin this afterpiece, other than that Herr *Stl.*, who just announced its content in the *German Library* of Herr Privy Councilor *Klotz*? –‡.[22]

But then what does the buffoon in the colorful little jacket get for being so obliging with his drum?[23] I do not recall that I promised him anything for it. He may simply drum for his own pleasure, and heaven knows where he gets all the things that the amiable young men in the streets who follow him with an admiring "Ah!" learn from him at first hand. He must have the spirit of divination, in spite of the maid in the story of the apostle.[24] For who else could have told him that the author of the *Dramaturgy* and its publisher are one and the same?[25] Who else could have uncovered to him the secret reasons why I attributed a sonorous voice to one actress and so extolled the work of another?[26] Admittedly, I was in love with both of them at the time, but I would never have thought a living soul could guess it. The ladies could not possibly have told him themselves, either, so I must be right about the spirit of divination. Indeed, woe to us poor writers when our noble gentlemen, the journalists and periodical writers, wish to plow with such calves![27] When, in forming their judgments, they not only draw on their customary learnedness and perspicacity but also avail themselves of little tricks drawn from the most secret magic – who can stand against them?

Inspired by his goblin, Herr *Stl.* writes: "I would also be able to advertise the second volume of the *Dramaturgy* if the author's treatise against the booksellers was not keeping him so busy that he could not finish the work on time."[28]

One should not call a goblin a liar when he really isn't one. What that evil thing has put into Herr *Stl.*'s head here is not entirely false. In fact, I had such a project in mind. I wanted to tell my readers why this work was interrupted so often, why it was only after two years, and with much trouble to boot, that I finished what I had promised to do in one year. I wanted to complain about piracy, by means of which they hit upon the most direct way to suffocate it at birth.[29] I wanted to make some observations about the adverse consequences of piracy in general. I wanted to propose the only way to prevent it.[30] – But would that then have been a treatise against the booksellers? Much rather one in their favor, at least for the upright men among them,

‡ Vol 9, p. 60.

and there are some. My good Herr *Stl.*, do not always trust your goblin so completely! You can see: such a hostile vermin only knows half of what it seems to know about the future. –

But now enough of answering the fool according to his folly, lest he think himself wise.[31] For the very same person says: do not answer the fool according to his folly, or you yourself will be just like him![32] That is: do not answer him according to his folly in such a way that the matter itself is forgotten in the process, for this would make you just like him. And so now I turn again to my serious reader, from whom I seriously beg pardon for these buffooneries.

It is the absolute truth: the only reason the issuance of these pages was hitherto so delayed, and why it will now cease completely, is the piracy that was intended to make them more available for common use. Before I say another word about this, allow me to put aside the suspicion of my own self-interest. The theater itself advanced the expenses for the work, in the hope of regaining at least a sizable portion from its sale.[33] I don't lose anything if this hope comes to naught. Moreover, I am not in the least bothered by the fact that I can no longer bring forth the material I gathered for its continuation. I remove my hand from this plow as gladly as I laid my hand to it. Klotz and company nevertheless wish I had never laid my hand to it, and we can easily find one among them who will keep the daily log of an unsuccessful enterprise to its end and show me what kind of *periodical use* I could and should have conferred upon such a *periodical paper*.

For I neither can nor wish to hide the fact that these last lines have been written nearly a year later than the date indicates. The sweet dream of founding a National Theater here in Hamburg has once again evaporated, and as far as I now can tell about this place, it may actually be the last place where such a dream will be realized.

But that, too, makes no difference to me! – In general, I would not want to give the impression that I consider it a great misfortune when endeavors in which I have taken part have been thwarted. The very fact that I took part in them indicates that they cannot have been of any special importance. But what if endeavors of broader importance could fail through the same hostilities that made mine fail? The world loses nothing because I was only able to bring two volumes of *Dramaturgy* to light instead of five or six. But it could lose something if someday a more useful work by a better writer were brought to a similar standstill, and if there really were people who expressly formed a plan so that even the most useful work initiated under similar circumstances should, and necessarily must, meet with failure.

In respect thereof, I do not hesitate, and consider it my duty, to denounce a particular conspiracy to the public. This very Dodsley and Company who took the liberty of pirating the *Dramaturgy* have for some time been circulating among the booksellers a written and printed document that reads, word for word:

Message to the messrs. Booksellers

With the assistance of various Gentleman Booksellers we have decided to forbid self-publishing from now on to those (like, for example, those several supposed businesses newly established in Hamburg and other places) who want to mingle in the book trade without the requisite qualifications, and we will reprint them without exception.[34] In addition, we will consistently reduce their established prices by half. These booksellers, who have joined this resolution and who have recognized that this kind of unauthorized interference would necessarily be detrimental to all booksellers, have resolved to establish a fund to support this proposal; to this end, they have already laid aside a goodly sum of money, with the request that they initially not be named, and yet at the same time with the promise to support it further. We anticipate the same toward the increase of the fund from the remaining group of well-intentioned booksellers, and we also highly recommend the services of our publishing house. We are unsurpassed with regard to quality of paper and printing; moreover, we will take care to keep a sharp eye on the countless number of blackmarketeers, to prevent each and every one from meddling and interfering in the book trade. We and the colleagues who have already joined us promise this much: that we will not reprint a single page from a legitimate bookseller without permission; but at the same time, we will be vigilant to ensure that as soon as a book is reprinted without permission from someone in our group, retaliatory measures will be inflicted not only on the illegitimate printers but also, and in no less measure, on those booksellers who undertake to sell their publications. We thus most respectfully request each and every one of the booksellers to get rid of every type of unauthorized reprint within one year after we have advertised the names of the Booksellers' Society membership, or to expect to see their own best publications sold at half price or far less. For those booksellers who are members of our group and from whom something might be pirated, we will provide a sizeable recompense based on the proportion and proceeds of the fund. And thus we hope that, with the assistance of well-meaning booksellers, any remaining impropriety in the book trade will quickly subside.

If circumstances permit, we will all come ourselves each year to the Easter book fair in Leipzig, and if not, we will still in that case give a commission. We commend ourselves to your good thoughts and remain your faithful colleagues,

J. Dodsley and Company

If this document contained nothing but an invitation to a more precise agreement among the booksellers, in order to prevent destructive piracy among themselves, then a man of letters could hardly deny them his approval. But how could it occur to reasonable and law-abiding people to give this plan such a reprehensible expansiveness? In order to put a stop to a couple of poor house thieves, they themselves want to become highway robbers? "*They will pirate those who pirate them.*" That may be, if the authorities will permit them to revenge themselves in this manner. But at the same time, they want to *forbid self-publishing*. Who are these people who want to forbid it? Do they have the courage to confess to this crime under their real names? Has self-publishing ever been forbidden anywhere? And how can it be forbidden? What law can infringe on the learned man's right to draw as much benefit from his own personal work as he possibly can? "*But they mingle in the book trade without the requisite qualifications.*" What are these requisite qualifications, anyway? To spend five years learning to tie up packages from some man who doesn't know how to do anything except tie packages? And who may not mingle in the book trade? Since when is the book trade a guild? What are its exclusive privileges? Who accorded those privileges to them?[35]

If Dodsley and Co. complete their piracy of the *Dramaturgy*, I beg them at least not to mutilate my work but rather to reproduce faithfully what they find written against them here. I will not blame them if they want to attach their defense – if any defense is possible.[36] Moreover, they may compose it (or have it composed by a man of letters who is low enough to lend them his pen) in any tone they like, even in that very interesting tone of the *Klotz* school, rich in all sorts of little histories and anecdotes and satires, without one word about the matter at hand. I will only declare in advance that it is a lie to insinuate at all that I speak so heatedly against them out of injured self-interest. I never had anything printed at my own cost and doubt I will ever do so in my life. As I already said, I know more than one honest man among the booksellers to whose management I willingly hand over such business. But none of them should think ill of me for showing my disdain and hatred for people in comparison to whom highwaymen and ambushers are truly not the worst among men. For each of these makes his *coup de main* for himself alone, while Dodsley and Co. want to rob as part of a gang.[37]

The best thing is that only the minority will likely accept their invitation. Otherwise, it would be time for men of letters to seriously consider undertaking the well-known Leibniz project.[38]

End of the Second Volume.

PARALIPOMENA[1]

[Drafts for discussions][2]

[1]

On the _____ *Miss Sara Sampson* was repeated.[3]

In the new edition of his *Progrés des Allemands* etc.,* the Baron of Bielfeld also sought to make this play known to foreigners through an extended synopsis.[4] The author must be obliged to him for this honor; but should he not make any objection to the Baron's criticism?

Herr von Bielfeld says: "*Sara Sampson* is indeed an original German play; yet the subject seems to have been taken or imitated from English novels, and the spirit as well as the taste of that nation dominates the play."[5]

What is this supposed to mean? The subject seems to have been taken from English novels? If you are going to deny someone's invention of something, is an "it seems" sufficient? Which English novel [. . .]

[2]

La Critique de L'Ecole des Femmes [*The Critique of the School for Wives*]
[Here Lessing translates into German a short passage from Scene 6 of Molière's play.][6]

Trublet[7]

"One must be much more rigorous with comedies than with tragedies. It is much easier to move an intelligent man, or even to make him cry, than it is to amuse him and make him laugh. The heart is always ready and willing for the emotions one wants to awaken in

* à Leide. 1767. 8. T. II. p. 343.

313

it; the mind, on the other hand, tends to resist humor. It seems that laughing at the wrong place would hurt our vanity much more than crying for no reason. The former is a sign of stupidity and the latter only of weakness, a weakness that itself is a form of goodness."[8]

[3]

On the fiftieth evening (Friday, the 24th of July), Molière's *School for Wives* was repeated.[9]

In the second half of 1661 and throughout 1662, Molière found his theater somewhat abandoned.[10] The entire city gravitated toward the Italians to see Scaramouche, who had returned to Paris.[11] If Molière did not want to play to an empty house, he had to find a way to attract the public with something new, something in the vein of the Italian farces. He thus offered his *School for Wives*; but the very public that had there laughed at and applauded the most tasteless farces and the dirtiest jokes, tossed out in barely coherent language, now responded to him sternly, as if it were prepared only to hear the purest morality and the most refined entertainment. Again he took up the challenge, and he welcomed criticism as long as one regularly visited his theater.

Nonetheless, he had it in his power the entire time to shame most of these critics, and ultimately he exercised this power in a brand-new way. Namely, he collected together the most tasteless among them, gave them voice through diverse and ridiculous original characters, mixed among them a few people with good taste, and created from their dialogue about his play another little play that he called the Critique of the first (*The Critique of the School for Wives*), and put it on immediately following that play.[12] In the following time period, more than one playwright imitated him in this new device, but never with notable success. For a mediocre play cannot ever win the reputation of being a good one with the help of an apologetic bodyguard; and a good play does not need one as it makes its way through all scornful attacks on the way to a more secure and forgiving future.

[4]

On the _____ *Olint and Sophronia* was repeated.[13]

On the presumed injustice that I am said to have inflicted upon H. v. C[ronegk] as a dramatic writer. Why would we want to boast to foreigners of treasures that we do not have? Thus says, for example, the *Journal encyclopédique*,[†] that his play *The Suspicious Man* found acclaim in our theater and has always been well-regarded.[14] That couldn't be further from the truth. It is an unbearable play and the dialogue is extremely dull.

The things that are said there about his *Olint and Sophronia* are even stranger.

"Encouraged by the acclaim given to his *Codrus*, he undertook another tragedy in which he wanted to reintroduce the chorus in the manner of the Greeks.[15] He wanted to see if that which Racine did so successfully with his *Athalie* in France could also succeed in Germany.[16] However, after overcoming tremendous obstacles and having already made

---

† Sept. 1761

considerable progress on his work, he suddenly gave it up, believing that his project could not succeed because of the nature of German music (*attendu la nature de la Musique allemande*). He believed that it was in no way fit to render the beauty of sentiments and the nobility of thoughts that he wanted to express.[‡,17] But it seems to us that he could have dispensed with the music altogether, as M. de Voltaire did with the chorus in his *Brutus*.[18] In any case, he gave up on the play; given the fragments he left behind that contain much beauty, it is sad that he did not put the finishing touch to his work. Germany might have been able to boast of a Christian tragedy that brought honor to its theater."[19]

How completely absurd! The German music! If only they had added that German poetry was unsuited to music!

And the whole thing is simply not true. Cronegk didn't give up on his work; he died in the middle of it.

What the journalist adds at the end is, to all appearances, also a lie: "Un Ecrivain Anglois qui a senti le mérite de cette Tragédie, se l'est appropriée. Sa piéce a paru sous ce titre: Olindo and Sophronia, a Tragedy taken from Tasso, by Abraham Portal, Esq. London. 1758."[20] That would make the good Mr. Portal a plagiarist who had never heard the name Cronegk. In 1758, Cronegk's *Olint* had not yet been published.[21]

[5]

On the sixty-fifth evening (Friday, the 14th of August), Herr Heufeld's *Julie* and Schlegel's *The Dumb Beauty* were repeated.[22]

The two plays that Herr Heufeld made himself known for in Vienna before his *Julie* were *Housekeeping* and *The Fashionable Lovers*.[23] I do not know anything more about them than their titles. But I have read his fourth play, the one he wrote after *Julie*.

It is called *The Birthday*, and it has three acts.[24] Its structure places it among what the French call "*pièces à tiroir*"; and its primary tone is that of a farce, even though its characters are far from belonging to the lowest class of persons.[25] It depicts various ridiculous characters who show up at a birthday that is being celebrated by a noble family in the manner customary in Vienna. The first act is composed of a series of morning visitors come to wish Frau von Ehrenwerth a happy birthday. The third act shows an evening's entertainment among roughly the same people, in which they play cards and gamble. The middle act consists of a little comedy called *Brother Philip's Sister*.[26]

[6]

71st Production. *Soliman the Second*.[27]

Did Favart make his alterations for critical reasons? Or did he merely make them to flatter his nation? Was it to make his Frenchwoman not only the liveliest, wittiest, and most entertaining girl, but also the most noble and generous? So that people would have to say: it's true, she is a foolish and thoughtless thing, but nonetheless she

---

‡ Il crut appercevoir qu'elle n'étoit nullement propre à rendre la beauté des sentiments et la noblesse des pensées qu'il vùoloit exprimer.

has the best heart? – Just as Boissy, in his *The Frenchman in London*, ended up making his dandy an honorable young man and thereby spoiled all of the good that the depiction of his follies could have effected.[28] Marmontel says of the role of the dandy in general (*Poetiq. Fr.* T. II, p. 395): "On s'amuse à recopier le Petit-Maître, sur lequel tous les traits du ridicule sont épuisés, et dont la peinture n'est plus qu'une école pour les jeunes, qui ont quelque disposition à le devenir."[29]

French playwrights today are in general the most calculating when it comes to flattering their nation. It is only through appeal to its vanity that they can protect their attempts. Proof of this can be seen in the *Siege of Calais* and more recently in – .[30]

At the same time, we Germans are sufficiently good-hearted fools to reprise these plays of theirs and let the callow praises of the French ring out on our German stages.

Their tragedies of this sort cannot possibly appeal to us; and their comedies of this sort must fail utterly. We have no Roxelanes and we have no dandies; where should our actors have seen examples of these types?[31] It's no wonder that they always play these roles badly. And that's a good thing!

[7][32]

The[§,33] actors were the first to openly support the grandchild of the great Corneille.[34] They put on a benefit performance of *Rodogune* for her, and people came in droves to reward the father of French theater in his descendant.[35] Mademoiselle Corneille was recommended to M. de Voltaire by Le Brun; he sent for her, took over her education, and provided something of a dowry for her through the sale of an edition of her grandfather's plays.[36]

M. de Voltaire's gesture was seen as extraordinary; it was praised in prose and verse, and the whole story was even disguised as a special Greek novel: (*La petite nièce d'Eschyle* 1761).[37]

The gesture is indeed praiseworthy, but it is not more praiseworthy because it was Corneille's granddaughter for whom Voltaire carried it out.[38] Rather, the honor that he could foresee would necessarily accrue to him as a result was its own kind of reward; and the dishonor that would reflect back on Fontenelle as a result may have had a bit of allure for Voltaire as well.[39]

M. de Voltaire was also given credit for an extraordinarily selfless and magnanimous gesture when he undertook to produce his Corneille commentaries. (*Journal Encyc.* Oct. 1761)[40] "L'exemple qu'il donne est unique; il abandonne pour ainsi dire son propre fonds, pour travailler au champ de son voisin et lui donner plus de valeur. Que ceux qui calomnient son coeur, admirent au moins la noblesse d'un procédé si rare. Il est ordinaire que les grands hommes s'étudient, mais ils n'ont pas coutume de se commenter. Dans le nombre presque infini des Éditeurs, des Commentateurs, des Compilateurs, on peut en citer beaucoup qui ont marqué de l'érudition; quelques-uns ont eu de l'esprit; très peu de goût: voici le premier qui a du génie,

§ "The Ephesian Matron" by Ogilby. Cibb. Vol. II. p. 267. A Poem. *The Ephesian Matron* by Charles Johnson. Ibid. Vol V. p. 342. A Farce.

et plus de goût, d'esprit et même d'érudition qu'aucun d'eux. Nous admirerons davantage l'auteur de *Rodogune*, de *Polieucte*, de *Cinna*, quand nous verrons toutes ses pièces enrichies des *Commentaires* que prépare l'auteur de *Mahomet*, d'*Alzire* et de *Mérope*; ils vont fortifier l'idée que nous nous formons de Corneille, et le rendre, s'il est possible, encore plus grand à nos yeux; ils feront relire le texte avec plus de plaisir et plus d'utilité."[41]

How off the mark this flattering prophecy has proved to be! How very differently this commentary has turned out! How easy it would be to believe that in this, too, Voltaire had very selfish intentions.

On[¶] Banks and his *Essex*, which is from 1682, and thus after Corneille's had appeared.[42] He appears not to have been familiar with the Frenchman's work, however.[43]

He stuck strictly to the historical circumstances, and although his play is very mediocre with respect to its arrangement and expression, nevertheless he had the artistry to incorporate very interesting situations, which have led to the play's long life in the theater.

Jones produced his Essex in 1753 (see Cibber's *Life* III, p. 175).[44] He wanted to make Banks's play conform better to the rules, and he made it colder. But his style is better, and his language is more poetic.

In 1761, Brooke's version came out.[45] He sought to use the best from both his predecessors (while distancing himself from the accusation of plagiarism) and to avoid their errors. It is said that he was able to combine the fire and pathos of Banks with the beautiful poetry of Jones.

Brooke was already well-known through a *Gustavus Vasa* that was, however, forbidden in London, because it was thought to contain various anti-government elements.[46]

Brooke ennobled the character of Essex and did not have him speak so heatedly to the queen in the final scene.[47] "Il a aussi fait tomber en demence la Comtesse de Rutland" (says the *Journal Encyl.* March 1761) "au moment que cet illustre [. . .] époux est conduit à l'échafaud: ce moment où cette Comtesse est un objet bien digne de pitié, a produit une très-grande sensation; et a été trouvé admirable à Londres: en France il eut paru ridicule, il auroit été sifflé, et l'on auroit envoyé la Comtesse avec l'Auteur aux Petites Maisons."[48] So much the worse for the French!

[8]

Canut[49]

Act II Scene 4

ULFO: *You fought the way one should when one fights over honor.*[50]

NB: The actor must not pronounce this as if *Ulfo* actually believed that Godewin fought at that time over honor.[51] He would contradict himself with what follows:

¶ From Samuel *Daniel's* "Philotas," which was the history of Essex under a different name. See Cibber Life Vol I. p. 147.

You make your venal blood the property of others
You live to your disgrace and just for foreign praise
You acted out of foolish fear, the way a slave would act.[52]

The actor must pronounce it as if the playwright had said:

You fought the way one should *only* fight when one is fighting over honor.

And this is what he really wanted to say.

[General observations][53]

Interruptions in dialogue

We mark them through dashes, or periods, which the French call "points poursuivans."

If we are to attribute this figure to the essence of the matter rather than to the laziness or embarrassment of the writer, then interrupted dialogue must at all times be filled, and filled easily.

Voltaire says (in his *Commentaire sur le Comte d'Essex* Act III Scene 2): "C'est une très grande négligence de ne point finir sa phrase, sa période, et de se laisser [ainsi] interrompre, surtout quand le personnage qui interrompt est un subalterne, qui manque aux bienséances en coupant la parole à son supérieur. Thomas Corneille est sujet à ce défaut dans toutes ses pièces."[54]

Who worries about respectability when the characters' emotion demands that they interrupt, or allow themselves to be interrupted?

In this respect Home understood the true beauties of dialogue better.[55] "No fault is more common among writers," (he says, in *Elements of Criticism*, Vol. II p. 284),[56] "than to prolong a speech after the impatience of the person to whom it is addressed ought to prompt him or her to break in. Consider only how the impatient actor is to behave in the meantime. To express his impatience in violent action without interrupting, would be unnatural; and yet to dissemble his impatience, by appearing cool where he ought to be highly inflamed, would be no less so."

Chorus[57]

In the ancient tragedies.

Among the modern English writers who have tried to reintroduce it, *Mason* in particular has made several attempts.[58] The first was his *Elfrida*, which I have, and which he prefaces with letters that give the reasons why he wants to write in this traditional manner.[59]

The second is his *Caractacus, a Dramatic Poem*, which was published in 1759.[60] On the occasion of this latter publication the editors of the *Monthly Review* (Vol. XX, p. 507) make some very pertinent arguments against the presumed advantages of the chorus, particularly in regard to two: (1) that it offers more frequent opportunities for poetic embellishments, and (2) that it is the most pleasant and appropriate means for conveying useful instruction to the spectator.[61] In the end, they very correctly observe that Mason's play would be better if it were less poetical.

Unstudied writers;

or those who were not raised to study the higher disciplines.

Henry Jones, the author of the new *Essex*, was a bricklayer.[62]

The author of the English *Olindo and Sophronia* is a blacksmith or steelworker.[63]

In England in general, it has never been uncommon to find such people who, working in the meanest crafts and worst circumstances, without any instruction, have made great accomplishments not only in writing but also in other disciplines. As, for example

Henry Wild, who taught oriental languages at Oxford in 1720; he was a tailor and known under the name of the Arabian tailor.[64]

Robert Hill, a tailor in Buckingham; in 1759 Spence wrote a comparison of him with the Italian Magliabechi, in order to draw a little more of the public's attention to him and possibly improve his circumstances thereby.[65] He taught himself Latin, Greek, and Hebrew (see *The Monthly Review* Vol. XX, p. 217).[66]

Delicacy[67]

An overly sensitive outrage over all language or events that do not conform to the strictest modesty and compunction is not always proof of a pure heart and a chaste imagination. Often the most bashful conduct and the most undisciplined thoughts are found in one person. It is only because they are all too aware of the latter that they assume a more disciplined exterior. Nothing betrays such people more than the fact that they are most insulted by coarse, crude language directly expressing obscenity and are far more forgiving of the most salacious thoughts as long as they are disguised in fine, inoffensive language.

And most certainly these are far more detrimental and corruptive of good morals.

There was an outcry over the word *whore* in my Minna.[68] The actor did not even want to dare speak it.[69] Nevertheless: I will not cut it, and I will use it again anywhere I believe it belongs.

But no one rails against Gellert's double entendres – the shoving of the kerchief and the like – in his *Lottery Ticket*.[70] Everyone just smiles with the author over them.

It is the same with Fielding and Richardson.[71] The coarse, crude expressions in the former's *Joseph Andrews* and *Tom Jones* were widely frowned upon, whereas the obscene thoughts that are not uncommon in *Clarissa* bothered no one.[72] This is the judgment of the British themselves.**,[73]

** The editors of *The Monthly Review* (Vol. XX, p. 132) when they rail against the fact that Rousseau held *Clarissa* to be one the best and most beautiful novels in any language: "In justice to the memory of a late very ingenious Writer, we cannot help taking notice here,

The reviewer need not be able to do better than that which he criticizes[74]

In general, criticizing means giving recognition to one's disapproval.

One can either appeal to feelings to express this disapproval, or one can support these feelings with justifications.

The man of taste does the former; the critic does the latter.

Which of these two should understand how to improve upon that which he criticizes?

A man is not master of his feelings; but a man is master of what he says about what he feels. If a man of taste dislikes something in a poem or a painting: does he first have to pause and become a poet or a painter before he can say: I don't like it? I find my soup too salty: am I not allowed to say it is over-salted until I can cook myself?

What are the justifications of the critic? Conclusions drawn from his own feelings that he has analyzed and compared with others' feelings, and then connected to the fundamental principles of the perfect and beautiful.

I do not see why a man should be more reserved with his conclusions than with his feelings. The critic does not merely feel that he doesn't like something; he appends his *because* to it. And should this *because* require him to do it better? When, in fact, this *because* ought to relieve him from having to do it better.

If, in fact, this *because* is a good and thorough *because*, he will easily derive from it what that which displeases him ought to be like in order to avoid displeasing him.

But this can badly seduce the critic into pointing out the beauty that could and should exist in place of the criticized flaw.

I say seduce: because one is seduced into doing things when one cannot be compelled, and into doing things that could turn out badly.

If the critic says to the dramatic writer: you should have constructed the complication of your story this way, instead of that way; you would have done better to resolve it this way rather than that way; then the critic has allowed himself to be seduced.

For no one could reasonably demand of him that he go so far. He has satisfied the requirements of his profession sufficiently when he simply says: your complication doesn't hold, the development is bad, for this and that reason. The playwright can figure out how it can be improved.

Because if he wants to help him, and the playwright wants to be helped, and he goes ahead and revises based on the suggestions of the critic: then it is true that the playwright and the reader should thank him if the revision is successful. But if it does not succeed?

---

how frequently we have been surprized to find persons, pretending to delicacy, so much offended at the coarse expressions they meet with in *Joseph Andrews* and *Tom Jones*; while the impure and obscene thoughts that occur in *Clarissa* have not given them the least umbrage. We would ask these very delicate persons, which they think of worse tendency, a coarse idea, expressed in vulgar language, in itself disgusting, or an idea equally luscious and impure, conveyed in words that may steal on the affections of the heart, without alarming the ear? On this occasion we cannot forbear exclaiming with the *confidous* Mrs. Slipslop 'Marry come up! People's ears are sometimes the nicest part about them.'" No doubt Slipslop says this in some English comedy, but it is taken from Molière, from the *Critique of the School for Wives*.

Then it doesn't take much for the whole blame to fall on the critic alone. And only in such a case – in order to justify his opinion – might he be required to shove the dabbler aside from the easel and take up brush and palette himself.

"Good luck with the work! We've waited for you right here, good man! When you are done, then we will compare!"

And who does not believe that they can compare!

Woe to him if he has only made a few improvements; when he has let it be enough to just do away with mistakes; when he has not succeeded in surprising us all with completely new, completely unexpected beauty!

What kind of a doctor is it, who merely makes a blind man see and does not simultaneously replace the dull gray eyes that nature gave him with beautiful blue or fiery black eyes!

"Was it worth the trouble? We were used to that mistake; and now we will need to get used to the improvement."

Perhaps we would not even have noticed the mistake, and the improvement is what made us notice it. We become indignant when we find that we should not have liked something that we have liked for so long.

In short, if the critic offends by criticizing, he offends twice as badly by improving the work.

Make it better! This may be the challenge the criticized writer makes of him, but not with the intention that it will be taken up. It is intended merely as a shield to deflect the critic's blows.

If the critic takes it up and is unsuccessful: his game is over.

If he takes it up and is successful – But who will concede to him that he is successful? No one in the world. Neither the artist, nor his colleagues in criticism.

Of all of these, it is not to be expected of the criticized artist; and the others – one crow will not peck out the eyes of another: its turn might come one day.

But the latter will damn him for the bad example: he has overplayed his hand; now people will expect such improving from all of them; for this he must be punished!

And in general, critics are the only kind of crows who give the lie to the proverb.

NOTES TO ESSAYS 1–104

Note: Within these notes, cross-references to other essays appear as a number in square brackets (e.g., [12] refers the reader to Essay 12; [12.3] refers the reader to note 3 of Essay 12).

Notice

1 Johann Elias Schlegel (1719–49): early eighteenth-century playwright and dramatic theorist. Lessing misquotes this passage from Schlegel's "Schreiben von Errichtung eines Theaters in Kopenhagen" ["Writings on the Establishment of a Theater in Copenhagen"] *Werke* 3: 252, and also misattributes it to Schlegel's "Gedanken zur Aufnahme des dänischen Theaters" ["Thoughts on the Improvement of the Danish Theater"]. See Eaton, *The German Influence in Danish Literature* 30–88.

Essay 1

1 Actually published 8 May 1767.
2 *Olint und Sophronia* (1760): five-act verse tragedy by German playwright Johann Friedrich von Cronegk (1731–58). The setting is Muslim-controlled Jerusalem during the time of the Crusades. Olint, a secret convert to Christianity, loves Sophronia, a Christian maiden. Ismenor, a "Mohammedan priest," has taken from the Christians an image of the Crucifixion and placed it in the city's mosque, believing that it will protect the city from Crusaders; Olint steals the image from the mosque and the sultan, Aladin, condemns all Christians to death if the thief is not caught. Attempting to save each other, as well as Jerusalem's Christians, Olint and Sophronia each claim responsibility for the theft. Clorinda (Clorinde), a Persian princess in love with Olint, is originally angered when she learns that Olint loves Sophronia but is later converted to Christianity by Sophronia. Clorinda seeks to save the condemned lovers, but a pardon from the sultan comes too late and they both perish. Johann Michael Böck and Susanna Mecour played the title roles. For the play's production history, see J. G. Robertson, *Lessing's Dramatic Theory* 54–7.
3 Kassian Anton von Roschmann-Hörburg completed the play in 1764.
4 The famous Italian poet Torquato Tasso (1544–95) tells the story of Olint and Sophronia in his epic poem *Gerusalemme Liberata* [*Jerusalem Delivered*] (1581), Bk. II, Ch. I – LIII. In his comparison of *Olint und Sophronia* to its source material, and in his analysis of Cronegk's

Codrus later in this essay, Lessing draws on Moses Mendelssohn's earlier review of Cronegk in the periodical they published jointly with Friedrich Nicolai, *Briefe, die neueste Litteratur betreffend* [*Letters Concerning the Newest Literature*], often referred to as the *Litteraturbriefe*. See Lessing, et al., *Briefe, die neueste Litteratur betreffend* XI: 167–88 (letters 190 and 191, dated 8 October 1761 and 15 October 1761).

5 Here Lessing lays out a few of the key criteria he will use throughout the *Hamburg Dramaturgy* to assess plays and performances: "having the appearance of truth" (*Wahrscheinlichkeit*); "illusory continuity" (*illusorische Stetigkeit*); and the need for an audience to "sympathize" (*sympathisieren*) with the action or characters.

6 For Tasso's tale of Olint and Sophronia, see [1.4]. Nisus and Euryalus: Trojan soldiers found in Book IX of the *Aeneid* (c. 30–19 BCE), the great unfinished epic poem by the Roman poet Virgil (also Vergil, in full Publius Vergilius Maro) (70–19 BCE). During a raid of an enemy's camp, Euryalus steals a helmet, which leads to his capture. Although Nisus heroically returns to rescue his friend, both are killed.

7 In Tasso's original, an image of the Virgin Mary has been taken from the Christians; Cronegk changes this to an image of the Crucifixion (*Olint und Sophronia* 267–8).

8 Ismenor was played by David Borchers.

9 Cronegk, *Olint und Sophronia* 268.

10 Evander: Olint's father; Serena: Sophronia's confidante.

11 Admiration (*Bewunderung*): term in dramatic theory that originated in Renaissance interpretations of Aristotle's *Poetics*; used in discussions of dramatic character and its effect on the spectator. For the significance of the term within Lessing's dramatic theory, see Nisbet, *Gotthold Ephraim Lessing* 211–16.

12 *Codrus* (1757): Cronegk's award-winning five-act verse tragedy; the titular main character, the legendary last king of Athens, sacrifices himself for his country.

13 Tr. note: Lessing uses the term *Vaterland* (literally, "fatherland") here and in the next sentence.

14 Elisinde and Philaide: Athenian noblewomen in Cronegk's play; Medon: Elisinde's son.

15 Bohemia and Spain: markedly Catholic countries.

Essay 2

1 Actually published 8 May 1767.

2 Lessing continues his discussion, from [1], of Johann Friedrich von Cronegk's *Olint und Sophronia*; for the plot, see [1.2]. For more on the role of conversion in Lessing's approach to "Christian tragedy," see Erickson, "Adapting Christian Tragedy for the Enlightenment Stage: Gotthold Ephraim Lessing's *Hamburgische Dramaturgie* (1767–1769)."

3 Natural causes: for the theological reasoning behind Lessing's emphasis on the dramaturgical necessity for natural causality, see Nisbet 396–7.

4 Lessing, on one hand, supported sentimental models of theater whose depictions of "natural" and universal behavior were meant to strengthen morality through a spectator's innate capacity for compassion. At the same time, however, Lessing had little patience for pedantic moralizing; see, for example, his letter to Nicolai (Letter 509) dated 11 October 1769, in which he condemns "wretched defenders of the theater, who seek with all their might to make it into a school of virtue" (*Werke und Briefe* 11/1: 629).

5 Sophronia's conversion of Clorinda occurs in fact in act 4, scene 4 (rather than in act 3, scene 4); see Cronegk 345–51. Tr. note: on the choice to translate *Mitleid* as "compassion" see [32.6].

6 Tasso: Cronegk's source; see [1.4]. Cronegk omits this detail about Clorinda's parentage.

7 Voltaire: pseudonym of French playwright, philosopher, and satirist François-Marie Arouet (1694–1778).

8 Zamor: "noble savage" who converts to Christianity in Voltaire's play *Alzire, ou les Américains* [*Alzire; or, The Americans*] (1736).

9 *Polyeucte* (1642): five-act verse tragedy by French poet and playwright Pierre Corneille (1606–84), widely regarded as the founder of neoclassical tragedy. The titular character, an Armenian lord, converts to Christianity and is martyred.

10 "purify passions through passions": first allusion to *catharsis*, a highly contested Aristotelian term variably defined as "purification," "purgation," "cleansing," or "clarification"; the purpose of tragedy, according to Aristotle. See [32], [74]–[83], and Aristotle, *Poetics* (Part VI).

11 Genius: Lessing did not subscribe to the increasingly popular "cult of genius" of the late eighteenth century. Unlike the later Romantics, he did not consider genius to be generative, but understood it rather as an indication of an individual's intuitive grasp of the laws of nature. For more on Lessing's understanding of genius and the authors who may have shaped it, see J. G. Robertson 449–58.

12 See [1.3].

13 Until late in the eighteenth century the lighting in German theaters was provided by candles; the *Lichtputzer* (here translated as "candlesnuffer") was responsible for maintaining those candles, trimming wicks to prevent them from smoking and extinguishing the flames when it was time for the candles to be changed. On lighting practices in the eighteenth-century German theater, see Maurer-Schmoock, *Deutsches Theater im 18. Jahrhundert* 65–75. David Garrick (1717–79): English actor, playwright, and entrepreneur; considered among the greatest dramatic artists of the century.

14 Konrad Ekhof (1720–78): German actor and theorist, known as "the father of German acting" and "the German Garrick"; a leading member of the Hamburg National Theater company. Ekhof exemplified an emerging, more naturalistic style of German acting that accorded with Lessing's ideas about the reform of the German theater (see Nisbet 367–69). Lessing uses a variant spelling of his name (Eckhof). In his discussion of the production, Lessing's criticism focuses mainly on the play's supporting roles; possibly because principle actress Susanna Mecour (Sophronia) refused Lessing permission to review her performances.

15 *Codrus*: see [1.12].

16 Lines spoken by Clorinda. See Cronegk 292; 293.

17 Ismenor: see [1.2].

18 A reference to antitheatrical critics such as the militant Lutheran German theologian Johann Melchior Götze, who in 1770 would deny the possibility of moral theater in his polemic *Theologische Untersuchung der Sittlichkeit der heutigen deutschen Schaubühne* [*Theological Investigation of the Morality of the Contemporary German Theater*]; for Lessing's theological dispute with Götze in 1777–78, see Nisbet 552–70.

Essay 3

1 Actually published 8 May 1767.

2 Lessing continues his discussion, from [2], of Konrad Ekhof's performance as Evander in Johann Friedrich Cronegk's *Olint und Sophronia*; for the plot, see [1.2].

3 Allusion to the biblical verse "For the mouth speaks out of that which fills the heart" (Matthew 12:34).

4 Mechanical mimicry: the eighteenth century witnessed a heated debate that placed a mechanistic approach to acting in opposition to a more intuitive approach; Lessing's acting theory draws from, and uniquely integrates, ideas from both sides. For an overview of the debate and its major participants, see Roach, *The Player's Passion*; for Lessing's negotiation of this debate, see the editor's second introductory essay in this volume (Baldyga, "We have actors, but no art of acting").

5 Lessing's discussion of the relationship between the actor's emotion and the legibility of emotional signs draws from a Cartesian understanding of the relationship between mind and body. See Descartes, *Selected Philosophical Writings* 160–212; 218–38.

6 Symbolic conclusion (*symbolischer Schluß*): knowledge stemming from the signs of things rather than from an intuitive understanding of the things themselves. For more on Lessing's distinction between the two forms of knowledge, see his "Abhandlung zur Fabel: I. Von dem Wesen der Fabel" ["Treatise on the Fable: I. On the Nature of the Fable"] (*Werke und Briefe* 4: 372–3); see also Nancy Cartwright, *The Dappled World* 37–42.

Essay 4

1   Lessing continues his evaluation, begun in [2], of Konrad Ekhof's performance of Evander in Cronegk's *Olint und Sophronia*, and in particular his ability to deliver "moral truisms," introduced in [3]. For the play's plot, see [1.2].

2   Chironomy: Lessing refers to the "hand language" of rhetoricians and actors in ancient Rome, as described in Quintilian, *The Institutes of Oratory* Bk. 11, Ch. 3, sec. 61–184.

3   This passage echoes Diderot's discussion of the lost art of pantomime in his theoretical essay *Entretiens sur Le Fils naturel [Conversations on the Natural Son]* (1757). See Diderot, *Entretiens sur Le Fils naturel* 139–45; for the English, see *Selected Writings on Art and Literature* 20–2.

4   Pantomimes: the ancient Roman term *pantomimus* (pantomime) indicated a masked performer who danced and imitated characters wordlessly, usually with musical accompaniment, in contrast to the unmasked *mimus* (mime) and *histrio* (actor), whose gestures supported and enhanced words that were spoken and sung.

5   Two uncompleted works of Lessing speak to his interest in gesture: "Abhandlung von den Pantomimen der Alten" ["Treatise on the Pantomime of the Ancients"] (dated between 1749 and 1750, *Werke und Briefe* 1: 711–24) and "Der Schauspieler: Ein Werk worinne [sic] die Grundsätze der ganzen körperlichen Beredsamkeit entwickelt werden" ["The Actor: A work in which the basic principles of a whole bodily expressivity will be developed"] (dated between 1750 and 1754, *Werke und Briefe* 3: 320–9). In his discussions of gesture, Lessing draws on a range of seminal eighteenth-century works of aesthetics and performance, a number of which he reviewed and translated, including the *Dissertation sur les Représentations Théâtrales des Anciens [Inquiry into the Theatrical Entertainments of the Ancients]* by the Abbé Du Bos; *Les Beaux-Arts Réduits à un Même Principe [The Fine Arts Distilled into a Few Principles]* by Charles Batteux; William Hogarth's *Analysis of Beauty*; and François (Francesco) Riccoboni's treatise *L'Art du théâtre [Art of the Theater]*.

6   For an analysis of Lessing's distinction between "natural signs" and conventionally agreed upon signs, see Wellbery, *Lessing's Laocoön* 191–203.

7   William Hogarth (1697–1764): English engraver and painter whose *Analysis of Beauty* (1753), a widely influential treatise on aesthetics in the pictorial and plastic arts, was translated into German in 1754 by Christlob Mylius. Lessing provided a preface to the second edition of this book (*Werke und Briefe* 3: 350ff.). In Chapter 17 ("Of Action"), Hogarth briefly addresses stage movement, explaining that stage action should be graceful and work in conjunction with, rather than against, stage dialogue.

8   Hogarth suggests chalking graceful curving lines on a flat surface and training the hand to follow them – an exercise that he describes as "an odd, but perhaps, efficacious method of acquiring a habit of moving in the lines of grace and beauty" (153).

9   *Port de bras*: ballet term indicating the movement and carriage of the arms; also an exercise meant to develop graceful arm movements.

10 The term Lessing uses, "*das Anschauende*" (translated here as "visible"), relates this passage to the eighteenth-century aesthetic concept of "*Anschaulichkeit*," (clarity or transparency). As Dorothea von Mücke notes, the "Project of *Anschaulichkeit*" aimed to remove the veil of artful representation in order to increase the reality effect of the artistic illusion (see von Mücke, *Virtue and the Veil of Illusion* 18; 40–60). See [3.6] for Lessing's distinction between symbolic and intuitive knowledge.

11 The lines that follow are from *Olint und Sophronia* 2.4; see Cronegk 311–2.

12 Sophie Friederike Hensel (née Sparmann) (1738–89): one of the leading German actresses of her day, as well as a playwright and librettist; Hensel toured for the majority of her career with the troupe of Konrad (Ernst) Ackermann (1712–71) and was hired by the Hamburg National Theater due to her status as a star performer. Known for her tragic neoclassical roles such as Semiramis, Merope, and Cleopatra, Hensel was also lauded for her performances of Lessing's Minna, Orsina, and Sara Sampson. Lessing and Hensel were not always on good terms, and traditionally the actress has been depicted as a divisive "diva" figure within the Hamburg company. Contemporary scholarship has begun only recently to explore more fully Hensel's contributions to the German theater; see, for example, Kord,

"Tugend im Rampenlicht: Friederike Sophie Hensel als Schauspielerin und Dramatikerin" ["Virtue in the Limelight: Friederike Sophie Hensel as actress and playwright"].

13 J. G. Robertson notes that Lessing's description of Hensel's declamation follows Sainte-Albine's description in *Le Comédien* of how actors should perform Act 2, Scene 5 of Racine's *Phèdre*; see J. G. Robertson 478–9; Sainte-Albine 198–207.

14 This speech, and the lines that follow, are from *Olint und Sophronia* 3.3; see Cronegk 331–2.

Essay 5

1 Lessing continues his discussion, from [4], of Sophie Hensel's performance as Clorinda in Johann Friedrich Cronegk's *Olint und Sophronia*; for the plot, see [1.2].

2 Lessing's aesthetics of "natural beauty," which predate the Romantic fascination with the sublime and the grotesque, are founded on ostensibly universal standards of order, proportion, and decorum. See Lessing, *Laokoon: oder über die Grenzen der Malerei und Poesie* (1766) (*Werke und Briefe* 5.2: 11–206). For an English translation, see Edward Allen McCormick, *Laocoön: An Essay on the Limits of Painting and Poetry*.

3 Tr. note: the word Lessing uses here is *Marquetenderin*, which translates best to the archaic English word "sutler," a merchant who sold goods from the back of a wagon to the army.

4 German critics received their view of Shakespeare as an indifferent actor from English biographers such as Nicholas Rowe, who wrote in his 1709 biographical preface to Shakespeare's works that "his admirable wit, and the natural turn of it to the stage, soon distinguish'd him, if not as an extraordinary Actor, yet as an excellent Writer" ("Some Account" 61–2).

5 *Hamlet* 3.2.

6 Lessing's argument is derived from the first part of Pierre Rémond de Sainte-Albine's seminal work of acting theory, *Le Comédien* [*The Actor*] (1747), specifically Chapter III, "Un Comédien peut-il avoir trop de Feu?" ["Can an actor have too much fire?"] (41–9). Lessing had planned a translation of *Le Comédien*, but instead published a detailed description in 1754 in his *Theatralische Bibliothek* under the title "Auszug aus dem *Schauspieler* des Herrn Remond von Sainte Albine" ["Excerpt from *The Actor* by Mr. Remond de Sainte Albine"] (*Werke und Briefe* 3: 304–11).

7 This statement represents another link between the *Hamburg Dramaturgy* and *Laokoon*, in which Lessing challenges the Latin dictum *ut pictura poesis* ("as is painting, so is poetry"), most famously employed by Horace in his *Ars Poetica*; there, as in this essay, Lessing argues that theatrical performance, as a "transitory painting," is responsible to different aesthetic criteria than either poetry or painting.

8 Tempesta: may refer to Dutch painter Pieter Mulier the Younger (1637–1701), nicknamed "Tempesta" for his paintings of stormy seas; J. G. Robertson, however, suggests that Lessing refers to Antonio Tempesta (1555–1630), known for his battle scenes (see J. G. Robertson 482). Gian Lorenzo Bernini (1598–1680): Italian architect and sculptor, considered synonymous with the Baroque style in architecture.

9 For an overview of eighteenth-century acting and its physiological grounding in "the passions of the soul," see Roach, *The Player's Passion*; for Lessing's acting theory and his discussion of the passions, see Baldyga, "Corporeal Eloquence and Sensate Cognition."

10 Seats in the gallery were inexpensive and typically would have been populated by servants and the working classes; the *parterre* audience would have been made up of students, merchants, lawyers, and literati.

11 *Le triomphe du temps passé* (1725): prose comedy by French actor and playwright Marc Antoine Le Grand (1673–1728).

12 Le Grand's *Le triomphe du temps* [*The Triumph of Time*] was staged in 1725 (Lessing's date appears to be an error); it was comprised of three one-act prose plays: *Le triomphe du temps passé* [*The Triumph of Times Past*], *Le triomphe du temps présent* [*The Triumph of the Present Time*], and *Le triomphe du temps futur* [*The Triumph of Future Time*]. *Les Amans ridicules* [*The Ridiculous Lovers*] (1711): five-act comedy in verse; performed by the Comédie Française but not published. Lessing draws his information about these works from the *Dictionnaire portatif historique*; see Léris 20; 439.

Essay 6

1 Lessing continues his discussion, from [3], of Johann Friedrich Cronegk's *Olint und Sophronia*; for the plot, see [1.2].

2 The author of the prologue and epilogue is unknown. Some historians attribute authorship to Johann Jakob Dusch (1725–87), others to Johann Friedrich Löwen (1727–71), the director of the Hamburg National Theater; see J. G. Robertson 56–8. Regardless of its provenance, this introduction to the theater's mission connects it to other eighteenth-century efforts to promote moral reform through the sentimental theater; a "civilized" populace was meant to espouse bourgeois ideological principles of moderation, compassion, and public citizenship (see Fischer-Lichte, "The Rise of the Middle Classes and the Theatre of Illusion" 146–70).

3 Tr. note: Both the prologue and the epilogue are written in rhymed couplets in the original.

4 Elisabeth Lucia Dorothea Löwen (1732–83) (frequently listed erroneously as Eleonore Luise Dorothea): daughter of the influential actor-manager Johann Friedrich Schönemann (1704–82) and wife of Johann Friedrich Löwen. A principal actress of the Hamburg theater.

5 See [6.2].

6 Solon (c. 630 – c. 560 BCE): Athenian statesman famous for legislative reforms; his name is synonymous with humane and democratic justice.

7 Themis: in Greek mythology the personification of justice.

8 Gaul: territory in modern-day Western Europe that was inhabited by the Celtic Gauls during the Roman era; here meant to imply France. Albion: archaic name for England.

9 Quintus Roscius Gallus (born c. 134–26, died 62 or 63 BCE): ancient Roman comic and tragic performer whose name later became an appellation for great actors.

10 James Quin: English actor (1693–1766), particularly noted for his performance of Falstaff. A leading actor of his time, Quin's popularity was challenged by the ascendency of David Garrick. The latter was seen as a pioneer of new acting methods, in comparison to which Quin's declamatory style appeared dated.

Essay 7

1 In this essay, Lessing refers to the prologue and epilogue, provided in [6], of the Hamburg National Theater's inaugural play, Johann Friedrich Cronegk's *Olint and Sophronia*; for the play's plot, see [1.2]. The idea of drama as "a supplement to the law" connects this passage to eighteenth-century debates concerning the relationship of theater and morality to the law; prominent participants include the Abbé Hédelin d'Aubignac, *La Pratique du Théâtre* [*The Whole Art of the Stage*] (1657); Jean-Jacques Rousseau, *Lettre à d'Alembert sur les spectacles* [*Letter to D'Alembert on the Theatre*] (1758); and, later, Friedrich Schiller, *Die Schaubühne als eine moralische Anstalt betrachtet* [*The Stage Considered as a Moral Institution*] (1784), among many others.

2 Tr. note: "*Bibliothek der schönen Wissenschaften*." In 1756, the journal's editor, C. F. Nicolai (1733–1811), held a contest for the best unpublished tragedy by a German author; Cronegk was posthumously awarded the prize for *Codrus*. Nicolai, a writer and bookseller, was a close friend of Lessing and of the philosopher Moses Mendelssohn (1729–86); all three were leading figures of the German Enlightenment. For more on their collaboration, see the editor's first introductory essay in this volume (Baldyga, "Missions, Misunderstandings, and Mythologies" 3). *Codrus* initiated a German revival of Alexandrine tragedies, whose popularity had declined as bourgeois dramas such as Lessing's *Miss Sara Sampson* (1755) gained popularity.

3 James Thomson (1700–48): Scottish poet and playwright whose work informed Lessing's understanding of English drama. Lessing translated Theophilus Cibber's biography of Thomson (*Werke und Briefe* 3: 282–99) and provided a preface to the 1756 German translation of his plays (*Werke und Briefe* 3: 755–61).

4 John Milton (1608–74): renowned English poet, theologian, and historian.

5 For more on the actor's need to be universally intelligible, see the editor's second introductory essay in this volume (Baldyga, "We have actors, but no art of acting").

6 Proteus: shape-changer from Greek mythology. From the Renaissance onward, this appellation was applied to actors who exhibited an uncanny ability to transform themselves and

who appeared to lose themselves within a role. See Roach, *The Player's Passion* 23–57. The term was applied to Garrick almost immediately upon his debut on the English stage.

7 Characters from Henry Fielding's novel, *The History of Tom Jones, a Foundling* (1749). The passage that follows is loosely paraphrased from Book XVI, Chap. 5, p. 794 (and not Book VI, as Lessing indicates in his footnote).

8 Although their specific function was contested by critics during the long eighteenth century, prologues and epilogues became an integral part of theatrical evenings, addressing debates over aesthetic concerns, recontextualizing older plays for new audiences, and often engaging social or political issues of the day. See Ennis and Bailey-Slagle, *Prologues, Epilogues, Curtain-raisers, and Afterpieces* 13–32.

9 Titus Maccius Plautus (c. 254 – c. 184 BCE): one of the two great Roman comic playwrights, the other being Terence.

10 Melpomene: in Greek mythology, the muse of tragedy.

11 John Dryden (1631–1700): preeminent English Restoration playwright, poet, literary critic, and dramatic theorist.

12 Lessing may be referring to the author of the prologue and epilogue of *Olint and Sophronia*, although this is by no means certain; see [6.2].

Essay 8

1 *Mélanide* (1741): five-act sentimental comedy in verse by French playwright Pierre-Claude Nivelle de La Chaussée (1692–1754).

2 *Mélanide* premiered in Hamburg in 1742 (under the direction of actress Sophie Charlotte Schröder, later Ackermann) and was produced regularly in Hamburg in subsequent decades. The German translator of the work is unknown. See Litzmann, *Friedrich Ludwig Schröder* 33; and Meyer, *Friedrich Ludwig Schröder* II/2: 44–7; 49; 52; and 118.

3 *Comédie larmoyante*: A sentimental drama of the eighteenth century that blurred the distinction between comedy and tragedy; the term was used by detractors of the genre and translated, by contemporary English commentators, as "whining comedies" (see, for example, Voltaire, "Preface to the Comedy of Nanine" 236). *Mélanide* is considered to exemplify the form. Lessing claims to have coined the word *weinerlich* (weeping or lachrymose) to translate the French term *larmoyant* in his preface to the "Abhandlungen von dem weinerlichen oder rührenden Lustspiele" (1754) ["Essays on the weepy or touching comedies"] (*Werke und Briefe* 3: 265; see also Grimm, *Deutsches Wörterbuch* 28: col. 903).

4 *Mélanide* opened at the Comédie-Française 12 May 1741 and remained in that theater's repertory throughout the eighteenth century (see Joannidès, *La Comédie-Française*).

5 The full (and correct) title of the work to which Lessing refers is *Mémoires de Mademoiselle Bontemps, ou de la Comtesse de Marlou* by Thomas-Simon Gueullette (1748); however, *Mélanide* does not appear to have been based on this work.

6 In *Mélanide*, young Rosalie is promised to a marquis, despite her love for Darviane. The conflict is resolved when Darviane is revealed to be the illegitimate son of the marquis and the eponymous Mélanide. In 3.2, Darviane confronts Rosalie about the arranged match and her feelings for him.

7 *Biblioteca teatrale italiana* II: 199ff. Collection of Italian plays and plays translated into Italian, compiled by Ottaviano Diodati between 1762–5, and supplemented with chapters in verse on dramatic theory and performance. Significant in part because of Diodati's use of the word *drammaturgia* to describe his project.

8 *Julie, oder Wettstreit der Pflicht und Liebe* (1766): three-act prose comedy by Viennese playwright, literary critic, director, and theater manager Franz von Heufeld (1731–95).

9 The two previous works were likely *Die Haushaltung nach der Mode, oder Was soll man für eine Frau nehmen?* [*Housekeeping à la mode, or What should one take for a wife?*] (1765) and *Die Liebhaber nach der Mode, oder Was soll man für einen Mann nehmen?* [*The Fashionable Lovers, or What should one take for a husband?*] (1766).

10 *Julie ou la nouvelle Héloïse, ou Lettres de deux amants* [*Julie, or the New Heloise, or Letters from Two Lovers*] (1761): wildly successful epistolary novel by the highly influential Swiss-born novelist, philosopher, and political theorist Jean-Jacques Rousseau (1712–78).

11 Lessing refers here to letters written by the philosopher and critic Moses Mendelssohn; see Lessing, Mendelssohn, and Nicolai, *Briefe, die neueste Litteratur betreffend* (Letters 166 through 171) X: 255–310. See [1.4].

12 In Rousseau's novel, lovers St. Preux and Julie, teacher and pupil respectively, are separated when Julie's father, the Baron d'Étange, marries her to Wolmar, a nobleman. Julie lives happily as a wife and mother until St. Preux is hired to tutor her children; although the affair is not rekindled, Julie eventually realizes that she still loves St. Preux. In Heufeld's play, Julie and her tutor resist their passion from the outset, Wolmar nobly releases Julie from her engagement, and her father allows the virtuous lovers to marry.

13 Here Lessing paraphrases rather than quotes Mendelssohn's text. See Lessing, Mendelssohn, and Nicolai, *Briefe, die neueste Litteratur betreffend* (Letter 167) X: 261.

14 Lessing, Mendelssohn and Nicolai, *Briefe, die neueste Litteratur betreffend* (Letter 167) X: 266–7.

Essay 9

1 Lessing continues, from [8], his discussion of Franz von Heufeld's stage adaptation of Jean-Jacques Rousseau's epistolary novel *Julie, or the New Heloise*.

2 Heufeld, *Julie* iv.

3 Champions of bourgeois drama argued that the private concerns of ordinary citizens were the most universally human, and thus the most compelling, subjects for a play, rather than the uncommon and exceptional deeds of public persons (as was the case in French neoclassical tragedies and the German baroque theater).

4 In fact, Rousseau's Julie is struck and bloodied by her enraged father (Part 1, Letter 63).

5 In Chapters 24 and 25 of *Laocoön*, Lessing explores the relationship between illusion, pleasure, and representations of attractive or repellent objects and argues that a theatrical representation of the disgusting invalidates any other intended emotional effect for the spectator; see Lessing, *Laokoon* 5/2: 169–82; for the English, see Lessing, *Laocoön* 126–37. See also Lessing's letter to Mendelssohn on the subject of illusion in the "Briefwechsel über das Trauerspiel" (Letter 115) dated 2 February 1757, *Werke und Briefe* 3: 711–14 (also 11/1: 165–69).

6 See *Laokoon* 5/2: 172–82; *Laocoön* 130–7; see also Lessing's letter to Mendelssohn dated 2 February 1757 (referenced in [1.5]).

7 As in the *tenebrismo* paintings of Caravaggio or Rembrandt.

8 *Der Schatz* [*The Treasure*] (1750): one-act prose comedy; Lessing's own adaptation of Plautus's comedy *Trinummus* [*The Three Pieces of Money*].

9 Giovanni Maria Cecchi (1517?–87): prolific Florentine playwright; frequently adapted Roman comedies.

10 *La Dote* [*The Dowry*] (1550): five-act prose comedy by Cecchi. Luigi Riccoboni (1675? – 1753): influential Italian author, theater reformer, and actor who directed the Comédie-Italienne in Paris. Riccoboni's *Réflexions historiques et critiques sur différents théâtres de l'Europe* [*An Historical and Critical Account of the Various Theaters in Europe*] (1738), the first comparative history of the European theater, influenced Lessing's own *Beyträge zur Historie und Aufnahme des Theaters* [*Contributions to the History and Improvement of the Theater*] (1750); see *Beyträge* preface and overview (*Werke und Briefe* 1: 723–33; 1330–6). In 1754, Lessing published (and may have translated) the majority of Riccoboni's *Histoire du théâtre italien* [*History of Italian Theater*] (1728–31) in his *Theatralische Bibliothek* [*Theatrical Library*] 2: 135–214. For Riccoboni's remarks on Cecchi's *La Dote*, see *Histoire du Théâtre Italien* 131–8.

11 *Le Tresor caché* [*The Hidden Treasure*] (1757): five-act prose comedy, first performed at the Théâtre Italien in 1745, by French diplomat and playwright Philippe Néricault Destouches

(1680–1754). Lessing provides a biography of Destouches in his *Theatralische Bibliothek*; see Lessing, "Leben des Herrn Nericault Destouches" ["Life of Mr. Nericault Destouches"] (*Werke und Briefe* 3: 312–18).

12 Philemon (born c. 368–60, died c. 267–63 BCE): writer of Athenian New Comedy; author of *Thesauros* [*Treasure*] (c. 300 BCE).

13 Tr. note: Lessing's term here, *Sykophant*, refers to the character in Plautus's play, in which the *sycophanta* is a "professional impostor."

Essay 10

1 *L'Obstacle imprévu, ou, L'obstacle sans obstacle* (1717): five-act prose comedy by Philippe Néricault Destouches. The German version used was *Das unvermuthete Hinderniss, oder das Hinderniss ohne Hinderniss* (1757); the translator is unknown.

2 *Le Trésor caché* (1745), *Le Tambour nocturne* (1736), and *La fausse Agnès, ou Le poète campagnard* (wr. 1727): comedies by Destouches; the latter two were translated by Luise Adelgunde Victorie Gottsched as *Das Gespenste mit der Trummel* [*The Ghost with the Drum*] and *Der Poetische Dorfjunker* [*The Poetical Village Squire*] in volumes 2 and 3, respectively, of J. C. Gottsched's *Die Deutsche Schaubühne* [*The German Stage*] (1741–5). *Le Tambour nocturne* was itself an adaptation of Joseph Addison's *The Drummer, or the Haunted House* (1715/16).

3 *Le Philosophe marié* (1727), *Le Glorieux* (1732), and *Le Dissipateur* (1733): comedies by Destouches. *Le Glorieux* was translated as *Der Ruhmredige* [*The Conceited Count*] by J. E. Schlegel (1761); *Le Dissipateur* was translated by L. A. V. Gottsched as *Der Verschwender* [*The Spendthrift*] (1741). An English version of *The Conceited Count* appears in Regnard, et al., *Heirs of Moliere* 89–196.

4 Herr Schulwitz: character in *Das Gespenste mit der Trummel* (M. Pincé in the original); Herr von Masuren: character in *Der Poetische Dorfjunker* (M. des Mazures in the original).

5 Lessing upholds the view that comedy is both moral and useful; its function is to heighten our ability to recognize the ridiculous and to avoid such behaviors in ourselves. If too moralistic, however, comedy no longer generates genuine laughter; conversely, if its characters are too ridiculous, they become merely repellent. See Lessing's letter to Nicolai (Letter 103) dated [13] November 1756, in the "Briefwechsel über das Trauerspiel," *Werke und Briefe* 3: 671 (also 11/1: 120); for an English version of the passage, see "Correspondence with Nicolai and Mendelssohn" 331.

6 *Die neue Agnese* (1768): one-act prose comedy, originally published anonymously, by Johann Friedrich Löwen.

7 Lessing here begins his synopsis of Voltaire's verse poem *Gertrude, ou, L'éducation d'une fille* [*Gertrude, or the Education of a Daughter*] (1763).

8 Lessing's animosity toward Voltaire in this and other essays can be attributed in part to an incident between the two authors. While still a young unknown, Lessing was lent a portion of a work in progress by the renowned French author; fearing piracy or an unauthorized translation, Voltaire demanded its return. See "Brief von Voltaire" ["Letter from Voltaire"] dated 1 January [1752], *Werke und Briefe* 11/1: 37–8; and Nisbet 92–3. Lessing was later denied the post of Royal Librarian by Voltaire's patron, Frederick II of Prussia; some historians speculate that the earlier incident may have been a contributing factor.

9 Charles-Simon Favart (1710–92): French dramatist, librettist, and director of the *opéra comique*; author of *Isabelle et Gertrude ou les Sylphes supposés* [*Isabelle and Gertrude, or the Supposed Sylphs*] (1765).

10 Gabalis: a master of the occult in the satirical novel *Le Comte de Gabalis, ou Entretiens sur les sciences secretes* [*The Count of Gabalis, or Conversations about the Secret Sciences*] (1670) by the Abbé de Montfaucon de Villars (1635–73). Sylph: folkloric, elemental being of the air.

11 Cordelia (or Cornelia/Cornelie) Felbrich left the company in November 1767, joining Karl Döbbelin's troupe in Berlin.

12 *Sémiramis* (1748): five-act verse tragedy. Sémiramis, Queen of Babylon, has colluded in the murder of her husband Ninus, whose ghost rises to demand justice. Queen Sémiramis seeks to marry a young general, Arzace, not knowing he is her long-lost son; the ghost of Ninus prevents the marriage by revealing their true relationship. In the final act of the play, Arzace fatally stabs his mother in his father's tomb, mistaking her for his enemy. The German translation was by J. F. Löwen (1755).

13 Lessing refers to the "Dissertation sur la tragédie ancienne et modern" ["Dissertation on Ancient and Modern Tragedy"] (1748), published as a preface to *Sémiramis*, in which Voltaire argues for the superiority of modern French tragedy over that of the ancients.

14 Here Lessing paraphrases – and occasionally takes phrases verbatim – from Voltaire; see "Dissertation sur la tragédie ancienne et modern" 157; for an English translation, see Voltaire, "Dissertation on Ancient and Modern Tragedy" 26–7. As theater became increasingly oriented toward the middle classes over the course of the eighteenth century, new dramatic modes such as bourgeois drama as well as new audience demographics necessitated a shift in theater-going practices that had favored aristocratic privilege. This shift included the elimination of the seventeenth-century practice of allowing (sometimes more than a hundred) socially important spectators to sit on the stage.

15 The ambitious staging called for by *Sémiramis* was not realized at its premiere, despite financial support from Louis XV.

16 The playwright and historian Jean-François Marmontel recounts that the ghost of Ninus had to struggle to make his way through the throng of spectators on the stage. The ensuing hilarity fueled Voltaire's campaign to remove spectators from the French stage, and the practice was abolished in 1759; see Marmontel, *Mémoires d'un père pour servir a l'instruction de ses enfants* 227. Chronicler Jean Louis Marie Dugas de Bois Saint-Just (1743–1820) adds that a sentinel in the background cried out "Messieurs, place à l'ombre, s'il vous plait, place à l'ombre" ["Gentleman, make way for the ghost, please, make way for the ghost"]; see Dugas de Bois Saint-Just, *Paris, Versailles, et les provinces* 5.

17 Titular characters in tragedies by Voltaire.

Essay 11

1 Lessing continues his discussion, from [10], of Ninus's ghost in *Sémiramis* and Voltaire's defense of this choice in the "Dissertation sur la tragédie ancienne et modern" ["Dissertation on Ancient and Modern Tragedy"] (1748). With *Sémiramis*, Voltaire challenged both the traditional rules of classical tragedy and new attitudes of the Enlightenment; see Niklaus, "Introduction" 39–137.

2 Voltaire, "Dissertation sur la tragédie" 159–60. In Francklin's translation of the "Dissertation," see 30–31.

3 The playwright's responsibility for historical accuracy has been a topic of debate since the classical era. In 1759, Lessing described the playwright as a "lord over history"; see *Briefe, die neueste Litteratur betreffend* (Letter 63) dated 18 October 1759, *Werke und Briefe* 4: 647. He maintains this view throughout the *Hamburg Dramaturgy*, repeatedly dismissing the need for historical accuracy.

4 Early in his career, in a letter to Mendelssohn, Lessing had argued that illusion was not necessary for dramatic effect; see "Briefwechsel über das Trauerspiel" (Letter 110) dated 18 December 1756, *Werke und Briefe* 3: 693–703 (also 11/1: 144–54). By the time of this writing, however, Lessing has developed a theory of illusionistic theater that stresses an "internal probability" (*innere Wahrscheinlichkeit*), in which the spectator's affective response is more important than a strict representation of reality.

5 Tr. note: we translate *Quelle des Schrecklichen* as "wellspring of terror" here; on Lessing's distinction between *Schrecken* (terror) and *Furcht* (fear), see [32.6].

6 See "Dissertation sur la tragédie" 160–1.

7 In fact, Voltaire intended for the ghost to appear in profound darkness, with dramatic lighting and sound effects; this staging was not always realized (see Niklaus 44). French

productions of the play would have been much more lavish than those of the Hamburg National Theater.

8 Again, Lessing's view of what constitutes an illusionistic performance differs from a contemporary understanding of realism. Ensemble performance developed with the rise of the modern stage director, considerably after Lessing's time.

9 The ghost of Hamlet's father does in fact appear to others in the first and fourth scenes of the play.

10 Lessing had argued previously against an "infectious" model of stage emotion, proposing instead a relationship of "sympathetic resonance" between actor and spectator. See for example his letter to Mendelssohn (Letter 115) dated 2 February 1757, *Werke und Briefe* 3: 711–15 (also 11/1: 165–69).

Essay 12

1 Lessing continues his critique, begun in [10], of Ninus's ghost in Voltaire's *Sémiramis*.

2 Lessing uses the word *Maschine* as a deliberate play on the term *deus ex machina*.

3 Tr. note: on our translation of *Mitleid* as "compassion" see [32.6].

4 As in [11], Lessing's criticism of Voltaire's ghost privileges the creation of poetic illusion over strict verisimilitude.

5 Another instance in which Lessing condemns sermonizing theater; see [2.4].

6 Tr. note: "punishment of good and evil" is a faithful translation of Lessing's *Bestrafung des Guten und Bösen*; we assume that Lessing intended his reader to interpret this phrase as "judgment of good and evil." As with many of his contemporaries, Lessing's metaphysical beliefs are grounded in the philosophical optimism of Gottfried Wilhelm Leibniz (1646–1716) and Christian Wolff (1679–1754).

7 The Hamburg National Theater was in fact rather small; see J. G. Robertson for a description of the theater and its dimensions (14–15). The first French productions of *Sémiramis* presented neither the four scene changes – nor the multitude of onstage characters and extras (a total of 48) – called for by Voltaire; see Niklaus 42–44; 47.

8 *Le Philosophe Marié* (1727): five-act verse comedy by Destouches. For an English translation (in prose), see that of John Kelly.

9 *Le Philosophe Marié* was produced annually at the Comédie Française until 1753; see Joannidès.

10 Lessing refers to *Des Herrn Nericault Destouches sämtliche theatralische Werke* (1756). *Le Philosophe Marié* was translated under a number of German titles; this particular translation (in alexandrines), *Der verehelichte Philosoph*, appears to have been by Johann Christian Krüger in collaboration with Konrad Ekhof; see H. Devrient 145; see also J. G. Robertson 62–3.

11 Céliante; Géronte: respectively, the sister-in-law and uncle of the titular married philosopher.

12 *Le Caffé, ou L'écossaise* (1760): five-act prose comedy by Voltaire. The translation used was that of Johann Joachim Christoph Bode (1731–93), *Das Caffeehaus, ein rührundes Lustspiel* [*The Coffeehouse, a moving comedy*] (1760), later published as *Das Caffeehaus, oder die Schottländerinn* [*The Coffeehouse, or the Scotch Woman*] (1765). For an English translation, see Francklin. Voltaire's play is set in a London inn, run by the landlord Fabrice. Its inhabitants are Lord Monrose, a Scottish nobleman condemned to death; an impoverished young lady, Lindane; and a scheming journalist, Frélon, who hopes to profit from the others' misfortunes. Lindane is revealed as the daughter of Monrose but is in love with Lord Murray (Murrai), whose family ruined hers. Murray's erstwhile mistress, Lady Alton, seeks revenge against Murray by having Lindane charged with treason. Thanks to the intervention of Freeport (Fréeport), a London merchant, Lindane is saved and reunited with her father. Murray obtains a pardon for Monrose and is allowed to marry Lindane.

13 Voltaire speciously presented *L'écossaise* as a translation of a play by "Monsieur Hume," meaning to cite Scottish playwright John Home (1722–1808), author of the controversial

tragedy *Douglas* (1757). A defense of *Douglas* by the Scottish moral philosopher and historian David Hume (1711–76) was prefaced to printed editions of Home's play. See Duckworth 243–44.

14 Don Marzio: the meddling slanderer in *La bottega del caffè* (c.1750), a comedy by Carlo Goldoni (1707–93).

15 Voltaire created Frélon (or Wasp, in some editions) to retaliate against critic Élie Catherine Fréron (1719–76), who attacked Voltaire and other members of the French Enlightenment in his periodical *L'Année littéraire* and other writings. See Duckworth 225–32.

16 Lessing frequently complains about the indifference of German audiences.

17 George Colman (the Elder) (1732–94): prominent English comic playwright and theater manager. *Le Caffé, ou L'écossaise* was originally translated as *The Coffee-House, or The Fair Fugitive* in 1760; Colman's adaptation, *The English Merchant*, was first performed and published in 1767. Lessing's critique of English conditions and characters in Voltaire's play and his praise of Colman's alterations are drawn almost verbatim from English criticism in *The Monthly Review*; see Anon., "The English Merchant, A Comedy" 224–5.

18 An error: Murray obtains Monrose's pardon in *L'écossaise*. In *The English Merchant*, Colman replaces Murray with a reformed rake (Lord Falbridge); he renames the father Sir William Douglas and the daughter Amelia.

19 *The English Merchant* was more sentimental than Colman's most popular comedies, *The Jealous Wife* (1761) and *The Clandestine Marriage* (1766) (a collaboration with David Garrick). Konrad Ernst Ackermann (1712–71): important German actor-manager who constructed a new theater in Hamburg in 1765, which was subsequently taken over by Johann Friedrich Löwen in order to form the Hamburg National Theater. Ackermann's company performed Bode's translation of *The Jealous Wife* in 1765.

20 In Colman's play, Freeport confesses that his generous actions were initiated by tender feelings for Amelia.

21 In multiple essays of the *Hamburg Dramaturgy*, Lessing discusses the English taste for action-packed plays and what he perceives as a German aversion to excessively complex plots.

22 William Congreve (1670–1729) and William Wycherley (c. 1640–1715): English comic playwrights.

23 *Il Caffè o La Scozzese* (1762): see Diodati I: 179–259. Diodati does not provide the translator's name; for more on the Italian translations of *The Scotch Wife*, see Pieri 170–4.

24 For the translator's justification of the scene's inclusion, see Diodati 181.

25 Frélon is banished in the Italian translation.

Essay 13

1 *Cénie* (1752): sentimental comedy by Françoise de Grafigny; see [20].

2 The "epidemic emergency," according to J. G. Robertson, was influenza (64).

3 For *The New Agnes*, see [10]. *Die Gouvernante* [*The Governess*] (c. 1763): a one-act comic operetta. Franz Anton Nuth (1698?–1788) and Joseph Felix von Kurz (Bernardon) (1717–84), both Viennese harlequins, each wrote a version of *Die Gouvernante*; see Schmid, *Chronologie des deutschen Theaters* 221; see also J. G. Robertson 64–5.

4 *La fausse Agnès, ou le poète campagnard* (wr. 1727): three-act prose comedy; literally, *The False Agnès, or the Country Poet*. Samuel Foote published an English translation under the title *The Young Hypocrite, or the Country Poet* in 1762. The German translation, *Der poetische Dorfjunker* (1741), included in volume 3 of J. C. Gottsched's *Die Deutsche Schaubühne* (1740–50), was by L. A. V. Gottsched; see [13.5].

5 Johann Christoph Gottsched (1700–66): prominent German critic, literary theorist, and major reformer of the theater, who advocated that the German theater should adopt French neoclassical models; also a mediocre playwright. Learned lady friend: Luise Adelgunde Victorie Gottsched (née Kulmus) (1713–62): prolific German translator, playwright, and satirist, known as the "inventor of Saxon comedy." Although L. A. V. Gottsched has been

eclipsed by her more famous husband, recent scholarly reevaluations have illuminated her significant contribution to German letters; see Kord, *Little Detours: Letters and Plays by Luise Gottsched*, and Brown, *Luise Gottsched the Translator*. Over the course of his career, Lessing grew increasingly hostile towards the work of J. C. Gottsched; see Letter 17 (dated 16 February 1759) of the *Briefe, die neueste Litteratur betreffend* (*Werke und Briefe* 4: 499–501).

6 Masure: character in *Der Poetische Dorfjunker* (M. des Mazures in the original).

7 Tr. note: the term Lessing uses here, *Virtuosin,* is a translation of the French term *virtuose,* which, in the original, later is made synonymous with a *savante,* or "learned woman." Destouches makes comic use of the word's double connotation (virtuous/worldly). Henriette: the titular hypocrite in L. A. V. Gottsched's translation, Angélique in the original.

8 Tr. note: L. A. V. Gottsched's substitution in German is *Wunder*, which translates as marvel, wonder, miracle, or prodigy. Our choice of "wonder" here allows for retention of Lessing's play on words in the next sentence.

9 Agnes: an appellation for an innocent young girl; the character type became associated with Molière's ingénue Agnès in *L'école des femmes* [*School for Wives*] (1662).

10 *Die stumme Schönheit* (1747): one-act alexandrine comedy by J. E. Schlegel. Tr. note: although a more accurate translation of Schlegel's title might be *The Silent Beauty,* translator Andrè Lefevere plays on the double meaning of "dumb" in his translation, *The Dumb Beauty;* see Schlegel and Lefevere. In Schlegel's play, Leonore, the daughter of a rich landowner, was given as an infant to the care of Mrs. Lovetotalk, a middle-class widow with a daughter of her own, Charlotte. Mrs. Lovetotalk switches the two girls, in the hopes that she can secure a wealthy husband for Charlotte, the silent beauty.

11 J. E. Schlegel's "Schreiben über die Komödie in Versen" ["Writings on Comedy in Verse"] (1740) defends the use of verse in comedy, a choice that runs counter to the dictates of French neoclassicism, which associated verse with tragedy and with characters drawn from the nobility.

12 Tr. note: in German, as in English, quadrille can refer both to a type of square dance and to a card game (specifically, a four-person version of ombre popular in the eighteenth century).

13 Mrs. Lovetotalk: Lefevere's English translation of "Frau Praatgern."

14 *Miss Sara Sampson* (1755): five-act prose tragedy by Lessing; considered the first German bourgeois tragedy (*bürgerliches Trauerspiel*). See *Werke und Briefe* 3: 431–526. The eponymous Sara was a highly coveted role and one for which Hensel was especially known.

15 Here Lessing apparently draws on his earlier medical studies. Shortly after the performance of *Miss Sara Sampson* (6 May 1767), Lessing asked his brother to forward a medical treatise from his library entitled "Von dem Zupfen der Sterbenden" ["On the Spasms of the Dying"]; see "Letter to Karl Lessing" (Letter 373) dated 22 May 1767, *Werke und Briefe* 11/1: 467.

16 Principal actress Karoline Schulze (later Schulze-Kummerfeld) (1745–1815) claims in her memoirs that Hensel stole this bit of business from her. Both actresses shared the same repertoire, including the role of Sara, and Hensel eventually succeeded in forcing Schulze to leave Hamburg. See Kummerfeld, "Aus dem Komödiantenleben des vorigen Jahrhunderts: Denkwürdigkeiten von Karoline Schulze" 360; 398–400; for Schulze-Kummerfeld's full account of her rivalry with Hensel at the Hamburg National Theater, see Schulze-Kummerfeld, *Lebenserinnerungen* 1: 221–9.

Essay 14

1 Lessing continues his discussion, from [13], of his bourgeois tragedy *Miss Sara Sampson* (1755). Some have stated, incorrectly, that the "French critic" was Denis Diderot (1753–84), philosopher, playwright, and editor of the *Encyclopédie*; the error stems from Lessing's mention of Diderot later in this essay. Jean-Marie Valentin identifies the author as Jean-Charles-Philibert Trudaine de Montigny; see *Dramaturgie de Hambourg* 391. Both Lessing and Diderot defended emerging middle-class modes of drama, and Lessing's dramatic theory is indebted to Diderot, whose work he translated as *Das Theater des Herrn Diderot* [*The*

Theater of M. Diderot] (1760); see *Werke und Briefe* 5/1: 10–230. Diderot intended to include a commissioned translation of *Sara* in an (unrealized) anthology of bourgeois tragedies; see Heitner, "Diderot's Own *Miss Sara Sampson*" 40–1.

2 This paragraph is paraphrased from the *Journal Étranger* review of *Sara* that Lessing references in his footnote.

3 Jean-François Marmontel (1723–99): French playwright, novelist, and critic. Lessing translates from Marmontel's discussion of popular versus heroic tragedy in his *Poétique françoise*.

4 *Poétique françoise* II: 49–51. Marmontel references the tragic figures of Barnwell and Beverley, from, respectively, George Lillo's *The London Merchant* (1731) and Edward Moore's *The Gamester* (1753), representative English bourgeois tragedies that were highly influential in both France and Germany.

5 *L'humanité, ou, le tableau de l'indigence* (1761/1777): five-act bourgeois tragedy by Pierre Louis Paul Randon de Boisset (1708–76). German translations were published in 1762 and 1764; for their titles and history, see J. G. Robertson 234.

6 The review suggests that many scenes, including that of Sara's death, would benefit from cutting and finds some to be improbable or dubiously motivated.

7 From Voltaire's defense of his comedy *L'enfant prodigue* [*The Prodigal Son*] (1736); see "Lettre á M. Berger."

8 *Le Joueur* (1696): five-act verse comedy by French playwright Jean-François Regnard (1655–1709). The theater may have used the German prose translation (possibly by J. C. Krüger) staged in Hamburg by Schönemann in 1747; see J. G. Robertson 66–7. A 1748 translation by Lessing and Christian Felix Weisse is not extant. Susanna Centlivre (1669–1723) provided an English adaptation, *The Gamester* (1708).

9 *Le Chevalier Joueur* [*The Gambling Knight*] (1697): five-act prose comedy by Charles-Rivière Dufresny or Du Fresny (1648–1724). Lessing's criticism of Regnard and Dufresny comes from French sources, one of which is the *Histoire du théâtre français depuis son origine jusqu'à présent* (1721), by historian brothers François (1698–1753) and Claude Parfaict (c.1705–77); see Parfaict, *Histoire du théâtre français* 15: 405; 409; see also, Léris, *Dictionnaire portatif historique* 254–5. Lessing draws frequently from the *Histoire du théâtre français*, as well as from the Parfaicts' *Histoire générale du théâtre français* (1735–49).

10 *The Married Philosopher:* see [12]. *L'amant auteur et valet* [*The Lover, Author and Servant*] (1740): one-act comedy by Pierre Cérou (1709–97), first performed at the Théâtre Italien. It is not known which of several German translations was used here; see J. G. Robertson 67–8.

11 *La Mère Coquette, ou, Les Amans Brouillés* (1665): five-act verse comedy by French playwright and librettist Philippe Quinault (1635–88). Lessing's criticism comes from Parfaict 9: 369–82. The German translation used was likely *Die bulhafftige Mutter* found in *Schau-Bühne Englischer und Frantzösischer Comödianten [. . .]* [*Theater of the English and French Players*] (1670). *L'avocat Patelin* [*The Lawyer Patelin*] (1706): three-act prose comedy by French theologian and playwright David-Augustin de Brueys (1640–1723). It was translated into German as *Der betrogene Lackenhändler* [*The Swindled Paint Merchant*] (1742) and *Der Advocat Patelin* (1762). An English translation, *The Village Lawyer* (1792), is attributed to both Colman the Elder and Charles Lyons.

12 In Quinault's play, the titular character, assuming her husband has died in slavery, attempts to marry her daughter's suitor. After many complications, a maid brings news that an old slave (bribed to claim the husband is dead) is, in fact, the missing husband.

13 *La Farce de maître Pierre Pathelin* [*The Farce of Master Pierre Pathelin*] (c.1470).

14 *Der Freigeist* (wr. 1749). Adrast, a freethinker, rejects the friendship of Theophan, a clergyman, believing him to be a hypocrite. Theophan is engaged to the pious Juliane, while Adrast (secretly in love with Juliane) is engaged to her more spirited sister Henriette. The sisters realize they prefer each other's fiancés (and Theophan realizes he prefers Henriette); their father, Lisador, happily rearranges the couples at play's end.

15 *Der Freigeist* (1757): five-act prose tragedy by German playwright Joachim Wilhelm von Brawe (1738–58), which contended with Cronegk's *Codrus* in Nicolai's 1756 competition for the best unpublished German tragedy.

16 Johann: Adrast's servant.

17 Johann Michael Böck (1743–93): principal actor who came to Hamburg with Ackermann's company. Friedrich Ludwig Schröder believed Theophan to be Böck's best role; see Meyer 1: 147.

18 *Der Schatz* (1761): pastoral one-act comedy by Alsatian poet, playwright, and translator Gottlieb Konrad Pfeffel (1736–1809).

19 *Der Eremit* (1761): one-act verse tragedy; also published as *Der Einsiedler* [*The Recluse*] (1761).

Essay 15

1 *Zaïre* (1732): five-act verse tragedy. The company used J. J. Schwabe's German translation in alexandrines, *Zayre* (1741). A tremendous international success, in Germany *Zaïre* was arguably the most popular of Voltaire's tragedies; see Jacobs 282–92. Zaïre, a slave to Orosmane (the Sultan of Jerusalem), has been raised Muslim, despite her Christian origins. Zaïre and Orosmane fall in love and prepare to marry. Liberated by Orosmane, Lusignan, the aged former king of Jerusalem, discovers that Zaïre and Nérestan, a French knight, are his children. Before he dies, Lusignan has Zaïre swear to become Christian and to hide her parentage; Zaïre is now torn between love and Christian filial duty. Orosmane becomes suspicious of her secrecy, then jealous when he intercepts a letter from Nérestan; Zaïre avows her fidelity but will not reveal her secrets. Orosmane kills her, and then, after Nérestan reveals himself as Zaïre's brother, kills himself.

2 Lessing quotes the majority of the "Avertissement" added by Voltaire to the 1738 edition of *Zaïre*.

3 Voltaire earlier claimed to have written the play in 22 days; see Jacobs 278.

4 *Polyeucte* (1643): five-act "Christian tragedy" in verse by Pierre Corneille, inspired by the Roman martyr Polyeuctus.

5 Lessing quotes from *Le Comédien* [*The Actor*] (1747), by French journalist and theorist Pierre Rémond de Sainte-Albine (1699–1778); see Sainte-Albine 208.

6 Gallantry: a swipe at Voltaire, who had previously criticized what he perceived to be an overemphasis on love in French tragedy and who, in order to avoid charges of hypocrisy, employed the term "gallantry" rather than "love" in his description of *Zaïre*. See Voltaire, *Discours sur la tragédie* 179–83; *A Discourse on Tragedy* 189–91; and Jacobs 399.

7 Tr. note: the term Lessing uses here, *Kanzleistil* – which we translate as "court-style" – refers to the style of bureaucratic writing found in chancery documents.

8 Voltaire never mentions a debt to *Othello*; this issue was (and continues to be) strongly debated; see Jacobs 302–11.

9 The quotation in Lessing's footnote comes from the prologue to Hill's *Tragedy of Zara* by actor, playwright, and theatrical manager Colley Cibber (1671–1757); see Hill xiv.

10 Christoph Martin Wieland (1733–1813) provided the first German overview of Shakespeare's work with his prose translation of 22 plays in eight volumes (1762–66). Critics have taken Wieland to task for his style, his errors in translation, and his alterations that purged the plays of their "less tasteful" elements; see Paulin, "Shakespeare and Germany" 317.

11 *Zaïre* premiered at the Comédie-Française in 1732.

12 Aaron Hill (1685–1750): English playwright and essayist, whose adaptation of *Zaïre*, *The Tragedy of Zara* (1736), was first performed in London in 1735 and staged at Drury Lane in 1736.

13 Sir Everard Fawkener (1694–1758): English merchant, diplomat, and statesman. Voltaire's "Épître Dédicatoire à M. Fakener [sic]" ["An Epistle Dedicatory to Mr. Falkener [sic]"] appeared with the 1732 printing of *Zaïre*; the "Seconde Lettre au même monsieur Fakener [sic]" ["A Second Letter to Mr. Falkener [sic]"] was appended to the second 1736 edition.

14 Joseph Addison (1672–1719): influential English essayist and playwright, known for his literary/social periodicals *The Tatler* and *The Spectator*, as well as for his classical tragedy *Cato* (1713).

15 Phèdre, Cleopatra: scholars remain uncertain as to which English plays Voltaire might be referencing here. Cato: a reference to Addison's tragedy (although the character does not in fact compare himself to a rock).

16 This paragraph is taken from the second letter to Fawkener; see Voltaire, "Seconde Lettre" 412–13; "A Second Letter to Mr. Falkener [sic]" 16.

17 Ben Jonson (1572?–1637), John Dryden, Nathaniel Lee (c.1649–92), Thomas Otway (1652–85), and Nicholas Rowe (1674–1718): all prominent English dramatists of the seventeenth century.

18 Eighteenth-century audiences were accustomed to musical entertainment between the acts of a play.

Essay 16

1 Lessing continues his discussion from [15] of *Zara* (Aaron Hill's translation of Voltaire's *Zaïre*).

2 Susanna Maria Cibber (1714–66): celebrated English singer and actor; much favored by Handel.

3 An error: Susanna Cibber was married to Colley Cibber's son, Theophilus (1703–58), also an actor and playwright.

4 Jeanne Cathérine Gaussin (also Gaussem) (1711–67): French actor famous for her performance of heroic plays; her first appearance at the Comédie-Française was in 1731. Voltaire's laudatory poem "Épître Dédicatoire à Mademoiselle Gossin [sic], Jeune Actrice" ["Dedicatory letter to Mlle. Gaussin, Young Actress"] was added to the 1732 edition of *Zaïre*.

5 Aaron Hill (c. 1715–39): nephew and namesake of the playwright; his performance of Osman (Orosman) on *Zara*'s opening night was a spectacular failure and he was removed from the cast.

6 From Voltaire's second letter to Fawkener; see Voltaire, "Seconde Lettre" 411; "A Second Letter" 15. See also [15.13].

7 Count Gasparo Gozzi (1713–86): Italian playwright, critic, poet, and translator whose collected works appeared in 12 volumes (1794–98). Not to be confused with his more famous brother, Carlo Gozzi.

8 For the plot of *Zaïre*, see [15.1].

9 The passage in Lessing's footnote is from G. Gozzi, *Zaira* 62.

10 In the original (as well as in the German translation) Orosman stabs himself, then orders safe conduct for Nérestan, who speaks the final lines of the play; see Voltaire, *Zaïre* 523.

11 Frederik Duim (1673–1754): Dutch playwright and author of the adaptation *Zaïre, bekeerde Turkinne* [*Zaïre, the Converted Turk*] (1735); possibly the father of Izaak Duim (1696–1782), a renowned actor.

12 See Duim's preface to his *Zaïre*, "Berecht aan den Lezer" ["Notice to the Reader"]; the quotation appears on the 26th page.

13 This sentence is also a quotation from Duim's preface, beginning at the bottom of the 26th page.

14 This paragraph is drawn from *Le Comédien* [*The Actor*] (1747), in which Sainte-Albine details the emotional and physical transitions that an actor playing Orosman must embody; see Sainte-Albine 208–14. See also [5.6] and [15.5].

Essay 17

1 *Sidney* (1745): three-act verse comedy by French playwright and poet Jean-Baptiste-Louis Gresset (1709–77). Translated anonymously into English as *Sidney, or, the Self-Murderer Reclaimed* (1801) and into German as *Sidnei, oder: der Schwermüthige* [*Sidney, or, the Melancholic*] (1751). Sidney, a rich young Englishman, has come to regret his libertine lifestyle, which led him to abandon his love, Rosalie (Rosamond, in the English); his empty existence and guilt have rendered him suicidal. Sidney's friend Hamilton tries to help him but fails. Rosalie

arrives to confront Sidney, but his friends learn that he has already drunk poison. Luckily, his faithful servant, Dumont, has substituted a harmless drink in its place. The estranged lovers are reunited.

2 See Gresset 53; for the English, see Anon., *Sidney* 196.

3 *La Famille* [*The Family*] (1736): one-act prose comedy by French playwright and novelist Thomas L'Affichard (1698–1753). The translation used by the Hamburg company, *Ist er von Familie?*, is unknown; a translation published in 1749 by Schönemann is entitled simply *Die Familie* [*The Family*]. See J. G. Robertson 71.

4 *Das Gespenst mit der Trommel* (1741): five-act prose comedy; a translation by L. A. V. Gottsched of *Le Tambour nocturne* [*The Nocturnal Drummer*] (1736) by Destouches, itself an adaptation of *The Drummer, or the Haunted House* (1715/16) by Joseph Addison; see [10.2].

5 *Démocrite amoureux* (1700): five-act verse comedy by Jean-François Regnard. The German translation in alexandrines used, *Demokrit, oder, Der lachende Philosoph* [*Democritus, or, the Laughing Philosopher*] (1749), was by actor-manager and playwright Heinrich Gottfried Koch (1703–75); see J. G. Robertson 72. In this essay, Lessing quotes liberally and often verbatim from the *Histoire du théâtre français* (see Parfaict 14: 164–70). Democritus, a misanthropic philosopher, exiles himself to a cave with his servant Strabo. They befriend a peasant, Thaler, and his daughter Criseis, with whom Democritus falls in love. Agelas, king of Athens, brings them all to his court and also falls in love with Criseis, who turns out to be the long-lost half-sister of Princess Ismene, his intended wife. Agelas marries Criseis, freeing Ismene to marry her love, Prince Agenor. Strabo falls in love with Ismene's servant Cleanthis, who is revealed to be his own forsaken wife. Most of this action occurs in the final act; the play deals primarily with Democritus's struggles to conceal his feelings.

6 Jeanne Olivier Bourgignon Beauval (c.1647–1720) and Pierre le Noir, sieur de la Thorillière (1656–1731): French actors; contemporaries of Molière.

Essay 18

1 *Les Fausses Confidences* (1737): three-act prose comedy by the noted French playwright, journalist, and novelist Pierre Carlet de Chamblain de Marivaux (1688–1763). The German translation used is unknown. Contemporary English translations have been provided by Bentley (*The False Confessions*) and Wertenbaker (*False Admissions*).

2 An error: Marivaux was 75.

3 Harlequin: Arlecchino, a character from Italian *commedia dell'arte*; Marivaux wrote extensively for the Théâtre Italien in Paris. Lessing exaggerates Marivaux's use of Harlequin, who appears in 13 of his 36 comedies.

4 Marivaux's distinct style came to be known as "marivaudage."

5 Callippides: proverbial Athenian actor who imitated running while remaining in place (either the 5th century BCE tragedian, or a mime of the same name).

6 In 1737, influential German actress-manager Friedericke Caroline Neuber ("die Neuberin") (1697–1760) staged *Die Verbannung des Hanswurst von der Bühne* [*The Expulsion of Harlequin from the Theater*]. Neuber partnered with J. C. Gottsched to develop a literary and morally respectable German-language theater. More so than Neuber, Gottsched objected to the improvised (and sometimes obscene) comedy of Hanswurst, the German Harlequin. Lessing, despite his own disapproval of lowbrow comedy, had defended Hanswurst while attacking Gottsched's French preferences; see *Briefe, die neueste Litteratur betreffend* (Letter 17) dated 16 February 1759, *Werke und Briefe* 4: 499–501. Tr. note: Lessing uses the Latin phrase *sub auspiciis Sr. Magnificenz* ("under the auspices of his Magnificence") to heighten his sarcastic jibe at Gottsched.

7 The brightly colored peasant costume of Hanswurst included an open jacket.

8 *Timon le Misanthrope* (1722) and *Le faucon et les oies de Bocace* [*Boccaccio's The Falcon and the Geese*] (1725): comedies written for the Théâtre Italien by Louis-François Delisle de La Drevetière (1682–1756).

9 Parasite: stock character of Roman comedy, a leechlike flatterer.

10 Reference to the tragicomic "satyr play" of ancient Greece, presented after a tragic trilogy and featuring mythological characters such as satyrs.

11 Lawyer and historian Justus Möser's (1720–94) essay, *Harlekin, oder Vertheidigung des Groteske-Komischen* [*Harlequin or a Defense of the Grotesquely Comical*] (1761), favorably reviewed by Lessing.

12 Möser has Harlequin say: "Herr Lessing, a man who possesses enough insight to one day become my eulogist, would perhaps object here that the exaggeration of figures is a sure means of undermining [the writer's] purpose, by misleading spectators to believe that they are far beyond the licentious ridicule of folly"; in a later edition, Möser added an erratum, claiming that he had misremembered statements by Lessing in the *Beiträge*. For both the original quotation and the correction, see Möser 46.

13 Johann Gottlieb Hensel (1728–87): husband of leading company member Sophie Hensel. Merschy: a minor actor in the company (first name and dates unavailable).

14 *Zelmire* (1762): five-act verse tragedy by French playwright and actor Pierre-Laurent Buirette de Belloy (also known as Dormont de Belloy) (1727–75). Polidore, king of Lesbos, thought murdered by his usurping son Azor, is being kept alive in a subterranean tomb by his daughter Zelmire, who gives him her breast milk. Azor has been killed by Prince Anténor, who now controls the island, supported by the head of the military, General Rhamnès. Zelmire's husband, Ilus, returns from battle and denounces her. Anténor attempts to stab Ilus, then frames Zelmire when she intervenes. Zelmire is finally cleared when Polidore is revealed and a Thracian soldier produces a note in which Azor identifies Anténor as his murderer. Anténor orders Rhamnès to kill Polidore, but the general kills Anténor instead.

15 *Le Siège de Calais* (1765): five-act "national tragedy" in verse. Depicts the heroism of self-sacrificing French burghers during the Hundred Years' War; the play became a sensation, due in part to the recent events of the Seven Years' War (1756–63).

16 Calais granted de Belloy honorary citizenship.

17 Albinus: referred to in Horace's *Ars Poetica* [*The Art of Poetry*].

18 "Good! you will be able to look after your means!": for the full quotation, in Latin and English, see Horace, *Satires, Epistles, and Ars Poetica* 476.

19 "When once this canker, this lust of petty gain has stained the soul": also from Horace, who questions how we can make poems worthy of posterity; see Horace, *Satires, Epistles, and Ars Poetica* 476–8.

20 Bartolus: Italian jurist Bartolo da Sassoferrato (1313/14–57), whose name became internationally synonymous with juridical excellence.

21 Jean-Baptiste-Jacques Elie de Beaumont (1710–86): prominent French jurist.

22 *Titus* (1760): five-act verse tragedy by de Belloy.

23 The play references the mythological story of Hypsipyle, Queen of Lemnos, as well as that of Pero and Cimon.

24 The critic to whom Lessing refers is unknown; see [18.26].

25 *Zaïre, Alzire, Mahomet* (wr. 1736): all tragedies by Voltaire.

26 The quoted passage is a paraphrase of an anonymous essay on *Zelmire* published in Pierre Rousseau's *Journal Encyclopédique* 14: 124 (original 1762 edition); 14: 37 (1967 reprint).

Essay 19

1 Lessing continues his discussion from [18] of an anonymous French essay on the subject of de Belloy's *Zelmire*.

2 Tr. note: the word Lessing uses here, *Wahrscheinlichkeit*, translates literally as: "the quality of seeming true." The term is most often translated as "probability" or "plausibility."

3 *Coup de théâtre*: term connoting a sudden and surprising plot development.

4 The tyrant: Prince Anténor. For the plot of *Zelmire*, see [18.14].

5 Ilus and Polidore, who is disguised as a Trojan soldier, go to battle with Anténor. Zelmire, weeping because she believes Polidore captured, does not recognize the disguised Polidore as he enters a tomb to hide. Polidore, looking toward the battle, fails to see Zelmire. Zelmire, attempting to save her father, reveals the location of the "Trojan Captain" to Rhamnès, inadvertently giving her father to the enemy.

6 Lessing paraphrases again from the *Journal Encyclopédique* 14: 126–7 (1762 edition); 14: 38 (1967 reprint).

7 For different theories regarding the translator's identity, see J. G. Robertson 73–4.

8 The alexandrine verse called for by neoclassicists naturally suits the cadence and construction of French; it pairs less well with German.

9 Antoine Houdar de la Motte (1672–1731): French playwright and theorist who challenged neoclassical principles, including the use of verse in tragedy; see la Motte, *Discours à l'occasion de la Tragédie d'Oedipe* 390–6.

10 David Isaac Borchers (1744–95): one of the strongest members of the Hamburg National Theater ensemble; the intuitive and highly versatile Borchers played young lovers, comic types, and, as Lessing indicates, even older roles. Although Borcher's career was affected by his volatile personality, he nonetheless gained recognition as Shakespearean performer. After his death, Borchers was memorialized for having "meticulously banned all obsession with declamation from his conversational tone (a rule Shakespeare put in Hamlet's mouth!)"; see "Ueber das Herzogliche Hoftheater zu Carlsruh in Oberschlesien" 521.

11 This criticism of "other young actors" hints at the increasing tension between Lessing and the Hamburg company; see the editor's first introductory essay in this volume (Baldyga, "Missions, Misunderstandings, and Mythologies" 7–8).

Essay 20

1 *Cénie* (1751): five-act sentimental comedy in prose by French playwright, novelist, and salonnière Françoise de Grafigny (Graffigny) (1695–1758); translated by L. A. V. Gottsched as *Cenie, oder die Grossmuth im Unglücke, ein moralisches Stück* [*Cenie, or Magnanimity in Misfortune, a moral play*] (1753). Dorimond's two nephews, Mericourt and Clerval, wish to marry his daughter Cénie. Mericourt seeks Cénie's fortune; Clerval, only her love. When Cénie, who loves Clerval, objects to her betrothal to Mericourt, he produces letters from her deceased mother revealing that Dorimond is not her father and that Cénie is in fact the daughter of her governess, Orphise. In the end, Cénie's father, Dorsainville (Orphise's long-lost husband), is rediscovered, enabling Cénie to marry Clerval.

2 Lessing quotes from the first page of L. A. V. Gottsched, "Vorrede."

3 Grafigny, *Cénie* 12; for the English, see Grafigny, *Cenia* 13.

4 "Alsdann werde ich meiner Güter erst recht genießen, wenn ich euch beide dadurch werde glücklich gemacht haben" (*Cenie*, trans. L. A. V. Gottsched 12).

5 "Frau Mutter! O welch ein süßer Namen!" (*Cenie*, trans. L. A. V. Gottsched 65); in the German text, the name Cenie is unaccented.

6 "Gnädiger Herr Vater! [. . .] Bin ich Ihrer Gnade wert!" (*Cenie*, trans. L. A. V. Gottsched 84).

7 Here Lessing critiques not Hensel's physical appearance but rather her forceful emotional expression, which he also censures in [5]; in contrast, Hensel is praised in [13] for giving a "delicate" and "picturesque" performance of femininity. It is assumed that this review exacerbated the already existing tension between Lessing and Hensel.

8 See Grafigny, *Cénie* 84; for the German, see Grafigny, *Cenie* 88; for the English, see Grafigny, *Cenia* 64.

9 "For this man, his limbs are all tongues": from the epigram "De Pantomimo" found in the anonymous *Anthologia Latina* (c. 500). The line continues, "It is the miracle of art which enables his fingers to speak when his mouth is silent"; see Kay 44; 136.

10 Friday: Lessing's mistake; the performance was on Monday. *Amalia* (1765): five-act prose comedy by German playwright Christian Felix Weisse (1726–1804), a friend of Lessing's

from their college days. Amalia learns that Freemann [sic], the man who jilted her five years earlier, has become impoverished through free-living. Having inherited wealth, Amalia disguises herself as a man (Manley) in order to find and aid him. In the final act, "Manley" tests Lady Freemann (who is not legally married to Freemann) by offering to return jewelry lost through gambling in exchange for her favors. Lady Freemann refuses, Freemann challenges "Manley," and Amalia reveals herself. Freemann wishes to marry the now wealthy Amalia, but she brings in Betty, the daughter he has by Lady Freemann, and insists that Freeman and Lady Freeman legitimize their relationship.

11 Madame Böck: Sophie Elisabeth Böck, née Schulz (c.1745–1800), married to J. M. Böck.

12 Novelistic: that is, fantastical; reflects eighteenth-century playwrights' views of the novel as not upholding standards of probability to which the theater ostensibly adhered.

13 In 5.5, "Manley" (Amalia in disguise) bluntly pressures Lady Freemann for sexual favors in exchange for discharging her debts. Lady Freemann refuses, thus proving her loyalty and love for Freemann; see [20.10]. Weisse did indeed revise this scene for the 1783 edition of his comedies.

14 Crébillonian capacity: allusion to Claude-Prosper Jolyot de Crébillon *fils* (1707–77), French libertine novelist and royal censor.

15 *Le Financier* (1762): a one-act prose comedy by French playwright and historian Germain-François Poullain de Saint-Foix (1698–1776). The German translation, *Der Finanzpachter* (1762), may have been by Christian August Wichmann (1735–1807); see J. G. Robertson 76.

Essay 21

1 *L'école des mères* (1744): five-act verse comedy by Nivelle de la Chaussée.

2 *L'école des mères* (1732): one-act prose comedy by Marivaux.

3 *Nanine* (1749): three-act verse comedy by Voltaire.

4 *Miles Gloriosus: The Braggart Captain* (c. 205 BCE); Roman comedy based on (unknown) Greek plays.

5 *Truculentus: The Churl* (c. 190 BCE); Roman comedy in the Greek style.

6 Grammarian: editor and commentator in the classical era.

7 A reference to the final line in Book I, Ch. 38 from the *De Officiis* of the great Roman rhetorician, statesman, philosopher, and scholar Marcus Tullius Cicero (106–43 BCE): "It is bad taste also to talk about one's self – especially if what one says is not true – and, amid the derision of one's hearers, to play 'The Braggart Captain'"; see Cicero *De Officiis* Book 1, section 137 (online); page 141 (print).

8 Plautus, *Miles Gloriosus* 2.1: "*Alazon* is the title of the comedy in Greek; in Latin we would say *Gloriosus*." Alazon: stock character of ancient Greek comedy; a braggart.

9 Thraso: another braggart soldier, from *The Eunuch* (161 BCE), by the Roman comic playwright Publius Terentius Afer (Terence) (c. 195 – c.159 BCE).

10 *Nanine* was originally published in 1749 with the first of these subtitles, *Le préjugé vaincu* [*Prejudice Overcome*]; the second, *L'homme sans préjugé* [*The Man without Prejudice*] was added later, perhaps to avoid confusion or comparison to Marivaux's *Le Préjugé vaincu* (1746); see Labriolle and Duckworth 22. Both subtitles appear singly or together in later editions.

11 *Pamela; or, Virtue Rewarded* (1741): popular epistolary novel by Samuel Richardson (1689–1761), in which a young servant, fending off rape and seduction, is rewarded by her master's proposal of marriage. Voltaire's play also centers on a *mésalliance* but otherwise does not resemble Richardson's novel. Lessing draws his statement directly from Léris, *Dictionnaire portatif*: "Le sujet de cette piece est tiré du Roman de *Pamela*" (313).

12 *Paméla en France* (1745) by French poet and playwright Louis de Boissy (1694–1758); *Paméla* (1743) by Nivelle de la Chaussée.

13 Loosely taken from Voltaire's preface to *L'enfant prodigue* 94.

14 From Voltaire's preface to *Nanine*, 72. Vulcan, Hector and Andromache: from Homer's *Iliad* (Books I and VI, respectively). Battle of Speyer (1703): disastrous German defeat by the

French during the War of Spanish Succession. Alcmena, Sosia: characters from Plautus's *Amphitryon*.

15 *Cénie:* see [20]. *The Father of the Family:* Diderot's *Le Père de famille* (1758), translated by Lessing in his collection *Das Theater des Herrn Diderot* (1760); see [14.1].

Essay 22

1 *Die kranke Frau* (1747): one-act comic afterpiece by Christian Fürchtegott Gellert (1715–69). Frau Stephan, envious of her sister-in-law's fashionable dress (an "Andrienne"), appears to be at death's door. Herr Stephan explores numerous remedies to restore her health; eventually, he is persuaded to purchase the dress in question, which results in Frau Stephan's immediate recovery.

2 Adrienne: Lessing's alternate spelling of "Andrienne." An eighteenth-century dress popularized through the stage; see J. G. Robertson 78.

3 Robe Ronde, Benedictine, Respectueuse: names of dresses; the latter two seem to be fictitious.

4 *Der Mann nach der Uhr, oder der ordentliche Mann* (1760), one-act prose comedy by German novelist, essayist, and playwright Theodor Gottlieb von Hippel the Elder (1741–96), from Königsberg (not Danzig).

5 *Vaterland:* an uncommon word for Lessing, which did not yet have the political associations that it would garner after the unification of Germany in 1871. Sara Figal explains that, "For some, the German *Vaterland* meant Prussia; for others, it included various constellations of German-speaking regions. . . . The German *Vaterland* was far from being clearly identifiable, whether by geographic, political, philosophical, linguistic, or ethnic identity markers" (72).

6 *Le Comte d'Essex* (1678): five-act verse tragedy by French playwright Thomas Corneille (1625–1709), the younger brother of Pierre Corneille; translated by L. Peter Stüven as *Der Graf von Essex* (1747). Based on the historical figure of Robert Devereux, 2nd earl of Essex (1567–1601), a famous favorite of Queen Elizabeth I, later executed by her after an attempted coup.

7 Calprenède: Gaultier de Coste, seigneur de La Calprenède (c. 1610–63), French playwright and novelist; his tragedy *Le Comte d'Essex* was published in 1638.

8 Lessing quotes freely here from T. Corneille's preface to *Le Comte d'Essex.*

9 David Hume discusses this incident in the fourth volume of his six-volume *History of England* (528–30). Lessing would have read Hume's history in English; a German translation of volume four would not appear until 1771. For the two-volume *History of Scotland* (1759) by Scottish historian William Robertson (1721–93), Lessing used the German translation published in 1762 by Matthias Theodor Christoph Mittelstedt.

10 Our quote here is taken from William Robertson, *History of Scotland* 2: 284–6, with original spelling retained. Lessing quotes from Mittelstedt 2: 301–3.

Essay 23

1 Lessing continues his discussion, from [22], of Thomas Corneille's *Le Comte d'Essex [The Earl of Essex]* (1678). Voltaire, in his collected works of Pierre Corneille, includes two plays by Thomas Corneille, including *Le Comte d'Essex*, which he critiques in his prefatory material entitled "*Le Comte d'Essex*, Tragédie de Thomas Corneille, 1678. Préface de l'Éditeur" (1761).

2 Voltaire, "*Le Comte d'Essex*" 1007; 1013.

3 Voltaire, "*Le Comte d'Essex*" 1004.

4 Lessing provides a loose translation of Hume; see *The History of England* 4: 515. We reproduce Hume's original.

5 Sir Walter Raleigh (1552?–1618): English courtier-explorer who competed with Essex for Elizabeth's favor. Sir Robert Cecil (1563–1612): the 1st earl of Salisbury, who became Elizabeth's chief minister.

6 Sir Henry Unton (1557?–96): English diplomat and member of Parliament; ambassador to France 1591–93.

7 Paragraph paraphrased from Hume 4: 562–63.

8 Voltaire, "*Le Comte d'Essex*" 1004.

9 See Hume 4: 475. Voltaire, "*Le Comte d'Essex*" 1013. Capture of Cadiz: in 1596, the Spanish port of Cadiz fell to a naval expedition led by Essex, Raleigh, and Charles Howard (1536–1624), commander of the English fleet against the Spanish Armada, later ennobled as the Earl of Nottingham.

10 Corneille, *Le Comte d'Essex* 3. Cobham: Henry Brooke (later Lord Cobham) (1527–97), brother-in-law of Robert Cecil.

11 Voltaire, "*Le Comte d'Essex*" 1006.

12 Corneille, *Le Comte d'Essex* 27.

13 Voltaire, "*Le Comte d'Essex*" 1012.

14 From Hume 4: 508.

15 Horace (originally Horatio) Walpole, 4th Earl of Orford (1717–97): English author in numerous genres. In his footnote, Lessing references the 1767 French translation of Walpole's novel *The Castle of Otranto* (1764), the preface of which takes issue with Voltaire's historical accuracy; see Walpole 23.

16 Voltaire, "*Le Comte d'Essex*" 1002. Robert Dudley (1532/33–88): created Earl of Leicester in 1564 by Queen Elizabeth I; stepfather of Essex.

17 The poet Arouet: Voltaire was born François-Marie Arouet; he was appointed a chamberlain of the court by Frederick II of Prussia in 1750.

18 Voltaire, "*Le Comte d'Essex*" 1017. *Hysteron proteron*: rhetorical device in which temporal order is reversed.

19 From Hume 4: 483–4.

Essay 24

1 Lessing continues his discussion, from [23], of Voltaire's critique of Thomas Corneille's *Le Comte d'Essex* [*The Earl of Essex*].

2 Voltaire makes comments about Elizabeth's age and nose in his preface to Corneille's play; see "*Le Comte d'Essex*" 1004.

3 French historian Paul Rapin de Thoyras (1661–1725) recounts Elizabeth's relationship with Essex in his *Histoire d'Angleterre* [*History of England*] 7: 508ff. As Rapin de Thoyras indicates, there was a 34-year age difference between the monarch and her young favorite.

4 "Eighty-year-old Elizabeth," in the first and some subsequent editions of the *Hamburg Dramaturgy.*

5 The Duchess of Irton [sic] is a fictional creation of Corneille. In *Terres tragiques* Jane Conroy suggests the name may have been inspired by Henry Ireton, son-in-law of Oliver Cromwell; see Conroy 309.

6 Voltaire, "*Le Comte d'Essex*" 1025.

7 Voltaire, "*Le Comte d'Essex*" 1010. Narcissus (Narcisse): an opportunistic advisor to the titular character in *Britannicus* (1669), a tragedy by French playwright and historiographer Jean Racine (1639–99), considered one of the masters of neoclassical tragedy.

8 Voltaire, "*Le Comte d'Essex*" 1013.

9 Voltaire, "*Le Comte d'Essex*" 1015.

10 This quotation is paraphrased; see Voltaire, "*Le Comte d'Essex*" 1016.

11 Voltaire, "*Le Comte d'Essex*" 1016–17.

12 This precise sentence does not appear in Voltaire's preface.

Essay 25

1 Lessing continues his discussion, from [23] and [24], of Voltaire's criticism of Thomas Corneille's *Le Comte d'Essex* [*The Earl of Essex*].

2 Paraphrased from Voltaire's preface to Corneille's play; see Voltaire *"Le Comte d'Essex"* 1021.

3 Voltaire, *"Le Comte d'Essex"* 1020.

4 Paraphrase of Voltaire, *"Le Comte d'Essex"* 1019.

5 Lessing's defensiveness here about the objectivity and fairness of his performance criticism reflects an increasing tension between him and the actors of the Hamburg National Theater. After this essay, Lessing abandons reviews of specific performances and discussions of the acting process in general and thereby relinquishes one of the original goals of his project. It is generally assumed that Lessing was responding to pressure from the company actors (most particularly Sophie Hensel) who were displeased with his criticism. See the editor's first introductory essay in this volume (Baldyga, "Missions, Misunderstandings, and Mythologies" 7–8).

Essay 26

1 *Die Hausfranzösin, oder die Mamsell* (1744): five-act prose comedy by L. A. V. Gottsched, which satirizes the Francophilia of the German upper-middle classes. In the play, Herr Germann, a widower, places his household under the control of a French governess, not knowing that she and her associates are actually criminals. See L. A. V. Gottsched, *Pietism in Petticoats and Other Comedies,* for a modern English translation.

2 The play was in fact performed regularly through the end of the century.

3 *The Last Will: Das Testament* (1745), five-act prose comedy printed in J. C. Gottsched, *Die Deutsche Schaubühne* [*The German Stage*] 6: 81–204.

4 Lessing's objections have to do with issues of both language and plot. Both French and German characters use oaths and coarse expressions, and various unsavory events occur (a teen-aged son sleeps in his governess's bed, a Frenchman is given a meal of bird excrement and vomits onstage, and the French villains kidnap Herr Germann's little daughter and threaten to sell her to a Parisian brothel).

5 See, for example, J. C. Gottsched, *Versuch einer critischen Dichtkunst* 521–2 (Vol. 2, Ch. 10, §26).

6 Johann Adolf Scheibe (1708–76): German-Danish composer and theorist who promoted emerging musical aesthetics of the Enlightenment. His works, including his weekly periodical *Critischer Musikus* (1736–40; expanded edition 1745), were influenced by the ideas of J. C. Gottsched.

7 See Scheibe, *Critischer Musikus*, Article 67 (8 December 1739); in the following paragraphs, Lessing's quotations are close to the original but not exact. *Polyeucte* (1642), *Mithridate* (1673): tragedies by P. Corneille and Racine, respectively.

8 Scheibe 614.

9 *Brutus* (1730), *Alzire* (1736): tragedies by Voltaire.

10 *Cato:* may refer to Joseph Addison's famous *Cato* (1713); J. C. Gottsched's adaptation of Addison, *Der sterbende Cato* [*The Dying Cato*] (1732); or L. A. V. Gottsched's translation of Addison, *Cato, ein Trauerspiel* [*Cato, a Tragedy*] (1735).

11 Scheibe 615–6. *Zaïre* (1732): tragedy by Voltaire.

12 *Le Faucon et les oies de Boccace* [*Boccaccio's the Falcon and the Geese*] (1725) by Delisle de la Drevetière. *La Double Inconstance* [*The Double Inconstancy*] (1723) by Marivaux. *L'enfant prodigue* [*The Prodigal Son*] (1738) by Voltaire.

13 *L'Avare* [*The Miser*] (1668) and *Le Malade Imaginaire* [*The Imaginary Invalid*] (1673) by Molière. *L'irrésolu* [*The Irresolute Man*] (1713) by Destouches. *Le Distrait* [*The Absent-Minded Lover*] (1697) by Regnard.

14 Scheibe 616.

15 Scheibe 616–17.

16 Scheibe 618.

17 Johann Wilhelm Hertel (1727–89): German musician, composer, and theorist. In 1767, in addition to the incidental music for *Olint and Sophronia*, Hertel provided the Hamburg

National Theater with music for C. F. Weisse's tragedies *Richard der Dritte* [*Richard the Third*] (1759) and *Romeo und Julie* (1767), and for the *divertissement* following J. F. Löwen's comic afterpiece, *Das Räthsel* [*The Puzzle*] (1765/66). Johann Friedrich Agricola (1720–74): German musician, composer, and theorist; a student of J. S. Bach, he was appointed court composer (1750) and musical director (1759) by Frederick II.

Essay 27

1 Lessing continues his discussion, from [26], of J. F. Agricola's score for Voltaire's *Sémiramis*; the music composed for this performance is lost. For details on the characters and plot of *Sémiramis*, and Lessing's analysis thereof, see [10–12].
2 Assur: Sémiramis's suitor, poisoner of her husband, and would-be-usurper of her realm.

Essay 28

1 *L'Héritier de Village* (1725): one-act prose comedy by Marivaux, translated by German actor, translator, and writer Johann Christian Krüger (1722–50) as *Der Bauer mit der Erbschaft*. First performed and published in 1747, the play was a great favorite in Hamburg and was one of the staples of the Hamburg National Theater repertoire. To date, this play has not been translated into English.
2 Character names in the French original are Blaise (Jürge), Claudine (Lise), Colin (Hans), and Colette (Grete).
3 Lessing misrenders Krüger's name as "Krieger" in the text. Krüger translated the French *patois* into *Plattdeutsch*, a dialect of the Hamburg region; our translation attempts to approximate that "low dialect" in English. We are grateful to Karen Jürs-Munby for assistance with the *Plattdeutsch* and to Savannah Reich for help in devising an English equivalent.
4 For the quotation in Lessing's footnote, see Marivaux, *L'Héritier de Village* 4–5. In the original, after Blaise tells his wife the coach is more comfortable, she asks, "You spent an *écu?*" to which Blaise responds: "Oh, very nobly. How much? I asked. One *écu*, he said. Here you go, look, take it. Just like that."
5 *Le Distrait* (1697): five-act verse comedy by Jean-François Regnard. An English version, under the title *The Absent-Minded Lover*, appears in Regnard et al., *The Heirs of Molière* 9–86. A German translation, *Der Zerstreute, oder der seine Gedanken nicht beysammen hat* [*The Absent-minded One, or he who does not have his wits about him*], was first produced in 1735; see J. G. Robertson 81.
6 See J. E. Schlegel, "Demokrit, ein Todtengespräch" ["Democrites, a Conversation among the Dead"] (1741) in *Johann Elias Schlegels Werke* 3: 188.
7 Tr. note: the modern use of the word *zerstreut* – "scattered" – to mean "absentminded" or "distracted" (after the French word *distrait*) dates from the beginning of the eighteenth century; see Grimm 31: col. 784.
8 For his discussion of *Le Distrait*, Lessing draws from and paraphrases criticism in the *Histoire du Théâtre Français*; see Parfaict 14: 71–81.
9 Conventional comedy: a comedy constructed according to neoclassical rules.
10 "Hence it is not enough to make your hearer grin with laughter . . .": from Horace, *Satires* I.x.7–8.
11 ". . . though even in that there is some merit": from Horace, *Satires* I.x.8.
12 This paragraph is directly paraphrased from Parfaict (81). Jean de la Bruyère (1645–96): French lawyer and writer; his masterpiece, *Les caractères de Théophraste, traduits du grec avec les caractères ou les moeurs de ce siècle* [*The Characters of Theophrastus, translated from the Greek, with The Characters or The Manners of This Century*] (1688), provided a satirical and moralistic critique of seventeenth-century France.
13 Lessing refers to criticism published in the *Mercure de France* (July, 1731) (qtd. in Parfaict 72–4).

14 A contentious point in neoclassical dramatic theory was the extent to which derision serves or detracts from comedy's potential moral function. Molière, who became a touchstone in these arguments, famously maintained that ridicule was the most effective means of correcting the defects of mankind; see Molière, "Preface to *Tartuffe*" 127. Lessing presents a counterview in [29].

15 J. J. Rousseau's antitheatrical polemic, the *Lettre à M. d'Alembert*, argues that, regardless of Molière's intentions, comedy cannot be moral if it hopes to succeed with audiences. For Rousseau's criticism of *The Misanthrope*, see *Politics and the Arts: Letter to M. d'Alembert on the Theatre* 36–45.

Essay 29

1 Lessing continues, from [28], his discussion of the function of comedy.

2 Lessing earlier addressed this distinction in a letter to Nicolai (Letter 103) dated 13 November 1756, *Werke und Briefe* 3: 671 (also 11/1: 120). Lessing's earlier plans to address comedy in a treatise or a series of remarks were unfulfilled. See letter to Mendelssohn (Letter 157) dated 14 September 1757, *Werke und Briefe* 11/1: 249; see also J. G. Robertson 389–90.

3 *Miser*: *L'Avare* (1668); *Gamester*: *Le Joueur* (1696); see [14].

4 *Das Räthsel, oder; Was dem Frauenzimmer am meisten gefällt* (1765/66): an afterpiece by J. F. Löwen that was followed by a musical *divertissement*; see [26.17]. Queen Bertha has sentenced the knight Robert to death; he can avoid this sentence by solving the riddle of what women find most pleasing. An old woman gives him the answer in exchange for his promise that he will repay her when she asks. When the answer saves his life, the old woman demands he marry her; he agrees, and she is magically revealed to be the Queen's daughter, who had been cursed by a fairy to live as an old woman until she could find a man to marry her.

5 *Ce qui plaît aux dames* (1764): a fairy-tale poem in verse by Voltaire, itself an adaptation of John Dryden's adaptation of Chaucer's *Wife of Bath's Tale*; an English version can be found in *Candide and Other Stories* 178–89. The Italian comedians: the actors of the Comédie-Italienne. *The Fairy Urgele*: an early comic opera, *La fée Urgele, ou, Ce qui plait aux dames* (1765), by Charles-Simon Favart, with music by the Italian composer Egidio Romualdo Duni (1708/9–75).

6 Pedrillo: Robert's servant in *The Puzzle*.

7 *Rodogune, Princesse des Parthes* [*Rodogune, Princess of Parthia*] (1644): a five-act verse tragedy by P. Corneille; it was performed, in a new German translation, for the Danish king, Christian VII (1749–1808), who visited Hamburg on multiple occasions. This translation, in alexandrines, *Rodogüne: Prinzessin der Parther*, was published in 1769. The translator may have been the actor Wilhelm Christian Dietrich Meyer, or, alternately, the playwright Friedrich Georg Behrmann; see J. G. Robertson 82–3; see also Knufmann 2684; 2712. The play's backstory: the Syrian king Demetrius (Démétrius) Nicanor was captured by the Parthians and reported dead, whereupon his queen, Cleopatra (Cléopâtre) married his brother (who then died in battle with a would-be usurper, Tryphon). Demetrius, however, is not actually dead and leads a Parthian army toward Syria, where he plans to revenge himself on Cleopatra by displacing her through marriage to the Parthian princess, Rodogune. Cleopatra's army ambushes that of Demetrius, kills him, and takes Rodogune captive. The play opens with the return of Cleopatra's twin sons, Antiochus and Seleucus (Séleucus), whom she had sent to Egypt for safety; they expect to learn now which is the elder and will therefore inherit the kingdom and marry Rodogune. Both sons fall in love with Rodogune. Cleopatra offers the crown to whichever brother will kill Rodogune. Rodogune offers to marry whichever brother will kill Cleopatra, but then confesses her love for Antiochus. Cleopatra pretends to accept their union but kills Seleucus when he will not aid her against them; she plans to poison Antiochus and Rodogune at their wedding. Rodogune is suspicious and challenges Cleopatra to drink from the wedding cup. Cleopatra, poisoned, curses their marriage and is led off to die.

8 See P. Corneille, "Examen de Rodogune" 98. Lessing will use *Rodogune* to address his criticisms of classical French tragedy; for his critique, Lessing will draw on P. Corneille's prefatory material to *Rodogune* and his "Examen," as well as Voltaire's criticism of the play in his *Commentaires sur Corneille* (1764). *Cinna* (1640) and *Le Cid* (1637): other tragedies by P. Corneille.

9 Appianus Alexandrinus (Appian of Alexandria) (fl. second century AD): Greek historian who wrote *Romaica*, a history of Rome organized according to the wars Rome had waged.

10 P. Corneille provides a version of Appianus's account as prefatory material to *Rodogune*; see P. Corneille, "Appian Alexandrin" 4–5. Lessing translates Corneille's version in consultation with Appian's original.

11 See P. Corneille, "Appian Alexandrin" 6–7.

12 See P. Corneille, "Appian Alexandrin" 7. *Trachiniae* [*The Women of Trachis*] (c. 458 BCE) by Sophocles: Deianira, attempting to win back her straying husband, Hercules, gives him a love charm. When it poisons him, she kills herself.

13 Here Lessing echoes Voltaire's critique of P. Corneille's justification for his play's title; see *Commentaires sur Corneille (II)* 483.

14 Cleopatra's name is mentioned twice in the opening exposition of the German translation.

Essay 30

1 Lessing continues, from [29], his discussion of Pierre Corneille's *Rodogune* (1644) and its relation to the historical account of Appianus Alexandrinus.

2 *Changeant*: fabric, usually cotton or silk, woven with contrasting colors to create an iridescent effect depending on the light and direction viewed.

3 Machiavellian maxims: proverbs of the Italian diplomat and author Niccolò Machiavelli (1469–1527); his famous treatise *The Prince* (1513) argues that a prince who wishes to maintain his position must learn how not to be good, and to use his goodness – or not – as necessity requires. The term "Machiavellian" now implies scheming, deceitfulness, cunning, and a lack of scruples. In these remarks, Lessing echoes both P. Corneille and Voltaire: P. Corneille describes Cleopatra as a "second Medea" in the play's preface ("Appian Alexandrin" 6), while Voltaire, in his criticism of the play, refers to "sentences in the style of Machiavelli" and calls Cleopatra a monster; see Voltaire, *Commentaires sur Corneille (II)* 498; 508; 550. Here and in the following essays, Lessing's critique of *Rodogune*'s plot and characters owes much to Voltaire's criticism of the play in his *Commentaires sur Corneille (II)* 478–560.

Essay 31

1 Lessing continues his discussion, begun in [29], of P. Corneille's tragedy *Rodogune*. For the plot of *Rodogune*, see [29.7]. Here and in the following essays, Lessing's critique of *Rodogune*'s plot and characters owes much to Voltaire's criticism of the play in his *Commentaires sur Corneille (II)* 478–560.

2 *Iphigenia in Tauris* (c. 413 BCE): tragedy by Euripides'. Lessing translates the title as *Iphigenia in Taurika*, following perhaps André Dacier's *Iphigenia Taurique*; see J. G. Robertson 171. Aristotle does not describe *Iphigenia* as a perfect tragedy *per se*, but uses the play to illustrate the best method for inciting pity and fear, as well as the best form of recognition and plot construction; see, respectively, Parts XIV, XVI, and XVII of S. H. Butcher's translation of *Poetics*. In Parts XVI and XVII, Aristotle also speaks favorably of a different *Iphigenia in Tauris* by Polyidus the Sophist.

3 In this paragraph, Lessing quotes rather freely from Corneille's introduction to *Rodogune*; see P. Corneille, "Appian Alexandrin" 7–8. *Helen* (412 BCE): play by Euripides, in which a phantom Helen is taken to Troy, while the real Helen languishes in Egypt until she is reunited with Menelaus after the war's end.

4 In the *Hamburg Dramaturgy*, Lessing repeatedly challenges Voltaire's need for historical accuracy in drama, as well as Voltaire's own accuracy as a historian; see, for example [23] and [24]. For Voltaire's comments on Rodogune's age, see *Commentaires sur Corneille (II)* 501.

5 Lessing alludes to French and German criticism identifying inaccuracies in Voltaire's historical works, in particular in his *Essai sur les moeurs et l'esprit des nations* [*Essay on the Manners and Spirit of Nations*] (1756); see J. G. Robertson 207.

Essay 32

1 Actually published 8 December 1767.

2 Lessing continues his discussion, begun in [29], of P. Corneille's tragedy *Rodogune*. For the plot of *Rodogune*, see [29.7]. Here, as in the preceding two essays, Lessing's critique of *Rodogune*'s plot and characters owes much to Voltaire's criticism of the play in his *Commentaires sur Corneille (II)* 478–560.

3 Thespis (fl. sixth century BCE): Athenian playwright (and reputedly the first actor in ancient Greece), commonly referred to as the inventor of tragedy.

4 According to an anecdote recounted by both Diogenes Laertius and Plutarch, after seeing Thespis perform, Solon equated fiction with the presentation of lies. See Diogenes, *Lives of Eminent Philosophers*, Chapter 2, and Plutarch, *Plutarch Lives I*, Chapter 29. For a more nuanced exploration of Solon's view of tragedy, see Fantuzzi 394–5.

5 The concept of "probability," derived from Aristotle, is a lynchpin of neoclassical dramatic theory; see, in Butcher's translation of Aristotle's *Poetics*, Part IX ("it is not the function of the poet to relate what has happened, but what may happen – what is possible according to the law of probability or necessity"); Part XXIV ("the poet should prefer probable impossibilities to improbable possibilities"); and Part XXV ("with respect to the requirements of art, a probable impossibility is to be preferred to a thing improbable and yet possible").

6 Tr. note: this is the first instance in the *Hamburg Dramaturgy* in which Lessing invokes the familiar Aristotelian coupling of *phobos* (fear) and *eleos* (pity). The terms Lessing uses in this essay, and in all of the subsequent essays until [74], are *Schrecken* and *Mitleid*; beginning in [74] he argues for the use of *Furcht* (fear) instead of *Schrecken* (terror). In [74] Lessing grounds his understanding of *Mitleid* in Mendelssohn's theory, outlined in his *Philosophische Schriften* [*Philosophical Writings*], that *Mitleid* involves the capacity to "share all sorts of suffering or pathos" with another person, hence the word (*mit* = with, + *Leid* = suffering, pain). "Compassion" in English has a similar etymological construction, hence our choice to use "compassion" for *eleos*/*Mitleid* instead of the conventional term "pity." Dahlstrom, Mendelssohn's translator, chooses "sympathy." See Mendelssohn, *Philosophical Writings* 141–2, and [74]. On Lessing's use of the term *Mitleid*, see Nisbet 400.

7 Line 1286 of "De syllabis" by Terentianus Maurus: "Books have their fates, according to their reader's understanding."

8 An honest Huron: Lessing refers to the protagonist of Voltaire's novella, *L'Ingénu* [*The Innocent*] (1767). French by birth, but raised by Hurons, the young man knows nothing of European civilization; after arriving in Paris, he is imprisoned in the Bastille for renouncing French suppression of religious freedom. Lessing may not have known that Voltaire was the author of *L'Ingénu*; see J. G. Robertson 171–2.

9 In chapter 12, the imprisoned "Huron" reads ancient Greek and French drama. He enjoys the Greek works, Molière, and Racine, but finds *Rodogune*'s verse unmoving and its plot confusing, improbable, and sometimes disgusting.

10 Some believe that Lessing refers to Francesco Scipione Maffei (1675–1755), the influential Italian playwright, critic, and archaeologist, who published his *Osservazioni sopra la Rodoguna* [*Observations on Rodogune*] (1700). J. G. Robertson, however, argues that Lessing refers instead to Count Pietro dei Conti di Calepio (1693–1762), the author of *Paragone della Poesia tragica d'Italia con quella de Francia* [*Comparison of Italian Tragic Poetry with that of France*] (1732); see J. G. Robertson 291–2.

11 A reference to Voltaire and the origins of his edited collection of P. Corneille's plays. Voltaire had indeed assumed guardianship of Marie Corneille, who was in fact not the impoverished granddaughter of Pierre Corneille but rather of his cousin (also named Pierre); through his herculean publishing efforts Voltaire succeeded in providing her with income and a handsome dowry. For the complete backstory and fuller literary context, see Williams, "Prelude to the First Edition" in *Commentaires sur Corneille (I)*. For Voltaire's opinion of *Rodogune*, see *Commentaires sur Corneille (II)* 475–560.

12 *Rodogune* was repeated on August 26, 1767, but Lessing provides no commentary on this performance, nor on the following half-dozen performances in 1768 and 1769.

13 Wolfenbüttel edition: *Rodogune, Prinzessin aus Parthien* (1691), translation by German playwright and opera librettist Friedrich Christian Bressand (c. 1670–99); for more on the new translation and possible identity of the translator, see [29.7].

Essay 33

1 Actually published 8 December 1767.

2 *Soliman second, ou les trois Sultanes* [*Soliman the Second, or the three Sultanas*] (1761): a three-act verse comedy by C. S. Favart. See [29.7] for a note on the Danish king. The German translation used was *Solimann der Zweyte, oder: Die drey Sultaninnen* (1765) by Rudolf Erich Raspe (1736–94).

3 The great Turkish sultan Suleiman the Magnificent (c. 1494–1566) did indeed marry his European concubine, Hürrem Sultan (c. 1505–58) (known in the West as Roxolana or Roxelane), violating long-standing tradition. Suleiman was the first sultan of that name but was sometimes mislabeled as the second from the mistaken belief that a previous Suleiman had reigned briefly in the fifteenth century; see L. Wolff 86. Although most accounts of Roxelane are conjecture rather than historical fact, the incident became a subject of great fascination in Europe. One of Lessing's earliest (unfinished) attempts at tragedy, *Giangir oder der verschmähte Thron* [*Giangir, or the Rejected Throne*] (1748), featured Roxelane. For more on the European literary preoccupation with Suleiman and Roxelane, as well as a translation of *Giangir*, see Yermolenko, *Roxolana in European Literature, History, and Culture* (2010); for a history of operatic depictions of Suleiman and Roxelane, see L. Wolff 79–107.

4 The historical Roxelane was neither French nor Italian but is believed to have been Ukrainian; see L. Wolff 94. In Marmontel's story, "Soliman II" (1760), three European slaves are procured to entice Soliman, whose concubines no longer interest him, but he eventually tires of both Elmire, a modest beauty, and Délia, a dazzling singer. He is then smitten by the saucy Roxelane, who orders him around and rebuffs him until, defying the laws and customs of his country, Soliman agrees to make her his wife. For an English translation of Marmontel's story, see *Marmontel's Moral Tales* 1–18.

5 Jean de La Fontaine (1621–95): renowned fabulist; author of the licentious *Contes et nouvelles en vers* [*Tales and Novels in Verse*] (1664–85). Jean-Baptiste Joseph Willart de Grécourt (1683–1743): libertine priest; author of many forms of light verse.

6 "Thank heaven, here is a human face!": Marmontel, "Soliman II" 43; *Marmontel's Moral Tales* 8.

7 "You are much better than a Turk should be: you even have something of a Frenchman about you – Really, these Turks are amusing – I undertake to teach this Turk how to live – I do not despair of making him into a Frenchman some day": Marmontel, "Soliman II" 48–50; *Marmontel's Moral Tales* 11–13.

8 See Marmontel, "Soliman II" 34, 50; *Marmontel's Moral Tales* 1, 18.

9 See Marmontel, "Préface," *Contes moraux* vi.

10 "the best example of a husband."

11 In her own time, Roxelane was accused of scheming and witchcraft, due to her unprecedented influence as a sultana and her power at court; most European accounts of Roxelane were based on these allegations; see L. Wolff 94; and Yermolenko, "The Greatest Empresse of the East" 233–6.

12 Suleiman had his first-born son Mustafa murdered in 1553; unsubstantiated rumor placed the blame on Roxelane's machinations; see L. Wolff 94; and Yermolenko, "The Greatest Empress of the East" 236.

13 Lessing's quote loosely paraphrases an anonymous critique, "Soliman Second," in the *Journal Encyclopédique* 13: 79. Lucretia: legendary figure of ancient Rome; a virtuous wife who committed suicide after having been raped. Socrates: considered synonymous with modesty and restraint.

Essay 34

1 Actually published 8 December 1767.

2 Lessing continues a discussion, begun in [33], on the proper treatment of historical characters; his critique centers on Marmontel's story "Soliman II," and its theatrical adaptation by Favart, *Soliman second* [*Soliman the Second*].

3 For Lessing's use of the term genius, see [2.11].

4 As Lessing indicates in his footnote, this statement on genius references the second Olympic ode by Pindar (c. 518–c. 438), lyric poet of ancient Greece. Richmond A. Lattimore's translation of the referenced lines reads: "The wise man knows many things in his blood; the vulgar are taught. They will say anything. They clatter vainly like crows against the sacred bird of Zeus"; see Pindar 8.

5 See Marmontel, "Soliman II" 43; *Marmontel's Moral Tales* 7–8.

6 See Marmontel, "Soliman II" 34; *Marmontel's Moral Tales* 2.

7 Above-mentioned French critics: in [33] Lessing quoted from an anonymous review, "Soliman Second," which appeared in the January 1762 issue of the *Journal Encyclopédique*.

8 This paragraph, roughly translated by Lessing, comes from the anonymous critique, "Soliman Second," in the *Journal Encyclopédique* 13: 71. In Marmontel's story, Roxelane has Délia sing for Soliman; she then asks Soliman for his handkerchief and gives it to Délia (Marmontel, "Soliman II" 51; *Marmontel's Moral Tales* 13–14). In Act 2 of Favart's play, Elmire dances while Roxelane and Délia sing; Soliman gives his handkerchief to Roxelane, who bestows it on Délia. Soliman then takes back the handkerchief and gives it to Elmire (*Soliman second* 41). In the same act, Roxelane seizes the pipe Soliman is smoking and hurls it toward the back of the theater (*Soliman second* 22).

Essay 35

1 Actually published 8 December 1767.

2 Lessing continues his discussion, begun in [33], of Favart's comedy *Soliman second* [*Soliman the Second*], an adaptation of Marmontel's story "Soliman II." Here Lessing responds to French criticism of stage business involving Roxelane's rejection of Soliman's handkerchief; see [34].

3 In Favart's play, Soliman responds "Quel mépris!" ["What contempt!"] after Roxelane hands the handkerchief over to Délia (*Soliman second* 41).

4 In [33], Lessing interrupts his analysis of Favart's changes to Marmontel's story ("I want to dwell on just one of these changes. But first I must quote the criticism that the French themselves made regarding this play").

5 Here we provide a translation of Lessing's rendering of Favart's text; Lessing appends a (mostly faithful) quotation of the original French in his footnote; see Favart, *Soliman second* 58–9.

6 See Lessing, "Fabeln und Fabelabhandlungen," *Werke und Briefe* 4: 362 ff.

7 See Lessing, "Fabeln und Fabelabhandlungen," *Werke und Briefe* 4: 376.

8 See Marmontel, "Préface" iv.

Essay 36

1 Actually published 15 December 1767.

2 Lessing continues his discussion, begun in [33], of Favart's comedy *Soliman second* [*Soliman the Second*], an adaptation of Marmontel's story "Soliman II." The "happy twist" in Favart's version is that Roxelane only acts in a flighty manner to test Soliman's love; see [35]. *Serva padrona*: reference to *La serva padrona* [*The Maid the Mistress*] (1733), a short *opera buffa*, with music by Giovanni Battista Pergolesi (1710–36) and libretto by Gennaro Antonio Federico. Serpina (Serbinette) cons her elderly master Uberto (Pimpinello) into marrying her and making her mistress of the household. For an English version, see Federico.

3 Reference to a story told in the *Satyricon* of Petronius Arbiter in Bk. IV, Ch. 111–112 (*The Satyricon of Petronius Arbiter* I: 254–8 and II: 259–61). A young widow known for her chastity so deeply mourns her husband that she intends to starve to death in his tomb but instead yields to the advances of a solicitous soldier who is supposed to be guarding the crosses of crucified thieves. During their dalliance, one of the bodies is stolen; to save the soldier's life, the widow offers her husband's body as a replacement. Lessing's interest in the story dates back to his university days, when he first developed the idea for a comic version of *The Widow of Ephesus* in which the widow is sympathetically portrayed. Lessing wrote the existing fragment around the time of the *Hamburg Dramaturgy*, but it was never completed; possibly because of his growing affection for Eva König (his future wife), the widow of his friend Engelbert König, who died in 1770; see Nisbet 409–12. For the extant portion of Lessing's play, see *Die Matrone von Ephesus* in *Werke und Briefe* 6: 147–77.

4 *La Matrone d'Ephese* (1702): one-act prose comedy by Houdar de la Motte. A German translation had recently appeared in 1766; see J. G. Robertson 331–2.

5 "If that governor had been a just man, he would have ordered the husband's body taken down and carried back into the vault, and crucified the woman"; see *The Satyricon of Petronius Arbiter* II: 261–2. Lycas (Lichas): character in *The Satyricon* who has been cuckolded.

6 Lessing does not provide further explicit commentary on the "Widow of Ephesus."

7 *Mérope* (1744): five-act verse tragedy. First staged in 1743, it was an immediate success and remained so throughout Voltaire's lifetime; for a comprehensive treatment of the play's composition and context, see Vrooman and Godden, "Introduction to *Mérope*" 91–210. The translator of the text used by the Hamburg company is unknown; for a plot synopsis of *Mérope*, see J. G. Robertson 86–7.

8 Voltaire may have begun work on *Mérope* as early as 1736. Maffei's *Merope* (1713), also a five-act verse tragedy, was performed at the Comédie-Italienne in 1717. Cirey: château of Voltaire's lover and patroness Émilie du Châtelet (1706–49), the French natural philosopher, mathematician, and physicist. Urania: the muse of astronomy.

9 Pierre Brumoy (1688–1742): French Jesuit humanist scholar. His internationally influential three-volume masterwork, *Théâtre des Grecs* [*The Theatre of the Greeks*], contained translations, summaries, and criticism of Greek tragedies.

10 René (Renatus) Joseph de Tournemine (1661–1739): Jesuit theologian and classical scholar; as Lessing suggests, the addition of Tournemine's letter was intended to circumvent criticism of *Mérope*. See Tournemine, "Lettre du Père de Tournemine"; "A Letter from the Jesuit Tournemine."

11 Euripides' *Cresphontes*, extant only in fragments. In the letter prefacing *Mérope*, Tournemine writes: "The Cresphontes of Euripides is lost; M. Voltaire has restored it to us"; see "Lettre du Père de Tournemine" 213; "A Letter" 240.

12 Unprecedented honor: Voltaire was the first French playwright to be called by the audience to appear and receive acclaim at the end of a performance; see Mouhy, *Tablettes dramatiques* 158.

13 For this anecdote about Corneille, see Raynal, *Anecdotes Littéraires* (1750) 2: 5.

14 Accounts of this incident vary: French chronicler and jurist Edmond Jean François Barbier (1689–1771) writes that the audience applauded for Voltaire for a quarter of an hour, while a contemporary anonymous police report included with Barbier's published journals claims that the audience demanded a thousand times for Voltaire to appear and that he kissed the hand of Mme. de Luxembourg in front of the crowd. See Barbier, *Chronique de la régence* 3: 431; and "Journal de Police" 8: 232.

15 Edward Young (1683–1765): English poet, playwright, and critic; famous for *The Complaint: or, Night Thoughts* (1742–45) and *Conjectures on Original Composition* (1759). Lessing's

reference is to a line from Young's poem "The Last Day (Book 1)"; see Young, *Poetical Works* II: 3.

16 Smyrnian schoolmaster: many early biographies of Homer claimed he was born in Smyrna; see A. D. Kelly, "Biographies of Homer."

17 During the eighteenth century, trained marmots were displayed at German fairgrounds and other locations.

18 Edmond Cordier de Saint Firmin (c. 1730–1816): French abbot and author. Marmontel claims to have been the second author called out in this manner, at the premiere of his 1748 play *Denys le Tyran*; see Marmontel, *Mémoires d'un père* 139.

19 Pulcinella: traditional *commedia dell'arte* character. *Mérope* generated a number of parodies, including *Mérope travestie* (1759), by Franco-Italian actor Antoine Fabio Sticotti (1708–72), which was performed by the actors of the Comédie-Italienne; see Vrooman and Godden 207–8.

20 The writer to whom Lessing refers here may well be French playwright and literary critic Jean-François de la Harpe (1739–1803), whose play *Pharamond* received a lukewarm reception at its premiere in August of 1765. Contemporary French writer and chronicler Louis Petit de Bachaumont (1690–1771) reports that the audience called for the author after the play had "mediocre success" on opening night, but he refused to appear; see Bachaumont, *Mémoires secrets* 424.

Essay 37

1 Actually published 15 December 1767.

2 Lessing continues his discussion, which extends from [36] to [50], of Voltaire's tragedy *Mérope* and its relationship to Maffei's original. For the plot of *Mérope*, see J. G. Robertson 86–7.

3 See Vrooman and Godden 94–100; 127–141.

4 In the following paragraph, Lessing quotes (very loosely) from Maffei's dedication of his *Merope* to Rinaldo I, Duke of Modena. See Maffei, *Teatro* xxxiv–xxxv; for an English translation from the Italian, see Maffei, "Preface."

5 Pausanius (fl. 143–76): ancient Greek geographer; this information is from his *Description of Greece* Bk. 4, Ch. 3, Sec. 7–8.

6 Apollodorus (second century BCE): ancient Athenian scholar; this information is from *The Library* Bk. 2, Ch. 8 (a compendium of Greek mythology attributed to Apollodorus but in fact composed several centuries later).

7 Gaius Julius Hyginus (fl. first century CE): Roman author; this information is drawn from *The Myths of Hyginus* Fab. 137.

8 Revelations and reversals of fortune: reference to Aristotle's concepts of *anagnorisis* and *peripeteia*; which he discusses extensively in *Poetics*.

9 *Cresphontes*: lost tragedy by Euripides. Plutarch (46–c. 199 CE): ancient Greek biographer and essayist. For the references that Lessing cites, see Aristotle, *Poetics* (Part XIV); and Plutarch, "On the Eating of Flesh (De esu carnium) II" 2. 5. Lessing's footnote refers to the collection *Euripidou Sōzomena Apanta* [*Extant Works of Euripides*] (1694) by English scholar Joshua Barnes (1654–1712). The fragment from Euripides' *Cresphontes* was indeed later found and published in 1856 by German classicist August Nauck (1822–92); see his *Tragicorum Graecorum Fragmenta* [*Fragments of Greek Tragedy*] 395–8 (Fragment 452–462).

10 See Cicero, *Tusculan Disputations I* 48 ("On the Contempt of Death").

11 Tournemine, "Lettre du Père de Tournemine" 213; "A Letter" 239–40.

12 Lessing is correct that Aristotle's comments are misrepresented and that Plutarch's are misattributed; see Vrooman and Godden 94–5.

13 See [32.6].

14 See Aristotle, *Poetics* (Part XIII).

15 André Dacier (1651–1722): influential French translator and interpreter of classical works; here Lessing refers to "Remarques sur le Chapitre XV" ["Notes on Chapter 15"] in Dacier's

1692 translation of and commentary on Aristotle's *Poetics*. See Aristotle and Dacier, *La poëtique d'Aristote* 224–5. Petrus Victorius (Pietro Vittori) (1499–1585): important Italian humanist and classicist; provided a commentary on Aristotle's *Poetics* in 1560 titled *Commentarii in primum librum Aristotelis De arte poetarum* [*Commentary on the First Book of Aristotle, De Arte Poetarum*].

Essay 38

1 Actually published 15 December 1767.
2 Lessing continues his discussion, which extends from [36] to [50], of Voltaire's tragedy *Mérope* and its relationship to Maffei's original. For the plot of *Mérope*, see J. G. Robertson 86–7. In [37], Lessing also addresses André Dacier's interpretation of Aristotle's discussion of plot in *Poetics*.
3 Michael Conrad Curtius (1724–1802): German historian and university professor; translated and commented on Aristotle in *Aristoteles Dichtkunst* [*Aristotle's Poetics*] (1753).
4 See Curtius 213–14.
5 Aristotle's *Poetics* is in fact an immensely challenging text; American classicist Gerald F. Else describes it as an "extraordinarily crabbed, difficult piece of writing" whose interpreters "have been content to let it remain a jungle of twisting paths intersected by an occasional clearing" (vii).
6 To support the argument that follows, Lessing draws from multiple sections of Aristotle's *Poetics*: for "composition of the plot," see Part VI; for the distinction between "simple" and "complex" plots, see Part X; for the "three main categories" of tragic incidents, see Part XI; for "reversal of fortune," "recognition," and "suffering," see Parts XI, XIV, and XVI.
7 πράξεως: *praxis* (act); σύνθεσις πραγμάτων: *synthesis pragmaton* (synthesis or ordering of events); see *Poetics* (Part VI).
8 περιπέτεια: *peripeteia* (reversal, change in fortune); ἀναγνώρισις: anagnorisis (recognition); πάθους: *pathos* (passion, suffering).
9 μύθος πεπλεγμένος: *mythos peplegménos*; ἁπλούς: *aplous*.
10 πάθη: *pathos* (suffering). Purpose of tragedy: a reference to *catharsis*; see [2.10]. Terror and compassion: see [32.6].
11 *Iphigenia in Tauris*: see [31.2].
12 There is no ancient play with the title of *Merope*; Lessing may be referring to Euripides' *Cresphontes*, or, as his later remarks here and in [39] suggest, to a hypothetical dramatic version of the myth.
13 The critic: Aristotle.

Essay 39

1 Actually published 15 December 1767.
2 Lessing continues his discussion, which extends from [36] to [50], of Voltaire's tragedy *Mérope* and its relationship to Maffei's original. For the plot of *Mérope*, see J. G. Robertson 86–7. Lessing's response to the Jesuit scholar Tournemine begins in [37].
3 Charles-Louis de Secondat, Baron de La Brède et de Montesquieu (1689–1755): French philosopher and political theorist. In his letter of 5 December 1750 to Count Octavien de Guasco, Montesquieu refers to the "despotic and turbulent spirit of Father Tournemine." De Guasco provides a footnote describing the bitter feud between Tournemine and Montesquieu, noting that Montesquieu took his revenge on Tournemine, "who was passionately fond of fame," by always asking "Who is this Father Tournemine? I have never heard of him"; see Montesquieu, *Lettres familières* (1771) 160; *Familiar Letters* 4: 63.
4 Euripides' lost play: *Cresphontes*, Euripides' version of *Merope*; only fragments remain.
5 Lessing provides the original French in his footnote; see "Lettre à Monsieur le Marquis Scipion Maffei" 217–8. For an English translation, see Voltaire, "A Letter to the Marquis Scipio Maffei" 245–6.

6 See Aristotle, *Poetics* (Part XIV); and Plutarch, "On the Eating of Flesh (De esu carnium) II" 2.5.

7 *Iphigenia in Tauris*: see [31.2]. *Helle*: mentioned in Aristotle's *Poetics* (Part XIV); the play's author is unknown.

8 Dacier: see [37.15]. *Peripeteia* (reversal, change in fortune): see *Poetics* (Parts XI, XIV, and XVI).

9 For the reference in Lessing's footnote, see Aristotle and Dacier, *La poëtique d'Aristote* 225–6; and Plutarch, "De capienda ex inimicis utilitate" ["How to profit by one's enemies"] 26.

10 Polybius (c. 200–c. 118 CE): Greek statesman and author of a history of Rome, who quotes from Euripides' *Cresphontes* in his *Histories* Book XII, § 26; see Polybius and Hultsch, *Histories of Polybius* 2: 110.

11 For the reference in Lessing's footnote, see Aristotle and Dacier, *La poëtique d'Aristote* 221. Pierre Corneille discusses Aristotle's reference to Merope in Euripides' *Cresphontes*, but does not make the remarks attributed to him by Dacier; see P. Corneille, "Sur la Tragédie" ["On Tragedy"] in his *Trois discours [Three Discourses]* 68; for the English, see P. Corneille, "Discourse on Tragedy" 13.

12 This claim appears in Maffei's dedication to the Duke of Modena. Lessing provides the Italian in his footnote; see Maffei, *Teatro del Sig. marchese Scipione* xxxvii–viii. For the English, see page 3 of the "Preface" in Ayre's translation of *Merope*.

13 Thomas Reinesius (1587–1667): German physician, philologist, and critic; the reference here is to a passage on Hyginus's fables in his 1640 *Variarum lectionum libri [. . .]* 372–5.

14 Christian Felix Weisse prefixed a translation of Hyginus's 88th fable ("Atreus") to his five-act tragedy *Atreus und Thyest* (1766).

15 See Hyginus, "Ino" (2nd fable), "Ino of Euripides" (4th fable), "Antiopa" (7th fable), and "Antiopa of Euripides" (8th fable) in *The Myths of Hyginus [Fabulae]*.

Essay 40

1 Actually published 22 December 1767.

2 Lessing continues his discussion, which extends from [36] to [50], of Voltaire's tragedy *Mérope* and its relationship to Maffei's original. For the plot of *Mérope*, see J. G. Robertson 86–7. Here Lessing continues to explore ancient sources of the Merope story; the question at hand is whether Hyginus's fable provides the plot of *Cresphontes*, Euripides' lost version of the story.

3 The edition of Hyginus's fables cited by Lessing in his footnote is that of German classicist and professor Johannes Gerhard Scheffer (Schefferus); for the original Latin, see Hyginus, Scheffer, and Munckerus, *Hygini Quae hodie extant* 123; 154–5. The error noted by Lessing is rectified in later editions, in which Merope's story (137th fable) is separated from that of Pentheus and Agave (184th fable); see, for example, Hyginus and Schmidt 116–17.

4 Joh. Bapt. Liviera: Giambattista Liviera (b. 1565); author of *Il Cresfonte* (1588). Pomponio Torelli, Count of Montechiarugolo (1539–1608): author of *La Merope* (1589). See Maffei, *Teatro del Sig. marchese Scipione* xxxviii; in his preface, Maffei gives *La Merope* the date of its second edition, 1598. For the English, see page 3 of the preface to Ayre's translation of *Merope*.

Essay 41

1 Actually published 22 December 1767.

2 Lessing continues his discussion, which extends from [36] to [50], of Voltaire's tragedy *Mérope* and its relationship to Maffei's original. For the plot of *Mérope*, see J. G. Robertson 86–7.

3 "Give way, Roman writers, give way, you Greeks / Something greater than Oedipus is being born."

4 This ode to Maffei's *Merope* by Italian classicist Leonardo Adami (1690–1719) modifies a pair of lines from the *Elegies* (Book II, poem 34b, l. 41–2) by Sextus Propertius (c. 55–c. 16 BCE), elegiac poet of ancient Rome; Adami puts "Oedipode" (Oedipus) in the place of "Iliade" (Iliad). Giulio Cesare Becelli recounts this story in his preface to Maffei's collected works; see Becelli viii.

5 Lessing's appears to have drawn this information from Becelli (x–xii).
6 "Lettre à Monsieur le Marquis Scipion Maffei, auteur de la Mérope Italienne, et de beaucoup d'autres ouvrages célèbres" ["A Letter to the Marquis Scipio Maffei, author of the Italian *Mérope* and many other famous works"] (1744). For more on the correspondence between Voltaire and Maffei, see Vrooman and Godden 100–7 and 159–62.
7 Here, and throughout this essay, Lessing loosely paraphrases from Voltaire's preface; see "Lettre à Maffei" 225–6; "A Letter to Maffei" 255–6.
8 Both the "Lettre de M. de La Lindelle à M. de Voltaire" ["A Letter from M. de La Lindelle to M. de Voltaire"] (1748) and the "Réponse de M. de Voltaire à M. de La Lindelle" ["The Answer of M. de Voltaire to Mr. de La Lindelle"] (1748) were published with *Mérope*.
9 M. de La Lindelle was indeed a pseudonym employed by Voltaire in order to address criticism of *Mérope*; both letters listed above were written by Voltaire. See Vrooman and Godden 155–59; 234.
10 Janus-head: the Roman god Janus was represented with two faces, one looking forward and the other back; the term "Janus-faced" now connotes insincerity or deceitfulness.
11 "Lettre à Maffei" 216–17; "A Letter to Maffei" 244–5.
12 "Lettre à Maffei" 225–6; "A Letter to Maffei" 256–7.
13 Nicolas Boileau-Despréaux (1636–1711): French poet and leading literary critic, author of the widely influential neoclassical treatise *L'Art poétique* (1674), who mocked Philippe Quinault for using a royal ring in his tragedy *Astarte* (1663), although in fact the ring was not used as a recognition device. Lessing provides Voltaire's original complaint in his footnote (see "Réponse de M. de Voltaire à M. de La Lindelle" 242–3; "The Answer of M. de Voltaire to Mr. de La Lindelle" 275). Rather than use a ring, Voltaire uses armor as a recognition device in *Mérope*, a change that was broadly criticized; see Vrooman and Godden 133–4. Voltaire also mentions Maffei's use of a ring in his preface; see "Lettre à Maffei" 225; "A Letter to Maffei" 255.
14 "Lettre à Maffei" 225; "A Letter to Maffei" 255–6. *Belles Nippes*: fancy clothes.
15 Nestorian blather: in the *Iliad*, Nestor, elderly king of Pylos, counsels the Greeks with stories of his youth; "Nestorian" now often implies a self-satisfied or senile prolixity.
16 "As in the poplar-shade a nightingale / Mourns her lost young . . . " Virgil, *Georgics* 4. 511–12. Maffei would deny that he used these lines in *Merope*; see Maffei, "Risposta alla Lettera del Signor di Voltaire" ["Response to the Letter of M. Voltaire"] 367.
17 "Lettre à Maffei" 229–30; "A Letter to Maffei" 261.
18 "Lettre à Maffei" 230; "A Letter to Maffei" 261–2.
19 "What at the top is a lovely woman ends below in a [black and ugly] fish": from Horace's *Ars Poetica*; for the full quotation, in Latin and English, see Horace, *Satires, Epistles, and Ars Poetica* 450–1.
20 *Persiflage*: light, contemptuous mockery, ironic banter.

Essay 42

1 Actually published 22 December 1767.
2 Lessing continues his discussion, which extends from [36] to [50], of Voltaire's tragedy *Mérope* and its relationship to Maffei's original. For the plot of *Mérope*, see J. G. Robertson 86–7. Here Lessing analyzes Maffei's *Merope* in response to Voltaire's criticism of the play; see [41].
3 Christoph Matthäus Pfaff (1686–1760) and Jacques Basnage de Beauval (1653–1723): Protestant theologians; Maffei supported the Catholic Church. Social pressure: Maffei gives his reasons for composing *Merope* in the dedicatory epistle prefacing his play; see Maffei, *Teatro del Sig. marchese Scipione Maffei* xxxi–xli.
4 For the quotation in Lessing's footnote, see Maffei, *Merope* in *Teatro del Sig. marchese Scipione Maffei* 10–11; for a (loose) English rendering see p. 9 of Ayre's translation of the play.
5 For the quotation in Lessing's footnote, see Maffei, *Merope* in *Teatro del Sig. marchese Scipione Maffei* xxxix; for the English, see the fourth page of Maffei's preface in Ayre's translation.
6 Ismene: Merope's confidant.

7　See Maffei, *Merope* in *Teatro del Sig. marchese Scipione Maffei* 62; for a (loose) English render-ing, see p. 50 of Ayre's translation of the play.

8　Reference to the "Lettre de M. de La Lindelle à M. de Voltaire" ["A Letter from M. de La Lindelle to M. de Voltaire"] (1748), which was in fact written by Voltaire himself; see [41.8] and [41.9].

9　Lessing's citation here is loose. See Voltaire, "Lettre de M. de La Lindelle" 240–1; "A Letter from M. de La Lindelle" 273.

10　Unbeknownst to Lessing, Maffei had, in fact, responded to Voltaire by publishing the "Ris-posta alla Lettera del Signor di Voltaire" ["Answer to the Letter of M. de Voltaire"] in the 1745 Veronese edition of *Merope*; Maffei replies to every point Voltaire makes in the "Letter to Maf-fei" – and then scrupulously examines Voltaire's *Mérope*. See Vrooman and Godden 354–5.

Essay 43

1　Actually published 22 December 1767.

2　Lessing continues his discussion, which extends from [36] to [50], of Voltaire's tragedy *Mérope* and its relationship to Maffei's original. For the plot of *Mérope*, see J. G. Robertson 86–7. Lessing has just wondered, in [42], whether Maffei responded to criticisms of *Merope* made by Voltaire (both as himself and as the pseudonymous M. de La Lindelle).

3　Lessing's translation is loose. See Voltaire, "Lettre de M. de La Lindelle à M. de Voltaire" 238; "A Letter from M. de La Lindelle to M. de Voltaire" 270.

4　"What doubt remains? Wretch that I am, and yet / I let myself be amused about a name, / As if there was no other Polidore" Maffei, *Merope* (Ayre trans.) 37; for the original Italian, see Maffei, *Teatro del Sig. marchese Scipione Maffei* 45.

5　Here again, Lessing's translation is loose. See "Lettre de M. de La Lindelle" 239; "A Letter from M. de La Lindelle" 271.

6　Lessing's footnote repeats a portion of the passage he has just cited from Lindelle. For the line from Voltaire, see his "Lettre à Monsieur le Marquis Scipion Maffei" 225–6; "A Letter to the Marquis Scipio Maffei" 256. Lessing correctly suspects that Lindelle and Voltaire are the same person; see [41.8] and [41.9].

7　For the text included in Lessing's footnote, see Maffei, *Teatro del Sig. marchese Scipione Maffei* 53; for the English, see p. 43 in Ayre's translation of *Merope*.

8　Lessing again takes minor liberties with his French source. See "Lettre de M. de La Lindelle" 239–40; "A Letter from M. de La Lindelle" 272.

9　Lessing gives the Italian original in his footnote; see Maffei, *Teatro del Sig. marchese Scipione Maffei* 65. In Ayre's translation, this speech is rendered: "Me, / My own service pays, I have enough reward / In seeing thee content. What wouldst thou give me? / I covet nothing: that alone to me / would be most grateful none have pow'r to give. / The heavy weight of years I would have lighten'd, / Which lye upon my head, and crouch me down, / And press me so [. . .]" (52–3).

Essay 44

1　Actually published 29 December 1767.

2　Lessing continues his discussion, which extends from [36] to [50], of Voltaire's tragedy *Mérope* and its relationship to Maffei's original. For the plot of *Mérope*, see J. G. Robertson 86–7. Beginning with [41], Lessing has been addressing criticisms of Maffei's *Merope* made by Voltaire (both as himself and as the pseudonymous M. de La Lindelle).

3　Lessing provides these lines in French in [41]; for the English see "The Answer of M. de Voltaire to Mr. de La Lindelle" 275. For Boileau's criticism of the ring recognition plot device, see [41.13].

4　Narbas: the old servant who takes Aegisthus from Messene; called Polydorus in Maffei's play.

5 Vulcan: Roman god of fire, forger of weapons for the gods.

6 Euricles: Merope's favorite, in Voltaire's play.

7 Voltaire, "Réponse de M. de Voltaire à M. de La Lindelle" 243; "The Answer of M. de Voltaire to Mr. de La Lindelle" 275.

8 See Voltaire, "Lettre de M. de La Lindelle à M. de Voltaire" 236; "A Letter from M. de La Lindelle to M. de Voltaire" 267–8.

9 For the Schlegel passage in Lessing's footnote, see "Gedanken zur Aufnahme des dänischen Theaters" in *Johann Elias Schlegels Werke* 3: 294.

10 Hédelin: François Hédelin, abbé d'Aubignac (1604–76), French cleric, playwright, and theater theorist, best known for his treatise *La Pratique du théâtre*. For Hédelin's discussion of the neoclassical principle of unity of place, see *La Pratique du théâtre* 93–4; *The Whole Art of the Stage* Bk 2, Ch. 6, p. 104.

11 "Unity of Place" is not discussed in Aristotle's *Poetics*; the rule was established with the codification of French neoclassicism. Corneille: Lessing refers to Pierre Corneille's discussion of unity of place, and his suggestion that a whole city could serve as one unified place, in "Sur les trois unités" ["Of the Three Unities"]; see P. Corneille, *Trois discours de P. Corneille* [*Three Discourses of P. Corneille*] 124. For an English translation, see "Of the Three Unities of Action" 129.

12 For the quotation in Lessing's footnote, see Hédelin, *La Pratique du théâtre* 94; for an English translation see *The Whole Art of the Stage* Bk 2, Ch. 6, p. 104.

Essay 45

1 Actually published 29 December 1767.

2 Lessing continues his discussion, which extends from [36] to [50], of Voltaire's tragedy *Mérope* and its relationship to Maffei's original. For the plot of *Mérope*, see J. G. Robertson 86–7. Here Lessing continues, from [41], a critique of Voltaire's *Mérope*, according to French neoclassical rules of playwriting. Unity of time: rule established with the codification of French neoclassicism that originated from Aristotle's statement in Part V of *Poetics* that "[t]ragedy endeavors, as far as possible, to confine itself to a single revolution of the sun, or but slightly to exceed this limit."

3 Pierre Corneille suggests a more flexible interpretation of the unity of time in "Sur les trois unités" ["Of the Three Unities"]; see *Trois discours de P. Corneille* [*Three Discourses of P. Corneille*] 116ff. For an English translation, see "Of the Three Unities of Action" 125ff.

4 Mayfly: insect known for its extremely short life span.

5 Lindelle: pseudonym of Voltaire; see [41.8] and [41.9]. For this criticism of Maffei, see Voltaire, "Lettre de M. de La Lindelle à M. de Voltaire" 236; "A Letter from M. de La Lindelle to M. de Voltaire" 267.

6 P. Corneille, *Trois Discours* 105; for an English translation, see "Of the Three Unities of Action" 119.

7 Euricles: Mérope's favorite, in Voltaire's play.

8 *Peto veniam exeundi*: "May I be excused?"

9 *Venez, Madame*: "Come, Madame."

10 Erox: Polyphontes' favorite, in Voltaire's play.

11 "Let us all hurry to the temple, where my dishonor awaits me"; Voltaire, *Mérope* 322.

12 "You come to drag the victim to the altar"; Voltaire, *Mérope* 323.

Essay 46

1 Actually published 29 December 1767.

2 Lessing continues his discussion, which extends from [36] to [50], of Voltaire's tragedy *Mérope* and its relationship to Maffei's original. For the plot of *Mérope*, see J. G. Robertson 86–7. Beginning with [41], Lessing has been critiquing Voltaire's *Mérope* according to French neoclassical rules of playwriting.

3 Unity of action: neoclassical rule limiting plays to a single plot; the only of the neoclassical unities actually drawn from Aristotle's *Poetics* (Part VIII). Lessing discusses Voltaire's treatment of the unity of place in [44], and of the unity of time in [45].

4 Lindelle: pseudonym of Voltaire; see [41.8] and [41.9]. Here and in the lines that directly follow, Lessing is paraphrasing Voltaire; see "Lettre de M. de La Lindelle à M. de Voltaire" 240; "A Letter from M. de La Lindelle to M. de Voltaire" 272–3.

5 This speech is in fact from III.i, rather than III.ii. See Maffei, *Teatro del Sig. marchese Scipione Maffei* 36–7; for the English, see p. 30 of the Ayre translation. "Lindelle" describes the interactions between Merope and Polyphontes as "scènes d'écolier" ("school boy scenes"); see "Lettre de M. de La Lindelle" 239; "A Letter from M. de La Lindelle" 271.

6 Voltaire, *Mérope* 259. In the Francklin translation: "heav'n / by slow and solemn steps, may bring down vengeance" (17).

7 Voltaire, *Mérope* 260. Francklin translates: "It must be so; this crime, and I have done" (18).

8 For the passage in Lessing's footnote, see Voltaire, *Mérope* 258; for the English, see p. 17 of the Francklin translation.

9 For the passage in Lessing's footnote, see Maffei, *Teatro del Sig. marchese Scipione Maffei* 33; for the English, see p. 27 of the Ayre translation.

10 Lessing paraphrases here. See "Lettre de M. de La Lindelle" 237; "A Letter from M. de La Lindelle" 269.

Essay 47

1 Actually published 29 December 1767.

2 Lessing continues his discussion, which extends from [36] to [50], of Voltaire's tragedy *Mérope* and its relationship to Maffei's original. For the plot of *Mérope*, see J. G. Robertson 86–7. Beginning with [41], Lessing has been addressing criticisms of Maffei's *Merope* made by Voltaire (both as himself and as the pseudonymous M. de La Lindelle). Here Lessing supports his statement, made at the end of [46], that Voltaire's Mérope is as much a "cannibal" (i.e. savage) as Maffei's Merope.

3 *coup de théâtre*: Lessing refers to Merope's recognition of Aegisthus; see [37]–[39].

4 In [39] and [40], Lessing discusses the relationship between Hyginus's fables and *Cresphontes*, Euripides' lost version of the Merope story.

5 See [44].

6 For the passage in Lessing's footnote, see Voltaire, *Mérope* 265–6; for the English, see pages 22–3 of the Francklin translation.

7 Chariton (fl. first century CE): ancient Greek novelist whose romance *Chaereas and Callirhoë* was published by Dutch classical scholar Jacques Philippe d'Orville (1696–1751) in 1750 as *Charitonis Aphrodisiensis de Chaerea et Callirrhoë amatoriam narrationum* [*The Loves of Chareas and Callirhoë, by Chariton of Aphrodisias*].

8 Both here and later, when Lessing cites Euripides, he is in fact referencing Hyginus, whose 137th fable may have summarized Euripides' *Cresphontes*.

9 See [40].

10 *Per combinazioni d'accidenti*: through a series of coincidences; see Maffei, *Teatro del Sig. marchese Scipione Maffei* xxxix.

11 Terror and compassion: see [32.6] for notes on our translation of the Aristotelian coupling of *phobos* (fear) and *eleos* (pity).

Essay 48

1 Actually published 5 January 1768.

2 Lessing continues his discussion, which extends from [36] to [50], of Voltaire's tragedy *Mérope* and its relationship to Maffei's original. For the plot of *Mérope*, see J. G. Robertson 86–7. In [47], Lessing criticizes both Maffei and Voltaire for hiding Aegisthus's true identity, which,

he argues, lessens the emotional effect for the spectator; Lessing extrapolates from available sources that in Euripides' version of the story Aegisthus's identity is known from the start.

3   Lessing's quotation of Diderot in the following paragraph combines several disparate passages from the French theorist's 1758 treatise *De la poésie dramatique* [*On Dramatic Poetry*], often referred to as the *Discours sur la poésie dramatique* [*Discourse on Dramatic Poetry*], published as an addendum to his comedy *Le Père de Famille* [*The Father of the Family*]. Lessing draws from his own 1760 translation of Diderot in *Das Theater des Herrn Diderot* [*The Theater of M. Diderot*], which is largely idiomatic rather than "mechanically literal" (see Nisbet 273); the page number to which he refers his reader in his footnote is in volume 2 of that work. Significant alterations made by Lessing in this excerpt are noted in [48.4], [48.5], and [48.6].

4   In Diderot's treatise, a hypothetical reader asks "Ce sont donc les personnages qu'il faut avoir en vue?" ("Then it is the characters we must keep in mind?"), to which the author responds "Je le crois" ("I think so") (292). Lessing follows Diderot's original in his 1781 reissue of his translation.

5   Diderot's text reads: "Le Poëte me ménage, par le secret, un instant de surprise; il m'eut exposé par la confidence à une longue inquiétude" ("By keeping the secret the poet treats me to an instant of surprise; by confiding it, he would have exposed me to prolonged anxiety") (293).

6   Diderot's final sentence in fact reads: "C'est ainsi que vous produirez en moi une attente violente de ce qu'ils deviendront, lorsq'ils pourront comparer ce qu'ils sont avec ce qu'ils ont fait ou voulu faire" ("This is how you produce in me a violent expectation of what they will become when they are able to compare what they are with what they have done or wanted to do") (297). For the passages Lessing cites, see Diderot, *De la poésie dramatique* 291–7; an excerpted English translation can be found in "Discourse on Dramatic Poetry" 64–5.

7   In Euripides: more properly, in Hyginus, whose 137th fable may have summarized Euripides' *Cresphontes*. "Web of little artifices": appears to be a loose reference to Diderot, who writes that the drama is "un tissu de loix particulieres dont on a fait des préceptes généraux" ("a tissue of particular rules, from which general precepts have been drawn"); *De la poésie dramatique* 298.

8   See Hédelin, *La Pratique du théâtre* 147; *The Whole Art of the Stage* Book 4, Ch. 1, p. 104.

9   Aristotle refers to Euripides as the "most tragic" of playwrights in *Poetics* (Part XIII).

10   The eighteenth century saw the emergence of multiple genres, such as Diderot's *genre sérieux* ("serious drama"), which challenged the strict separation of dramatic forms. Here, however, Lessing's purpose is to challenge the efficacy of rigid neoclassical rules rather than to advocate for a specific mixed or intermediate genre.

Essay 49

1   Actually published 5 January 1768.

2   Lessing continues his discussion, which extends from [36] to [50], of Voltaire's tragedy *Mérope* and its relationship to Maffei's original. For the plot of *Mérope*, see J. G. Robertson 86–7. In [47] and [48], Lessing faults both Maffei and Voltaire for deviating from their classical source material by hiding Aegisthus's true identity; here Lessing continues, from [48], a defense of Euripides' prologues, which had been criticized by modern critics for revealing the plot in advance.

3   *Ion*, *Hecuba*: tragedies by Euripides.

4   Terror and compassion: see [32.6] for notes on our translation of the Aristotelian coupling of *phobos* (fear) and *eleos* (pity).

5   William Whitehead (1715–85): English playwright and poet laureate; adapted *Ion* as *Creusa, Queen of Athens* (1754).

6   Calamitous catastrophe: unhappy ending (not all Greek tragedies ended unhappily); see Aristotle, *Poetics* (Part XIII). Stagirite: Aristotle was born in Stagira, Macedonia.

7 Almost no biographical information about Euripides exists; for the sources of the claim that Euripides collaborated with the philosopher Socrates, see Lefkowitz 30–1.

8 Narbas: in Voltaire's *Mérope*, the old servant who takes Aegisthus from Messene.

9 Lessing refers to the play's printed form, in which characters' names precede their lines. This criticism, of course, is not strictly fair. Lessing has been analyzing audience reception, but here (and for the remainder of this essay), he shifts to a discussion of the reader's experience.

10 For the full exchange between mother and son, see Voltaire, *Mérope* 271; Francklin's translation reads: "Knowst thou ought of Narbas, / Or of Aegisthus? Never hath that name / Yet reach'd thine ear? What rank, condition, friends, / Who was thy father?" (28).

11 Voltaire, *Mérope* 271; Francklin's translation reads "Polycletes, madam, / A poor old man: to Narbas, or Aegisthus, / Of whom thou speak'st, I am a stranger" (28).

Essay 50

1 Actually published 5 January 1768.

2 Lessing continues his discussion, which extends from [36] to [50], of Voltaire's tragedy *Mérope* and its relationship to Maffei's original. For the plot of *Mérope*, see J. G. Robertson 86–7. In [47] and [48], Lessing faults both Maffei and Voltaire for deviating from their classical source material by hiding Aegisthus's true identity; in [49] Lessing points out that in Voltaire's play, Aegisthus's name appears in the list of characters and above his lines, thus presumably spoiling the suspense for the reader.

3 Giulio Cesare Becelli (1686–1750): Veronese scholar and critic; provided a preface to Maffei's *Merope*. See "Al lettore" ["To the Reader"] in *Teatro del Sig. marchese Sciopone Maffei* xxvii.

4 See the "Notice" for Lessing's original intentions. Lessing had ceased to discuss acting and actors' performances after [25], presumably due to pressure from the Hamburg National Theater company members; the focus of the *Hamburg Dramaturgy* would continue to shift as the theater company began to fail, publication difficulties ensued, and Lessing became more engrossed with his studies of antiquity.

5 Aristotle, *Poetics* (Part XVIII).

6 The title of Euripides' lost play is not *Merope*, but *Cresphontes*; its plot may have been summarized in "Merope," the 137th fable of Hyginus.

7 Pamiso: the Pamisos, a river in Messenia.

8 Narbas: in Voltaire's *Mérope*, the old servant who takes Aegisthus from Messene.

9 Johann Balhorn (c. 1550–c. 1604): printer in Lübeck so famous for introducing errors into his editions that "to ballhorn" [*verballhornen* (sic)] became a term for making detrimental "improvements" to a text (in current usage, *verballhornen* refers to the coinage of new words either by mistake or for the purpose of parody).

10 *Corpus delicti*: "body of the offense," evidence.

11 Euricles: Mérope's favorite, in Voltaire's play.

12 Lindelle: pseudonym of Voltaire, see [41.8] and [41.9]. For this criticism, see Voltaire, "Lettre de M. de La Lindelle à M. de Voltaire" 239–40; "A Letter from M. de La Lindelle to M. de Voltaire" 271–2.

13 "[T]his long stretch of five acts which is tremendously difficult to complete without episodes": Voltaire uses this phrase to issue a backhanded compliment to Maffei. See the "Lettre à Monsieur la Marquis Scipion Maffei" 217; "A Letter to the Marquis Scipio Maffei" 245.

Essay 51

1 Actually published 5 January 1768.

2 *Le Philosophe Marié* (1727): five-act verse comedy by Destouches; see [12]. For *The New Agnes*, see [10].

3 François Antoine de Chevrier (1721–62): French playwright and critic, author of the *L'Observateur des Spectacles* [*The Theatrical Observer*] (1762). Jean-Galbert de Campistron (1656–1723): French playwright, author of *Le Jaloux Désabusé* [*The Disillusioned Jealous One*] (1709), a five-act verse comedy.

4 From Act 2, Sc. 2 of *Le Jaloux Désabusé*; see Campistron 145–7. Compare to Act 1, Sc. 2 of Destouches's play; see *The Married Philosopher*, 3–6. Tr. note: we have translated Lessing's rendition of the text, which is a very free adaptation of the French rhymed couplets into German prose.

5 Ariste: the married philosopher; Mélite: his wife; the Marquis: Mélite's would-be suitor. In the English translation, the characters are renamed Young Bellefleur, Melissa, and Sir Harry Sprightly, respectively.

6 Terror and compassion: see [32.6] for notes on our translation of the Aristotelian coupling of *phobos* (fear) and *eleos* (pity).

7 Lessing refers here to the four-volume luxury edition of Destouches's works, *Oeuvres Dramatiques de Néricault Destouches* (1757).

8 See Destouches, *Oeuvres Dramatiques* 1: ix-x.

Essay 52

1 Actually published in early 1768.

2 *Der Triumph der guten Frauen* (1748): five-act comedy in prose by J. E. Schlegel. For the plot, see J. G. Robertson 87.

3 *Der geschäftige Müßiggänger* (1741): five-act prose comedy by J. E. Schlegel, published in 1743 in the fourth volume of J. C. Gottsched's *Deutsche Schaubühne* [*The German Stage*].

4 Possibly a jab at Johann Heinrich Schlegel, J. E. Schlegel's brother, who published his collected works and who defends *The Busy Idler* in his preface to the play; see *Johann Elias Schlegels Werke* 2: 47–50.

5 *Der Geheimnißvolle* (1746; pub. 1747): five-act prose comedy by J. E. Schlegel. In a prologue to the play, Schlegel cites the description of Timante from Act 2, Scene 4 of Molière's *Misanthrope* as the model for his main character; see J. E. Schlegel, *Der Geheimnißvolle* 185–6.

6 Lessing refers to the titular character in *Der Mistrauische* [sic] [*The Suspicious Man*] (1760): five-act prose comedy by J. F. Cronegk.

7 The play was produced in Hamburg in 1751.

8 Moses Mendelssohn, in his letter of 31 January 1765; see Lessing, Mendelssohn, and Nicolai, *Briefe, die neueste Litteratur betreffend* (Letter 312) XXI: 132–3.

9 Mendelssohn; see Lessing, Mendelssohn, and Nicolai, *Briefe, die neueste Litteratur betreffend* (Letter 312) XXI: 135–6.

Essay 53

1 Actually published in early 1768.

2 Claude-Henri de Fusée, abbé de Voisenon (1708–75): French playwright and author of libertine novels.

3 "But the author left 81 of the original verses in their entirety": see Chevrier, *Observateur des Spectacles* 1: 211.

4 Tr. note: the translation here is that of Allan Bloom; for the full passage, see J. J. Rousseau, *Politics and the Arts: Letter to M. d'Alembert on the Theatre* 103. For the original French, see J. J. Rousseau, *Lettre à d'Alembert Sur Les Spectacles* 213–14.

5 In Bloom's translation: "And it is not to a woman that I refuse the talents of men, but to women"; see J. J. Rousseau, *Politics and the Arts: Letter to M. d'Alembert* 48. For the French, see J. J. Rousseau, *Lettre à d'Alembert* 100.

6 Rousseau writes: "J'honore d'autant plus volontiers ceux de l'auteur de Cénie en particulier, qu'ayant à me plaindre de ses discours, je lui rends un hommage pur et désintéressé,

comme tous les éloges sortis de ma plume" (100); in Bloom's translation: "I am all the more willing to praise the talents of the author of *Cénie* in particular, because I have suffered from her words and can thus render her a pure and disinterested homage, as are all those issued from my pen" (48). For more on the relationship between the two authors, see Showalter, *Madame de Graffigny* [sic] *and Rousseau.*

7 Not Charles Simon Favart, but rather his collaborator and wife, Marie-Justine-Benoîte Favart (née Duronceray) (1727–72), a celebrated actress and singer.

8 That is, Chevrier claims that the Abbé de Voisenon, rather than Marie-Justine-Benoîte Favart, was the author of *Annette et Lubin* (1762), a one-act vaudeville verse comedy. A published edition from 1782 lists Mme. Favart and Voisenon as coauthors and additionally notes that Mme. Favart played the lead role.

9 *L'École des femmes* (1662): five-act verse comedy. The translation used was *Die Frauen-Schule* (1752) by F. S. Bierling.

10 *L'École des maris* [*The School for Husbands*] (1661): three-act verse comedy.

11 "The Maxims of Marriage, or the Duties of the Married Woman, with her Daily Practice": a "useful tract" that Arnolphe, the main character, gives to Agnès, his intended bride; see Molière, *The School for Wives* 130–1.

12 Abbé Nicolas-Charles-Joseph Trublet (1697–1770): French essayist and literary theorist, known for his friendship with Antoine Houdar de la Motte and Fontenelle. Bernard le Bouyer (or Bovier) de Fontenelle (1657–1757): playwright, moralist, and philosopher of the French Enlightenment, also the nephew of Pierre and Thomas Corneille. For the quotation given by Lessing, see Trublet, *Essais* 4: 222.

13 Paul Scarron (1610–60): French playwright and novelist, author of *La précaution inutile* [*The Useless Precaution*], a translation of the Spanish novella by Doña Maria de Zayas y Sotomayor; Scarron's version was published in *Les Nouvelles tragi-comiques de M. Scarron* (1655–57). Gianfrancesco Straparola (c.1480–1557): Italian author, whose popular two-part collection of novellas, *Le piacevoli notti* [*The Nights of Straparola*] (lit. "Pleasant Nights") (1550–53), introduced numerous folktales into European literature. In *Le piacevoli notti*, a group of men and women tells stories, in the manner of Boccaccio's *Decameron*, over a succession of nights – Lessing refers to the fourth story told on the fourth night; see Straparola, *Le Piacevoli* 1: 231–41; *Nights of Straparola* 1: 199–207.

14 See Voltaire, *La Vie de Molière* 419–20.

15 Molière responded to his critics in the form of a one-act prose comedy, *La Critique d'école des femmes* [*The Critique of the School for Wives*] (1663), from which Lessing quotes in his footnote; for the English, see Molière, *The Critique of the School for Wives* 199.

16 Horace: a handsome younger man who pursues Agnès.

Essay 54

1 Actually published early in 1768.

2 *School for Mothers*, see [21]. *Le Comte d'Essex* [*The Earl of Essex*]: five-act verse tragedy by French playwright Thomas Corneille; see [22].

3 *Domestica facta*: domestic affairs; a reference to the *Ars Poetica* [*The Art of Poetry*] of Horace; see *Satires, Epistles, and Ars Poetica* 474–5.

4 John Banks (c. 1652/3–1700): English playwright.

5 *The Unhappy Favourite* went through multiple printings in the seventeenth century, was staged repeatedly in the eighteenth century, and spawned many adaptations and imitations; see Wykes 90.

6 Calprenède, see [22.7]. Claude Boyer (1618–98): French poet and playwright. The younger Corneille: Thomas Corneille, see [22.6]. Lessing appears to have drawn this information from Léris 120–1.

7 *Philotas* (1605): tragedy by English poet, historian, and playwright Samuel Daniel (1562–1619); Lessing refers to a later 1611 edition. Lessing's assertion about the play's relationship to the historical Essex is drawn from Theophilus Cibber, who writes, "it was reported that

the character of Philotas was drawn for [sic] the unfortunate earl of Essex, which obliged the author to vindicate himself from this charge, in an apology printed at the end of the play"; see *The Lives of the Poets of Great Britain and Ireland* 147–8. (Lessing slightly misrenders Cibber's title in his footnote). Contemporary scholarship is disinclined to believe Daniel's disavowal; see Bergeron 100–4.

8 Various sources have been suggested for Banks's play, beginning with *The Secret History of the most renowned Queen Elizabeth and the Earl of Essex* (1680), which was in fact a translation of Thomas Corneille's *Comte d'Essex* (1678). Another suggested source, an anonymous chapbook entitled *History of the Most Renowned Queen Elizabeth and her Great Favourite, the Earl of Essex* (1700?), was originally believed to have been published in 1650, but is actually an abbreviated version of *The Secret History*. For more on the origins of Banks's play, see Wykes 79–81.

9 Tr. note: The lengthy quote that follows is Lessing's translation of the plot description of *The Earl of Essex* from the second volume of the anonymous compilation *A Companion to the Theatre* (99–105). (Lessing also slightly misrenders this title). We have restored the original English (with original orthography and punctuation) except where Lessing deviates significantly from his source, in which cases our translation of Lessing's alteration is interpolated in square brackets (including his addition of the act breaks), and the difference explained in these endnotes.

10 Tr. note: the bracketed text is a translation of Lessing's free expansion of the scene; the (far briefer) original English reads "like Reproaches; on which the Queen, inflamed with Wrath, gives him a Blow. He lays his Hand on his Sword, and it is in vain that"; see *A Companion to the Theatre* 2: 102.

11 Tr. note: the original reads "there to wait their Trial. But the Queen, in spite of all can be said to her"; see *A Companion to the Theatre* 2: 103.

12 Tr. note: this last sentence is Lessing's addition, and not in the original; see *A Companion to the Theatre* 2: 103.

Essay 55

1 Actually published early in 1768.

2 In [54], Lessing begins his analysis of *The Unhappy Favourite: or, The Earl of Essex* (1682) by John Banks. Here he continues the play's synopsis, drawn from *A Companion to the Theatre* 2: 99–105 (the passage quoted in this essay begins on 2: 103), so that his reader might compare Banks's play to Thomas Corneille's *Le Comte d'Essex* (1678). We have restored the original English except where Lessing deviates significantly from his source, in which case a retranslation of Lessing's changes back into English is interpolated in square brackets.

3 Tr. note: in the original, the following is in place of the text in brackets: "Instead of bearing his Message to the Queen, she represents him as insolent, disdaining to receive any Favour from her; and daring all that her Power and Indignation can inflict: To heighten her Displeasure against him, an unlucky Accident contributes: His Wife hearing he was condemn'd to die, quite desperate with Grief, flies to the Queen, reveals the Secret of their Marriage, and begs her Husband's Life. Never did publick Indignation, or secret Despair, rise to a greater Height than in the Behaviour, and Breast of this Princess; she spurns the Countess from her, and" (*A Companion to the Theatre* 2: 103–4).

4 For the relationship between the *Essex* of Banks and that of T. Corneille, see [54.8].

5 See [22] and [23].

6 In Pierre Corneille's *Le Cid* (1636), the play's hero fights a duel to avenge his father's honor after the latter receives a slap to the face.

7 Georges de Scudéry (1601–67): French playwright, poet, novelist, and rival of Pierre Corneille. François Le Métel de Boisrobert (1592–1662): French abbé, playwright, and poet. Both were participants in the famous literary controversy sparked by the success of *Le Cid*.

8 Amphitryon, Sosia: see [55.13]. For the quotation provided by Lessing, see Voltaire, "*Le Cid*" in *Commentaires sur Corneille (II)* 60.

9 This definition is that of François Hédelin d'Aubignac; see Hédelin, *La Pratique du théâtre* 133; *The Whole Art of the Stage* Bk 4, Ch. 5, p. 145–6.

10 See P. Corneille, *Trois discours* 63–72; "Discourse on Tragedy" 10–16.

11 See [55.14].

12 Lessing's footnote refers to Robert Garnier (1544/5–90), lawyer, playwright, and poet, whose *Bradamante* (1582; originally misdated by Lessing as 1682) is considered the first important French tragicomedy; for Lessing's first quotation see Hédelin, *La Pratique du théâtre* 133; *The Whole Art of the Stage* Bk 4, Ch. 5, p. 144–5. Lessing's comment about "historians of French theater" refers to the brothers Parfaict; his second quotation draws selectively from their *Histoire du théâtre français* 3: 454–6.

13 In Plautus's play, Jupiter sleeps with Alcmena by impersonating her husband (the titular Amphitryon), who is away at war; Jupiter's efforts are supported by Mercury, who disguises himself as Amphitryon's slave Sosia. For a further plot synopsis, see Plautus, "Introduction to *Amphitryon, or Jupiter in Disguise.*"

14 From Plautus's prologue to *Amphitryon*. Henry Thomas Riley's translation reads: "I'll make this to be a mixture – a Tragi-comedy. For me to make it entirely to be a Comedy, where Kings and Gods appear, I do not deem right. What then? Since here the servant has a part as well, just as I said, I'll make it to be a Tragi-comedy"; see Plautus, *The Comedies of Plautus* 2: 5.

Essay 56

1 Actually published early in 1768.

2 In [54], Lessing begins his analysis of *The Unhappy Favourite: or, The Earl of Essex* (1682) by John Banks; here he continues, from [55], to address criticism of Banks's choice to include a moment in which Queen Elizabeth slaps the titular character.

3 More accurately, Voltaire's sentence reads: "Les acteurs mêmes sont très embarrassés à donner ce soufflet, ils font le semblant" ("The actors themselves are too embarrassed to give the blow; they pretend to do so"); see Voltaire, "*Le Cid*" in *Commentaires sur Corneille (II)* 60.

4 Diego (Don Diègue): character in Pierre Corneille's *Le Cid*; the father of Rodrigo (Don Rodrigue), later called "The Cid." See [55.6].

5 The venerable Don Diego is struck by the Count of Gormas, Don Gomez (Gomès).

6 For the demographic make up of the gallery, see [5.10].

7 To avenge the insult done to his father, Rodrigo duels with – and kills – Count Gormas, the father of his beloved, Ximena (Chimène).

8 *Pundonor*. "punto de honor" (point of honor).

9 These lines, suppressed by Corneille, do not appear in modern editions of the play. The first mention of these lines, in 1637, is slightly different from Lessing's. Voltaire, in his edited collection of Corneille's works, gives them as, "Les satisfactions n'apaisent point une âme; / Qui les reçoit a tort, qui les fait se diffame; / Et de pareils accords, l'effet le plus commun / Est de déshonorer deux hommes au lieu d'un" ("Reparations appease no soul; / Whoever receives them wrongly, defames himself. / And the most common effect from such agreements, / Is to dishonor two men instead of one"); see Voltaire "*Le Cid*" in *Commentaires sur Corneille (II)* 63–4.

10 A reference to Louis XIII's 1626 edict, one of many attempts by French monarchs to control dueling, starting in the sixteenth century and continuing into the eighteenth.

11 This information and that which follows is drawn from Hume, *The History of England* 4: 483–4.

12 Queen Elizabeth withdrew from Essex his monopoly on the import of sweet wines; see Hume 505–6.

Essay 57

1 Actually published early in 1768.

2 In [54], Lessing begins his analysis of *The Unhappy Favourite: or, The Earl of Essex* (1682) by John Banks, in comparison to Thomas Corneille's *Le Comte d'Essex* (1678). Here he continues to address criticism of Banks's choice to include a moment in which Queen Elizabeth slaps the titular character; see [55] and [56].

3 For the quotation in Lessing's footnote, see Banks 34–5.

4 Gascon: a boaster or braggart, the natives of Gascony being reputedly very boastful. Calprenède was not, in fact, born in Gascony, but in nearby Dordogne.

5 Suffolk: the "young sister of Suffolk" is a fictional creation of Thomas Corneille in his version of *Essex*. Here Lessing appears to be drawing from Voltaire's criticism of his play; see Voltaire, "*Comte d'Essex*" in *Commentaires sur Corneille (I)* 1008.

6 Nottingham: the Countess of Nottingham; in Banks's play, she has been rejected by Essex. Tr. note: Banks's original English is an elevated and formal blank verse; Lessing's German prose translation uses much plainer diction, a choice he explains in [59]. Because Lessing discusses his translation choices later, we have re-translated Lessing's adaptation back into English. To compare this version to the original, see Banks, *The Unhappy Favourite: or, the Earl of Essex* 3.1.

7 Tr. note: here the Queen has a long speech, which Lessing omits.

8 Rutland: Countess, secretly married to Essex.

Essay 58

1 Actually published early in 1768.

2 In [54], Lessing begins his analysis of *The Unhappy Favourite: or, The Earl of Essex* (1682) by John Banks, in comparison to Thomas Corneille's *Le Comte d'Essex* (1678); here Lessing continues, from [57], his translation and discussion of Act 3, Scene 1 from Banks's play. Rutland: a countess.

3 Tr. note: on the translation, see [57.6]. In the following, Lessing not only changes the tone and diction of the text, but also departs from Banks's original dialogue in significant ways. For comparison, see Banks, *The Unhappy Favourite* 3.1.

Essay 59

1 Actually published early in 1768.

2 In [54], Lessing begins his analysis of *The Unhappy Favourite: or, The Earl of Essex* (1682) by John Banks; regarding Lessing's adaptation of Banks's text, see translator's note [57.6].

3 *Ampullae & sesquipedalia verba*: from Horace's *Ars poetica*, translated by Fairclough as "bombast and Brobdingnagian words"; see *Satires, Epistles, and Ars Poetica* 459. Diderot uses the same phrase in his *Entretiens sur Le Fils naturel* [*Conversations on the Natural Son*] (1757) just before the passage Lessing cites in the next paragraph. See Diderot, *Entretiens sur Le Fils naturel* 165; *Selected Writings on Art and Literature* 34. The "Entretiens" contain many of Diderot's ideas regarding the form and function of emerging genres such as "serious drama" and bourgeois tragedy and influenced Lessing's own theories of drama and performance, including those outlined here. For Lessing's translation of this text and others, see *Das Theater des Herrn Diderot* [*The Theater of M. Diderot*] (1760) in *Werke und Briefe* 5/1: 10–230.

4 *Entretiens sur Le Fils naturel* 165; English translation taken from Geoffrey Bremner in Diderot, *Selected Writings on Art and Literature* 34–5.

5 *Hecuba* (424 BCE): Euripidean tragedy.

6 Pomposity and bombast: charges frequently leveled against the language of baroque tragedy.

7 Lessing draws this and the following information from a review of Henry Jones's *Earl of Essex* in the English literary journal *The Monthly Review* (March 1753: 225–9). Henry Jones (1721–70): Irish-born poet and playwright. Henry Brooke (1703–83): Irish-born novelist and playwright; his *Earl of Essex*, published in 1761, was previously performed in Dublin in 1749.

8 Ben Jonson (1572?–1637): English playwright, poet, and literary critic. In *The Monthly Review*, the anonymous author provides the epilogue (by an unknown author) to Jones's *Essex*, which contains the lines, "Can he believe th'example of Old Ben, / Who chang'd (like him) the trowel for the pen, / will in his favour move your critic bowels?" (228). Jonson and Jones did indeed both begin as bricklayers.

9 James Ralph (1705?–62): (possibly) American-born English poet, playwright, and dramatic critic of indifferent success; later a historian and political writer. Authored *The Fall of the Earl of Essex* (1731).

10 For Lessing's footnote, see the *Journal encyclopédique* 11: 120–1. The anonymous *Journal* author describes how Rutland becomes hysterical when Essex is led to his execution; he observes that although London audiences found this moment admirable, Parisian spectators would find it ridiculous and would wish to see both character and author sent to the insane asylum.

Essay 60

1 Actually published early in 1768.

2 In [54], Lessing begins his analysis of *The Unhappy Favourite: or, The Earl of Essex* (1682) by John Banks; at the end of [59], Lessing promises a discussion "in passing" of "a Spanish *Essex.*" This essay begins a long description and discussion of that play, in which Lessing often quotes at length (and not always accurately) from the play, whose full title Lessing provides in his footnote. Its author has subsequently been identified as Spanish playwright Antonio Coello (1611–52).

3 Joseph Padrino: prolific eighteenth-century publisher. Printed editions of the play have considerable variance in orthography, punctuation, and word usage; see Schmiedel 21–30.

4 The play was first produced in Madrid in 1633 by the company of Manuel Álvarez Vallejo.

5 For the quotations in Lessing's footnote, see Coello 3.

6 Coello 3.

7 Comic character: the *gracioso* (fool) was a stock character in seventeenth-century Spanish drama.

8 For the first part of the footnote quotation, see Coello 1; the second part of the quotation appears on page 2.

9 Coello 4.

10 Duke of Alanzon: Hercule-François, duc d'Anjou, later duc d'Alençon (1554–84); youngest son of Henri II of France and Catherine de Médicis, brother to three kings of France, and suitor of Elizabeth I.

11 "I made you owner (master) of my honor"; see Coello 5.

12 Coello 6.

Essay 61

1 Actually published early in 1768.

2 In [54], Lessing begins his analysis of *The Unhappy Favourite: or, The Earl of Essex* (1682) by John Banks; here Lessing continues, from [60], his extended synopsis and discussion of a "Spanish Essex" (Antonio Coello's *Dar la vida por su Dama*, 1633), from which Lessing often quotes at length (and not always accurately). The "she" in Lessing's first sentence refers to Blanca, a (fictional) lover of the Earl of Essex.

3 For the quotation in Lessing's footnote, see Coello 7–8.

4 For the quotation in Lessing's footnote, see Coello 8.

5 The Duke (of Alanzon): in England to negotiate the marriage of Elizabeth to the youngest brother of the King of France.

6 Cosme: Essex's servant; a comic fool.

7 For the quotation in Lessing's footnote, see Coello 9.

Essay 62

1 Actually published early in 1768.

2 In [54], Lessing begins his analysis of *The Unhappy Favourite: or, The Earl of Essex* (1682) by John Banks; here Lessing continues, from [60], his extended synopsis and discussion of a

"Spanish Essex" (Antonio Coello's *Dar la vida por su Dama*, 1633), from which Lessing often quotes at length (and not always accurately). The Duke in Lessing's first sentence refers that of Alanzon, who is in England to negotiate the marriage of Elizabeth to the youngest brother of the King of France.

3 Blanca: (fictional) lover of the Earl of Essex.
4 For the quotation in Lessing's footnote, see Coello 9–10.
5 For the quotation in Lessing's footnote, see Coello 10.
6 For the quotation in Lessing's footnote, see Coello 10.
7 For the quotation in Lessing's footnote, see Coello 10.
8 For the quotation in Lessing's footnote, see Coello 10.
9 For the quotation in Lessing's footnote, see Coello 11.
10 For the quotation in Lessing's footnote, see Coello 11–12.
11 Lessing refers to hybrid plays popular with traveling troupes in the seventeenth and early eighteenth centuries, which featured great figures of the past and present. These serio-comic works condensed literary tragedies both domestic and foreign (including Spanish plays of love and honor), adding to them the improvisation and ribaldry of Italian *commedia dell'arte*. Such plays were irksome to eighteenth-century theater reformers such as Lessing and J. C. Gottsched, and historians typically follow their lead, describing these works as bombastic, sensational, and gory, as well as comically obscene. Tr. note: the phrase Lessing uses here, *Staats- und Helden-Actionen*, is a variant on the more familiar label *Haupt- und Staatsaktionen* ["head and state actions"] – the most common translation of this generic designation is "chief and state plays"; others include "main and state action," "monarch and state action," and "political action plays."
12 Lope Félix de Vega Carpio, commonly referred to as Lope de Vega (1562–1635): major playwright of the Spanish Golden Age. Lessing provides this statement by Lope in the foot-note that follows; see also [62.14].
13 Cristóbal de Virués (c. 1550 – c. 1614): Spanish poet, playwright, and soldier.
14 For the quotation in Lessing's footnote, see Vega, *Arte Nuevo de Hazer Comedias* (1609) in *Rimas* 375–7; *The New Art of Writing Plays* 31.
15 Miguel de Cervantes Saavedra (1547–1616): renowned Spanish novelist, poet, and play-wright; author of *Don Quixote* (1605, 1615). Lessing's quotation is from his "Prologo al lector" ["Prologue to the Reader"] in *Ocho comedias y ocho entremeses nuevos* [*Eight New Plays and Interludes*] (7).

Essay 63

1 Actually published early in 1768.
2 In [54], Lessing begins his analysis of *The Unhappy Favourite: or, The Earl of Essex* (1682) by John Banks; here Lessing continues, from [60], his extended synopsis and discussion of a "Spanish Essex" (Antonio Coello's *Dar la vida por su Dama*, 1633), from which Lessing often quotes at length (and not always accurately).
3 Cosme: Essex's servant; a comic fool.
4 Blanca: the (fictional) lover of the Earl of Essex. Flora: Blanca's chambermaid.
5 For the quotation in Lessing's footnote, see Coello 13.
6 For the quotation in Lessing's footnote, see Coello 13.
7 For the quotation in Lessing's footnote, see Coello 13.
8 For the quotation in Lessing's footnote, see Coello 13.
9 Irene: a musician; the character never appears onstage.
10 Coello 14.
11 *Redondilla*: Spanish four-line octosyllabic stanza with the rhyme scheme ABBA. Lessing provides the Spanish in his footnote.
12 For the song (the *mote*) quoted by Lessing in his footnote, see Coello 14; for the larger quotation (the *glosa*), see pages 14–15. The "Boscán and Garcilaso" alluded to at the end of

Lessing's footnote are Juan Boscán (Joan Boscà i Almogàver) (c.1490–1542) and Garcilaso de la Vega (1503–36), poets (Catalan and Spanish, respectively) whose works were published together posthumously in 1543; their naturalization of Italian verse forms had a lasting influence on Spanish Golden Age poetry.

13 This is a paraphrase of the Queen's dialogue; see Coello 15.

Essay 64

1 Actually published early in 1768.

2 In [54], Lessing begins his analysis of *The Unhappy Favourite: or, The Earl of Essex* (1682) by John Banks; here Lessing continues, from [60], his extended synopsis and discussion of a "Spanish Essex" (Antonio Coello's *Dar la vida por su Dama*, 1633), from which Lessing quotes at length (and not always accurately).

3 For the first part of the quotation in Lessing's footnote, see Coello 15; for the second, see Coello 16.

4 *Coup de théâtre*: term connoting a sudden and surprising plot development.

5 For the quotation in Lessing's footnote, see Coello 16.

6 For the quotation in Lessing's footnote, see Coello 17.

7 For the quotation in Lessing's footnote, see Coello 18.

Essay 65

1 Actually published early in 1768.

2 In [54], Lessing begins his analysis of *The Unhappy Favourite: or, The Earl of Essex* (1682) by John Banks; here Lessing continues, from [60], his extended synopsis and discussion of a "Spanish Essex" (Antonio Coello's *Dar la vida por su Dama*, 1633), from which Lessing quotes at length (and not always accurately).

3 For the quotation in Lessing's footnote, see Coello 19.

4 For the quotation in Lessing's footnote, see Coello 19–20.

5 For the quotation in Lessing's footnote, see Coello 21–2.

Essay 66

1 Actually published in early 1768.

2 In [54], Lessing begins his analysis of *The Unhappy Favourite: or, The Earl of Essex* (1682) by John Banks; here Lessing continues, from [60], his extended synopsis and discussion of a "Spanish Essex" (Antonio Coello's *Dar la vida por su Dama*, 1633), from which Lessing quotes at length (and not always accurately).

3 For the quotation in Lessing's footnote, see Coello 23.

4 An apparently treasonous letter written by Essex; actually intended to trap traitors plotting against the queen. See [61].

5 Roberto: Blanca's treasonous uncle; see [61].

6 For the quotation in Lessing's footnote, see Coello 24.

7 This line belongs in fact to Cosme, rather than Essex. For the quotation in Lessing's footnote, see Coello 26.

Essay 67

1 Actually published in early 1768.

2 In [54], Lessing begins his analysis of *The Unhappy Favourite: or, The Earl of Essex* (1682) by John Banks; here Lessing continues, from [60], his extended synopsis and discussion of a "Spanish Essex" (Antonio Coello's *Dar la vida por su Dama*, 1633), from which Lessing quotes at length (and not always accurately).

3 For the quotation in Lessing's footnote, see Coello 27.
4 For the quotation in Lessing's footnote, see Coello 28.
5 For the quotation in Lessing's footnote, see Coello 29.
6 For the quotation in Lessing's footnote, see Coello 29.
7 For the quotation in Lessing's footnote, see Coello 29.
8 For the quotation in Lessing's footnote, see Coello 29.
9 Lessing does not provide the Spanish for this final passage; for the original, see Coello 30.

Essay 68

1 Actually published in early 1768.
2 In [54], Lessing begins his analysis of *The Unhappy Favourite: or, The Earl of Essex* (1682) by John Banks; here Lessing continues, from [60], his extended synopsis and discussion of a "Spanish Essex" (Antonio Coello's *Dar la vida por su Dama*, 1633), from which Lessing quotes at length (and not always accurately).
3 For the quotation in Lessing's footnote, see Coello 31.
4 For the quotation in Lessing's footnote, see Coello 31.
5 For the quotation in Lessing's footnote, see Coello 31.
6 *Virginia* (1750): five-act unrhymed verse tragedy by Spanish playwright and critic Agustín de Montiano y Luyando (1697–1764), proponent of the French neoclassical model and author of *Discurso sobre las Tragedias españolas* [*Discourse on Spanish Tragedies*] (1750–53). In 1754, Lessing published a lengthy selection from *Virginia* in his *Theatralische Bibliothek*, drawn not from the original Spanish but from a French translation by Nicolas-Gabriel Vaquette d'Hermilly (1705?–78); see *Werke und Briefe* 3: 302. *Virginia* is considered to have influenced Lessing's tragedy *Emilia Galotti* (1772); see Nisbet 487.
7 For Lessing's remarks on the play, see *Werke und Briefe* 3: 300–3. For Lessing's excerpt in full, see Lessing, "Auszug aus dem Trauerspiele Virginia des Don Augustino [sic] de Montiano y Luyando" ["Excerpt from the Tragedy *Virginia* by Don Agustín de Montiano y Luyando"] in *Gotth. Ephr. Lessings Theatralische Bibliothek* 1: 117–208.
8 Montiano y Luyando's second tragedy was *Ataúlfo* (1753). Pedro Calderón de la Barca (1600–81): Spanish playwright and poet, considered, with Lope de Vega, the greatest of Spanish Golden Age playwrights.
9 Decorum: the French neoclassical rule of bienséance (propriety), which called for civility and an adherence to perceived social norms of behavior.
10 Hanswurst: see [18.6]. Generally, Lessing supported neither the mixing of genres, nor the antics of the German clown Hanswurst; here his (qualified) support of the "Spanish Hanswurst" allows him to criticize, as he does in this paragraph, both the "cold uniformity" of French neoclassical theater and the aristocratically dominated social structure it upholds.

Essay 69

1 Actually published in early 1768.
2 Lessing continues his discussion, begun in [68], of the mixture of comedy and tragedy in Spanish Golden Age drama.
3 See [62].
4 Old Comedy: Lope de Vega appears to refer to the classical comedy of both Greece and Rome; in contemporary usage, the term refers to ancient Greek comedy (c. fifth century BCE), considered synonymous with the work of Aristophanes (c. 450–c. 388 BCE). Lessing discusses Plautus's *Amphitryon* at the end of [55].
5 Menander (c. 342–c. 292 BCE): Hellenistic playwright, chief representative of Athenian New Comedy. Plutarch criticizes Old Comedy through Aristophanes, its only extant representative, in "A Comparison Between Aristophanes and Menander" (extant only in fragments), for combining "tragic, comic, pompous, and prosaic elements, obscurity, vagueness, dignity, and elevation, loquacity and sickening nonsense" (465).

6 Lucius Annaeus Seneca (Seneca the Younger) (c. 4 BCE–65 CE): Roman orator, statesman, Stoic philosopher, and tragic playwright. Pasiphae's minotaur: in Greek mythology, a monster with the body of a man and the head of a bull; the offspring of Pasiphae, wife of the Cretan king Minos, and a bull.

7 Lessing may have translated this passage not from the Spanish but from a French translation of Lope de Vega's poem entitled "Nouvelle Pratique de Théatre, accommodée à l'usage présent d'Espagne, adressée à l'Académie de Madrid e traduite de l'espagnol de Lopez [sic] de Vega" ["The New Practice of Theater, accommodated to the current usage in Spain, addressed to the Academy of Madrid and translated from the Spanish of Lope de Vega"]; see Lope de Vega, "Nouvelle Pratique" 255 ff.; and J. G. Robertson 299–300. For the Spanish quoted in Lessing's footnote, see Lope de Vega, *Arte Nuevo de Hazer* [sic] *Comedias* in *Rimas* 371–3; for an English translation see Lope de Vega, *The New Art of Writing Plays* 29–30.

8 Lessing refers to Christoph Martin Wieland, see [15.10].

9 See Wieland, *Geschichte des Agathon* 2: 192–3; for an English version of the novel, see Wieland, *The History of Agathon* 4: 1–2.

10 Gothic taste: refers to the baroque style of the seventeenth century; see Grimm 8: col. 1008. Although generally derided by eighteenth-century critics, its value would be readdressed at the end of the century by authors such as Wieland and Goethe. *Haupt- und Staatsaktionen*: see [62.11].

11 Aristotle describes a plot as having two parts, the complication and the resolution; his term for the latter is *lusis* (λύσις), usually translated as "unraveling." See *Poetics* (Part XVIII).

12 The Hanswurst character, popularized by the Viennese actor and manager Joseph Anton Stranitzky (1676–1726), remained an important figure in the theater of Vienna, capital of the Holy Roman Empire, long after its popularity declined elsewhere.

13 See Wieland, *Geschichte des Agathon* 2: 193–5; *The History of Agathon* 4: 2–5.

14 Lessing cuts off midsentence for his parenthetical digression; he picks up his thought again at the beginning of [70].

15 Chew on the ***: part of the attraction of "trivial" novels of the time was their anonymity, which allowed the public the added entertainment of speculating about their authorship.

Essay 70

1 Actually published spring of 1768; performances mentioned by Lessing occurred in 1767.

2 In [69], Lessing provides an excerpt from Christoph Martin Wieland's novel *Geschichte des Agathon* [*The History of Agathon*] (1766–67), which (somewhat ironically) supports the mixing of tragic and comic genres, as a means of expanding on Lope de Vega's defense of tragicomedy in his *Arte Nuevo de Hacer Comedias* [*The New Art of Writing Plays*] (1609). Lessing's discussion of the mixing of genres in Spanish Golden Age drama begins in [68].

3 Imitation of nature: in the *Hamburg Dramaturgy*, Lessing's dramatic theory negotiates between a mimetic representation of reality and one that is more subjective, in which the function of theatrical illusion is affective rather than strictly representational. For a detailed discussion of this negotiation, see Nisbet 324; 395–403.

4 Wieland was not only a novelist, poet, and translator, but also a professor of philosophy and literary critic; in 1773, he founded the literary periodical *Der teutsche Merkur* [*The German Mercury*].

5 See Wieland, *Geschichte des Agathon* 2: 193; *The History of Agathon* 4: 3.

6 For Lessing's use of *gotische* (gothic), see [69.10].

7 *Haupt- und Staatsaktionen*: see [62.11].

8 *Die Brüder, oder die Schule der Väter* [*The Brothers, or The School for Fathers*] (1763): five-act comedy by Karl Franz Romanus (1731–87), freely adapted from *L'École des pères* [*The School for Fathers*] (1705) by French actor and playwright Michel Baron (Boyron) (1653–1729); for the relationship between Romanus's comedy and that of Baron, see J. G. Robertson 155; 321–2; 327–8. *L'Oracle* [*The Oracle*] (1740): one-act comedy by Germain François Poullain de Saint-Foix (1698–1776). The German translation used, *Das Orakel*, was most

likely Schönemann's, which was staged in 1747 and published in 1752; see J. G. Robertson 89–90.

9 *Adelphi (or Adelphoe)* [*The Brothers*] (160 BCE): Terence's Latin adaptation of Menander's Greek comedy of the same name. Micio and Demea are brothers of different temperaments. Demea, a country-dweller, is married and has two sons; his elder son, Aeschinus, has been adopted by Micio, who lives in the city. Aeschinus, raised indulgently by Micio, has impregnated (and promised to marry) Pamphila, the daughter of the widow Sostrata. Ctesipho, Aeschinus's younger brother, despite having been raised strictly by Demea, visits the city and falls in love with a "music girl" (*psaltria*) belonging to Sannio, a pimp. Aeschinus, on his brother's behalf, steals the girl from Sannio. Comedy ensues as both Aeschinus and Syrus, Micio's slave, seek to hide Ctesipho's involvement in the affair. Ultimately, however, Demea discovers Ctesipho carousing; initially enraged, Demea is soothed by Micio and vows to change. Aeschinus marries Pamphila, Ctesipho is allowed to keep the (now legally purchased) music girl, Syrus and his wife are freed, and Micio is convinced to marry Sostrata.

10 *L'École des Maris* (1661); see [53]. Middle-aged brothers Sganarelle and Ariste have promised to care for Isabelle and Léonor, orphaned sisters; each of the brothers hopes to marry his ward. Ariste, near 60, gives Léonor considerable liberty; Sganarelle, despite being 20 years his brother's junior, keeps his own ward, Isabelle, under strict control. Isabelle, through various machinations, nevertheless manages to secure a marriage with a handsome young neighbor, Valère, and Léonor, disgusted by the young fools she has encountered, pledges to marry Ariste.

11 In *La Vie de Molière* (1739); Lessing provides Voltaire's comments in the final paragraph of this essay.

12 *Primus autem sapientiae gradus est falsa intelligere, secundus [vera] cognoscere:* "The first step toward wisdom is to understand what is false; the second, to ascertain what is true." An aphorism from the first book of the *Divinae institutiones* [*The Divine Institutes*] of (Lucius Caecilius Firmianus) Lactantius (c. 240–c. 320), an early Church Father and Christian apologist known as the "Christian Cicero"; see Lactantius, *Divinae institutiones* 94; *The Divine Institutes* 39.

13 Lessing applies this polemical approach in his earlier writings, as well as in the *Hamburg Dramaturgy*.

14 "Aristotle tends to look for a fight in his books. And he does this not rashly and by chance, but by a fixed method and with a plan, for [he does this] after others' perceptions have become unsteady, etc." According to J. G. Robertson, this quotation is from *Aristotelis Artis rhetoricae* (1598), a commentary on Aristotle's *Rhetoric* by Aemilius Portus (also Aemil, Émile, or Emilio Porto) (1550–1614/15), an Italian humanist and professor of Greek and Rhetoric; see J. G. Robertson 345.

15 See Voltaire, "*L'École des Maris*" in *La Vie de Molière* 419–20.

Essay 71

1 Actually published spring of 1768.

2 Lessing continues, from [70], a critique of Voltaire's comparison of Terence's *The Brothers* with Molière's *The School for Husbands*; for the plots of these plays, see [70.9] and [70.10] respectively. Voltaire's early schooling was at the Jesuit College of Louis-le-Grand in Paris (1704–11), where his classical education would have included the reading of Terence, albeit with the more scabrous material redacted; see Valentin 197–200.

3 See Voltaire, "L'École des Maris" in *La Vie de Molière* 420.

4 Pamphila does in fact remain offstage.

5 "Throughout the entire play, each character is preserved – gentle Micio, severe Demea, the greedy pimp." From the commentary on *The Brothers* by the Roman grammarian and rhetorician Aelius Donatus (fl. fourth century BCE); see Donatus, *Publii Terentii* 240.

6 His cousin: an error; should read "his brother."

7 The quotation that Lessing provides in his footnote can be found in Terence, *Adelphi* l. 859–60; for both the Latin and English, see Barsby 2: 349–51.

8 The quotation that Lessing provides in his footnote can be found in Terence, *Adelphi* l. 984–91; for both the Latin and English, see Barsby 2: 364–7.

9 "Here Terence shows that Demea pretends his character has changed, rather than that [Demea] has actually changed"; see Donatus, *Publii Terentii* 334.

10 For a direct translation of the Latin, see Barsby 2: 345.

11 "He seems to have calmed down a bit more quickly than is called for by even these uncertain circumstances. But this is also characteristic: for those who are angry with just cause often come quickly to logical reasoning, once they set aside their rage"; see Donatus, *Publii Terentii* 320.

12 "Watch not what is said, but with what gesture it is said, and you will see that Demea, at this point, has neither restrained his temper, nor come back to himself"; see Donatus, *Publii Terentii* 320.

Essay 72

1 Actually published spring of 1768.

2 In [70], Lessing begins a discussion of Terence's comedy *The Brothers*, which he continues here; for a plot synopsis, see [70.9].

3 The quotation that Lessing provides in his footnote can be found in Terence, *Adelphi* l. 835–53; for both the Latin and English, see Barsby 2: 346–9.

4 Tr. note: for an English translation directly from the Latin text, see Barsby 2: 347–9.

5 "Demea speaks this line with such a facial expression that he seems to be smiling against his will. But then with 'Unfortunately, I feel,' he speaks again with an angry and bitter countenance"; see Donatus, *Publii Terentii* 322.

6 Traditional histories describe Roman theater as entering a decline, in both quality and popularity, during the Roman Empire, after having flourished during the time of the Republic; for a counterview, see Goldberg, "The Fall and Rise of Roman Tragedy."

7 Anne Lefèvre Dacier (1647–1720): distinguished French classicist, renowned throughout Europe for her translations of Greek and Latin texts. With her husband, André Dacier, she produced the Delphin series of editions of Latin classics; her prose translation of *Adelphi/ Brothers*, with accompanying dissertation on Terence, appears in the three-volume collection *Les Comedies de Terence* (1691); see Vol. 2: 251–445.

8 Tr. note: Lessing, in his original essay, subsequently quotes in his footnote from the German translation of Terence's play by Johann Samuel Patzke (1727–87), which was published in Halle in 1753 in the volume *Des Publius Terenzius Lustspiele aus dem lateinischen übersetzt [The Comedies of Publius Terentius, translated from the Latin]*. Lessing's aim is to demonstrate how wooden and unfunny that translation is; because his argument rests on subtle differences between his own German translation and that of Patzke, we refer the reader to the original rather than include another translation of the scene. See Patzke 447–8.

9 Lessing refers to K. F. Romanus, author of *Die Brüder [The Brothers]*.

10 Lysimon: Romanus's name for Demea.

11 Frontin: the servant of Lysimon's nephew. (Terence's original has two pairs of brothers; Romanus changes the younger set to cousins.) For this exchange, see Romanus 117.

12 J. G. Robertson believes that the dramaturgical choices that Lessing criticizes, here and in later essays, should more accurately be applied to *L'École des pères [The School for Fathers]*, Michel Baron's adaptation of Terence, which, Robertson says, Romanus has used for his own adaptation, rather than the Latin original; see J. G. Robertson 154–5.

Essay 73

1 Actually published spring of 1768; performances mentioned by Lessing occurred in 1767.

2 In [70], Lessing begins a discussion of Terence's *The Brothers*; for a plot synopsis, see [70.9]. Here he continues, from [72], a comparison of Terence's comedy with K. F. Romanus's *Die Brüder [The Brothers]*; see [70.8].

3 Lysimon: Romanus's name for Terence's Demea.

4 Romanus's *Die Brüder* was repeated on August 11 and October 7, 1767, and on January 5, 1768 (in Hanover). Lessing resumes his discussion of the play in [96].

5 See [70.8].

6 *Le dénouement imprévu* (1727): one-act prose comedy by Marivaux; first performed in 1724. The German translation, *Der unvermuthete Ausgang*, was by J. C. Krüger.

7 Peter (Pierre in Marivaux's original): M. Argante's gardener.

8 *Richard der Dritte* (1759/65): five-act verse tragedy by C. F. Weisse. *Herzog Michel* (1750; pub. 1757): one-act verse comedy by J. C. Krüger; a highly popular *Nachspiel* (afterpiece), it was performed five times by the Hamburg National Theater company.

9 William Shakespeare's *Life and Death of King Richard III* (c. 1593); the play was introduced in Germany through four anonymously translated scenes that appeared in the *Neue Erweiterungen der Erkenntnis und des Vergnügens* [*New Expansions of Knowledge and Pleasure*] (1756). Scholars disagree whether Weisse's statement regarding his ignorance of Shakespeare's play is credible.

10 See Weisse 9.

11 Virgil's apocryphal response to charges that he plagiarized Homer. See Donatus, *The Life of Virgil*, paragraph 46.

12 *Camera obscura* (lit. dark room): boxlike device, a precursor to the photographic camera, which projected images of external objects onto a flat surface, used from the Renaissance onward as a composition tool for artists.

13 Here, and in the next paragraph, Lessing responds to German professor, editor, literary critic, and translator Christian Heinrich Schmid (1746–1800), author of *Theorie der Poesie nach den neuesten Grundsätzen und Nachricht von den besten Dichtern nach den angenommenen Urtheilen* [*Theory of Poetry, according to the most recent principles and Information about the Best Poets, according to accepted judgments*] (1767). Schmid objected, in his *Zusätze zur Theorie der Poesie: Sammlung 1* [*Supplements to the Theory of Poetry: Anthology 1*] (1767), to Lessing's critical approach in the *Hamburg Dramaturgy*, complaining that Lessing focused on exposing authors' errors rather than on teaching audiences how to admire their works (see 1: 38). Schmid would continue his critique of Lessing in all four volumes of these "supplements;" in the third volume, Schmid defends himself at length against this essay, which he perceived as a personal attack (see 3: 74; 88–95). A critic of dubious merit, Schmid was criticized harshly not only by Lessing but also Wieland, Herder, and Goethe, among others.

14 Schmid makes this accusation on page 45 of his first *Zusätze* [*Supplements*] (Lessing's claim, in his footnote, to have "just now remembered" Schmid's commentary seems rather disingenuous); for Lessing's views on *Amalia*, see [20]. The end of this essay may also serve as an apologia to Weisse, Lessing's childhood friend, for the harshness of the criticism that follows in the next several essays.

Essay 74

1 Actually published spring of 1768.

2 Lessing continues his discussion, from [73], of C. F. Weisse's *Richard der Dritte*. In this essay and in the six that follow, however, Lessing is less concerned with Weisse's tragedy than he is with parsing Aristotle's tragic theory. Lessing does not provide a systemic interpretation of Aristotle, either in the *Hamburg Dramaturgy* or elsewhere, and scholars disagree about the extent to which Lessing's knowledge of Aristotle was authoritative.

3 See Aristotle's *Poetics* (Part XIII). Tr. note: The terms Lessing uses here for Aristotle's *eleos* and *phobos* are *Mitleid* and *Schrecken*, which we translate here as "compassion" and "terror." Because Lessing's argument in this essay depends on his understanding of how one person can feel what another is feeling, the latinate term "compassion" seems a more suitable translation of *Mitleid* than either "pity," the most common English translation, or "sympathy," which in modern English usually connotes a feeling toward another person rather than a sharing of feelings. For more on the challenges of translating the term *Mitleid*, see [32.6] and

Thomas Martinec's essay "The Boundaries of 'Mitleidsdramaturgie': Some Clarifications." Lessing discusses the term *phobos* (terror/fear) later in this essay.

4 Prosper Jolyot de Crébillon (Crébillon père) (1674–1762): French playwright whose tragedies, modeled after Seneca, specialized in extreme violence and horror. In his preface to *Atrée et Thyeste* [*Atreus and Thyestes*] (1707), Crébillon specifically states that tragedy evokes pity through terror.

5 The philosopher: Aristotle.

6 Here Lessing translates Aristotle's *phobos* as *Furcht* (fear) and not as *Schrecken* (terror). Lessing also makes this choice and defends it in the "Briefwechsel über das Trauerspiel" ["Correspondence on Tragedy"] (1755–57), taking issue with both André Dacier's French translation and the German translation of Curtius; see Lessing's letter to Nicolai (Letter 122) dated 2 April 1757, *Werke und Briefe* 3: 715–16 (also 11/1: 178–182). "Terror" was the standard translation of *phobos* in eighteenth-century France and Germany. Given Lessing's emphasis on *Furcht*, both here and in his earlier writing, it is curious that Lessing uses *Schrecken* (terror) in earlier essays of the *Hamburg Dramaturgy* (see, for example, [32]); this choice may be explained in part by the existence of the paired terms "pity and terror" as an established phrase in dramatic theory.

7 In his footnote, Lessing refers to Christian Ernst Schenk (1733–1807), who published his *Komisches Theater* [*Comic Theater*] (1759) anonymously. For the passage quoted by Lessing, see Schenk 35–6.

8 *Letters on Sentiments*: "Briefe über die Empfindungen," first published by Moses Mendelssohn in 1755. This work, together with Nicolai's "Abhandlung vom Trauerspiele" [sic] ["Discourse on Tragedy"] (1757), influenced Lessing's thinking on theatrical affect in the "Briefwechsel über das Trauerspiel" ["Correspondence on Tragedy"] (1755–57). Mendelssohn revised his thoughts on the subject in the "Rhapsodie oder Zusätze zu den Briefen über die Empfindung" ["Rhapsody or Additions to the *Letters on Sentiments*"] in his *Philosophische Schriften* [*Philosophical Writings*] (1761), from which Lessing draws this quotation. See Mendelssohn, "Rhapsodie; oder, Zusätze zu den Briefen über die Empfindungen" in *Philosophische Schriften* 2: 4–6; for an alternate English translation of the passage, see Mendelssohn, "Rhapsody or Additions to the *Letters on Sentiments*" in *Philosophical Writings* 141–2.

9 Electra: titular Sophoclean tragic character.

10 Philoctetes: titular Sophoclean tragic character.

11 Oedipus: titular Sophoclean tragic character. Monime, Mithridates: tragic characters from Racine's *Mithridate*. Desdemona, Othello: from Shakespeare's *Othello*.

12 Mérope, Aegisthus: from Voltaire's tragedy *Mérope*, which Lessing discusses over the course of 15 essays, beginning with [36].

Essay 75

1 Actually published spring of 1768.

2 In [74], Lessing begins his analysis of Aristotle's statement in *Poetics* that tragedy should evoke *eleos* (compassion) and *phobos* (terror/fear); at the end of the essay, he cites Moses Mendelssohn's thoughts on "mixed sentiments," in which Mendelssohn (the "modern philosopher" referred to in the next sentence) argues that all tragic passions originate in compassion.

3 André Dacier; see [37.15].

4 Lessing refers to Aristotle's *Rhetoric* (divided into three books) and his *Nicomachean Ethics* (divided into ten books). Lessing may not, in fact, have deeply studied any of Aristotle's works other than *Poetics*; J. G. Robertson notes, for example, that the frequent invocations in Lessing's writings of Aristotle's *Rhetoric*, *Nicomachean Ethics*, and *Politics* are "vaguely general, or based on second-hand sources" (345).

5 Stagirite: Aristotle was born in Stagira, Macedonia.

6 The Greek line in Lessing's footnote, and the passage that he quotes here in this essay, are from *Rhetoric* 2.5.12. The Latin quotation in Lessing's footnote, from Aemilius Portus

(Aemil Porto), translates as: "Finally, to speak plainly, those fearful things become pitiable when they have come or are about to come into the sphere of other people." Lessing's alternate suggestion reads: "those things are fearful, when they have happened – or are about to happen – to others."

7 Lessing's emphasis on the familiarity of a character's circumstances echoes eighteenth-century critics such as Marmontel and Diderot, who advocated for the development of middle-class drama; see, for example, [14].

8 For the quotation in Lessing's footnote, see P. Corneille, *Trois discours* 10; for an English translation, see P. Corneille, "First Discourse on the Uses and Elements of Dramatic Poetry" 140.

9 In [2], Lessing critiques martyr-dramas, and specifically P. Corneille's *Polyeucte*. Prusias, Phocas, Cleopatra: characters in, respectively, *Nicomède* (1651), *Héraclius* (1647), and *Rodogune* (1644). Lessing discusses *Rodogune*, and Cleopatra in particular, in [29]–[32].

10 Here Lessing draws from P. Corneille's second discourse, "Sur la Tragédie" ["On Tragedy"] in *Trois discours* 60–2; for an English translation of the passage, see P. Corneille, "Discourse on Tragedy" 8–9.

Essay 76

1 Actually published spring of 1768.

2 In [74], Lessing begins his analysis of Aristotle's statement in *Poetics* that tragedy should evoke *eleos* (compassion) and *phobos* (terror/fear); at the end of [75], he quotes Pierre Corneille's view that Aristotle's intention was *not* to assert that both fear and compassion needed to be present simultaneously for the cleansing of tragic emotion (*catharsis*).

3 In his commentary accompanying his 1692 translation of *Poetics*, André Dacier sharply criticizes P. Corneille's interpretation of Aristotle.

4 Tr. note: we translate Lessing's term *vermischte Empfindung* as "mixed sensation"; see Guyer, "Eighteenth Century German Aesthetics" (Section 4: "Mendelssohn, Winckelmann, and Lessing: Mixed Emotions").

5 Tr. note: the term Lessing uses here, *Affekt*, is unusual, and appears to be a terminologically conscious choice, drawing on not just Aristotle but also Spinoza; see Goetschel, *Spinoza's Modernity: Mendelssohn, Lessing, and Heine* (esp. Ch. 12). Hence, we retain the English cognate "affect" (and resist the temptation to narrow its definition through a term like "emotion").

6 See Aristotle's *Poetics* (Part XIII).

7 *Hominibus gratum*: that which is pleasing to people; *ce que peut faire quelque plaisir*: that which can give some pleasure (from Dacier's translation).

8 Theodore Goulston (c. 1575–1632): English physician who published a Latin translation of Poetics in 1623, titled *Aristotelis de Poetica liber*. Φιλανθρωπον: philanthropon. The Latin phrase *quod humanitatis sensu tangat* translates as "that which moves [a person] through a sense of humanity"; see *Aristotelis de Poetica liber* 166.

9 From Curtius's commentary on his 1753 translation of Aristotle's *Poetics*; see Curtius, *Aristoteles Dichtkunst* 191.

10 Mendelssohn, *Philosophische Schriften* 1: 146; *Philosophical Writings* 74.

Essay 77

1 Actually published spring of 1768.

2 Lessing continues his discussion, begun in [74], of Aristotle's *Poetics*; exploring in particular Aristotle's statement that tragedy should evoke *eleos* (compassion) and *phobos* (terror/fear).

3 Lessing apparently possessed a corrupted edition of the *Poetics*; his "word for word" quotation is therefore inaccurate. In Butcher's English translation, Aristotle's text reads: "Tragedy . . . is an imitation of an action . . . in the form of action, not of narrative; through pity and fear

effecting the proper purgation of these emotions"; see Aristotle, *Poetics* (Part VI). On Lessing's corrupted edition, see Anderson, "A Note on Lessing's Misinterpretation of Aristotle."

4 "[O]f an action – that, without help from the narration, by means of compassion and terror"; see Aristotle and André Dacier, *La poëtique d'Aristote* 70–1.

5 Curtius, *Aristoteles Dichtkunst* 12.

6 Lessing errs here; in [75] he quotes from the eighth chapter of Aristotle's *Rhetoric*, rather than the ninth. The passage in Lessing's footnote reads, in the translation by J. H. Freese,

> And since sufferings are pitiable when they appear close at hand, while those that are past or future, ten thousand years backwards or forwards, either do not excite pity at all or only in a less degree, because men neither expect the one nor remember the other, it follows that those who contribute to the effect by gestures, voice, dress, and dramatic action generally, are more pitiable.

7 Here, and in earlier writings, Lessing seeks a middle ground when addressing the moral purpose of tragedy. He avoids on the one hand a strict adherence to moral sensualism and on the other a moralistic rubric conforming to social norms. Feeling and reason are both required for theater to achieve its moral purpose. Although, according to Aristotle, tragedy is meant to evoke compassion and fear, the spectator's emotion requires regulation. An audience member should be neither overwrought nor insensible, and the arousal of theatrical emotion must be coupled with an understanding of the natural law that is responsible for its arousal; see Baldyga, "Corporeal Eloquence and Sensate Cognition" 179–80.

8 Curtius, *Aristoteles Dichtkunst* 156–7.

9 Lessing had already made this assertion in a letter to Nicolai (Letter 103) dated [13] November 1756, *Werke und Briefe* 3: 668–73 (also 11/1: 116–22); for an English translation of this passage, see "Correspondence with Nicolai and Mendelssohn" 329ff.

10 An allusion to the novel *Don Quixote* (1605) by Miguel de Cervantes. The title character, an elderly knight, has become delusional after reading chivalric romances; in his eyes, quotidian objects become fantastical. He is accompanied by his decidedly unromantic squire, Sancho Panza.

11 *Τῶν τοιούτων παθημάτων: ton toiouton pathimaton* (of such passions/sufferings).

12 *Τοιούτων*: such as these. *τούτων*: these.

Essay 78

1 Actually published spring of 1768.

2 In [74], Lessing begins a discussion of Aristotle's *Poetics*; exploring in particular Aristotle's statement that tragedy should evoke *eleos* (compassion) and *phobos* (terror/fear). Here, Lessing continues, from [77], his examination of *Poetics* (Part VI).

3 In Book 8 of his *Politics* (Sections 1339a–1342b), Aristotle discusses the role of music in the education of the young; for Lessing's specific reference, see *Politics* (Section 1341b).

4 See P. Corneille, *Trois discours* 51; for an English translation directly from the French, see P. Corneille, "Discourse on Tragedy" 2.

5 See *Poetics* (Part XIII).

6 See P. Corneille, *Trois discours* 51; for an English translation of the passage, see P. Corneille, "Discourse on Tragedy" 2–3.

7 Here Lessing echoes earlier arguments in the "Briefwechsel über das Trauerspiel" ["Correspondence on Tragedy"] (1755–57), in which he connects such reasoning to a "false concept of compassion"; see his letter to Nicolai (Letter 122) dated 2 April 1757, *Werke und Briefe* 3: 716 (also 11/1: 178).

8 André Dacier; see [37.15].

9 For the original French, see Aristotle and André Dacier, *La poëtique d'Aristote* 78–9. Oedipus, Philoctetes, Orestes: tragic characters in ancient Greek drama.

10 The Stoic: Lessing refers to the Roman Emperor Marcus Aurelius (121–180 CE), known for his *Meditations* (167 CE) in Greek on Stoic philosophy. In Book 11 of *Meditations* (to

which Dacier refers), Marcus Aurelius states that tragedies were created to help us endure the "things we all have to go through"; the pleasure incurred through that stage, he writes, allows one to resist anger on the stage of life (148–9).

11 Curtius, "Abhandlung von der Absicht des Trauerspiels" in *Aristoteles Dichtkunst*.

Essay 79

1 Actually published spring of 1768.

2 In [74], Lessing digresses from a discussion, which he begins in [73], of C. F. Weisse's tragedy *Richard der Dritte* in order to explore Aristotle's statement in *Poetics* that tragedy should evoke *eleos* (compassion) and *phobos* (terror/fear); see [74.3].

3 Tr. note: Lessing uses the word *Schrecken* (terror) in the first part of this sentence and then reverts back to *Furcht* (fear); see [74.6].

4 νέμεσις, νεμεσᾶν: *némesis, nemesán*; here *némesis* translates to "indignation," following Aristotle's usage in *Rhetoric* 2.9.1.

5 μιαρόν: *miarón*; morally repulsive, filthy, distasteful, disgusting. English translators of Aristotle often render *miarón* with a variation on "shock." See Aristotle, *Poetics* (Part XIII).

6 Here Lessing references Enlightenment thinking that portrayed nature as a miniaturized version of God's law, as, for example, in Leibniz's monadology; despite such references, however, Lessing's approach to the theater is always primarily empirical. For an overview of Leibniz's ideas and on Lessing's employment of them, see Martinson 46–50.

7 In an earlier letter to Mendelssohn, Lessing argued that admiration is not a sufficient goal for tragedy, writing that the pleasure evoked by tragedy should be specific to its genre rather than evoking "all kinds of pleasure" without distinction. See his letter to Mendelssohn (Letter 110) dated 18 December 1756, *Werke und Briefe* 3: 694 (also 11/1: 145); for an English translation, see "Correspondence with Nicolai and Mendelssohn" 334.

Essay 80

1 Actually published spring of 1768.

2 In [79], Lessing discusses C. F. Weisse's tragedy *Richard der Dritte*; at the end of the essay, he argues that the effects of tragedy must be specific to that genre.

3 In [74]–[79], Lessing provides an in-depth analysis of Aristotle's assertion in *Poetics* that tragedy should evoke *eleos* (compassion) and *phobos* (terror/fear); see [74.3].

4 Lessing refers to an internationally respected drama of high literary merit, rejecting centuries-old German performance traditions. Like other German theater reformers in the eighteenth century, Lessing sought to upgrade the status of the theater from lowbrow entertainment to a respectable art form suitable for the German middle classes; see, in this volume, Baldyga, "Missions, Misunderstandings, and Mythologies" (3–6); and Maurer-Schmoock 87–149.

5 Charles de Marguetel de Saint-Denis, seigneur de Saint-Évremond (or Évremont) (1614?–1703): French soldier and amateur essayist who lived in exile in England and Holland; author of numerous works of dramatic theory inflected by his exposure to English theater. See Saint-Évremond, *Sur les tragédies* in *Oeuvres en prose* 3: 31–2.

6 *Sir Politick Would-be* (1705): five-act prose comedy "in the English style," inspired by Ben Jonson's *Volpone*; collaboratively written in French c. 1662–5 by Saint-Évremond; George Villiers, 2nd Duke of Buckingham; and Ludovic Stewart, Sieur d'Aubigny. *Les Opéra* (1705): five-act prose comedy written c. 1676 that satirized the contemporary French obsession with opera.

7 See Voltaire, *Appel à toutes les nations de l'Europe* 95–6. This essay served as "an integral part of Voltaire's campaign against foreign, and particularly English, literary influence" (Williams, "Introduction to *Appel à toutes les nations de l'Europe*" 21).

8 *Cyrus* and *Clélie*: reference to *Artamène, ou le grand Cyrus* [*Artamène, or Cyrus the Great*] (1649–53) and *Clélie, histoire romaine* [*Clélie, a Roman History*] (1654–60), courtly novels

(each issued in ten volumes) authored by Madeleine de Scudéry (1607–1701), a prominent French novelist, salonnière, and philosopher.

9 *Sertorius* (1662), *Othon* (1665), *Suréna* (1674), and *Attila* (1667): tragedies by P. Corneille.

10 Voltaire ardently advocated, in numerous writings, for the reform of French theater archi-tecture, which, in the early eighteenth century, retained the long and narrow shape of the tennis courts from which the French theaters had been adapted; see, for example, Voltaire's "Dissertation sur la tragédie ancienne et moderne" ["Dissertation on Ancient and Modern Tragedy"] (1748).

11 See Voltaire, *Appel à toutes les nations de l'Europe* 96–8. This passage was included in editions subsequent to the original.

12 See Aristotle, *Poetics* (Part XIV). The final line ends differently in *Poetics*; Butcher's transla-tion reads, "But to produce this effect by the mere spectacle is a less artistic method, and dependent on extraneous aids" (see Part XIV). Lessing's ending appears to refer back to Part VI of *Poetics*, in which Aristotle discusses the role of spectacle in dramatic poetry: "of all the parts, [Spectacle] is the least artistic, and connected least with the art of poetry. . . . [The] production of spectacular effects depends more on the art of the stage machinist than on that of the poet" (Butcher's translation).

13 Lessing's footnote quotation from T. Cibber is accurate; dashes indicate textual elisions.

14 See [10.14].

15 See [11] and [12] for Lessing's comparison of Shakespeare and Voltaire's use of ghosts.

Essay 81

1 Actually published spring of 1768.

2 Lessing continues, from [80], his criticism of French theater.

3 Dominique Bouhours (1628–1702): French Jesuit priest, author, and literary critic, who stated in his *Entretiens d'Ariste et d'Eugène* [*Conversations between Ariste and Eugene*] (1671) that Germans rarely possess a *bel esprit*, contributing to a polemical discussion in Ger-many regarding French cultural superiority. See Bouhours, "Le Bel Esprit" in *Les Entretiens d'Ariste et d'Eugène* 302–3; for the English, see Bouhours, "The Bel Esprit from The Con-versations of Aristo and Eugene" 221. The French mercenary soldier Riccaut, a minor character in Lessing's *Minna von Barnhelm* (1767), is generally regarded as a satirical response to Bouhours.

4 Hédelin: Abbé Hédelin d'Aubignac; Dacier: André Dacier.

5 "[Q]uelque moderation, quelque favorable interpretation" (some moderation, some favorable interpretation): for this, and the quotation that follows, see P. Corneille, *Trois discours* 63; for an English translation, see P. Corneille, "Discourse on Tragedy" 9.

6 Rodrigue, Chimène: characters from P. Corneille's *Le Cid* (1637). In this paragraph, Less-ing paraphrases from Corneille's second discourse; see P. Corneille, *Trois discours* 60–1; for an English translation, see P. Corneille, "Discourse on Tragedy" 8. (Ed. note: the English translation of the passage paraphrased by Lessing mistakenly references "Rodogune and Chimene" instead of "Rodrigue and Chimène.")

7 Cleopatra (Cléopâtre), Prusias, Phocas: tragic characters from, respectively, *Rodogune* (1644), *Héraclius* (1647), and *Nicomède* (1651).

8 See P. Corneille, *Trois discours* 62–3; for an English translation, see P. Corneille, "Discourse on Tragedy" 9.

9 See P. Corneille, *Trois discours* 51; for an English translation, see P. Corneille, "Discourse on Tragedy" 2–3. See also Lessing's discussion of catharsis in [78].

10 For Lessing's criticism of André Dacier's *La poëtique d'Aristote*, see [78].

11 For the quotation in Lessing's footnote, see André Dacier, "Remarques sur le Chapitre VI" ["Notes on Chapter 6"] in *La poëtique d'Aristote* 80.

12 Prosper Jolyot de Crébillon (Crébillon père); see [74.4].

Essay 82

1 Actually published spring of 1768.
2 Lessing continues, from [81], his refutation of French neoclassical theory by way of a point-by-point critique of Pierre Corneille's interpretation of Aristotle's *Poetics*. Tr. note: Lessing uses the word *gräßlich* here (horrible, dreadful, awful) to translate Aristotle's *miarón* (repulsive, shocking); see [79.5].
3 Lessing is paraphrasing here. See P. Corneille *Trois discours* 55; for an English translation, see P. Corneille, "Discourse on Tragedy" 4–5.
4 For the quotation in Lessing's footnote, see P. Corneille, *Trois discours* 63; for an English translation directly from the French, see P. Corneille, "Discourse on Tragedy" 10.
5 "Here are two or three methods that perhaps Aristotle could not have foreseen, because there were no examples of these in the theater of his time." P. Corneille, *Trois discours* 63; see also P. Corneille, "Discourse on Tragedy" 10.
6 Antiochus, Rodogune; Héraclius, Pulchérie, and Martian: noble young lovers in P. Corneille's tragedies *Rodogune* (1644) and *Héraclius* (1647), respectively. Cleopatra (Cléopâtre), Antiochus's mother, attempts to murder him (after having killed her other son); Phocas, a usurper, attempted to slaughter an entire royal family.
7 P. Corneille, *Trois discours* 63–4; see also P. Corneille, "Discourse on Tragedy" 10.
8 In P. Corneille's "Christian tragedy" *Polyeucte* (1643), the titular character, an Armenian prince, converts to Christianity and is martyred. Severus (Sévère), a Roman soldier, attempts to save him, but he is executed by his father-in-law Felix (Félix), the Roman governor of Armenia. His death inspires Felix and his daughter Pauline, Polyeucte's wife, to convert to Christianity.
9 P. Corneille, *Trois discours* 64; see also P. Corneille, "Discourse on Tragedy" 10–11.
10 For the argument summarized by Lessing in this paragraph, see P. Corneille, *Trois discours* 59–60; for an English translation, see P. Corneille, "Discourse on Tragedy" 7–8.
11 See Lessing's in-depth analysis, in [74]–[79], of Aristotle's statement in *Poetics* that tragedy should evoke *eleos* (compassion) and *phobos* (terror/fear).
12 Abbé Jean-Baptiste Du Bos (Dubos) (1670–1742): French diplomat, historian, and critic. His widely influential aesthetic treatise *Réflexions critiques sur la poésie et sur la peinture* [*Critical Reflections on Poetry and Painting*] (1719) was partially translated by Lessing; see [4.5]. Du Bos was an important contributor to discussions of theatrical emotion, arguing that the primary function of the arts was to stimulate the emotions, and that all emotions thus raised are inherently pleasurable. For the remarks referenced by Lessing here, see Dubos, *Réflexions critiques* 1: 108–113; Dubos, *Critical reflections* 1: 96–100.
13 Narcissus (Narcisse): the tutor of the titular character in Racine's tragedy *Britannicus* (1669).

Essay 83

1 Actually published Easter (March) 1769; for the large interval between the publication dates of [82] and [83], see Nisbet 391. Performances mentioned by Lessing occurred in 1767.
2 Lessing concludes a refutation, begun in [81], of French neoclassical theory by way of a point-by-point critique of Pierre Corneille's interpretation of Aristotle.
3 Lessing paraphrases here. See P. Corneille, *Trois discours* 27; for an English translation directly from the French, see P. Corneille, "First Discourse: On the Uses and Elements of Dramatic Poetry" 144.
4 *Proairesis*: reasoned choice; Aristotle introduces this term in his *Nicomachean Ethics* (see in particular Book 3, Chapter II).
5 P. Corneille, *Trois discours* 28; see also P. Corneille, "First Discourse" 144.
6 *Le Menteur* (1642): five-act verse comedy by P. Corneille, based on a comedy by Mexican-born Spanish playwright Juan Ruiz de Alarcón (1581–1639), *La Verdad sospechosa* [*The Suspicious Truth*] (1634) (mistakenly attributed by Corneille to Lope de Vega).

7 Dorante: the central character of *La Menteur*. For the argument of Corneille that Lessing paraphrases here, see P. Corneille, *Trois discours* 28; P. Corneille, "First Discourse" 144.

8 René Le Bossu (1631–80): distinguished French critic, whose theoretical work, *Traité du poème épique* [*Treatise on Epic Poetry*] (1675), is referenced by André Dacier in his edition of Aristotle's *Poetics*.

9 Aristotle and André Dacier 233.

10 Lessing's multi-essay analysis of Aristotle, spanning essays [73]–[83], is prompted by his discussion of C. F. Weisse's *Richard der Dritte* (1759/65), which he begins in [73] and returns to in [74] and [79].

11 *Herzog Michel*: see [73.8].

12 Krüger's play is based on a story, *Das ausgerechnete Glück* [*The Calculated Fortune*] by Johann Adolf Schlegel (1731–93), published in vol. 4 (1747) of the weekly Bremen-based periodical *Neue Beiträge zum Vergnügen des Verstandes und Witzes* [*New Contributions for the Pleasure of Reason and Wit*], which is generally referred to as the *Bremer Beiträge* [*Bremen Contributions*] (1744–59). Schlegel's story was itself based on La Fontaine's fable "La laitière et le pot au lait" ["The Milkmaid and the Pot of Milk"].

13 Krüger died in 1750 at the age of 27.

14 *Die Candidaten, oder die Mittel zu einem Amte zu gelangen* [*The Candidates, or the Means to an Office*] (1748): five-act prose comedy.

15 Johann Friedrich Löwen published Krüger's collected plays as *Johann Christian Krügers Poetische und Theatralische Schriften* [*Johann Christian Krüger's Poetry and Theatrical Writings*] (1763). *Die Geistlichen auf dem Lande* [*The Clergymen in the Country*] (1743): three-act prose comedy.

16 Graue Kloster (Grey Monastery): the oldest secondary school in Berlin; founded in 1574, it took its name from the medieval Greyfriars monastery that originally occupied its site.

17 *La femme qui a raison* (1758): three-act verse comedy by Voltaire. The German translation, *Die Frau, welche Recht hat*, was first published in 1762; the translator is unknown. *La famille* [*The Family*] (1736): see [17].

18 Voltaire did in fact stage performances at his estates Les Délices and Ferney (in and just outside of Geneva, respectively), but the original one-act version *La femme qui a raison* appears to have been first performed in 1748 at the court theater of Lunéville (where Voltaire was in residence), by the acting troupe of Duke Stanislas Leszczynski, the former King of Poland.

19 The three-act version of *La femme qui a raison* was first performed in 1758 at Carouge (a small city on the outskirts of Geneva). The play was staged throughout the provinces but was not performed in Paris in Voltaire's lifetime.

20 François-Louis-Claude Marin (Marini) (1721–1809) and Antoine Le Bret (1717–92): lesser French playwrights.

21 In *La femme qui a raison*, a brother and sister, with the assistance of their mother, outwit their father in order to marry the people they love. For more on the play, see Goulbourne and Waddicor, "Introduction to *La femme qui a raison*" 255–94.

22 *Mot pour rire*: punchline.

23 *Sidney* (1745): see [17]. *L'aveugle clairvoyant* (1716): one-act verse comedy by Marc Antoine Le Grand. This program actually occurred on July 31 rather than July 24.

24 *L'aveugle clairvoyant* (1650): five-act verse comedy by Brosse (or La Brosse) (first name unknown).

25 *Der sehende Blinde* (1752), a translation in alexandrines, possibly by Karl August Suabe; see J. G. Robertson 92.

Essay 84

1 Actually published Easter (March) 1769; performances mentioned by Lessing occurred in 1767.

2 *Le Père de famille* (1758): five-act bourgeois drama in prose by Denis Diderot. Lessing's translation was published anonymously in 1760, with the play's accompanying essay *De la poésie Dramatique* [*On Dramatic Poetry*], often referred to as the *Discours sur la poésie dramatique* [*Discourse*

on Dramatic Poetry] (1758). See *Das Theater des Herrn Diderot* [*The Theater of M. Diderot*] in *Werke und Briefe* 5/1: 10–230; Lessing's name was added to the second edition. Lessing quotes extensively from his own largely idiomatic translation of Diderot's essay in [48].

3 The play was in fact a theatrical success when it was first performed in Paris in 1761 but was attacked by French critics. It had 12 performances at the Hamburg National Theater. Lessing's critical engagement with Diderot, which dates back to his 1751 review of Diderot's *Lettre sur les sourds et muets* [*Letter on the Deaf and Dumb*] (*Werke und Briefe* 2: 127–35), significantly influenced his own dramatic and performance theory, as well as his playwriting. Diderot's advocacy for new illusionistic theater practices appealed to Lessing, as the latter sought to undermine the supremacy of French neoclassicism in the German theater. Lessing's admiration of Diderot is hardly slavish, however, as his criticism in the *Hamburg Dramaturgy* demonstrates.

4 Diderot's essay *Entretiens sur Le Fils naturel* [*Conversations on the Natural Son*] was appended to his five-act bourgeois drama in prose *Le Fils naturel* [*The Natural Son*] (1757); the essay provides the theoretical background for Diderot's experimental play, in the form of a dialogue between the author and his protagonist Dorval. For Lessing's (originally anonymous) translation of both play and essay, see *Das Theater des Herrn Diderot* [*The Theater of M. Diderot*] in Werke und Briefe 5/1: 10–230.

5 *The Indiscreet Jewels* (1748): Diderot's satirical, politically subversive, and enormously popular erotic novel, which was published anonymously and suppressed by the authorities; Diderot later claimed to regret writing the novel and officially apologized to the police but would go on to add three new chapters between 1770 and 1775. A German translation, *Die Verräther* [*The Traitors*], would be published in 1793 by Carl Friedrich Cramer.

6 Because Diderot's later work echoes ideas found in *Les bijoux indiscrets*, Lessing points out that Diderot cannot disavow the novel without seeming to have plagiarized it.

7 In Diderot's novel, the sultan Mangogul of the Congo is given a magic ring that can make women's "jewels" (genitals) speak their secrets aloud; eventually, the sultan's principled and keen-minded favorite, Mirzoza, becomes disgusted by what she learns of other women and asks for a respite from their company. Mangogul and Mirzoza (as Lessing well knows) represent Louis XV, the king of France (1710–74), and his mistress Madame de Pompadour (1721–64), a prominent patron of literature and the arts. The origins of *Les bijoux indiscrets* date back to a medieval French *fabliau* (short comic tale in verse), *Le Chevalier qui fit les cons parler* [*The Knight Who Made Cunts Speak*], attributed to the *jongleur* Guerin (or Garin).

8 Selim: believed to represent Louis-François-Armand du Plessis, Duke de Richelieu (1696–1788), soldier, diplomat, and grandnephew of Cardinal de Richelieu. Ricaric: possibly Antoine Houdar de la Motte, although, as a leader of the "Moderns," his views align more with those of Selim.

9 The topic of theater is introduced in Chapter 37; the discussion from which Lessing quotes significantly follows in Chapter 38, "Entretiens sur les lettres" ["A Conversation about Literature"], and is contextually situated within the aftermath of the seventeenth-century literary quarrel between the "Ancients" and the "Moderns." For the entire exchange, see Diderot, "Entretiens sur les lettres" in *Les bijoux indiscrets*; for the English, see "A Conversation about Literature" in *The Indiscreet Jewels* 160–70 (Lessing's quotation begins on page 163).

10 Here, and throughout the chapter, Diderot substitutes fantastical "exotic" names for those of figures from the contemporary French literary scene.

11 Eurisope: Euripides. Azophe: Sophocles.

12 Polipsile: Philoctetes, titular character of Sophoclean tragedy. Alindala: island on which Philoctetes was exiled. Ibrahim (Neoptolemus), Forfanti (Odysseus): also characters in Philoctetes.

Essay 85

1 Actually published Easter (March) 1769.

2 Lessing continues, from [84], a long quotation from Chapter 38 ("A Conversation about Literature") of Diderot's erotic novel *The Indiscreet Jewels* (1748). The conversation, which

here critiques the (French neoclassical) theater, takes place between Mongogul, the sultan of the Congo; Selim, a courtier; Ricaric, an academic; and Mirzoza, the sultan's favorite, whose words begin this essay. Lessing's translation is loose in several places. For more about the novel and the allegorical identity of these characters, see [84]. For the entire exchange, see Diderot, "Entretiens sur les lettres" in *Les bijoux indiscrets*; for the English, see "A Conversation about Literature" in *The Indiscreet Jewels* 160–70 (the section quoted in this essay begins on page 165).

3 Cinna, Maximus (Maxime), Aemilia (Emilie); Sertorius: characters from P. Corneille's tragedies *Cinna* (1641) and *Sertorius* (1662), respectively.

4 Charles Palissot de Montenoy (1730–1814): French playwright and satirist who attacked, through plays and essays, the writers of the *Encyclopédie* (one of the major works of the Enlightenment; Diderot and Jean Le Rond d'Alembert were its chief editors).

5 *Le Fils naturel* (1757); see [84.4]. Palissot targets the play specifically in his *Petites lettres sur de grands philosophes* [*Little Letters on Great Philosophers*] (1757). The plot is as follows: Dorval, wealthy but illegitimate, is staying with Clairville (his best friend) and Constance (Clairville's sister), who are also hosts to Rosalie (Clairville's fiancée), whose father is abroad. Dorval loves Rosalie, who also has feelings for him, as does Constance. Dorval, who is tormented by guilt, rescues Clairville from attackers; Clairville offers Dorval Constance's hand in marriage. A devastated Rosalie learns that her father has lost his fortune; Dorval decides to transfer his fortune secretly to her and then retire from the world. Constance persuades Dorval that she cares only about his virtue (rather than birth or fortune) and that they should work to reunite Rosalie and Clairville before pursuing their own happiness. Rosalie's father (Lysimond) returns and is revealed to be Dorval's father as well; Lysimond gives each couple his blessing.

6 *Le Père de famille* (1758); see [84.2].

7 Constance's name was changed to Theresa in Lessing's translation; she is "philosophical" in that her arguments are based on reason rather than emotion (as opposed to Dorval, who is brooding and idealistic). Lessing refers here to Constance and Dorval's climactic conversation in Act Four, Scene 3. See Diderot, *Le Fils naturel* 74–85; for the English, see Diderot, *The Illegitimate Son* 40–3.

8 *Entretiens sur le Fils naturel* [*Conversations on the Natural Son*] (1757); see [84.4].

Essay 86

1 Actually published Easter (March) 1769.

2 Lessing continues his discussion, from [84] and [85], of Diderot's dramatic theory. At the end of [85], he begins a critique of Diderot's *Entretiens sur le Fils naturel* [*Conversations on the Natural Son*] (1757); see also [84.4].

3 The eighteenth century saw the introduction of a number of "middle genres" situated between the extremes of tragedy and comedy but differentiated from the "mixed" genre of tragicomedy. In his theory, Diderot seeks to establish a new "serious" genre, with "serious comedy" focusing on virtue and human duties. See Diderot, *Entretiens sur le Fils naturel* 184–5; Diderot, "Conversations on *The Natural Son*" 46–51. See also Diderot, *De la Poésie Dramatique* 229–34; Diderot, "Discourse on Dramatic Poetry" 57–9.

4 See Diderot, *Entretiens sur le Fils naturel* 208–9; "Conversations on *The Natural Son*" 60.

5 For Palissot's criticism of *Le Fils naturel*, see *Petites Lettres sur de grands Philosophes* 18–73.

6 *The Misanthrope* (1666): generally considered Molière's masterwork. *Non plus ultra*: the pinnacle of achievement. Lessing, in his footnote, provides an excerpt from Molière's one-act comedy *L'Impromptu de Versailles* [*The Versailles Impromptu*] (1663), a self-referential response to his critics in which Molière and his company are rehearsing a new play for the king; the "rehearsal" is repeatedly interrupted, allowing Molière to comment on contemporary playwriting and performance. See Molière, *L'Impromptu de Versailles* 30–1; Molière, *The Versailles Impromptu* 221–2. Tr. note: Lessing has excerpted this quotation from Palissot's *Petites Lettres*, replicating Palissot's textual errors, which we have corrected.

7 The eccentric man: refers to Destouches' comedy *L'homme singulier* [*The Singular Man*] (1754). The hypocrite of social virtues: Palissot's original reads "le Tartuffe de société" ("the Tartuffes of social conventions"), referring to Molière's titular hypocrite (the comment that religious hypocrites are "out of fashion" is Lessing's). For this list of characters, see Palissot 69–70.

8 The new comic genres of the eighteenth century deviated from earlier comedies that offered characters up for ridicule, presenting instead exemplary characters that provided a model to follow rather than behavior to be eschewed.

9 Perfect character: as evidenced in his discussions of Aristotle, Lessing's dramatic and performance theory, which insists on a "sympathetic resonance" between actors and spectators, necessitates that characters be consistent but neither totally good nor totally bad in order for them to have the proper emotional effect on an audience.

10 Lessing extensively discusses Terence's comedy *The Brothers* in essays [70]–[73]; see [70.9] for a plot synopsis.

11 Micio, Demea: brothers of different temperaments; each is raising a son.

12 Tr. note: our English translation is of Lessing's (fairly accurate) translation of the French into German; for the original, see Diderot, *De la Poésie Dramatique* 310–11.

Essays 87 and 88

1 Actually published Easter (March) 1769.

2 Lessing continues his discussion, begun in [84], of Diderot's dramatic theory. In [85] and [86], he addresses criticisms of Diderot's play *Le Fils naturel* [*The Natural Son*] (1757) made by Charles Palissot de Montenoy in his *Petites lettres sur de grands philosophes* [*Little Letters on Great Philosophers*] (1757).

3 Lessing paraphrases here; see Palissot, *Petites lettres* 45.

4 For the plot of *Le Fils naturel*, see [85.5].

5 This digression reflects Lessing's revived interest in studies of antiquity, which he resumed in the summer of 1768 and which generated his *Briefe, antiquarischen Inhalts* [*Antiquarian Letters*] (1768–69) and *Wie die Alten den Tod gebildet* [*How the Ancients Portrayed Death*] (1769); see Nisbet 413–22.

6 *Heauton Timorumenos* [*The Self Tormentor*]: comedy by Terence, modeled on a play by Menander that now exists only in fragments. Tr. note: with "Heauton Timorumenos" Diderot seems to be referring simultaneously to the title of Terence's play and to the central character, Menedemus, the father who torments himself.

7 See Diderot, *Entretiens sur Le Fils naturel* 190–1; for an English translation directly from the French, see Diderot "Conversations on *The Natural Son*" 50.

8 The following are references made by Lessing in his extended footnote. Anne Lefèvre Dacier; see [72.7]. George Colman (the Elder): Colman's blank verse translation, *The Comedies of Terence*, with accompany commentary, appeared in 1765; Lessing provides Colman's original English. Adrian (Hadrianus) Barlandus (von Baarland) (1486–1538): professor and classicist from the Netherlands who published a commentary on Terence's comedies in 1530. *Glossa interlinealis*: intertextual or marginal notes. Jodocus Badius Ascensius (1462–1535): Flemish humanist and pioneering printer who published an edition of Terence's comedies in 1493. Chremes, Clitipho: characters from *Heauton Timorumenos* (father and son, neighbors of Menedemus, the titular "self-tormentor"). Julius Caesar Scaliger (Giulio Cesare Scaligero, or Scaligeri) (1484–1558): Italian-born French classical scholar whose posthumous *Poetice* [*Poetics*] (1561) widely influenced neoclassical theorists of the baroque period. Eugraphius (sixth century): Roman grammarian who authored a commentary on Terence. Gabriele Faerno (1510–61): Italian humanist whose commentary on Terence appeared in 1565. Diphilus (born c. 350 BCE): playwright who lived most of his life in Athens; a major influence on Plautus and Terence. Aediles: ancient Roman magistrates in charge of festivals and games (as well as other public works). Luscius Lavinius: ancient Roman comic playwright, considered a rival of Terence. Gnaeus Naevius (c. 270–c. 201

BCE): one of the earliest playwrights of ancient Rome. *duplex quae ex argumento facta est duplici* ("a double play crafted from a double plot"): this reading is found in the Codex Bembo, a manuscript collection of Terence's writing, which belonged to Cardinal Pietro Bembo (1470–1547). *simplex quae ex argumento facta est duplici* ("a single play crafted from a double plot"): this is the reading of Tanneguy Lefèvre (Faber) (1615–72) and of Richard Bentley (1662–1742) in their editions of Terence (printed 1671 and 1726, respectively). *simplex quae ex argumento facta est simplici* ("a single play crafted from a single plot"): Lessing's reading is doubtful; Boris Dunsch suggests that Lessing is being "characteristically self-ironic and only half-serious," and that his translation, "although possible metrically, must be regarded as desperate" (103).

9 ὦ Μένανδρε καὶ βίε, πότερος ἄρ ὑμῶν πότερον ἐμιμήσατο: "Menander and life, which of you imitated which?" This assessment of Menander is attributed to Aristophanes of Byzantium; see Goldberg, *The Making of Menander's Comedy* 109.

10 See Diderot, *Entretiens* 191–2; Diderot, "Conversations" 50.

11 *Non se pejus cruciaverit*: "never tortured himself worse." Lessing translates this passage from Diderot's French, rather than from Latin; for the original Latin (with accompanying English translation), see Horace, *Satires* (I.ii.12–22) in *Satires, Epistles, and Ars Poetica* 18–21.

12 "Now all these things are done in grief, from a persuasion of their truth and propriety and necessity; and it is plain that those who behave thus do so from a conviction of its being their duty; for should those mourners by chance drop their grief, and either act or speak for a moment in a more calm or cheerful manner, they presently check themselves and return to their lamentations again, and blame themselves for having been guilty of any intermissions from their grief; and parents and masters generally correct children not by words only but by blows, if they show any levity by either word or deed when the family is under affliction, and, as it were, oblige them to be sorrowful. [. . .] What does that man say in Terence who punishes himself, the Self-tormentor?" (Tr. by C. D. Yonge from Cicero, *Cicero's Tusculan Disputations* 118–19).

13 Dorval: the title character of *The Natural Son*.

14 Lessing's translation here is loose; see Diderot, *Le Fils naturel* 76; for an English translation directly from the French, see Diderot, *The Illegitimate Son* 40–1.

15 See Diderot, *Entretiens* 192; Diderot, "Conversations" 51.

16 Serious drama: see [86.3].

Essay 89

1 Actually published Easter (March) 1769.

2 Lessing continues his discussion, begun in [84], of Diderot's dramatic theory. In the previous essay, Lessing critiques Diderot's statement that tragic characters are individualized and comic characters are types. The assertion to which Lessing refers is Diderot's statement that characters in the serious genre occupy a middle ground, that they will always be less individual than tragic characters but may sometimes approach the universality of comic characters. For "serious genre," see [86.3]. For a contextualization of Lessing's extended digression into antiquity in this series of essays, see [87/88.5].

3 Herodotus (c. 484–c. 430/420 BCE): ancient Greek author who wrote an account of the Greco-Persian wars entitled *The Histories* (c. 425 BCE); considered the first historian of Western civilization.

4 Alcibiades (c. 450–404 BCE): cunning, flamboyant, and unscrupulous ancient Athenian statesmen and military commander who changed sides several times during the course of the Peloponnesian War (431–404 BCE).

5 Agathon (c. 445–c. 400 BCE): Athenian tragic playwright, of whose work fewer than 40 lines have survived. No fragment of *The Flower* (dated between 416 and 406 BCE) is extant. The play's Greek title is given variably as *Anthos* (flower) and *Antheus*; the latter is used by those who believe that the title refers to a character's name.

6 Lessing notes in the subsequent paragraph that he provides his own translation of this passage from *Poetics* (Part IX). Although he claims "to have remained as close to the exact words as possible," he appears to have been working from a corrupted version of Poetics; see [77.3]. For an English translation directly from the Greek, see Butcher.

7 καθόλον: kathólon (whole).

8 See Diderot, *Entretiens sur Le Fils naturel* 191; Diderot, "Conversations on *The Natural Son*" 50.

9 οὗ στοχάζεται ἡ ποίησις ὀνόματα ἐπιτιθεμένη: "it is this universality at which poetry aims in the names she attaches to the personages." Tr. Butcher in Aristotle, *Poetics* (Part IX).

10 "[A] general thing is that which every man of such and such a character has had to say or do, either probably or necessarily; this is the object of poetry, even when it imposes names on its characters." See Aristotle and André Dacier, *La poëtique d'Aristote* [*The Poetics of Aristotle*] 126.

11 Lessing has added the phrase "or necessity," which Curtius's translation does not contain; see Curtius, *Aristoteles Dichtkunst* [*Aristotle's Poetics*] 19.

12 *Lors même*: "even when."

13 For the quotation in Lessing's footnote, see André Dacier, "Remarques sur le Chapitre IX" ["Notes on Chapter 9"] in *La poëtique d'Aristote* 132–3. For Curtius's commentary, see "Anmerkungen zu Aristoteles Dichtkunst" ["Remarks on Aristotle's Poetics"] 150–1.

14 οὗ στοχάζεται: "at which [poetry] aims."

Essay 90

1 Actually published Easter (March) 1769.

2 Lessing continues his discussion of Aristotle's views on dramatic character in *Poetics* (Part IX). Lessing's analysis of Aristotle was triggered by Diderot's statement, in [83], that tragic characters are individualized and comic characters are types. At the end of [89], Lessing explores the statement that dramatic poetry aspires to the universal, and questions how this aspiration might relate to the names of dramatic characters. For a contextualization of Lessing's extended digression into antiquity in this series of essays, see [87/88.5].

3 "In Comedy this is already apparent: for here the poet first constructs the plot on the lines of probability, and then inserts characteristic names – unlike the lampooners who write about particular individuals." Tr. Butcher in Aristotle, *Poetics* (Part IX).

4 "This point is already rendered apparent in comedy, because comic poets, having arranged their subject according to verisimilitude, afterward impose on their characters whatever names they please and do not imitate satiric poets, who are attached only to the particular"; see Aristotle and André Dacier, *La poëtique d'Aristote* [*The Poetics of Aristotle*] 126.

5 See Curtius, *Aristoteles Dichtkunst* [*Aristotle's Poetics*] 20.

6 *Tels noms qu'il leur plaît*: "whatever names they please."

7 τὰ τυχόντα ὀνόματα: "randomly occurring names"; οὕτω: "thus" or "so."

8 οὗ στοχάζεται ἡ ποίησις ὀνόματα ἐπιτιθεμένη: "it is this universality at which poetry aims in the names she attaches to the personages." Tr. Butcher in Aristotle, Poetics (Part IX).

9 This passage comes from Donatus's commentary on Terence's comedy *The Brothers*; see Donatus, *Publii Terentii, Carthaginensis Afri, Comoediae* 244. Lessing extensively discusses the play in essays [70]–[73].

10 "The names of the characters, in comedies at any rate, must be chosen intentionally and in such a way that we can figure out what they mean. Indeed, it is absurd to openly invent a comedic plot: by either giving an unfitting name to a character or by giving a character a role that is different from its name." The following translations pertain to Lessing's footnote. *Absurdum est* [. . .]: "It is absurd to openly provide a comedic plot that invents an unfitting name for a character. *aperte argumentum* [. . .]: "to plainly invent a comedic plot and give an unfitting name to a character."

11 In the following translation, the meaning of names has been given in brackets: "Hence we have a faithful slave named *Parmeno* [stand fast]; an unfaithful slave named either *Syrus*

[Syrian] or *Geta* [Goth]; a soldier named *Thraso* [bold] or *Polemon* [warrior]; a youth named *Pamphilus* [beloved by all]; a matron named *Myrrhina* [myrtle]; and a boy named *Storax* [a fragrant bush] because of his smell, or *Circus* [a circular racing track], because of his sport and gestures; and more of the same. In this lies the greatest error of the poet, if he uses some name that is antithetical and opposite, that fights against itself, unless he has assigned the name as a joke due to its *antiphrasis*, like the moneylender in Plautus called *Misargyrides* [money-hater's son]." Misargyrides: character in Plautus's comedy *Mostellaria*.

12 ἐπὶ μὲν τῆς κωμῳδίας ἤδη τοῦτο δῆλον γέγονεν: "In Comedy this is already apparent"; see note 3 above.

13 Pyrgopolinices: title character of Plautus's play *Miles Gloriosus* [*The Braggard Soldier*], whose name in fact means "the much-conquering tower"; see Plautus, *Miles Gloriosus* 69.

14 Artotrogus: the parasite (sycophant) in Plautus's *Miles Gloriosus*, whose name means "bread-eater"; see Plautus, *Miles Gloriosus* 69.

15 Pheidippides ("sparing a horse"): character from Aristophanes' comedy *The Clouds* (423 BCE).

16 New Comedies: ancient Athenian comedy has traditionally been divided into Old, Middle, and New; contemporary scholars have indicated the ways in which these categories are unsatisfactory, and occasionally misleading, although they continue to be used (see Olson 1–32). Aristophanes (c. 450–c. 388 BCE) is representative of Old Comedy, which combined political, artistic, and philosophical criticism with savage personal attacks and scatological humor. Antiphanes (c. 408–c. 330 BCE) is representative of Middle Comedy, which is considered a transitional genre; it had less political commentary and fewer personal attacks, and also saw the emergence of stock characters. Menander (c. 342–c. 292 BCE) is representative of New Comedy, which gently satirized domestic life and eschewed politics and obscenity. As Lessing states in the following footnote about Hurd, Aristotle died around the time that Menander's first play was produced, but he would have seen other early examples of New Comedy.

17 Richard Hurd (1720–1808): English bishop and scholar; authored moral works and literary criticism and published multiple editions of Horace's works. Hurd published Horace's *Ars Poetica* [*Art of Poetry*] in 1749, with English commentary and notes. His subsequent editions of Horace added additional works, also supplemented by his own commentary; to each printing (1751, 1753, 1757, and 1766) Hurd added a new critical dissertation (culminating with four dissertations in the edition of 1766). Lessing owned the two-volume second edition, *Q. Horatii Flacci Epistolae ad Pisones et Augustum* [*Q. Horace Flaccus's Letters to Pisones and Augustus*] (1766); in his footnote, Lessing quotes (in English) from the second dissertation ("Dissertation on the Provinces of the Drama"). Lessing's quotation from Aristotle's *Nicomachean Ethics* is actually from Chapter 8 of Book IV (rather than Chapter 14). Eusebius of Caesarea (c. 260–c. 337): Greek historian and early Christian bishop, whose world history, or *Chronographia*, contains a list of Olympic victors (used by the Greeks as a dating system). Philemon (c. 368–c. 264 BCE): playwright of Athenian New Comedy; a rival of Menander. *Cocalus*: one of Aristophanes' final works (not extant). *Life of Aristophanes*: Lessing quotes from an anonymous text (XXVII Koster) in the collection of Byzantine treatises known as the *Prolegomena on Comedy*. "Κώκαλον ἐν ᾧ εἰσάγει φθοράν καὶ ἀναγνωρισμὸν καὶ τἄλλα πάντα ἅ ἐζήλωσε Μένανδρος": Jeffrey Henderson's translation reads "*Cocalus*, in which he introduced rape and recognition and all the other elements that Menander emulated" (Aristophanes, *Fragments* 8–9).

Essay 91

1 Actually published Easter (March) 1769.

2 Lessing continues, from [89], his discussion of Aristotle's views on dramatic character; at the end of [90], Lessing considers to what extent ancient Greek comedy made use of the names of real people. For a contextualization of Lessing's extended digression into antiquity in this series of essays, see [87/88.5].

3 Sophists: ancient Greek scholars and lecturers of the fifth and fourth centuries BCE; most were itinerant professional teachers. Plato and Aristotle portrayed the sophists (known for employing moral skepticism) as ethically suspect and avaricious, leading to the association of sophistry with clever, but fallacious, argumentation. Aristophanes lampoons Socrates in his comedy *Clouds* (423 BCE), portraying him (unfairly) as embodying the negative traits of the Sophists.

4 This incident is related by the Roman rhetorician Claudius Aelianus (Aelian) (c. 170–c. 235) in his *Various History* (Book II, Chapter 13).

5 For "Old Comedy," see [90.16]. The following are references in Lessing's footnote. The *Margites* (eighth century BCE) is a bawdy epic poem attributed to Homer; Margites is the titular (foolish) hero. Μαργίτης (Margites); μάργης (margis: mad, gluttonous, lustful). Pherecrates (fifth century BCE): ancient Athenian comic playwright.

6 The following references pertain to Lessing's footnote. Contrary to Lessing's statement, explicit satire of public persons and events is considered an essential feature of Old Comedy, although the work of the earliest comic playwrights is not extant. Cratinus (died c. 420 BCE): highly successful ancient Athenian comic playwright. Aristophanes' *Eirēnē* [*Peace*] (421 BCE): comedy staged during the Peloponnesian War; Aristophanes' claim occurs during the play's *parabasis* (during which the playwright or choral leader directly addressed the audience).

7 The following references pertain to Lessing's footnote. For the quotation from André Dacier, see Aristotle and Dacier 63. Epicharmus (Epicharmos) (c. 530 BCE–c. BCE BCE) and Phormis (fifth century BCE); Crates (Krates) (fifth century BCE): early comic playwrights in Syracuse and Athens, respectively. Cleon (d. 422 BCE), Hyperbolus (d. 411 BCE), Pericles (c. 495 BCE–429 BCE): politicians of ancient Athens lampooned by Aristophanes.

8 Until quite recently, it was generally believed that legislation in ancient Athens forbade the slanderous comedic representation of actual persons; see Halliwell, "Comic Satire," for the source of this belief and a detailed account of the lack of evidence for its support.

9 The following references pertain to Lessing's footnote. For the illegality of comic ridicule, see note 8. Ctesippus (Ktesippus): son of Chabrias (fourth c. BCE), an Athenian general, who was said to have sold the stones of his father's monument in order to fund his luxurious lifestyle; mentioned by Menander in his *Orge* [*Anger*] (321 BCE). See *Menandri et Philemonis Reliquiae* 137; for an English translation, see *Menander, the principal fragments* 417.

10 Lessing's multi-essay analysis of Aristotle was triggered in [83] by Diderot's statement that tragic characters are individualized and comic characters are types.

Essay 92

1 Actually published Easter (March) 1769.

2 Lessing continues, from [89], his discussion of Aristotle's views on dramatic character, which was triggered by Lessing's analysis, in [83], of Diderot's statement that tragic characters are individualized and comic characters are types. At the end of [91], Lessing asserts that "Diderot must comprehend something completely different under the idea of universality of a character than Aristotle did."

3 For a list of Richard Hurd's multiple editions of Horace, and his four appended commentaries (dissertations), see [90.17].

4 Lessing's suggestion would be taken up by Johann Joachim Eschenburg (1743–1820), a German scholar, translator, and friend of Lessing; his *Horazens Episteln an die Pisonen und an den Augustus* [*Horace's Epistles to Pisones and Augustus*] (1772), incorporates the translations of these passages that Lessing provides here. Eschenburg is best known for producing the first German translation of the complete plays of Shakespeare (a continuation and revision of Wieland's earlier translation), which appeared in 13 volumes as *William Shakespear's Schauspiele* [*William Shakespeare's Plays*] (1775–82).

5 See Horace and Richard Hurd, 163–243.

6 Tr. note: Hurd uses the term "species" to denote different types of literature; Lessing translates "species" into *Gattung*, which we render with the more common modern English term "genre."

7 *L'Avare* [*The Miser*] (1668): five-act prose comedy.

8 Nero: character in Racine's tragedy *Britannicus* (1669). We provide Hurd's original English rather than retranslating Lessing's German translation; see Hurd, "Dissertation on the Provinces of the Drama" 183.

9 Tr. note: the rest of this essay is a quotation from Hurd, which we have taken directly from "Dissertation on the Provinces of the Drama" 183–6.

10 One of Molière's inspirations for *The Miser* was Plautus's *Aulularia* [*The Little Pot, or The Pot of Gold*].

11 These lines are from "Of the Nature and State of Man with Respect to Himself As an Individual," the second of four epistles in the philosophical poem "The Essay on Man" (1733–34), by English poet and satirist Alexander Pope (1688–1744); see Pope, *The Works of Alexander Pope* 3: 63.

12 Hurd, "Dissertation" 183–6.

Essay 93

1 Actually published Easter (March) 1769.

2 The entirety of this essay is a quotation, continued from [92], from Richard Hurd's "Dissertation on the Provinces of the Drama." Lessing has brought Hurd into his discussion of Aristotle's views on dramatic character, begun in [89], which was triggered by Lessing's analysis, in [83], of Diderot's statement that tragic characters are individualized and comic characters are types. For Richard Hurd's dramatic commentaries (dissertations), which were appended to his multiple editions of Horace, see [90.17]. Tr. note: we provide Hurd's original English; see "Dissertation" 186–9.

3 Hurd references (and Lessing cites in his footnote) a comment about the sculptor Silarion (Seilanion) from the celebrated (if not always accurate) 37-volume *Naturalis Historiae*, known as *Naturalis historia* [*The Natural History*] (77 CE) by Roman scholar Pliny the Elder (Gaius Plinius Secundus) (23–79 CE); in Book 34 ("Statuaria/Bronze Statuary") Pliny writes that "Seilanion cast a portrait of [the sculptor] Apollodoros . . . a severe critic of his own work, who often broke up a finished statue, being unable to reach the ideal he aimed at. . . . This characteristic Seilanion rendered, and made his bronze not a portrait of an individual, but a figure of Vexation itself" (for the full quotation, in English and Latin, see Pliny 66–9).

4 Charles Le Brun (1619–90): court painter and theorist who provided detailed representations of and instructions for depicting "the passions of the soul"; author of the influential *Conférence de M. Le Brun sur l'expression générale et particulière* [*Discourse by Monsieur Le Brun on General and Specific Expressions*] (1698), translated into English (or, more accurately, adapted) by John Williams as *A Method to Learn to Design the Passions* (1734).

5 *The Characters* [*Charaktēres*]: a series of character sketches of moral types based on Aristotle's studies; a surviving work of the Peripatetic philosopher Theophrastes (c. 372–c. 287 BCE), who succeeded Aristotle as the head of the Lyceum in Athens.

6 The following references pertain to Lessing's footnote. The English playwright Ben Jonson is particularly known for his "comedies of humour," a dramatic genre that takes its name from medieval and Renaissance medical theory in which a body's health depended on the balance of its "humours" (blood, phlegm, yellow bile, and black bile). (Ed. note: here and in our translation of the footnote we use Jonson's English spelling of "humor" for the sake of consistency and clarity.) Jonson's characters are usually "unbalanced" caricatures governed by a particular humour that determines their dispositions. *Every Man in His Humour* (1598) was popular in both the seventeenth and eighteenth centuries. The less successful *Every Man Out of His Humour* (1599) functioned as one of Jonson's contributions to the "war of the theaters," a literary conflict in which Jonson and his fellow playwrights John Marston

and Thomas Dekker satirized each other in their comedies; although the conflict dealt in part with the nature and purpose of theater, another factor was the significant commercial rivalry between Jonson and Marston. The quotation (given in its original English) is from the prologue to *Every Man Out of His Humour*; see Jonson 118–19. Lessing's translation of "humour" as "mood" (*Laune*), which he says he now regrets, first appears in his essay "Von Johann Dryden und dessen dramatischen Werken" ["On John Dryden and his dramatic works"] (1759; Lessing gives the date as 1758) in the *Theatralische Bibliothek* [*Theatrical Library*]; see *Werke und Briefe* 4: 130–79. καθ᾽ ἕκαστον: "individually." Grex: "flock" in Latin.

7 Thomas Randolph (1605–34/5): English poet and playwright, a member of the "Sons of Ben" (also called the "Tribe of Ben"), who were professed followers of Ben Jonson's dramatic style; Randolph's comedy *The Muse's Looking Glass* (1630) was a moral satire inspired by Jonson.

Essay 94

1 Actually published Easter (March) 1769.

2 Lessing has brought Hurd into his discussion, begun in [89], of Aristotle's views on dramatic character, which was triggered by Lessing's analysis, in [83], of Diderot's statement that tragic characters are individualized and comic characters are types. A large portion of [92] and the entirety of [93] consists of a passage from Richard Hurd's "Dissertation on the Provinces of the Drama" (186–9). For Richard Hurd's dramatic commentaries (dissertations), which were appended to his multiple editions of Horace, see [90.17].

3 The long quotation that follows is drawn from Hurd's "Notes on the Art of Poetry." Tr. note: we provide Hurd's original English; see "Notes" 252–7.

4 The two points that follow are from Horace's *Ars Poetica* [*The Art of Poetry*] (for the full quotation, in Latin and English, see Horace, *Satires, Epistles, and Ars Poetica* 476–7).

5 *Ad veritatem vitae propius accedere*: "to accommodate themselves more to the reality of life." Hurd is citing Horace, who in turn cites Cicero; see Cicero, *De Oratore* [*On the Orator*] I (Liber Primus); for an English translation, see Cicero "De Oratore" 204. Horace's citation of Cicero is not exact; our translation is from this English source.

6 For the text in Lessing's footnote, see Cicero, *De Oratore* [*On the Orator*] II (Liber Secundus); for an English translation, see Cicero "De Oratore" 240. Horace's citation of Cicero is not exact.

7 The Philosopher: Plato. Book Ten of *The Republic* outlines Plato's argument about artistic representation's distance from universal truth; see *The Republic* 329.

8 The great critic: Aristotle. Butcher's translation reads: "Poetry . . . is a more philosophical and a higher thing than history"; see *Poetics* (Part IX).

9 Butcher's translation reads: "for poetry tends to express the universal, history the particular," see *Poetics* (Part IX).

10 Butcher's translation is practically identical to Hurd's; see Aristotle, *Poetics* (Part XXV).

11 In his footnote, Lessing quotes from André Dacier's translation of Aristotle, *La poëtique d'Aristote* [*The Poetics of Aristotle*] (1692).

12 Hurd, "Notes on the Art of Poetry" 252–7.

Essay 95

1 Actually published Easter (March) 1769.

2 In the previous three essays, Lessing has been quoting Richard Hurd, as a means of illuminating Aristotle's views on dramatic character, which Lessing begins discussing in [89]; here Hurd introduces Euripides' *Electra* in order to continue an examination of whether characters should be drawn from real life or idealized. For Hurd's dramatic commentaries (dissertations), which were appended to his multiple editions of Horace, see [90.17]. The

long quotation that follows is drawn from Hurd's "Notes on the Art of Poetry." Tr. note: we provide Hurd's original English; see "Notes" 257–60.

3 In Greek mythology, Electra unites with her brother Orestes to murder their mother (Clytemnestra) and her lover (Aegisthus), who killed their father (Agamemnon). In Euripides' version of the story, after the murder of Agamemnon, Clytemnestra and Aegisthus marry Electra off to a peasant.

4 Both Euripides and Sophocles include a scene in which Electra at first fails to recognize Orestes, who was exiled by Clytemnestra and Aegisthus.

5 Hurd, "Notes on the Art of Poetry" 257–60.

6 Lessing's examination of Hurd's views on Aristotle stems from Lessing's analysis, in [83], of Diderot's statement that tragic characters are individualized and comic characters are types.

7 *Καθολον: kathólon* (whole).

8 See [93] for Hurd's criticism of Ben Jonson's "comedies of humour."

9 *Fermenta cognitionis*: food for thought. Tr. note: literally "ferment of knowledge"; that is, a leavening that will allow future knowledge to rise.

Essay 96

1 Actually published Easter (March) 1769.

2 The second performance of Romanus's *Die Brüder* [*The Brothers*] at the Hamburg National Theater in fact occurred on August 11, 1767; for more about the play, see [70.8].

3 "They say that this play was produced second, at a point when the writer's name was not well known; and so it was announced as 'The Brothers of Terence,' rather than 'Terence's The Brothers,' because up to that point, the writer was recommended more by the name of the play than the play by the name of the writer." From Donatus's commentary on the play; see Donatus, *Publii Terentii* 293.

4 For the state of German dramatic literature in the mid-eighteenth century, see the editor's first introductory essay in this volume (Baldyga, "Missions, Misunderstandings, and Mythologies," 5).

5 A belief reminiscent of those held by Lessing's father, Johann Gottfried Lessing (1693–1770), a Lutheran pastor who published numerous theological works; see Nisbet 11–13.

6 In his footnote, Lessing references Plutarch's *Comparationis Aristophanis Et Menandri Compendium* [*Summary of a Comparison between Aristophanes and Menander*] in *Plutarchi Chaeronensis quae extant opera, cum Latine interpretatione* [*Extant Works of Plutarch of Chaeronea, with Latin interpretation*] (1572), edited by Henricus Stephanus. Lessing's page citation is incorrect; the statement to which he refers can be found on page 1568 (not 1588).

7 In these next paragraphs, Lessing refers specifically to the young German professor and dilettante literary critic, Christian Adolf Klotz (1738–71), who had criticized Lessing's *Laokoon* (in 1768), and, in early 1769, in his journal *Deutsche Bibliothek der schönen Wissenschaften* [*German Library of Liberal Arts and Sciences*], the first volume of collected essays from the *Hamburg Dramaturgy* (Klotz 9: 41–60). Lessing's two-volume polemical response to Klotz, the *Briefe antiquarischen Inhalts* [*Antiquarian Letters*] (1768–69) thoroughly demolished the critic's reputation, leading Klotz's biographer to write that Klotz "threw a pea at Lessing and was answered by an avalanche of stones"; see von Murr 95–6.

8 Genius: see [2.11].

9 Loosely quoted from Klotz, *Deutsche Biblothek* 9: 42–3.

10 See Lessing's remarks "Der Rezensent braucht nicht besser machen zu können, was er tadelt" ["The reviewer need not be able to do better than that which he criticizes"] in the "Paralipomena" (320–1 of this volume).

11 Hurd writes, "Comedy succeeds best when the scene is laid at home, tragedy for the most part when abroad"; see "Dissertation on the Provinces of the Drama" 191.

12 This quotation is actually from William Warburton's commentary on Pope's *Imitation of Horace* Epistle I, verse 282 (Pope, *The Works of Alexander Pope, Esq.* 4: 182). Lessing appears

to have drawn the quotation, which we provide in the original English, from Hurd's "Dissertation on the Provinces of the Drama" 191–2.

Essay 97

1 Actually published Easter (March) 1769.
2 At the end of [96], Lessing proposes to address Karl Franz Romanus's comedy *Die Brüder* [*The Brothers*] and the ways in which it differs from Terence's *Adelphi* [*The Brothers*]. He then begins to question the need for comedy to reflect contemporary customs, and whether authors should adapt classical plays accordingly.
3 See *Poetics* (Part IX).
4 Aeschylus's *Persians* (472 BCE): the only extant ancient Greek tragedy drawn from current events (rather than myth), which dramatizes the aftermath of the defeat of the Persians by the Greeks in 480 BCE. Although it is true that *Persians* does not exhibit strict historical fidelity, Aeschylus nonetheless employs specifics of Persian culture, history, and customs.
5 See [70.9] for the plot of Terence's play.
6 Tr. note: a later edition of Romanus's play bears the subtitle *Die Schule der Väter* [*The School for Fathers*].
7 "Learn how to be a father from those who *really* know!" (Act 1, Sc. 1). Tr. John Barsby, from Terence, *Adelphi/The Brothers* 2: 265.
8 Romanus, *Die Brüder* 41.
9 "If you're going to concern yourself with both, you might as well demand the return of the one you gave me" (Act 1, Sc. 1). Tr. John Barsby, from Terence, *Adelphi/The Brothers* 2: 265.

Essay 98

1 Actually published Easter (March) 1769.
2 Lessing continues from [97] his discussion, begun in [96], of the differences between Romanus's comedy *Die Brüder* [*The Brothers*] and Terence's *Adelphi* [*The Brothers*]. Terence's play has two pairs of brothers: Micio and Demea (Philidor and Lysimon in *Die Brüder*), and Demea's sons Aeschinus and Ctesipho (Leander and Lycast in *Die Brüder*). Romanus changes the younger set to cousins. See [70.8] for the origins of *Die Brüder* and [70.9] for the plot of Terence's play.
3 The citations given by Lessing in his footnotes do not align with the 1763 edition available through our Works Cited. In our edition, this line (which Lessing alters slightly) and the following line can be found in Act I, Sc. 2; see Romanus 9.
4 See Romanus 10.
5 "It's thanks to him that I'm alive. The wonderful fellow! He saw everything else as second to my interests. He took upon himself the insults, the gossip, my troubles, my misdeeds" (Act 2, Sc. 5). Tr. by John Barsby, in Terence, *Adelphi/The Brothers* 2: 281. Tr. note: Lessing's Latin text, which we give here, varies from Barsby's edition, most significantly substituting "*amorem*" (love) for "*laborem*" (troubles).
6 Citalise: Lycast's love interest; Romanus's substitute for the unnamed "music girl" in Terence's play.
7 In *Die Brüder*, the reprobate cousin Lycast threatens to stay with Damis, an unsavory character who does not appear in the play, if his virtuous cousin Leander (the "German Aeschinus") will not house him; see Romanus 19–20.
8 For an English translation of the quotation in Lessing's footnote, see Terence, *Adelphi/The Brothers* 2: 281–3.
9 "He counted out the money on the spot, and gave us half a mina on top to spend on the party" (Act 3, Sc. 3). Tr. John Barsby, in Terence, *Adelphi/The Brothers* 2: 295.
10 *Psaltria*: music-girl. "our Ctesipho": Lycast.
11 In our edition, these lines appear in Act 1, Sc. 5; see Romanus 16–17.

12 Terence's play is a Roman adaptation of Menander's Greek comedy of the same name.

13 "I only hope he is. As long as he doesn't come to any harm, I'd like him to get himself so exhausted that for the next three days he can't get out of bed at all" (Act 4, Sc. 1). Tr. John Barsby, in Terence, *Adelphi/The Brothers* 2: 309.

14 "CTE: He'll ask me where I've been. 'I haven't seen you all day,' he'll say. What shall I tell him? / SYR: Can't you think of anything? / CTE: Nothing at all. / SYR: So much the worse for you. Don't you people have clients, friends, guest-friends? / CTE: Yes, we do. What of it? / SYR: So you can say you've been offering your services to them. / CTE: When I haven't? It can't be done." Tr. John Barsby in Terence, *Adelphi/The Brothers* 2: 311.

Essay 99

1 Actually published Easter (March) 1769.

2 Lessing continues from [98] his discussion, begun in [96], of the differences between Romanus's comedy *Die Brüder* [*The Brothers*] and Terence's *Adelphi* [*The Brothers*]. Terence's play has two pairs of brothers: Micio and Demea (Philidor and Lysimon in *Die Brüder*), and Demea's sons Aeschinus and Ctesipho (Leander and Lycast in *Die Brüder*). Romanus changes the younger set to cousins. See [70.8] for the origins of *Die Brüder*, and [70.9] for the plot of Terence's play.

3 "What is this whim? What is this unexpected extravagance?" (Act 5, Sc. 8). Tr. John Barsby in Terence, *Adelphi/The Brothers* 2: 365.

4 "To support from time to time" (Act 5, Sc. 8). Tr. John Barsby in Terence, *Adelphi/The Brothers* 2: 365.

5 Diphilus (born c. 350 BCE): playwright of ancient Athens; a major influence on Plautus and Terence.

6 *The Dying Companions*: Lessing's translation of *Synapothnescontes*; see note 7 below.

7 "*Synapothnescontes* [*Joined in Death*] is a comedy by Diphilus [. . .]. At the beginning of the Greek version there is a young man who abducts a girl from a pimp [. . .]. Our author has taken it over for his *The Brothers* [. . .]" (Prologue). Tr. John Barsby in Terence, *Adelphi/The Brothers* 2: 255.

8 "Menander writes that he wants to die, Terence that he wants to escape." From Donatus's commentary on the play; see Donatus, *Publii Terentii* 268.

9 Peter Nannius (Petrus Nannius, Pieter Nanninck) (1500–57): Dutch humanist scholar who published numerous ancient Greek and Roman works, with accompanying commentary. For the Latin quoted in Lessing's footnote, see Nannius, *Symmiktōn* 53–4; for an English translation, see J. G. Robertson 329.

10 "To say nothing of what he's done in the past, look at his latest exploit [. . .]. He's broken down a door and forced his way into someone else's house [. . .]. Everybody is protesting that it's outrageous behavior. The number of people who spoke of it, Micio, as I came into town! The whole population is talking about it" (Act 1, Sc. 2). Tr. John Barsby in Terence, *Adelphi/The Brothers* 2: 261.

11 Lessing paraphrases here; see Romanus 5.

12 *Scholia*: commentary.

Essay 100

1 Actually published Easter (March) 1769.

2 Lessing continues from [99] his discussion, begun in [96], of the differences between Romanus's comedy *Die Brüder* [*The Brothers*] and Terence's *Adelphi* [*The Brothers*]. Terence's play has two pairs of brothers: Micio and Demea (Philidor and Lysimon in *Die Brüder*) and Demea's sons Aeschinus and Ctesipho (Leander and Lycast in *Die Brüder*). Romanus changes the younger set to cousins. See [70.8] for the origins of *Die Brüder* and [70.9] for the plot of Terence's play.

3 Tr. note: here we translate Lessing's German rendering of the Latin that he provides in his footnote; for Barsby's English translation directly from the original, see Terence, *Adelphi/The Brothers* 2: 357–61.

4 The critic: Samuel Patrick (1684–1748), an English schoolmaster, classical scholar, and lexicographer.

5 Patrick's criticism is quoted in the 1765 edition of Terence by George Colman (the Elder); see Terence and Colman, *Comedies of Terence* 415. Our English is taken from that source. Colman's quotation of Patrick is not entirely faithful; see Patrick, *Terence's Comedies* 2: 113–15. The final line is Lessing's addition, for the sake of rhetorical flourish.

6 George Colman (the Elder).

7 "In Menander's play, the old man is not upset about the marriage. Thus Terence invented it himself"; see Donatus, *Publii Terentii* 331.

8 Our English here is taken from Lessing's source; see Terence and Colman, *The Comedies of Terence* 415.

9 In classical Greek and Latin, a deponent verb has a passive or middle voice form but an active meaning. *Gravo* (active) means "to burden" or "vex," but *gravor* (passive/middle) is often used as if it were a deponent verb, in which case it would mean "to be/feel burdened." Lessing is debating whether Donatus is using a middle verb, *gravor*, or the passive of *gravo*, and thus whether the old man (Micio) is the subject or object of the sentence.

10 Although *de nuptiis gravari* is indeed nonstandard usage in classical Latin, Lessing's interpretation of Donatus is somewhat fanciful.

11 "Terence invented it himself!"

Essays 101, 102, 103, and 104

1 Actually published Easter (March) 1769.

2 Dodsley and Company: English publishing company belonging to Robert and James Dodsley, whose name was used by Leipzig publisher Engelbert Benjamin Schwickert to sell unauthorized copies of the *Hamburg Dramaturgy*. Lessing had attempted to publish his essays on his own, as partner in the printing enterprise of his friend Johann Joachim Christoph Bode (1730/1–93), but their efforts were severely hampered by the piracy rampant in German publishing at the time, as well as their inability to match the distribution capacities of the major publishers. For more on Lessing's conflicts with publishers, see Nisbet 379–82; and Reemtsma 22–33.

3 From the prologue to Terence's *Andria/Woman of Andros*: "When the playwright first turned his mind to writing." Tr. John Barsby, in *Terence* 1: 51.

4 Principal (*Prinzipal*): leading actor; in the eighteenth century often functioning as an actor-manager.

5 Allusion to Matthew 20: 6–7: "And about five o'clock he went out and found others standing around; and he said to them, 'Why are you standing here idle all day?' They said to him, 'Because no one has hired us.'"

6 Lessing's ostensibly self-effacing statement serves in fact as an introduction to his defense of criticism and also takes aim at the emerging generation of proto-Romantic writers, the forerunners of the *Sturm und Drang* ("Storm and Stress") movement, who, by the late 1760s, increasingly eschewed rules of art in favor of intuitive "genius." Lessing is credited with a much-cited, but unverifiable, remark that he would slap anyone who called him a genius so hard that they would think they were slapped twice. (There are several colorful phrasings of this remark, which originated in the early nineteenth century, perhaps in the *British Monthly Magazine*; see the anonymous account, "Anecdotes of German Authors and Authoresses residing at Weimar in Saxony" 41.) Despite Lessing's complaints about the literary aesthetics of the new generation, he was not entirely unsupportive of younger writers, who were, like Lessing, admirers of Shakespeare; in 1768, for example, he and Bode published the famously gruesome five-act tragedy *Ugolino* by German poet, playwright, and critic Heinrich Wilhelm von Gerstenberg (1737–1823).

7 Allusion to the revolutionary treatise on rhetoric, *Conjectures on Original Composition* (1759), by English poet Edward Young (1683–1765), in which the author states that "Rules, like crutches, are a needful aid to the lame, tho' an impediment to the strong" (28). The treatise, which privileged originality over imitation and argued in part that genius is as important as learning, was widely popular in Germany and influenced later Romantic writers. Young's quotation appears in an essay by the young German professor and mathematician Thomas Abbt (1738–66); it was published in 1761 in the *Briefe, die neueste Litteratur Betreffend* [*Letters Concerning the Newest Literature*], of which Lessing was a coeditor. See Abbt, "Review of Möser" 327.

8 In 1750, the prolific Venetian playwright Carlo Goldoni famously pronounced to patrons of the Sant' Angelo Theater that he would provide them with 16 new plays in the coming year, a promise that he fulfilled.

9 Shandy: the father of the titular character in the nine-volume novel *Tristram Shandy* (1759–66) by the English novelist Laurence Sterne (1713–67); in the novel, Tristram describes his father's appreciation for the Italian poet, translator, and bishop Giovanni della Casa (1503–56), famous for his conduct manual *Galateo: overo de' costumi* [*Galateo: Or, The Rules of Polite Behavior*] (1558).

10 Lessing's footnote provides an edited version of the original English; see Sterne, *The Life and Opinions of Tristram Shandy, Gentleman* 2: 42–4.

11 Isaac Casaubon (Causaubonus) (1559–1614): Swiss theologian and leading classical scholar; commentator on numerous Greek and Roman authors. In his footnote, Lessing quotes from Casaubon's commentary on *The Deipnosophistai* [*The Gastronomers*], a 15-book dialogue by the ancient Greek rhetorician and grammarian Athenaeus (fl. 200 CE); see Casaubon 414. For an English translation of Lessing's footnote, see J. G. Robertson 120.

12 Archons ("the ruling ones"): chief judicial officers and leaders of ancient Greek city-states.

13 Lione (Leone) Allacci (Leo Allatius) (c. 1586–1669): Greek antiquarian scholar, theologian, and important Vatican librarian who provided a catalog of Italian plays (with their authors and composers, as well as the date and location of their premieres) in his *Drammaturgia* [*Dramaturgy*] (1666); a revised and expanded version was published in 1755. Unlike Allacci, Lessing had always intended that his "dramaturgy" would be more than merely a "register" of plays; see the "Notice" preceding Lessing's essays, in which he articulates his original goals for the *Hamburg Dramaturgy* project. See J. G. Robertson for Italian and French precedents that may have influenced Lessing and for the manner in which Lessing's essays effectively changed the meaning of the word "dramaturgy" (122–3).

14 Terence's *Didascaliae*: production notes preceding the playwright's works, which provide information regarding the original performances. *Breviter & eleganter scriptas*: "briefly and elegantly written"; see Casaubon 415.

15 See "Notice" 36.

16 For more on eighteenth-century German acting and Lessing's acting theory, see the editor's introductory essays in this volume.

17 For more on the difficulties of the short-lived Hamburg National Theater, see the editor's first introductory essay in this volume (Baldyga, "Missions, Misunderstandings, and Mythologies").

18 *Stoicheia* [*Elements*]: foundational treatise on geometry by the ancient Greek mathematician Euclid (born c. 300 BCE).

19 Fermentation of taste: another criticism of the emerging generation of writers who championed intuitive genius; see [101–4.6].

20 Lessing resumes his battle with Christian Adolf Klotz, and with Klotz's periodical, the *Deutsche Bibliothek der schönen Wissenschaften* [*German Library of Liberal Arts and Sciences*], which had negatively reviewed the first volume of the collected essays of the *Hamburg Dramaturgy*; see [96.7]. "A barrel for our critical whales!": Lessing's allegorical jibe at the *Deutsche Bibliothek* draws on a diversionary tactic used by sailors seeking to avert the attention of whales; writing of the sperm whale, Dutch amateur marine biologist Adriaen Coenen wrote in 1585 that seamen "throw tremendously large barrels into the sea with

which they try to stop the beast from approaching because he starts to play with these barrels" (Coenen, et al. 44).

21 The little whale: a reference to Klotz, who was at that time a professor of philosophy and rhetoric in Halle, a city known for the harvesting of salt.

22 Herr *Stl.*: an (unknown) author writing for Klotz's *Deutsche Bibliothek*, suspected by Lessing of being Klotz himself. Herr Privy Councilor: in 1766, Frederick the Great awarded Klotz the title *Geheimrat* (Privy Councilor).

23 Another jab at Klotz; here he is compared to the German fool Hanswurst, who sported a brightly colored jacket.

24 A reference to the biblical Acts of the Apostles, in which Paul exorcises a fortune-telling slave-girl of "a spirit of divination" (Acts 16: 16–18).

25 The original edition of the *Hamburg Dramaturgy* that was printed by Lessing does not list Lessing as a publisher.

26 The *Deutsche Bibliothek* review of the *Hamburg Dramaturgy* suggests "secret reasons" (*geheimen Ursachen*) for Lessing's praise of principal actress Elisabeth Löwen and ingénue Cordelia Felbrich; see Klotz, *Deutsche Bibliothek* 9: 59.

27 Reference to the biblical Book of Judges, in which Samson discovers that his wife has divulged the answer to a riddle posed by Samson to her people: "And he said to them, 'If you had not plowed with my heifer, you would not have found out my riddle'" (Judges 14: 12–18).

28 His goblin: the "spirit of divination" providing Klotz with his information. See Klotz, *Deutsche Bibliothek* 9: 60.

29 Piracy, here, refers to the unauthorized reprinting of works by unscrupulous publishers. See [101–4.2].

30 An indication of Lessing's ideas concerning book manufacture and distribution can be found in his unpublished fragment entitled *Leben und leben lassen: Ein Projekt für Schriftsteller und Buchhändler* [*Live and Let Live: A Plan for Writers and Booksellers*] (written in the 1770s).

31 Allusion to the biblical Proverbs 26: 5: "Answer fools according to their folly, or they will be wise in their own eyes."

32 Proverbs 26: 4.

33 The Hamburg National Theater offered subscriptions to the *Hamburg Dramaturgy*; for more on the distribution of Lessing's journal, see J. G. Robertson 123.

34 The reprints threatened here would be unauthorized, pirated reissues of already-published works. Booksellers at the time printed only as many books as they anticipated they would sell; if a work was popular, other booksellers might (illegally) reprint the work before the original publisher had a chance to produce a subsequent edition. For more on the state of publishing in the eighteenth-century German Lands, see Pamela E. Selwyn, *Everyday Life in the German Book Trade.*

35 In his review of the *Hamburg Dramaturgy* and its pirated edition, Friedrich Nicolai, a long-time bookseller (and Lessing's friend), gives his opinion on the necessary qualities and training for a bookseller; see Selwyn 30–1.

36 Schwickert did both; he reprinted Lessing's essay in full and added a response in which he defended his actions. See Schwickert, "Intermezzo" in *Werke und Briefe* 6: 927–9.

37 *Coup de main*: surprise attack.

38 In his "De vera ratione reformandi rem literariam meditationes" ["On the True Way to Renew the Book Trade"] (1668), the great German philosopher and mathematician Gottfried Wilhelm Leibniz (1646–1716) had proposed to the Archbishop Elector of Mainz that a coalition of scholars take over the printing and distribution of their own works, thereby shutting out the middleman.

NOTES TO THE
PARALIPOMENA

1 Paralipomena: "things omitted or neglected that are added as a supplement." These items consist of notes found amongst Lessing's papers. Most are in conversation with existing essays in the *Hamburg Dramaturgy*; a few are preparatory notes on plays he intended to revisit when they were remounted. The notes are organized in their presumed (but not uncontested) chronological order; see Bohnen, "Textgrundlage" in *Werke und Briefe* 6: 1072.

2 Drafts for Discussions (*Entwürfe zu Besprechungen*): these first eight items follow the order in which they are arranged in the collection of Lessing's works edited by Karl Lachmann and Franz Muncker (subtitles and numbers in brackets are theirs); see Lessing, *Sämtliche Schriften* [*Complete Works*] 15: 38–48.

3 These comments are associated with the Hamburg National Theater's first repeat performance of Lessing's *Miss Sara Sampson* on July 20, 1767, which Lessing mentions in [73]; Lessing discusses the first performance in [13] and [14]. Repeat performances followed on Feb. 22, 1767; Sept. 12, 1768; and Feb. 23, 1769.

4 Jakob Friedrich Freiherr von Bielfeld (1717–70): German statesman and author; Bielfeld in fact includes the entirety of an anonymous French translation of *Miss Sara Sampson* in his *Progrès des Allemands dans les Sciences, les Belles-Lettres et les Arts, particulièrement dans la Poësie, l'Eloquence, et le Théatre* [*The Progress of the Germans in Science, Literature, and the Arts: Particularly in Poetry, Eloquence, and Theater*] (1752; revised and expanded 1767.)

5 Numerous English tragedies have been suggested (some more convincingly than others) as source material for *Miss Sara Sampson*, including George Lillo's *The London Merchant* (1731), Thomas Shadwell's *The Squire of Alsatia* (1688), and Charles Johnson's *Caelia* (1733); the plot is indeed drawn from Shadwell and Johnson. Lessing may also have been influenced by classical sources, as well as by Samuel Richardson's enormously successful epistolary novel *Clarissa* (1747–48; translated into German in 1748–49). See Nisbet 196–9; and Paul Kies, "The Sources and Basic Model of Lessing's 'Miss Sara Sampson.'"

6 Lessing evokes *The Critique of the School for Wives* (1663) in his discussion, in [53], of Molière's *L'École des femmes* [*The School for Wives*] (1662); for an English translation of the passage, see Molière, *Tartuffe and Other Plays* 193. For Lessing's German translation, see *Werke und Briefe* 6: 697–8.

7 Here Lessing translates a passage from the Abbé Trublet's *Essais sur divers sujets de litterature et de la morale* [*Essays on Several Subjects of Literature and Morality*] (1735). Lessing questions an observation by Trublet on French drama in [53].

8   See Trublet 4: 215.

9   Lessing discusses *L'École des femmes* [*The School for Wives*] in [53].

10 This paragraph is a free translation from Voltaire's *Life of Molière*; see Voltaire, "L'École des Femmes" in *La Vie de Molière* 423–4.

11 Scaramouche (in Italian, Scaramuccia): Italian *commedia dell'arte* character, developed by the famous Italian actor Tiberio Fiorillo (also Fiorilli, or Fiurelli) (c. 1608–94), a co-manager of the Comédie-Italienne in Paris; the Italian company, which shared performance spaces with Molière's troupe, decamped to Italy in July 1659, returning in January 1662.

12 See "Paralipomena" note 6.

13 These comments are associated with the third performance of Cronegk's *Olint und Sophronia* on August 12, 1767; Lessing discusses the first performance in essays [1]–[5] and critiques Cronegk in [7]. A repeat performance followed on May 4, 1768.

14 *Der Mistrauische* [sic] [*The Suspicious Man*] (French title: *Le Défiant*) (1765): five-act prose comedy by Cronegk. For the assessment referenced by Lessing, see Anon., "Des Freyherrn Johann Friedrich von Cronegk Schriften" in the *Journal encyclopédique* 196 (page 88 in the original).

15 *Codrus* (1757): five-act verse tragedy by Cronegk; see [7.2].

16 *Athalie* (1691): five-act verse tragedy by Racine, based on the biblical story of Athaliah in 2 Kings 11 and 2 Chronicles 22–3; Racine's play included a chorus of young girls.

17 For the quotation in Lessing's footnote, see "Des Freyherrn Johann Friedrich von Cronegk Schriften" in the *Journal encyclopédique* 197 (92 in the original).

18 *Brutus* (1730): five-act verse tragedy by Voltaire; the play includes a chorus of nonspeaking senators. Audiences apparently laughed at the chorus in Voltaire's earlier *Oedipe* [*Oedipus*] (1718); see Voltaire, *Discours sur la tragédie* 176; for the English, see Voltaire, "A Discourse on Tragedy" 87–8.

19 See "Des Freyherrn Johann Friedrich von Cronegk Schriften" in the *Journal encyclopédique* 197 (91–2 in the original). For Lessing's thoughts on "Christian tragedy," see essays [1] and [2].

20 "An English writer who perceived the merit of this tragedy has appropriated it. His play appeared under the title: 'Olindo and Sophronia, a Tragedy taken from Tasso, by Abraham Portal, Esq. London. 1758.'" *Olindo and Sophronia*: a five-act verse tragedy by Abraham Portal (1726–1809), an English playwright of Huguenot origin. Portal cites as his source Torquato Tasso's *Gerusalemme Liberata* [*Jerusalem Delivered*]; see [1.4].

21 The original, unfinished version of Cronegk's *Olint und Sophronia* was first published in 1760; a completed version was published in 1764. See [1.2].

22 August 14, 1767 saw the first repeat performance of both Franz von Heufeld's *Julie* and J. E. Schlegel's *Die stumme Schönheit* [*The Dumb Beauty*]. Heufeld's *Julie* was first performed on April 17, 1767; Lessing uses that occasion to discuss the play in [8] and [9]. Subsequent performances followed on Sept. 1 and Nov. 17, 1767; and April 6, July 26, and Aug. 25, 1768. Schlegel's *Die stumme Schönheit* was first performed on May 5, 1767; see [13]. Subsequent performances followed on Oct. 29, 1767; and Jan. 2, Jan. 5, and Feb. 13, 1769.

23 *Die Haushaltung nach der Mode, oder Was soll man für eine Frau nehmen?* [*Housekeeping à la mode, or What should one take for a wife?*] and *Die Liebhaber nach der Mode, oder Was soll man für einen Mann nehmen?* [*The Fashionable Lovers, or What should one take for a husband?*]; Lessing alludes to these plays in [8].

24 *Der Geburtstag*: Heufeld also produced a two-act version; see note 26.

25 *Pièces à tiroir* ("plays that belong in a drawer"): a comic genre consisting of loosely affiliated scenes that are thematically linked, often with an actor playing multiple roles.

26 *Die Schwester des Bruder Philipps* [*Brother Philip's Sister*] also appears as a standalone one-act with a slightly altered title: *Die Tochter des Bruder Philipps* [*Brother Philip's Daughter*] (1769). *Der Geburtstag* [*The Birthday*] was also published in a two-act version that omits the Brother Philip insert.

27 These comments are associated with the first repeat performance of C. S. Favart's comedy *Soliman second, ou les trois Sultanes* [*Solomon the Second, or the three Sultanas*] on August 24, 1767. Lessing uses the first performance on July 3, 1767 to critique both Favart's play and its source, Jean-François Marmontel's story "Soliman II"; here Lessing picks up his criticism of Favart's depiction of the sultana Roxelane, whom Favart has made a Frenchwoman. See Essays [33]–[36]. Subsequent repetitions took place on Nov. 11, 1767; and Jan. 8 and 19, Feb. 25, July 20, Nov. 18, and Dec. 12, 1768.

28 *Le François à Londres* [*The Frenchman in London*] (1727): one-act prose comedy by Louis de Boissy.

29 "We amuse ourselves by copying the dandy, on whom all the features of ridicule are worn out, and whose portrait is nothing but a school for those young men who have some disposition to become one." See Jean-François Marmontel, *Poétique Françoise* 2: 276. (Ed. note: the page numbers in our edition differ from those of Lessing's.)

30 *Le Siège de Calais* [*Siege of Calais*]: tragedy by Dormont de Belloy; see [18.15].

31 Roxelanes: flighty, insolent flirts; see "Paralipomena" note 27.

32 These notes relate to Lessing's discussion, in [32], of Voltaire's criticism of Pierre Corneille's tragedy *Rodogune*, which Lessing addresses in [29]–[32]. Lessing's information is drawn in part from an entry in the *Journal Encyclopédique*; see Anon., "Lettre de Mr. [sic] de Voltaire, à Mr. [sic] l'Abbé d'Olivet."

33 Lessing's footnote seems to relate to his discussion, in [36], of C. S. Favart's theatrical adaptation of Marmontel's story "Soliman II" (see "Paralipomena" note 27); in that essay, Lessing lists Antoine Houdar de la Motte's one-act comedy *La Matrone d'Ephese* [*The Ephesian Widow*] as an example of an unsuccessful adaptation (of the story of the Widow of Ephesus in the *Satyricon*). Lessing's first footnote reference is to "The Ephesian Matron: or Widow's Tears" (1668), a heroic poem by the Scottish-born printer, poet, translator, and failed theatrical entrepreneur John Ogilby (1600–76); see Cibber, *Lives of the Poets of Great Britain and Ireland* 2: 267. His second footnote reference is to *The Ephesian Matron* (1730), a one-act farce by English playwright Charles Johnson (c.1660–1744); see Cibber, *Lives* 5: 342.

34 Marie Françoise Corneille was in fact not the granddaughter of the playwright Pierre Corneille, but of his cousin (also named Pierre).

35 The Comédie Française gave a benefit performance of Pierre Corneille's *Rodogune* on March 10, 1760; although the proceeds went to Marie's father, Jean François Corneille, a portion was put toward her schooling. (Marie Corneille was not in fact a direct descendant of the famous French playwright; see "Paralipomena" note 34.)

36 The French poet Ponce Denis Ecouchard Le Brun (1729–1807) sent a poem with an accompanying letter to Voltaire in 1760, asking him to help the impoverished Marie Corneille (see "Paralipomena" note 34); Voltaire took the young woman in and secured her dowry through his multi-volume edited collection of P. Corneille's plays. For the full story, see Williams, "Prelude to the First Edition" in *Commentaires sur Corneille (I)* 27–88.

37 Although some praised Voltaire's actions, there was also considerable gossip and scurrilous speculation concerning his motives; see Williams, "Prelude" 31–40. *La petite nièce d'Eschyle* [*The grand-niece of Aeschylus*]: an "Athenian history translated from a Greek manuscript" by the Chevalier Jean-Florent-Joseph Neufville de Brunaubois-Montador (1707–70?); the pamphlet tells Marie Corneille's story using Greek names (Pierre Corneille becomes Aeschylus, Voltaire Sophocles, Marie Corneille Cléonyme, and so forth). See the anonymous entry "La petite nièce d'Eschyle" in the *Journal Encyclopédique* Vol. 11, Book 1 (Jan 1761): 144–5.

38 Corneille's granddaughter: see "Paralipomena" note 34.

39 Dishonor: Voltaire privately excoriated Bernard le Bovier de Fontenelle, who, as the nephew of Pierre and Thomas Corneille, should have borne responsibility for the well-being of Marie Corneille; see Williams, "Prelude" 35–6.

40 For the original, see the editor's introduction to Voltaire's letter about his Corneille commentaries in the *Journal Encyclopédique* (Anon., "Lettre de Mr. [sic] de Voltaire, à Mr. [sic] l'Abbé d'Olivet" 114–15.) For a translation, see "Paralipomena" note 41.

41 "The example that he gives is unique; he abandons, so to speak, his own turf to work his neighbor's field and give it more value. Let those who slander his heart at least admire the nobility of such a rare practice. It is common that great men study one another, but they rarely comment on one another. Among the almost infinite numbers of Publishers, Commentators, Compilers, one can name many who have displayed some erudition; some have had wit; very few have had taste: here is the first one who has shown genius and has had more taste, wit, and even erudition than any of them. We shall admire even more the author of *Rodogune*, *Polyeucte*, and *Cinna* when we see all these plays enriched by the *Commentaries* prepared by the author of *Mahomet*, *Alzire*, and *Mérope*; they will strengthen the idea that we form of Corneille and make him, if at all possible, even greater in our minds; they will make us re-read the text with more pleasure and usefulness."

42 Reference to *The Unhappy Favourite: or, The Earl of Essex* (1682), by English playwright John Banks; discussed by Lessing in [54]–[59]. Thomas Corneille's *Le Comte d'Essex* appeared in 1678; see [22]–[25]. Lessing's footnote refers to Samuel Daniel's tragedy *Philotas*, mentioned in [54] as potentially the first dramatization of Essex's story; see [54.7]. Lessing slightly misrenders the title of Theophilus Cibber's *Lives of the Poets of Great Britain and Ireland* (1753); for the entry on Samuel Daniel, see Cibber, *Lives* 1: 145–9.

43 For the suggested sources of Banks's play see [54.8].

44 The *Earl of Essex* by Irish-born playwright Henry Jones is mentioned in [59]. For Cibber's entry on Henry Jones, see *Lives* 3: 174–7.

45 The *Earl of Essex* by Irish-born playwright Henry Brooke is mentioned in [59].

46 Henry Brooke's *Gustavus Vasa* (1739) was one of the first plays to be banned for its political content after the institution in 1737 of the Licensing Act in England.

47 That is, the final scene between Essex and Queen Elizabeth I (in Act Four); see Brooke 40–4.

48 "He also had the Countess of Rutland tumble into madness, at the moment when this illustrious [. . .] husband was led to the gallows: this moment when the Countess is an object worthy of pity produced a great sensation and was found admirable in London: in France, it would have appeared ridiculous, it would have been booed and the Countess would have been sent, along with the Author, to the Petites Maisons." For the original, see Anon., "The Earl of Essex, a Tragedy" 120–1. Les Petites Maisons: insane asylum founded in 1557.

49 *Canut* (1747): five-act verse tragedy by Johann Elias Schlegel, performed by the Hamburg National Theater on Sept. 23, 1767.

50 J. E. Schegel, *Canut* 24.

51 This note of Lessing's is reminiscent of his discussions of acting in [3]–[5].

52 J. E. Schegel, *Canut* 26.

53 General Observations (*Allgemeine Bemerkungen*): the following five items follow the order in which they are arranged in the collection of Lessing's works edited by Karl Lachmann and Franz Muncker (the subtitle in brackets is theirs); see Lessing, *Sämtliche Schriften* [*Complete Works*] 15: 59–65.

54 "It is a very great carelessness not to finish his sentence and to allow him to be interrupted, especially when the person who interrupts is a subordinate, who lacks propriety by cutting off the speech of his superior. Thomas Corneille is prone to this error in all his plays"; see Voltaire, "Le Comte d'Essex" in *Complete Works of Voltaire* 55: 1015.

55 Henry Home, Lord Kames (1696–1782): Scottish lawyer and philosopher.

56 *Elements of Criticism* (1762): a highly influential multi-volume work on aesthetics, for which Home is best known. Lessing provides Home's original English.

57 These remarks are associated with Lessing's intention to discuss the third performance of Cronegk's *Olint und Sophronia*; see "Paralipomena" note 13. In Lessing's record

of performances by the Hamburg National Theater, there are two notes next to this evening; the first refers to Portal's *Olindo and Sophronia* (see "Paralipomena" note 20). In the second, Lessing writes "Reintroduction of the chorus" and refers to Richard Hurd's "Notes on the Art of Poetry," which specifically mentions William Mason's historical tragedies *Elfrida* and *Caractacus* (see "Paralipomena" note 58). For Hurd's thoughts on the function of the chorus, see "Notes on the Art of Poetry" 129–32. Lessing's notes here also relate to his remarks, in [7], about English playwrights' usage of prologues and epilogues.

58 William Mason (1725–97): English clergyman, poet, and playwright. Both his historical tragedies, *Elfrida* (1752) and *Caractacus* (1759), were "written on the model of the ancient Greek tragedy" and employed a chorus.

59 William Mason's *Elfrida, a Dramatic Poem* (see "Paralipomena" note 58), to which the playwright appends his "Letters: Concerning the following Drama."

60 See "Paralipomena" note 57.

61 These remarks can be found in the "Review of *Caractacus, a Dramatic Poem*" in *The Monthly Review* 20: 507–12.

62 Henry Jones was indeed originally a bricklayer; see "Paralipomena" note 44 and [59.8].

63 Lessing refers to Abraham Portal, who was in fact a goldsmith and silversmith as well as an author; see "Paralipomena" note 20.

64 Henry Wild (1684–1721), the "Arabick Taylour": autodidactic English tailor who mastered not only Arabic but also Latin, Greek, Hebrew, Syriac, and a number of other languages; he was not admitted to Oxford but did translation work and teaching at the Bodleian Library. 1720 is the year that he moved to London.

65 Robert Hill (1699–1777), "the famous Buckingham Taylor": penurious autodidactic English tailor whose struggles to acquire learning were described by Joseph Spence (1699–1768), the English clergyman and scholar, in *A Parallel; in the Manner of Plutarch: between a most celebrated Man of Florence; and One, scarce ever heard of in England* (1759). Antonio Magliabechi (Magliabecchi) (1633–1714): autodidactic Italian goldsmith, classical scholar, ducal librarian, and famous bibliophile.

66 For a brief outline of Hill's abilities, see *The Monthly Review* 20: 217–19.

67 These notes are connected to Lessing's criticism, in [59], of overly "fastidious" or "bombastic" dramatic language, as well as to the initial reception of Lessing's *Minna von Barnhelm* (see "Paralipomena" notes 68 and 69).

68 Minna: Lessing's highly successful five-act prose comedy, *Minna von Barnhelm, oder das Soldatenglück [Minna von Barnhelm, or, the Soldier's Happiness]*, was premiered by the Hamburg National Theater in 1767 and had either 14 or 15 repeat performances (see J. G. Robertson 33); it was the company's most performed play. The word *Hure* (whore) was not then associated with prostitution but with the ruination of an unmarried girl; for the offending line, spoken by the servant Just in Act 1, Scene 12, see Lessing, *Minna von Barnhelm* in *Werke und Briefe* 6: 27; for an English translation, see Lessing, *Minna von Barnhelm* 22.

69 Lessing's brother Karl, in his letter of March 22, 1768, mentions that the word "whore" presented difficulties for the actor in the Berlin production of *Minna* as well; see "Brief von Karl Lessing" in *Werke und Briefe* 11/1: 512.

70 *Das Loos in der Lotterie [The Lottery Ticket]* (1746): five-act prose comedy by C. F. Gellert (1715–69). "[S]hoving of the kerchief": in Gellert's play, the self-styled *galant* Herr Simon, who wishes to accompany the object of his fancy while she dresses, claims that he knows where to stuff a kerchief in a lady; see Gellert, *Das Loos in der Lotterie* 252.

71 Henry Fielding (1701–54) and Samuel Richardson (1689–1761): two of the most important English novelists of the early eighteenth century.

72 *Joseph Andrews (The History of the Adventures of Joseph Andrews and of His Friend Mr. Abraham Adams)* (1742) and *The History of Tom Jones, a Foundling* (1749): bawdy novels by Fielding. *Clarissa; or, The History of a Young Lady* (1747–48): Richardson's epistolary novel about a virtuous young woman who is lured from her home, held prisoner, and eventually raped by an evil aristocrat.

73 References in Lessing's footnote: For Jean-Jacques Rousseau's comment about *Clarissa*, see his *Lettre à d'Alembert sur les Spectacles* 170; for the English, see J. J. Rousseau, *Politics and the Arts* 82. Mrs. Slipslop: character in Henry Fielding's *Joseph Andrews* who is prone to malapropisms such as *confidous* ("confident"). For Mrs. Slipslop's remark about ears, see Fielding, *Joseph Andrews* 34. In Molière's *Critique of the School for Wives*, female theatrical spectators of affected delicacy are described as "more chaste in their ears than in all the rest of their bodies" (180).

74 These remarks relate to Lessing's defense of his critical method and to his critique of the *Deutsche Bibliothek der schönen Wissenschaften* [German Library of Liberal Arts and Sciences] of Christian Adolf Klotz; see [96] and [101–104].

WORKS CITED

Abbt, Thomas. "Review of Möser, J.: *Harlekin, oder Vertheidigung des Groteske-Komischen.*" 1761. Letter 204. In Lessing, et al. *Briefe, die neueste Literatur betreffend* 11/12: 327–44. Print.

Addison, Joseph. *Cato, a Tragedy, by Mr. Addison.* London: Printed for the company, 1730. Print.

———. *The Drummer, or the Haunted House.* London: Company of Booksellers, 1733. Print.

Aelianus, Claudius (Aelian). *Various History.* Trans. Thomas Stanley. London: Printed for Thomas Dring, 1665. Print.

Anderson, Michael. "A Note on Lessing's Misinterpretation of Aristotle." *Greece and Rome* 15.1 (1968): 59–62. Print.

Anon. "Anecdotes of German Authors and Authoresses Residing at Weimar in Saxony." *The Monthly Magazine; or, British Register* 11.69 (1801): 40–3. Print.

——— "Art. 32: Review of Henry Jones's 'Earl of Essex'." *The Monthly Review* March 1753: 225–9. Print.

——— *A Companion to the Theatre: Or, a View of Our Most Celebrated Dramatic Pieces: In Which the Plan, Characters, and Incidents of Each Are Particularly Explained: Interspersed with Remarks Historical, Critical, and Moral.* 2 vols. Dublin: Printed by S. Powell, 1751. Print.

———."The Earl of Essex a Tragedy, &c. Le Comte d'Essex, Tragédie représentée depuis peu à Londres sur le Théâtre de Drury-Lane." In *Journal encyclopédique.* Ed. Pierre Rousseau. Vol. 11, Bk. 2 (March 1761): 117–22. Geneva: Slatkine Reprints, 1967. 204–5. Print.

———. "The English Merchant, a Comedy, as It Is Acted at the Theatre Royal in Drury-Lane." In *Monthly Review, or, Literary Journal, 1752–1825.* Ed. Ralph Griffiths. Vol. 36 (March 1767). London: Hurst, Robinson, and Co., 1767. 224–9.

———. "Des Freyherrn Johann Friedrich von Cronegk Schriften. Erste Band. Leipzig, 1760, Bey Johan Christoph Posch, &c." In *Journal encyclopédique.* Ed. Pierre Rousseau. Vol. 12, Bk. 6 (September 1761): 85–97. Geneva: Slatkine Reprints, 1967. 196–9. Print.

———. "Journal de Police sous Louis XV (1742–1743)." In *Chronique de la régence et du règne de Louis XV (1718–1763) ou Journal de Barbier.* Ed. Barbier, Edmond [E. J. F.]. Vol. 8. Paris: G. Charpentier et Cie., 1885. 129–348. Print.

———. "Lettre de Mr. de Voltaire, à Mr. l'Abbé d'Olivet, du 20 Aout 1761." In *Journal encyclopédique.* Ed. Pierre Rousseau. Vol. 12, Bk. 7 (October 1761): 113–26. Geneva: Slatkine Reprints, 1967. 287–90. Print.

———. "La petite nièce d'Eschyle, Histoire Athènienne, traduite d'un manuscrit Grec & Fragmens de l'Histoire Anecdote des Gens de Lettres, 1761." In *Journal encyclopédique.* Ed. Pierre Rousseau. Vol. 11, Bk. 1 (January 1761): 144–5. Geneva: Slatkine Reprints, 1967. 84–5. Print.

————. *Sidney, or, the Self-Murderer Reclaimed: A Tragi-Comedy: From the French of Gresset.* [In *Select Translations and Imitations from the French of Marmontell and Gresset.* By an Officer of the Army; Who Fought for America, Under Gen. Wolfe, at the Taking of Quebec]. New York: Samuel Campbell, 1801. Print.

————. "Soliman Second, Comédie nouvelle, par Mr. Favart, à Paris chez Duchesne 1762." In *Journal encyclopédique ou universal.* Ed. Pierre Rousseau. Vol. 13 (January 1762): 79–93. Geneva: Slatkine Reprints, 1967. 68–72. Print.

———— "Ueber das Herzogliche Hoftheater zu Carlsruh in Oberschlesien (Aus einigen Briefen an die Herausgeber)." *Ruebezahlider Schlesische Provinzialblätter* 22.12 (1795): 519–24. Print.

————. "Zelmire, Tragédie en cinq actes, représentée pour la première fois, par les Comédiens François ordinaires du Roi, le 6 Mai, 1762. Par Mr. de Belloy. A Paris, chez Duchesne." In *Journal encyclopédique ou universal.* Ed. Pierre Rousseau. Vol. 14 (July 1762): 101–27. Geneva: Slatkine Reprints, 1967. 32–8. Print.

Apollodorus. *Apollodorus, the Library, with an English Translation by Sir James George Frazer, F.B.A., F.R.S.* 2 vols. Cambridge, MA: Harvard University Press, 1921. Perseus Digital Library. www.perseus.tufts.edu/hopper/text?doc=Perseus:text:1999.01.0022:text=Library. Print & Web. 2 January 2014.

Aristophanes. *Fragments.* Trans. Jeffrey Henderson. Loeb Classical Library. Vol. 502. Cambridge, MA: Harvard University Press, 2007. Print.

————. *Peace.* In *The Complete Greek Drama.* Ed. Eugene O'Neill, Jr. Vol. 2. New York: Random House, 1938. 671–732. Print.

Aristotle. *Nicomachean Ethics.* Trans. H. Rackham. *Aristotle in 23 Volumes.* Vol. 19. Cambridge, MA: Harvard University Press, 1934. Perseus Digital Library. www.perseus.tufts.edu/hopper/text?doc=urn:cts:greekLit:tlg0086.tlg010.perseus-eng1. Print & Web. 8 July 2014.

————. *Poetics by Aristotle.* Trans. S. H. Butcher. 1902. *The Internet Classics Archive.* Web. 25 October 2012.

————. *Politics.* Trans. H. Rackham. *Aristotle in 23 Volumes.* Vol. 21. Cambridge, MA: Harvard University Press, 1944. Perseus Digital Library. www.perseus.tufts.edu/hopper/text?doc=urn:cts:greekLit:tlg0086.tlg035.perseus-eng1:8.1341b. Print & Web. 11 June 2017.

————. *Rhetoric.* Trans. J. H. Freese. *Aristotle in 23 Volumes.* Vol. 22. Cambridge, MA: Harvard University Press, 1926. Perseus Digital Library. http://data.perseus.org/texts/urn:cts:greekLit:tlg0086.tlg038.perseus-eng1. Print & Web. 26 May 2014.

————, and André Dacier. *La poëtique d'Aristote, Traduite en François, avec des remarques.* Paris: Claude Barbin, 1692. Print.

————, Theodore Goulston, et al. *Aristotelis De poetica liber.* Trans. Theodore Goulston. Cambridge: John Hayes & Thomas Dawson, 1696. Print.

————, and Aemil Porto. *Aristotelis, Artis Rhetoricæ, Sive De Arte Dicendi Libri Iii: A Æmilio Porto, Francisci Porti Cretensis F. in Antiquissima & Celeberrima Heidelbergensi Academia Ordinario Languæ Græcæ Prosessore, Noua Interpretatione Illustrati, Et Nunc Primùm in Lucem Emissi.* Spiræ: Apud Bernardum Albinum, 1598. Print.

Aubignac, Abbé d'. *La Pratique du Théâtre.* Vol. 1. Amsterdam: J. F. Bernard, 1715. Print.

Bachaumont, Louis Petit de, and Jules Amédée Désiré Ravenel. *Mémoires secrets de Bachaumont de 1762 à 1781.* Vol. 1. Paris: Brissot-Thivars, 1830. Print.

Baldyga, Natalya. "Corporeal Eloquence and Sensate Cognition: G. E. Lessing, Acting Theory, and Properly Feeling Bodies in Eighteenth-Century Germany." *Theatre Survey* 58.2 (2017): 162–85. Print.

Banks, John. *The Unhappy Favourite: Or, the Earl of Essex: A Tragedy: Acted at the Theatre Royal, by Their Majesty's Servants: Written by John Banks.* London: Printed for Richard Bentley and Mary Magnes, 1685. Print.

Barbier, Edmond [E. J. F.]. *Chronique de la régence et du règne de Louis XV (1718–1763) ou Journal de Barbier.* Vol. 3. 8 vols. Paris: G. Charpentier et Cie., 1885. Print.

Baron, (Monsieur Michel). *L'École des Pères.* In *Le Theatre de Mr. Baron: augmenté de deux pieces qui n'avoient point encore été imprimées, & de diverses poeśies du même auteur.* 1736. Vol. 2. Paris: La Compagnie des Libraires Associés, 1742. 295–427. Print.

Barsby, John, trans. and ed. *Terence.* 2 vols. *The Loeb Classical Library.* Cambridge, MA: Harvard University Press, 2001. Print.

Batteux, Charles. *Les Beaux Arts Reduits a un Même Principe.* Paris: Durand, 1746. Print.

Becelli, Giulio Cesare. "Al lettore." In *Teatro del Sig. marchese Scipione Maffei cioè la tragedia, la comedia e il drama, non più stampato: aggiunta la spiegazione d'alcune antichità pertinenti al teatro.* Verona: Tumermani, 1730. vii–xxx. Print.

Bell, Edward. "Preface." *Selected Prose Works of G. E. Lessing.* Ed. Edward Bell. London: George Bell and Sons, 1889. Print.

Belloy, Pierre-Laurent Buirette de. *Le Siège de Calais.* Paris: Chez Duchesne, 1765. Print.

———. *Zelmire.* Amsterdam: H. Constapel, 1765. Print.

Bentley, Eric. *The Classic Theatre, Vol. 4: Six French Plays.* New York: Doubleday, 1961. Print.

Bergeron, David Moore. *Textual Patronage in English Drama, 1570–1640.* Burlington, VT: Ashgate, 2006. Print.

Bielfeld, Jakob Friedrich (Freiherr von). *Progrès des Allemands dans les Sciences, les Belles-Lettres et les Arts, particulièrement dans la Poësie, l'Eloquence, & le Théatre.* 3rd ed. Vol. 2. Leide: Samuel & John Luchtmans, 1767. Print.

Bohnen, Klaus. "Textgrundlage." In *Werke und Briefe in zwölf Bänden.* Ed. Barner, Wilfried, Klaus Bohnen, et al. Vol. 6. Frankfurt-am-Main: Deutscher Klassiker Verlag, 1985–2003. 1072. Print.

Bois-Saint-Just, Jean Louis M. Dugast de. *Paris, Versailles, et les provinces au dix-huitième siècle: anecdotes, par un ancien officier aux Gardes-françaises.* 4th ed. Vol. 1. Paris: H. Nicolle, 1817. Print.

Boisset, Pierre Louis Paul Randon de. *Die Menschlichkeit oder Schilderung der Dürftigkeit.* Dresden & Warsaw: Gröllische Buchhandlung, 1761. Print.

———. *L'humanité ou le tableau de l'indigence. Drame en cinq actes et en prose.* Paris: Ruault, 1777. Print.

Boissy, Louis de. *Le François à Londres.* Paris: Chez les Frères Barbou, 1727. Print.

———. *The Frenchman in London.* London: S. Crowder and H. Woodgate, 1755. Print.

———. *Paméla en France: ou la vertu mieux eprouvee; comedie en vers et en trois actes [. . .].* Paris: chez la Veuve Duchesne, 1766.

Bouhours, Dominique. "The Bel Esprit from *The Conversations of Aristo and Eugene.*" 1671. Trans. Donald Schier. *The Continental Model: Selected French Critical Essays of the Seventeenth Century, in English Translation.* Ed. Scott Elledge and Donald Schier. Minneapolis: University of Minnesota Press, 1960. 206–27. Print.

———. *Les Entretiens d'Ariste et d'Eugène.* Paris: Sebastien Mabre-Cramoisy, 1671. Print.

Brawe, Joachim Wilhelm von. *Der Freygeist, ein Trauerspiel in fünf Aufzügen.* Danzig, 1767. Print.

Bressand, Friedrich Christian. *Rodogune, Prinzessin aus Parthien. Trauer=Spiel aus des P. Corneille Französischem übersetzt.* Wolfenbüttel, 1691. Print.

Brooke, Henry. *The Earl of Essex.* Dublin: Wilson and Smith, 1761. Print.

Brosse. *L'aveugle clairvoyant: comédie représentée sur le Théâtre Royal devant leurs Majestez.* Paris: T. Quinet, 1650. Print.

Brown, F. Andrew. *Gotthold Ephraim Lessing.* New York: Twayne, 1971. Print.

Brown, Hilary. *Luise Gottsched the Translator.* Rochester, NY: Camden House, 2012. Print.

Brueys, David Augustin de. *L'Avocat Patelin: comédie en trois actes et en prose.* Paris: Hachette & Co., 1854. Print.

———, and J. C. S. *Der Advocat Patelin: ein Lust-Spiel in drey Aufzügen, aus dem Französischen übersetzt von J.C.S.* Danzig: Daniel Ludwig Wedel, 1762. Print.

Calepio, Pietro dei Conti di. *Paragone della Poesia tragica d'Italia con quella de Francia.* Zurich: M. Rordorf, 1732. Print.

Campistron, Jean-Galbert de. *Le Jaloux Désabusé, comédie en cinq actes et en vers.* 1709. *Oeuvres Choisies de Campistron.* Paris: P. Didot L'Aîné & F. Didot, 1810. 127–98. Print.

Cartwright, Nancy. *The Dappled World: A Study of the Boundaries of Science.* Cambridge: Cambridge University Press, 2010. Print.

Casaubon, Isaac, Athenaeus, Dominicus Baudius, and Erricus Memmius. *Isaaci Casauboni Animadversionum in Athen. Dipnosophistas Libri XV: Opus Præclarum in Lucem Iam Ante Editum: Quo Non Solum Athenæi Libri Quindecim [. . .] recensentur, Illustrantur, Emendantur:Verùm Etiam Multorum Aliorum Scriptorum Loci Multi Quâ Explicantur, Quâ Corriguntur.* Lugduni: Harsy & Ravaud, 1621. Print.

Cecchi, Giovanni M. *La Dote: Commedia.* Florence: n.p., 1750. Print.

Centlivre, Susanna, and Jean François Regnard. *The Gamester: A Comedy as It Is Acted at the Theatre-Royal by His Majesty's Servants.* London: Lowndes, Bathoe, and Horsfield, 1767. Print.

Cérou, Pierre. *L'amant, Auteur et Valet: Comédie en un Acte, en Prose.* Paris: Duchesne, 1762. Print.

———, and Christian Leberecht Martini. *Der Liebhaber, als ein Schriftsteller und Bedienter: Ein Lustspiel von einer Handlung.* Vienna, 1778. Print.

Cervantes Saavedra, Miguel de. "Prologo al Lector." *Ocho Comedias y Ocho Entremeses Nuevos.* Madrid: por la viuda de Alonso Martin, 1615. 5–10. Print.

Chariton, and Jacques Phillipe d'Orville, et al. *Charitonis Aphrodisiensis De Chaerea Et Callirrhoë Amatoriarum Narrationum Libri VIII: Graece Et Latine.* 1750. Lipsiae: Sumtu E. B. Schwickerti, 1783. Print.

Chevrier, François Antoine. *L'Observateur des Spectacles, ou Anecdotes Théâtrales: ouvrage périodique. Tome premier contenant les mois de Janvier, Fevrier et Mars 1762.* Vol. 1. 2 vols. LaHaye, 1762. Print.

———. *L'Observateur des Spectacles, ou Anecdotes Théâtrales: ouvrage périodique. Tome second contenant les mois d'Avril, Mai et Juin 1762.* Vol. 2. 2 Vols. LaHaye, 1762. Print.

Cibber, Theophilus. *The Lives of the Poets of Great Britain and Ireland.* 5 vols. London: Printed for R. Griffiths, 1753. Print.

Cicero, Marcus Tullius. *Cicero's Tusculan Disputations: Also, Treatises on the Nature of the Gods, and on the Commonwealth.* Trans. C. D. Yonge. New York: Harper & Brothers, 1877. Print.

———. *De Officiis.* With an English Translation. Ed. and Trans. Walter Miller. Cambridge, MA: Harvard University Press, 1913. Perseus Digital Library. www.perseus.tufts.edu/hop per/text?doc=Perseus%3atext%3a2007.01.0048. Print & Web. 13 February 2015.

———. "De Oratore." www.thelatinlibrary.com. Web. 27 July 2017.

———. "De Oratore [On the Orator]." Trans. J. S. Watson. In *Cicero on Oratory and Orators, with His Letters to Quintus and Brutus.* London: Bell & Daldy, 1871. 142–401. Print.

Coello, Antonio. *Comedia Famosa. Dar La Vida Por Su Dama. De Don Luis Coello.* Valencia: en la Imprenta de José Tomás de Orga, 1780. Print.

Coenen, Adriaen, et al. *The Whale Book: Whales and Other Marine Animals as Described by Adriaen Coenen in 1585.* London: Reaktion, 2003. Print.

Colman, George. *The Village Lawyer: A Farce, in Two Acts, as Performed at the Theatres Royal in London and Dublin, with Universal Applause.* Dublin: T. Mcdonnel, 1792. Print.

———, and Johann J. C. Bode. *Die Eifersüchtige Ehefrau: Ein Lustspiel.* Hamburg, 1764. Print.

———, and Thomas Price. *Critical Edition of the Jealous Wife and Polly Honeycombe, by George Colman, the Elder (1732–1794).* Lewiston, NY: Edwin Mellen Press, 1997. Print.

———, and Henry W. Wells. *The English Merchant.* Dublin: W. W. Smith et al., 1767. Print.

Conroy, Jane. *Terres tragiques: l'Angleterre et l'Ecosse dans la tragédie française du XVIIe siècle.* Tübingen: G. Narr, 1999.

Corneille, Pierre. "Appian Alexandrin." In *Rodogune, Princesse des Parthes: tragédie, accompagnée de notes par E. Geruzez.* 1644. Paris: Librairie Hachette et Cie, 1900. 4–9. Print.

————. *The Cid*. 1636. Trans. John Cairncross. *The Cid, Cinna, the Theatrical Illusion.* New York: Penguin Books, 1975. 23–112. Print.

————. "Discourse on Tragedy." 1660. Trans. Henry Hitch Adams and Baxter Hathaway. In *Dramatic Essays of the Neoclassic Age.* Ed. Henry Hitch Adams and Baxter Hathaway. New York: Columbia University Press, 1950. 2–34. Print.

————. "Discourses." 1660. Trans. Arlin Hiken Armstrong. In *Dramatic Theory and Criticism: Greeks to Grotowski.* Ed. Bernard F. Dukore. New York: Holt, Rinehart and Winston, 1974. 226–38. Print.

————. "Examen de Rodogune." In *Rodogune, Princesse des Parthes: tragédie, accompagnée de notes par E. Geruzez.* 1644. Paris: Librairie Hachette et Cie, 1900. 95–102. Print.

————. "First Discourse: On the Uses and Elements of Dramatic Poetry [Premier Discours. De L'utilité et des Parties du Poème Dramatique]." 1660. Trans. Beatrice Stewart Mac-Clintock. In *European Theories of the Drama: An Anthology of Dramatic Theory and Criticism from Aristotle to the Present Day, in a Series of Selected Texts, with Commentaries, Biographies, and Bibliographies.* Ed. Barrett H. Clark. Cincinnati: Steward & Kidd Company, 1918. 139–47. Print.

————. *Les chef-D'oeuvres de P. Corneille. Savoir, Le Cid, Horace, Cinna, Polyeucte, Pompee, Rodogune. Avec le jugement des savans a la suite de chaque piece.* Ed. J. G. Dupré. Nouvelle ed. Oxford: chez Jaques Fletcher, 1746. *Eighteenth Century Collections Online.* Gale. Web.

————. "Of the Three Unities of Action." 1660. Trans. Donald Schier. In *The Continental Model: Selected French Critical Essays of the Seventeenth Century in English Translation.* Ed. Scott Elledge and Donald Schier. Minneapolis: University of Minnesota Press, 1960. 117–31. Print.

————. *Polyeucte Martyr, Tragedie Chretienne.* In *Les chef-D'oeuvres de P. Corneille.* 209–80. Web. 4 June 2014.

————. *Polyeucte: Or, the Martyr.* Trans. Thomas Constable. New York: P. F. Collier, 1909. Print.

————. *Rodogune: Or the Rival Brothers: A Tragedy: Done from the French of Mons. Corneille: Humbly Inscribed to the Right Honourable Philip Earl of Chesterfield.* Trans. S. Aspinwall. London, 1765. *Eighteenth Century Collections Online.* Gale. Web. 24 October 2013.

————. *Rodogune, Princesse des Parthes: tragédie, accompagnée de notes par E. Geruzez.* 1644. Paris: Librairie Hachette et Cie, 1900. Print.

————. *Rodogune, Prinzessin der Parther: ein Trauerspiel in Fünf Ackten.* Hamburg and Bremen: Bey Johann Henrich Cramer, 1769. Print.

————. *Trois discours de P. Corneille: Oeuvres de P. Corneille, avec Commentaires, Notes, Remarques, et Jugements Littéraires.* Vol. 10. 11 vols. Paris: Ledoyen, 1830. Print.

Corneille, Thomas. *Le Comte d'Essex, Tragedie par T. Corneille.* Paris: Chez Thomas Amaury, 1678. Print.

————. "Au Lecteur [Preface to *Le Comte d'Essex*]." In *Le Comte d'Essex, Tragedie par T. Corneille.* Paris: Chez Thomas Amaury, 1678. Print.

————. *Der Graf von Essex, ein Trauerspiel, aus dem Französischen des Herrn Thomas Corneille übersetzet, von Herrn L. Peter Stüven aus Hamburg.* Trans. L. Peter Stüven. Vienna: Krauß, 1761. Print.

Crébillon, Prosper Jolyot de. *Atrée et Thyeste.* Paris: Pierre Ribou, 1709. Print.

Creffield, C. A. "Zimmern, Helen." *Oxford Dictionary of National Biography.* Oxford: Oxford University Press, 2004. Print.

Cronegk, Johann Friedrich von. *Des Freyherrn Johann Friedrich von Cronegk Schriften.* Vol. 1. Leipzig: bey Johann Christoph Posch, 1760. Print.

————. *Der Mistrauische.* In *Des Freyherrn Johann Friedrich von Cronegk Schriften* 1: 23–177. Print.

————. *Olint und Sophronia.* In *Des Freyherrn Johann Friedrich von Cronegk Schriften* 1: 281–352. Print.

Curtius, Michael Conrad. *Aristoteles Dichtkunst, ins Deutsche übersetzet, Mit Anmerkungen, und besondern Abhandlungen, versehen.* Hannover: Johann Christoph Richter, 1753. Print.

————. "Abhandlung von der Absicht des Trauerspiels." In *Aristoteles Dichtkunst, ins Deutsche übersetzet, Mit Anmerkungen, und besondern Abhandlungen, versehen.* 389–96. Print.

D'Aubignac, Abbé. *La Pratique du Théâtre*. Vol. 1. Amsterdam: J. F. Bernard, 1715. Print.

Delisle de la Drevetière, Louis-François. *Le faucon et les oies de Bocace: comédie en trois actes et en prose. Petite bibliothèque des théâtres*. Paris: Au Bureau de la petite bibliothèque des théâtres, 1783. Print.

———. *Timon le misanthrope, comédie en trois actes, précédée d'un prologue. Par le sieur De L'Isle.* Dublin, 1749. Print.

Descartes, René. *Selected Philosophical Writings*. Trans. John Cottingham, Robert Stoothoff, and Dugald Murdoch. Cambridge, UK: Cambridge University Press, 1988. Print.

Destouches, Philipe Néricault. *The Conceited Count*. In Regnard, et al., *The Heirs of Molière*. 89–196. Print.

———. *Le Dissipateur*. 1733. In *Œuvres choisies de Destouches* 2: 81–255. Print.

———. *La fausse Agnès, ou le poète campagnard*. Paris: chez la Veuve Duchesne, 1770. Print.

———. *Das Gespenste mit der Trummel, oder Der wahrsagende Ehemann. Ein Lustspiel des Herrn Addisons, nach dem Französischen des Herrn Destouches übersetzt*. 1741. Trans. Luise Adelgunde Victorie Gottsched. In *Die Deutsche Schaubühne*. Ed. J. C. Gottsched. 2: 231–358. Print.

———. *Le Glorieux*. 1732. In *Œuvres choisies de Destouches* 1: 169–350. Print.

———. *L'irresolu, comédie en vers et en cinq actes*. Vienna: Dans l'Imprimerie de Ghelen, 1763. Print.

———. *The Married Philosopher*. Trans. John Kelly. London: T. Worrall, 1732. Print.

———. *L'Obstacle imprévu, ou, L'obstacle sans obstacle*. 1717. Paris: La Compagnie des libraires, 1788. Print.

———. *Œuvres choisies de Destouches*. 3 Vols. Paris: L. de Bure, 1826. Print.

———. *Oeuvres dramatiques de Néricault Destouches*. 4 vols. Paris: de l'Imprimerie Royale, 1757. Print.

———. *Le Philosophe marié*. 1727. *Œuvres choisies de Destouches*. 1: 1–168. Print.

———. *Der Poetische Dorfjunker*. 1741. Trans. Luise Adelgunde Victorie Gottsched. In *Die Deutsche Schaubühne*. Ed. J. C. Gottsched. 3: 443–558. Print.

———. "Preface to *Le Dissipateur*." In *Œuvres choisies de Destouches*. 2: 82–7. Print.

———. *Der Ruhmredige, Ein Lustspiel in Versen, in Fünf Aufzügen. Von Hn. Professor Schlegeln, aus des Herrn Nericault Destouches [. . .] Französischem Übersetzt*. Trans. Johann Elias Schlegel. Vienna: zu finden in Kraußischen Buchladen, 1761. Print.

———. *Le Tambour nocturne*. 1736. In *Œuvres choisies de Destouches*. 3: 206–371. Print.

———. *Le Tresor Caché*. In *Oeuvres dramatiques de Néricault Destouches*. 4 vols. Paris: de l'Imprimerie Royale, 1757. 4: 259–351. Print.

———. *Der Verschwender*. 1741. Trans. Luise Adelgunde Victorie Gottsched. In *Die Deutsche Schaubühne*. Ed. J. C. Gottsched. 3: 63–194. Print.

———. *The Young Hypocrite, or The Country Poet*. Trans. Samuel Foote et al. *The Comic Theatre: Being a Free Translation of All the Best French Comedies*. Vol.1. London: D. Leach, 1762. 1–108. Print.

———, and Johann D. Schleuen. *Des Herrn Nericault Destouches Sämtliche Theatralische Werke: aus dem Französischen Übersetzt*. Leipzig and Göttingen: Luzac, 1756. Print.

Devrient, Hans. *Johann Friedrich Schönemann und seine Schauspielergesellschaft. Ein Beitrag zur Theatergeschichte des 18. Jahrhunderts. Theatergeschichtliche Forschungen 11*. Hamburg and Leipzig: L. Voss, 1895. Print.

Dibdin, Charles, and Mme. Marie-Justine-Benoîte Favart. *Annette and Lubin: A Comic Opera in One Act*. London: Printed for G. Kearsly, 1778. Print.

Diderot, Denis. *Les bijoux indiscrets*. 2 vols. Paris: Au Monomotapa, 1748. Print.

———. "Conversations on *The Natural Son*." Trans. Geoffrey Bremner. *Selected Writings on Art and Literature*. London and New York: Penguin Books, 1994. 4–79. Print.

———. *De la Poésie dramatique, à Monsieur Grimm [Discours sur la poésie dramatique]*. In *Oeuvres de Théatre de M. Diderot, Avec un Discours sur la Poésie Dramatique*. 2: 229–394. Print.

———. "From 'Discourse on Dramatic Poetry' to Mr. Grimm." Trans. Barbara Kerslake. In *Sources of Dramatic Theory*. 1758. Ed. Michael J. Sidnell. Vol. 2. Cambridge: Cambridge University Press, 1994. 57–68. Print.

———. *Entretiens sur Le Fils naturel*. In *Oeuvres de Denis Diderot*. 4: 109–238. Print.

———. *Le Fils naturel*. In *Oeuvres de Denis Diderot*. 4: 10–108. Print.

———. *The Illegitimate Son*. Trans. Kiki Gounaridou. In *Two Plays by Denis Diderot*. New York: Peter Lang, 2011. 7–53. Print.

———. *The Indiscreet Jewels*. Trans. Sophie Hawkes. New York: Marsilio, 1993. Print.

———. *Lettre sur les sourds et muets*. Paris: [publisher unknown], 1751. Print.

———. *Oeuvres de Denis Diderot*. 6 vols. Paris: Desrey & Deterville, 1798. Print.

———. *Oeuvres de Théatre de M. Diderot, Avec un Discours sur la Poésie Dramatique*. 2 vols. Paris: chez la Veuve Duchesne, 1771. Print.

———. "On Dramatic Poetry." In *European Theories of Drama, with a Supplement on the American Drama*. Ed. Barrett H. Clark. New York: Crown Publishers Inc., 1947. 286–99. Print.

———. "The Paradox of the Actor." Trans. Geoffrey Bremner. In *Selected Writings on Art and Literature*. London and New York: Penguin Books, 1994. 100–59. Print.

———. *Le Père de Famille*. In *Oeuvres de Théatre de M. Diderot, Avec un Discours sur la Poésie Dramatique*. 2: 1–226. Print.

———. "Von der dramatischen Dichtkunst. An meinen Freund Herrn Grimm." Trans. G. E. Lessing. In *Das Theater des Herrn Diderot: Aus dem Französischen. Zweyter Theil*. Vol. 2. Berlin: Christian Friedrich Voß, 1760. 229–480. Print.

Diderot, Denis, and Carl Friedrich Cramer. *Die Verräther, nach Diderot*. Trans. Carl Friedrich Cramer, with preface by Gotthold Ephraim Lessing. 2 vols. Monomotapa [i.e. Braunschweig]: Vieweg, 1793. Print.

Diodati, Ottaviano. *Biblioteca teatrale italiana/ scelta e disposta da Ottaviano Diodati, con un suo capitolo in verso per ogni tomo, correlativo alle cose teatrali, per servire di trattato completo di drammaturgia*. 12 vols. Lucca: Gio della Valle, 1762. Print.

Diogenes Laertius. *Lives of Eminent Philosophers*. Trans. Robert Drew Hicks. London: W. Heinemann, 1925. Perseus Digital Library. www.perseus.tufts.edu/hopper/text?doc=Perseus%3A text%3A1999.01.0258%3Abook%3D1%3Achapter%3D2. Print & Web. 1 September 2016.

Donatus, Aelius. *Life of Virgil*. Trans. David Scott Wilson-Okamura. 1996. Rev. 2005, 2008. www.virgil.org/vitae/a-donatus.htm. Web. 15 May 2017.

———. *Publii Terentii, Carthaginensis Afri, Comoediae N. VI*. Frankfurt: in Bibliopolio Heringiano, 1623. Print.

Dubos, Abbé (Jean-Baptiste). *Réflexions Critiques sur la Poësie et sur la Peinture*. Geneva: Slatkine Reprints, 1967. Print.

———, and Thomas Nugent. *Critical Reflections on Poetry, Painting and Music. With an Inquiry into the Rise and Progress of the Theatrical Entertainments of the Ancients. Written in French by the Abbé Du Bos, . . . Translated into English by Thomas Nugent, gent. From the Fifth Edition Revised, Corrected, and Inlarged by the Author*. 3 Vols. London: Printed for John Nourse, 1748. Print.

Duckworth, Colin. "Introduction to *L'Écossaise*." In *Complete Works of Voltaire (Les Oeuvres complètes de Voltaire)*. 50: 221–338. Print.

Dugas de Bois Saint-Just, Jean Louis Marie. *Paris, Versailles et les provinces, au 18e siècle: anecdotes sur la vie privée de plusieurs ministres, évêques, magistrats célèbres, hommes de lettres, et autres perssonnages connus sous les règnes de Louis XV et de Louis XVI*. Paris: Le Normant, 1809. Print.

Duim, Frederik. *Zaïre, bekeerde Turkinne, treurspel*. Amsterdam: Pieter Aldewerelt, 1753. Print.

Dunsch, Boris. "Some Notes on the Understanding of Terence, *Heuton Timorumenos 6: Comoedia duplex, argumentum simplex*, and Hellenistic Scholarship." In *Classica et Mediaevalia*. Copenhagen: Museum Tusculanum Press, U. Copenhagen, 1999. 97–131. Print.

Eaton, John W. *The German Influence in Danish Literature in the 18th Century: The German Circle in Copenhagen, 1750–1770*. Cambridge, UK: Cambridge University Press, 1929. Print.

Else, Gerald F. "Preface." In *Aristotle's Poetics: The Argument*. Cambridge, MA: Harvard University Press, 1963. vii–xii. Print.

Ennis, Daniel J., and Judith Bailey-Slagle. "Introduction." In *Prologues, Epilogues, Curtain-Raisers, and Afterpieces: The Rest of the Eighteenth-Century London Stage*. Ed. Daniel J. Ennis and Judith Bailey-Slagle. Newark, DE: University of Delaware Press, 2007. 13–32. Print.

Erickson, Peter. "Adapting Christian Tragedy for the Enlightenment Stage: Gotthold Ephraim Lessing's *Hamburgische Dramaturgie* (1767–1769)." *Lessing Yearbook* 42 (2015): 145–50. Print.

Euripides, and Joshua Barnes. *Euripidou sōzomena apanta = Euripidis Quae Extant Omnia.* Cantabrigiae (Cambridge): Green, 1694. Print.

Fantuzzi, Maria Noussia. *Solon the Athenian, the Poetic Fragments.* Boston: Brill, 2010. Print.

Favart, Charles-Simon. *The Fairy Urgele: Or, What Pleases the Ladies: a Marionette Opera in Four Acts, after the French of C. S. Favart. Produced and performed by the Collegium musicum of North Texas State University, translated, edited, and Directed by Cecil Adkins.* Trans. Cecil Adkins. Denton: North Texas State University, 1972. Print.

———. *Isabelle et Gertrude, Ou Les Sylphes Supposés. Théâtre Choisi de Favart.* Vol. 2. Paris: Leopold Collin, 1809. 1–53. Print.

———. *Soliman second, ou les trois Sultanes.* Nouvelle édition. Paris: Chez Didot l'ainé, 1772. Print.

———. *Solimann der Zweyte oder die drey Sultaninnen: Ein Lustspiel in drey Aufzügen.* Trans. Rudolf Erich Raspe. Münster: Perrenon, 1777. Print.

———, and Egidio Duni. *La fée Urgele, ou, Ce qui plait aux dames.* Avignon: Chez Louis Chambeau, 1769. Print.

Favart, Madame, and Mr. C. H. Fusée de Voisenon. *Annette et Lubin, comédie, en un acte en vers.* 1762. Nouvelle édition. Toulouse: Chez Broulhiet, 1782. Print.

Federico, Gennaro Antonio. *La serva padrona, comedia in due atti. = The Maid the Mistress, a Comedy of Two Acts, as It Is Now Performing at the Theatre of Edinburgh. Translated from the Italian, by David Erskine Baker.* Edinburgh, 1763. *Eighteenth Century Collections Online.* Gale. Web. 13 December 2013.

Fielding, Henry. *The History of the Adventures of Joseph Andrews, and His Friend Mr. Abraham Adams.* London: A. Millar, 1749. Print.

———. *The History of Tom Jones, a Foundling.* London: A. Millar, 1749. Print.

Figal, Sara E. *Heredity, Race, and the Birth of the Modern.* New York: Routledge, 2008. Print.

Fischer-Lichte, Erika. "The Rise of the Middle Classes and the Theatre of Illusion." In *History of European Drama and Theatre.* Trans. Jo Riley. New York: Routledge, 2004. 146–70. Print.

Gellert, Christian Fürchtegott. *Das Loos in der Lotterie: ein Lustspiel.* In *C. F. Gellerts Sämtliche Schriften.* Vol. 2. Leipzig: Weid'mannische Buchhandlung, 1853. 201–301. Print.

———. *Die Kranke Frau.* In *C. F. Gellerts Lustspiele.* Leipzig: Johann Wendler, 1763. 291–324. Print.

Goetschel, Willi. *Spinoza's Modernity: Mendelssohn, Lessing, and Heine.* Madison: University of Wisconsin Press, 2004. Print.

Goeze, Johann Melchior. *Theologische Untersuchung der Sittlichkeit der heutigen deutschen Schaubühne, überhaupt [. . .].* Hamburg: bey Johan Christian Brandt, 1770. Print.

Goldberg, Sander M. "The Fall and Rise of Roman Tragedy." *Transactions of the American Philological Association* 126 (1996): 265–86. Print.

———. *The Making of Menander's Comedy.* Berkeley and Los Angeles: University of California Press, 1980. Print.

Goldoni, Carlo, and Robert Cornthwaite. *The Coffee Shop.* Lyme, NH: Smith and Kraus, 1995. Print.

———, and Roberta Turchi. *La Bottega Del Caffè.* Venice: Marsilio, 1994. Print.

Gottsched, Johann Christoph, ed. *Die Deutsche Schaubühne: Nach den Regeln und Exempeln der Alten Griechen und Römer eingerichtet.* 6 vols. Leipzig: Bernhard Christoph Breitkopf, 1740–1745. Print.

———. *Versuch einer critischen Dichtkunst.* Leipzig: Bernhard Christoph Breitkopf, 1730. Berlin: Holzinger, 2013. Print.

Gottsched, Luise Adelgunde Victorie. *Cato, ein Trauerspiel, aus dem Englischen des Herrn Addisons übersetzt.* Trans. Luise Adelgunde Victorie Gottsched. Leipzig: Bernhard Christoph Breitkopf, 1735. Print.

———. *Die Hausfranzösin, Oder Die Mammsell: Ein Deutsches Lustspiel, in Fünf Aufzügen.* Leipzig: Bernhard Christoph Breitkopf, 1749. Print.

———. *Das Testament, ein deutsches Lustspiel in fünf Aufzügen.* In Gottsched, J. C. *Die Deutsche Schaubühne* 6: 81–204. Print.

———. "Vorrede." In *Cenie, oder die Großmuth im Unglücke: Ein moralisches Stück, in fünf Aufzügen.* Trans. Luise Adelgunde Victorie Gottsched. Vienna, 1753. 1–7. Print.

Gottsched, Louise A. V., Thomas Kerth, and John R. Russell. *The French Housekeeper, or The Mamsell.* In *Pietism in Petticoats and Other Comedies.* Columbia, SC: Camden House, 1994. 139–210. Print.

———. *The Last Will.* In *Pietism in Petticoats and Other Comedies.* Columbia, SC: Camden House, 1994. 211–80. Print.

Goulbourne, Russell, and Mark Waddicor. "Introduction to *La femme qui a raison.*" In *Complete Works of Voltaire (Les Oeuvres complètes de Voltaire).* 30A: 255–294. Print.

Gozzi, Gasparo. *Zaira.* In *Opere in versi e in prosa.* Vol. 3. Venice: Bartolommeo Ochhi, 1758. 5–62. Print.

Grafigny, (Mme.) Françoise d'Issembourg d'Happoncourt de. *Cenia: or, the suppos'd daughter. Translated from the French of Madam d'Happoncourt de Grafigny, by a French gentleman.* London: Printed for W. Reeve, 1752. Print.

———. *Cénie.* Vienna: Ghelen, 1768. Print.

———. *Cenie, oder die Großmuth im Unglücke: Ein moralisches Stück, in fünf Aufzügen.* Trans. Luise Adelgunde Victorie Gottsched. Vienna, 1753. Print.

Gresset, Jean B. L. *Sidney: Comédie en Trois Actes, en Vers.* 1745. In *Petite Bibliotheque des Théatres. Vol 16: Chef-d'oeuvres de Gresset.* Paris: Chez Bélin & Brunet, 1787. 1–53. Print.

Grimm, Jacob, and Wilhelm Grimm. *Deutsches Wörterbuch von Jacob Grimm und Wilhelm Grimm.* 32 vols. Leipzig: S. Hirzel, 1854–1962. Print.

Gueullette, Thomas Simon. *Memoires De Mademoiselle Bontemps, ou de la Comtesse De Marlou.* Amsterdam: J. Catuffe, 1738. Print.

Guyer, Paul. "18th Century German Aesthetics." In *The Stanford Encyclopedia of Philosophy.* Ed. Edward N. Zalta. Winter 2016 Edition. https://plato.stanford.edu/archives/win2016/entries/aesthetics-18th-german/. Web. 28 January 2017.

Halliwell, Stephen. "Comic Satire and Freedom of Speech in Classical Athens." *The Journal of Hellenic Studies* 111 (1991): 48–70. Print.

Hédelin, François (Abbé d'Aubignac). *La Pratique du Théâtre.* Vol. 1. Amsterdam: J. F. Bernard, 1715. Print.

———. *The Whole Art of the Stage Containing Not Only the Rules of the Drammatick Art, But Many Curious Observations about It, Which May be of Great Use to the Authors, Actors, and Spectators of Plays: Together with Much Critical Learning about the Stage and Plays of the Antients / Written in French by the Command of Cardinal Richelieu by Monsieur Hédelin, Abbot of Aubignac, and Now Made English.* 1684. New York: Benjamin Blom, 1968. Print.

Heitner, Robert R. "Diderot's Own *Miss Sara Sampson.*" *Comparative Literature* 5.1 (1953): 40–9. Print.

———. *German Tragedy in the Age of Enlightenment.* Berkeley: University of California Press, 1963. Print.

Heufeld, Franz von. *Der Geburtstag. Ein Lustspiel von drey Aufzügen.* 2nd ed. Vienna: Johann Thomas Edl. von Trattnern, 1767. Print.

———. *Der Geburtstag. Ein Lustspiel in zween Aufzügen.* Vienna, 1769. Print.

———. *Die Haushaltung nach der Mode, oder Was soll man für eine Frau nehmen? Ein Lustspiel Von 3 Aufzügen.* Vienna: J. P. Krauß, 1765. Print.

———. *Julie, oder Wettstreit der Pflicht und Liebe: Ein Lustspiel von drey Aufzügen.* Vienna: 1766. Print.

———. *Die Liebhaber nach der Mode, oder Was soll man für einen Mann nehmen? Ein Lustspiel Von 3 Aufzügen.* Vienna: J. P. Krauß, 1766. Print.

———. *Die Tochter Des Bruder Philipps. Ein Lustspiel in Einem Aufzug.* Vienna, 1769. Print.

Hill, Aaron. *The Tragedy of Zara.* 1736. London: T. Lowndes, 1769. Print.

Hill, John. *The Actor: A Treatise on the Art of Playing. Interspersed with Theatrical Anecdotes, Critical Remarks on Plays, and Occasional Observations on Audiences.* 1750. New York: Benjamin Blom, 1971. Print.

Hippel, Theodor Gottlieb von, and Erich Jenisch. *Der Mann Nach Der Uhr; Oder, Der Ordentliche Mann: Lustspiel in Einem Aufzuge.* Halle/Saale: M. Niemeyer, 1928. Zeno.org. Print & Web. 13 February 2015.

Hogarth, William. *The Analysis of Beauty, Written with a View of Fixing the Fluctuating Ideas of Taste.* London: Strahan, 1772. Print.

———. *Zergliederung der Schönheit, die schwankenden Begriffe von dem Geschmack festzusetzen.* Trans. Christlob Mylius. Berlin and Potsdam: Voß, 1754. Print.

Home, Henry, Lord Kames. *Elements of Criticism.* 1761. Vol. 2. 2 vols. New York: S. Campbell & Son et al., 1823. Print.

Home, John. *Douglas.* Edinburgh: Oliver and Boyd, 1972. Print.

Homer. *The Iliad.* Trans. A. T. Murray. London: W. Heinemann, 1924. Perseus Digital Library. www.perseus.tufts.edu/hopper/text?doc=Perseus:text:1999.01.0134. Print & Web. 14 February 2015.

Horace (Quintus Horatius Flaccus). *Satires, Epistles, and Ars Poetica.* Trans. H. Ruston Fairclough. Cambridge, MA: Harvard University Press, 1926. Print.

———, and Richard Hurd. *Q. Horatii Flacci Epistolae ad Pisones, Et Augustum: With an English Commentary and Notes: To Which Are Added Critical Dissertations, by the Reverend Mr. Hurd.* 5th ed. 3 vols. London: W. Bowyer and J. Nichols, 1776. Print.

Hume, David. *The History of England: From the Invasion of Julius Caesar, to the Revolution in 1688.* Vol. 4. New York: Innskeep and Bradford, 1810. Print.

Hurd, Richard. "Dissertation on the Provinces of the Drama." In Horace and Hurd. *Q. Horatii Flacci Epistolae ad Pisones, Et Augustum: With an English Commentary and Notes: To Which Are Added Critical Dissertations, by the Reverend Mr. Hurd.* 2: 163–247. Print.

———. "Notes on the Art of Poetry." In Horace and Hurd. *Q. Horatii Flacci Epistolae ad Pisones, Et Augustum: With an English Commentary and Notes: To Which Are Added Critical Dissertations, by the Reverend Mr. Hurd.* 1: 37–277. Print.

Hyginus Gaius Julius. *The Myths of Hyginus [Fabulae].* Trans. Mary Grant. In *University of Kansas Publications in Humanistic Studies, No. 34.* Lawrence: University of Kansas Press, 1960. www.theoi.com/Text/HyginusFabulae3.html#137. Print & Web. 2 January 2014.

———, Johannes Scheffer, and Thomas Munckerus. *Hygini Quae hodie extant, adcurante Joanne Scheffero Argentoratensi, qui simul adjecit notas, hic admodum necessarias, cum indice verborum locutionumque rariorum, & dissertatione, de vero hujus operis auctore. Accedunt & Thomae Munckeri in fabulas Hygini Annotationes.* Hamburgi: ex officina Gothofredi Schultzen prostant, 1674. Print.

———, and Moritz Schmidt. *Hygini Fabulae.* Jenae: apud Hermannum Dufft, 1872. Print.

Jacobs, Eva. "Introduction to *Zaïre*." In *Complete Works of Voltaire (Les Oeuvres complètes de Voltaire).* 8: 277–382. Print.

Joannidès, Alexandre. *La Comédie-Française de 1680 à 1900: Dictionnaire général des pièces et des auteurs.* Paris: Librairie Plon, 1901. Print.

Jonson, Ben. *Every Man Out of His Humor.* Ed. Helen Ostovich. Manchester: Manchester University Press, 2001. Print.

Kay, Nigel M. *Epigrams from the Anthologia Latina: Text, Translation and Commentary.* London: Duckworth, 2006. Print.

Kelly, Adrian D. "Biographies of Homer." In *The Homer Encyclopedia.* Ed. Margalite Finkelberg. Hoboken, NJ: Wiley, 2011. Print.

Kies, Paul P. "The Sources and Basic Model of Lessing's 'Miss Sara Sampson'." *Modern Philology* 24.1 (August 1926): 65–90. Print.

Klotz, Christian Adolf. *Deutsche Bibliothek der schönen Wissenschaften.* Vol. 9. Halle: bey Johann Justinus Gebauer, 1769. Print.

Kord, Susanne. *Little Detours: Letters and Plays by Luise Gottsched.* Rochester, NY: Camden House, 2000. Print.

———. "Tugend im Rampenlicht: Friederike Sophie Hensel als Schauspielerin und Dramatikerin." *The German Quarterly* 66.1 (1993): 1–19. Print.

Knufmann, Helmut. "Das deutsche Übersetzungswesen des 18. Jahrhunderts im Spiegel von Übersetzer- und Herausgebervorreden." *Börsenblatt für den Deutschen Buchhandel – Frankfurter Ausgabe* 91 (1967): 2676–716. Print.

Krüger, Johann Christian. *Die Candidaten, oder die Mittel zu einem Amte zu gelangen, in fünf Handlungen.* In *Johann Christian Krügers Poetische und Theatralische Schriften.* 290–415. Print.

———. *Herzog Michel, ein Lustspiel von einer Handlung, in Versen.* 1757. Print. [also in: *Johann Christian Krügers Poetische und Theatralische Schriften.* 447–69. Print.].

———. *Johann Christian Krügers Poetische und Theatralische Schriften.* Ed. Johann Friedrich Löwen. Leipzig: bey M. G. Weidmanns Erben und Reich, 1763. Print.

———, and Joachim Bark. *Die Geistlichen auf dem Lande: Ein Lustspiel in drey Handlungen, aus der frühen Aufklärung.* Stuttgart: Klett, 1980. Print.

Kummerfeld, Karoline. "Aus dem Komödiantenleben des vorigen Jahrhunderts: Denkwürdigkeiten von Karoline Schulze." 1793. Ed. Hermann Uhde. In *Historisches Taschenbuch.* Ed. W. H. Riehl. Leipzig: F. A. Brockhaus, 1873. 359–415. Print.

Kurz, Johann Felix Joseph (von). *Die Hofmeisterinn: ein musicalisches Lustspiel; mit Tänzen von Kindern und pantominischen Auftritten vermischet.* Vienna: Krauß, 1769. Print.

Labriolle, Marie-Rose de, and Colin Duckworth. "Introduction to *Nanine.*" In *Complete Works of Voltaire (Les Oeuvres complètes de Voltaire).* 31B: 3–61. Print.

Lactantius, Samuel Brandt. *The Divine Institutes: Book 1 (Of the False Worship of the Gods).* Trans. William Fletcher. In *The Ante-Nicene Fathers: Translations of the Writings of the Fathers Down to A.D. 325.* Vol. 7. Ed. Alexander Roberts, James Donaldson, and A. Cleveland Coxe. Buffalo, NY: Christian Literature Publishing Co., 1886. 7: 9–39. Print.

———, and Georg von Laubmann. *Divinae institutiones.* In *Corpus Scriptorum Ecclesiasticorum Latinorum. Vol 19: L. Caeli Firmiani Lactanti Opera Omnia […] Pars 1.* Vindobonae: F. Tempsky, 1890. Print.

L'Affichard, Thomas. *La Famille. Comédie en un Acte.* In *Théâtre de Monsieur L'Affichard.* Paris: Chez Jacques Clousier, 1746. 64–123. Print.

La Motte, Antoine Houdar de. "Discours à l'occasion de la Tragédie d'Oedipe." In *Oeuvres de Monsieur Houdar de la Motte.* Vol. 4. Paris: Chez Prault L'aîné, 1754. 377–96. Print.

———. *La Matron d'Ephese.* In *Oeuvres de Monsieur Houdar de la Motte.* Vol. 5. Paris: Chez Prault l'aîné, 1754. 465–510. Print.

Le Brun, Charles. *Conférence de M. Le Brun sur l'expression générale et particulière.* Paris: E. Picart, 1698. Print.

Le Grand, Marc Antoine. *L'aveugle clair-voyant.* Naples: Jean Gravier, 1777. Print.

———. *Le triomphe du temps passé.* Paris: J. P. van Ghelen, 1754. Print.

———. *Der sehende Blinde: ein Nachspiel in Versen.* Trans. Karl August Suabe. Dresden, 1752. Print.

Lefkowitz, Mary. *Euripides and the Gods.* New York: Oxford University Press, 2016. Print.

Leibniz, Gottfried Wilhelm. "De vera ratione reformandi rem literariam meditationes (1668)." In *Oeuvres de Leibniz.* Ed. Foucher de Careil and Louis Alexandre. Vol. 7. Paris: Librairie de Firmin Didot Frères, Fils et Cie, 1875. 20–3. Print.

Léris, Antoine de. *Dictionnaire portatif historique et littéraire des théâtres.* Paris: C. A. Jombert, 1763. Print.

Lessing, Gotthold Ephraim. "Abhandlung von den Pantomimen der Alten." 1750. *Werke und Briefe* 1: 711–21. Print.

———. "Abhandlungen von dem weinerlichen oder rührenden Lustspiele." 1754. *Werke und Briefe* 3: 259–318. Print.

————. "Des Abts du Bos Ausschweifung von den Theatralischen Vorstellungen der Alten." 1755. *Werke und Briefe* 3: 651–61. Print.

————. "Auszug aus dem *Schauspieler* des Herrn Remond von Sainte Albine." 1754. *Werke und Briefe* 3: 304–11. Print.

————. "Auszug aus dem Trauerspiele Virginia des Don Augustino de Montiano y Luyando." *Gotth. Ephr. Lessings Theatralische Bibliothek.* Vol. 1. Berlin: Voß, 1754. 117–208. Print.

————. *Beyträge zur Historie und Aufnahme des Theaters.* 1750. *Werke und Briefe* 1: 725–950.

————. "Brief an Karl Lessing." 22 May 1767. Letter 373. *Werke und Briefe* 11/1: 466–8. Print.

————. "Brief an Mendelssohn." 13 November 1756. Letter 104. *Werke und Briefe* 3: 673–75; also 11/1: 122–4. Print.

————. "Brief an Mendelssohn." 18 December 1756. Letter 110. *Werke und Briefe* 3: 693–703; also 11/1: 144–54. Print.

————. "Brief an Mendelssohn." 2 February 1757. Letter 115. *Werke und Briefe* 3: 711–14; also 11/1: 165–9. Print.

————. "Brief an Nicolai." 13 November 1756. Letter 103. *Werke und Briefe* 3: 668–73; also 11/1: 116–22. Print.

————. "Brief an Nicolai." 2 April 1757. Letter 122. *Werke und Briefe* 3: 715–18; also 11/1: 178–82. Print.

————. "Brief von Voltaire." 1 January 1752. Letter 29. *Werke und Briefe* 11/1: 37–8. Print.

————. *Briefe, antiquarischen Inhalts.* 1768–1769. *Werke und Briefe* 5/2: 353–618. Print.

————. *Briefe, die neueste Litteratur betreffend.* 1759–1765. *Werke und Briefe* 4: 453–777. Print.

————. "Briefwechsel über das Trauerspiele zwischen Lessing, Mendelssohn, und Nicolai (1755–1757)." 1789. *Werke und Briefe* 3: 662–736. Print.

————. "Correspondence with Nicolai and Mendelssohn 1756–1757." Trans. Henry Hitch Adams and Baxter Hathaway. In *Dramatic Essays of the Neoclassic Age.* Ed. Henry Hitch Adams and Baxter Hathaway. New York: Columbia University Press, 1950. 328–40. Print.

————. "Dramatic Notes [*The Hamburg Dramaturgy*]." Trans. Helen Zimmern. *Selected Prose Works of G. E. Lessing.* Ed. Edward Bell. London: George Bell and Sons, 1889. 227–493. Print.

————. *The Dramatic Works of G. E. Lessing.* Trans. Ernest Albert Bell. London: George Bell and Sons, 1878. Print.

————. *Dramaturgie de Hambourg.* Ed. and Trans. Jean-Marie Valentin. [Paris]: Klincksieck, 2010. Print.

————. "Einleitung." Hogarth, William. *Zergliederung der Schönheit, die schwankenden Begriffe von dem Geschmack festzusetzen.* 2nd ed. Trans. Christlob Mylius. Berlin and Potsdam: Voß, 1754. Print.

————. "Fabeln und Fabelabhandlungen." 1759. *Werke und Briefe* 4: 295–411. Print.

————. "Giangir. Oder der verschmähte Thron" (Versuch eines Trauerspiels). 1748. *Werke und Briefe* 1: 243–7. Print.

————. *Hamburgische Dramaturgie. Werke und Briefe* 6: 182–713.

————. "Des Hrn. Ludewig Riccoboni Geschichte Der Italiänischen Schaubühne." In *Gotth. Ephr. Lessings Theatralische Bibliothek.* Vol. 2. Berlin: Voß, 1754. 135–214. Print.

————. *Laocoön: An Essay on the Limits of Painting and Poetry.* Trans. Edward Allen McCormick. Baltimore: Johns Hopkins University Press, 1984. Print.

————. *Laokoon: oder über die Grenzen der Malerei und Poesie.* 1766. *Werke und Briefe* 5/2: 11–206. Print.

————. "Leben des Herrn Nericault Destouches." 1754. *Werke und Briefe* 3: 312–18. Print.

————. "Leben und Leben Lassen: Ein Projekt für Schriftsteller und Buchhändler." ca. 1774/75. *Werke und Briefe* 10: 233–9. Print.

————. *Die Matrone von Ephesus*. Fragment, ca. 1767. *Werke und Briefe* 6: 147–77. Print.

————. *Miß Sara Sampson*. 1757. *Werke und Briefe* 3: 431–526. Print.

————. *Minna von Barnhelm*. Trans. Kenneth J. Northcott. Chicago: University of Chicago Press, 1972. Print.

————. *Minna von Barnhelm, oder das Soldatenglück*. 1767. *Werke und Briefe* 6: 9–110. Print.

————. *Nathan the Wise*. Trans. Edward Kemp. London: Nick Hern, 2003. Print.

————. *Sämtliche Schriften*. Ed. Karl Lachmann and Franz Muncker. 3rd ed. Vol. 15. 23 vols. Stuttgart: J. G. Göschen, 1900. Print.

————. "Der Schauspieler: Ein Werk worinne die Grundsätze der ganzen körperlichen Beredsamkeit entwickelt werden." 1750–1754. *Werke und Briefe* 3: 320–9. Print.

————. "Die Schauspielkunst (Riccoboni-Übersetzung)." 1750. *Werke und Briefe* 1: 885–935. Print.

————. "Von Johann Dryden und dessen dramatischen Werken." 1759. *Werke und Briefe* 4: 130–79. Print.

————. *Werke und Briefe in zwölf Bänden*. Ed. Wilfried Barner with Klaus Bohnen, et al. 12 vols. Frankfurt am Main: Deutscher Klassiker Verlag, 1985–2003. Print.

————. *Wie die Alten den Tod gebildet*. 1769. *Werke und Briefe* 6: 715–78. Print.

————. *Das Theater des Herrn Diderot*. 1760. *Werke und Briefe* 5/1: 10–230. Print.

Lessing, Gotthold Ephraim, Moses Mendelssohn, and Friedrich Nicolai. *Briefe, die neueste Litteratur betreffend*. 24 issues. Berlin and Stettin: bey Friedrich Nicolai, 1759–1766. Print & Web.

Lessing, Karl. "Brief von Karl Lessing." 22 March 1768. Letter 412. *Werke und Briefe*. 11/1: 509–12. Print.

Litzmann, Berthold. *Friedrich Ludwig Schröder. Ein Beitrag zur deutschen Litteratur- und Theatergeschichte*. Vol. 1. Hamburg and Leipzig: Leopold Voß, 1890. Print.

Lope de Vega. *The New Art of Writing Plays*. Trans. William T. Brewster. New York: Printed for the Dramatic Museum of Columbia University, 1914. Print.

————. "Nouvelle Pratique de Théatre, accommodée à l'usage présent d'Espagne, adressée à l'Académie de Madrid e traduite de l'espagnol de Lopez de Vega." In *Pièces fugitives d'histoire et de littérature anciennes et modernes*. Ed. Anthelme de Tricaud. Part 2. Paris: Chez Jean Cot, 1704. 2: 248–64. Print.

————, and Felipe B. Pedraza Jiménez. *Arte Nuevo de Hazer Comedias. Rimas: 2. Edición crítica de las rimas de Lope de Vega*. Vol. 2. 2 vols. Cuenca: Universidad de Castilla-La Mancha, 1994. 355–93. Print.

Löwen, Johann Friedrich. "Geschichte des deutschen Theaters." In *Johann Friedrich Löwens Schriften*. Vol. 4. Hamburg: Bock, 1766. 3–66. Print.

————. *Die neue Agnese, ein Lustspiel in einem Aufzuge*. Vienna: zu finden beym Logenmeister, n.d. Print.

————. *Das Räthsel, oder Was dem Frauenzimmer am meisten gefällt. Ein Lustspiel, in einem Aufzuge, mit einem Divertissement*. In *Johann Friedrich Löwens Schriften*. Vol. 4. Hamburg: Bock, 1766. 339–67. Print.

————. "Vorläufige Nachricht von der auf Ostern 1767 vorzunehmenden Veränderung des Hamburgischen Theaters." 1766. In Lessing, G. E. *Werke und Briefe* 6: 906–11. Print.

Maffei, Scipione. "Osservazione sopra la Rodoguna (1700)." In *Rime e prose del Sig. marchese Scipione Maffei*. Venice: S. Coleti, 1719. 165–85. Print.

————. "Preface." In *Merope, a Tragedy: By the Marquis Scipio Maffei: Translated from the Original Italian, by Mr. Ayre*. Trans. William Ayre. London: J. Chrichley et al., 1740. Print.

————. "Risposta alla Lettera del Signor di Voltaire." 1745. In *Complete Works of Voltaire (Les Oeuvres complètes de Voltaire)*. 17: 355–87. Print.

————. *Merope, a Tragedy: By the Marquis Scipio Maffei. Translated from the Original Italian, by Mr. Ayre*. Trans. William Ayre. London: J. Chrichley et al., 1740. Print.

Maffei, Scipione and Giulio Cesare Becelli. *Teatro del Sig. marchese Scipione Maffei cioè la tragedia, la comedia e il drama, non più stampato: aggiunta la spiegazione d'alcune antichità pertinenti al teatro.* Verona: Tumermani, 1730. Print.

Marcus Aurelius. *Meditations.* Trans. Gregory Hays. New York: Modern Library, 2002. Print.

Marivaux, Pierre C. C. de. *Der Bauer mit der Erbschaft.* Trans. Johann Christian Krüger. *Sammlung einiger Lustspiele aus dem Französischen des Herrn von Marivaux.* Vol. 1. Hannover: bey Joh. Adolph Gerckens sel. Witwe, 1747. Print.

———. *Le Denouement Imprevu.* In *Le Theatre de Monsieur de Marivaux, de L'academie Française. Nouvelle Édition.* 3: 55–86. Print.

———. *La double inconstance, comedie en trois Actes.* Paris: Chez François Flahault, 1740. Print.

———. *The Double Inconstancy.* Trans. Nicholas Wright. In *Marivaux: Plays.* Introduced by Claude Schumacher. London: Methuen, 1988. 39–106. Print.

———. *L'école des Mères.* In *Le Theatre de Monsieur de Marivaux, de L'academie Française. Nouvelle Édition.* 4: 357–94. Print.

———. *Les Fausses Confidences.* In *Le Theatre de Monsieur de Marivaux, de L'academie Française. Nouvelle Édition.* 4: 79–166. Print.

———. *L'heritier de Village.* In *Le Theatre de Monsieur de Marivaux, de L'academie Française. Nouvelle Édition.* 2: 3–44. Print.

———. *Marivaux: Plays.* Introduced by Claude Schumacher. London: Methuen, 1988. Print.

———. *Le Theatre de Monsieur de Marivaux, de L'academie Française. Nouvelle Édition.* 4 vols. Amsterdam and Leipzig: Chez Arkstee & Merkus, 1754. Print.

———. *Der unvermuthete Ausgang. Ein Lustspiel in einer Handlung.* In *Sammlung einiger Lustspiele aus dem Französischen des Herrn von Marivaux übersetzt.* Trans. Johann Christian Krüger. Vol. 2. Hannover: Johann Christoph Richter, 1749. 464–510. Print.

———, and Timberlake Wertenbaker. *False Admissions.* Woodstock, IL: Dramatic Pub. Co, 1989. Print.

Marmontel, Jean François. *Marmontel's Moral Tales.* Trans. George Saintsbury. London: George Allen, 1895. Print.

———. *Mémoires d'un père pour servir a l'instruction de ses enfants.* In *Oeuvres Posthumes de Marmontel, historiographe de France [. . .].* Vol. 1. Paris, 1805. Print.

———. *Poetique Françoise.* Vol. 2. 2 vols. Paris: Lesclapart, 1763. Print.

———. "Préface." In *Contes moraux et pieces choisies de M. Marmontel.* Vol. 1. Leipzig: Chez S. L. Crusius, 1791. iii–xiv. Print.

———. "Soliman II." In *Contes moraux et pieces choisies de M. Marmontel.* Vol. 1. Leipzig: Chez S. L. Crusius, 1791. 34–56. Print.

Martinec, Thomas. "The Boundaries of 'Mitleidsdramaturgie': Some Clarifications Concerning Lessing's Concept of 'Mitleid'." *Modern Language Review* 101.3 (2006): 743–58. Print.

Martinson, Steven D. "Lessing and the European Enlightenment." In *A Companion to the Works of Gotthold Ephraim Lessing.* Ed. Barbara Fischer and Thomas C. Fox. Rochester, NY: Camden House, 2005. 41–64. Print.

Mason, Haydn T. "Voltaire vs. Shakespeare: The Lettre à L'Académie Française (1776)." *Nineteenth Century Studies* 18.2 (1995). 173–84. Print.

Mason, William. *Caractacus: Written on the Model of the Ancient Greek Tragedy.* 1759. *The Works of William Mason, M. A. in Four Volumes.* Vol. 2. London: T. Cadell and W. Davies, Strand, 1811. 77–174. Print.

———. *Elfrida, a Dramatic Poem: Written on the Model of the Antient Greek Tragedy.* London: J. and P. Knapton, 1752. Print.

———. "Letters: Concerning the Following Drama." In *Elfrida, a Dramatic Poem: Written on the Model of the Antient Greek Tragedy.* London: J. and P. Knapton, 1752. i–xv. Print.

Maurer-Schmoock, Sybille. *Deutsches Theater im 18. Jahrhundert.* Tübingen: Max Niemeyer Verlag, 1982. Print.

Menander. *Menander, the Principal Fragments: With an English Translation by Francis G. Allinson.* Trans. Francis. G Allinson. *Loeb Classical Library.* London: William Heinemann, 1921. Print.

415

———. *Menandri Et Philemonis Reliquiæ, Quotquot Reperiri Potuerunt.* Ed. H. Grotius and Johannes Clericus. Amsterdam: T. Lombrail, 1709. Print.

Mendelssohn, Moses. *Philosophical Writings.* Trans. and Ed. Daniel O. Dahlstrom. Cambridge: Cambridge University Press, 1997. Print.

———. *Philosophische Schriften.* Vol. 1–2. 2 vols. Berlin: Bey Christian Friedrich Voß, 1761. Print.

Meyer, Friedrich Ludwig Wilhelm. *Friedrich Ludwig Schröder.* Vol. 1 and 2. 3 vols. Hamburg: Hoffmann & Campe, 1819. Print.

Milton, John. *Paradise Regain'd: A Poem, in Four Books: To Which Is Added, Samson Agonistes: And Poems upon Several Occasions, with a Tractate of Education.* London: Printed for J. Tonson, 1713. Print.

Mittelstedt, Matthias Theodor Christoph. *Herrn William Robertsons Geschichte von Schottland unter den Regierungen der Königinn Maria, und des Königes Jacobs VI. bis auf dessen Erhebung auf den englischen Thron.* Vol. 2. Braunschweig: in der Meyerischen Buchhandlung, 1762. Print.

Molière. *L'Avare.* Paris: Chez Duchesne, 1784. Print.

———. *The Critique of the School for Wives.* 1663. In *Tartuffe and Other Plays.* Trans. Donald M. Frame. New York: Signet Classic, 1967. 169–201. Print.

———. *Die Frauen-Schule.* In *Des Herrn Moliere Sämmtliche Lustspiele.* Trans. F. S. Bierling. Vol. 2. Hamburg: bey Christian Herold, 1752. Print.

———. *L'Impromptu de Versaille, Comédie en un Acte, avec une notice et des notes.* 1663. Paris: Librairie des Bibliophiles, 1890. Print.

———. *Le malade imaginaire.* Vienna: Chez Jean Pierre van Ghelen, 1753. Print.

———. "Preface to *Tartuffe.*" 1669. Trans. Henri Van Laun. In *The Dramatic Works of Molière, Rendered into English by Henri Van Laun.* Vol. 4. Edinburgh: William Patterson, 1876. 125–30. Print.

———. *The School for Wives.* 1662. In *Tartuffe and Other Plays.* Trans. Donald M. Frame. New York: Signet Classic, 1967. 97–168. Print.

———. *The Versailles Impromptu.* 1663. Trans. Donald M. Frame. *Tartuffe and Other Plays.* New York: Signet Classic, 1967. 203–34. Print.

Montesquieu, Charles de Secondat, Baron de, and Octavien de Guasco. *Familiar Letters.* In *The Complete Works of M. de Montesquieu: Translated from the French: In Four Volumes.* Vol. 4. London: Printed for T. Evans, in the Strand, and W. Davis, in Piccadilly, 1776. Print.

———. *Lettres Familières du Président de Montesquieu. Nouvelle édition, revue, corrigée, et augmentée de plusieurs Lettres.* 1771. Print (n.p.). https://books.google.com/books?id=jgyR5JHwHEMC&dq=Lettres+familieres+Montesquieu+Tournemine&source=gbs_navlinks_s

The Monthly Review. Vol. 20. Review of *Caractacus, a Dramatic Poem: Written on the Model of the Antient* [sic] *Greek Tragedy. By the Author of Elfrida.* London: Printed for R. Griffiths, 1759: 507–12. Print.

The Monthly Review. Vol. 8, Art. 32. Review of Henry Jones's *Earl of Essex.* London: printed for R. Griffiths, 1753. 225–29. Print.

The Monthly Review. Vol. 20. Review of *A Letter from Mr. Rousseau, of Geneva, to Mr. d'Alembert [. . .].* London: Printed for R. Griffiths, 1759: 115–34. Print.

The Monthly Review. Vol. 20. Review of *A Parallel: In the Manner of Plutarch: Between a Most Celebrated Man of Florence: And One, Scarce ever Heard of in England: By the Reverend Mr. Spence.* London: Printed for R. Griffiths, 1759: 217–19. Print.

Montiano y Luyando, Agustín de. *Virginia: Discurso sobre las Tragedias españolas.* Vol. 1. Madrid: Mercurio, 1750. 123–255. Print.

Morley, John, ed. *The Works of Voltaire: A Contemporary Version.* Trans. William F. Fleming. In 21 vols. A Critique and Biography by John Morley, notes by Tobias Smollett. New York: E. R. DuMont, 1901. http://oll.libertyfund.org/titles/783. Print & Web. 26 June 2014.

Möser, Justus. *Harlekin, oder Vertheidigung des Groteske-Komischen.* Bremen: Johann Heinrich Cramer, 1777. Print.

Mouhy, Charles de Fieux, Chevalier de. *Tablettes dramatiques: contenant l'abrégé de l'histoire du théâtre français, l'établissement des théâtres à Paris, un dictionnaire des pièces et l'abrégé de l'histoire des auteurs et des acteurs*. Paris: Sebastien Jorry, 1752. Print.

Mücke, Dorothea von. *Virtue and the Veil of Illusion*. Stanford: Stanford University Press, 1991. Print.

Muncker, Franz. *Bremer Beiträger II*. Berlin: W. Spemann, 1889. Vol. 44 of *Deutsche National-Litteratur*. Ed. Joseph Kürschner. 163 vols. 1882–1893. Print.

Murr, Christoph Gottlieb von. *Denkmal zur Ehre des sel. Herrn Klotz, nebst einigen Briefen*. Frankfurt and Leipzig, 1772. Print.

Nannius, Petrus. *Summiktōn, Sive Miscellaneorum Decas Una*. Lovanii: ex off. Servatii Sasseni, 1548. Print.

Nauck, August. *Tragicorum Graecorum Fragmenta. Recensuit Augustus Nauck*. Lipsiae (Leipzig): B. G. Teubneri, 1856. Print.

Nicolai, Friedrich. "Abhandlung vom Trauerspiele." *Bibliothek der schönen Wissenschaften und der freyen Künste* 1.1 (1757): 17–68. Print.

Niklaus, Robert. "Introduction." In Voltaire, *Complete Works of Voltaire (Les Oeuvres complètes de Voltaire)* 30A: 39–137. Print.

Nisbet, Hugh Barr. *Gotthold Ephraim Lessing: His Life, Works, and Thought*. Oxford: Oxford University Press, 2013. Print.

Nivelle de la Chaussée, Pierre Claude. *L'école des mères: Comédie nouvelle [. . .] en cinq actes et en vers*. Paris: Chez Prault Fils, 1749. Print.

———. *Mélanide: Comédie Nouvelle*. Paris: Chez Prault Fils, 1741. Print.

———. *Melanide, ein Lustspiel in fünf Aufzügen. Aus dem Französischen des Herrn de la Chaussee übersetzt*. In Schönemann, J. F. *Neue Sammlung von Schauspielen*. Vol. 1. Hamburg: n.p., 1754. 1–72. Print. Rpt. in *German and Austrian Drama*. Ed. Rita B. Belasco and James E. Walsh. Woodbridge, CT: Research Publications, 1984. Reel: 50, No. 1964. Microform.

———. *Pamela*. In *Oeuvres de Monsieur Nivelle de la Chaussée, de l'Académie Françoise. Nouvelle Édition [. . .]*. Vol. 4. Paris: Chez Prault Fils, 1742. 1–90. Print.

Olson, S. Douglas. *Broken Laughter: Select Fragments of Greek Comedy*. Oxford: Oxford University Press, 2007. Print.

Palissot de Montenoy, Charles. *Petites Lettres sur de grands Philosophes*. Paris, 1757. Print.

Parfaict, François, and Claude Parfaict. *Histoire du théâtre français*. 15 vols. Paris: Le Mercier et Saillant, 1749. Print.

Paulin, Roger. "Shakespeare and Germany." In *Shakespeare in the Eighteenth Century*. Ed. Fiona Ritchie and Peter Sabor. Cambridge: Cambridge University Press, 2012. Print.

Pausanius. *Description of Greece, with an English Translation by W.H.S. Jones, Litt.D., and H.A. Ormerod, M.A., in 4 Volumes*. Cambridge, MA: Harvard University Press, 1918. Perseus Digital Library. www.perseus.tufts.edu/hopper/text?doc=urn:cts:greekLit:tlg0525.tlg001. perseus-eng1:4.3. Print & Web. 2 January 2014.

Pergolesi, Giambattista, and Gennaro Antonio Federico. *La Serva Padrona: Intermezzi*. Milan: Ricordi, 1973. Print.

Petronius Arbiter. *The Satyricon of Petronius Arbiter/ Complete and unexpurgated translation by W.C. Firebaugh, in which are incorporated the forgeries of Nodot and Marchena, and the readings introduced into the text by De Salas: illustrations by Norman Lindsay*. 2 vols. New York: Boni & Liveright, 1922. Print & Web.

Pieri, Marzia. "Translating for the Audience: Plautus's *Captivi* by Accademici Intronati (Siena 1530) and Goldoni's Adaptation of Voltaire's *L'Écossaise* (Venezia 1761)." In *Theatre Translation in Performance*. Ed. Silvia Bigliazzi, Peter Kofler, and Paola Ambrosi. New York: Routledge, 2013. 165–79. Print.

Pindar, and Richmond A. Lattimore. *The Odes of Pindar*. Trans. Richmond A. Lattimore. Chicago: University of Chicago Press, 1942. Print.

Pfeffel, Gottlieb Konrad. *Der Einsiedler, ein Trauerspiel in Versen von einem Aufzuge*. 1761. 3rd ed. Carlsruhe: Macklot, 1771. Print.

————. *Der Schatz, ein Schäferspiel von einem Aufzuge.* Frankfurt am Main: bey Johann Gottlieb Garbe, 1761. Print.

Plato. *Laws.* Trans. R. G. Bury. *Plato in Twelve Volumes.* 1926. Vol. 10 and 11. *The Loeb Classical Library.* Cambridge, MA: Harvard University Press, 1967 and 1968. Perseus Digital Library. www.perseus.tufts.edu/hopper/text?doc=urn:cts:greekLit:tlg0059.tlg034.perseus-eng1. Print & Web. 11 July 2014.

————. *Leges.* [Greek]. In *Platonis Opera.* Ed. John Burnet. Vol. 5. Oxford: Oxford University Press, 1903. 624–969. Perseus Digital Library. http://data.perseus.org/texts/urn:cts:greekLit:tlg0059.tlg034. Print & Web. 11 July 2014.

————. *The Republic.* Trans. R. E. Allen. New Haven: Yale University Press, 2006. Print.

Plautus, Titus Maccius. *Amphitryon: Or, Jupiter in Disguise.* Trans. Henry Thomas Riley. In *The Comedies of Plautus.* Vol. 2. 2 vols. London: G. Bell and Sons, 1913. 1–62. Perseus Digital Library. www.perseus.tufts.edu/hopper/text?doc=Perseus%3Atext%3A1999.02.0092%3Aact%3Dintro%3Ascene%3D1. Print & Web. 4 March 2014.

————. "Introduction to *Amphitryon: Or, Jupiter in Disguise.*" Trans. Henry Thomas Riley. In *The Comedies of Plautus.* Vol. 2. London: G. Bell and Sons, 1912. 2–8. Perseus Digital Library. https://books.google.com/books?id=1egIAAAAQAAJ&printsec=frontcover&dq=editions:hLs4zlSbPjEC&hl=en&sa=X&ved=0ahUKEwjE7aCigrbRAhXHKMAKHROyAxgQ6AEIJDAC#v=onepage&q&f=false. Print & Web. 9 January 2017.

————. *Miles Gloriosus: Or, the Braggart Captain.* Trans. Henry Thomas Riley. In *The Comedies of Plautus.* Ed. Henry Thomas Riley. Vol. 1. 2 vols. London: G. Bell and Sons, 1912. 67–144. Perseus Digital Library. www.perseus.tufts.edu/hopper/text?doc=Perseus%3Atext%3A1999.02.0103%3Aact%3D2%3Ascene%3D1. Print & Web. 13 February 2015.

————. *Truculentus: Or, the Churl.* Trans. Henry Thomas Riley. In *The Comedies of Plautus.* Vol. 2. 2 vols. London: G. Bell and Sons, 1913. 209–54. Perseus Digital Library. www.perseus.tufts.edu/hopper/text?doc=Perseus:text:1999.02.0111. Print & Web. 13 February 2015.

Pliny (the Elder). "Bronze Statuary (Book 34)." Trans. K. Jex-Blake. In *The Elder Pliny's Chapters on the History of Art.* London: Macmillan and Co., Ltd., 1896. 6–81. Print.

Plutarch. "De capienda ex inimicis utilitate." Trans. Frank Cole Babbitt. In *Moralia.* Ed. Frank Cole Babbitt. Vol. 2. Cambridge, MA: Harvard University Press, 1928. 6–40. Perseus Digital Library. www.perseus.tufts.edu/hopper/text?doc=Perseus:text:2008.01.0157:section=7&highlight=merope. Print & Web. 4 January 2018.

————. *Comparationis Aristophanis Et Menandri Compendium [Summary of a Comparison between Aristophanes and Menander].* Trans. Harold North Fowler. *Plutarch's Moralia.* Vol. 10. Cambridge, MA: Harvard University Press, 1936. Perseus Digital Library. www.perseus.tufts.edu/hopper/text?doc=urn:cts:greekLit:tlg0007.tlg122.perseus-eng1:intro. Print & Web. 18 March 2017.

————. "On the Eating of Flesh (De esu carnium) II." Trans. Harold Cherniss and William C. Helmbold. In *Moralia.* Vol. 12. Cambridge, MA: Harvard University Press, 1957. 563–79. Perseus Digital Library. www.perseus.tufts.edu/hopper/text?doc=Perseus%3Atext%3A2008.01.0381%3Asection%3D1. Print & Web. 3 January 2014.

————. *Plutarch Lives: I, Theseus and Romulus, Lycurgus and Numa, Solon and Publicola.* Trans. Bernadotte Perrin. Vol. 1. Cambridge, MA: Harvard University Press, 1914. Perseus Digital Library. www.perseus.tufts.edu/hopper/text?doc=Perseus%3Atext%3a2008.01.0063. Print & Web. 1 September 2016.

————. *Plutarchi Chaeronensis quae extant opera: Cum Latina interpretatione: Ex vetustis codicibus plurima nunc primum emendata sunt, ut ex Henrici Stephani Annotationibus intelliges, quibus & suam quorundam libellorum interpretationem adiunxit. Variorum Plutarchi scriptorum tomus tertius.* Geneva: Stephanus, 1572. Print.

Polybius, and Fridericus (Friedrich Otto) Hultsch. *The Histories of Polybius.* Trans. Evelyn Shuckburgh. Vol. 2. 2 vols. London and New York: Macmillan and Co., Ltd., 1889. Print.

Pope, Alexander. "The Essay on Man." 1733–1734. In *The Works of Alexander Pope, Esq.: Volume 3. Containing His Moral Essays.* Vol. 3. London: A. Millar, and J. and R. Tonson, 1757. 1–167. Print.

————. "Preface to Edition of Shakespeare." 1725. In *Eighteenth Century Essays on Shakespeare*. Ed. David Nichol Smith. Glasgow: James MacLehose & Sons, 1903. 106–21. Print.

————, and William Warburton. *The Works of Alexander Pope, Esq.: Volume 4, Containing His Satires, &c*. Vol. 4. 9 vols. London: A. Millar, 1757. Print.

Poullain de Saint-Foix, Germain François. *L'Oracle, comédie [etc.]*. Paris, 1740. Print.

————. *The Oracle: A Comedy of One Act: As It Is Acted at the Theatre-Royal in Covent-Garden*. Trans. S. Cibber. London: R. and J. Dodsley, 1763. Print.

Propertius. *Elegies*. Ed. Lucian Mueller. Leipzig: Teubner, 1898. Perseus Digital Library. www. perseus.tufts.edu/hopper/text?doc=Perseus%3Atext%3A2008.01.0494%3Abook%3D2%3 Apoem%3D34b. Print & Web. 20 November 2016.

————. "Sextus Propertius, The Elegies: A New Translation." Trans. A. S. Kline. In *Poetry in Translation*. A. S. Kline, 2000–2018. Web. 20 November 2016. www.poetryintranslation. com/PITBR/Latin/Prophome.htm.

Quinault, Philippe. *Die bulhafftige Mutter. Schau-Bühne Englischer und Frantzösischer Comödianten [. . .]*. Ed. Christian Schad and Ottmar Lautenschlager. Frankfurt: Schiele, 1670. 431–536. Print.

————. *La Mère Coquette: Ou, Les amans brouillés, comédie en cinq actes et en vers*. Paris: Chez P. Fr. Guiffier, 1769. Print.

Quintilian (Marcus Fabius Quintilianus). *Institutes of Oratory*. Trans. John Selby Watson. London: George Bell and Sons, 1891. Print.

Rapin de Thoyras, Paul, Jean Leclerc, and Thomas Rymer. *Histoire d'Angleterre [. . .] Nouvelle édition augmentée des notes de M. Tindal [. . .]*. Vol. 7. 16 vols. La Haye: s.n, 1749.

Raynal, Abbé (Guillaume-Thomas-François). *Anecdotes littéraires: ou, Histoire de ce que est arrivé le plus singulier & de plus intéressant aux écrivains françois, depuis le renouvellement des lettres sous François I, jusqu' à nos jours*. Vol. 2. 2 vols. Paris: Durand, 1750. Print.

Reemtsma, Jan Philipp. *Lessing in Hamburg*. Munich: Beck, 2007. Print.

Regnard, Jean-François. *The Absent-Minded Lover*. In Regnard, et al., *The Heirs of Molière*. 9–86. Print.

————. *Le Distrait: Comédie en cinq actes, en vers*. Paris: Michel Lévy frères, 1874. Print.

————. *Der Spieler, ein Lustspiel des Herrn Regnard*. Trans. Johann Christian Krüger. In *Sechs Schauspiele aus dem Französischen übersetzt*. Ed. Johann Friedrich Schönemann. Braunschweig und Hamburg, 1748. 270–381. Print.

Regnard, Jean-François, Philippe Néricault Destouches, Pierre Nivelle de la Chaussée, and Jean-Louis Laya. *The Heirs of Molière: Four French Comedies of the 17th and 18th Centuries*. Trans. and Ed. Marvin Carlson. New York: Martin E. Segal Theatre Center, 2003. Print.

————, and John Dunkley. *Le Joueur*. Geneva: Droz, 1986. Print.

Reinesius, Thomas. *Variarum Lectionum Libri III [. . .]*. Altenburg: Otto Michael, 1640. Print.

Riccoboni, François (Francesco). *L'art du Théâtre: Suivi d'une Lettre de M. Riccoboni Fils à M*** au Sujet de L'art du Théâtre*. Geneva: Slatkine Reprints, 1971. Print.

Riccoboni, Luigi (Louis). *Histoire du Théâtre Italien: depuis la Decadence de la Comedie Latine [. . .]*. Paris: A. Cailleau, 1730. Print.

————. *An Historical and Critical Account of the Theatres in Europe*. T. Waller, London, 1741. Print.

————. *Reflexions historiques et critiques sur les differens theatres de l'Europe: avec les Pensées sur la déclamation*. Amsterdam: Aux depens de la Compagnie, 1740. Print.

Roach, Joseph R. *The Player's Passion: Studies in the Science of Acting*. Ann Arbor: University of Michigan Press, 1993. Print.

Robertson, John George. *Lessing's Dramatic Theory*. New York: Benjamin Blom, 1936. Cambridge University Press, 1965. Print.

Robertson, William. *The History of Scotland During the Reigns of Queen Mary and of King James VI [. . .] in Two Volumes*. 4th ed. Vol. 2. 2 vols. London: A. Millar, 1761. Print.

Romanus, Karl Franz. *Die Brüder, oder die Schule der Väter. Ein Lustspiel in fünf Aufzügen*. Vienna: J. P. Krauß, 1763. Print.

Rousseau, Jean-Jacques. *Julie, Ou, La Nouvelle Héloïse*. Ed. Henri Coulet. Paris: Gallimard, 1993. Print.

———. *Lettre à d'Alembert Sur Les Spectacles (1758). Oeuvres Complètes de J. J. Rousseau.* Vol. 16. *Sciences, Arts, et Belles-Lettres.* Vol. 2. Paris: Poinçot, 1791. Print.

———. *Politics and the Arts: Letter to M. d'Alembert on the Theatre.* Trans. Allan Bloom. Glencoe, IL: The Free Press, 1960. Print.

Rousseau, Jean-Jacques, Philip Stewart, and Jean Vaché. *Julie, Or, the New Heloise: Letters of Two Lovers Who Live in a Small Town at the Foot of the Alps.* Hanover: Dartmouth College, 1997. Print.

Rousseau, Pierre, ed. *Journal encyclopédique ou universal.* 76 vols. Bouillon etc: de l'Imprimerie du journal, 1760–1793. Geneva: Slatkine Reprints, 1967. Print.

Rowe, Nicholas. "Some Account of the Life, etc. of Mr. William Shakespear." 1709. In *Eighteenth Century Essays on Shakespeare.* Ed. David Nichol Smith. Glasgow: James MacLehose & Sons, 1903. 59–82. Print.

Sainte-Albine, Pierre Rémond de. *Le Comédien: Ouvrage Divisé en deux Parties.* Paris: Desaint & Saillant, 1747. Print.

Saint-Évremond, Charles de Marguetel de Saint-Denis. *Oeuvres en prose.* Ed. R. Ternois. 4 vols. Paris: M. Didier, 1962–1969. Print.

Scarron, Paul. "La Précaution Inutile." In *Les Nouvelles Tragi-comiques de M. Scarron.* Paris: Chez Iean Ribou, 1666. 1–92. Print.

———. "The Useless Precaution." Trans. Thomas Brown, Mr. Savage and others. In *The Whole Comical Works of Mons. Scarron.* Vol. 2. London: J. & J. Knapton, et al., 1727. 29–82. Print.

Scheibe, Johann Adolph. *Critischer Musicus.* Article 67. Leipzig: Breitkopf, 1745. 611–18. Print.

Schenk, Christian Ernst. *Komisches Theater von S***: Erster Theil.* Vol. 1. Breslau: bey Carl Gottfried Meyer, 1759. Print.

Schiller, Friedrich von. "Die Schaubühne als eine Moralische Anstalt Betrachtet." (1784). In *Sämtliche Werke.* Vol. 2. Stuttgart and Tübingen: J. G. Cotta, 1812. 392–408. Print.

Schiller, Friedrich. "The Stage as a Moral Institution." In *Essays Aesthetical and Philosophical.* Vol. 8. Boston: S. E. Cassino, 1884. 339–45. Print.

Schlegel, Johann Elias. *Canut: Ein Trauerspiel in Versen, und fünf Aufzügen.* Vienna: Krauß, 1770. Print.

———. "Demokrit. Ein Todtengespräch." 1741. In *Johann Elias Schlegels Werke.* 3: 177–202. Print.

———. "Gedanken zur Aufnahme des dänischen Theaters." 1747. In *Johann Elias Schlegels Werke.* 3: 259–98. Print.

———. *Der Geheimnißvolle, ein Lustspiel in fünf Aufzügen.* 1746. In *Johann Elias Schlegels Werke.* 2: 183–322. Print.

———. *Der geschäfftige Müßiggänger, ein Lustspiel in fünf Aufzügen.* 1741. In *Johann Elias Schlegels Werke.* 2: 45–182. Print.

———. *Johann Elias Schlegels Werke.* Ed. Johann Heinrich Schlegel. 5 vols. Copenhagen and Leipzig: im Verlag der Mummischen Buchhandlung, 1761–1770. Frankfurt-Am-Main: Athenaeum, 1971. Print.

———. "Schreiben über die Komödie in Versen." In *Johann Elias Schlegels Werke.* 3: 65–95. Print.

———. "Schreiben von Errichtung eines Theaters in Kopenhagen." In *Johann Elias Schlegels Werke.* 3: 251–58. Print.

———. *Die stumme Schönheit, ein Lustspiel in einem Aufzuge.* In *Johann Elias Schlegels Werke.* 2: 469–520. Print.

———. *Der Triumph der guten Frauen, ein Lustspiel in fünf Aufzügen.* In *Johann Elias Schlegels Werke.* 2: 323–448. Print.

Schlegel, Johann Elias, and Andrè Lefevere. *The Dumb Beauty.* In *German Theater before 1750.* Ed. Gerald Gillespie. New York: Continuum, 1992. 215–44. Print.

Schmid, Christian Heinrich. *Chronologie des deutschen Theaters.* Leipzig: 1775. Print.

———. *Theorie der Poesie nach den neuesten Grundsätzen und Nachricht von den besten Dichtern nach den angenommenen Urtheilen.* Leipzig: Siegfried Lebrecht Crusius, 1767. Print.

———. *Zusätze zur Theorie der Poesie und Nachrichten von den besten Dichtern: 1. Sammlung.* Vol. 1. 4 vols. Leipzig: Siegfried Lebrecht Crusius, 1767. Print.

————. *Zusätze zur Theorie der Poesie und Nachrichten von den besten Dichtern: 3. Sammlung.* Vol. 3. 4 vols. Leipzig: Siegfried Lebrecht Crusius, 1769. Print.

Schmiedel, Donald Emerson. "'El Conde de Sex' by Antonio Cello: A Critical Edition and Study." Ph.D. Dissertation. University of Southern California, 1967. Print.

Schulze-Kummerfeld, Karoline. *Lebenserinnerungen der Komödiantin Karoline Schulze-Kummerfeld.* Ed. Emil Benezé. 2 vols. Berlin: Selbstverlag der Gesellschaft für Theatergeschichte, 1915. Print.

Schwickert, Engelbert Benjamin. "Intermezzo." 1769. In Lessing, G. E. *Werke und Briefe in zwölf Bänden.* 6: 927–9. Print.

Selwyn, Pamela E. *Everyday Life in the German Book Trade.* University Park, PA: Pennsylvania State University Press, 2000. Print.

Showalter, English. *Madame de Graffigny and Rousseau: Between the two discours.* Oxford: Voltaire Foundation, 1978. Print.

Spence, Joseph. *A Parallel: In the Manner of Plutarch: Between a Most Celebrated Man of Florence: And One, Scarce Ever Heard of in England: By the Reverend Mr. Spence.* London: William Robinson, 1758. Print.

Sterne, Laurence. *The Life and Opinions of Tristram Shandy, Gentleman.* Vol. 2. 2 vols. Basil: Legrand, 1792. Print.

Storey, Ian C. *Fragments of Old Comedy, Volume 1: Alcaeus to Diocles.* Ed. and Trans. Ian C. Storey. Cambridge, MA: Harvard University Press, 2011. Print.

Straparola, Giovanni Francesco. *The Nights of Straparola.* 1550/1553. Trans. W. G. Waters. 2 vols. London: Lawrence and Bullen, 1894. Print.

————, and Giuseppe Rua. *Le Piacevoli Notti di M. Giovanfrancesco Straparola, da Caravaggio: Nelle Quali Si Contengono le Favole con i loro Enimmi da Dieci Donne e Duo Giovani Raccontate.* 2 Vols. Bologna: Romagnoli-dall'Acqua, 1899. Print.

Tasso, Torquato, and Luigi Bonfigli. *Gerusalemme Liberata.* Bari: Laterza, 1930. Print.

————, Edward Fairfax, and Henry Morley. *Jerusalem Delivered.* Lexington, Kentucky: Forgotten Books, 2010. Print.

Terence. *Adelphi/The Brothers.* Trans. and Ed. John Barsby. In *Terence.* 2: 243–367. Print.

————. *Andria/Woman of Andros.* Trans. and Ed. John Barsby. In *Terence.* 1: 41–170. Print.

————. *Heauton Timorumenos/The Self-Tormentor.* Trans. and Ed. John Barsby. In *Terence.* 1: 176–303. Print.

————. *Terence.* Trans. and Ed. John Barsby. 2 vols. *The Loeb Classical Library.* Cambridge, MA: Harvard University Press, 2001. Print.

————, and George Colman (the Elder). *The Comedies of Terence, Translated into Familiar Blank Verse.* London: T. Becket et al., 1765. Print.

————, and Anne Le Fèvre Dacier. "Publii Adelphi Terentii/ Les Adelphes de Terence." In *Les Comedies de Terence, traduite en françois par Madame D***; avec des remarques.* Vol. 2. Amsterdam: Chez J. Ollier, 1691. 251–445. Print.

————, and Aelius Donatus, Eugraphius, and Friedrich Lindenbrog. *Publii Terentii, Carthaginensis Afri, Comoediae N. VI.* Frankfurt: in Bibliopolio Heringiano, 1623. Print.

————, and Samuel Patrick. *Terence's Comedies, translated into English Prose [. . .] Revised and Corrected by S. Patrick.* 1745. Trans. Samuel Patrick. 3 ed. Vol. 2. 2 vols. London: J. Oswald, 1767. Print.

————, and Johann Samuel Patzke. *Die Brüder.* Trans. Johann Samuel Patzke. In *Des Publius Terenzius Lustspiele aus dem lateinischen übersetzt, und Theils mit den wichtigsten Anmerkungen der Frau Dacier, theils auch mit eignen Anmerkungen begleitet von Johann Samuel Patzke.* Halle: Carl Hermann Hemmerde, 1753. 366–462. Print.

Terentianus Maurus. "De syllabis." In *De litteris, syllabis, pedibus, et metris.* Ed. Laurentius Santenius. London: H. Bohn, 1825. 14–59. Print.

Tournemine, R[ené] J[oseph de]. "A Letter from the Jesuit Tournemine to Father Brumoy, on the Tragedy of Merope." 1738. Trans. Thomas Francklin. In *The Dramatic Works of Mr. de Voltaire.* Vol. 3. Salisbury, UK: Newbery et al., 1762. 239–43. Print.

———. "Lettre du Père de Tournemine, Jésuite, au Père Brumoy, sur la tragédie de *Mérope*." In Voltaire, *Complete Works of Voltaire (Les Oeuvres complètes de Voltaire)*. 17: 213–15. Print.

Trublet, Nicolas Charles Joseph. *Essais sur divers sujets de litterature et de la morale*. 4 vols. Paris, 1762. Geneva: Slatkine Reprints, 1968. Print.

[Trudaine de Montigny, Jean-Charles-Philibert]. "*Miss Sara Sampson*, Tragèdie bourgeoise de M. Lessing." In *Journal Étranger*. 1761. Vol. 7. Geneva: Slatkine Reprints, 1968. 666–75. Print.

Valentin, Jean-Marie. *Les Jésuites et le théâtre (1554–1680): contribution à l'histoire culturelle du monde catholique dans le Saint-Empire romain germanique*. Paris: Desjonquères, 2001. Print.

Victorius (Pietro Vittori), and Aristotle. *Commentarii in Primum Librum Aristotelis De Arte Poetarum*. Florence: In officina Iuntarum, Bernardi Filiorum, 1560. Print.

Villars, Nicolas P. H. M. *Comte De Gabalis*. Paterson, NJ: The Brothers, 1914. Print.

Virgil, and Robert Fitzgerald. *The Aeneid*. New York: Random House, 1983. Print.

———. "Georgics 4." In *Bucolics, Aeneid, and Georgics of Vergil*. Ed. J. B. Greenough. Boston: Ginn & Co, 1900. Perseus Digital Library. www.perseus.tufts.edu/hopper/text?doc=Perseus%3Atext%3A1999.02.0058%3Abook%3D4%3Acard%3D494. Print & Web. 15 January 2014.

Voltaire (François-Marie Arouet). "The Answer of Mr. de Voltaire to Mr. de la Lindelle." Trans. Thomas Francklin. In *The Dramatic Works of Mr. de Voltaire*. 1762. 3: 274–6. Print.

———. *Appel à toutes les nations de l'Europe, des jugements d'un écrivain anglais; ou manifeste au sujet des honneurs du pavillon entre les théâtres de Londres et de Paris*. 1761. In *Complete Works of Voltaire (Les Oeuvres complètes de Voltaire)*. 51B: 55–100. Print.

———. "Avertissement." *Zaïre*. 1732. In *Complete Works of Voltaire (Les Oeuvres complètes de Voltaire)*. 8: 391. Print.

———. *Le Caffé, Ou L'Écossaise: Comédie, Par Mons. Hume, Traduite En Français*. 1760. In *Complete Works of Voltaire (Les Oeuvres complètes de Voltaire)*. 50: 361–468. Print.

———. *Ce qui plaît aux dames*. 1764. In *Complete Works of Voltaire (Les Oeuvres complètes de Voltaire)*. 57B: 21–62. Print.

———. "Le Cid." *Commentaires sur Corneille (II)*. 1764. In *Complete Works of Voltaire (Les Oeuvres complètes de Voltaire)*. 54: 38–108. Print.

———. *The Coffee-House: Or, The Scotch Woman*. Trans. Thomas Francklin. In *The Dramatic Works of Mr. de Voltaire*. 1762. 7: 121–225. Print.

———. *Commentaires sur Corneille (I)*. 1764. In *Complete Works of Voltaire (Les Oeuvres complètes de Voltaire)*. 53. Print.

———. *Commentaires sur Corneille (II)*. 1764. In *Complete Works of Voltaire (Les Oeuvres complètes de Voltaire)*. 54. Print.

———. *The Complete Works of Voltaire (Les Oeuvres complètes de Voltaire)*. Ed. Nicholas Cronk, et al. 143 vols. Oxford: Voltaire Foundation, 1968–2013. Print.

———. "*Le Comte d'Essex*, Tragédie de Thomas Corneille, 1678. Préface de l'Éditeur." *Commentaires sur Corneille*. Vol. 3. *Andromède-Le Comte d'Essex*. 1761. In *Complete Works of Voltaire (Les Oeuvres complètes de Voltaire)*. 55: 1001–27.

———. "A Discourse on Tragedy." Trans. William F. Fleming. In *The Works of Voltaire: A Contemporary Version*. Ed. John Morley. 19: 174–92. http://oll.libertyfund.org/titles/666#lf0060-19p2_head_033. Print & Web. 17 October 2017.

———. *Discours sur la tragédie*. In *Complete Works of Voltaire (Les Oeuvres complètes de Voltaire)*. 5: 156–83. Print.

———. "Dissertation on Ancient and Modern Tragedy." 1748. Trans. Thomas Francklin. In *The Dramatic Works of Mr. de Voltaire*. 1761. 2: 3–38. Print.

———. "Dissertation sur la tragédie ancienne et moderne." In *Complete Works of Voltaire (Les Oeuvres complètes de Voltaire)*. 30A: 139–64. Print.

———. *The Dramatic Works of Mr. de Voltaire*. 7 vols. Trans. Thomas Francklin. London: Newbery et al., 1761–65. Print.

———. *L'Enfant prodigue*. 1738. In *Complete Works of Voltaire (Les Oeuvres complètes de Voltaire)*. 16: 98–234. Print.

————. "An Epistle Dedicatory to Mr. Falkener [sic], an English Merchant, Since Ambassador at Constantinople, with the *Tragedy of Zaïre*." Trans. William F. Fleming. In *The Works of Voltaire. A Contemporary Version*. Ed. John Morley. 10: 16. <http://oll.libertyfund.org/titles/2240>. Print & Web. 26 June 2014.

————. "Épître Dédicatoire à Mademoiselle Gossin [sic], Jeune Actrice." In *Complete Works of Voltaire (Les Oeuvres complètes de Voltaire)*. 8: 406–7. Print.

————. "Épître Dédicatoire à M. Fakener [sic]." In *Complete Works of Voltaire (Les Oeuvres complètes de Voltaire)*. 8: 392–504. Print.

————. *Essai sur les mœurs et l'esprit des nations*. 1756. In *Complete Works of Voltaire (Les Oeuvres complètes de Voltaire)*. Vols. 21–27. Print.

————. *La femme qui a raison*. 1758. In *Complete Works of Voltaire (Les Oeuvres complètes de Voltaire)*. 30A: 295–367. Print.

————. *Gertrude, ou l'éducation d'une fille*. In *Œuvres complètes de Voltaire*. Ed. Louis Moland. Vol. 10. Paris: Garnier Fréres, 1877–1885. 26–9. Print.

————. *L'Ingénu*. 1767. In *Complete Works of Voltaire (Les Oeuvres complètes de Voltaire)*. 63C: 187–328. Print.

————. *The Ingenu*. Trans. Roger Pearson. *Candide and Other Stories*. Oxford: Oxford University Press, 2006. 190–253. Print.

————. "A Letter from Mr. de la Lindelle to Mr. de Voltaire." Trans. Thomas Francklin. In *The Dramatic Works of Mr. de Voltaire*. 1762. 3: 266–73. Print.

————. "A Letter to the Marquis Scipio Maffei, Author of the Italian MEROPE and Many other Celebrated Performances." Trans. Thomas Francklin. In *The Dramatic Works of Mr. de Voltaire*. 1762. 3: 244–65. Print.

————. "Lettre á M. Berger, 24 Octobre 1736." In *Complete Works of Voltaire (Les Oeuvres complètes de Voltaire)*. 88: 95–6. Print.

————. "Lettre à Monsieur le Marquis Scipion Maffei, auteur de la Mérope Italienne, et de beaucoup d'autres ouvrages célèbres." 1744. In *Complete Works of Voltaire (Les Oeuvres complètes de Voltaire)*. 17: 216–33. Print.

————. "Lettre de M. de La Lindelle à M. de Voltaire." 1748. In *Complete Works of Voltaire (Les Oeuvres complètes de Voltaire)*. 17: 234–41. Print.

————. *Mérope*. 1744. In *Complete Works of Voltaire (Les Oeuvres complètes de Voltaire)*. 17: 211–387. Print.

————. *Merope*. Trans. Thomas Francklin. In *The Dramatic Works of Mr. de Voltaire*. 1762. 4: 2–90. Print.

————. *Nanine*. 1749. In *Complete Works of Voltaire (Les Oeuvres complètes de Voltaire)*. 31B: 74–179. Print.

————. "Préface." *Nanine*. 1749. In *Complete Works of Voltaire (Les Oeuvres complètes de Voltaire)*. 31B: 63–73. Print.

————. "Préface de l'éditeur." *L'Enfant prodigue*. 1738. In *Complete Works of Voltaire (Les Oeuvres complètes de Voltaire)*. 16: 93–97. Print.

————. "Preface to the Comedy of Nanine." In *Critical Essays on Dramatic Poetry, with Notes by the Translator*. London: Printed for L. Davis and C. Reymers, 1761. 234–41. Print.

————. "Réponse de M. de Voltaire à M. de La Lindelle." 1748. In *Complete Works of Voltaire (Les Oeuvres complètes de Voltaire)*. 17: 242–3. Print.

————. "A Second Letter to Mr. Falkener [sic]." Trans. William F. Fleming. In *The Works of Voltaire: A Contemporary Version* 10: 16. http://oll.libertyfund.org/titles/2240. Print & Web. 26 June 2014.

————. "Seconde Lettre au même monsieur Fakener [sic]." In *Complete Works of Voltaire (Les Oeuvres complètes de Voltaire)*. 8: 408–18. Print.

————. *Sémiramis*. 1748. In *Complete Works of Voltaire (Les Oeuvres complètes de Voltaire)*. 30A: 167–254. Print.

————. *Semiramis*. Trans. Thomas Francklin. In *The Dramatic Works of Mr. de Voltaire*. 1761. 2: 40–140. Print.

————. *Semiramis, ein Trauerspiel in Versen und fünf Aufzügen, vom Herrn Sekretär Löwen, aus den Werken des Herrn von Voltaire übersetzt [. . .].* 1755. Trans. Johann Friedrich Löwen. Vienna: zu finden in Kraußischen Buchladen, 1764. Print.

————. *La Vie de Molière: avec de petits sommaires de ses pièces.* 1739. In *Complete Works of Voltaire (Les Oeuvres complètes de Voltaire).* 9: 323–463. Print.

————. "What Pleases the Ladies." Trans. Roger Pearson. In *Candide and Other Stories.* 1763/4? Oxford: Oxford University Press, 2006. 178–89. Print.

————. *Zaïre.* 1732. In *Complete Works of Voltaire (Les Oeuvres complètes de Voltaire).* 8: 430–523. Print.

————. *Zayre. Ein Lustspiel, des Herrn von Voltaire, aus dem Französischen übersetzt.* Trans. Joh. Joach. Schwabe. In *Die Deutsche Schaubühne.* Ed. J. C. Gottsched. 2: 359–426. Print.

————, and Johann J. C. Bode. *Das Caffeehaus, der die Schottländerinn.* Vienna, 1765. Print.

Vrooman, Jack R., and Janet Godden. "Introduction to *Mérope*." In *Complete Works of Voltaire (Les Oeuvres complètes de Voltaire).* 17: 91–210. Print.

Walpole, Horace. *The Castle of Otranto.* 1764. New York: Dover Books, 2004. Print.

Weisse, Christian Felix. *Amalia.* In *Lustspiele von C. F. Weiße.* Vol. 2. Leipzig: Dykische Buchhandlung, 1783. 3–126. Print.

————. *Richard der Dritte, ein Trauerspiel in fünf Aufzügen.* In *Quellenschriften zur Hamburgischen Dramaturgie.* Ed. Daniel Jacoby and August Sauer. Berlin: B. Behr's Verlag, 1904. Print.

————, and Karl Schüddekopf. *Briefe Von Ch. F. Weiße an K. W. Ramler.* Braunschweig, 1886–1888. Print.

Wellbery, David E. *Lessing's Laocoön: Semiotics and Aesthetics in the Age of Reason.* Cambridge: Cambridge University Press, 1984. Print.

Wieland, Christoph Martin. *Geschichte des Agathon.* Vol. 2. 2 vols. Frankfurt and Leipzig, 1767. Print.

————. *The History of Agathon, by Mr. C.M. Wieland: Translated from the German original, with a preface by the translator.* Vol. 4. 4 Vols. London: printed for T. Cadell, 1773. Print.

Williams, David. "Introduction to *Appel à toutes les nations de l'Europe*." In Voltaire, *The Complete Works of Voltaire (Les Oeuvres complètes de Voltaire).* 51B: 19–54. Print.

————. "Prelude to the First Edition." *Commentaires sur Corneille (I).* In Voltaire, *The Complete Works of Voltaire (Les Oeuvres complètes de Voltaire).* 53: 27–88. Print.

Wolff, Larry. *The Singing Turk: Ottoman Power and Operatic Emotions on the European Stage from the Siege of Vienna to the Age of Napoleon.* Stanford: Stanford University Press, 2016. Print.

Wykes, David. "The Barbinade and the She-Tragedy: On John Banks's *The Unhappy Favourite*." In *Augustan Studies: Essays in Honor of Irvin Ehrenpreis.* Ed. Douglas Lane Patey and Timothy Keegan. Newark: University of Delaware Press, 1985. 79–94. Print.

Yermolenko, Galina. "The Greatest Empresse of the East." *The Muslim World* 95 (2005): 231–48. Print.

————. *Roxolana in European Literature, History, and Culture.* Burlington, VT: Ashgate, 2010. Print.

Young, Edward. *Conjectures on Original Composition.* London: A. Millar and R. and J. Dodsley, 1759. Print.

————. *The Poetical Works of Edward Young.* Vol. 2. London: William Pickering, 1852. Print.

Zimmern, Helen, trans. "Dramatic Notes." In *Selected Prose Works of G. E. Lessing.* Ed. Edward Bell. London: George Bell and Sons, 1889. 227–493. Print.

————. *The Dramatic Works of G. E. Lessing.* Trinity College: Cambridge, 1878. Print.

SUBJECT INDEX

acting 2–5, 7–8, 10, 11, 36–7, 38, 42–8,
66, 77–8, 79, 86, 98–9, 100–2, 126, 183,
229–33, 253, 306, 317–18, 324–7, 334,
344, 360, 394, 400; acting theory 2, 7, 10,
11, 13–21, 24, 49–50, 306–7, 326, 336,
381; external approach 16–18, 21; internal
approach 15–18, 21, 77, 79–80, 337;
judgment of 2, 11, 13–17, 36–7, 41, 55–6,
58, 60, 63, 68, 71–2, 74, 80, 82, 83, 87,
88, 92, 100–2, 306–7, 309, 340, 344, 395;
training 4–5, 7, 11, 13–14, 16–17, 20–1,
24, 46
actors 3–9, 11–19, 21, 24, 35–7, 41–7, 49–51,
58, 61, 63–4, 66, 68, 69, 71, 74, 77–80, 83,
87, 88, 92, 98–9, 100–2, 167, 176, 181,
183, 229, 230, 233, 254, 266, 304, 306–7,
316–19, 334, 336, 337, 339–40, 344, 348,
360, 362, 383; English 18, 56, 77, 324, 327,
328, 337; French 4, 64, 77, 82, 84, 98–9,
181, 266, 337–9, 370; German 3–6, 7–9,
11–14, 17, 18, 20, 26, 35–6, 50, 82, 92,
233, 306–7, 316, 324–5, 327, 333, 338,
340, 344; Italian 62, 74, 82, 111, 314, 329,
346, 397; *see also* under individual names
in name index
adaptation 5, 9, 23, 59, 63, 68–70, 73, 80–1,
112–20, 131–3, 167–8, 169–72, 175, 177,
261–2, 293–304, 329, 338, 346, 351, 359,
372, 398; cross-cultural 9, 24, 69, 131, 143,
151, 315–16, 333; from myth 37–8, 143–7,
151, 315–16, 360; from novel 59, 60–1,
177–8, 362; from short story 37–8, 111,
120–8, 129, 138, 177, 261, 346, 349–51,
362, 380, 398

admiration 39, 84, 101, 110, 116, 119, 130,
236, 239, 251, 284, 323, 377
aesthetics of compassion (*Mitleidsaesthetik*)
18–20, 25, 374
affect 15–19, 32, 58, 107, 242–3, 244, 331,
370, 374–5; *see also* emotion
afterpieces 10, 61, 74, 93, 111, 304, 309, 328,
342, 345, 346, 373
amateur, novice 58, 105
American Conservatory Theatre 27
Amsterdam Theater 79
Ancient Greece 5, 9–10, 90, 122, 123, 130,
138, 140, 146, 160, 224, 350–1; Athens
9–10, 42, 53, 81, 132, 159, 258, 279, 28,
383, 387–8, 392; audience 83, 132, 159,
228, 252; mythology 131–2, 139–40,
159–6, 238, 241, 248, 352; plays, theater 5,
10, 52, 53, 63–4, 85, 87, 90, 118, 130, 132,
135–6, 137–8, 140, 146, 156, 159, 162,
163–5, 192, 226, 256, 275, 279, 287–9,
294, 306, 308, 341, 348, 351, 352, 353,
358, 359; *see also* comedy, New Comedy;
comedy, Old Comedy; individual author
names in name index
Ancient Rome 90, 122, 144, 341, 355;
audience 83, 228, 252; mythology 15,
357; plays, theater 53, 233, 342, 370, 372,
383–4; Romans 122, 129, 132, 137–8,
350–2, 354; *see also* Comedy, Roman
comedy; individual author names in
name index
ancients and antiquity 45–6, 50, 63–4, 65, 67,
85, 90, 103, 112, 117, 118, 129, 131, 132,
134–6, 137, 138, 144, 145–7, 151, 152,

154, 156, 159–61, 162, 163–5, 167, 191,
223, 224, 226, 230, 232, 237, 248, 262–6,
273, 285, 291, 294, 308, 318–19, 325, 331,
341, 347, 351–2, 355, 359–60, 376, 383
antitheatricalism 18, 20, 40–2, 324, 346
audience 3, 6, 7–10, 12, 26, 36–7, 40, 41, 42,
46, 50, 53, 56, 59, 61, 64, 69, 70, 79, 81,
84, 86, 90, 92–3, 95, 98, 99, 100, 103, 104,
106, 112, 142–4, 147, 152, 224, 225, 237,
252–4, 258, 294, 319, 323, 326, 329, 331,
332, 337, 339, 346, 351–2, 373, 376, 383,
387, 397; expectations 8, 105, 144, 162,
163, 164, 165–6, 167, 168, 183; reception
10, 15–19, 24, 109, 130–1, 132, 159,
161–3, 183–5, 234, 250, 257–8, 264–5,
267, 299, 303, 359–60; responsibility of
307, 333
authenticity 16–18, 24, 37, 118, 124–5;
see also truth; verisimilitude

ballet 5, 9, 10, 66, 325
baroque 224, 326, 329, 365, 370, 383
behavior 14, 35, 40, 55, 100, 126, 128, 146,
158, 160, 184, 259, 260, 273, 323, 330,
383, 392; *see also* manners; nature, natural
behavior
Beredsamkeit des Körpers [corporeal
eloquence] 5, 14, 17, 19, 21, 325
Berliner Ensemble 27
Biblical references 305, 309, 310, 324, 393,
395, 397
body language *see* gesture
bombast 44, 59, 190–2, 365, 367
bourgeois drama (or bourgeois tragedy) 4, 11,
15, 24, 25, 26, 72–3, 327, 329, 331, 334,
335, 365, 375, 380–1
burlesque 57

catastrophe 163, 165, 182, 359
catharsis (purification) 21, 40, 135, 244–8,
256, 259–60, 324, 353, 375–6
cause and effect 114, 118, 121, 123, 169,
225, 250
chance 85, 114, 141, 148–9, 160, 161, 165,
224, 226, 358, 371
character 60, 68, 75, 82, 89, 97–8, 99, 100,
122–8, 144, 163, 165, 171, 181, 185,
191, 224, 228–9, 323, 350; and actors 41;
construction of 49, 60, 102, 110, 118–19,
122–3, 124, 128, 145, 157–9, 162, 173,
185–6, 192, 259–60, 267–90, 299, 383;
mixed (*gemischte Charaktere*) 26, 186;
motivation 38–9, 40, 79, 99, 125, 153–4,

155, 165, 168, 181, 185; names of 33, 59,
82–3, 97, 98, 117, 123, 138, 148, 166–7,
274–81, 360; rank of 72, 144, 182, 183,
191–2, 195, 222, 223, 237, 315; types 62,
74, 83, 91, 172–3, 270, 276, 278, 316, 334
chorus 103, 112, 156, 191, 314, 315, 318–19,
397, 400
Christian tragedy 37–9, 40, 53, 75, 79, 84,
315, 323, 336, 379
coincidence *see* chance
colonialism 27
Comédie Française 24, 326, 328, 332, 336,
337, 398
Comédie-Italienne *see* Théâtre Italien
comédie larmoyante (weeping comedy) 57, 328;
see also sentimental drama
comedy: comedies of humor (humour) 285,
388–9; form and function of comedy 55,
61, 62–3, 68–9, 70, 92–3, 102–4, 109–11,
127, 129, 147, 171, 172–4, 177, 183–4,
246, 258, 260, 267–86, 290, 293–304,
313–14, 330, 346; Middle Comedy 279,
386; New Comedy 62, 223, 270–2,
278–81, 291–2, 298–301, 303–4, 330, 369,
371, 386, 392; Old Comedy 223, 279–81,
386, 387, 369; Roman comedy 61–2, 83,
90–1, 92, 182, 223, 227–33, 268, 270–3,
278, 283, 284, 291–304, 306, 341, 342,
364, 369, 371; Saxon comedy of types 5,
333; sentimental comedy 5, 87–8, 91, 328,
340; serious comedy 91–2; *see also* farce;
laughter
commedia dell'arte 129, 338, 352, 367, 397
compassion (*Mitleid*) 7, 10, 14, 18–21, 24, 25,
32, 34, 40, 48, 52, 67, 72, 79, 92, 95, 107,
113, 118, 119, 124, 132, 135, 136, 144,
147, 157, 159, 161, 162, 165, 171, 184–5,
209, 236–50, 252–3, 255–60, 299, 323,
327, 332, 347, 348, 373, 374, 376
complication 41, 67, 79, 81, 82, 99, 114,
116–17, 167, 222, 224, 225, 234–5, 269,
270, 320, 335, 370
confidant/confidante 41, 99, 149, 152, 155,
162, 165, 213–14, 220, 221, 323, 355
connoisseur 7, 36, 50, 53, 58, 74, 79, 81, 87,
89, 90, 99, 103
consistency (also inconsistency) 40, 81, 124,
147, 152–3, 155, 181, 185, 186, 223, 266,
304, 383, 388
corporeal eloquence *see Beredsamkeit des
Körpers*
costumes 9, 38, 71, 82–3, 93, 98, 104, 251,
265–6, 338, 342

coup de théâtre 85, 137, 159, 206, 339, 358, 368
criticism 1, 7, 70, 101, 110, 111, 165, 224,
    236, 238, 254, 288, 292, 232, 292–3,
    305–8, 390; art of 36, 65, 73, 79, 83, 85,
    101, 226–8, 244, 307–8, 320–1, 344;
    function of 7, 23–6, 99, 101, 122, 236,
    292, 305–9, 320–1
critics/theorists 36, 41, 55, 59, 61, 62, 69,
    75, 76, 80, 81, 90, 98, 104, 122, 130, 133,
    136, 152, 161–3, 164, 228, 229, 230–3,
    309, 339, 359; Dutch 79, 270, 383; English
    13–14, 17, 192, 243, 282–4, 290, 303, 304,
    318, 319, 365, 386, 393, 394; female 93;
    French 2, 13–14, 16, 17, 18, 20, 21, 72–3,
    75, 80, 84, 85–6, 95, 98, 110, 120, 122,
    125, 126, 130, 133, 138, 142–51, 152, 154,
    155, 157, 158, 161–3, 169, 175–7, 182–3,
    191, 192, 193, 227–8, 240–3, 245–8, 254,
    255–61, 262–82, 286–7, 290, 313, 314–15,
    317, 334, 345, 347, 348, 349, 350, 351,
    352–3, 354, 357, 358, 359, 360, 362–5,
    372, 377, 378, 379, 380–1; German 2–7, 9,
    10, 11, 13–14, 19, 59, 83, 120, 172–4, 192,
    224–5, 238, 243, 245, 252, 254, 276–7,
    292–3, 309–10, 312, 313, 348, 361, 367,
    370, 373, 390, 394; Italian 119–20, 133,
    166, 271–2, 306, 329, 348, 353, 356, 360,
    383; role of 55, 226; Spanish 202, 223–6,
    367, 369–70; Swiss 11, 306, 329, 394
customs 5, 68, 70, 76–8, 81, 93, 120, 128,
    146, 152, 173, 220, 244, 261, 264, 273,
    293–4, 297, 304, 305, 349, 391

dance 46, 71, 78, 111, 334
Danish theater 35, 70, 151–2, 322
decency, propriety 49, 61, 72, 74, 115, 158,
    186, 192, 228, 279, 319–20, 369, 384;
    see also decorum
deception 65, 186, 266; *see also* dissimulation;
    illusion
declamation (or vocal delivery) 5, 16, 37,
    43–4, 45, 47, 48–50, 56, 58, 61, 63, 58, 77,
    80, 86–8, 101, 102, 157, 191, 229, 230,
    250, 253, 265–6, 326, 327, 340
decorum 10, 50, 52, 92, 179, 222, 279, 293,
    319–20, 326, 369; lack of 158, 179, 319;
    see also decency, propriety; indecency,
    impropriety
deus ex machina 225, 332
Deutsches Theater 26
dialectics 24
dialogue 191, 192, 250, 263–5, 266, 318
discretion *see* taste

disguise 89
disgust 39, 49, 51, 61, 92, 102, 110, 113, 116,
    119, 121, 125, 128, 172, 203, 258, 263,
    320, 329, 377; causes of, in theater 116;
    feeling of 113, 121, 250, 258, 377; *see also*
    miarón
dissimulation 15, 183, 229, 318
domestic tragedy 3, 5; *see also* bourgeois
    tragedy
dramatic theory 1–3, 8, 10, 13, 223, 262–70,
    283–7, 334, 357, 365, 370, 373–4, 381;
    see also Aristotle, dramatic theory
dramaturg 23, 26–8, 119, 120; development
    of 26–8; history of 25; origin of, as staff
    position 23; *Reichsdramaturg* 26
dramaturgy 394; education and 27;
    transnational 27, 35, 70; trends in 27–8
Dutch playwriting 11, 337
Dutch theater 70

emotion 7, 13–21, 55, 66, 72–3, 88, 100,
    103–7, 118–19, 145, 159, 162, 163, 169,
    184, 191, 224, 226–7, 230–1, 235, 238,
    244, 246–8, 250–1, 257–60, 273, 313, 318,
    320, 324, 326, 329, 359, 379; and actors
    42–5, 47–8, 58, 79, 80, 183, 337, 340;
    complex 239; deficiency of 227; excess of
    49–50, 227; infectious nature of emotion
    15, 19, 20, 67, 332; mixed emotions
    ("mixed sensation") 224, 238–9, 242–3,
    249, 257, 284, 374–5; *see also* passions
emotional signs 15–18, 43–5, 101, 238, 324
emotional transparency 15–16
England 23, 56, 319; English audiences 68,
    70, 80, 192, 366; English character 68, 254;
    Theater in Drury-Lane 76, 336
English language/verse 86–7, 365
English plays 4, 5, 11, 56, 68, 69, 75–7, 81,
    178–93, 256, 308, 317, 335, 362–9, 396, 399
English playwrights 2, 5, 15, 23, 24, 25, 28,
    49, 50, 66, 67, 75–7, 165, 178, 181–3,
    185–6, 190–3, 224, 253, 255–6, 285, 286,
    290, 317, 318–19, 326, 336, 340, 359,
    363, 365, 373, 387, 389, 393, 400; *see also*
    individual names in name index
English playwriting 86, 151–2, 157, 178, 181,
    308–9, 337
English theater 9, 14, 77, 151–2, 178, 308–9,
    327–8
Enlightenment 2, 15, 21, 323, 331, 344, 377;
    French 331, 333, 362, 382; German 23, 24,
    26, 308, 327, 344, 377
epilogues 53–6, 327, 328, 365, 400

episodic 69, 82, 117, 169, 264, 265, 293–4, 299, 360
expert *see* connoisseur

fable 67, 85, 122, 127, 129, 138, 139–40, 159–60, 324, 350, 354, 358, 380
farce 9, 61, 74, 82, 109, 147, 176, 183–4, 225, 262, 282, 314, 315–16, 335
fatherland *see* nation; *Vaterland*
fear 21, 52, 53, 54, 66, 73, 92, 97, 107, 113, 114, 116, 127, 132, 158, 162, 168, 181, 184, 237–50, 252, 253, 255–6, 258–9, 299, 318, 347, 348, 374, 375, 376, 377; *see also* terror
fool (character of) 56, 62, 64, 80, 82, 83, 84, 92, 108, 111, 176, 194–5, 203, 213–14, 222, 225, 253, 260, 268, 272, 285, 309–10, 316, 366, 387, 395
France: French audiences 80, 83, 128, 130–1, 142, 143, 147, 156, 168, 182, 193, 266, 366; French character 68, 84, 98, 120, 121, 124, 128, 142–3, 145, 156, 167, 173, 195, 254, 315–16, 349; French nation 73, 83, 119, 120, 145, 255, 306, 315–16, 335, 345
francophilia 11, 192, 307, 344, 378
French comedy 62, 68, 73–4, 80–3, 87–90, 103, 108–10, 120–9, 169–72, 175–8, 227–8, 234–5, 252, 260, 261–2, 267, 282–3, 313, 314, 315–16, 335, 337, 338, 341, 344, 345, 350, 351, 360–1, 396, 370–1, 377
French language/verse 86–7, 98, 108, 175, 191, 340
French plays 4, 8, 9, 10, 67–9, 151–69, 172, 175–8, 181–6, 190, 227–8, 234–5, 363–4, 370
French playwrights 4, 6, 8, 9, 10, 15, 51, 62, 67–8, 74, 80, 82–4, 87, 91, 93–8, 108–10, 125–9, 130–1, 148–69, 171–2, 175–8, 181–6, 190–2, 227–8, 233, 234, 252, 254–60, 262–74, 275, 281–3, 308–9, 316, 335, 337, 338, 341, 344, 345, 350, 352, 355, 360–5, 370; *see also* individual names in name index
French playwriting 6, 63–4, 86, 90–1, 95–7, 126, 143, 150–6, 175–7, 181–4, 190, 191, 195, 222, 262–6, 308–9
French theater (state of) 10, 14, 57, 62, 64, 81, 83–4, 111, 128, 151, 191, 252–4, 262, 266, 308–9, 378
French tragedy 4, 8, 9, 57, 63–5, 75–7, 84, 85–7, 93, 95–102, 103, 105–7, 111–20, 129–34, 137, 142–5, 147–69, 176, 178,

181–5, 190–1, 235, 237, 238, 252–4, 255–60, 263–6, 282, 314, 315–16, 323, 331, 339–40, 343, 347, 348, 351, 363–5, 397, 399

gallantry 75, 95, 121, 143, 252–3, 336
gallery 50, 184, 326
gender: performance of 89, 101, 126, 340–1; roles 93, 95, 101, 114, 115, 117, 121, 124, 128, 129, 158–9, 173, 184, 196–7, 209, 228; *see also* women, depiction of
genius 25, 32, 37, 40, 49, 52, 55, 65, 68, 73, 84, 92, 104, 113–14, 119, 122–5, 131, 145, 148, 152, 162, 163, 168, 175, 192, 235, 252–3, 263, 282, 286, 291–2, 305, 308, 324, 350, 393, 394, 399
genre 39, 55, 57, 64, 81, 91, 92, 103, 127, 163, 177, 182, 183, 192, 205, 244, 246, 251, 252, 268, 270, 274–5, 282, 328, 359, 365, 369, 370, 377, 382, 383, 384, 386, 388, 397; mixed 57, 92, 163–4, 177, 181–2, 202, 222–6, 359, 369–70, 382
German comedy 3, 4, 5, 7, 13, 63, 89, 92, 93, 102–3, 111, 172–4, 175, 227, 233, 234, 236, 261, 291–301, 314, 315, 319, 334, 340–1, 344, 346, 361, 370, 378, 400
German domestic tragedy 3, 4, 5, 7, 13, 72–3, 313, 327, 334–5, 396
German language/verse 3, 4, 5, 6, 10, 11, 86–7, 98
German plays 3–5, 9, 10, 37, 59, 60–1, 63, 74, 80–1, 82, 173–5, 202, 227, 233, 234, 235–7, 249–51, 313, 335, 338
German playwrights 3–5, 10, 15, 37, 63, 74, 81, 172, 223–4, 227, 235–7, 261, 291–301, 335, 361, 367, 370, 387; *see also* individual names in name index
German playwriting 1, 3–5, 13–14, 84, 86, 172–4, 202, 213, 227, 291, 327
German theater 1–12, 13–14, 53, 82, 84, 92, 93, 169, 224, 252, 291–2, 305, 316, 338, 381
German tragedy 3, 5, 37–42, 49–50, 73, 78, 139, 235–7, 249–51, 261, 314, 315, 322, 327, 334, 335, 336, 349, 373, 377, 393
Germany 10, 14, 68, 82, 83–4, 93, 102, 119, 291; German audience 3–4, 6–10, 50, 68–9, 70, 250, 252, 261, 307; German character 5, 57, 68, 78–9, 80, 83, 120, 145, 173, 192, 307, 316, 378; German people 192, 225, 228, 252
gesture 16, 18, 21, 24, 26, 37, 44–8, 49, 50, 61, 71, 72, 77, 80, 87, 88, 100, 230, 231, 262, 266, 265–6, 325, 337, 372, 376, 386

ghosts 21, 24, 56, 64–7, 81, 107, 254, 331, 332
God (or gods) 38, 46, 52, 53, 54, 65, 67, 75, 85, 92, 124, 130, 138, 140, 142, 163, 165, 168, 223, 225, 237, 250, 355, 357, 377
gothic 224, 226, 370
grotesque 83, 287, 326, 339
Guthrie Theater 27

Hamburg 3–10, 11, 26, 28, 35, 53, 57, 103, 306, 310, 328, 333, 334, 335, 336, 345, 346
Hamburg Dramaturgy 1–2, 5, 8–10, 13–19, 23–7, 31–4, 119, 167, 309, 312, 326, 331, 333, 348, 306, 309–10, 351, 360, 370, 371, 373, 374, 381, 390, 393, 394, 395, 396; film and 26; German politics and 25–6; legacy of 23–8; music and 25
Hamburg National Theater 1–11, 13, 23, 24, 35–7, 305–7, 310, 327, 332, 333, 334, 338, 340, 344, 345, 360, 373, 381, 390, 394, 395, 396, 400; administration and management 1, 4–7, 105; company 1, 4–5, 7–9, 10, 324, 325, 340, 344, 360, 373, 400
Hanswurst 4, 222, 225, 309, 338, 369–70, 395; *see also* Harlequin
Harlequin 4, 9, 82–3, 147, 333, 338–9; *see also* Hanswurst
Haupt- und Staatsaktionen (chief and state plays, state and hero plays) 4, 202, 224, 226, 367
hero/heroine 39, 48, 54, 72, 73, 75, 76, 78, 84, 96, 98, 99, 103, 104, 112, 114, 117, 121, 125, 130, 143, 144, 152, 168, 181, 183, 185–6, 191, 202, 236, 245, 249, 258–9, 270, 274; heroic sentiments 38–9, 115
history 65, 84, 85, 94–8, 112–15, 117–20, 122–3, 131, 133, 145, 176, 178, 181, 184–5, 186, 193, 225, 235, 250, 275–6, 280–2, 287, 289, 294, 306, 329, 342, 343, 347, 349, 386, 389; historical accuracy in drama 65, 81, 85, 94, 95–8, 115–19, 120, 122–3, 133, 185–6, 192–3, 285, 294, 317, 331, 342, 348, 391
horror 40, 66, 114, 237, 238, 251, 374

illusion 15, 21, 24, 37, 50, 64, 65, 66, 85, 92, 128, 130, 147, 184, 260, 264–6, 294, 323, 325, 327, 329, 331, 332, 370, 381
imagination 16, 17, 18, 47, 65, 69, 119, 124, 143, 145, 172, 229, 246, 253, 254, 271, 282, 319
imitation 16, 17, 18, 43–4, 51, 84, 125, 134, 186, 224, 226, 244, 246, 251, 263–6, 271, 279, 284, 286–7, 324, 370, 375, 394

indecency, impropriety 61, 66, 131, 160, 183, 279, 299, 311; *see also* decorum, lack of
interruptions 103, 229, 253, 318, 399
Italian language 32, 57, 78
Italian plays (also Italian opera, intermezzi) 4, 5, 9, 11, 62, 69, 129, 131, 142–51, 157–8, 166–9, 182, 314, 333, 352
Italian playwrights 62, 79, 138, 140, 154, 159–61, 162, 166–9, 182, 305, 337, 348, 394; *see also* individual names in name index
Italian playwriting 69, 78, 140–51, 182
Italy 4, 69, 79, 119, 142, 319, 322, 326, 328, 397; Italian audiences 142, 144, 147; Italian character 69, 120, 143, 144, 167; Italian nation 83, 142, 144, 145

Jews 26
jokes 61, 92, 232, 279, 291, 314, 386

kathólon see universality
Kulturbund Deutscher Jüden (Cultural Association of German Jews) 26

laughter 52, 53, 56, 63, 74, 81, 90, 91, 92, 108, 109, 110, 111, 121, 124, 147, 172, 182, 183–4, 192, 224, 227, 232, 261, 262, 291, 301, 313–14, 330, 345, 397; *see also* jokes
law 52, 54–5, 67, 76, 84, 121, 127, 183–4, 281, 311, 327; lawyers 74, 145, 335, 339, 345, 399
literary manager 27; *see also* dramaturg
Literary Managers and Dramaturgs of the Americas, the 27

manners 66, 71, 80, 83, 95, 108, 128, 144, 222, 223, 283, 284, 285, 288, 293, 345, 348
masks 87, 126, 183, 193, 194, 203, 216, 325
masterpiece 26, 36, 57, 64, 68, 77, 100, 112, 119, 130, 132, 137, 144, 145, 226, 239, 266, 306, 308, 309
method acting 21
miarón (indignation/shock/abomination) 125, 250, 257–8, 259, 377, 379
middle-class characters in drama 15, 173, 334, 344
Mitleidsaesthetik see aesthetics of compassion
mixed sensation *see under* emotion
morals (or morality) 4, 14–16, 19–20, 21, 40, 54, 56, 70, 73, 85, 89, 110, 111, 120–2, 123, 125, 127–8, 131, 134, 138, 145, 146, 165, 173, 224, 238, 245, 251, 264, 268,

284, 287, 288, 319, 345, 377, 386, 387, 388, 396; moral behavior/moral character 4, 14–15, 110, 158, 165, 242, 259–60, 268, 307; morality in theater 4, 14–16, 19–20, 21, 40, 41–8, 51–7, 63, 67, 73, 83, 89, 110, 111, 127, 131, 134, 138, 146, 165, 238, 242, 245, 251, 259–60, 268, 287–8, 306, 314, 319, 323, 324, 327, 330, 338, 340, 346, 376, 389; moral unity 153–4

music 9, 19, 25, 36, 58, 77, 86, 103–7, 176, 191, 246, 307, 315, 337, 344–5, 346, 351, 376

mythology 92, 131–2, 139–40, 146, 159–60, 253, 339, 352

narration 37, 56, 65, 74, 110, 115, 117, 163–4, 177, 244–5, 375–6

National Socialism 26

national theater 10, 307

nation and nationalism 2, 8, 23, 25, 27, 37, 52, 63, 65, 68, 72, 73, 83, 84, 85, 93, 98, 131, 142, 143, 144–5, 151, 182, 222, 223, 225, 254, 255, 262, 266, 291, 307, 308, 313, 315, 316, 339, 342, 348

nature 18, 61, 72, 73, 76, 106, 165, 181, 191–2, 223–4, 226–8, 229, 242, 259, 266, 269, 284–9, 293, 295, 298, 376, 377; art *vs.* nature 58, 62, 74, 101, 130, 142, 202, 222, 226–8; imitation of 16–18, 224, 226–7, 263–6, 325, 370; natural (or unnatural) behavior 38, 40, 42–5, 49, 55, 59, 60, 67, 77, 79, 86, 91, 99, 110, 114–16, 119, 135, 141, 143, 154, 168, 169, 184, 192–3, 318, 323, 326; natural (or unnatural) reaction 159, 184

necessity 39, 104, 106, 115, 148, 155, 227, 275, 276, 296, 299, 323, 348, 384, 385

némesis (indignation) 125, 184, 249, 257, 377

Neoclassicism 2, 4, 5, 8, 19, 23, 24, 222–3, 329, 333, 334, 340, 343, 345, 346, 348, 355, 357, 358, 359, 369, 381, 383

novels 56, 57, 59, 60, 89, 91, 96, 119, 178, 225–6, 262–6, 305–6, 313, 316, 319, 328, 329, 330, 341, 343, 348, 349, 358, 362, 370, 376, 377–8, 381, 382, 394, 396, 400

opera 4, 28, 63, 64, 69, 78, 111, 142, 176, 330, 346, 349, 351, 377

operetta (or comic opera) 63, 69, 111, 129, 176, 333, 351

painting 24, 50, 61, 128, 235, 242, 254, 283–7, 305, 307, 320, 326, 329, 379

pantomime 5, 9, 20–1, 45–6, 250, 325, 340

parasite (character of, in drama) 83, 278, 339, 386

parterre 42, 50, 64, 128, 130–1, 142, 143, 168, 193, 291, 326; *see also* audience

passions 15–19, 21, 37, 40, 42, 43–5, 48, 49–50, 51, 52, 75, 76, 77, 82, 87, 101, 104, 106–7, 111, 112, 113, 115, 118–19, 127, 140, 144, 158, 159, 185, 191, 195, 239, 244–6, 253, 256, 283–4, 286, 304, 324, 326, 374, 388; *see also* affect; emotion

pastoral 4, 74, 336

pathos (suffering) 61, 65, 73, 135–6, 146, 238, 243, 248, 257, 193, 317, 348, 353

patriotism 7, 35, 39, 52

pedantry 60, 63, 77, 146, 157, 228, 255, 266, 308, 323

philanthropy 242–3, 246, 375

piracy (by publishers) 9, 11, 31, 309–12, 330, 393, 395

pity *see* compassion

plagiarism 73, 167–8, 235, 262, 315, 317, 373, 381

Plattdeutsch 33, 108, 345

plausibility (or implausibility) 68, 82, 153, 339; *see also* probability, probable

playwrights 36, 37, 39, 40, 41, 42, 48–9, 55–6, 59, 66, 73, 76, 110, 114–15, 116, 130, 173, 185, 191–2, 250–1, 253, 269, 275–7, 280–2, 284, 287–9, 294; female 5, 11, 81, 86, 102–3, 175–6, 330, 333–4, 338, 340, 344, 362; *see also* under individual author names in name index

playwriting, art of 62, 66, 67, 72, 73, 74, 76, 92–3, 97–9, 105–7, 114–15, 118–20, 128, 133, 134–6, 145–69, 175, 183, 185, 192, 229–30, 296, 299, 300–1, 307–9; *see also* under specific countries

plot 55, 61, 62, 67, 69, 79, 82, 90, 98, 99, 111, 116, 117, 119, 127, 131, 133, 134–7, 139, 140–1, 148, 156, 159–61, 162–3, 167, 169, 170, 178, 181, 191, 224, 226, 241–2, 252, 261, 267, 268, 269, 270–1, 275, 277, 278, 280, 285, 293–4, 299, 333, 339, 344, 347, 348, 353, 358, 359, 370, 384

poetic justice 67, 69, 249

poetry (also dramatic poetry) 3, 24, 50, 65, 75, 81, 97, 100, 104, 106, 117, 118, 130, 144, 145, 192–3, 204–5, 246, 249, 250, 264, 275–7, 278, 286–7, 307, 315, 317, 326, 367–8, 378, 385

principles *see* rules

proairesis (reasoned choice) 260, 379

probability, probable (or improbability) 32, 85, 89, 93, 94, 113, 118–19, 120, 123, 125, 128, 149, 152, 153, 157, 184, 228, 240, 248, 269, 275–7, 282, 294, 303, 331, 335, 339, 341, 348, 385; *see also* plausibility
prologues 51, 54, 56, 121, 146, 163–5, 166, 172, 270–2, 304, 309, 327, 328, 359, 400
propriety *see* decency, propriety; decorum
prose 57, 68, 70, 86–7, 175, 275, 316, 336, 361, 365, 372
Providence *see* God

reason 20, 36, 39, 44, 45, 55, 59, 65, 76, 87, 107, 134, 148, 175, 237, 247, 250, 258, 269, 291, 292–3, 376, 379
recognition (*anagnorisis*) 114, 132, 135–6, 137–8, 141, 143, 146, 150–1, 159–61, 169, 181, 347, 352, 353, 354, 355, 358, 386
reconciliation 81, 185, 258
Reichsdramaturg 26
religion 38–9, 40–2, 53–4, 65, 75, 84–5, 103, 258, 264; Catholicism 39, 323, 355; Christianity, Christians 26, 38–9, 40, 46, 48, 53–4, 55, 84–5, 258, 322–3, 336, 371, 379, 386; Islam, Muslims 26, 38–9, 40, 53, 55, 85, 322–3, 336; religious tolerance 25, 26, 53–4, 55
resolution (of plot) 56, 74, 82, 117, 162, 163, 167, 183, 224, 225, 264–5, 293, 320, 370
reversal (*peripeteia*) 132, 135–6, 137–8, 299, 352–4
ridicule 110, 285, 339, 346, 383, 398
ridiculous 51, 55, 63, 65, 74, 81, 87, 95, 104, 125, 129, 149, 166, 172, 177, 183–4, 223, 225, 229, 265, 271, 272, 273, 279, 281, 285, 314, 315, 330, 399
romantic 39, 119, 222, 260, 266, 269, 376
Romanticism 25, 26, 324, 326, 393, 394
rules (of playwriting) 4, 76, 79, 81, 82, 85, 87, 99, 104, 117, 122, 127, 132, 134–7, 144, 151–7, 162–5, 167, 223, 240, 244, 250, 255, 257, 260, 263–4, 279, 282, 292, 299, 308, 317, 331, 345, 348, 357–8, 359, 393, 394

Saitenmetapher [String metaphor] 19
satire, satirists 51, 56, 108, 129, 143, 151, 261, 262, 272, 276–8, 280, 312, 323, 330, 333, 344, 345, 377, 378, 381, 382, 385, 386, 387, 388, 389
Satyr plays 83, 339
scenic design (or scenic decoration) 4, 253–4; *see also* staging practices

sensate cognition 18, 20
sensibility 15–16, 18–20, 32, 89, 119, 122, 129, 376
sentimental drama 5, 15, 20, 21, 323, 328, 333
sentimental philosophy 15, 333
sentiments 17, 20, 39, 40, 42, 43, 58, 69, 72, 74, 88, 92, 99, 126, 144, 186, 238, 243, 252, 315, 374
serious drama (or serious comedy) 62, 91, 92, 103, 262, 266, 267, 269, 274, 359, 365, 382, 384
Seven Years' War, the (1756–63) 23, 339
signs 15–18, 45, 89, 101, 150, 159, 175, 238, 324; universal/natural 16–18, 45–6, 325
Spanish character 195
Spanish plays 4, 156, 182, 193–223, 366, 367, 369, 379
Spanish playwrights 182, 193, 202, 222–3, 366, 367, 369, 379; *see also* individual names in name index
Spanish playwriting 182, 195, 202, 213, 222–3, 369–70
spectacle 253–4, 378
spectator *see* audience
stage violence 61, 181–5, 329, 364, 374
staging practices 2, 4, 41, 61, 64, 66, 67, 72, 104, 105–7, 126, 130–1, 147, 151–2, 154–5, 229–30, 253–4, 324, 331, 332, 350, 351, 352
Sturm und Drang [Storm and Stress] 25, 393
sublime 85, 107, 176, 192, 263, 326
suffering *see* pathos
surprise 61, 86, 105–7, 149, 161–7, 224, 237, 249, 339, 359, 360
sycophant (character of) 90, 278, 330, 386
symbolic conclusion (*symbolischer Schluß*) 44, 324
sympathetic vibration or resonance 19, 65, 67, 332, 383
sympathy 15, 17–19, 21, 37, 49, 65, 67, 72–3, 106–7, 109, 125, 195, 243, 251, 323, 332, 348, 373, 401

taste 2, 6, 7, 8, 10, 36, 44, 57, 63, 64, 65, 67, 76, 82, 85, 101, 105, 120, 143–5, 164–5, 178, 224, 225, 226, 233, 252, 255, 263, 271, 284, 306, 308, 314, 320, 370, 394; English 8, 68, 70, 76, 80, 81, 313, 333, 399; French 8, 24, 59, 68, 70, 73, 80, 128, 142, 143–4, 147, 156, 167, 195, 235, 399; German 8, 9, 10, 11, 12, 42, 50, 68, 69, 70, 78, 80, 108, 202, 213, 224–5, 255, 308, 333, 370, 394; Italian 69, 78, 83, 142,

143–5, 147, 156, 167; Spanish 156, 195, 202, 223; among women 75, 93, 175

terror 52, 65, 66, 92, 118, 119, 125, 132, 135, 161, 165, 171, 236–9, 243, 245, 249, 252, 331, 348, 351, 373–4; *see also* fear

theater: 18th c. German 1–12, 13–14; corruption of 35–7; instructive, teaching, didactic 10, 14, 24, 111, 115, 122–3, 125, 256, 267, 275, 278, 306, 319; and law 52, 54, 327; reform/improvement/ development of 1–5, 10, 11, 13–15, 19, 35–7, 40–2, 54, 305, 367, 377; as school for morals 39, 40, 51–4, 111, 127, 245

Théâtre Italien (Comédie-Italienne) 62, 74, 82, 111, 314, 329, 335, 338, 346, 351, 352, 397

titles (of plays) 33, 62, 74, 81, 90–1, 93, 109, 112–13, 138, 234, 261, 269

tradition 65, 66, 82, 85, 139, 233, 318, 331, 349, 377

tragedy: form and function 24, 39, 40, 42, 55, 63–4, 72–3, 75, 78, 79, 85, 95, 97–8, 100, 103–4, 117, 118–19, 127, 132–8, 144, 145–69, 171, 181, 183–4, 191, 192, 236–61, 263–6, 275–6, 280–3, 285–6, 290, 293–4, 299, 308–9, 313–14, 331, 335, 376; *see also* under Ancient Greece; Ancient Rome; ancients and antiquity; rules

tragicomedy 81, 181–2, 223–5, 364

translation 3, 5, 11, 13, 20, 31–4, 57, 68, 69–70, 76–7, 78, 81, 83, 86, 87–8, 98, 108–9, 113, 120, 134, 142, 147, 167–8, 190–1, 233, 237, 239, 243, 245, 261, 262, 270, 275, 277, 282, 285, 301, 304, 333–4, 335, 336, 337, 338, 340, 345, 346, 349, 353, 361, 365, 372, 374, 381

truth 53, 54, 65, 67, 73, 81, 95–7, 98, 107, 115, 122, 132, 133, 144, 181, 191, 229,

258, 260, 264, 274, 282, 286–7, 289; appearance of 37, 40, 42, 45, 48, 50, 61, 80, 85, 323, 331, 332, 339; poetic 42, 190; *see also* authenticity; versimilitude

Turkey: Turkish character 120–2, 124, 126–7; Turkish nation 122

unity of action 135, 154, 156–7, 358

unity of place 79, 81, 151–3, 156–7, 357

unity of time 60, 85, 93, 153–4, 156–7

universal 16, 44, 45, 56, 81, 85, 111, 122, 127–8, 237, 275–82, 283, 285, 290–1, 307

universality (*kathólon*) 21, 65, 265, 274–82, 286–91, 329, 384, 385, 387

Vaterland [fatherland] 93, 297, 300, 323, 342; *see also* nation

verisimilitude 147, 173, 183, 332, 385; *see also* authenticity; truth

verse 47, 57, 68, 70, 76, 86–7, 98, 111, 119, 120, 175, 191, 262, 275, 291, 368; Alexandrine 5, 11, 120, 327, 332, 334, 336, 338, 340, 380; blank 77, 365, 383; rhyme 57, 70, 77, 86, 119, 120, 175, 265, 307, 327, 361, 367; versification 70, 86–7, 110, 191; versifiers 57, 145, 254–5; *see also* under English language/verse; French language/verse; German language/verse

Vienna 41, 59, 142, 315, 328, 333, 370

vocal delivery *see* declamation

Wanderbühnen [travelling theater troupes] 4

Women: depiction of 95–6, 98–9, 101–2, 114–17, 126, 128, 129, 141, 158–60, 184–6, 190–3, 209, 228, 242; on stage 61–2, 101, 181, 184–5

Yale University 27

NAME INDEX

Note: Titles in the list below appear in English translation only; to locate titles in the original foreign language, see the Title Index.

Abbt, Thomas 394
Ackermann, Konrad (Ernst) 4–6, 9, 11, 68–9, 325, 333, 336
Ackermann, Sophie Charlotte (nee Schröder) 11, 328
Adami, Leonardo 142, 334
Addison, Joseph 76, 81, 330, 336, 337, 338, 344
Aelianus, Claudius (Aelian) 387
Aeschylus 294, 391, 398
Agathon 225, 275, 370, 384
Agricola, Johann Friedrich Agricola 105, 107, 345
Alarcón, Juan Ruiz de 379
Albrecht, Heinrich Cristoph 25
Alcibiades 275, 384
Alençon, Henri-François, duc d' 366
Allacci, Lione 306, 394
Anderson, Michael 376
Antiphanes 386
Apollodorus 131, 284, 352
Appianus Alexandrinus (Appian of Alexandria) 112, 115, 347
Arbiter, Petronius 351
Aristophanes 279–81, 369, 386, 387, 390
Aristophanes of Byzantium 384
Aristotle 2, 25, 93, 159, 163, 227, 236–60, 293, 306, 370, 371, 383; commentaries on 133–4, 137, 138, 237–9, 241, 243, 245, 247–9, 255–6, 260, 270, 276–7, 280, 286–8, 352–4, 374–8, 380, 385, 387, 389; on (universal v. particular) dramatic character 275–83, 290; dramatic theory 132–8, 159, 165, 167, 236–49, 275–83, 308, 348, 352–3; on emotion 21; French intepretations/misunderstanding of 2, 23, 151–2, 132, 133–4, 136, 137, 151–2, 240–2, 245–9, 255–61, 308–9, 357, 378–80; on historical truth in drama 85, 275, 293–4, 348; *Nichomachean Ethics* 279, 374, 379, 386; *Poetics* 2, 23, 132, 134, 137, 237, 239–49, 275–81, 287, 308, 323, 324, 347–8, 352–4, 357–60, 370, 373–80, 385, 389, 391; *Politics* 246, 374, 376; *Rhetoric* 239–40, 245, 249, 371, 374; on tragedy 117, 132–7, 165, 236–49
Ascensius, Jodocus Badius 270, 383
Athenaeus 394
Ayre, William 354, 355, 356, 358

Bach, Johann Sebastien 345
Bachaumont, Louis Petit de 352
Bailey-Slagle, Judith 328
Baldyga, Natalya 1–22, 324, 326, 327, 340, 344, 376–7, 390, 394
Balhorn, Johann 168, 360
Banks, John 178, 181–2, 185–6, 190–3, 317, 362, 363, 365, 399
Barbier, Edmond Jean François 351
Barlandus, Adrian 270, 283
Barnes, Joshua 132, 352

433

Baron (Boyron), Michel 370, 372
Barsby, John 270, 371–2, 391–3
Bartolus (Bartolo da Sassoferrato) 84, 339
Batteux, Charles 325
Beaumont, Jean-Baptiste-Jacques Elie de
  84, 339
Beauval, Jeanne Olivier Bourgignon 82,
  338, 355
Becelli, Giulio Cesare 166–7, 354, 360
Behrmann, Wilhelm Christian Dietrich 346
Bell, Edward 28, 30–1, 34
Belloy, Pierre-Laurent Buirette de 83–5, 89,
  339, 398
Bembo, Cardinal Pietro 384
Bentley, Eric 338
Bentley, Richard 384
Bergeron, David Moore 363
Bernini 50, 326
Bharatamuni: *Natyasastra* 27
Bielfeld, Jakob Friedrich (Freiherr von)
  313, 396
Bierling, F. S. 362
Bly, Mark 27–8
Boccaccio 338, 344, 362
Böck, Johann Michael 12, 74, 322, 336, 341
Böck, Sophie Elisabeth 89, 341
Bode, Johann Joachim Christoph 68, 332, 393
Bodmer, Johann Jakob 335
Bohnen, Klaus 34, 396
Boileau-Despréaux, Nicolas 143, 151, 355–6
Boisrobert, François le Métel de 181, 363
Boisset, Pierre Louis Paul Randon de 335
Boissy, Louis de 91, 316, 341, 398
Borchers, David 87, 323, 340
Borkenstein, Hindrich 11
Boscán, Juan 205, 367
Bouhours, Dominique 254, 378
Boyer, Claude 178, 362
Brawe, Joachim Wilhelm von 74, 335
Brecht, Bertolt 26
Breitinger, Johann Jakob 11
Bremner, Geoffrey 365
Bressand, F[riedrich] C[hristian] 120, 349
Brockman, Beatrix 33
Brockmann, Stephen 33
Brooke, Henry (1703–83) 192–3, 365, 317, 399
Brooke, Henry (Lord Cobham) (1527–97)
  96, 343
Brosse (La Brosse) 262–2, 380
Brown, Hilary 11, 334
Brueys, David-Augustin de 74, 335
Brumoy, Pierre 129–30, 351
Bruyère, Jean de la 110, 345

Bubbers, Adolf Siegmund 6
Butcher, S. H. 280, 347–8, 375, 378, 385, 389

Calderón de la Barca, Pedro 222, 369
Calepio, Pietro dei Conti di 348
Callippides 82, 338
Calprenède, Gaultier de Coste, seigneur de la
  93–4, 178, 185, 342, 362, 365
Campistron, Jean-Galbert de 169–72, 361
Caravaggio 329
Cartwright, Nancy 324
Casa, Giovanni della (John de la Casa) 305, 394
Casaubon, Isaac 306, 394
Cato 76, 270, 274, 276, 281, 337
Cecchi, Giovanni Maria 62, 329
Cecil, Sir Robert 95–6, 99–100, 342–3
Centlivre, Susanna 335
Cérou, Pierre 74, 335
Cervantes Saavedra, Miguel de 202, 367, 376
Chabrias 281, 387
Chariton 160, 358
Charles II 23
Châtelet, Émilie du (Marquise du Châtelet)
  129, 351
Chaucer 346
Chevrier, François Antoine 169–71, 175–6,
  361–2
Christian VII, King of Denmark 111, 120, 346
Cibber, Colley 75, 77, 336
Cibber, Susanna Maria 77, 337
Cibber, Theophilus 178, 253, 317, 327, 337,
  362–3, 378, 398, 399
Cicero [Marcus Tullius] 90, 132, 273, 341,
  352, 384, 389; *On Duties* 90, 341; *On
  Oratory* 286, 287, 389; *Tusculan Disputations*
  273, 352, 384
Cleon 280, 387
Cleopatra 8, 76, 112–16, 119, 241, 255,
  258–60, 325, 337, 346–7, 375, 378, 379
Clytemnestra 133, 289, 390
Cobham, Lord *see* Brooke, Henry
Coello, Antonio 366–9
Coenen, Adriaen 394–5
Colman (the Elder), George 68–9, 270,
  303–4, 333, 335, 383, 393; *The Clandestine
  Marriage* 333; *The English Merchant* 68–9,
  333; *The Jealous Wife* 69, 333; translation
  of Terence 270, 303–4, 383, 393; *The
  Village Lawyer* 74, 92, 335
Congreve, William 69, 333
Conroy, Jane 343
Cordier de Saint Firmin, Edmond 131, 352
Corneille, Marie 349, 398

Corneille, Pierre 4, 8–9, 40, 93–7, 111–20, 130, 152–5, 176, 178, 181–90, 240–7, 255–65, 308–9, 316–23, 336, 342–51, 354–7, 362–4, 375–82, 398–9; "Appian Alexandrin" 347; and Aristotle's dramatic theory 138, 241, 243, 245, 255–6, 260, 375–8, 380; *Attila* 253, 378; *Cinna* 111, 265, 317, 347, 382, 399; "Examination of Rodogune" 347; and French Neoclassicism 240–2, 245–9, 255–61, 357, 378–80; *Héraclius* 257–8, 375–9; *Le Cid* 111, 176, 181–2, 184, 255, 347, 363–4, 378; *The Liar* 260, 379; *Mélite* 240; *Nicomede* 375, 378; *Othon* 253, 378; *Polyeucte* 40, 75, 103, 258, 317, 323, 336, 344, 375, 379, 399; *Rodogune* 9, 111–20, 256–60, 316–17, 346–9, 375–9, 398–9; *Sertorius* 253, 378, 382; *Suréna* 240, 253, 378; *Three Discourses* 240, 246–8, 255–61, 354, 357, 364, 375–6, 378–9, 380; Voltaire's commentaries on 181–2, 183, 347–9, 363–5, 398

Corneille, Thomas 93, 95, 318, 342–3, 362–5, 398–9; *The Earl of Essex* 93–102, 178, 182, 186, 190, 342–4, 362–5, 399

Cramer, Carl Friedrich 381

Crates 280, 387

Cratinus 280, 387

Crébillon, Claude-Prosper Jolyot de (fils) 341

Crébillon, Claude-Prosper Jolyot de (père) 237, 256, 374, 378

Cronegk, Johann Friedrich von 37–9, 41, 49, 54–5, 172, 315, 322–3, 361, 397; *Codrus* 39, 41, 55, 314, 323, 335, 397; *Olint and Sophronia* 20, 37–9, 41, 105, 314, 322, 344, 39, 399; *The Suspicious Man* 314, 361, 392

Ctesippus 281, 387

Curtius, Michael Conrad 134, 243, 245, 248–9, 276–7, 353, 374, 375, 376–7, 385; *Aristotle's Poetics* 353, 376–7, 385; "Treatise on the Purpose of Tragedy" 249, 377

Dacier, André 133–4, 137–8, 233, 239, 241, 245, 247, 248, 255–6, 260, 270, 276–7, 280, 287–8, 347, 352–4, 372, 374–80, 385, 387, 389; *Aristotle's Poetics* 133–4, 137, 138, 239, 241, 245, 247–8, 255–6, 260, 270, 276–7, 280, 287–8, 352–4, 374–6, 378, 380, 385, 387, 389

Dacier, Anne Le Fèvre 233, 270, 372, 383

Dahlstrom, Daniel O. 348

D'Alembert, Jean le Rond 382

Daniel, Samuel 178, 317, 362–3, 399

D'Aubignac, Abbé Hédelin *see* Hédelin, François

Dekker, Thomas 389

Delisle de la Drevetière, Louis-François 338, 344

Descartes, René 17, 324

Destouches, Philippe Néricault 68–70, 81, 91, 268, 329–30, 334, 338, 344, 360–1, 383; comic character types in 62, 171, 267–8; *Complete Works* 332; *The Conceited Count* 62, 330; *Dramatic Works of* 361; *The Hidden Treasure* 62, 329; *The Irresolute Man* 103, 344; *The Married Philosopher* 62, 68, 74, 87, 169–72, 330, 332, 360–1; *The Nocturnal Drummer* 62, 330, 338; *The Singular Man* 268, 383; *The Spendthrift* 62, 330; *The Unexpected Obstacle* 62, 330; *The Young Hypocrite, or The Country Poet (La fausse Agnès)* 62, 69, 330, 333

Devereux, Robert, 2d Earl of Essex 342

Devrient, Hans 332

Diderot, Denis 15, 24–5, 73, 262, 380–90; acting theory 18, 20; and Aristotle's dramatic theory 161–3; on character 267–76, 282–2, 290, 375; *Conversations on the Natural Son* 20, 191, 262, 266–74, 281–2, 325, 365, 381–5; criticism of French theater 191, 262–6; *Discourse on Dramatic Poetry, to Mr. Grimm* 161–3, 359, 380–3; *Encyclopedia* 334–5, 382; *The Father of the Family* 20, 262, 266, 342, 359, 380, 382; *The Indiscreet Jewels* 262, 381–2; Lessing's translation of (*Das Theater des Herrn Diderot*) 334, 342, 359, 365, 381; *Letter on the deaf and dumb* 20, 381; *The Natural Son* 20, 262, 266–9, 273–4, 365, 381–5; *Paradox of the Actor* 20; on plot construction 161–3

Diodati, Ottaviano 57, 69, 328, 333

Diogenes Laertius 118, 348

Diphilus 271, 299–300, 383, 392

Döbbelin, Karl 11, 330

Dodsley, James 304, 310–12, 393

Dodsley, Robert 304, 310–12, 393

Donatus, Aelius 228–33, 278, 291, 300–1, 304, 371–3, 385, 390, 392–3; *Life of Virgil* 373; *Works of Terence* 228–33, 278, 291, 300–1, 304, 371–2, 385, 390, 392–3

D'Orville, Jacques Philippe 160, 358

Dryden, John 57, 77, 328, 337, 346, 389

Dubos, Abbé (Jean-Baptiste) 259, 379

Ducis, Jean François 23

Duckworth, Colin 333, 341

Dudley, Robert (Earl of Leicester) 96, 343

Dufresny (Du Fresny), Charles-Rivière 73, 335

Dugas de Bois Saint-Just, Jean Louis Marie 331
Duim, Frederik 79, 337
Duim, Izaak 337
Duni, Egidio Romualdo 376
Dunsch, Boris 384
Dusch, Johann Jakob 327

Eaton, J. W. 322
Ekhof, Konrad 7, 11–12, 14, 16, 18, 20, 24, 74, 100, 324; description of acting 7, 41–2, 47, 58, 61, 80, 88; *The Married Philosopher* 68, 332; "Rules for Acting" 14
Elizabeth I, Queen of England 93–102, 178, 186, 191, 195–6, 209, 249, 342–3, 363–7, 399
Ennis, Daniel J. 328
Epicharmus 387
Erickson, Peter 33, 323
Eschenburgh, Johann Joachim 387
Euclid 308, 394
Eugraphius 271, 383
Euripides 42, 117, 130, 132, 136, 140, 146, 159–67, 192, 256, 287–9, 347, 351–4, 358–60, 381, 389, 390; *Cresphontes* 131–3, 138–40, 146, 159–60, 351–60; *Electra* 117, 288–9, 389–90; *Hecuba* 164, 192, 359, 365; *Helen* 117, 347; *Ion* 164–5, 359; *Iphigenia in Tauris* 117, 136–8, 347, 353–4
Eusebius of Caesarea 386

Faerno, Gabriele 271–2, 383
Fairclough, H. Ruston 365
Fantuzzi, Maria Noussia 348
Favart, Charles-Simon 63, 122, 125–8, 176, 315, 330, 346, 349–50, 362, 398; *The Fairy Urgele* 111, 346; *Isabelle and Gertrude* 63, 330; *Soliman the Second* 120–9, 349–51, 315–16, 398
Favart, Mme. Marie-Justine-Benoîte 362
Fawkener, Everard 76, 336–7
Federico, Gennaro Antonio 351
Felbrich, Cordelia (or Cornelia/Cornelie) 63, 330, 395
Fielding, Henry 319, 400–1
Figal, Sara 342
Fiorillo, Tiberio (Fiorilli/Fiurelli) 397
Fischer-Lichte, Erika 327
Fontenelle, Bernard le Bouyer (or Bovier) de 177, 316, 362, 398
Foote, Samuel 333
Francklin, Thomas 332, 358
Frederick II of Prussia (Frederick the Great) 6, 11, 330, 343, 345, 395
Fréron, Élie Catherine 68, 333

Garcilaso de la Vega 205, 367–8
Garnier, Robert 182, 364
Garrick, David 18, 23, 41, 54–6, 324, 327–8, 333
Gaussin, Jeanne Cathérine 77, 337
Gellert, Christian Fürchtegott 5, 92, 319, 342, 400
Gemmingen-Hornberg, Otto Heinrich 25
Gerstenberg, Heinrich Wilhelm von 393
Gnaeus Naevius 383
Godden, Janet 351–2, 355–6
Goebbels, Joseph 26
Goethe, Johann Wolfgang von 9, 25, 370, 373
Goetschel, Willi 375
Goldberg, Sander M. 372, 384
Goldoni, Carlo 68, 305, 333, 394
Gottsched, Johann Christoph (J. C.) 4–5, 11, 70, 82–3, 254, 338, 344, 367; *Attempt at a Critical Poetics* 344; *The German Stage* 5, 69–70, 102, 330, 333, 344, 361
Gottsched, Luise Adelgunde Victorie (Luise A. V.) 333–4; *The French Housekeeper* 102, 344; *The Ghost with the Drum* 81, 330; *The Last Will* 102, 344; *The Poetical Village Squire* 330; *The Spendthrift* 330; as translator 70, 81, 87–8, 333–4, 338, 340, 344
Götze, Johann Melchior (Goeze) 324
Goulbourne, Russell 380
Goulston, Theodore 243, 375
Gozzi, Carlo 337
Gozzi, Gasparo 78, 337
Grafigny, (Mme.) Françoise d'Issembourg d'Happoncourt de 87, 175–6, 333, 340
Grécourt, Jean-Baptiste Joseph Willart de 120, 349
Green-Rogers, Martine Kei 28
Gresset, Jean B. L. 80, 261, 337–8
Grimm, Jacob 328, 345, 370
Grimm, Wilhelm 328, 345, 370
Guasco, Octavien de 353
Guerin (Garin) 381
Gueullette, Thomas Simon 328
Guyer, Paul 375

Halliwell, Stephen 387
Hamann, Johann Georg 25
Havel, Václav 27
Hédelin, François (Abbé d'Aubignac) 20, 152, 163, 182, 255, 357, 359, 363–4, 378; *The Whole Art of the Stage* 20, 152, 163, 182, 327, 357, 359, 363–4
Hegel, Georg Wilhelm Friedrich 25
Heitner, Robert R. 335
Henderson, Jeffrey 386

Hensel, Johann Gottlieb 83, 339
Hensel, Sophie 16, 53, 72, 88, 325–6, 334;
description of acting 47, 72, 88; and the
Hamburg National Theater 6, 7; objection
to criticism 7, 11
Herder, Johann Gottfried 25, 373
Hernilly, Nicolas-Gabriel Vaquette d' 369
Herodotus 275, 384
Hertel, Johann Wilhelm Hertel 105, 344
Heufeld, Franz von 59, 61, 315, 328, 397
Hill, Aaron (1685–1750) 76–8, 336–7
Hill, Aaron (the younger, 1715–39) 78, 337
Hill, John 17
Hill, Robert 319, 400
Hippel, Theodor Gottlieb von 93, 175, 342
Hitler, Adolph 26
Hogarth, William 16, 46, 325
Home, Henry, Lord Kames 399
Home, John 318, 332
Homer 92, 130, 146–7, 224, 235, 352, 373,
387; *The Iliad* 92, 341, 354–5; *Margites*
280, 387
Horace (Quintus Horatius Flaccus) 163,
271–2, 282–3, 339, 345, 355; *Art of Poetry*
272, 282, 283, 286, 326, 339, 355, 362,
365, 384, 386, 389; *Satires* 272, 339, 345,
355, 362, 365, 384, 389
Howard, Charles (Earl of Nottingham) 96, 343
Hultsch, Fridericus (Friedrich Otto) 354
Hume, David 68, 94–5, 333, 342–3, 364
Hurd, Richard 279, 282–90, 386, 400; on
Aristotle's dramatic theory 279, 282–90; on
character types 282–90; "Dissertation on
the Provinces of the Drama" 279, 282, 290,
386, 388; "Notes on the Art of Poetry"
282, 389–90, 400; on poetry *vs.* history 287;
on universality in dramatic poetry 286–90
Hürrem Sultan *see* Roxelane
Hyginus (Gaius Julius Hyginus) 132,
138–42, 159–60, 352, 354, 358–60
Hyperbolus 280, 387

Ibsen, Henrik 25

Jacobs, Eva 336
James VI, King of Scotland 96
Joannidés, Alexandre 328, 332
Johnson, Charles 316, 396, 398
Jones, Henry 192–3, 365, 317, 399
Jonson, Ben 32, 192, 337, 365, 377, 388, 389,
390; *Every Man in his Humour* 285, 388;
Every Man out of his humour 285, 388–9
Jürs, Hans-Joachim 33
Jürs-Munby, Karen 33

Kay, N. M. 340
Kelly, Adrian D. 352
Kelly, John 332
Kemp, Edward 28
Kies, Paul P. 396
Klotz, Christian Adolf 292, 309, 310, 312,
390, 394–5, 401
Knigge, Adolph Freiherr von 25
Knufmann, Helmut 346
Koch, Heinrich Gottfried 11, 338
König, Engelbert 351
König, Eva 351
Kord, Susanne 11, 325, 334
Krüger, Johann Christian 4, 11, 108, 261,
335, 345, 373, 380; *The Candidates* 261,
380; *The Clergymen in the Country* 261,
380; *Duke Michael* 235, 261, 373, 380;
The Farmer with the Inheritance 345; *The
Married Philosopher* 68, 332; *The Unforeseen
Denouement* 234, 373
Kummerfeld, Karoline *see* Schulze-
Kummerfeld, Karoline
Kurz, Joseph Felix von (called Bernardon) 333

Labriolle, Marie Rose de 341
Lachmann, Karl 396, 399
Lactantius 371
L'Affichard, Thomas 80, 261, 338
La Fontaine, Jean de 120, 349, 380
La Harpe, Jean-François de 352
La Motte, Antoine Houdar de 86–7, 129,
340, 351, 362, 381, 398; *The Ephesian
Widow* 129, 351, 398
Lattimore, Richmond A. 350, 417
Le Bossu, René 260, 380
Le Bret, Antoine 261, 380
Le Brun, Charles 16, 284, 388
Le Brun, Ponce Denis Ecouchard 316, 398
Lee, Nathaniel 77, 337
Lefevere, Andrè 334
Lefèvre, Tanneguy 384
Le Grand, Marc Antoine 51, 261–2, 280, 326,
371, 380
Leibniz, Gottfried Wilhelm 312, 332, 377, 395
Léris, Antoine de 326, 335, 341, 362
Lessing, Gotthold Ephraim 1–12, 13–21,
23–8, 31–4, 74; career of 1–5, 7–9, 11,
13, 23–4, 327, 329, 330, 334–5, 338, 351,
360, 365, 369, 371, 377, 381, 383, 390,
393, 394, 400; *Emilia Galotti* 13, 369;
impact of 2, 10, 23–8, 327, 328, 334, 387,
390, 393; *Laocöon* 326, 329, 390; *Minna
von Barnhelm* 3, 7, 11, 13, 319, 325, 378,
400; *Miss Sara Sampson* 3–5, 7, 13, 72, 73,

234, 313, 325, 327, 334–5, 396; *Nathan the Wise* 13, 26, 28
Lessing, Johann Gottfried 390
Lessing, Karl 8, 12, 334, 400
Leszczynski, Duke Stanislas 380
Lillo, George 15, 335, 396
Lindelle, M. de la (Voltaire) 143, 147–59, 169, 355
Litzmann, Berthold 328
Liviera, Giambattista 140, 354
Lope de Vega 202, 223, 367, 369–70, 379; *New Art of Writing Plays* 202, 223, 226, 367, 370; *The New Practice of Theater* 370; *Rhymes* 202, 367, 370
Louis XV, King of France 306, 331, 381
Löwen, Elisabeth Lucia Dorothea 51, 395; description/criticism of acting 58, 68, 71–2, 88, 101
Löwen, Johann Friedrich 4–11, 14, 111, 261, 327, 330, 331, 345–6, 380; *History of the German Theater* 11–12; *The New Agnes* 63, 69, 169, 330, 333, 360; *Preliminary Announcement* 10–11; *The Puzzle* 111, 345–6
Lucretia 122, 350
Luscius Lavinius 383
Lyons, Charles 335

Machiavelli, Niccoló 114, 347
Maffei, (Francesco) Scipione 129, 131, 137–48, 150–1, 154–5, 157–62, 166–9, 348, 351; *Merope* 129, 131, 140–69, 351; *Observations on Rodogune* 348; "Response to the Letter from M. de Voltaire" 355–6
Magliabechi, Antonio (Magliabecchi) 319, 400
Marcus Aurelius 248, 376–7
Marin (Marini), François-Louis-Claude 261, 380
Marivaux, Pierre [C. C.] de 82, 90, 108, 234, 338, 341, 344–5, 373; *The Double Inconstancy* 103, 344; *The False Confessions* 82–3, 338; *The Farmer Inherits a Fortune* 108, 345; *The School for Mothers* 341; *The Unforeseen Denouement* 234, 373
Marmontel, Jean François 24–5, 72–3, 111, 120–8, 131, 316, 331, 335, 349, 375, 398; *Denys the Tyrant* 352; *French Poetics* 316, 335, 398; *Marmontel's moral tales* 349, 350; *Memoirs of a Father* 331, 352; *Soliman II* 120–9, 315–16, 349, 350, 398
Marston, John 388–9
Martinec, Thomas 374
Martinson, Steven D. 377

Mary, Queen of Scotland 196
Mason, William 23–4, 318, 400
Maurer-Schmoock, Sybille 324, 377
McCormick, Edward Allen 326
Mecour, Susanna 7, 322, 324
Medea 114, 133, 347
Melpomene 56, 328
Menander 232, 270–2, 279, 281, 291–2, 298–301, 303–4, 369, 371, 383–4, 386–7, 390, 392–3; *Andria* 271; *Anger* 387; *The Brothers* 371; *Colax* 271; *Eunuchus* 271; *Perinthia* 271; *Principle Fragments* 281, 387
Mendelssohn, Moses 3, 19, 238, 243, 327, 346, 348, 361, 377; on compassion 13–14, 19, 238, 243, 348, 361, 374, 375; *Letters Concerning the Newest Literature* 3, 323, 329, 331, 334, 338, 361, 394; *Letters on Sentiments* 238, 243, 374; *Philosophical Writings* 348, 374–5; *Rhapsody* 374; on Rousseau's *Julie* 59
Merschy, (Herr) 83, 339
Meyer, F. L. W. 328, 336
Meyer, Wilhelm Christian Dietrich 346
Miller, Arthur 25
Milton, John 56, 327
Mittelstedt, Matthias Theodor Christoph 342
Molière 25, 32, 62, 70, 74, 91, 110–11, 172, 176–7, 227–8, 267, 282–3, 313–14, 320, 330; *Critique of The School for Wives* 177, 313, 314, 320, 362, 396, 401; *The Imaginary Invalid* 103, 344; *The Misanthrope* 110, 172, 267, 346, 361, 382; *The Miser* 103, 111, 344, 346, 388; *The School for Husbands* 176, 227–8, 362, 371; *The School for Wives* 176–7, 314, 334, 362, 396–7; *Tartuffe* 346; *The Versailles Impromptu* 267, 382; Voltaire's criticism of 177, 227–8
Montesquieu, Charles de Secondat, baron de 131, 353
Montiano y Luyando, Agustín de 222, 369
Moore, Edward 335
Möser, Justus 83, 339, 394
Mouhy, Charles de Fieux, Chevalier de 351
Mücke, Dorothea von 325
Mulier, Pieter the Younger 326
Müller, Heiner 27
Muncker, Franz 396, 399
Murr, Christoph Gottlieb von 390
Mylius, Christlob 10, 325

Nannius, Petrus 392
Napoleon 25
Nauck, August 352

Neuber, Friedericke Caroline 4, 11, 13–14, 82–3, 103, 338
Neufville de Brunaubois-Montador, Chevalier Jean-Florent-Joseph de 398
Nicolai, Friedrich 3, 19, 24, 327, 335, 346, 361, 374, 376–7, 395; *Letters Concerning the Newest Literature* 3, 323, 329, 331, 334, 338, 361, 394; *Library of the Literary Arts* 327, 390, 394, 401; *Treatise on Tragedy* 374
Niklaus, Robert 331–2
Nisbet, H. B. 11–13, 20, 25, 323–4, 330, 348, 351, 359, 369–70, 379, 383, 390, 393, 396
Nivelle de la Chaussée, Pierre Claude 57, 90, 178, 328, 341
Nottingham, Earl of (Charles Howard) 96, 343
Nuth, Franz Anton 333

Ogilby, John 316, 398
Olson, S. Douglas 386
Otway, Thomas 77, 337

Padrino, Joseph 193, 366
Palissot de Montenoy, Charles 266–9, 382–3
Parfaict, Claude 335, 338, 345, 364
Parfaict, François 335, 338, 345, 364
Patrick, Samuel 393
Patzke, Johann Samuel 233, 372
Paulin, Roger 336, 379
Pausanius 131, 352
Pergolesi, Giambattista 351
Pericles 280, 387
Pfeffel, Gottlieb Konrad 74, 336
Phèdre 76, 326, 337
Pherecrates 280, 387
Philemon 62, 279, 330, 386–7
Philip the Second (King of Spain) 223
Phormis 280, 387
Pieri, Marzia 333
Pindar 123, 350
Piscator, Erwin 26
Plato 20, 281, 287, 387, 389
Plautus (Titus Maccius Plautus) 56, 61–2, 90, 182, 223, 272, 278, 283, 328, 329, 341–2, 364, 369, 383, 386, 388, 392; *Amphitryon* 182, 223, 342, 364, 369; *The Braggart Captain* 90, 278, 341, 386; *The Churl* 90, 341; *The Little Pot* 388; *Mostellaria* 386; *The Three Pieces of Money* 61–2, 329
Plessis, Louis-François-Armand de, Duc de Richelieu 381
Pliny (the Elder) 388
Plutarch 132, 137–8, 223, 291, 348, 352, 354, 369, 390, 400

Polybius 138, 354
Polyidus the Sophist 347
Pompadour, Mme. de 381
Pope, Alexander 293, 388, 390
Portal, Abraham 315, 397, 400
Porto, Aemil (Aemilius Portus) 371, 375
Poullain de Saint-Foix, Germain François 341, 370
Propertius (Sextus Propertius) 354
Proteus 56, 327
Pulcinella 131, 352

Quin, James 54, 56, 327
Quinault, Philippe 74, 335, 355
Quintilian (Marcus Fabius Quintilianus) 325

Racine, Jean 4, 99, 164, 192, 255–6, 282, 308, 314, 343–4, 348, 374, 379, 388, 397; *Athalie* 314, 397; *Britannicus* 259, 343, 379, 388; *Mithridate* 102, 238, 344, 374; *Phédre* 326
Rackham, H. 279
Raleigh, Sir Walter 95, 96, 178–80, 342, 343
Ralph, James 193, 366
Randolph, Thomas 286, 389
Rapin de Thoyras, Paul 98, 343
Raspe, Rudolf Erich 349
Raynal, Abbé 351
Reemtsma, Jan Philip 11, 393
Regnard, Jean François 73, 81, 109–11, 330, 335, 338, 344–5; *The Absent-Minded Lover* 103, 109–10, 344–5; *Democritus* 81, 338; *The Gamester* 73, 111, 335, 346
Reich, Savannah 33
Reinesius, Thomas 139, 354
Reinhardt, Max 26
Rembrandt 329
Riccoboni, François (Francesco) 16, 21, 62, 325
Riccoboni, Luigi (Louis) 329
Richardson, Samuel 319, 341, 396, 400
Riley, Henry Thomas 364
Rinaldo I, Duke of Modena 352
Roach, Joseph R. 324, 326, 328
Robertson, John George (J.G.) 11, 26, 322, 324, 326–7, 332–3, 335, 338, 340–2, 345–8, 351–61, 370–2, 374, 380, 392, 394–5, 400
Robertson, William 94, 342
Romanus, Karl Franz 10, 227, 233, 291, 293–4, 370, 372–3, 390–2; *The Brothers* 10, 227, 233–4, 291, 293–301, 370–3, 390–2
Roschmann-Hörburg, Kassian Anton von 322
Roscius (Quintus Roscius Gallus) 53, 327

Rousseau, Jean-Jacques 20, 59, 61, 110, 175–6, 319, 329, 346, 361–2, 401; *Julie, or, the New Heloise* 59–61, 329; *Letter to d'Alembert* 175, 327, 361, 401
Rousseau, Pierre 339
Rowe, Nicholas 77, 326, 337
Roxelane (Hürrem Sultana) 122–3, 128, 316, 349–51, 398

Sainte-Albine, Pierre Rémond de 17, 80, 326, 336–7
Saint-Évremond, Charles de Marguetel de Saint-Denis 252, 377
Saint-Foix, Germain François Poullain de 89, 227, 234, 341, 370; *see also* Poullain de Saint-Foix, Germain François
Saxe-Meiningen, Duke of 9
Scaliger, Julius Caesar 270, 383
Scarron, Paul 177, 362
Schefferi, Joannis (Johannes Gerhard Scheffer) 140, 354
Scheibe, Johann Adolph 103, 344
Schenk, Christian Ernst 237, 374
Schiller, Friedrich 25, 29, 327
Schlegel, Johann Adolf 380
Schlegel, Johann Elias 4–5, 35, 70–1, 109, 151, 172, 315, 322, 334, 357, 361, 397, 399; *The Busy Idler* 172, 361; *Canut* 317, 399; *The Conceited Count* 330; *The Mysterious Man* 172, 361; *The Silent Beauty* 70–2, 315, 334, 397; "Thoughts on the Improvement of the Danish Theater" 322, 357; *The Triumph of the Good Women* 172, 361; "Writings on Comedy in Verse" 334; "Writings on the Establishment of a Theater in Copenhagen" 322
Schlegel, Johann Heinrich 361
Schlösser, Rainer 26
Schmid, Christian Heinrich 236, 333, 373
Schönemann, Johann Friedrich 4, 20, 227, 327, 335, 338, 371
Schröder, Friedrich Ludwig 11, 328, 336
Schröder, Sophie Charlotte *see* Ackermann, Sophie Charlotte
Schulze-Kummerfeld, Karoline 12, 334
Schwabe, J. J. 336
Schwickert, Engelbert Benjamin 393, 395
Scudéry, Georges 181, 363
Scudéry, Madeleine de 378
Selwyn, Pamela E. 395
Seneca, Lucius Annaeus (Seneca the Younger) 223–4, 370, 374

Seyler, Abel 6, 11
Shadwell, Thomas 396
Shakespeare, William 2, 5, 23–5, 28–9, 49–50, 66–7, 75–7, 224, 235, 253, 256, 286, 326, 336, 340, 373–4, 378, 387, 393; "bardolatry" and 24; *Hamlet* 21, 24, 48–50, 56, 66, 326, 332, 340; Jubilee (1769) 23; *Othello* 75–6, 238, 336, 374; *Richard the Third* 235; *Romeo and Juliet* 75; Voltaire and 23, 24, 66–7, 75, 76
Shaw, George Bernard 25, 30
Silarion (Seilanion) 284, 388
Smith, Daniel 33
Socrates 42, 122, 165, 279–81, 350, 360
Solon 52, 118, 327, 348
Sophocles 53, 112, 117, 256, 287–9, 347, 381, 390, 398
Spence, Joseph 319, 400
Spinoza 375
Stanislavski, Konstantin 25, 30
Stephanus, Henricus 390
Sterne, Laurence 305–6, 394
Stewart, Ludovic 377
Storey, Ian C. 280
Stranitzky, Joseph Anton 370
Straparola, Giovanni Francesco 362
Stüven, L. Peter 342
Suabe, Karl August 380
Süleyman I 349–50

Tasso, Torquato 37–8, 40–1, 315, 322–3, 397
Tempesta, Antonio 50, 326
Terence (Publius Terentius Afer) 91, 223, 227–31, 233, 268, 270–3, 278, 284, 291, 293–306, 328, 341, 371–3, 385; *The Brothers* 301, 371–2, 390, 391–3; *Didascaliae* (production notes) 306, 394; *The Eunuch* 341; *The Self Tormentor* 270–3, 383–4; *Woman of Andros* 271, 393
Terentianus Maurus 348
Thalia 53
Themis 52, 327
Theophrastes 388
Thespis 118, 348
Thomson, James 56, 327
Thorillière, Pierre le Noir, sieur de la 82, 338
Tieck, Ludwig 25, 28, 30
Tillemann, Johann Martin 6
Torelli, Pomponio 140, 354
Tournemine, René Joseph de 130, 132–3, 136–7, 351–3
Trublet, Nicolas-Charles-Joseph 176–7, 313, 362, 396–7

Trudaine de Montigny, Jean-Charles
  Philibert 334
Tynan, Kenneth 27

Unton, Sir Henry 96, 343

Vallejo, Manuel Álvarez 366
Victorius (Pietro Vittori) 133, 353
Villars, Nicolas P. H. M. (Abbé de
  Montfaucon de) 330
Villiers, George 377
Virgil, (Publius Vergilius Maro) 38, 144, 323,
  355, 373
Virués, Cristóbal de 202, 367
Voisenon, C.H. Fusée De 175, 361–2
Voltaire 6, 8, 10, 23–30, 40, 63–79, 90–118,
  129–31, 137–47, 149–69, 177, 181–3,
  227–33, 252–6, 261, 315–18, 323, 328,
  330–3, 335–7, 341–3, 346–9, 351, 355–8,
  360, 364–5, 371, 377–8, 380, 397–9,
  398; *Alzire, or, The Americans* 63, 84, 103,
  317, 323, 339, 344, 399; and audience
  on stage 64, 254, 331; *Brutus* 63, 103,
  315, 344, 397; *Caesar* 63; *The Café, or
  the Scottish Woman* 68–9, 332–3; *Call
  to all Nations of Europe* 252–3, 377–8;
  Commentaries on Corneille 181–2, 183,
  347–9, 363–5, 398; criticism of Maffei
  143–69, 353–8; *Discourse on Tragedy*
  336, 397; "Dissertation on Ancient and
  Modern Tragedy" 63–4, 331, 378; "The
  Earl of Essex" 95–102, 318, 342–4, 399;
  Essay on the Manners and Spirit of Nations
  348; *Gertrude, or the Education of a Daughter*
  63, 330; and ghosts in drama 64–7, 107,
  254, 331–2; *The Innocent* 348; Lessing's
  criticism of 40, 63–7, 68–9, 75–9, 90–2,
  95–100, 107, 111, 117–18, 129–31, 137,
  142–62, 165–9, 177, 181–3, 227–8,
  229, 233, 252–6, 261, 316–17, 330, 332,
  343, 347–8, 357; "Letter from M. de
  la Lindelle" 143–58, 169, 355; "Letter
  from Voltaire" 330; "Letter to Maffei"
  137, 142–50, 353, 355–6; "Letter to Mr.
  Berger" 73, 335; *The Life of Molière* 227–8,
  362, 371, 397; *Mahomet* 84–5, 317, 339,
  399; *Mérope* 8, 64, 129–31, 142–5, 150–69,
  351; *Nanine* 10, 90, 91, 108, 129, 234,
  328, 341; *Oedipus* 397; *The Prodigal Son*
  103, 335, 341, 344; "Response to M. de
  la Lindelle" 143, 150–1, 355, 356, 357;
  Sémiramis 8, 63–7, 103, 105, 107, 254, 325,
  331–2, 345; and Shakespeare 23–4, 28,
  66–7, 75–7, 256; *What Pleases the Ladies*
  345–6; *The Woman who is Right* 261, 380;
  Zaïre 63–4, 75–9, 84, 103, 336–9, 344
Vrooman, Jack R. 351–2, 355–6

Waddicor, Mark 380
Wagner, Richard 25, 30
Walpole, Horace 96, 343
Warburton, William 390
Wegener, Paul 26
Weisse, Christian Felix 5, 89, 139, 235–6,
  335, 340–1, 345, 354, 373, 377, 380;
  Amalia 89, 236, 340–1, 373; *Atreus und
  Thyest* 354; Lessing's harsh criticism of 5,
  373; *Richard III* 235–7, 249–51, 261, 345,
  373, 377, 380; as translator 335
Wellbery, David E. 325
Wertenbaker, Timberlake 338
Whitehead, William 165, 359
Wichmann, Christian August 341
Wieland, Christoph Martin 76, 336, 370,
  373, 387; as critic 224, 226, 370, 373; *The
  History of Agathon* 224–6, 370; translation
  of Shakespeare 76, 336, 370, 387
Wild, Henry 319, 400
Williams, David 349, 377, 398
Williams, John 388
Wolff, Christian 332
Wycherley, William 69, 333
Wykes, David 362–3

Yermolenko, Galina 349–50
Yonge, C. D. 384
Young, Edward 130, 351–2, 394

Zayas y Sotomayor, Doña Maria de 362
Zimmern, Helen 25, 30–1, 33

TITLE INDEX

Note: English-language titles in the list below are alphabetized without articles; foreign-language titles are alphabetized with articles. Works originally published in a foreign language appear with their original title first followed by an English translation in brackets.

"Abhandlungen von dem weinerlichen oder rührenden Lustspiele" ["Essays on the weepy or touching comedies"] (Lessing, G. E.) 328

Abhandlung vom Trauerspiele [Treatise on Tragedy] (Nicolai, F.) 374

"Abhandlung von den Pantomimen der Alten" ["Treatise on the Pantomime of the Ancients"] (Lessing, G. E.) 20, 325

"Abhandlung von der Absicht des Trauerspiels" ["Treatise on the Purpose of Tragedy"] (Curtius, C.) 249, 377

"Abhandlung zur Fabel: I. Von dem Wesen der Fabel" ["Treatise on the Fable: I. On the Nature of the Fable"] (Lessing, G. E.) 324

Actor, The: or, A Treatise on the Art of Playing (Hill, J.) 17

Adelphi (or Adelphoe) [The Brothers] (Menander) 298–301, 303–4, 371, 392, 393

Adelphi (or Adelphoe) [The Brothers] (Terence) 227–33, 268, 291, 293–304, 371–2, 391–3

Aeneid (Virgil) 323

"Al Lettore" ["To the Reader"] (Becelli, C.) 166–7, 360

Alzire, ou les Américains [Alzire; or, The Americans] (Voltaire) 63, 84, 103, 317, 323, 339, 344, 399

Amalia (Weisse, C.) 89, 236, 340–1, 373

Amphitryon (Plautus) 182, 223, 342, 364, 369

Analysis of Beauty, The (Hogarth, W.) 46, 325

Andria (Menander) 271

Andria [Woman of Andros] (Terence) 271, 304, 393

Annette et Lubin [Annette and Lubin] (Mme. Favart & Voisenon, C. H. F. de) 176, 362

Anthologia Latina 340

Appel à toutes les nations de l'Europe, des jugements d'un écrivain anglais; ou manifeste au sujet des honneurs du pavillon entre les théâtres de Londres et de Paris [Call to all Nations of Europe . . .] (Voltaire) 252–3, 377–8

"Appian Alexandrin" (Corneille, P.) 112–15, 347

Aristoteles Dichtkunst [Aristotle's Poetics] (Curtius, C. M.) 134, 243, 245, 248–9, 276–7, 353, 374, 375, 376–7, 385

Aristotelis Artis rhetoricæ [Aristotle's Art of Rhetoric] (Aristotle & Porto, A.) 371

Aristotelis de poetica liber [Aristotle's Poetics] (Goulston, T.) 243, 375

Ars Poetica [Art of Poetry] (Horace) 272, 282, 283, 286, 326, 339, 355, 362, 365, 384, 386, 389

Artamène (Scudéry, M. de) 252, 377

Arte Nuevo de Hazer Comedias [The New Art of Writing Plays] (Lope de Vega) 202, 223, 226, 367, 370

Ataúlfo (Montiano y Luyando, A. de) 369
Athalie (Racine, J.) 314, 397
Atrée et Thyeste [*Atreus and Thyestes*]
 (Crébillon, P. J. de) 374
Atreus und Thyest [*Thyestes*] (Weisse, C. F.) 354
Attila (Corneille, P.) 253, 378
Aulularia [*The Little Pot*] (Plautus)
 283–4, 388
"Aus dem Komödiantenleben des vorigen
 Jahrhunderts: Denkwürdigkeiten von
 Karoline Schulze" ["Memoirs of Karoline
 Schulze"] (Schulze-Kummerfeld, K.) 334
"Auszug aus dem Schauspieler des Herrn
 Remond von Sainte Albine" ["Excerpt
 from The Actor by Mr. Remond von
 Sainte Albine"] (Lessing, G. E.) 17, 326
"Auszug aus dem Trauerspiele Virginia des
 Don Augustino de Montiano y Luyando"
 ["Excerpt from the Tragedy Virginia by
 Don Augustino de Montiano y Luyando"]
 (Lessing, G. E.) 369

*Beyträge zur Historie und Aufnahme des
 Theaters* [*Contributions to the History and
 Improvement of the Theater*] (Lessing, G. E.)
 3, 14, 329
Biblioteca teatrale italiana [*Theatrical Library*]
 (Diodati, O.) 57, 69, 328, 333
Bibliothek der schönen Wissenschaften [*Library
 of the Literary Arts*] (Nicolai, F.) 327, 390,
 394, 401
Bradamante (Garnier, R.) 182, 364
Bremer Beiträge [*Bremen Contributions*] 380
Briefe, antiquarischen Inhalts [*Antiquarian
 Letters*] (Lessing, G. E.) 383
Briefe, die neueste Litteratur betreffend [*Letters
 Concerning the Newest Literature*] (Lessing,
 G. E., Mendelssohn, M. & Nicolai, F.) 3,
 59, 323, 329, 331, 334, 338, 361, 394
Briefe über die Empfindungen [*Letters on Sentiments*]
 (Mendelssohn, M.) 238, 243, 374
"Brief von Voltaire" ["Letter from Voltaire"]
 dated 1 January [1752] (Voltaire) 330
"Briefwechsel über das Trauerspiel"
 ["Correspondence on Tragedy"] (Lessing,
 G. E.) 28, 329, 330, 331, 374, 376
Britannicus (Racine, J.) 259, 343, 379, 388
Bruder Philipps Schwester [*Brother Philip's Sister*]
 (Heufeld, F. von) 315, 397
Brutus (Voltaire) 63, 103, 315, 344, 397

Caelia (Johnson, C.) 396
Caesar (Voltaire) 63

Canut (Schlegel, J. E.) 317, 399
Caractacus (Mason, W.) 318, 400
Castle of Otranto, The (Walpole, H.) 96, 343
Cato 103, 336–7, 344
Cénie (Grafigny, F. de) 32, 69, 87, 92, 175–6,
 333, 340, 342, 362
Ce qui plaît aux dames [*What Pleases the
 Ladies*] (Voltaire) 111, 346
Chaereas and Callirrhoë (Chariton & d'Orville,
 J. P.) 160, 358
Chronographia (Eusebius of Caesarea) 386
Cinna (Corneille, P.) 111, 265, 317, 347,
 382, 399
Clandestine Marriage, The (Colman, G. [the
 Elder] & Garrick, D.) 333
Clarissa (Richardson, S.) 319–20, 396, 400–1
Clélie (Scudéry, M. de) 252, 377
Clouds (Aristophanes) 386–7
Cocalos (Aristophanes) 279, 386
Codex Bembo (Bembo, P.) 384
Codrus (Cronegk, J. F. von) 39, 41, 55, 314,
 323, 335, 397
Colax (Menander) 271
Comedies of Terence, The (Colman, G. [the
 Elder]) 270, 303–4, 383, 393
Commentaires sur Corneille [*Commentaries on
 Corneille*] (Voltaire) 181–2, 183, 347–9,
 363–5, 398
*Commentarii in primum librum Aristotelis
 De arte poetarum* [*Commentary on the
 First Book of Aristotle, De Arte Poetarum*]
 (Victorius, P.) 133, 353
Companion to the Theatre, A 178, 363
Conceited Count, The (Destouches, P. N.)
 62, 330
Conjectures on Original Composition (Young, E.)
 351, 394
Contes moraux [*Marmontel's moral tales*]
 (Marmontel, J. F.) 349–50
"Correspondence with Nicolai and
 Mendelssohn" (Lessing, G. E.) 330,
 376, 377
Cresphontes (Euripides) 131–3, 138–40, 146,
 159–60, 351–60
Creusa, Queen of Athens (Whitehead, W.)
 165, 359
Critischer Musikus [*Critical Musician*] (Scheibe,
 J. A.) 103, 344

Dar la vida por su dama [*To Die for One's Lady*]
 (Coello, A.) 193–223, 366–9
Das ausgerechnete Glück [*The Calculated
 Fortune*] (Schlegel, J. A.) 380

Das Caffeehaus, ein rührendes Lustspiel [*The Coffeehouse, a moving comedy*] (Bode, J. J. C.) 68, 332

Das Caffeehaus, oder die Schottländerinn [*The Coffeehouse, or the Scotch Woman*] (Bode, J. J. C.) 332

Das Gespenste mit der Trummel [*The Ghost with the Drum*] (Gottsched, L. A. V.) 81, 330

Das Loos in der Loterie [*The Lottery Ticket*] (Gellert, C. F.) 319, 400

Das Orakel (Schönemann, J. F.) 227, 370

Das Räthsel, oder, Was dem Frauenzimmer am meisten gefällt [*The Puzzle, or, What Pleases the Ladies*] (Löwen, J. F.) 111, 345–6

Das Testament [*The Last Will*] (Gottsched, L. A. V.) 102, 344

Das Theater des Herrn Diderot [*The Theater of M. Diderot*] (Lessing, G. E.) 334, 342, 359, 365, 381

Decameron (Boccacio) 362

"De Capienda Ex Inimicis Utilitate" ["How to profit by one's enemies"] (Plutarch) 138, 354

Deipnosophistai, The (Athenaeus) 394

De la Poésie Dramatique, à Monsieur Grimm (Discours sur la poésie dramatique) [*Discourse on Dramatic Poetry, to Mr. Grimm*] (Diderot, D.) 161, 359, 380–3

Démocrite amoureux [*Democritus*] (Regnard, J.F.) 81, 338

Demokrit, oder der lachende Philosoph [*Democritus, or the laughing philosopher*] (Koch, H.G.) 338

Denys le Tyran [*Denys the Tyrant*] (Marmontel, J.F.) 352

De Officiis [*On Duties*] (Cicero) 90, 341

De Oratore [*On Oratory*] (Cicero) 286, 287, 389

Der Bauer mit der Erbschaft [*The Farmer Inherits a Fortune*] (Marivaux, P. [C. C.] de & Krüger, J. C. [trans.]) 345

Der betrogene Lackenhändler [*The Swindled Paint Merchant*] 335

Der Einsiedler [*The Recluse*] (Pfeffel, G.K.) 336

Der Eremit [*The Hermit*] (Pfeffel, G.K.) 74, 336

Der Freigeist [*The Freethinker*] (Brawe, J. W. von) 74, 335

Der Freigeist [*The Freethinker*] (Lessing, G. E.) 74, 335

Der Geburtstag [*The Birthday*] (Heufeld, F. von) 315, 397

Der Geheimnißvolle [*The Mysterious Man*] (Schlegel, J. E.) 172, 361

Der geschäftige Müßiggänger [*The Busy Idler*] (Schlegel, J. E.) 172, 361

Der Graf von Essex [*The Earl of Essex*] (Corneille, T. & Stüven, L. P.) 342

Der Junge Gelehrte [*The Young Scholar*] (Lessing, G. E.) 11

Der Mann nach der Uhr, oder der ordentliche Mann [*The Man of the Clock, or the Regular Man*] (Hippel, T. G. von) 93, 175, 342

Der Mistrauische [*The Suspicious Man*] (Cronegk, J. F. von) 314, 361, 397

Der Poetische Dorfjunker [*The Poetical Village Squire*] (Gottsched, L. A. V.) 330

Der Ruhmredige [*The Conceited Count*] (Schlegel, J. E.) 330

Der Schatz [*The Treasure*] (Lessing, G.E.) 62, 329

Der Schatz [*The Treasure*] (Pfeffel, G. K.) 74, 336

"Der Schauspieler: Ein Werk worinne [sic] die Grundsätze der ganzen körperlichen Beredsamkeit entwickelt werden" ["The Actor: A work in which the basic principles of a whole bodily expressivity will be developed"] (Lessing, G. E.) 21, 325

Der Triumph der Guten Frauen [*The Triumph of the Good Women*] (Schlegel, J. E.) 172, 361

Der unvermuthete Ausgang [*The Unforeseen Denouement*] (Krüger, J.C.) 234, 373

Der verehelichte Philosoph [*The Married Philosopher*] (Krüger, J.C. & Ekhof, K.) 68, 332

Der Verschwender [*The Spendthrift*] (Gottsched, L. A. V.) 330

"Des Herrn Jacob Thomson Sämtliche Trauerspiele" ["The Complete Tragedies of Mr. Jacob Thomson"] (preface) (Lessing, G. E.) 327

Des Herrn Nericault Destouches sämtliche theatralische Werke [*Complete Works of Destouches*] (Destouches, P. N.) 332

Des Publius Terenzius Lustspiele aus dem lateinischen übersetzt [*The Comedies of Publius Terentius, translated from the Latin*] (Patzke, J. S.) 233, 372

"De Syllabis" ["On syllables"] (Terentianus Maurus) 348

Deutsche Bibliothek der schönen Wissenschaften [*German Library of Liberal Arts and Sciences*] (Klotz, C. A.) 292, 309, 390, 394, 401

Dictionnaire portatif historique [*Portable historical dictionary*] (Léris, A. de) 326, 335

Didascaliae (Terence) 306, 394

Die Brüder, oder die Schule der Väter [*The Brothers, or The School for Fathers*] (Romanus, K. F.) 10, 227, 233–4, 291, 293–301, 370–3, 390–2

Die bulhafftige Mutter [*The Flirtatious Mother*] 335

Die Candidaten, oder die Mittel zu einem Amte zu gelangen [*The Candidates, or the Means to an Office*] (Krüger, J. C.) 261, 380
Die Deutsche Schaubühne [*The German Stage*] (Gottsched, J. C.) 5, 69–70, 102, 330, 333, 344, 361
Die Geistlichen auf dem Lande [*The Clergymen in the Country*] (Krüger, J. C.) 261, 380
Die Gouvernante [*The Governess*] (Kurz, J. F. von) 333
Die Gouvernante [*The Governess*] (Nuth, F. A.) 69, 333
Die Hausfranzösin, oder die Mamsell [*The French Housekeeper, or the Mamsell*] (Gottsched, L. A. V.) 102, 344
Die Haushaltung nach der Mode, oder Was soll man für eine Frau nehmen? [*Housekeeping à la mode, or What should one take for a wife?*] (Heufeld, F. von) 315, 328, 397
Die kranke Frau [*The Sick Woman*] (Gellert, C. F.) 92, 342
Die Liebhaber nach der Mode, oder Was soll man für einen Mann nehmen? [*The Fashionable Lovers, or What should one take for a husband?*] (Heufeld, F. von) 315, 328, 397
Die neue Agnese [*The New Agnes*] (Löwen, J. F.) 63, 69, 169, 330, 333, 360,
Die Schaubühne als eine moralische Anstalt betrachtet [*The Stage Considered as a Moral Institution*] (Schiller, F.) 327
"Die Schauspielkunst" ["The Art of Acting"] (Lessing, G. E.) 325
Die stumme Schönheit [*The Silent Beauty*] (Schlegel, J. E.) 70–2, 315, 334, 397
Die Verräther [*The Traitors*] (Cramer, C. F.) 381
Discours sur la Tragedie [*Discourse on Tragedy*] (Voltaire) 336, 397
Discurso sobre las tragedia españolas [*Discourse on Spanish Tragedies*] (Montiano y Luyando, A. de) 369
"Dissertation on the Provinces of the Drama" (Hurd, R.) 279, 282, 290, 386, 388
"Dissertation sur la tragédie ancienne et modern" ["Dissertation on Ancient and Modern Tragedy"] (Voltaire) 63–4, 331, 378
Dissertation sur les Représentations Théâtrales des Anciens [*Inquiry into the Theatrical Entertainments of the Ancients*] (Dubos, Abbé) 325
Divinae institutiones [*The Divine Institutes*] (Lactantius) 371
Don Quixote (Cervantes, M. de) 367, 376
Douglas (Home, J.) 68, 333
Dowry, The (Cecchi, G. M.) 62, 329

Dramaturgische Blätter [*Dramaturgical Pages*] (Knigge, A. F. von) 25, 28
Drummer, The, or the Haunted House (Addison, J.) 330, 338
Dumb Beauty, The (Schlegel, J. E., and Lefevere, A. [trans.]) 70–2, 315, 334, 397

Earl of Essex (Brooke, H.) 192–3, 365, 317, 399
Earl of Essex (Jones, H.) 192–3, 365, 317, 399
"On the Eating of Flesh (De esu carnium) II" (Plutarch) 132, 137, 352, 354
Eirene (Aristophanes) 280, 387
Electra (Euripides) 117, 133, 288–9, 389–90
Electra (Sophocles) 117, 289, 390
Elegies (Propertius) 354
Elements of Criticism (Home, H.) 318, 399
Elfrida (Mason, W.) 318, 400
Emilia Galotti (Lessing, G. E.) 13, 369
Encyclopédie (d'Alembert, J. & Diderot, D.) 334, 382
"English Merchant, A Comedy, The" 333
English Merchant, The (Colman, G. [the Elder]) 68–9, 333
Entretiens d'Ariste et d'Eugène [*Conversations between Ariste and Eugène*] (Bouhours, D.) 378
Entretiens sur Le Fils naturel [*Conversations on the Natural Son*] (Diderot, D.) 20, 191, 262, 266–74, 281–2, 325, 365, 381–5
Ephesian Matron, The (Johnson, C.) 316, 398
"Ephesian Matron, The: or Widow's Tears" (Ogilby, J.) 316, 398
Essais sur divers sujets de litterature et de la morale [*Essays on diverse literary subjects and on morals*] (Trublet, N. C. J.) 396
Essai sur les moeurs et l'esprit des nations [*Essay on the Manners and Spirit of Nations*] (Voltaire) 348
"Essay on Man" (Pope, A.) 284, 388
Eunuchus (Menander) 271
Eunuchus [*The Eunuch*] (Terence) 271–2, 341
Every Man in his Humour (Jonson, B.) 285, 388
Every Man out of his Humour (Jonson, B.) 285, 388–9
"Examen de Rodogune" ["Examination of Rodogune"] (Corneille, P.) 112, 347

"Fabeln und Fabelabhandlungen" ["Fables and Essays on the Fable"] (Lessing, G. E.) 127–8, 350
False Agnès, The, or the Country Poet (Destouches, P. N.) 62, 69, 333
Flower (Agathon) 275, 384

Gamester, The (Moore, E.) 73, 335
"Gedanken zur Aufnahme des dänischen
    Theaters" ["Thoughts on the
    Improvement of the Danish Theater"]
    (Schlegel, J. E.) 35, 151–2, 322, 357
Georgics (Virgil) 355
Gertrude, ou, L'éducation d'une fille [*Gertrude,
    or the Education of a Daughter*] (Voltaire)
    63, 330
Gerusalemme Liberata [*Jerusalem Delivered*]
    (Tasso, T.) 322, 397
Geschichte des Agathon [*History of Agathon*]
    (Wieland, C. M.) 224–6, 370
"Geschichte des deutschen Theaters"
    ["History of the German Theater"]
    (Löwen, J. F.) 11–12
Giangir oder der verschmähte Thron [*Giangir, or
    the Rejected Throne*] (Lessing, G. E.) 349
Glossa interlinealis (Ascensius) 270, 383
Governess, The (Kurz, J. F. von) 69, 333
Governess, The (Nuth, F. A.) 69, 333
"Grammatik der Schauspielkunst" ["Rules
    for Acting"] (Ekhof, K.) 14
Gustavus Vasa (Brooke, H.) 317, 399

Hamlet (Shakespeare, W.) 21, 24, 48–50, 56,
    66, 326, 332, 340
Heauton Timorumenos / The Self-Tormentor
    (Terence) 270–3, 383–4
Hecuba (Euripides) 164, 192, 359, 365
Helen (Euripides) 117, 347
Helle 137, 354, 369
Héraclius (Corneille, P.) 257–8, 375–9
Herzog Michel [*Duke Michael*] (Krüger, J. C.)
    235, 261, 373, 380
Hidden Treasure, The (Destouches, P. N.)
    62, 329
Histoire d'Angleterre [*History of England*]
    (Rapin de Thoyras, P.) 98, 343
*Histoire du théâtre français depuis son origine
    jusqu'à présent* [*History of French Theater
    from its origins to the present*] (Parfaict, C. &
    Parfaict, F.) 182, 335, 338, 345, 364
Histoire du Théâtre Italien [*History of Italian
    Theater*] (Riccoboni, L.) 329
Histoire générale du théâtre français [*General
    History of French Theater*] (Parfaict, C. &
    Parfaict, F.) 335
Histories, The (Herodotus) 384
Histories of Polybius, The (Polybius & Hultsch)
    138, 354
History of England (Hume, D.) 94, 95,
    342, 364

History of Scotland (Robertson, W.) 94, 342
*Hygini Quae hodie extant, adcurante Joanne
    Scheffero Argentoratensi [...]* (Schefferi, J.)
    140, 354

Il Caffè o La Scozzese [*The Coffee House*]
    (Goldoni, C.) 68, 333
Il Cresfonte [*Cresphontes*] (Liviera, G.) 140, 354
Iliad, The (Homer) 92, 341, 354–5
Imitation of Horace (Pope, A.) 390
Institutes of Oratory, The (Quintilian) 325
Ion (Euripides) 164–5, 359
Iphigenia in Tauris (Euripides) 117, 136–8,
    347, 353–4
Isabelle et Gertrude ou les Sylphes supposés
    [*Isabelle and Gertrude, or the Imagined
    Sylphs*] (Favart, C. S.) 63, 330

Jealous Wife, The (Colman, G. [the Elder])
    69, 333
Joseph Andrews (Fielding, H.) 319–20, 400–1
Journal Encyclopédique [*Encyclopedic Journal*]
    (Rousseau, P. [ed]) 122, 193, 314, 316,
    339–40, 350, 366, 397–9
Journal Étranger [*Foreign Journal*] 72, 335
Julie, oder Wettstreit der Pflicht und Liebe [*Julie,
    or the Conflict between Duty and Love*]
    (Heufeld, F. von) 59–61, 315, 328, 397
*Julie ou la nouvelle Héloïse, ou Lettres de deux
    amants* [*Julie, or the New Heloise*] (Rousseau,
    J. J.) 59–61, 329

Komisches Theater (Schenk, C. E.) 237, 374

La Critique d'École des femmes [*The Critique
    of the School for Wives*] (Molière) 177, 313,
    314, 320, 362, 396, 401
La Double Inconstance [*The Double Inconstancy*]
    (Marivaux, P. [C. C.] de) 103, 344
La Famille [*The Family / Is he a member of the
    Family?*] (L'Affichard, T.) 80, 261, 338, 380
La Farce de Maître Pierre Pathelin [*The Farce of
    Master Pierre Pathelin*] 335
La fausse Agnès, ou Le poète campagnard [*The
    Young Hypocrite, or, The Country Poet*]
    (Destouches, P. N.) 69, 330, 333
La fée Urgele, ou, Ce qui plait aux dames [*The
    Fairy Urgele, or, What Pleases the Ladies*]
    (Favart, C. S.) 111, 346
La Femme qui a raison [*The Woman who is
    Right*] (Voltaire) 261, 380
"La laitière et le pot au lait" ["The Milkmaid and
    the Pot of Milk"] (La Fontaine, J. de) 380

L'Amant auteur et valet [*The Lover, Author and Servant*] (Cérou, P.) 74, 335

La Matron d'Ephese [*The Matron of Ephesus*] (La Motte, H. de) 129, 351, 398

La Mère Coquette, ou, Les Amans Brouillés [*The Coquette Mother*] (Quinault, P.) 74, 335

La Merope (Torelli, P.) 140, 354

L'Année littéraire [*The Literary Annual*] (Fréron, É. C.) 333

Laokoon: oder über die Grenzen der Malerei und Poesie [*Laocoon: An Essay on the Limits of Painting and Poetry*] (Lessing, G. E.) 326, 329, 390

La Petite Nièce d'Eschyle [*The grand-niece of Aeschylus*] (Neufville de Brunaubois-Montador, J. F. J. de) 316, 398

La Pratique du Théâtre [*The Whole Art of the Stage*] (Hédelin, F.) 20, 152, 163, 182, 327, 357, 359, 363–4

La Précaution inutil [*The useless precaution*] (Scarron, P.) 177, 362

L'Art du théâtre [*Art of the Theater*] (Riccoboni, F.) 21, 325

La Serva Padrona [*The Maid the Mistress*] (Pergolesi, G.) 129, 351

La Siège de Calais [*The Siege of Calais*] (Belloy, P. B. de) 83, 316

L'Avare [*The Miser*] (Molière) 103, 111, 344, 346, 388

L'Aveugle clairvoyant [*The Seeing Blindman*] (Brosse) 261, 380

La Vie de Molière [*The Life of Molière*] (Voltaire) 227–8, 362, 371, 397

L'Avocat Patelin [*The Village Lawyer*] (Brueys, D. A. de) 74, 92, 129, 335

Laws (Plato) 281

"Leben des Herrn Nericault Destouches" ["Life of Mr. Nericault Destouches"] (Lessing, G. E.) 330

"Leben des Thomson" ["Thomson's Life"] (Lessing, G. E.) 327

Lebenserinnerungen [*Memoirs*] (Schulze-Kummerfeld, K.) 12, 334

Le Caffé, ou L'écossaise [*The Café, or the Scottish Woman*] (Voltaire) 68–9, 332–3

Le Chevalier Joueur [*The Gambling Knight*] (Dufresny, C. R.) 335

Le Chevalier qui fit les cons parler [*The Knight Who Made Cunts Speak*] (Geurin) 381

Le Cid [*The Cid*] (Corneille, P.) 111, 176, 181–2, 184, 255, 347, 363–4, 378

L'École des femmes [*The School for Wives*] (Molière) 176–7, 314, 334, 362, 396–7

L'École des maris [*The School for Husbands*] (Molière) 176, 227–8, 362, 371

L'École des mères [*The School for Mothers*] (Marivaux, P. [C. C.] de) 341

L'École des mères [*The School for Mothers*] (Nivelle de la Chaussée, P. C.) 90, 178, 341, 362

L'École des pères [*The School for Fathers*] (Baron [Boyron], M.) 370, 372

Le Comédien [*The Actor*] (Sainte-Albine, P. R. de) 80, 326, 336–7

Le Comte d'Essex [*The Earl of Essex*] (Calprenède, G.) 93–4, 178, 185, 342

Le Comte d'Essex [*The Earl of Essex*] (Corneille, T.) 93–102, 178, 182, 186, 190, 342–4, 362–5, 399

"Le Comte d'Essex" [*"The Earl of Essex"*] (Voltaire) 95–102, 318, 342–4, 399

Le Comte de Gabalis, ou Entretiens sur les sciences secretes [*The Count of Gabalis, or Conversations about the Secret Sciences*] (Villars, Abbé de) 63, 330

Le Dénouement Imprévu [*The Unforeseen Denouement*] (Marivaux, P. [C. C.] de) 234, 373

Le Dissipateur [*The Spendthrift*] (Destouches, P. N.) 62, 330

Le Distrait [*The Absent-Minded Lover*] (Regnard, J.F.) 103, 109–10, 344–5

Le Faucon et les oies de Bocace [*Boccaccio's The Falcon and the Geese*] (Delisle de la Drevetière, L.) 83, 103, 338, 344

Le Fils naturel [*The Natural Son*] (Diderot, D.) 20, 262, 266–9, 273–4, 365, 381–5

Le Financier [*The Financier*] (Poullain de Saint-Foix, G. F.) 89, 341

Le François à Londres [*The Frenchman in London*] (Boissy, L. de) 316, 398

Le Glorieux [*The Conceited Count*] (Destouches, P. N.) 62, 330

Le Jaloux Désabusé [*The Disillusioned Jealous One*] (Campistron, J. de) 169–71, 361

Le Joueur [*The Gamester*] (Regnard, J. F.) 73, 111, 335, 346

Le Malade Imaginaire [*The Imaginary Invalid*] (Molière) 103, 344

Le Menteur [*The Liar*] (Corneille, P.) 260, 379

Le Misanthrope [*The Misanthrope*] (Molière) 110, 172, 267, 346, 361, 382

L'Enfant prodigue [*The Prodigal Son*] (Voltaire) 103, 335, 341, 344

Le Père de Famille [*The Father of the Family*] (Diderot, D.) 20, 262, 266, 342, 359, 380, 382

Le Philosophe marié [*The Married Philosopher*] (Destouches, P. N.) 62, 68, 74, 87, 169–72, 330, 332, 360–1

Le piacevoli Notti [*The Nights of Straparola*] (Straparola, G. F.) 177, 362

Les Beaux-Arts Réduits à un Même Principe [*The Fine Arts Distilled into a Few Principles*] (Batteux, C.) 325

Les Bijoux indiscrets [*The Indiscreet Jewels*] (Diderot, D.) 262–6, 381–2

Les Fausses Confidences [*The False Confessions*] (Marivaux, P. [C. C.] de) 82–3, 338

Le Tambour nocturne [*The Nocturnal Drummer*] (Destouches, P. N.) 62, 330, 338

Le Trésor caché [*The Hidden Treasure*] (Destouches, P. N.) 62, 329–30

Le Triomphe du temps passé [*The Triumph of Times Past*] (Le Grand, M. A.) 51, 326

"Letter to Karl Lessing" (Letter 373) dated 22 May 1767 (Lessing, G. E.) 334

Letter to Nicolai (Letter 509) dated 11 October 1769 (Lessing, G. E.) 323, 330, 346, 374, 376

Lettre à d'Alembert sur les spectacles [*Letter to D'Alembert on the Theatre*] (Rousseau, J. J.) 175, 327, 361, 401

"Lettre à M. Berger" ["Letter to M. Berger"] (Voltaire) 73, 335

"Lettre à Monsieur le Marquis Scipion Maffei" ["A Letter to the Marquis Scipio Maffei"] (Voltaire) 137, 142–50, 353, 355–6

"Lettre de M. de la Lindelle" ["Letter from M. de la Lindelle"] (Voltaire) 143–58, 169, 355–60

"Lettre de Mr. [sic] de Voltaire, à Mr. [sic] l'Abbé d'Olivet" ["Letter from Mr. de Voltaire to Mr. Abbé d'Olivet"] 398–9

"Lettre du Père de Tournemine" ["A Letter"] (Tournemine, R. J. de) 130, 132–3, 136–7, 351–3

Lettres familières [*Familiar Letters*] (Montesquieu, C.) 137, 353

Lettre sur les sourds et les mouets [*Letter on the deaf and dumb*] (Diderot, D.) 20, 381

L'Héritier de Village [*The Farmer Inherits a Fortune*] (Marivaux, P. [C. C.] de) 108, 345

L'Homme singulier [*The Singular Man*] (Destouches, P. N.) 268, 383

L'Humanité, ou, le tableau de l'indigence [*Humanity, or, The Picture of Indigence*] (Boisset, P. L. P. R. de) 73, 335

Life and Opinions of Tristram Shandy, Gentleman, The (Sterne, L.) 305–6, 394

Life of Virgil (Donatus, A.) 373

L'Impromptu de Versailles [*The Impromptu at Versailles*] (Molière) 267, 382

L'Ingénu [*The Innocent*] (Voltaire) 348

L'Irrésolu [*The Irresolute Man*] (Destouches, P. N.) 103, 344

Lives of Eminent Philosophers (Diogenes Laertius) 118, 348

Lives of the Poets of Great Britain and Ireland, The (Cibber, T.) 178, 253, 317, 327, 362–3, 378, 398, 399

L'Observateur des Spectacles (Chevrier, F. A. de) 169, 175, 361

L'Obstacle imprévu, ou, L'obstacle sans obstacle [*The Unexpected Obstacle, or the Obstacle without Obstacle*] (Destouches, P. N.) 62, 330

London Merchant, The (Lillo, G.) 335, 396

L'Oracle [*The Oracle*] (Poullain de Saint-Foix, G. F.) 227, 234, 370

Mahomet (Voltaire) 84–5, 317, 339, 399

Mannheimer Dramaturgie [*Mannheim Dramaturgy*] (Gemmingen-Hornberg, O. H.) 25

Margites (Homer) 280, 387

Meditations (Marcus Aurelius) 376

Mélanide (Nivelle de la Chaussée, P. C.) 57, 93, 328

Mélite (Corneille, P.) 240

Mémoires de Mademoiselle Bontemps, ou de la Comtesse de Marlou [*Memoirs of Mlle. Bontemps*] (Gueullette, T.) 57, 328

Mémoires d'un père pour servir a l'instruction de ses enfants [*Memoirs of a Father*] (Marmontel, J. F.) 331, 352

Menandri Et Philemonis Reliquiæ, Quotquot Reperiri Potuerunt [*Menander, the Principle fragments*] (Menander) 281, 387

Merope (Maffei, [F.] S.) 131, 138, 141–69, 351–60

Mérope (Voltaire) 8, 64, 129–31, 142–5, 150–69, 351–60

Messingkauf Dialogues, The (Brecht, B.) 26

Miles Gloriosus [*The Braggart Captain*] (Plautus) 90, 278, 341, 386

Minna von Barnhelm (Lessing, G. E.) 3, 7, 11, 13, 319, 325, 378, 400

Miss Sara Sampson (Lessing, G. E.) 3–5, 7, 13, 72, 73, 234, 313, 325, 327, 334–5, 396

"Miss Sara Sampson, Tragèdie bourgeoise de M. Lessing" ["Miss Sara Sampson, bourgeois tragedy by Mr. Lessing"] ([Trudaine de Montigny, J.]) 72, 422

Mithridate (Racine, J.) 102, 238, 344, 374

Monthly Review, The 318–19, 333, 365, 400
Mostellaria (Plautus) 386
"Mr. James Thomson" (Cibber, T.) 327
Myths of Hyginus, The (Hyginus) 131–2,
  138–42, 159–60, 352, 354, 358, 359, 360

Nanine (Voltaire) 10, 90, 91, 108, 129, 234,
  328, 341
Nathan the Wise (Lessing, G. E.) 13, 26, 28
Naturalis historia (Pliny the Elder) 388
Neue Hamburgische Dramaturgie [*New Hamburg
  Dramaturgy*] (Albrecht, H. C.) 25
Nichomachean Ethics (Aristotle) 239, 279, 374,
  379, 386
Nicomede (Corneille, P.) 375, 378
"Nisus and Euryalus" (Virgil) 38, 323
"Notes on the Art of Poetry" (Hurd, R.)
  282–90, 389–90, 400
"Nouvelle Pratique de Théatre" ["The New
  Practice of Theater"] (Lope de Vega) 370

Oedipus (Sophocles) 135, 238, 248, 253, 354,
  374, 376
Oedipus (Voltaire) 397
Oeuvres dramatiques de Néricault Destouches
  [*Dramatic Works of Néricault Destouches*]
  (Destouches, P. N.) 171–2, 361
Olindo and Sophronia (Portal, A.) 315, 319,
  397, 400
Olint und Sophronia [*Olint and Sophronia*]
  (Cronegk, J. F. von) 20, 37–57, 322,
  397, 399
Olympia (Pindar) 123, 350
Orge [*Anger*] (Menander) 387
Osservazioni sopra la Rodoguna [*Observations
  on Rodogune*] (Maffei, [F.] S.) 348
Othello (Shakespeare) 75–6, 238, 336, 374
Othon (Corneille, P.) 253, 378

Paméla (Nivelle de la Chaussée, P. C.) 91, 341
Pamela, or, Virtue Rewarded (Richardson, S.)
  91, 341
Paméla en France (Boissy, L.) 91, 341
Paradoxe sur le comédien [*Paradox of the Actor*]
  (Diderot, D.) 20
*Paragone della Poesia tragica d'Italia con quella di
  Francia* [*Comparison of Italian Tragic Poetry
  with that of France*] (Calepio, P.) 348
*A Parallel; in the Manner of Plutarch: between a
  most celebrated Man of Florence; and One, scarce
  ever heard of in England* (Spence, J.) 400
Perinthia (Menander) 271
Persians (Aeschylus) 294, 391

Petites Lettres sur de grands Philosophes [*Little
  letters on great Philosophers*] (Palissot de
  Montenoy, C.) 267–9, 382–3
Pharamond (La Harpe, J. de) 352
Phédre (Racine, J.) 326
Philoctetes (Sophocles) 238, 248, 374, 376, 381
Philosophische Schriften [*Philosophical Writings*]
  (Mendelssohn, M.) 348, 374–5
Philotas (Daniel, S.) 178, 317, 362–3, 399
Plutarch Lives I (Plutarch) 348
Poetics (Aristotle) 2, 23, 132, 134, 137, 237,
  239–49, 275–81, 287, 308, 323, 324,
  347–8, 352–4, 357–60, 370, 373–80, 385,
  389, 391
Poetique d'Aristote [*Aristotle's Poetics*] (Dacier,
  A.) 133–4, 137, 138, 239, 241, 245, 247–8,
  255–6, 260, 270, 276–7, 280, 287–8,
  352–4, 374–6, 378, 380, 385, 387, 389
Poétique françoise [*French poetics*] (Marmontel,
  J. F.) 316, 335, 398
Politics (Aristotle) 246, 374, 376
Polyeucte (Corneille, P.) 40, 75, 103, 258, 317,
  323, 336, 344, 375, 379, 399
"Preface to Tartuffe" (Molière) 346
Prince, The (Machiavelli, N.) 347
*Progrès des Allemands dans les Sciences, les
  Belles-Lettres et les Arts* [*The Progress of the
  Germans in Science, Literature, and the Arts*]
  (Bielfeld, J. F. F. von) 313, 396
Prolegomena on Comedy ("*Life of
  Aristophanes*") 386
"Prologo al Lector" ["Prologue to the
  Reader"] (Cervantes, M. de) 202, 367
Publii Terentii [*Works of Terence*] (Donatus, A.)
  228–33, 278, 291, 300–1, 304, 371–2, 385,
  390, 392–3

*Réflexions Critiques sur la Pöesie et sur la
  Peinture* [*Critical Reflections on Poetry,
  Painting, and Music*] (Dubos, Abbé) 259, 379
*Réflexions historiques et critiques sur différents
  théâtres de l'Europe* [*An Historical and
  Critical Account of the Theaters in Europe*]
  (Riccoboni, L.) 329
"Réponse de M. de Voltaire à M. de la
  Lindelle" ["Answer from Mr. de Voltaire
  to Mr. de la Lindelle"] (Voltaire) 143,
  150–1, 355, 356, 357
"Review of Möser" (Abbt, T.) 394
"Rhapsodie oder Zusätze zu den Briefen
  über die Empfindung" ["Rhapsody or
  Additions to the Letters on Sentiments"]
  (Mendelssohn, M.) 238, 243, 374

Rhetoric (Aristotle) 239–40, 245, 249, 371–7
Richard der Dritte [*Richard the Third*] (Weisse,
  C. F.) 235–7, 249–51, 261, 345, 373,
  377, 380
Richard the Third (Shakespeare, W.) 235
Ridiculous Lover, The (Le Grand, M. A.) 51, 326
Rimas [*Rhymes*] (Lope de Vega) 202, 367, 370
"Risposta alla Lettera del Signor di Voltaire"
  ["Response to the letter from Mr. de
  Voltaire"] (Maffei, [F.] S.) 355–6
Rodogune, Princesse des Parthes [*Rodogune,
  Princess of Parthia*] (Corneille, P.) 9,
  111–20, 241, 256–60, 316–17, 346–9,
  375–9, 398–9
Romeo and Juliet (Shakespeare, W.) 75
Romeo und Julie [*Romeo and Juliet*] (Weisse,
  C. F.) 345

Satires (Horace) 272, 339, 345, 355, 362, 365,
  384, 389
Satyricon of Petronius Arbiter, The (Arbiter, P.) 351
*Schau-Bühne Englischer und Frantzösischer
  Comödianten* [*Theater of the English and
  French Players*] 335
"Schreiben über die Komödie in Versen"
  ["Writings on Comedy in Verse"]
  (Schlegel, J. E.) 70, 334
"Schreiben von Errichtung eines
  Theaters in Kopenhagen" ["Writings
  on the Establishment of a Theater in
  Copenhagen"] (Schlegel, J. E.) 35, 322
Selected Philosophical Writings (Descartes, R.) 324
Sémiramis (Voltaire) 8, 63–7, 103, 105, 107,
  254, 325, 331–2, 345
Sertorius (Corneille, P.) 253, 265, 378, 382
Sidney (Gresset, J.) 80, 261, 337–8, 380
"Soliman II" (Marmontel, J. F) 120–9,
  315–16, 349–51, 398
Soliman second, ou les trois Sultanes [*Solomon
  the Second, or the three Sultanas*] (Favart,
  C. S.) 120–9, 349–51, 315–16, 398
"Some Account" (Rowe, N.) 326
Squire of Alsatia, The (Shadwell, T.) 396
Stoicheia [*Elements*] (Euclid) 308, 394
Suréna (Corneille, P.) 240, 253, 378
Symmiktōn (Nannius, P.) 300, 392
Synapothnescontes (Diphilus) 299–300, 392

Theatralische Bibliothek [*Theatrical Library*]
  (Lessing, G. E.) 3, 222, 326, 329–30,
  369, 389
Théâtre des Grecs [*Theater of the Greeks*]
  (Brumoy, P.) 130, 351
*Theologische Untersuchung der Sittlichkeit der
  heutigen deutschen Schaubühne* [*Theological

*Investigation of the Morality of the Contemporary
  German Theater*] (Götze, J. M.) 324
*Theorie der Poesie nach den neuesten
  Grundsätzen und Nachricht von den besten
  Dichtern nach den angenommenen Urtheilen
  [*Theory of Poetry, according to the most
  recent principles and Information about the
  Best Poets, according to accepted judgments*]
  (Schmid, C. H.) 373
Thesauros [*Treasure*] (Philemon) 330
Timon le Misanthrope (Delisle de la Drevetière,
  L.) 338
Titus (Belloy, P. de) 84, 328, 339
Tom Jones (Fielding, H.) 56, 319–20, 328, 400
Trachiniae [*The Women of Trachis*] (Sophocles)
  112, 347
Tragedy of Zara, The (Hill, A.) 76–8, 336
Trinummus [*The Three Pieces of Money*]
  (Plautus) 61–2, 329
Triumph of Time, The (Le Grand, M. A.) 51, 326
Trois discours de P. Corneille [*Three Discourses
  of P. Corneille*] (Corneille, P.) 240, 246–8,
  255–61, 354, 357, 364, 375–6, 378–9, 380
Truculentus [*The Churl*] (Plautus) 90, 341
Tusculan Disputations (Cicero) 273, 352, 384

Ugolino (Gerstenberg, H. W. von) 393
"Un Comédien peut-il avoir trop de Feu?"
  ["Can an actor have too much fire?"]
  (Sainte-Albine, P. R. de) 326
Unhappy favourite, The: or, the Earl of Essex
  (Banks, J.) 178–93, 317, 362–9, 399
Utopia (More, T.) 41

Various History (Aelianus, C.) 387
Versuch einer critischen Dichtkunst [*Attempt at a
  Critical Poetics*] (Gottsched, J. C.) 344
Village Lawyer, The (Colman, G. [the Elder]/
  Lyons, C.) 74, 92, 335
Virginia (Montiano y Luyando, A. de) 222, 369
"Von dem Zupfen der Sterbenden" ["On the
  Spasms of the Dying"] 334
"Vorläufige Nachricht" ["Preliminary
  Announcement"] (Löwen, J. F.) 10–11

"Widow of Ephesus, The" 129, 351, 398
Wie die Alten den Tod gebildet [*How the Ancients
  Portrayed Death*] (Lessing, G. E.) 383

Young Hypocrite, The, or the Country Poet
  (Foote, S.) 69, 333

Zaïre (Voltaire) 63–4, 75–9, 84, 103,
  336–9, 344
Zelmire (Belloy, P. de) 83–6, 89, 339–40

Printed in Great Britain
by Amazon

22187509R00262